To our families and students

— A.H. W.M. J.D.

Cambridge Business Publishers

MANAGERIAL ACCOUNTING, Al L. Hartgraves, Wayne J. Morse, and James R. Davis.

10 Digit ISBN 1-934319-18-X
13 Digit ISBN 978-1-934319-18-5

Bookstores & Faculty: to order this book, contact the company via email **customerservice@cambridgepub.com** or call 800-619-6473.

Students & Retail Customers: to order this book, please visit the book's website and order directly online.

Printed in Canada
10 9 8 7 6 5 4 3 2 1

Business Insight	Research Insight
• A Century of Innovation Sets Corning Apart • FedEx and UPS Stage Battle—Customer is Sure to Win • GM Code of Ethics: "Winning with Integrity"	• Managerial Accounting is a Key to Success • Working Principles for Corporations
• Alliance Alters USPS Cost Structure • Aircraft Diversity is a Cost Driver	• Don't Base Decision on the Purchase Price • Regression Finds "Big Tree" Premium
• HP's High-Volume, Low-Price Break-Even Point • CVP Analysis Using Financial Statements • Operating Leverage Makes XM- Sirius Merger Attractive • Think Customer Value Not Sales Volume	• Careless Financial Management is a Primary Cause of Business Failure • Determining the Cash Break-Even Point for Delaying Retirement
• Using Cost Analysis to Decide Whether to Outsource Public Services • Delta Airline Adopts Theory of Constraints for Technical Operations	• Benefits of Outsourcing
• Software for Job Costing • Weaknesses in the Job Cost Business Model • Service Contractors Learn Poor Cost Measurement Can Really Hurt • Process Costing in a Japanese Dyestuffs Plant	• Inventory Levels and Company Financial Performance
• Blue Cross and Blue Shield of Florida Ensures Adequate Product Pricing with Activity-Based Management • Managing the Drivers of Customer Profitability • Using ABC to Justify Capital Equipment	• The History of ABC
• Computer Software Aids Telephone Service Cost Allocation • Cost Allocations for College Services • The History of Lean Production • Mercedes Benz Produces Smart Car Using Just-in-Sequence Production	• Survey Documents Benefits of Lean Production Strategy
• Internet Driven Virtual Value Chain at Dell • Cost-based Pricing Advocated for Medical Groups • Target Costing and New Product Development • Quality Parts Yield Product Success • Intel Benchmarks Performance	
• Fort Collins Budgets for Outcomes • Going Broke Getting Rich • Budgetary Slack May Provide Flexibility for Innovation and Improve Control in Unstructured Environments • The Heart of Every Decision	• Data Warehousing Gives Managers Control
• Ethics and Responsibility Accounting • GE's Six Sigma • Flexibility in Standard Costing • Multiple Cost Drivers • Chrysler Hits Financial Pothole Because of Sales Variances	
• Citigroup's Transfer-Pricing Problems • Methods Used to Evaluate IT Projects at Harrah's • Balanced Scorecard Software	• Transfer Pricing and External Competition • Evidence Supports EVA • Balanced Scorecard Yields Results
• Energy Reduction as a Corporate Goal Fosters Green Investments • Manager Behavior and Expected Vehicle Value • Investment Returns are Not Always Quantifiable	• Where the Errors are • Size and Education Matter in Capital Budgeting

Managerial Accou

AL L. HARTGRAVES
Emory University

WAYNE J. MORSE
Rochester Institute of Technology

JAMES R. DAVIS
Clemson University/Anderson University

PREFACE

Welcome to *Managerial Accounting*. Our book presents managerial accounting in the context of a big-picture, decision oriented, business setting. It integrates traditional coverage with cutting-edge topics such as lean accounting, activity-based management, customer profitability analysis, and value chain analysis. It does this with an eye toward the general business student since a book is not useful if it is not read. An overriding aim of our book is to engage students to read further and understand the materials presented.

APPROACH

Managerial accounting focuses on using financial and nonfinancial information by managers and associates of a firm to make strategic, organizational, and operational decisions. Our book provides a framework for identifying and analyzing decision alternatives and for evaluating success or failure in accomplishing such organizational goals. Although accountants are important in the managerial accounting process, managerial accounting is more about managerial tools than processes. In our era of global competition, continuous improvement, process reengineering, and employee empowerment, the tools of managerial accounting are used by decision makers at all levels, rather than just by "managers." One goal of our book is to introduce students to this reality.

Our book is written for all students—not just accounting students. We place managerial accounting in a broad business context, relating it to other business areas. We also avoid details that are appropriate for advanced cost accounting books. Like the trunk of a tree, our book serves as a strong base for students' future knowledge growth and as a means of unifying the branches of business management.

EMPHASIS

We emphasize the use of managerial accounting information for decision making within the context of organizational strategy. The organization and content of our book reflect our belief that students who understand the big picture are better learners, are better decision makers, and are better able to apply what they learn.

The following illustrate the big picture, decision orientation, of our book.

- **Strategic Focus** Our book uses concepts from the management literature such as strategic position analysis and value chain analysis. Strategic position analysis considers the consequences of managerial decisions on how a business competes in the marketplace (such as with low price/cost, product differentiation and innovation, and market niche). Those decisions affect managers' need for and use of accounting information. It also places managerial decision making within the context of a company's internal and external value chains. Examples include:

  Chapter 1 pages 8–10
  Chapter 8 pages 252–256

- **Activity-Cost Concepts Emphasize Decisions** Activity concepts are presented not only within the context of product costing but also within the context of improved decision making about products, customers, budgets, and performance assessment. This decision orientation provides a framework for understanding the use of activity-cost concepts for activity-based management. It aids students in *thinking outside the product costing box*. Examples include:

  Chapter 2 pages 42–44
  Chapter 6 pages 191–193
  Chapter 9 page 290

- **Deemphasize distinction between Product and Period Costs** The accounting distinction between product and non-product costs (introduced early in most books) is not the central theme of *Managerial Accounting*. Instead we focus on analysis of the complete value chain for both manufacturing and nonmanufacturing organizations, rather than presenting managerial accounting within the context of product costing for a manufacturing organization. This book successfully avoids the product/period cost trap.

Although the focus of this book is on decision making tools, an important element of any managerial accounting text is product costing. In this edition, traditional product costing techniques are presented in Chapters 5, 6, and 7, after the introduction of key managerial accounting concepts (Chapter 2–Cost Behavior and Cost Estimation; Chapter 3–Cost-Volume-Profit Analysis; Chapter 4–Relevant Costs for Decision Making). Chapter 5 presents traditional product costing techniques; Chapter 6 deals with indirect overhead cost assignment, including activity-based costing; and Chapter 7 discusses service department cost allocation, along with lean production and just-in-time concepts.

ETHICS

Managerial ethics receives extensive coverage. For example, ethics is introduced in the context of measurement and management in Chapter 1 and discussed further in Chapters 4 and 9. "Business Insight" features and numerous end-of-chapter problems and cases in Chapters 1, 3, 8, 9, 10, and 11 include a variety of decision situations involving ethical dilemmas. The following excerpt is from Chapter 9:

Ethics

Because most wrongful activities related to budgeting are unethical, rather than illegal, organizations often have difficulty dealing with them. However, when managers' actions cross the gray area between ethical and fraudulent behavior, organizations are not reluctant to dismiss employees or even pursue legal actions against them.[4]

Although most managers have a natural inclination to be conservative in developing their budgets, at some level the blatant padding or building slack into the budget becomes unethical. In an extreme case, it might even be considered theft if an inordinate level of budgetary slack creates favorable performance variances that lead to significant bonuses or other financial gain for the manager. Another form of falsifying budgets occurs when managers include expense categories in their budgets that are not needed in their operations and subsequently use the funds to pad other budget categories. The deliberate falsification of budgets is unethical behavior and is grounds for dismissal in most organizations.

Ethical issues might also arise in the reporting of performance results, which usually compares actual data with budgeted data. Examples of unethical reporting of actual performance data include misclassification of expenses, overstating revenues or understating expenses, postponing or accelerating the recording of activities at the end of the accounting period, or creating fictitious activities. The views of the former CEO of **Phillips Petroleum** on this type of behavior and the competitive environment from which it is often motivated are summarized in the following Business Insight.

UNIQUE PEDAGOGY

Managerial Accounting includes several special features specifically designed to engage students and help them succeed in this course.

Business Insights

Students appreciate and become more engaged when they can see the real world relevance of what they are learning in the classroom. We have included a generous number of current, real world examples throughout each chapter in Business Insight boxes. The following is a representative example:

BUSINESS INSIGHT **Intel Benchmarks Performance**

Intel Corporation divides its benchmarks into two types, component and system. *Component benchmarks* measure the performance of specific parts of a computer system, such as a microprocessor or hard disk drive. *System benchmarks* typically measure the performance of the entire computer system. The performance obtained will almost certainly vary from benchmark performance for a number of reasons. First, individual components must usually be tested in a complete computer system, and it is not always possible to eliminate the considerable effects that differences in system design and configuration have on benchmark results. For instance, vendors sell systems with a wide variety of disk capabilities and speeds, system memory, and video and graphics capabilities, all of which influence how the system components perform in actual use. Differences in software, including operating systems and compilers, also affect component and system performance. Finally, benchmark tests are typically written to be exemplary for only a certain type of computer application, which might or might not be similar to what is being compared.

A benchmark is, at most, only one type of information that an organization might use during the purchasing or manufacturing process. To get a true picture of the performance of a component or system being considered, the organization should consult industry sources, publicly available research reports, and even government publications of related information.[6]

Decision Making Orientation

One primary goal of a managerial accounting course is to teach students the skills needed to apply their accounting knowledge to solve real business problems and make informed business decisions. With that goal in mind, Managerial Decision boxes in each chapter encourage students to apply the material presented to solving actual business scenarios. The following is a representative example:

MANAGERIAL DECISION **You are the Division Manager**

As manager of a division responsible for both production and sales of products and, hence, division profits, you are looking for ways to leverage the profits of your division to a higher level. You are considering changing your cost structure to include more fixed costs and less variable costs by automating some of the production activities currently performed by people. What are some of the considerations that you should keep in mind as you ponder this decision? [Answer, p. 81]

Research Insights

Academic research plays an important role in the way business is conducted, accounting is performed, and students are taught. It is important for students to recognize how modern research and modern business practice interact. Therefore, we periodically incorporate relevant research to help students understand the important relation between research and modern business. The following is a representative example:

RESEARCH INSIGHT **Transfer Pricing and External Competition**

Researchers found that a firm can glean benefits from discussing transfer-pricing problems with external suppliers. Though transfer prices above marginal cost introduce interdivision coordination problems, they also reduce a firm's willingness to pay outside suppliers. Knowing that costly internal transfers will eat into demand, the supplier is more willing to set lower prices. Such supplier discounts can make decentralization worthwhile for the firm. The benefit of decentralization is shown to be robust in both downstream and upstream competition.[2]

[2] "Anil Arya and Brian Mittendorf, "Interacting Supply Chain Distortions: The Pricing of Internal Transfers and External Procurement," *The Accounting Review*, May 2007.

Mid-Chapter and Chapter-End Reviews

Managerial accounting can be challenging—especially for students lacking business experience or previous exposure to business courses. To reinforce concepts presented in each chapter and to ensure student comprehension, we include mid-chapter and chapter-end reviews that require students to recall and apply the managerial accounting techniques and concepts described in each chapter. The following is a representative example:

MID-CHAPTER REVIEW

Tigertec Company manufactures golf clubs using a traditional process involving significant hand tooling and finishing. A European machine company has proposed to sell Tigertec a new highly automated machine that would reduce significantly the labor cost of producing its golf clubs. The cost of the machine is $1,000,000, and would have an expected life of 5 years, at the end of which it would have a residual value of $100,000. It has an estimated operating cost of $10,000 per month. The direct labor cost savings per club from using the machine is estimated to be $5 per club. In addition, one monthly salaried manufacturing manager, whose salary is $6,000 per month would no longer be needed. The Vice President of Manufacturing earns $10,000 per month. Also, the new machine would free up about 5,000 square feet of space from the displaced workers. Tigertec's building is held under a 10-year lease that has eight years remaining. The current lease cost is $1 per square foot per month. Tigertec may be able to use the space for other purposes, and it has received an offer to rent it to a nearby related company for $3,500 per month.

Required:

a. Identify all of the costs described above as either "relevant" or "irrelevant" to the decision to acquire the new machine.

b. Assuming the new machine would be used to produce an average of 5,000 clubs per month, prepare a differential analysis of the relevant costs of buying the machine and using it for the next five years, versus continuing to use hand labor.

c. In addition to the quantitative analysis in requirement b., what qualitative considerations are important for making the right decision?

Solution

a.

Relevant costs:	Irrelevant costs:
Cost of machine	Building lease cost
Residual value of machine	Vice President's salary
Operating cost of machine	
Direct labor savings	
Cost of manager	
Opportunity cost of renting released space	

Excellent Assignments

Excellent assignment material is a must-have component of any successful textbook (and class). We went to great lengths to create the best assignments possible. We tried to include assignments that reflect our belief that students should be trained in analyzing accounting information to make business decisions, as opposed to working on mechanical computations. Assignments encourage students to analyze accounting information, interpret it, and apply the knowledge gained to a business decision. There are five categories of assignments: **Discussion Questions**, **Mini Exercises**, **Exercises**, **Problems**, and **Cases**. The following is a representative example:

E3-21. Alternative Production Procedures and Operating Leverage (LO3, 5)

Paper Mate

Assume Paper Mate is planning to introduce a new executive pen that can be manufactured using either a capital-intensive method or a labor-intensive method. The predicted manufacturing costs for each method are as follows:

	Capital Intensive	Labor Intensive
Direct materials per unit	$ 5.00	$ 6.00
Direct labor per unit	$ 5.00	$12.00
Variable manufacturing overhead per unit	$ 4.00	$ 2.00
Fixed manufacturing overhead per year	$2,440,000.00	$700,000.00

Paper Mate's market research department has recommended an introductory unit sales price of $30. The incremental selling costs are predicted to be $500,000 per year, plus $2 per unit sold.

Required

a. Determine the annual break-even point in units if Paper Mate uses the:
   1. Capital-intensive manufacturing method.
   2. Labor-intensive manufacturing method.

b. Determine the annual unit volume at which Paper Mate is indifferent between the two manufacturing methods.

c. Management wants to know more about the effect of each alternative on operating leverage.
   1. Explain operating leverage and the relationship between operating leverage and the volatility of earnings.
   2. Compute operating leverage for each alternative at a volume of 250,000 units.
   3. Which alternative has the higher operating leverage? Why?

CHANGES TO THE 5TH EDITION

The revisions made in the 5th edition are substantial. In addition to the new pedagogy and the updating of vignettes, examples, and assignments, we have reorganized and streamlined the book based on adopter and reviewer feedback. Some of the more significant content changes include:

- All chapters now include a chapter outline, a mid chapter review with solution, and a managerial decision question with suggested answer. Mini exercises have also been added to chapter assignment materials, and many of the other exercises and problems have been expanded to include critical thinking requirements.
- Chapter 2: The section on potential errors with the unit-level approach was deleted because it is more appropriate for an advanced text. The appendix on least-squares regression using a spreadsheet was also deleted.
- Chapter 3: The appendix on sales mix analysis from the 4th edition has been incorporated into the chapter and the section on profitability analysis and unit and nonunit cost drivers has been moved to Appendix 3A.
- Chapter 4: Includes expanded coverage of the make-or-buy decision with emphasis on outsourcing as a major business strategy.
- Chapter 5: The illustration of job costing, presented in Chapter 6 of the 4th edition, has been simplified. The appendix on journal entries from the 4th edition has been eliminated in favor of the use of T-accounts incorporated into the body of the chapter. The illustration of absorption and variable costing, presented in Chapter 8 of the 4th edition, has been simplified to focus on essentials important to all business students and moved to Appendix 5A.
- Chapter 6: The activity based costing and activity based management topics that spanned Chapters 5 and 7 in the 4th edition have been consolidated into a single chapter. In addition, a major new section on customer profitability analysis has been added.

- Chapter 7: This chapter continues to include the topic of service department cost assignment, but in this edition it also includes the topic of just-in-time inventory management (from Chapter 8 in the 4th edition), expanded and modified to emphasize the growing trend toward lean production and lean accounting. The appendix illustrating the algebra method of service department cost allocation was deleted.
- Chapter 8: This chapter presents the topic of value chain management and analysis (from Chapter 5 in the 4th edition) along with the related product management models, including target costing, continuous improvement and benchmarking (which were covered in Chapter 9 in the 4th edition) .
- Chapter 9: The illustration of operational budgeting, presented in Chapter 11 of the 4th edition, has been simplified. The illustration of budgeting in a manufacturing organization, a chapter appendix in the 4th edition, has also been simplified and incorporated into the chapter.
- Chapter 10: The discussion of responsibility accounting, Chapter 12 in the 4th edition, has been streamlined. The illustration of variance analysis for variable costs has been simplified. Materials on variable overhead variances and the fixed overhead budget variance have been moved from a chapter appendix in the 4th edition into the body of the text. The illustration of variance analysis for revenue centers has been simplified.
- Chapter 11: The topics of segment reporting, transfer pricing, and balanced scorecard, presented in Chapter 13 of the 4th edition, have been updated and moved to Chapter 11.
- Chapter 12: The chapter on capital budgeting, Chapter 10 in the 4th edition, has been moved to the end of the book.
- Appendix A: The appendix on the managerial reporting of cash flows is no longer in the book but is available for download from the book's Website. The appendix on managerial analysis of financial statements is now Appendix A.

ANCILLARY MATERIALS

Our book is part of a comprehensive and carefully prepared teaching package that includes various forms of assistance to both instructors and students. For this edition, we created and carefully verified the teaching support materials to ensure consistency between the book and its supplements.

Key supplements follow:

- **Solutions Manual,** prepared by the authors, contains detailed solutions to all assignments.
- **PowerPoint Slides**, enhance the classroom presentation of book materials.
- **Test Bank**, is a collection of problems, questions, and exercises designed to save time in preparing and grading periodic and final exams.
- **Book Website**, overseen by the authors, contains further instructor resources and key teaching links.

ACKNOWLEDGMENTS

We are indebted to the following instructors who provided us with revision suggestions for this and/or prior editions of our book:

Helen Adams, *University of Washington*
William David Albrecht, *Bowling Green State University*
James L. Bierstaker, *Villanova University*
Susan Borkowski, *LaSalle University*
A. Faye Borthick, *Georgia State University*
Gary Bridges, *University of Texas—San Antonio*
Stephen Brown, *Emory University*
Gene Bryson, *University of Alabama—Hunstville*
Tom Clausen, *University of Illinois—Springfield*
Douglas Clinton, *Northern Illinois University*
Gary Colbert, *University of Colorado—Denver*
Vicki Dickinson, *University of Florida*
Paul M. Fischer, *University of Wisconsin-Milwaukee*
Benjamin P. Foster, *University of Louisville*
David P. Franz, *San Francisco State University*
Mark Friedman, *University of Miami*

Peter Frischmann, *Idaho State University*
Margaret Gagne, *Marist College*
Karen Geiger, *Arizona State University*
John Giles, *North Carolina State University*
Judith Harris, *Nova Southeastern University*
John Hassell, *Indiana University—Indianapolis*
Eleanor G. Henry, *Southeast Missouri State University*
James W. Hesford, *Cornell University*
Jay S. Holmen, *University of Wisconsin—Eau Claire*
David R. Honodel, *University of Denver*
Ronald Huefner, *SUNY Buffalo*
Eric N. Johnson, *Indiana University—Indianapolis*
Paul Juras, *Wake Forest University*
Anthony Craig Keller, *Missouri State University*
Charles Kile, *Middle Tennessee State University*
Larry N. Killough, *Virginia Tech University*
John Koeplin, *University of San Francisco*
William Lathen, *Boise State University*
Elliot Levy, *Bentley College*
Donna Losell, *University of Toronto*
Linda M. Marquis, *Northern Kentucky University*
Otto B. Martinson, *Old Dominion University*
Michael J. Meyer, *Ohio University*
Dale Morse, *University of Oregon*
Ramesh Narasimhan, *Montclair State University*
Larry Paquette, *Francis Marion University*
Gordon Potter, *Cornell University*
Barbara Reider, *University of Montana*
Maryanne Rouse, *University of South Florida*
Jack Ruhl, *Western Michigan University*
Jane Saly, *University of St. Thomas*
Jeffrey Schatzberg, *University of Arizona*
Lewis Shaw, *Suffolk University*
Henry Smith, III, *Otterbein College*
Charles Stanley, *Baylor University*
Audrey Taylor, *Western Washington University*
Pierre L. Titard, *Southeastern Louisiana State University*
Leslie Turner, *Northern Kentucky University*
Sheila Viel, *University of Wisconsin-Milwaukee*
Wallace Wood, *University of Cincinnati*
Elisa Zuliani, *University of Toronto*

Appreciation is extended to the Institute of Certified Management Accountants for permission to use adaptations of problems from past Certified Management Accounting Examinations—these materials are identified as "CMA Adapted." We are also indebted to the American Institute of Certified Public Accountants for permission to use materials from the Uniform CPA exam—these materials are identified as "CPA Adapted." We appreciate the tolerance and feedback of our students as we tested many of the new ideas and assignments for this book. Finally, we appreciate the encouragement, support, and detailed suggestions for improvement provided by George Werthman and his colleagues at Cambridge Business Publishers, including Jill Fischer, Keith Chasse, Deborah Golden, and Terry McQuade. Working with them has been a pleasure. To assist us in continuously improving our book to better fits your needs and the needs of your students, comments and suggestions are welcome.

Al L. Hartgraves
Atlanta, GA

Wayne J. Morse
Rochester, NY

James R. Davis
Clemson, SC

July 2008

ABOUT THE AUTHORS

The author team of Hartgraves, Morse, and Davis provides relevant experience, award-winning teaching, and scholarly insights as a foundation for this leading textbook on managerial accounting.

AL L. HARTGRAVES is Professor of Accounting at the Goizueta Business School at Emory University in Atlanta, Georgia with a primary teaching focus in the Executive MBA programs and other executive programs. He has also been a frequent Guest Professor at Johannes Kepler University in Linz, Austria and at the Helsinki School of Economics and Business Administration in Finland. His published scholarly and professional articles have appeared in The Accounting Review, Accounting Horizons, Management Accounting, Journal of Accountancy, Journal of Accounting and Public Policy and many other journals. Students at Goizueta Business School have selected him on seven occasions to receive the Distinguished Educator Award. In 2002 he received Emory University's highest teaching award, The Scholar/Teacher Award, and he was recognized as the Accounting Educator of the Year by the Georgia Society of CPAs. He has been recognized as an Outstanding Faculty Member in two editions of The Business Week Guide to the Best Business Schools. He is a Certified Public Accountant (inactive) and a Certified Management Accountant, having received the Certificate of Distinguished Performance on the CMA exam. He received his Ph.D. from Georgia State University.

WAYNE J. MORSE, a hiking and canoeing enthusiast, is Professor of Accounting at the Saunders College of Business at Rochester Institute of Technology. An author or co-author of more than fifty published papers, monographs, and textbooks, he was a founding member of the Management Accounting section of the American Accounting Association. His most notable writings are in the areas of learning curves, human resource accounting, and quality costs. He was a member of the IMA Committee on Research and an AICPA Board of Examiners subcommittee, and he has served on the editorial boards of Advances in Accounting, Trends in Accounting Education, Issues in Accounting Education, and Management Accounting Research. A Certified Public Accountant, he received his Ph.D. from Michigan State University. Prior to joining RIT, he was on the faculty of the University of Illinois, Duke University, the University of Tennessee, Clarkson University, and the University of Alabama-Huntsville.

JAMES R. DAVIS is Professor of Accounting in the Division of Business at Anderson University and Professor Emeritus of the School of Accountancy at Clemson University. A co-author of three textbooks, he has authored or co-authored numerous journal articles and professional meeting proceedings. His primary areas of interest are managerial accounting, information systems, and professional ethics. He has served on several editorial boards and professional committees and has been very active with the ICMA Examination Project. He is a Certified Management Accountant and has held numerous offices in local IMA Chapters. He received his Ph.D. from Georgia State University. His international experience has included several teaching and consulting positions in New Zealand and Portugal, the most recent being a visiting lecturer at Universidade de Algarve in Faro, Portugal.

BRIEF CONTENTS

CONTENTS

Chapter 1
Managerial Accounting: Tools for Decision Making 2

Chapter 2
Cost Behavior, Activity Analysis, and Cost Estimation 26

Chapter 3
Cost-Volume-Profit Analysis and Planning 58

Chapter 4
Relevant Costs and Benefits for Decision Making 94

Chapter 5
Product Costing: Job and Process Operations 128

Chapter 6

Activity-Based Costing, Customer Profitability, and Activity-Based Management 174

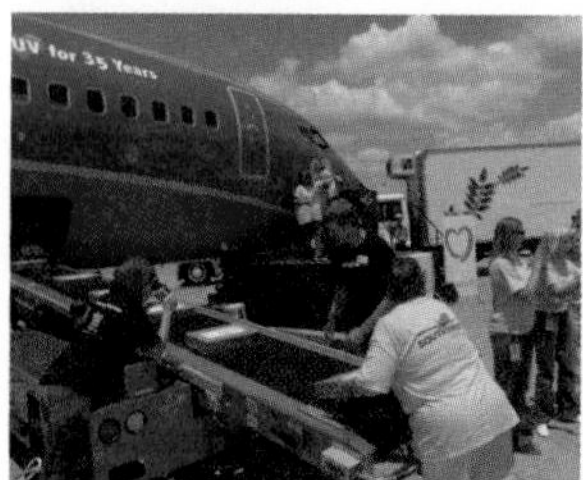

Chapter 7

Additional Topics in Product Costing 218

Chapter 8

Pricing and Other Product Management Decisions 250

Chapter 9
Operational Budgeting and Profit Planning 286

Chapter 10
Standard Costs and Performance Reports 328

Chapter 11
Segment Reporting, Transfer Pricing, and Balanced Scorecard 368

Chapter 12
Capital Budgeting Decisions 408

Appendix A
Managerial Analysis of Financial Statements 456

Chapter 1

Managerial Accounting: Tools for Decision Making

LEARNING OBJECTIVES

LO1 Contrast financial and managerial accounting and explain how managerial accounting is used by internal decision makers. (p. 4)

LO2 Explain how an organization's mission, goals, and strategies affect managerial accounting. (p. 7)

LO3 Discuss the factors determining changes in the nature of business competition. (p. 13)

LO4 Differentiate among structural, organizational, and activity cost drivers. (p. 14)

LO5 Explain the nature of the ethical dilemmas managers and accountants confront. (p. 16)

MISSIONS, GOALS, AND STRATEGIES

The automobile industry is experiencing some rough times. With fuel costs increasing, sales sagging, profits crashing, and auto plants closing this hardly seems like the time to start a new automobile company. Nevertheless, newly organized Carbon Motors Corporation is revving up to fill their stated *mission* of building "the world's first purpose-built law enforcement patrol vehicle." By following a *strategy* focused on the needs of this narrow market segment or niche, marketing directly to government agencies, and utilizing innovative manufacturing approaches, management believes Carbon Motors can accomplish its profitability *goal* with an annual sales volume between 10,000 and 80,000 units.

According to Carbon Motors Chief Executive Officer (CEO) William Santana Li, current police cars are basically "a retail passenger car with some lights on it" purchased through a local car dealer and then modified with between $5,000 and $35,000 of aftermarket equipment that was not designed, engineered, or manufactured by an automaker. Starting from scratch, Carbon Motors developed a set of criteria they believe reflects the needs and wants of the law enforcement personnel. They then designed a product to meet 95 percent of these criteria.

To achieve profitability at their anticipated scale of operations with competitive pricing, they plan to contain costs by selling directly to law

Courtesy of Carbon Motors Corporation

enforcement agencies (rather than through dealers) and avoid inventory carrying costs by building only to fill customer orders. Management believes that direct sales to government agencies will also allow Carbon Motors to avoid major media advertising costs required for sales to the general public. Also avoided are the costs of annual "face-lifts" that are the norm for passenger vehicles. And, to the extent possible, Carbon Motors plans to minimize investments in manufacturing facilities and all of the issues associated with operating such facilities. Instead, the production of many of the components included in completed vehicles will be accomplished by contract manufacturing. Carbon Motors will then assemble the final product at facilities under development near Atlanta, Georgia.

Although CEO Li and other members of the top-management team have many years of experience at established automobile companies, they are sober about the challenges they face. Fortunately, given the company's stage of development and lack of current sales, Carbon Motors Corporation is a privately held company without public stock. Being privately held relieves management of many issues related to shareholder expectations, such as current profits. Management must still, of course, meet the expectations of private investors and use accounting concepts as tools to accomplish the mission of Carbon Motors. We start this chapter by considering how companies use financial and managerial accounting and by examining the all important mission, goals, and strategies that provide broad guidelines for all members of the management team.[1]

[1] Gary S. Vasilash, "Creating a New Car Company," *Fleet Owner*, December 2007, p.96; Gary S. Vasilash, Creating a New Car Company. *Automotive Design and Production*, May 2006, pp.46-47; John Toon, "First Responders: Carbon Motors and Georgia Tech to Collaborate on Development of World's First "Purpose-Built" Law Enforcement Vehicle," http://gtresearchnews.gatech.edu/newsrelease/carbon.htm, April 21, 2006; www.carbonmotors.com.

This chapter provides an overview of the factors that make managerial accounting increasingly important to successful businesses. We begin by distinguishing between financial and managerial (also called *management*) accounting and by investigating how competitive strategy affects the way organizations, such as Carbon Motors, use managerial accounting information. Next, we explore how the emergence of global competition and changes in technology have increased the need to understand managerial accounting concepts. We also provide an overview of factors that influence costs in an organization and how these factors have changed in recent years. Finally, we examine the interrelationships among measurement, management, and ethics.

INTERNAL USES OF ACCOUNTING INFORMATION

Financial Accounting

LO1 Contrast financial and managerial accounting and explain how managerial accounting is used by internal decision makers.

Financial accounting is an information-processing system that generates general-purpose reports of financial operations (income statement and statement of cash flows) and financial position (balance sheet) for an organization. Although financial accounting is used by decision makers inside and outside the firm, financial accounting typically emphasizes external users, such as security investors, analysts, and lenders. Adding to this external orientation are external financial reporting requirements determined by law and generally accepted accounting principles.

Financial accounting is also concerned with keeping records of the organization's assets, obligations, and the collection and payment of cash. An organization cannot survive without converting sales into cash, paying for purchases, meeting payroll, and keeping track of its assets.

The **income statement** is a summary of economic performance during a period of time, showing the revenues generated by operations, the expenses matched to those revenues, and any gains and losses attributed to the period. The **statement of cash flows** is a summary of resource inflows and outflows stated in terms of cash. This statement summarizes cash flows from operating, investing, and financing activities. The **balance sheet** is a picture of the economic position of an organization at a specific time, showing the organization's assets and the claims on those assets. Complete financial statements also include a **statement of owners' equity** that summarizes changes in owner's equity and detailed footnotes summarizing accounting policies. These financial statements, typically prepared quarterly and annually, report on the past activities of the organization.

Equity investors, creditors, and others rely on financial statements to help evaluate the amount, timing, and uncertainty of future cash flows. These statements also provide a basis for interested parties to contract on audited financial numbers. For instance, creditors may use financial statements to design loan covenants, owners may use the statements for determining performance-based pay for their managers, and franchisors may assess royalties from franchisees on these numbers. Thus, financial accounting information helps create value by aiding firms in accessing outside funding and in contracting with interested parties.

Managers often use income statements and balance sheets as a starting point in evaluating and planning the firm's overall activities. Managers learn a great deal by performing a comparative analysis of their firm and competing firms. Corporate goals are often stated using financial accounting numbers such as net income, or ratios such as return on investment and earnings per common share. However, internal decision makers often find the information provided in financial statements of limited value in managing day-to-day operating activities. They often complain that financial accounting information is too aggregated, prepared too late, based on irrelevant past costs, and not action oriented. For example, the costs of all items produced and sold or all services rendered are summarized in a single line in most financial statements, making it impossible to determine the costs of individual products or services. Financial accounting procedures, acceptable for costing inventories as a whole, often produce misleading information when applied to individual products. Even when they are accurately determined, the costs of individual products or services are rarely detailed enough to provide the information needed for decisions concerning the factors that influence costs. Financial accounting reports, seldom prepared more than once a month, are not timely enough for use in the management of day-to-day activities that cause excess costs. Finally, financial accounting reports are mainly based on historical costs rather than on current or future costs. Managers are more interested in future costs than in historical costs such as last year's depreciation. While financial accounting information is useful in making some management decisions, its primary emphasis is not on internal decision making.

Managerial Accounting

Managers are constantly faced with the need to understand and control costs, make product decisions, coordinate resources, and guide and motivate employees. **Managerial accounting** provides an information framework to organize, evaluate, and report proprietary data in light of an organization's goals. This information is directed to managers and other employees within the organization. Managerial accounting reports can be designed to meet the information needs of internal decision makers. Top management may need only summary information prepared once a month for each business unit. An engineer responsible for hourly production scheduling may need continuously updated and detailed information concerning the cost of alternative ways of producing a product.

Because of the intensity of competition and the shorter life cycles of new products and services, managerial accounting is crucial to an organization's success. All managers must understand the financial implications of their decisions. While accountants are available to assist in obtaining and evaluating relevant information, individual managers are responsible for requesting information, analyzing it, and making the final decisions. The increased use of accounting information is further examined in the Research Insight box that follows.

RESEARCH INSIGHT **Managerial Accounting Is a Key to Success**

After studying several highly competitive, world-class companies, noted managerial accounting guru Robin Cooper observed that "with the emergence of the lean enterprise and increased global competition, companies must learn to be more proactive in the way they manage costs. For many, survival is dependent upon their abilities to develop sophisticated cost management systems that create intense pressure to reduce costs." He also observed that "as cost management becomes more critical to a company's survival, two trends emerge. First, new forms of cost management are required, and second, more individuals in the firm become actively involved in the cost management process." Cooper suggests that with the growing number of managers involved in the cost management process, there is an increased need for managerial accounting information (and people who know how to use it).[2]

Managerial accounting information exists to serve the needs of management. Hence, it is subject to a cost-benefit analysis and should be developed only if the perceived benefits exceed the costs of development and use. Also, while financial measures are often used in managerial accounting, they are not used to the exclusion of other measures. Money is simply a convenient way of expressing events in a form suitable to summary analysis. When this is not possible or appropriate, nonfinancial measures are used. Time, for

---

[2] Robin Cooper, "Look Out, Management Accountants," *Management Accounting*, May 1996, pp. 20–26.

example, is often an important element of quality or service. Hence, many performance measures focus on time, for example:

- Internet vendors such as Amazon.com and Netflix track delivery time.
- Fire departments and police departments measure the response time to emergency calls.
- Airlines, such as United Airlines as well as the Federal Aviation Administration monitor the number of on-time departures and arrivals.

No external standards (such as requirements of the Securities and Exchange Commission) are imposed on information provided to internal users. Consequently, managerial accounting information may be quite subjective. In developing a budget, management is more interested in a subjective prediction of next year's sales than in an objective report on last year's sales. The significant differences between financial and managerial accounting are summarized in Exhibit 1.1.

EXHIBIT 1.1 Differences Between Financial and Managerial Accounting

Financial Accounting	Managerial Accounting
Information for internal *and* external users	Information for internal users
General-purpose financial statements	Special-purpose information and reports
Statements are highly aggregated	Information is aggregated or detailed, depending on need
Relatively long reporting periods	Reporting periods are long or short, depending on need
Report on past decisions	Oriented toward current and future decisions
Follows generally accepted accounting principles	Not constrained by generally accepted accounting principles
Must conform to external standards	No external standards
Emphasizes objective data	Encourages subjective data, if relevant

Strategic Cost Management

Most businesses are under constant pressure to reduce costs to remain competitive. A 2007 study by the accounting firm KPMG reported that more than 80 percent of survey participants viewed an efficient cost structure as a source of long-term competitive advantage.[3]

During recent years, the rapid introduction of improved and new products and services has shortened the market lives of products and services. Some products, such as personal computers, can be obsolete within two or three years after introduction. At the same time, the increased use of complex automated equipment makes it difficult to change production procedures after production begins. Combining short product life cycles with automated production results in an environment where most costs are determined by decisions made before production begins (decisions concerning product design and production procedures).

In response to these trends, a strategic approach to managerial accounting, referred to as *strategic cost management* has emerged. Strategic cost management is a blending of three themes:

1. **Strategic position analysis**—an examination of an organization's basic way of competing to sell products or services.
2. **Cost driver analysis**—the study of factors that cause or influence costs.
3. **Value chain analysis**—the study of value-producing activities, stretching from basic raw materials to the final consumer of a product or service.[4]

We define **strategic cost management** as making decisions concerning specific cost drivers within the context of an organization's business strategy, internal value chain, and position in a larger value chain stretching from the development and use of resources to final consumers. Strategic position analysis is considered in this chapter as part of an organization's strategy. Cost driver analysis is also introduced in this chapter and examined further in Chapter 2. Value chain analysis is discussed in Chapter 8.

---

[3] Rethinking Cost Structures: Creating a Sustainable Cost Advantage, KPMG, 2007, p. 60.

[4] John K. Shank, "Strategic Cost Management: New Wine, or Just New Bottles?" *Journal of Management Accounting Research,* Fall 1989, p. 50.

ORGANIZATIONS: MISSIONS, GOALS, AND STRATEGIES

LO2 Explain how an organization's mission, goals, and strategies affect managerial accounting.

An organization's **mission** is the basic purpose toward which its activities are directed. Carbon Motors' current mission is to build "the world's first purpose-built law enforcement patrol vehicle." Starbucks' mission is to "establish Starbucks as the premier purveyor of the finest coffee in the world while maintaining our uncompromising principles while we grow."[5] Organizations vary widely in their missions. One benefit of a mission statement is to help focus all the activities of an organization. For instance, the former chairman and CEO of Coca-Cola stated that the mission of The Coca-Cola Company is "to create value over time for the owners of our business." He went on to say:

> Our society is based on democratic capitalism. In such a society, people create specific institutions to help meet specific needs. Governments are created to help meet social needs. . . Businesses such as ours are created to meet economic needs. The common thread between these institutions is that they can flourish only when they stay focused on the specific need they were created to fulfill. When institutions try to broaden their scope beyond their natural realms, when for example they try to become all things to all people, they fail.[6]

The CEO of Coca-Cola believed that Coca-Cola best contributes to society and helps government and other organizations fulfill their missions by staying focused on shareholder value. He believed focusing on economics keeps a company financially healthy, and a healthy company fills its responsibilities. Conversely, a bankrupt company is incapable of paying taxes, employing people, serving customers, supporting charitable institutions, or making other contributions to society.

We frequently distinguish between organizations on the basis of profit motive. **For-profit organizations** have profit as a primary objective, whereas **not-for-profit organizations** do not have profit as a primary objective. Clearly, the Coca-Cola Company is a for-profit organization, whereas the City of Chicago and the Red Cross are not-for-profit organizations. (The term *nonprofit* is frequently used to refer to what we have identified as not-for-profit organizations.) Regardless of whether a profit motive exists, organizations must use resources wisely. Every dollar United Way spends for administrative salaries is a dollar that cannot be used to support charitable activities. Not-for-profit organizations, including governments, can go bankrupt if they are unable to meet their financial obligations. All organizations, for-profit and not-for-profit, should use managerial accounting concepts to ensure that resources are used wisely.

A **goal** is a definable, measurable objective. Based on the organization's mission, management sets a number of goals. For-profit organizations have some measure of profitability or shareholder value as one of their stated or implicit goals. The mission of a paper mill located in a small town is to provide quality paper products in order to earn a profit for its owners. The paper mill's goals might include earning an annual profit equal to 10 percent of average total assets, maintaining annual dividends of $2 per share of common stock, developing a customer reputation for above-average quality and service, providing steady employment for area residents, and meeting or exceeding environmental standards.

A clear statement of mission and well-defined goals provides an organization with an identity and unifying purpose, thereby ensuring that all employees are heading in the same direction. Having developed a mission and a set of goals, employees are more apt to make decisions that move the organization toward its defined purpose.

A **strategy** is a course of action that will assist in achieving one or more goals. Much of this text will focus on the financial aspects of selecting strategies to achieve goals. For example, if an organization's goal is to improve product quality, possible strategies for achieving this goal include investing in new equipment, implementing additional quality inspections, prescreening suppliers, reducing batch size, redesigning products, training employees, and rearranging the shop floor. Managerial accounting information will assist in determining which of the many alternative strategies for achieving the goal of quality improvement are cost effective. The distinction between mission, goals, and strategies is illustrated in Exhibit 1.2.

---

[5] www.starbucks.com

[6] Roberto Goizueta, "Why Shareholder Value?" *CEO Series Issue No. 13,* February 1997, Center for the Study of American Business, Washington University in St. Louis, p. 2.

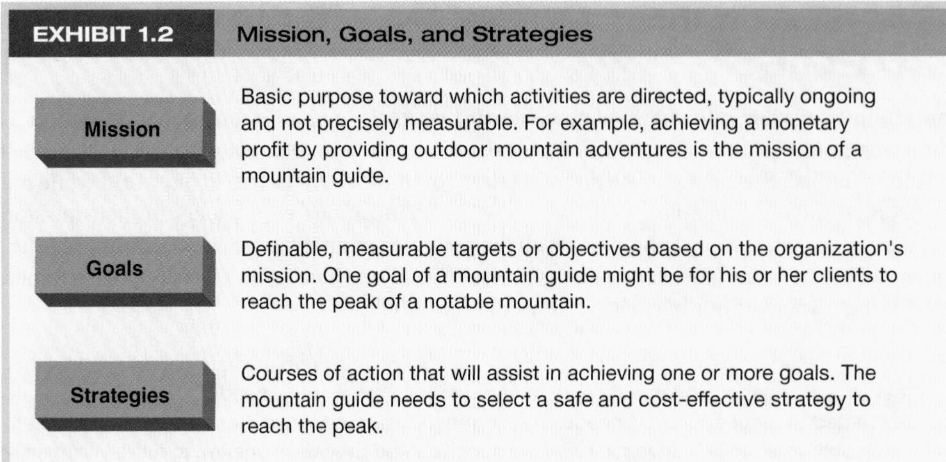

EXHIBIT 1.2
Mission, Goals, and Strategies
Mission
Basic purpose toward which activities are directed, typically ongoing and not precisely measurable. For example, achieving a monetary profit by providing outdoor mountain adventures is the mission of a mountain guide.
Goals
Definable, measurable targets or objectives based on the organization's mission. One goal of a mountain guide might be for his or her clients to reach the peak of a notable mountain.
Strategies
Courses of action that will assist in achieving one or more goals. The mountain guide needs to select a safe and cost-effective strategy to reach the peak.

Strategic Position Analysis

In competitive environments, managers must make a fundamental decision concerning their organization's goal for positioning itself in comparison to competitors. This goal is referred to as the organization's **strategic position**. Much of the organization's strategy depends on this strategic positioning goal. Michael Porter, a highly regarded expert on business strategy, has identified three possible strategic positions that lead to business success:[7]

1. Cost leadership
2. Product or service differentiation
3. Market niche

According to Porter, cost leadership

> requires aggressive construction of efficient-scale facilities, vigorous pursuit of cost reductions from experience, tight cost and overhead control, avoidance of marginal customer accounts, and cost minimization in areas like R&D [research and development], service, sales force, advertising, and so on. A great deal of managerial attention to cost control is necessary to achieve these aims. Low cost relative to competitors becomes the theme running through the entire strategy, though quality, service, and other areas cannot be ignored.[8]

Achieving cost leadership allows an organization to achieve higher profits selling at the same price as competitors or by allowing the firm to aggressively compete on the basis of price while remaining profitable. One of the first companies to successfully use a cost leadership strategy was **Carnegie Steel Company**.

> Carnegie's operating strategy was to push his own direct costs below his competitors so that he could charge prices that would always ensure enough demand to keep his plants running at full capacity. This strategy prompted him to require frequent information showing his direct costs in relation to those of his competitors. Possessing that information and secure in the knowledge that his costs were the lowest in the industry, Carnegie then mercilessly cut prices during economic recessions. While competing firms went under, he still made profits. In periods of prosperity, when customers' demands exceeded the industry's capacity to produce, Carnegie joined others in raising prices.[9]

Southwest Airlines and **Dell** are current examples of successful businesses competing with a strategy of cost leadership. Although **Amazon.com** uses the Internet to differentiate itself from traditional booksellers, its primary strategic position is price leadership.

Conversely, while an organization might compete primarily on the basis of price, management must take care to ensure their product or service remains attuned to changing customer needs and preferences. In the early twentieth century, **General Motors** employed a differentiation strategy, focusing on the rapid

---

[7] Michael E. Porter, *Competitive Strategy* (New York: The Free Press, 1980), p. 35.

[8] Porter, p. 35.

[9] H. Thomas Johnson and Robert S. Kaplan, *Relevance Lost: The Rise and Fall of Management Accounting* (Boston: Harvard Business School Press, 1987), pp. 33–34.

introduction of technological change in new automobile designs to overcome the market dominance of the Model T produced by **Ford Motor Company**. While successfully following a cost leadership strategy for years, Ford made the mistake of excluding other considerations such as vehicle performance and customer desires for different colors.[10] The following Business Insight box reports on **Corning Corporation**'s strategy of product differentiation to achieve a competitive advantage.

BUSINESS INSIGHT **A Century of Innovation Sets Corning Apart**

Corning Incorporated, whose mission is to be "the world leader in specialty glass and ceramics," is a textbook example of a successful company with a strategy of product differentiation based on researching, developing, and manufacturing innovative products. The lengthy list of new products developed by Corning scientists and engineers include: A glass envelope for Thomas Edison's light bulb in 1870; heat-resistant Pyrex glass in 1915; processes for mass-producing television tubes in 1947; low-loss fiber optic cable in 1970; ceramic bases for automotive catalytic converters in 1972; LCD glass for flat-panel displays in 1984; and aluminum titanate filters for diesel vehicles in 2005.

To facilitate their product differentiation strategy Corning employs 1,700 scientists to work on hundreds of exploratory projects and is investing $300 million to refurbish and expand its research labs near Corning, New York. According to UBS analyst Nikos Theodosopoulos, "they're not afraid to invest and lose money for many years." Corning avoids outsourcing and owns dozens of factories producing thousands of different products. Its executives believe that retaining control of research and manufacturing provides a competitive advantage. Their strategy is to keep an array of products in the pipeline and, once a market develops, to quickly produce in volumes that keep rivals from getting traction.

Corning's strategy has produced major winners. The company is the world's largest producer of liquid-crystal-display glass used in flat-panel televisions and computers, which produced more than 90 percent of Corning's 2007 profit of $2.2 billion. Corning's strategy also carries risks. Its investments in the development and production of optical fiber placed the company in financial difficulty after the dot com collapse of the early 2000s. Looking ahead, predicting the market for diesel filters will reach $2 billion by 2011, Corning is ramping up production to profitably fill that anticipated demand. Oh yes, Corning still produces fiber-optic cable and the company's development of bendable fiber-optic cable was cited by *Time Magazine* as one of the best inventions of 2007.[11]

The third possible strategic position according to Porter, focuses on a specific market niche such as a buyer group, segment of the product line, or geographic market and

> rests on the premise that the firm is thus able to serve its narrow strategic target more effectively or efficiently than competitors who are competing more broadly. As a result, the firm achieves either differentiation from better meeting the needs of the particular target, or lower costs in serving the target, or both. Even though the focus strategy does not achieve low costs or differentiation for the market as a whole, it does achieve one or both of these positions vis-à-vis its narrow market target.[12]

Carbon Motors is following a market niche strategy. Other examples of organizations successfully following a market niche strategy include regional breweries that cater to local tastes and **Learjet**, which follows a focused strategy in designing and building corporate aircraft, leaving the market for larger passenger aircraft to firms such as **Boeing** and the market for smaller private planes to firms such as **Piper Aircraft**.

The Research Insight box on the following page considers cost leadership and product or service differentiation among the working principles for twenty-first century corporations.

---

[10] William J. Abernathy and Kenneth Wayne, "Limits of the Learning Curve," *Harvard Business Review*, September–October 1974, pp. 109–119

[11] Sara Silver, Corning's Biggest Bet Yet? Diesel-Filter Technologies," *The Wall Street Journal*, March 7, 2008, pp. B1-B2; Nancy Kelly, "Corning's Renaissance," *American Ceramic Society Bulletin*, February 2008; "Best Inventions of The Year," *Time Magazine*, November 12, 2007, www.corning.com.

[12] Porter, pp. 38–39.

RESEARCH INSIGHT **Working Principles for Corporations**

A *Business Week* editorial reinforced the importance of competing on the basis of a business strategy of price or differentiation. However, recognizing the transitory nature of differentiation in a competitive environment, the editorial used the term "innovation" in place of "differentiation." According to Business Week, the first three working principles of the twenty-first century corporation follow:[13]

1. *Everything gets cheaper faster.* "The Net destroys corporate pricing power. It allows customers, suppliers, and partners to compare prices from 100 or 1,000 sources, not just two or three, and erases market inefficiencies. It rapidly commoditizes all that is new, reducing prices fast."
2. *Cutting costs is the answer.* "In an economic universe of downward pressure on margins, one path to profitability will be to reduce expenses."
3. *Innovation builds profits.* "There is one way for corporations to circumvent principle No. 1 and raise prices. In an information economy, companies can gain an edge through new ideas and products." This advantage is temporary, so corporations following this strategy must innovate rapidly and continuously.

The editorial asserts that human capital is the only asset. In a twenty-first century corporation, creativity is the sole source of growth and wealth. Consequently, the "value of education rises exponentially in an economy based on ideas and analytic thinking."

Managerial Accounting and Goal Attainment

A major purpose of managerial accounting is to support the achievement of goals. Hence, determining an organization's strategic position goal has implications for the operation of an organization's managerial accounting system.

Careful budgeting and cost control with frequent and detailed performance reports are critical with a goal of cost leadership. When the product is difficult to distinguish from that of competitors, price is the primary basis of competition. Under these circumstances, everyone in the organization should continuously apply managerial accounting concepts to achieve and maintain cost leadership. The managerial accounting system should constantly compare actual costs with budgeted costs and signal the existence of significant differences. A simplified version of a *performance report* for costs during a budget period is as follows:

Budgeted (planned) Costs	Actual Costs	Deviation from Budget	Percent Deviation
$560,000	$595,000	$35,000 unfavorable	6.25

Frequent and detailed comparisons of actual and budgeted costs are less important when a differentiation strategy is followed. This is especially true when products have short life cycles or production is highly automated. In these situations, most costs are determined before production begins and there is little opportunity to undertake cost reduction activities thereafter.

With short product lives or automated manufacturing, exceptional care must go into the initial design of a product or service and the determination of how it will be produced or delivered. Here, detailed cost information assists in design and scheduling decisions. A simplified version of the predicted costs of producing a specialty product is as follows:

Engineering and scheduling (12 hours @ $70)	$ 840
Materials (detail omitted)	3,500
Equipment setup (2.5 hours @ $100)	250
Machine operation (9.5 hours @ $90)	855
Materials movement	150
Packing and shipping	675
Total	$6,270

[13] Based on "The Twenty-First Century Corporation," *Business Week,* August 28, 2000, p. 278.

When a differentiation strategy is followed, it often pays to work closely with customers to find ways to enhance the perceived value of a product or service. This leads to an analysis of costs from the customer's viewpoint. The customer may not want a costly feature. Alternatively, the customer may be willing to pay more for an additional feature that will reduce subsequent operating costs.

In designing its 777 aircraft, Boeing invited potential customers to set up offices in Boeing plants and to work with Boeing employees designing the aircraft. Many design changes were made to reduce customer costs. United Airlines, for example, convinced Boeing to move the location of the 777's fuel tanks to reduce servicing costs.

Planning, Organizing, and Controlling

The process of selecting goals and strategies to achieve these goals is often referred to as **planning**. The implementation of plans requires the development of subgoals and the assignment of responsibility to achieve subgoals to specific individuals or groups within an organization. This process of making the organization into a well-ordered whole is called **organizing**. In organizing, the authority to take action to implement plans is delegated to other managers and employees.

Developing an **organization chart** illustrating the formal relationships that exist between the elements of an organization is an important part of organizing. An organization chart for Crown Department Stores is illustrated in Exhibit 1.3. The blocks represent organizational units, and the lines represent relationships between the units. Authority flows down through the organization. Top management delegates authority to use resources for limited purposes to subordinate managers who, in turn, delegate to their subordinates more limited authority for accomplishing more structured tasks. Responsibility flows up through the organization. People at the bottom are responsible for specific tasks, but the president is responsible for the operation of the entire organization.

EXHIBIT 1.3 Crown Department Stores' Organization Chart

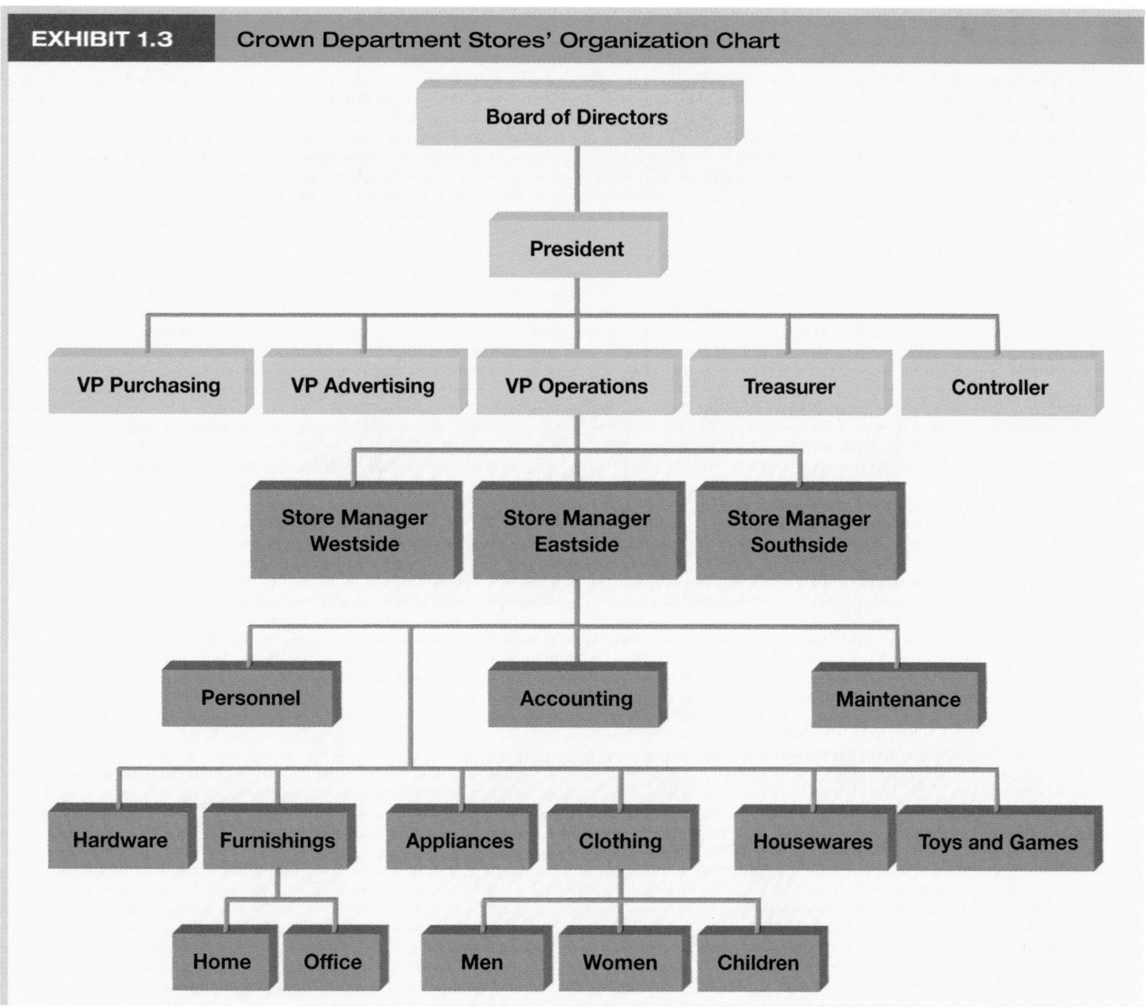

A distinction is often made between line and staff departments. *Line departments* engage in activities that create and distribute goods and services to customers. *Staff departments* exist to facilitate the activities of line departments. In Exhibit 1.3, we see that Crown Department Stores has two levels of staff organizations—corporate and store. The corporate staff departments are Purchasing, Advertising, Treasurer, and Controller. Staff departments at the store level are Personnel, Accounting, and Maintenance. All other units are line departments. A change in plans can necessitate a change in the organization. For example, Crown's plan to discontinue the sale of hardware and add an art department during the coming year will necessitate an organizational change.

Controlling is the process of ensuring that results agree with plans. A brief example of a performance report for costs was presented previously. In the process of controlling operations, actual performance is compared with plans.

With a cost leadership strategy and long-lived products, if actual results deviate significantly from plans, an attempt is made to bring operations into line with plans, or the plans are adjusted. The original plan is adjusted if it is deemed no longer appropriate because of changed circumstances.

With a differentiation strategy and short-lived products, design and scheduling personnel will consider previous errors in predicting costs as they plan new products and services. Hence, the process of controlling feeds forward into the process of planning to form a continuous cycle coordinated through the management accounting system. This cycle is illustrated in Exhibit 1.4.

EXHIBIT 1.4 Planning, Organizating, & Control Cycle

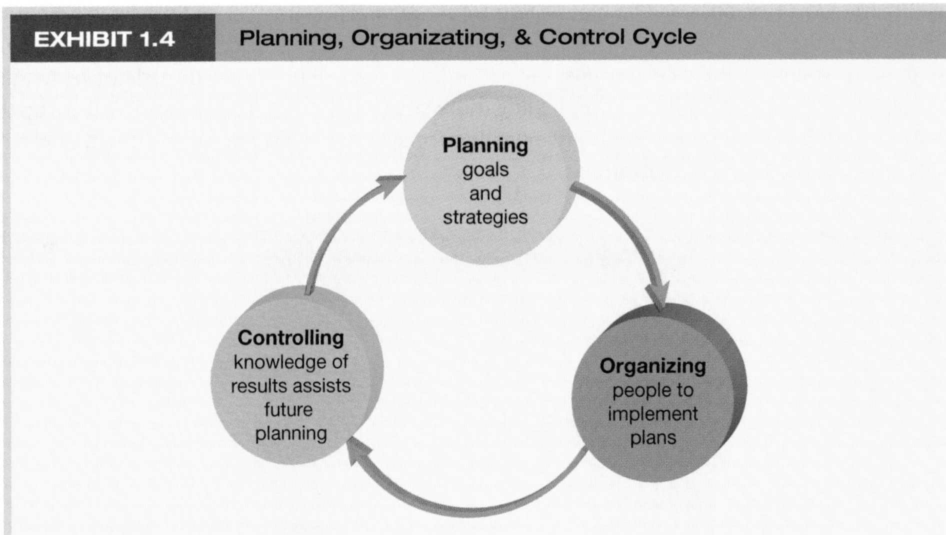

MID-CHAPTER REVIEW

The previous discussion has focused on understanding the difference between financial and managerial accounting and the broader context of managerial accounting within a company.

Required:

Identify the statements and phrases from the following list that are primarily relevant to managerial accounting, as opposed to financial accounting:

1. Preparing periodic financial statements
2. A company's strategic position
3. Calculates earnings per share for stockholders
4. Summarizes information about past events
5. Is not based on generally accepted accounting principles
6. Must conform to external standards
7. Helping managers make decisions is its primary purpose
8. Encourages use of selective data, if relevant
9. Is tailored to the needs of the company and its managers
10. Cost driver analysis

Solution

2, 5, 7, 8, 9, and 10

Competition and Its Key Dimensions

LO3 Discuss the factors determining changes in the nature of business competition.

The move away from isolated national economic systems toward an interdependent global economic system has become increasingly pronounced. International treaties, such as the North American Free Trade Agreement and the General Agreement on Tariffs and Trade, merely recognize an already existing and inevitable condition made possible by advances in telecommunications (to move data), computers (to process data into information), and transportation (to move products and people).

The labels of origins on goods (Japan, Germany, Canada, Taiwan, China, and so forth) only scratch the surface of existing global relationships. Behind labels designating a product's final assembly point are components from all over the world.

The move toward a global economy has heightened competition and reduced selling prices to such an extent that there is little or no room for error in managing costs or pricing products. Moreover, customers are not just looking for the best price. Well-informed buyers routinely search the world for the product or service that best fits their needs on the three interrelated dimensions of price/cost, quality, and service; hence, these are the three key dimensions of competition.

To customers, *price/cost* includes not only the initial purchase price but also subsequent operating and maintenance costs. To compete on the basis of price, the seller must carefully manage costs. Otherwise, reduced prices might squeeze product margins to such an extent that a sale becomes unprofitable. Hence, price competition implies cost competition.

Quality refers to the degree to which products or services meet the customer's needs. *Service* includes things such as timely delivery, helpfulness of sales personnel, and subsequent support. The Business Insight box below takes a look at how Federal Express and United Parcel Service compete on the basis of quality, service, and price.

BUSINESS INSIGHT **FedEx and UPS Stage Battle—Customer Is Sure to Win**

To increase customer service in the express delivery business, Federal Express introduced a personal computer-based system that lets even its smallest customers go online to order pickups, print shipping labels, and track deliveries. "We have to stay ahead of the competition" was the theme of remarks describing this service by FedEx's chief information officer. Almost immediately, United Parcel Service announced a similar service. Responding to a reporter's question, the vice president of marketing at UPS, commented, "There's no question we track FedEx, just like they track us."

Both companies invest heavily in equipment and infrastructure to continue to meet increasingly tight delivery deadlines. This includes sorting hubs for air shipments and investments in new aircraft. FedEx even entered into an arrangement with the U.S. Postal Service to ship some USPS packages while the USPS placed FedEx boxes in selected Post Office buildings. A recent article in *Business Week* reports that UPS gained at least a temporary advantage by utilizing information technology to integrate its traditional strengths in ground transportation with its overnight air transportation system. According to the article, "UPS, like FedEx, still uses planes to make most (overnight) deliveries. But in the past two years, its logisticians have also figured out how to make quick mid-distance deliveries—as far as 500 miles in one night—by truck, which is much less expensive than by air." While both companies battle to improve or at least maintain profitability, customers benefit from continuously improving quality and service at lower and lower costs.[14]

Managers of successful companies know they compete in a global market with instant communications. Because the competition is hungry and always striving to gain a competitive advantage, world-class companies must continuously struggle to improve performance on these three interrelated dimensions: price/cost, quality, and service. Throughout this text, we examine how firms successfully compete on these three dimensions.

[14] Based on David Greising, "Watch Out for Flying Packages," *Business Week* (November 14, 1994), p. 40; and Charles Haddad, "Ground Wars: UPS's Rapid Ascent Leaves FedEx Scrambling," *Business Week*, May 21, 2001.

COST DRIVERS

LO4 Differentiate among structural, organizational, and activity cost drivers.

An **activity** is a unit of work. To serve a customer at a restaurant such as Outback Restaurants, a waiter or waitress might perform the following units of work:

- Seat customer and offer menu
- Take customer order
- Send order to kitchen
- Bring food to customer
- Serve and replenish beverages
- Determine and bring bill to customer
- Collect money and give change
- Clear and reset table

Each of these is an activity, and the performance of each activity consumes resources that cost money. To manage activities and their costs, it is necessary to understand how costs respond to **cost drivers**, which are the factors that cause or influence costs.

The most basic cost driver is customer demand. Without customer demand for products or services, the organization cannot exist. To serve customers, managers and employees make a variety of decisions and take numerous actions. These decisions and actions, undertaken to satisfy customer demand, drive costs. While these cost drivers may be classified in a variety of ways, we believe that dividing them into the three categories of structural, organizational, and activity cost drivers, as summarized in Exhibit 1.5, provides a useful foundation for the study of managerial accounting.

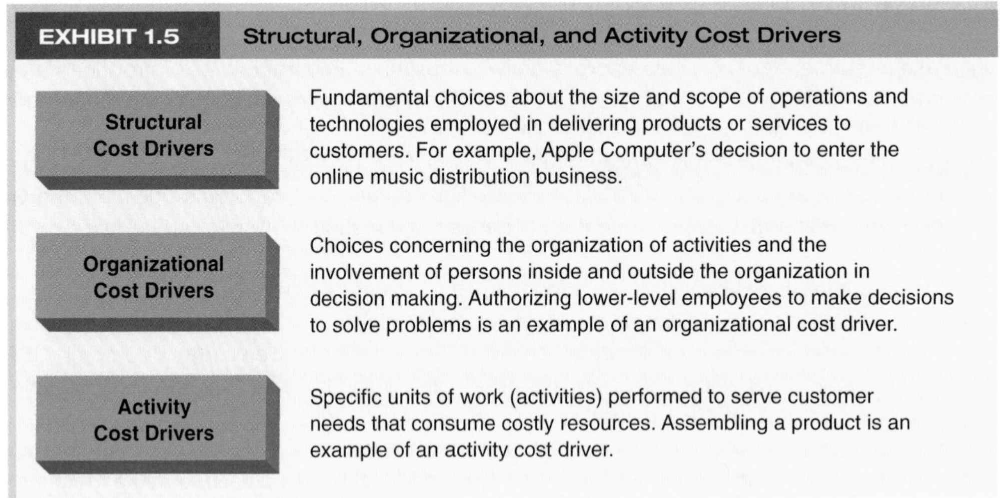

EXHIBIT 1.5 Structural, Organizational, and Activity Cost Drivers
Structural Cost Drivers
Fundamental choices about the size and scope of operations and technologies employed in delivering products or services to customers. For example, Apple Computer's decision to enter the online music distribution business.
Organizational Cost Drivers
Choices concerning the organization of activities and the involvement of persons inside and outside the organization in decision making. Authorizing lower-level employees to make decisions to solve problems is an example of an organizational cost driver.
Activity Cost Drivers
Specific units of work (activities) performed to serve customer needs that consume costly resources. Assembling a product is an example of an activity cost driver.

Structural Cost Drivers

The types of activities and the costs of activities performed to satisfy customer needs are influenced by an organization's size, its location, the scope of its operations, and the technologies used. Decisions affecting structural cost drivers are made infrequently, and once made, the organization is committed to a course of action that will be difficult to change. For a chain of discount stores such as Target, possible structural cost drivers include:

- *Determining the size of stores.* This affects the variety of merchandise that can be carried and operating costs.
- *Determining the type of construction.* While a lean warehouse type of construction is less expensive, it is not an appropriate setting for selling high-fashion clothing.
- *Determining the location of stores.* Locating in a shopping mall can cost more and subject the store to mall regulations but provides for more customer traffic and shared advertising.

- *Determining types of technology to employ in stores.* A computerized system for maintaining all inventory and sales data requires a large initial investment and fixed annual operating costs while providing more current information. However, the computerized inventory and sales systems can be less expensive at high sales volumes than a less costly system relying more on clerks taking physical inventory.

Organizational Cost Drivers

Like structural cost drivers, organizational cost drivers influence costs by affecting the types of activities and the costs of activities performed to satisfy customer needs. Decisions that affect organizational cost drivers are made within the context of previous decisions affecting structural cost drivers. In a manufacturing organization, previous decisions about plant, equipment, and location are taken as a given when decisions impacting organizational cost drivers are made. Examples of organizational cost drivers at a manufacturing organization such as **Harley-Davidson** include making decisions regarding:

- *Working closely with a limited number of suppliers.* This can help achieve proper materials in the proper quantities at the optimal time. Developing linkages with suppliers can also result in suppliers' initiatives that improve the profitability of both organizations.
- *Providing employees with cost information and authorizing them to make decisions.* This helps improve decision speed and reduce costs while making employees more customer oriented. Production employees may, for example, offer product design suggestions that reduce manufacturing costs or reduce defects.
- *Reorganizing the existing equipment in the plant so that sequential operations are closer.* This more efficient layout reduces the cost of moving inventory between workstations.
- *Designing components of a product so they can fit together only in the correct manner.* This can reduce defects as well as assembly time and cost.
- *Manufacturing a low-volume product on low-speed, general-purpose equipment rather than high-speed, special-purpose equipment.* Assuming the special-purpose equipment is more difficult and costly to set up for a new job, this decision can increase operating time and operating cost while reducing setup time and setup cost.

Activity Cost Drivers

Activity cost drivers are specific units of work (activities) performed to serve customer needs that consume costly resources. Several examples of activities in a restaurant were mentioned previously. The customer may be outside the organization, such as a client of an advertising firm, or inside the organization, such as an accounting office that receives maintenance services. Because the performance of activities consumes resources and resources cost money, the performance of activities drives costs.

The basic decisions concerning which available activities will be used to respond to customer requests precede the actual performance of activities. At the activity level, execution of previous plans and following prescribed activities are important. All of the examples of structural and organizational cost drivers involved making decisions. In the following list of activity cost drivers for a manufacturing organization, note the absence of the decision-oriented words.

- *Placing a purchase order for raw materials*
- *Inspecting incoming raw materials*
- *Moving items being manufactured between workstations*
- *Setting up a machine to work on a product*
- *Spending machine time working on a product*
- *Spending labor time working on a product*
- *Hiring and training a new employee*
- *Packing an order for shipment*
- *Processing a sales order*
- *Shipping a product*

In managing costs, management makes choices concerning structural and organizational cost drivers. These decisions affect the types of activities required to satisfy customer needs. Because different types of activities have different costs, management's decisions concerning structural and organizational cost drivers ultimately affect activity costs and profitability. Good decision making at the level of structural and organizational cost drivers requires an understanding of the linkages among the types of cost drivers and the costs of different activities.

MANAGERIAL DECISION **You are the CEO**

How can you use information about structural, organizational, and activity cost drivers to help you in impementing the organization's strategy? [Answer, p. 18]

ETHICS IN MANAGERIAL ACCOUNTING

LO5 Explain the nature of the ethical dilemmas managers and accountants confront.

Ethics deals with the moral quality, fitness, or propriety of a course of action that can injure or benefit people. Ethics goes beyond legality, which refers to what is permitted under the law, to consider the moral quality of an action. Because situations involving ethics are not guided by well-defined rules, they are often subjective.

Although some actions are clearly ethical (working a full day in exchange for a full day's pay) and others are clearly unethical (pumping contaminants into an underground aquifer used as a source of drinking water), managers are often faced with situations that do not fall clearly into either category such as the following:

- Accelerating shipments at the end of the quarter to improve current earnings.
- Keeping inventory that is unlikely to be used so as to avoid recording a loss.
- Purchasing supplies from a relative or friend rather than seeking bids.
- Basing a budget on an overly optimistic sales forecast.
- Assigning some costs of Contract A to Contract B to avoid an unfavorable performance report on Contract A.

Many ethical dilemmas involve actions that are perceived to have desirable short-run consequences and highly probable undesirable long-run consequences. The ethical action is to face an undesirable situation now to avoid a worse situation later, yet the decision maker prefers to believe that things will work out in the long run, be overly concerned with the consequences of not doing well in the short run, or simply not care about the future because the problem will then belong to someone else. In a situation that is clearly unethical, the future consequences are known to be avoidable and undesirable. In situations involving questionable ethics, there is some hope that things will work out:

- Next year's sales will more than make up for the accelerated shipments.
- The obsolete inventory can be used in a new nostalgia line of products.
- The relative or friend may charge more but provides excellent service.
- A desire to have more confidence in the sales staff.
- Making up for the cost shift by working extra hard and more efficiently with the remaining work on Contract B.

When forced to think about the situation, most employees want to act in an ethical manner. The problem faced by personnel involved in measurement and reporting is that while they may question the propriety of a proposed action, and the arguments may be plausible, they want to be team players, and their careers can be affected by "whistle-blowing." Of course, careers are also affected when individuals are identified as being involved in unethical behavior. The careers of people who fail to point out unethical behavior are also affected, especially if they have a responsibility for measurement and reporting.

Major ethical dilemmas often evolve from a series of small compromises, none of which appears serious enough to warrant taking a stand on ethical grounds. **WorldCom** is such a case, in which managers deferred expenses inappropriately over several periods to meet profit forecasts, expecting to recognize them at later time when sales improved. Unfortunately, these small compromises establish a pattern of behavior that is increasingly difficult to reverse. The key to avoiding these situations is recognizing the early warning signs of situations that involve questionable ethical behavior and taking whatever action is appropriate.

Codes of ethics are developed by professional organizations to increase members' awareness of the importance of ethical behavior and to provide a reference point for resisting pressures to engage in actions of questionable ethics. These professional organizations include the American Bar Association, the American Institute of Certified Public Accountants, the American Medical Association, and the Institute of Management Accountants (IMA).

Many corporations have established codes of ethics. General Motors Corporation's code of ethics, "Winning with Integrity" is presented in the following Business Insight box. One of the important goals of corporate codes of ethics is to provide employees with a common foundation for addressing ethical issues. An addendum to its code of ethics, a basic rule of thumb used by General Motors is that employees should never do anything they would be ashamed to explain to their families or to see in the front page of the local newspaper.

BUSINESS INSIGHT **GM Code of Ethics: "Winning with Integrity":**

- GM hires, promotes, trains and pays based on merit, experience, or other work-related criteria and strives to create work environments that accept and tolerate differences while promoting productivity and teamwork.
- GM endeavors to protect the health and safety of each employee by creating and maintaining a healthy, injury-free work environment.
- All GM employees have an obligation to protect GM's assets, including information, and to ensure their proper use.
- Providing false or misleading information in any GM business record is strictly prohibited.
- As a general rule, GM employees should accept no gift, entertainment, or other gratuity from any supplier to GM or bidder for GM's business.
- GM employees must immediately disclose any situation that could result in an actual or potential conflict of interest, involving the employee or any member of his household, such as investing in a supplier, dealer, customer, or competitor.
- GM and all its employees must comply with all laws, including the U.S. Foreign Corrupt Practices Act, competition laws, and export control laws.
- To protect GM's reputation for integrity, it must communicate clearly and accurately to the public.[15]

CHAPTER-END REVIEW

Classify each of the following as a structural, organizational, or activity cost driver.

a. Meals served to airplane passengers aboard Northwest Airlines.
b. General Motors' decision to manufacture the Saturn® automobile in completely new facilities.
c. Zenith's decision to sell its computer operations and focus on the core television business.
d. Number of tax returns filed electronically by H&R Block.
e. Number of passenger cars in a Via train.
f. Coors' decision to expand its market area east from the Rocky Mountains.
g. Boeing's decision to invite airlines to assist in designing the model 777 airplane.
h. DaimlerChrysler's decision to use cross-disciplinary teams to design a new automobile.
i. St.Jude Hospital's decision to establish review committees on the appropriateness and effectiveness of medical procedures for improving patient care.
j. Harley-Davidson's efforts to restructure production procedures to reduce inventories and machine setup times.

---

[15] http://www.gm.com/corporate/responsibility/reports/05/300_company/3_thirty/331.html.

Solution

a. Activity cost driver
b. Structural cost driver
c. Structural cost driver
d. Activity cost driver
e. Activity cost driver
f. Structural cost driver
g. Organizational cost driver
h. Organizational cost driver
i. Organizational cost driver
j. Organizational cost driver

GUIDANCE ANSWER

MANAGERIAL DECISION **You are the CEO**

It is important that an organization's cost structure be aligned with its strategy. If your goal is to be a cost leader (such as Wal-Mart or Costco), you will want to make sure that the structural cost drivers, such as the type of buildings acquired and the displays used are consistent with this strategy. As the CEO of Wal-Mart you would not permit many of the costs that would be incurred in an organization such as Tiffany or Nordstrom.

DISCUSSION QUESTIONS

Q1-1. Contrast financial and managerial accounting on the basis of user orientation, purpose of information, level of aggregation, length of time period, orientation toward past or future, conformance to external standards, and emphasis on objective data.

Q1-2. What three themes are a part of strategic cost management?

Q1-3. Distinguish between a mission and a goal.

Q1-4. Describe the three strategic positions that Porter views as leading to business success.

Q1-5. Distinguish between how managerial accounting would support the strategy of cost leadership and the strategy of product differentiation.

Q1-6. Why are the phases of planning, organizing, and controlling referred to as a *continuous cycle*?

Q1-7. Identify three advances that have fostered the move away from isolated national economic systems toward an interdependent global economy.

Q1-8. What are the three interrelated dimensions of today's competition?

Q1-9. Differentiate among structural, organizational, and activity cost drivers.

Q1-10. What is the link between performing activities and incurring costs?

Q1-11. How can top management establish an ethical tone in an organization?

Q1-12. Describe how pressures to have desirable short-run outcomes can lead to ethical dilemmas.

MINI EXERCISES

M1-13. Management Accounting Terminology (LO1-5)
Match the following terms with the best descriptions. Each description is used only once.

Terms

1. Ethics
2. Mission
3. Controlling
4. Goal
5. Not-for-profit organization
6. Quality
7. Balance sheet
8. Income statement
9. Organizational cost driver
10. Financial accounting
11. Activity cost driver
12. Structural cost driver
13. Managerial accounting
14. Resources
15. Product differentiation

Description

a. Designing components so they are easily assembled
b. The Starlight Foundation raising money to grant wishes for terminally ill children
c. Prepared as of a point in time
d. Accounting for external users
e. Increase year 2008 sales by 10 percent over year 2007 sales
f. Shows the results of operations for a period of time
g. Packing an order for shipment
h. Deciding to build a factory away from a highway but near a railroad
i. The degree to which a new television meets a buyer's expectations
j. Used internally to make decisions
k. Consumed by activities
l. The propriety of taking some action
m. Reduces customer price sensitivity
n. Basic purpose toward which activities are directed
o. Comparing the budget with the actual results

M1-14. Financial and Managerial Accounting (LO1)

Indicate whether each phrase is more descriptive of financial accounting or managerial accounting.

a. May be subjective
b. Often used to state corporate goals
c. Typically prepared quarterly or annually
d. May measure time or customer satisfaction
e. Future oriented
f. Subject to cost-benefit analysis
g. Keeps records of assets and liabilities
h. Highly aggregated statements
i. Must conform to external standards
j. Special-purpose reports
k. Decision-making tool
l. Income statement, balance sheet, and statement of cash flows

M1-15. Missions, Goals, and Strategies (LO2)

Identify each of the following as a mission, goal, or strategy.

a. Budget time for study, sleep, and relaxation
b. Provide shelter for the homeless
c. Provide an above-average return to investors
d. Protect the public
e. Locate fire stations so that the average response time is less than five minutes
f. Overlap police patrols so that there are always police cars on major thoroughfares
g. Achieve a 12 percent market share
h. Lower prices and costs
i. Select the most scenic route to drive between Las Vegas and Denver
j. Graduate from college

M1-16. Line and Staff Organization (LO2)

Presented are the names of several departments often found in a merchandising organization such as Kohl's Department Store.

Kohl's Department Store (KSS)

a. Maintenance
b. Home Furnishings
c. Store Manager
d. Payroll
e. Human Resources
f. Advertising

Required

Identify each as a line or a staff department.

M1-17. Line and Staff Organization (LO2)

Presented are the names of several departments often found in a manufacturing organization such as Kimberly-Clark.

Kimberly-Clark (KMB)

a. Manager, Plant 2
b. Design Engineering
c. President
d. Controller
e. Property Accounting
f. Sales Manager, District 1

Required

Identify each as a line or a staff department.

M1-18. Classifying Cost Drivers (LO4)

Classify each of the following as structural, organizational, or activity cost drivers.

a. Oneida Silversmiths reorganizes production facilities from a layout in which all similar types of machines are grouped together to one in which a set of machines is designated for the production of a particular product and that set of machines is grouped together.

b. A cable television company decides to start offering telephone service.

Xerox Corporation (XRX)

c. Xerox Corporation decides to stop making personal computers.

Canon (CAJ)

d. Canon decides to start making high-volume photocopy equipment to compete head-to-head with Xerox.

e. The number of meals a cafeteria serves.

f. The number of miles a taxi is driven.

g. A company eliminates the position of supervisor and has each work group elect a team leader.

Toyota (TM)

h. Toyota empowers employees to halt production if a quality problem is identified.

i. The number of tons of grain a ship loads.

j. Crossgate Mall decides to build space for 80 additional stores.

M1-19. Classifying Cost Drivers (LO4)

Mesa Construction managers provide design and construction management services for various commercial construction projects. Senior managers are trying to apply cost driver concepts to their firm to better understand Mesa's costs.

Required

Classify each of the following actions or decisions as structural, organizational, or activity cost drivers.

a. The decision to be a leader in computer-assisted design services.

b. The decision to allow staff architects to follow a specific project through to completion.

c. The daily process of inspecting the progress on various construction projects.

d. The process of conducting extensive client interviews to assess the exact needs for Mesa services.

e. The decision to expand the market area by establishing an office in another state.

f. The decision to begin building projects with Mesa staff rather than relying on subcontractors.

g. The process of receiving approval from government authorities along with appropriate permits for each project.

h. The decision to organize the workforce into project teams.

i. The decision to build a new headquarters facility with areas for design and administration as well as storage and maintenance of construction equipment.

j. The process of grading building sites and preparing forms for foundations.

EXERCISES

E1-20. Financial and Managerial Accounting (LO1)

Procter & Gamble (PG)

Assume Michelle Jones has just been promoted to product manager at Procter & Gamble. Although she is an accomplished sales representative and well versed in market research, her accounting background is limited to reviewing her paycheck, balancing her checkbook, filing income tax returns, and reviewing the company's annual income statement and balance sheet. She commented that while the financial statements are no doubt useful to investors, she just doesn't see how accounting can help her be a good product manager.

Required

Based on her remarks, it is apparent that Michelle's view of accounting is limited to financial accounting. Explain some of the important differences between financial and managerial accounting and suggest some ways managerial accounting can help Michelle be a better product manager.

E1-21. Developing an Organization Chart (LO1)

Develop an organization chart for a three-outlet bakery chain with a central baking operation and deliveries every few hours. Assume the business is incorporated and that the president has a single staff assistant. Also assume that the delivery truck driver reports to the bakery manager.

E1-22. Identifying Monetary and Nonmonetary Performance Measures (LO2)

Identify possible monetary and nonmonetary performance measures for each of the following situations. One nonmonetary measure should relate to quality, and one should relate to time.

Cornell University

a. Cornell University wishes to evaluate the success of last year's graduating class.

Cook County Hospital

b. Cook County Hospital wishes to evaluate the performance of its emergency room.

c. L.L. Bean wishes to evaluate the performance of its telephone order–filling operations. L.L. Bean

d. Hilton Hotels wishes to evaluate the performance of registration activities at one of its hotels. Hilton Hotels (HLT)

e. United Parcel Service wishes to evaluate the success of its operations in Knoxville. United Parcel Service (UPS)

E1-23. Identifying Monetary and Nonmonetary Performance Measures (LO2)

Identify possible monetary and nonmonetary performance measures for each of the following situations. One nonmonetary measure should relate to quality, and one should relate to time.

a. AOL's evaluation of the performance of its Internet service in Huntsville. AOL

b. Time Warner Cable's evaluation of the performance of new customer cable installations in Rochester. Time Warner Cable (TWTC)

c. Dell Computer's evaluation of the performance of its logistical arrangements for delivering computers to residential customers. Dell Computer (DELL)

d. Amazon.com's evaluation of the performance of its Web site. Amazon.com (AMZN)

e. Emory University's evaluation of the success of its freshman admissions activities. Emory University

E1-24. Identifying Information Needs of Different Managers (LO2)

Jerry Damson operates a number of auto dealerships for Acura and Honda. Identify possible monetary and nonmonetary performance measures for each of the following situations. One nonmonetary measure should relate to quality, and one should relate to time. Acura Honda (HMC)

a. An individual sales associate.

b. The sales manager of a single dealership.

c. The general manager of a particular dealership.

d. The corporate chief financial officer.

e. The president of the corporation.

E1-25. Activities and Cost Drivers (LO4)

For each of the following activities, select the most appropriate cost driver. Each cost driver may be used only once.

Activity		Cost Driver
1. Pay vendors	*a.*	Number of different kinds of raw materials
2. Evaluate vendors	*b.*	Number of classes offered
3. Inspect raw materials	*c.*	Number of tables
4. Plan for purchases of raw materials	*d.*	Number of employees
5. Packaging	*e.*	Number of operating hours
6. Supervision	*f.*	Number of units of raw materials received
7. Employee training	*g.*	Number of new customers
8. Clean tables	*h.*	Number of vendors
9. Machine maintenance	*i.*	Number of checks issued
10. Opening accounts at a bank	*j.*	Number of customer orders

CASES

C1-26. Goals and Strategies (LO2)

a. What is your instructor's goal for students in this course? What strategies has he or she developed to achieve this goal?

b. What is your goal in this course? What strategies will help you achieve this goal?

c. What is your goal for this semester or term? What strategies will help you achieve this goal?

d. What is your employment goal? What strategies will help you achieve this goal?

C1-27. Product Differentiation (LO3)

You are the owner of Lobster's Limited. You have no trouble catching lobsters, but you have difficulty in selling all that you catch. The problem is that all lobsters from all vendors look the same. You do catch high-quality lobsters, but you need to be able to tell your customers that your lobsters are better than those sold by other vendors.

Required

a. What are some possible ways of distinguishing your lobsters from those of other vendors?

b. Explain the possible results of this differentiation.

C1-28. Ethics and Short-Term Borrowing (LO5)

Ethel, a secretary, is in charge of petty cash for a local law firm. Normally, about $200 is kept in the petty cash box. When Ethel is short on cash and needs some for lunch or to pay her babysitter, she sometimes takes a few dollars from the box. Since she is in charge of the box, nobody knows that she takes the money, and she always replaces it within a few days.

Required

a. Is Ethel's behavior ethical?

b. Assume that Ethel has recently had major problems meeting her bills. She also is in charge of purchasing supplies for the office from petty cash. Last week when she needed $12 for the babysitter, she falsified a voucher for the amount of $12. Is this behavior ethical?

C1-29. Ethics and Travel Reimbursement (LO5)

Scott takes many business trips throughout the year. All of his expenses are paid by his company. Last week he traveled to Rio De Janeiro, Brazil, and stayed there on business for five days. He is allowed a maximum of $28 per day for food and $100 per day for lodging. To his surprise, the food and accommodations in Brazil were much less than he expected. Being upset about traveling last week and having to sacrifice tickets he'd purchased to a Red Sox baseball game, he decided to inflate his expenses a bit. He increased his lodging expense from $50 per day to $75 per day and his food purchased from $10 per day to $20 per day. Therefore, for the five-day trip, he overstated his expenses by $175 total. After all, the allowance was higher than the amount he spent.

Required

Assume that the company would never find out that he had actually spent less. Are Scott's actions ethical? Are they acceptable?

C1-30. Ethics and False Claims Act (LO5)

The U.S. Government passed the Federal False Claims Act to encourage persons to bring forward evidence of fraudulent charges on government contracts. Under the provisions of the Act, whistle-blowers receive up to 25 percent of any money recovered as a result of evidence they bring forth. To date, the largest settlement under the terms of the Act was a $7.5 million reward to a former employee of a defense contractor who filed a suit after leaving his former employer to accept a position as a price analyst for the Department of Defense.

Required

Evaluate the likely impact of the Federal False Claims Act on corporations doing business with the U.S. government. Do you believe the Act is a good idea?

C1-31. Costs and Ethics of Unlimited Returns (LO5)

Is it possible to have too much emphasis on pleasing final customers? Many manufacturers of consumer electronics argue that the answer is yes. Many firms comment that there is an escalation of problems with returns, and they think of this as a joint problem of consumer and retailer ethics. Some companies are unhappy with the product return policies of some discount retail stores that guarantee a full refund, no questions asked, any time a product is returned, no matter how long since the date of purchase.

Generous return policies have resulted in televisions being returned the Monday after a Superbowl, camcorders being returned shortly after a wedding, and radar detectors being returned after a long trip. One supplier complained about receiving a two-year-old cordless telephone (that had obviously been chewed by a dog) from a retailer who gave the customer a complete refund. Thus, many returns to small manufacturers are not related to defective products.

In an attempt to reduce returns, many small companies are opening customer assistance phone numbers to supply the kind of technical expertise that is not available from sales personnel at discount stores. But, according to one expert, the cost of customer assistance services will ultimately be passed along to customers in the form of higher prices.

Required

a. Does an unlimited return policy pose an ethical problem? Is it unethical to buy a product with the intention of returning it? Is it unethical to return a product that has been subject to abuse?

b. Over an extended period of time, what are the likely consequences of unlimited returns on small manufacturers, small retail stores, large manufacturers, discount superstores, and customers?

C1-32 Ethical Issues with Supplier-Buyer Partnerships (LO5)

John Snyder was excited to learn of his appointment as Circuit Electronics Corporation's new vendor sales representative to Household Appliance, Inc. For the past four years, Circuit Electronics has supplied all of the electric switches used in Household's washers and dryers. As Circuit Electronics' vendor sales representative, John Snyder's job involves the following tasks.

1. Working with Household engineers to design electric switches that can be manufactured to meet Household's cost and quality requirements.
2. Assisting Household in resolving any problems related to electric switches.

3. Monitoring the inventory levels of electric switches at Household and placing orders for additional switches when appropriate.

This appointment will require John to move to Stutgart, Germany, for two years. Although John has mixed feelings about the move, he is familiar with the success of the program in improving Circuit Electronics' financial performance. He is also very much aware of the fact that the two previous vendor sales representatives received promotions at the end of their appointments.

As John toured the Household factory in Stutgart with his predecessor, Janet Smith, his excitement turned to concern. It became apparent that Circuit Electronics had not been supplying Household with the best available switches at the lowest possible costs. Although the switches were adequate, they were more likely to wear out after five or six years of use than would switches currently on the market (and being used by Household's competitors). Furthermore, when the switches in transit by ship from North America to Europe were counted, it also appeared that the inventory level of electric switches would soon be more than enough to satisfy Household's needs for the next four months.

Required

If you were John, what would you do?

C1-33. Expected Values of Questionable Decisions **(LO5)**

The members of the jury had to make a decision in a lawsuit brought by the State of Alabama against Exxon Mobil. The suit revolved around natural-gas wells that Exxon drilled in state-owned waters. After signing several leases obligating Exxon to share revenues with Alabama, company officials started questioning the terms of the agreement that prohibited deducting several types of processing costs before paying the state royalties.

Exxon Mobil (XOM)

During the course of the trial, a memo by an in-house attorney of Exxon Mobil came to light. The memo noted that Royal Dutch/Shell, which had signed a similar lease, interpreted it "in the same manner as the state." The memo then presented arguments the company might use to claim the deduction, estimated the probability of the arguments being successful (less than 50 percent), and proceeded to consider whether Exxon should obey the law using a cost-benefit analysis. According to the memo, "If we adopt anything beyond a 'safe' approach, we should anticipate a quick audit and subsequent litigation." The memo also observed that "our exposure is 12 percent interest on underpayments calculated from the due date, and the cost of litigation." Deducting the questionable costs did, indeed, result in an audit and a lawsuit. Source: *Business Week.*[16]

Royal Dutch/Shell (RDS-B)

Required

If you were a member of the jury, what would you do? Why?

C1-34. Management Decisions Affecting Cost Drivers **(LO4)**

An avid bicycle rider, you have decided to use an inheritance to start a new business to sell and repair bicycles. Two college friends have already accepted offers to work for you.

Required

a. What is the mission of your new business?
b. Suggest a strategic positioning goal you might strive for to compete with area hardware and discount stores that sell bicycles.
c. Identify two items that might be long-range goals.
d. Identify two items that might be goals for the coming year.
e. Mention two decisions that will be structural cost drivers.
f. Mention two decisions that will be organizational cost drivers.
g. Identify two activity cost drivers.

C1-35. Success Factors and Performance Measurement **(LO2)**

Three years ago, Vincent Chow completed his college degree. The economy was in a depressed state at the time, and Vincent managed to get an offer of only $35,000 per year as a bookkeeper. In addition to its relatively low pay, this job had limited advancement potential. Since Vincent was an enterprising and ambitious young man, he instead started a business of his own. He was convinced that because of changing lifestyles, a drive-through coffee establishment would be profitable. He was able to obtain backing from his parents to open such an establishment close to the industrial park area in town. Vincent named his business The Cappuccino Express and decided to sell only two types of coffee: cappuccino and decaffeinated.

As Vincent had expected, The Cappuccino Express was very well received. Within three years, Vincent had added another outlet north of town. He left the day-to-day management of each site to a manager and turned his attention toward overseeing the entire enterprise. He also hired an assistant to do the record keeping and other selected chores.[17]

---

[16] Mike France, "When Big Oil Gets Too Slick," *Business Week,* April 9, 2001, p. 70.

[17] Based on Chee W. Chow, "Instructional Case: Vincent's Cappuccino Express—A Teaching Case to Help Students Master Basic Cost Terms and Concepts Through Interactive Learning," *Issues in Accounting Education,* Spring 1995, pp. 173–190.

Required

a. Develop an organization chart for The Cappuccino Express.

b. What factors can be expected to have a major impact on the success of The Cappuccino Express?

c. What major tasks must Vincent undertake in managing The Cappuccino Express?

d. What are the major costs of operating The Cappuccino Express?

e. Vincent would like to monitor the performance of each site manager. What measure(s) of performance should he use?

f. If you suggested more than one measure, which of these should Vincent select if he could use only one?

g. Suppose that last year, the original site had yielded total revenues of $146,000, total costs of $120,000, and hence, a profit of $26,000. Vincent had judged this profit performance to be satisfactory. For the coming year, Vincent expects that due to factors such as increased name recognition and demographic changes, the total revenues will increase by 20 percent to $175,200. What amount of profit should he expect from the site? Discuss the issues involved in developing an estimate of profit.

Chapter 2

Cost Behavior, Activity Analysis, and Cost Estimation

LEARNING OBJECTIVES

LO1 Identify basic patterns of how costs respond to changes in activity cost drivers. (p. 28)

LO2 Determine a linear cost estimating equation. (p. 35)

LO3 Identify and discuss problems encountered in cost estimation. (p. 40)

LO4 Describe and develop alternative classifications for activity cost drivers. (p. 41)

GLOBAL SOURCING LEADS TO COST LEADERSHIP, PRICE LEADERSHIP, AND SALES LEADERSHIP

In the second quarter of 2007, little known Vizio of Irvine, California, sold more than 600,000 television sets in North America making it the market leader in the U.S. with 12 percent market share. Samsung, the former market leader, moved to second place with 11 percent of the market. How did Visio, a firm founded in 2003, manage to overtake a well established company such as Samsung and do it in such a short period of time?

According to Vizio CEO, William Wang, the answer is by being low-cost, which allows the company to underprice competitors. Commenting on Vizio's strong 2007 performance, Riddhi Patel, an analyst with iSuppli, observed that consumers with a $1,000 budget "could probably buy a premium brand 32- or 37- inch, or they could buy a Vizio 47-inch for the same amount."

According to a story in *USA Today*, Vizio's success is an example of the global character of a streamlined enterprise. With just 85 employees in the United States and only a small number in other countries, Vizio does no manufacturing. Instead, it uses carefully coordinated suppliers from around the world. One of its products contains an LCD panel from South Korea, electronic components from China, and processors from the United

Courtesy of Wal-Mart

States with final assembly in Mexico. This strategy allows Visio to operate without major investments in plant and equipment and all the associated costs that do not vary with volume. Instead, they negotiate for the best volume-based prices with contract manufacturers.

To further contain costs to the final consumer, Vizio engages in almost no advertising (their 2007 advertising budget was $35 million with sales approaching $1 billion), and primarily sells televisions through retailers such as Costo and Sam's Clubs that seek a 10 percent gross margin, rather than the more typical 25 percent.

Although analyst such as Patel believe Vizio has a quality product, Ross Young, President of Display Sear, notes that, "A Vizio set isn't likely to have the latest features, the most sophisticated signal-processing chips, or cutting-edge high-resolution."

In analyzing Vizio's success, it is apparent that the firm is following a cost leadership strategy. Such a strategy necessarily requires a thorough understanding of cost behavior, the topic of this chapter. What's more, firms such as Samsung must manage their costs to ensure their price premium remains acceptable to customers while they compete on the basis of quality or leadership in product features valued by consumers. The common theme for both types of firms is that a detailed knowledge of cost behavior is a key to their success.[1] In this chapter, we develop an understanding of cost behavior

[1] Based on: David J. Lynch, "Flat-panel TVs Display Effects of Globalization," *USA Today*, 1B-2B, May 8, 2007; Michelle Kessler, "Vizio's Unexpected Flat-Panel King, *USA Today*, August 21, 2007; Erica Ogg and Michael Kanellos, "The Secret of Vizio's Success, *c/net News.com*, August 20, 2007; Moon Ihlwan, "Will LCD TV's follow the PC Model?" *Business Week*, August 23, 2007

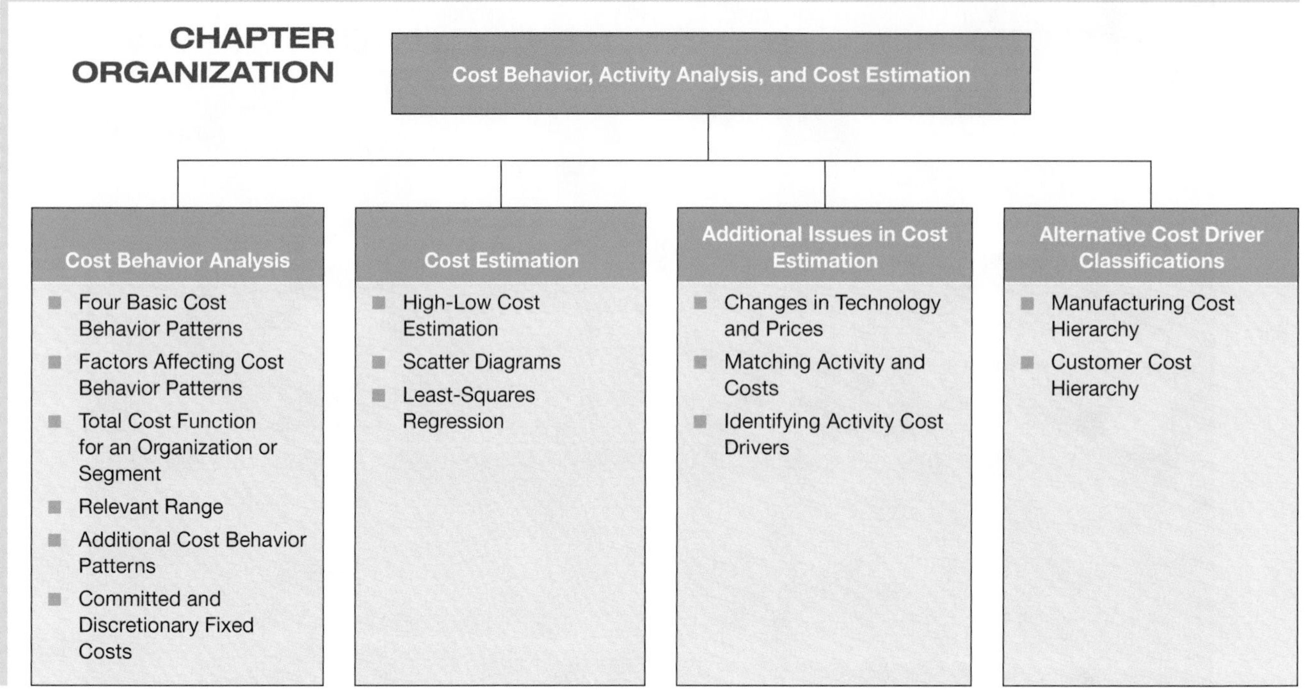

COST BEHAVIOR ANALYSIS

This chapter introduces **cost behavior**, which refers to the relationship between a given cost item and the quantity of its related cost driver. Cost behavior, therefore, explains how the total amount for various costs respond to changes in activity volume. Understanding cost behavior is essential for estimating future costs. In this chapter we examine several typical cost behavior patterns and methods for developing cost equations that are useful for predicting future costs.

Four Basic Cost Behavior Patterns

LO1 Identify basic patterns of how costs respond to changes in activity cost drivers.

Although there are an unlimited number of ways that costs can respond to changes in cost drivers, as a starting point it is useful to classify cost behavior into four categories: variable, fixed, mixed, and step. Graphs of each are presented in Exhibit 2.1. Observe that total cost (the dependent variable) is measured on the vertical axis, and total activity for the time period (the independent variable) is measured on the horizontal axis.

1. **Variable costs** change in total in direct proportion to changes in activity. Their total amount increases as activity increases, equaling zero dollars when activity is zero and increasing at a constant amount per unit of activity. The higher the variable cost per unit of activity, the steeper the slope of the line representing total cost. With the number of pizzas served as the activity cost driver for Pizza Hut restaurants, the cost of cheese is an example of a variable cost.
2. **Fixed costs** do not change in response to a change in activity volume. Hence, a line representing total fixed costs is flat with a slope (incline) of zero. With the number of Pizza Hut pizzas sold as the cost driver, annual depreciation, property taxes, and property insurance are examples of fixed costs. While fixed costs may respond to structural and organizational cost drivers over time, they do not respond to short-run changes in activity cost drivers.
3. **Mixed costs** (sometimes called **semivariable costs**) contain a fixed and a variable cost element. Total mixed costs are positive (like fixed costs) when activity is zero, and they increase in a linear fashion (like total variable costs) as activity increases. With the number of pizzas sold as the cost driver, the cost of electric power is an example of a mixed cost. Some electricity is required to provide basic lighting, while an increasing amount of electricity is required to prepare food as the number of pizzas served increases.
4. **Step costs** are constant within a narrow range of activity but shift to a higher level when activity exceeds the range. Total step costs increase in a steplike fashion as activity increases. With the number

EXHIBIT 2.1 Cost Behavior Patterns

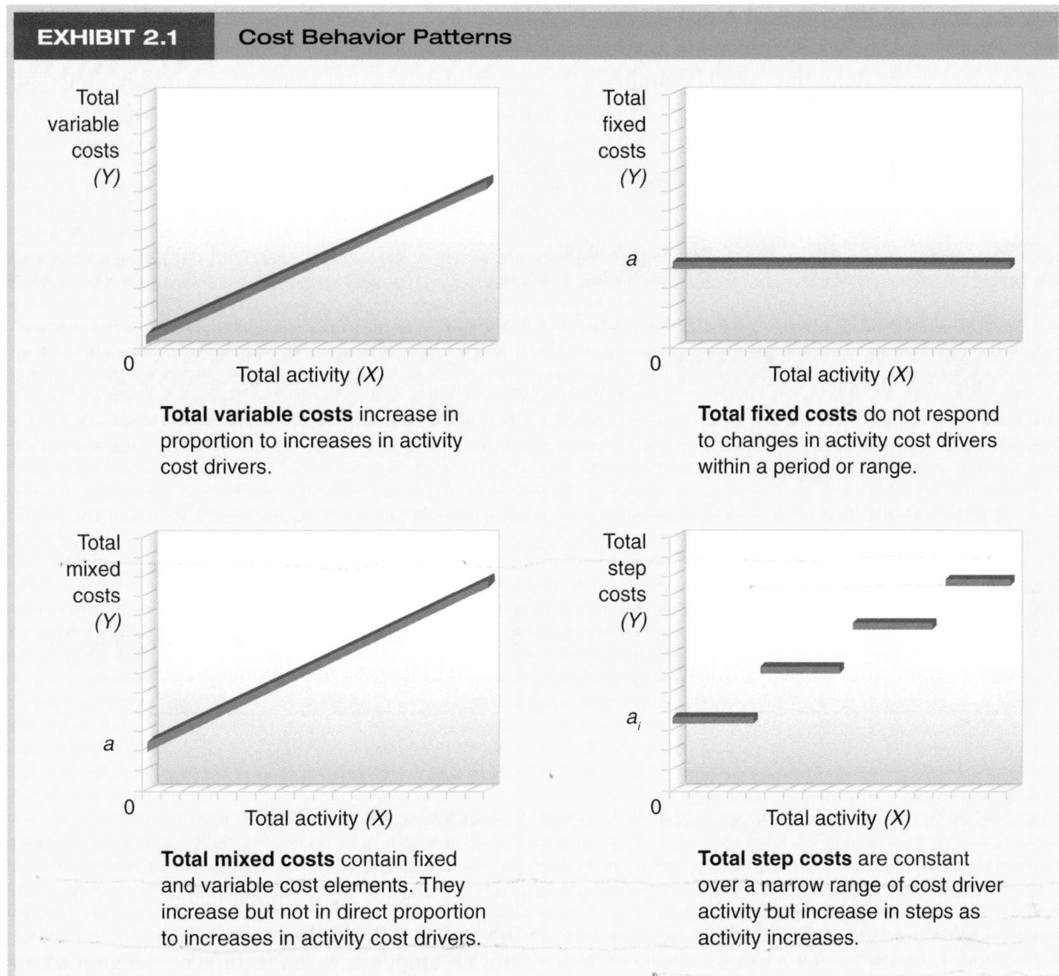

Total variable costs increase in proportion to increases in activity cost drivers.

Total fixed costs do not respond to changes in activity cost drivers within a period or range.

Total mixed costs contain fixed and variable cost elements. They increase but not in direct proportion to increases in activity cost drivers.

Total step costs are constant over a narrow range of cost driver activity but increase in steps as activity increases.

of pizzas served as the cost driver, employee wages is an example of a step cost. Up to a certain number of pizzas, only a small staff needs to be on duty. Beyond that number, additional employees are needed for quality service and so forth.

The relationship between total cost (*Y* axis) and total activity (*X* axis) for the four cost behavior patterns is mathematically expressed as follows:

Variable cost: Y = bX

where

b = the variable cost per unit, sometimes referred to as the slope of the cost function.

Fixed cost: Y = a

where

a = total fixed costs. The slope of the fixed cost function is zero because fixed costs do not change with activity.

Mixed cost: Y = a + bX

where

a = total fixed cost element
b = variable cost element per unit of activity.

Step cost: $Y = a_i$

where

a_i = the step cost within a specific range of activity, identified by the subscript i.

The total cost function of most organizations has shifted in recent years toward more fixed costs and fewer variable costs, making it increasingly important for organizations to manage their fixed costs. Some organizations have done this by outsourcing activities rather than performing the activities internally. This avoids the many fixed costs of infrastructure in exchange for a variable cost per unit of activity. The Business Insight box below considers how an alliance between the United States Postal Service and Federal Express (FedEx) helps keep down the cost of postage by shifting fixed costs.

BUSINESS INSIGHT **Alliance Alters USPS Cost Structure**

"The Postal Service delivers Main Street, and FedEx provides an air fleet," proclaimed the Postmaster General when announcing an alliance between the United States Postal Service (USPS) and FedEx. Under terms of the alliance, FedEx transports express mail, priority mail, and some first-class mail on its fleet of over 650 aircraft. The projected costs to the USPS are approximately $6.3 billion over the seven-year contract period. FedEx will also locate overnight service collection boxes at selected post offices across the United States.

It is predicted that USPS will save a billion dollars in transportation costs over the life of the contract. A major aspect of the alliance is that it moves USPS from a fixed-cost transportation network toward a variable cost network. "This is a unique opportunity to turn some fixed costs into variable costs," said the president of the Association for Postal Commerce. "It is using someone else's fixed costs." The chairman and chief executive officer of FedEx added that the system allows "the Postal Service to grow unconstrained without having to put in big [transportation] networks."[2]

Factors Affecting Cost Behavior Patterns

The four cost behavior patterns presented are based on the fundamental assumption that a unit of final output is the primary cost driver. The implications of this assumption are examined later in this chapter.

Another important assumption is that the time period is too short to incorporate changes in strategic cost drivers such as the scale of operations. Although this assumption is useful for short-range planning, for the purpose of developing plans for extended time periods, it is more appropriate to consider possible variations in one or more strategic cost drivers. When this is done, many costs otherwise classified as fixed are better classified as variable.

Even the cost of depreciable assets can be viewed as variable if the time period is long enough. Assuming that the number of pizzas served is the cost driver, for a single month the depreciation on all Pizza Hut restaurants in the world is a fixed cost. Over several years, if sales are strong, a strategic decision will be made to open additional restaurants; if sales are weak, strategic decisions will likely be made to close some restaurants. Hence, over a multiple-year period, the number of restaurants varies with sales volume, making depreciation appear as a variable cost with sales revenue as the cost driver.

Total Cost Function for an Organization or Segment

To obtain a general understanding of an organization, to compare the cost structures of different organizations, or to perform preliminary planning activities, managers are often interested in how total costs respond to a single measure of overall activity such as units sold or sales revenue. This overview can be useful, but presenting all costs as a function of a single cost driver is seldom accurate enough to support decisions concerning products, services, or activities. Doing so implies that all of an organization's costs can be manipulated by changing a single cost driver. This is seldom true.

In developing a total cost function, the independent variable usually represents some measure of the goods or services provided customers, such as total student credit hours in a university, total sales revenue in a store, total guest-days in a hotel, or total units manufactured in a factory. The resulting cost function is illustrated in Exhibit 2.2.

[2] "USPS-FedEx Alliance Could Save $1 Billion in Transportation Costs," *Federal Times*, January 15, 2001, p. 4.

EXHIBIT 2.2 Total Cost Behavior

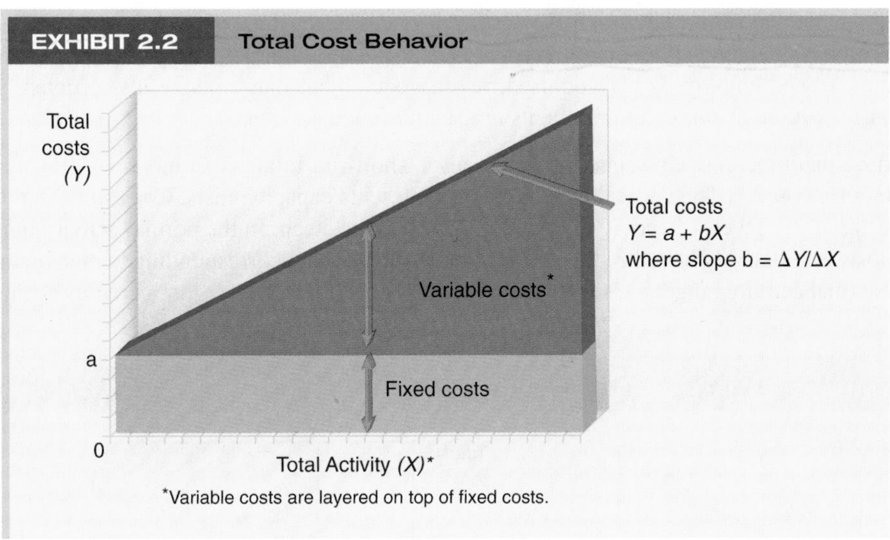

*Variable costs are layered on top of fixed costs.

The equation for total costs is:

$$\mathbf{Y = a + bX}$$

(Also Mix Cost see p. 29)

where

Y = total costs
a = vertical axis intercept (an approximation of fixed costs)
b = slope (an approximation of variable costs per unit of X)
X = value of independent variable

In situations where the variable, fixed, and mixed costs, and the related cost functions, can be determined, a total cost equation can be useful in predicting future costs for various activity levels. However, generally, a total cost equation is useful for predicting costs in only a limited range of activity. The **relevant range** of a total cost equation is that portion of the range associated with the fixed cost of the current or expected capacity. For example, assume that a **Dairy Queen** ice cream shop's only fixed cost is the depreciation on its ice cream making machines, and that it is able to produce a maximum of 50 gallons of ice cream per day with a single ice cream making machine. If it has four machines in operation, and if it can readily adjust its fixed capacity cost by increasing or decreasing the number of ice cream machines, the relevant range of activity for the shop's current total cost equation is 151 to 200 gallons. In the future, if the shop expects to operate at more than 200 gallons per day, the current total cost equation would not predict total cost accurately, because fixed costs would have to be increased for additional machines. Conversely, if it expects to operate at 150 gallons or less, it may reduce the number of machines in the shop, thereby reducing total fixed costs.

Relevant Range

The use of straight lines in accounting models of cost behavior assumes a linear relationship between cost and activity with each additional unit of activity accompanied by a uniform increment in total cost. This uniform increment is known as the *variable cost of one unit*.

Economic models show a nonlinear relationship between cost and activity with each incremental unit of activity being accompanied by a varying increment in total cost. Economists identify the varying increment in total cost as the **marginal cost** *of one unit*.

It is useful to relate marginal costs to the following three levels of activity:

1. *Below the activity range for which the facility was designed*, the existence of excess capacity results in relatively high marginal costs. Having extra time, employees complete assignments at a leisurely pace, increasing the time and the cost to produce each unit above what it would be if employees were more pressed to complete work. Frequent starting and stopping of equipment may also add to costs.
2. *Within the activity range for which the facility was designed*, activities take place under optimal circumstances and marginal costs are relatively low.

3. *Above the activity range for which the facility was designed,* the existence of capacity constraints again results in relatively high marginal costs. Near capacity, employees may be paid overtime wages, less-experienced employees may be used, regular equipment may operate less efficiently, and old equipment with high energy requirements may be placed in service.

Based on marginal cost concepts, the economists' short-run total cost function is illustrated in the first graph in Exhibit 2.3. The vertical axis intercept represents capacity costs. Corresponding to the high marginal costs at low levels of activity, the initial slope is quite steep. In the normal activity range, where marginal costs are relatively low, the slope becomes less steep. Then, corresponding to high marginal costs above the normal activity range, the slope of the economists' total cost function increases again.

EXHIBIT 2.3 Economic and Accounting Cost Structures

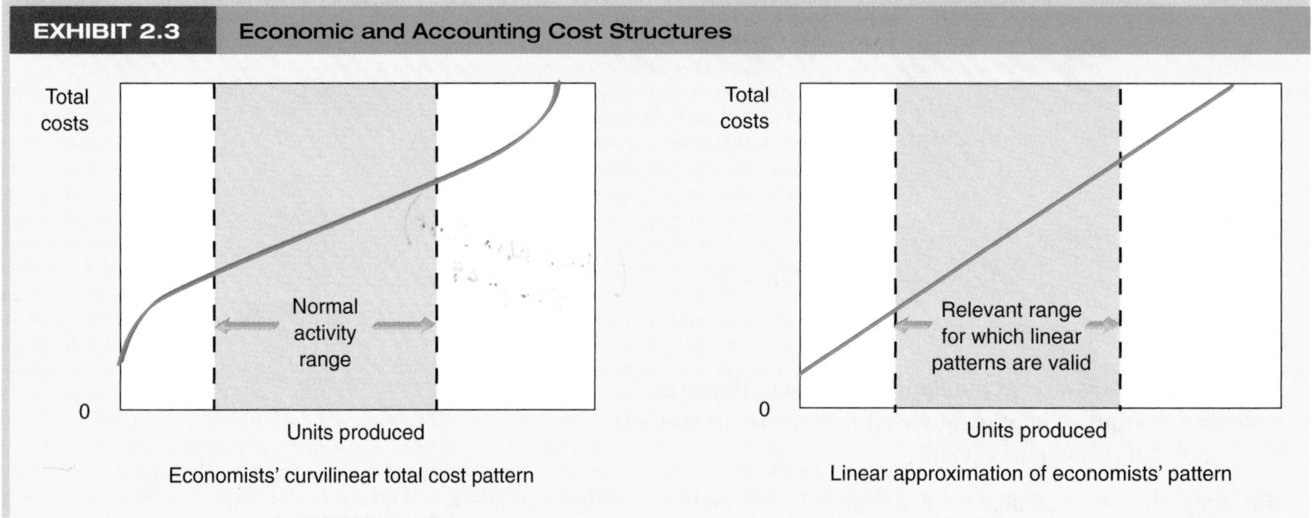

If the economists' total cost curve is valid, how can we reasonably approximate it with a straight line? The answer to this question is in the notion of a *relevant range.* A linear pattern may be a poor

RESEARCH INSIGHT Don't Base Decision on the Purchase Price

When buying a printer, it is tempting to base the decision on the purchase price of the printer, or on the price of the printer and the cost of replacement cartridges. That would be a mistake according to David Stone who analyzed the yield on ink cartridges and the three-year cost of operating and owning printers with recommended ink cartridges under light- and heavy-duty operation for general printing.

The first step in Stone's analysis was determining the average cost of a standard printed page using ink cartridges recommended for five widely used printers. The low-cost winner for printing in black was the HP Officejet K5400dtn Color printer using the HP 74XL black cartridge at 1.4 cents per page ($34.99 cost of cartridge divided by the average yield of 2,450 pages per cartridge). With three additional cartridges required for color printing, the HP Officejet K5400dtn Color printer was also the low-cost color printer at 5.9 cents per page. For color printing, the Kodak EasyShare 5300 All-in-One, with the advantage of only requiring one color ink cartridge, came in second at 6.9 cents per page.

Looking at three-year total ownership costs with light-duty general printing, the Lexmark X3550 was the low-cost leader. Although the per page costs of cartridges used in the Lexmark X3550 was higher than either the HP Officejet K5400dtn or the Kodak EasyShare 5300, the low purchase price of the Lexmark X3550 gave it the lowest three-year total cost for light-duty printing. For heavy-duty general printing, the HP Officejet K5400dtn or the Kodak EasyShare 5300 took top honors with three-year costs of $562.20 and $657.19, respectively.[3]

[3] M. David Stone, "The True Cost of Printer Ink," *PC Magazine*, October 2, 2007, pp.67-71; www.pcworld.com

approximation of the economists' curvilinear pattern over the entire range of possible activity, but a linear pattern as illustrated in the right-hand graph in Exhibit 2.3 is often sufficiently accurate within the range of probable operations. The range of activity within which a linear cost function is valid is called the **relevant range**. Linear estimates of cost behavior are valid only within the relevant range. Extreme care must be exercised when making comments about cost behavior outside the relevant range.

Additional Cost Behavior Patterns

Although we have considered the most frequently used cost behavior patterns, remember that there are numerous ways that costs can respond to changes in activity. Avoid the temptation to automatically assume that the cost in question conforms to one of the patterns discussed in this Chapter. As illustrated by the Research Insight box on page 32, it is important to think through each situation and then select a behavior pattern that seems logical and fits the known facts.

Particular care needs to be taken with the vertical axis. So far, all graphs have placed *total* costs on the vertical axis. Miscommunication is likely if one party is thinking in terms of *total* costs while the other is thinking in terms of *variable* or *average* costs. Consider the following cost function:

Total costs = $3,000 + $5X

where

X = customers served

The total, variable, and average costs at various levels of activity are computed here and graphed in Exhibit 2.4 on the following page. As the number of customers served increases, total costs increase, the variable costs of each unit remain constant, and the average cost decreases because fixed costs are spread over a larger number of units.

Customers Served	Total Costs	Average Cost*	Variable Costs per Customer
100	$3,500	$35.00	$5.00
200	4,000	20.00	5.00
300	4,500	15.00	5.00
400	5,000	12.50	5.00
500	5,500	11.00	5.00

*Total costs/customers served

To predict total costs for the coming period, management will use the first graph in Exhibit 2.4. To determine the minimum price required to avoid a loss on each additional customer served, management is interested in the variable costs per customer, yet if a manager inquired as to the cost of serving a customer, a financial accountant would probably provide average cost information, as illustrated in the third graph in Exhibit 2.4. The specific average cost would likely be a function of the number of customers served during the most recent accounting period.

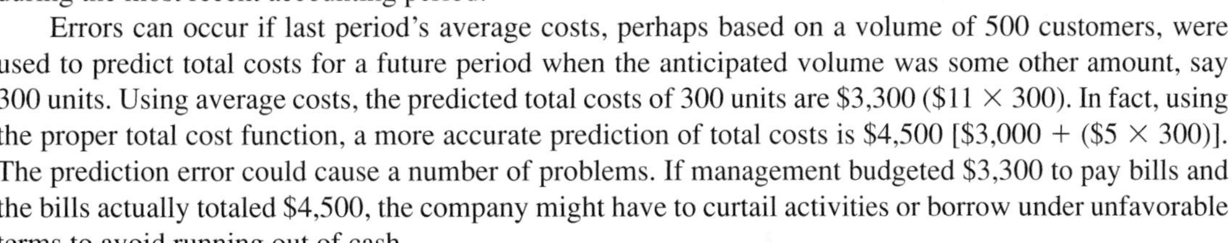

Errors can occur if last period's average costs, perhaps based on a volume of 500 customers, were used to predict total costs for a future period when the anticipated volume was some other amount, say 300 units. Using average costs, the predicted total costs of 300 units are $3,300 ($11 × 300). In fact, using the proper total cost function, a more accurate prediction of total costs is $4,500 [$3,000 + ($5 × 300)]. The prediction error could cause a number of problems. If management budgeted $3,300 to pay bills and the bills actually totaled $4,500, the company might have to curtail activities or borrow under unfavorable terms to avoid running out of cash.

Committed and Discretionary Fixed Costs

Fixed costs are often classified as *committed* or *discretionary,* depending on their immediate impact on the organization if management attempts to change them. **Committed fixed costs**, sometimes referred to as **capacity costs**, are the fixed costs required to maintain the current service or production capacity or to

EXHIBIT 2.4 Total Costs, Variable Costs, and Average Costs

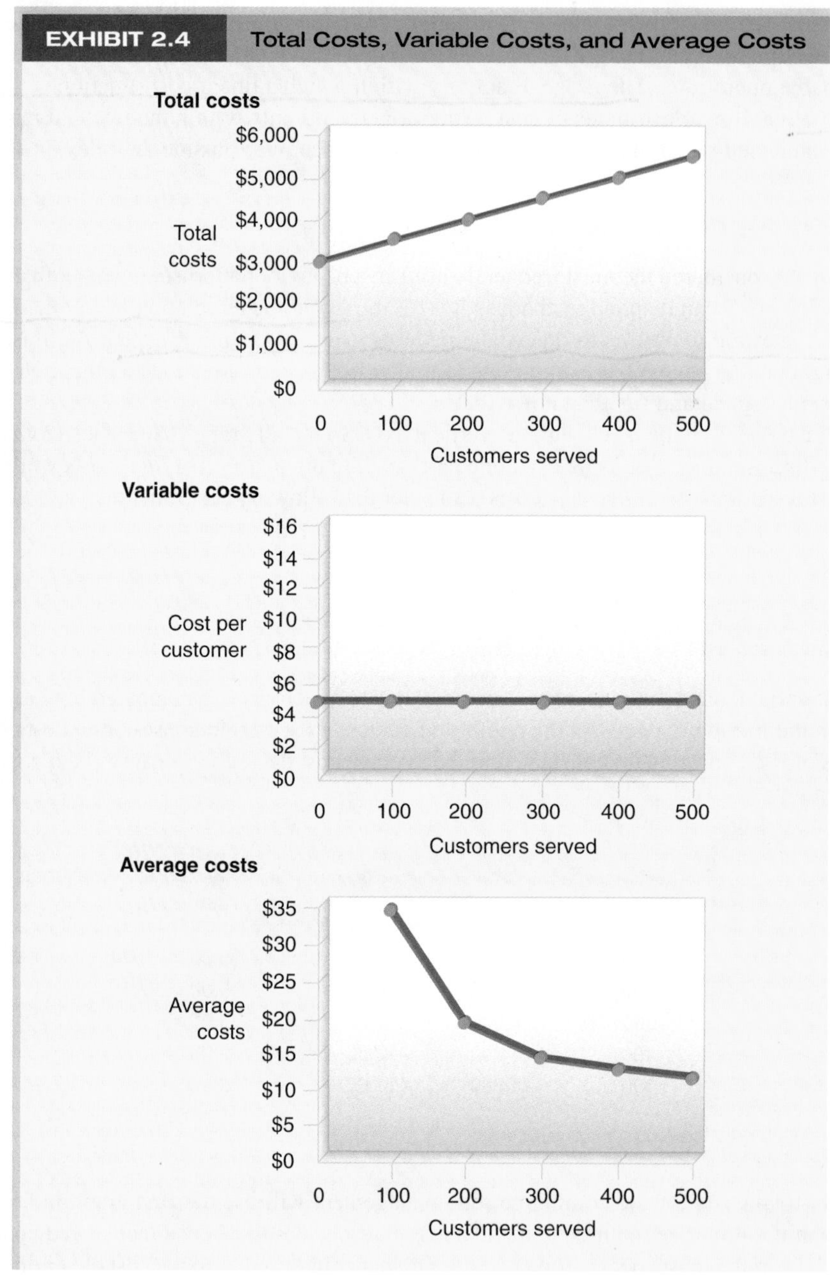

fill previous legal commitments. Examples of committed fixed costs include depreciation, property taxes, rent, and interest on bonds.

Committed fixed costs are often the result of structural decisions about the size and nature of an organization. For example, years ago the management of Santa Fe Railroad made decisions concerning what communities the railroad would serve. Track was laid on the basis of those decisions, and the Santa Fe Railroad now pays property taxes each year on the railroad's miles of track. These property taxes could be reduced by disposing of track. However, reducing track would also diminish the Santa Fe's capacity to serve.

Discretionary fixed costs, sometimes called **managed fixed costs**, are set at a fixed amount each period at the discretion of management. It is possible to reduce discretionary fixed costs without reducing production or service capacity in the short term. Typical discretionary fixed costs include advertising, maintenance, charitable contributions, employee training, and research and development.

Maintenance expenditures for discretionary fixed costs are frequently regarded as investments in the future. Research and development, for example, is undertaken to develop new or improved products that can be profitably produced and sold in future periods. During periods of financial well-being, organizations may make large expenditures on discretionary cost items. Conversely, during periods of financial stress, organizations likely reduce discretionary expenditures before reducing capacity costs. Unfortunately, fluctuations in the funding of discretionary fixed costs may reduce the effectiveness of long-range programs. A high-quality research staff may be difficult to reassemble if key personnel are laid off. Even the contemplation of layoffs may reduce the staff's effectiveness. In all periods, discretionary costs are subject to debate and are likely to be changed in the budgeting process.

MID-CHAPTER REVIEW

Identify each of the following cost behavior patterns as variable, committed fixed, discretionary fixed, mixed, or step.

a. Total cost of bakery products used at a McDonald's restaurant when the number of meals served is the activity cost driver.
b. Total cost of operating the Mayo Clinic when the number of patients served is the cost driver.
c. Total property taxes for a Midas Muffler Shop when the number of vehicles serviced is the cost driver.
d. Total cost of motherboards used by Apple Computer when the number of computers manufactured and shipped is the cost driver.
e. Total cost of secretarial services at Indiana University with each secretary handling the needs of ten faculty members and where part-time secretarial help is not available. The number of faculty is the cost driver.
f. Total advertising costs for International Business Machines (IBM).
g. Automobile rental costs at Alamo in Orlando, Florida, when there is no mileage charge. The cost driver is the number of miles driven.
h. Automobile rental cost at Hertz in Dallas, Texas, which has a base charge plus a mileage charge. The cost driver is the number of miles driven.
i. Salaries paid to personnel while conducting on-campus employment interviews for Champion International. Number of on-campus interviews is the cost driver.
j. The cost of contributions to educational institutions by Xerox Corporation.

Solution

a. Variable cost
b. Mixed cost
c. Committed fixed cost
d. Variable cost
e. Step cost
f. Discretionary fixed cost
g. Fixed cost (Without knowing the purpose of renting the car, the cost cannot be classified as committed or discretionary.)
h. Mixed cost
i. Step cost
j. Discretionary fixed cost

COST ESTIMATION

LO2 Determine a linear cost estimating equation.

Cost estimation, the determination of the relationship between activity and cost, is an important part of cost management. In this section, we develop equations for the relationship between total costs and total activity.

To properly estimate the relationship between activity and cost, we must be familiar with basic cost behavior patterns and cost estimating techniques. Costs known to have a variable or a fixed pattern are readily estimated by interviews or by analyzing available records. Sales commission per sales dollar, a variable cost, might be determined to be 15 percent of sales. In a similar manner, annual property taxes might be determined by consulting tax documents.

Mixed (semivariable) costs, which contain fixed and variable cost elements, are more difficult to estimate. According to a basic rule of algebra, two equations are needed to determine two unknowns. Following this rule, at least two observations are needed to determine the variable and fixed elements of a mixed cost.

High-Low Cost Estimation

The most straightforward approach to determining the variable and fixed elements of mixed costs is to use the **high-low method of cost estimation**. This method utilizes data from two time periods, a *representative* high-activity period and a *representative* low-activity period, to estimate fixed and variable costs. Assuming identical fixed costs in both periods, any difference in total costs between these two periods is due entirely to variable costs. The variable costs per unit are found by dividing the difference in total costs by the difference in total activity:

$$\textbf{Variable costs per unit} = \frac{\textbf{Difference in total costs}}{\textbf{Difference in activity}}$$

Once variable costs are determined, fixed costs, which are identical in both periods, are computed by subtracting the total variable costs of either the high or the low activity period from the corresponding total costs.

$$\textbf{Fixed costs} = \textbf{Total costs} - \textbf{Variable costs}$$

Assume a mail-order company such as **Lands' End** wants to develop a monthly cost function for its packaging department and that the number of shipments is believed to be the primary cost driver. The following observations are available for the first four months of 2009.

		Number of Shipments	Packaging Costs
(Low-activity period)	January	6,000	$17,000
	February	9,000	26,000
(High-activity period)	March	12,000	32,000
	April.	10,000	20,000

Equations for total costs for the packaging department in January and March (the periods of lowest and highest activity) follow:

January: $17,000 = a + b (6,000 shipments)

March: $32,000 = a + b (12,000 shipments)

where

a = fixed costs per month

b = variable costs per shipment

Solving for the estimated variable costs:

$$b = \frac{\text{Difference in total costs}}{\text{Difference in activity}}$$

$$b = \frac{\$32{,}000 - \$17{,}000}{12{,}000 - 6{,}000}$$

$$= \$2.50$$

Next, the estimated monthly fixed costs are determined by subtracting variable costs from total costs of *either* the January or March equation:

a = Total costs − Variable costs

January: a = $17,000 − ($2.50 per shipment × 6,000 shipments)
= $2,000

or

March: a = $32,000 − ($2.50 per shipment × 12,000 shipments)
= $2,000

The cost estimating equation for total packaging department costs is

Y = $2,000 + $2.50X

where

X = number of shipments
Y = total costs for the packing department

The concepts underlying the high-low method of cost estimation are illustrated in Exhibit 2.5.

Cost prediction, the forecasting of future costs, is a common purpose of cost estimation. Previously developed estimates of cost behavior are often the starting point in predicting future costs. Continuing the mail-order example, if 5,000 shipments are budgeted for June 2009, the predicted June 2009 packaging department costs are $14,500 [$2,000 + ($2.50 per shipment × 5,000 shipments)].

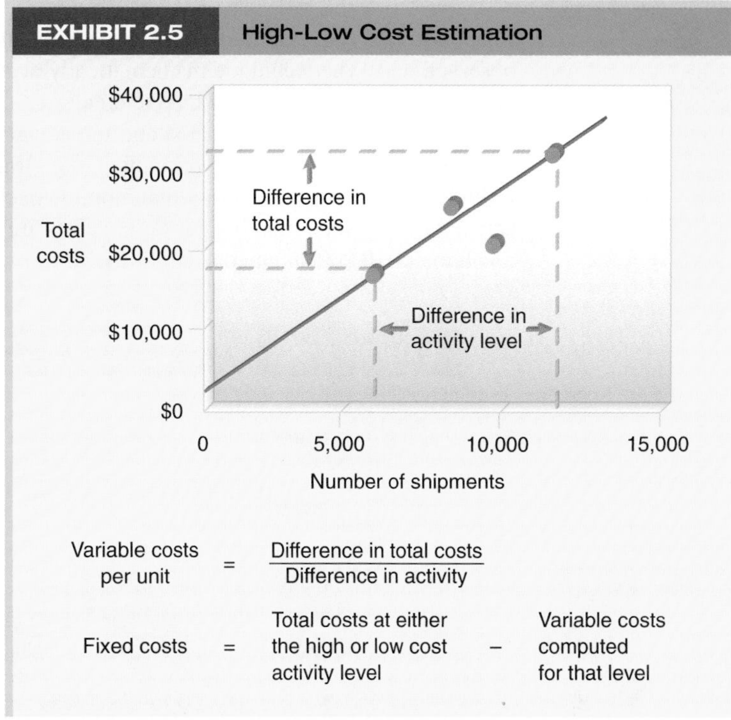

Scatter Diagrams

A **scatter diagram** is a graph of past activity and cost data, with individual observations represented by dots. Plotting historical cost data on a scatter diagram is a useful approach to cost estimation, especially when used in conjunction with other cost-estimating techniques. As illustrated in Exhibit 2.6, a scatter diagram helps in selecting high and low activity levels representative of normal operating conditions. The periods of highest or lowest activity may not be representative because of the cost of overtime, the use of less efficient equipment, strikes, and so forth. If the goal is to develop an equation to predict costs under normal operating conditions, then the equation should be based on observations of normal operating conditions. A scatter diagram is also useful in determining whether costs can be reasonably approximated by a straight line.

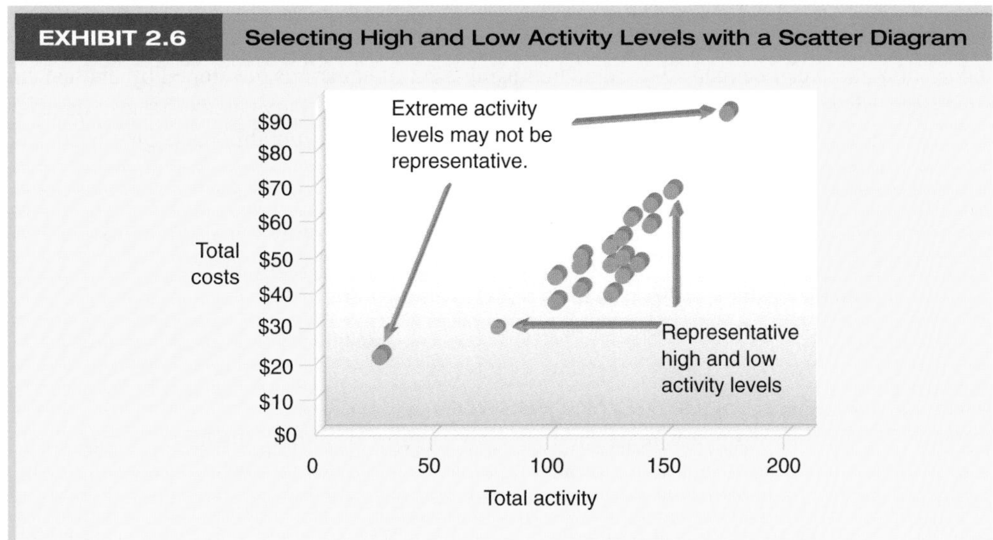

Scatter diagrams are sometimes used alone as a basis of cost estimation. This requires the use of professional judgment to draw a representative straight line through the plot of historical data. Typically, the analyst tries to ensure that an equal number of observations are on either side of the line while minimizing the total vertical differences between the line and actual cost observations at each value of the independent variable. Once a line is drawn, cost estimates at any representative volume are made by studying the line. Alternatively, an equation for the line may be developed by applying the high-low method to any two points on the line.

Least-Squares Regression

Least-squares regression analysis uses a mathematical technique to fit a cost-estimating equation to the observed data. The technique mathematically accomplishes what the analyst does visually with a scatter diagram. The least-squares technique creates an equation that minimizes the sum of the vertical squared differences between the estimated and the actual costs at each observation. Each of these differences is an estimating error. Using the packaging department example, the least-squares criterion is illustrated in Exhibit 2.7. Estimated values of total monthly packaging costs are represented by the straight line, and the actual values of total monthly packaging costs are represented by the dots. For each dot, such as the one at a volume of 10,000 shipments, the line is fit to minimize the vertical squared differences.

EXHIBIT 2.7 Least-Squares Criterion

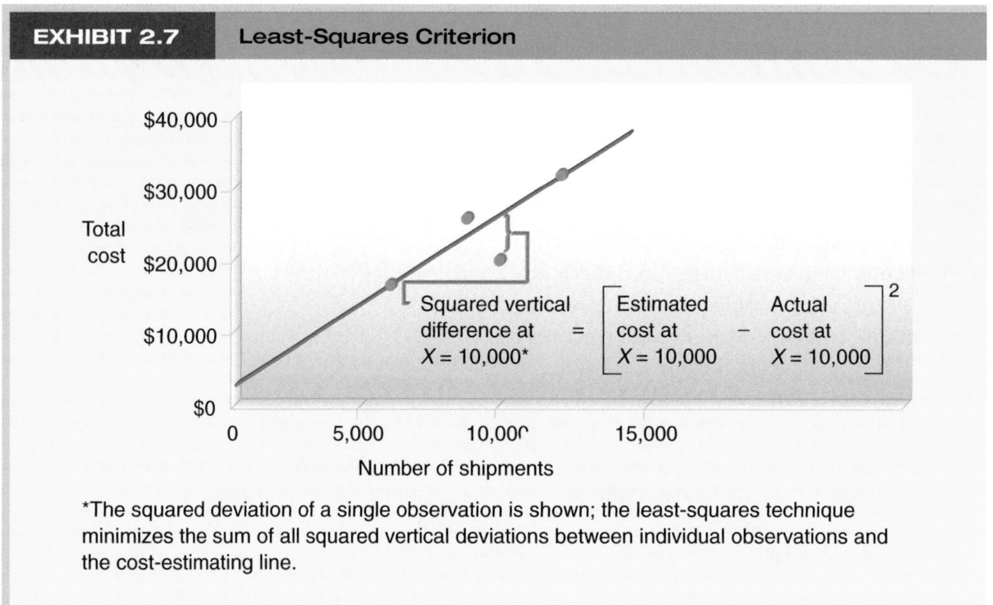

*The squared deviation of a single observation is shown; the least-squares technique minimizes the sum of all squared vertical deviations between individual observations and the cost-estimating line.

Values of *a* and *b* can be manually calculated using a set of equations developed by mathematicians or by using spreadsheet software packages such as Microsoft Excel®. Many calculators also have built-in functions to compute these coefficients. The least-squares equation for monthly packaging costs is:

$$Y = \$3{,}400 + \$2.20X$$

Using the least-squares equation, the predicted June 2009 packaging department costs with 5,000 budgeted shipments are $14,400 [$3,400 + ($2.20 per shipment × 5,000 shipments)]. Recall that the high-low method predicted June 2009 costs of $14,500. Although this difference is small, we should consider which prediction is more reliable.

Advantage of Least-Squares Regression

Mathematicians regard least-squares regression analysis as superior to both the high-low and the scatter diagram methods. It uses all available data, rather than just two observations, and does not rely on subjective judgment in drawing a line. Statistical measures are also available to determine how well a least-squares equation fits the historical data. These measures are often contained in the output of spreadsheet software packages.

In addition to the vertical axis intercept and the slope, least-squares regression calculates the coefficient of determination. The **coefficient of determination** is a measure of the percent of variation in the dependent variable (such as total packaging department costs) that is explained by variations in the independent variable (such as total shipments). Statisticians often refer to the coefficient of determination as R-squared and represent it as R^2.

The coefficient of determination can have values between zero and one, with values close to zero suggesting that the equation is not very useful and values close to one indicating that the equation explains most of the variation in the dependent variable. When choosing between two cost-estimating equations, the one with the higher coefficient of determination is generally preferred. The coefficient of determination for the packaging department cost estimation equation, determined using least-squares regression analysis, is 0.68. This means that 68 percent of the variation in packaging department costs is explained by the number of shipments.

Managers, Not Models, Are Responsible

Although computers make least-squares regression easy to use, the generated output should not automatically be accepted as correct. Statistics and other mathematical techniques are tools to help managers make decisions. Managers, not mathematical models, are responsible for decisions. Judgment should always be exercised when considering the validity of the least-squares approach, the solution, and the data. If the objective is to predict future costs under normal operating conditions, observations reflecting abnormal operating conditions should be deleted. Also examine the cost behavior pattern to determine whether it is linear. Scatter diagrams assist in both of these judgments. Finally, the results should make sense. When the relationships between total cost and several activity drivers are examined, it is possible to have a high R-squared purely by chance. Even though the relationship has a high R-squared, if it "doesn't make sense" there is probably something wrong.

Simple and Multiple Regression

Least-squares regression analysis is identified as "simple regression analysis" when there is only one independent variable and as "multiple regression analysis" when there are two or more independent variables. The general form for simple regression analysis is:

$$\mathbf{Y = a + bX}$$

The general form for multiple regression analysis is:

$$\mathbf{Y = a + \Sigma b_i X_i}$$

In this case, the subscript i is a general representation of each independent variable. When there are several independent variables, i is set equal to 1 for the first, 2 for the second, and so forth. The total variable costs of each independent variable is computed as b_iX_i, with b_i representing the variable cost per unit of independent variable X_i. The Greek symbol sigma, Σ, indicates that the costs of all independent variables are summed in determining total variable costs.

As an illustration, assume that Walnut Desk Company's costs are expressed as a function of the unit sales of its two products: executive desks and task desks. Fixed costs are $18,000 per month and the variable costs are $250 per executive desk and $120 per task desk. The mathematical representation of monthly costs with two variables is:

$$\mathbf{Y = a + b_1X_1 + b_2X_2}$$

where

$$\begin{aligned} \mathbf{a} &= \mathbf{\$18{,}000} \\ \mathbf{b_1} &= \mathbf{\$250} \\ \mathbf{b_2} &= \mathbf{\$120} \\ \mathbf{X_1} &= \textbf{unit sales of executive desks} \\ \mathbf{X_2} &= \textbf{unit sales of task desks} \end{aligned}$$

During a month when 105 executive desks and 200 task desks are sold, Walnut Desk Company's estimated total costs are:

$$\begin{aligned} \mathbf{Y} &= \mathbf{\$18{,}000 + \$250(105) + \$120(200)} \\ &= \mathbf{\$68{,}250} \end{aligned}$$

In addition to estimating costs, multiple regression analysis can be used to determine the effect of individual product features on the market value of a product or service. The following Research Insight box reports a study that estimated the impact of mature trees on the selling price of single-family homes.

RESEARCH INSIGHT **Regression Finds "Big Tree" Premium**

While most real estate professionals believe that, all else being equal, homes with mature trees (defined as having a diameter of nine inches or more) are preferred to homes without mature trees, it is difficult to estimate the value of mature trees. The Council of Tree and Landscape Appraisers recommends a cost-based approach for the valuation of trees. While this is possible for small trees, it is difficult to value mature trees. To better determine the market value of mature trees, a recent study used multiple regression analysis to analyze the impact of mature trees on the selling prices of homes in Baton Rouge, Louisiana. Independent variables included the size and age of the house, the presence of other house amenities such as a garage, porch, or fireplace, days on the market, location, and the presence of mature trees. The study revealed that the presence of mature trees increased the selling price of a home by 1.856 percent. The researchers conclude that an appraiser "would be supported in adding approximately 2 percent to the value of a single-family house that has mature trees."[4]

MANAGERIAL DECISION **You are the Purchasing Manager**

Your department has been experiencing increased activity in recent periods as the company has grown, and you have observed that the average cost per purchase order processed has been declining, but not at a constant rate. You have been given an estimate by the production manager of the number of purchase orders that will be processed next period and have been asked by the accounting department to provide within one hour an estimate of the cost to process those orders. How can the scatter diagram method help you to meet this deadline? [Answer, p. 46]

ADDITIONAL ISSUES IN COST ESTIMATION

LO3 Identify and discuss problems encountered in cost estimation.

We have mentioned several items to be wary of when developing cost estimating equations:

- Data that are not based on normal operating conditions.
- Nonlinear relationships between total costs and activity.
- Obtaining a high R-squared purely by chance.

Additional items of concern include:

- Changes in technology or prices.
- Matching activity and cost within each observation.
- Identifying activity cost drivers.

Changes in Technology and Prices

Changes in technology and prices make cost estimation and prediction difficult. When telephone companies changed from using human operators to using automated switching equipment to place long-distance telephone calls, cost estimates based on the use of human operators were of little or no value in predicting future costs. Care must be taken to make sure that data used in developing cost estimates are based on the existing technology. When this is not possible, professional judgment is required to make appropriate adjustments.

[4] Jonathan Dombrow, Mauricio Rodriguez, and C. F. Sirmans, "The Market Value of Mature Trees in Single-Family Housing Markets," *Appraisal Journal,* January 2000, p. 39.

Only data reflecting a single price level should be used in cost estimation and prediction. If prices have remained stable in the past but then uniformly increase by 20 percent, cost-estimating equations based on data from previous periods will not accurately predict future costs. In this case, all that is required is a 20 percent increase in the prediction. Unfortunately, adjustments for price changes are seldom this simple. The prices of various cost elements are likely to change at different rates and at different times. Furthermore, there are probably several different price levels included in the past data used to develop cost-estimating equations. If data from different price levels are used, an attempt should be made to restate them to a single price level.

Matching Activity and Costs

The development of accurate cost-estimating equations requires the matching of the activity to related costs within each observation. This accuracy is often difficult to achieve because of the time lag between an activity and the recording of the cost of resources consumed by the activity. Current activities usually consume electricity, but the electric bill won't be received and recorded until next month. Driving an automobile requires routine maintenance for items such as lubrication and oil, but the auto can be driven several weeks or even months before the maintenance is required. Consequently, daily, weekly, and perhaps even monthly observations of miles driven and maintenance costs are unlikely to match the costs of oil and lubrication with the cost-driving activity, miles driven.

In general, the shorter the time period, the higher the probability of error in matching costs and activity. The cost analyst must carefully review the database to verify that activity and cost are matched within each observation. If matching problems are found, it may be possible to adjust the data (perhaps by moving the cost of electricity from one observation to another). Under other circumstances, it may be necessary to use longer periods to match costs and activity.

Identifying Activity Cost Drivers

Identifying the appropriate activity cost driver for a particular cost requires judgment and professional experience. In general, the cost driver should have a logical, causal relationship with costs. In many cases, the identity of the most appropriate activity cost driver, such as miles driven for the cost of automobile gasoline, is apparent. In other situations, where different activity cost drivers might be used, scatter diagrams and statistical measures, such as the coefficient of determination, are helpful in selecting the activity cost driver that best explains past variations in cost. When scatter diagrams are used, the analyst can study the dispersion of observations around the cost-estimating line. In general, a small dispersion is preferred. If regression analysis is used, the analyst considers the coefficient of determination. In general, a higher coefficient of determination is preferred. The relationship between the activity cost driver and the cost must seem logical, and the activity data must be available.

ALTERNATIVE COST DRIVER CLASSIFICATIONS

LO4 Describe and develop alternative classifications for activity cost drivers.

So far we have examined cost behavior and cost estimation using only a unit-level approach, which assumes changes in costs are best explained by changes in the number of units of product or service provided customers. This approach may have worked for Carnegie Steel Company, but it is inappropriate for multiproduct organizations, such as General Electric. The unit-level approach becomes increasingly inaccurate for analyzing cost behavior when organizations experience the following types of changes:

- From labor-based to automated manufacturing,
- From a limited number of related products to multiple products, with variations in product volume and complexity (and related costs), and
- From a set of similar customers to a diverse set of customers.

Exhibit 2.8 illustrates the composition of total manufacturing costs for the past century, illustrating changes in the percentage of manufacturing costs for three major cost categories.

EXHIBIT 2.8 Changing Composition of Total Manufacturing Costs

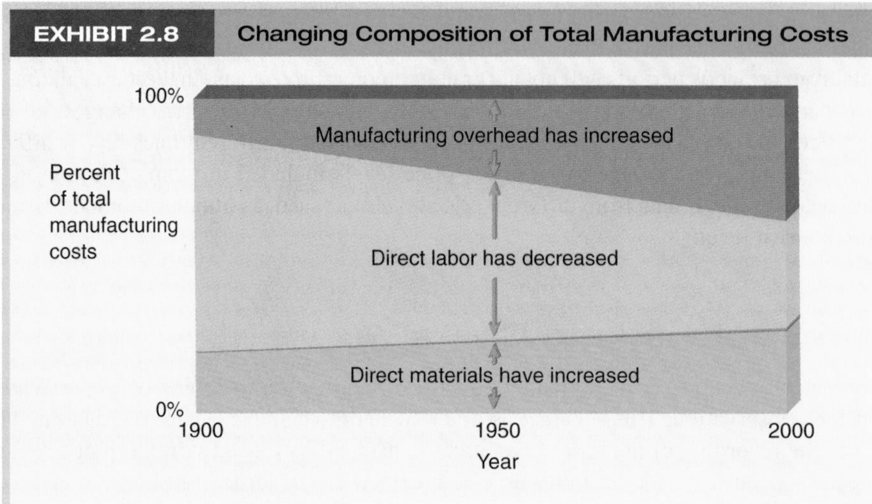

1. **Direct materials**, the cost of primary raw materials converted into finished goods, have increased slightly as organizations purchase components they formerly fabricated. The word "direct" is used to indicate costs that are easily or directly traced to a finished product or service.
2. **Direct labor**, the wages earned by production employees for the time they spend converting raw materials into finished products, has decreased significantly as employees spend less time physically working on products and more time supporting automated production activities.
3. **Manufacturing overhead**, which includes all manufacturing costs other than direct materials and direct labor, has increased significantly due to automation, product diversity, and product complexity.

Changes in the composition of manufacturing costs have implications for the behavior of total costs and the responsiveness of costs to changes in cost drivers. Because direct materials and direct labor vary directly with the number of units, they are easy to measure. In the past, when manufacturing overhead was relatively small, it was possible to assume units of product or service was the primary cost driver. This is no longer true. Units of final product is no longer an adequate explanation of changes in manufacturing overhead for many organizations.

The past tendency to ignore overhead, while focusing on direct materials and direct labor, led one researcher to describe overhead-causing activities as "the hidden factory."[5] To better understand the hidden factory, several researchers have developed frameworks for categorizing cost-driving activities. The crucial feature of these frameworks is the inclusion of nonunit cost drivers. Depending on the characteristics of a particular organization, as well as management's information needs, there are an almost unlimited number of cost driver classification schemes. We consider two frequently applied cost driver classification schemes: one based on a manufacturing cost hierarchy and a second based on a customer cost hierarchy. We also illustrate variations of each.

Manufacturing Cost Hierarchy

The most well-known framework, developed by Cooper[6] and Cooper and Kaplan[7] for manufacturing situations, classifies activities into the following four categories.

1. A **unit-level activity** is performed *for each unit* of product produced. Oneida Silversmiths manufactures high-quality eating utensils. In the production of forks, the stamping of each fork into the prescribed shape is an example of a unit-level cost driver.

[5] Jeffrey G. Miller and Thomas E. Vollmann, "The Hidden Factory," *Harvard Business Review*, September-October 1985, pp. 142–150.
[6] Robin Cooper, "Cost Classification in Unit-Based and Activity-Based Manufacturing Cost Systems," *The Journal of Cost Management*, Fall 1990, pp. 4–14.
[7] Robin Cooper and Robert S. Kaplan, "Profit Priorities from Activity-Based Costing," *Harvard Business Review*, May-June 1991, pp. 130–135.

2. A **batch-level activity** is performed *for each batch* of product produced. At Oneida Silversmiths, a batch is a number of identical units (such as a fork of a specific design) produced at the same time. Batch-level activities include setting up the machines to stamp each fork in an identical manner, moving the entire batch between workstations (i.e., molding, stamping, and finishing), and inspecting the first unit in the batch to verify that the machines are set up correctly.
3. A **product-level activity** is performed *to support* the production of *each different type of product*. At Oneida Silversmiths, product-level activities for a specific pattern of fork include initially designing the fork, producing and maintaining the mold for the fork, and determining manufacturing operations for the fork.
4. A **facility-level activity** is performed *to maintain* general manufacturing capabilities. At Oneida Silversmiths, facility-level activities include plant management, building maintenance, property taxes, and electricity required to sustain the building.

Several additional examples of the costs driven by activities at each level are presented in Exhibit 2.9.

EXHIBIT 2.9 Hierarchy of Activity Costs

Activity Level	Reason for Activity	Examples of Activity Cost
1. Unit level	Performed for each unit of product produced or sold	• Cost of raw materials • Cost of inserting a component • Utilities cost of operating equipment • Some costs of packaging • Sales commissions
2. Batch level	Performed for each batch of product produced or sold	• Cost of processing sales order • Cost of issuing and tracking work order • Cost of equipment setup • Cost of moving batch between workstations • Cost of inspection (assuming same number of units inspected in each batch)
3. Product level	Performed to support each different product that can be produced	• Cost of product development • Cost of product marketing such as advertising • Cost of specialized equipment • Cost of maintaining specialized equipment
4. Facility level	Performed to maintain general manufacturing capabilities	• Cost of maintaining general facilities such as buildings and grounds • Cost of nonspecialized equipment • Cost of maintaining nonspecialized equipment • Cost of real property taxes • Cost of general advertising • Cost of general administration such as the plant manager's salary

When using a cost hierarchy for analyzing and estimating costs, total costs are broken down into the different cost levels in the hierarchy, and a separate cost driver is determined for each level of cost. For example, using the above hierarchy, the costs that are related to the number of units produced (such **as** direct materials or direct labor) may have direct labor hours or machines hours as the cost driver; whereas, batch costs may be driven by the number of setups of production machines or the number of times materials are move from one machine to another. Other costs may be driven by the number of different products produced. Facility-level costs are generally regarded as fixed costs and do not vary unless capacity is increased or decreased.

Customer Cost Hierarchy

The manufacturing hierarchy presented is but one of many possible ways of classifying activities and their costs. Classification schemes should be designed to fit the organization and meet user needs. A merchandising organization or the sales division of a manufacturing organization might use the following hierarchy.

1. **Unit-level activity**: performed for each unit sold.
2. **Order-level activity**: performed for each sales order.
3. **Customer-level activity**: performed to obtain or maintain each customer.
4. **Facility-level activity**: performed to maintain the general marketing function

This classification scheme assists in answering questions concerning the cost of individual orders or individual customers.

If an organization sells to distinct market segments (for profit, not for profit, and government), the cost hierarchy can be modified as follows:

1. Unit-level activity
2. Order-level activity
3. Customer-level activity
4. **Market-segment-level activity**: performed to obtain or maintain operations in a segment.
5. Facility-level activity

The market-segment-level activities and their related costs differ with each market segment. This classification scheme assists in answering questions concerning the profitability of each segment.

Finally, an organization that completes unique projects for different market segments (such as buildings for IBM and the U.S. Department of Defense) can use the following hierarchy to determine the profitability of each segment:

1. **Project-level activity**: performed to support the completion of each project.
2. Market-segment-level activity
3. Facility-level activity

The possibilities are endless. The important point is that both the cost hierarchy and the costs included in the hierarchy be tailored to meet the specific circumstances of an organization and the interests of management.[8] The following Business Insight box considers a possible cost hierarchy for the airline industry, with a closer examination of aircraft types as a cost driver.

BUSINESS INSIGHT **Aircraft Diversity is a Cost Driver**

Cost hierarchies can be developed for almost any type of organization. The cost hierarchy for airlines might include seat miles, airports served, number of flights, point-to-point or hub and spoke scheduling, age of aircraft, and number of aircraft types. The diversity of aircraft impacts costs such as maintenance, parts inventories, ability to substitute aircraft and crew on a scheduled flight, pilot training, and crew assignments. Consider the differences between US Airways and AirTran in fleet complexity.

US Airways, formed through a series of mergers (the latest with America West), flies a wide variety of regional, national, and international routes. Because of its history of mergers and complex route structure, US Airways operates more than 450 aircraft consisting of 15 types, ranging from the De Havilland Dash 8-100 with 37 seats to the Airbus A330-300 with 266 seats. Although US Airways is striving to reduce the diversity of its fleet, which has been called a "hodgepodge," restructuring fixed assets takes many years. In the interim, US Airways struggles with high costs related to the number of aircraft types.

AirTran operates approximately 130 aircraft consisting of only two types, Boeing B717 and B737, from a single manufacturer. AirTran was the launch customer for the B717 that management regards as "ideally suited for the short-hall, high-frequency service that we primarily operate." Explaining the addition of the B737 to AirTran's fleet, management noted that Boeing discontinued the production of the B717 in 2006. By focusing on two types of Boeing aircraft, AirTran benefits from many efficiencies and avoids the types of costs US Airways incurs by having so many different types of planes.[9]

---

[8] George Foster and Mahendra Gupta, "Marketing Cost Management and Management Accounting," *Journal of Management Accounting Research*, 6, Fall 1994, pp. 43-77.

[9] Christopher Palmeri, "A Cautionary Tale for Airline Mergers, *Business Week*, March 17, 2008, p. 66 and information in annual reports of AirTran and US Airways found at www.airtran.com and www.usairways.com.

CHAPTER-END REVIEW

Assume a local Subway reported the following results for April and May:

	April	May
Unit sales	2,100	2,700
Cost of food sold	$1,575	$2,025
Wages and salaries	1,525	1,675
Rent on building	1,500	1,500
Depreciation on equipment	200	200
Utilities	710	770
Supplies	225	255
Miscellaneous	113	131
Total	$5,848	$6,556

Required

a. Identify each cost as being fixed, variable, or mixed.

b. Using the high-low method, estimate an equation for the cost of food, wages and salaries, rent on building, and total monthly costs.

c. Predict total costs for monthly volumes of 1,000 and 2,000 units.

d. Predict the average cost per unit at monthly volumes of 1,000 and 2,000 units. Explain why the average costs differ at these two volumes.

Solution

a. Fixed costs are easily identified. They are the same at each activity level. Variable and mixed costs are determined by dividing the total costs for an item at two activity levels by the corresponding units of activity. The quotients of the variable cost items will be identical at both activity levels. The quotients of the mixed costs will differ, being lower at the higher activity level because the fixed costs are being spread over a larger number of units.

Cost	Behavior
Cost of food sold	Variable
Wages and salaries	Mixed
Rent on building	Fixed
Depreciation on equipment	Fixed
Utilities	Mixed
Supplies	Mixed
Miscellaneous	Mixed

b. The cost of food sold was classified as a variable cost. Hence, the cost of food may be determined by dividing the total costs at either observation by the corresponding number of units.

$$\mathbf{b = \frac{\$1{,}575 \text{ total variable costs}}{2{,}100 \text{ units}}}$$

$$\mathbf{= \$0.75X}$$

Wages and salaries were previously classified as a mixed cost. Hence, the cost of wages and salaries is determined using the high-low method.

(variable cost)

$$\mathbf{b = \frac{\$1{,}675 - \$1{,}525}{2{,}700 - 2{,}100}}$$

$$\mathbf{= 0.25X}$$

(fixed cost)

$$\mathbf{a = \$1{,}525 \text{ total cost} - (\$0.25 \times 2{,}100) \text{ variable cost}}$$

$$\mathbf{= \$1{,}000}$$

Rent on building was classified as a fixed cost.

$$\mathbf{a = \$1{,}500}$$

Total monthly costs most likely follow a mixed cost behavior pattern. Hence, they can be determined using the high-low method.

$$
\begin{aligned}
b &= \frac{\$6{,}556 - \$5{,}848}{2{,}700 - 2{,}100} \\
&= \$1.18X \\
a &= \$5{,}848 - (\$1.18 \times 2{,}100) \\
&= \$3{,}370 \\
\text{Total costs} &= \$3{,}370 + \$1.18X
\end{aligned}
$$

where

$$X = \text{unit sales}$$

c. and *d.*

Volume	Total Costs	Average Cost per Unit
1,000	\$3,370 + (\$1.18 × 1,000) = \$4,550	\$4,550/1,000 = \$4.550
2,000	\$3,370 + (\$1.18 × 2,000) = \$5,730	\$5,730/2,000 = \$2.865

The average costs differ at 1,000 and 2,000 units because the fixed costs are being spread over a different number of units. The larger the number of units, the smaller the average fixed cost per unit.

GUIDANCE ANSWER

MANAGERIAL DECISION You are the Purchasing Manager

One of the quickest methods for gaining a general understanding of the relationship between a given cost and its cost driver is to graph the relationship using data from several recent periods. As purchasing manager you could probably quickly obtain information about the amount of the total purchasing department costs and number of purchase orders processed for each of the most recent eight or ten periods. By graphing these data with costs on the vertical axis and number of purchase orders on the horizontal axis, you should be able to visually determine if there is an obvious behavioral pattern (variable, fixed, or mixed). Since costs have been declining as volume has increased, this would suggest that there are some fixed costs, and that they have been declining on a per unit basis as they are spread over an increasing number of purchase orders. Using two representative data points in the scatter diagram, you can plot a cost curve on the graph, and then use the data for those two points to calculate the estimated fixed and variable costs using the high-low cost estimation method. Using these cost estimates, you can predict the total cost for next period. This method may not give you a precise estimate of the cost, but coupled with your subjective estimate of cost based on your experience as manager of the department, it should give you more confidence than merely making a best guess. Hopefully, you will have an opportunity before presenting your budget for the next period to conduct additional analyses using more advanced methods.

DISCUSSION QUESTIONS

Q2-1. Briefly describe variable, fixed, mixed, and step costs and indicate how the total cost function of each changes as activity increases within a time period.

Q2-2. Why is presenting all costs of an organization as a function of a single independent variable, although useful in obtaining a general understanding of cost behavior, often not accurate enough to make specific decisions concerning products, services, or activities?

Q2-3. Explain the term "relevant range" and why it is important in estimating total costs.

Q2-4. How are variable and fixed costs determined using the high-low method of cost estimation?

Q2-5. Distinguish between cost estimation and cost prediction.

Q2-6. Why is a scatter diagram helpful when used in conjunction with other methods of cost estimation?

Q2-7. Identify two advantages of least-squares regression analysis as a cost estimation technique.

Q2-8. Why is it important to match activity and costs within a single observation? When is this matching problem most likely to exist?

Q2-9. During the past century, how have direct materials, direct labor, and manufacturing overhead changed as a portion of total manufacturing costs? What is the implication of the change in manufacturing overhead for cost estimation?

Q2-10. Distinguish between the unit-, batch-, product-, and facility-level activities of a manufacturing organization.

MINI EXERCISES

M2-11. Classifying Cost Behavior (LO1)

Classify the total costs of each of the following as variable, fixed, mixed, or step. Sales volume is the cost driver.

a. Salary of the department manager
b. Memory chips in a computer assembly plant
c. Real estate taxes
d. Salaries of quality inspectors when each inspector can evaluate a maximum of 1,000 units per day
e. Wages paid to production employees for the time spent working on products
f. Electric power in a factory
g. Raw materials used in production
h. Automobiles rented on the basis of a fixed charge per day plus an additional charge per mile driven
i. Sales commissions
j. Depreciation on office equipment

M2-12. Classifying Cost Behavior (LO1)

Classify the total costs of each of the following as variable, fixed, mixed, or step.

a. Straight-line depreciation on a building
b. Maintenance costs at a hospital
c. Rent on a photocopy machine charged as a fixed amount per month plus an additional charge per copy
d. Cost of goods sold in a bookstore
e. Salaries paid to temporary instructors in a college as the number of course sessions varies
f. Lumber used by a house construction company
g. The costs of operating a research department
h. The cost of hiring a dance band for three hours
i. Laser printer paper for a department printer
j. Electric power in a restaurant

M2-13. Classifying Cost Behavior (LO1)

For each of the following situations, select the most appropriate cost behavior pattern (as shown in the illustrations on the next page) where the lines represent the cost behavior pattern, the vertical axis represents costs, the horizontal axis represents total volume, and the dots represent actual costs. Each pattern may be used more than once.

a. Variable costs per unit
b. Total fixed costs
c. Total mixed costs
d. Average fixed costs per unit
e. Total current manufacturing costs
f. Average variable costs
g. Total costs when employees are paid $10 per hour for the first 40 hours worked each week and $15 for each additional hour.
h. Total costs when employees are paid $10 per hour and guaranteed a minimum weekly wage of $200.
i. Total costs per day when a consultant is paid $200 per hour with a maximum daily fee of $1,000.
j. Total variable costs
k. Total costs for salaries of social workers where each social worker can handle a maximum of 20 cases
l. A water bill where a flat fee of $800 is charged for the first 100,000 gallons and additional water costs $0.005 per gallon
m. Total variable costs properly used to estimate step costs
n. Total materials costs
o. Rent on exhibit space at a convention

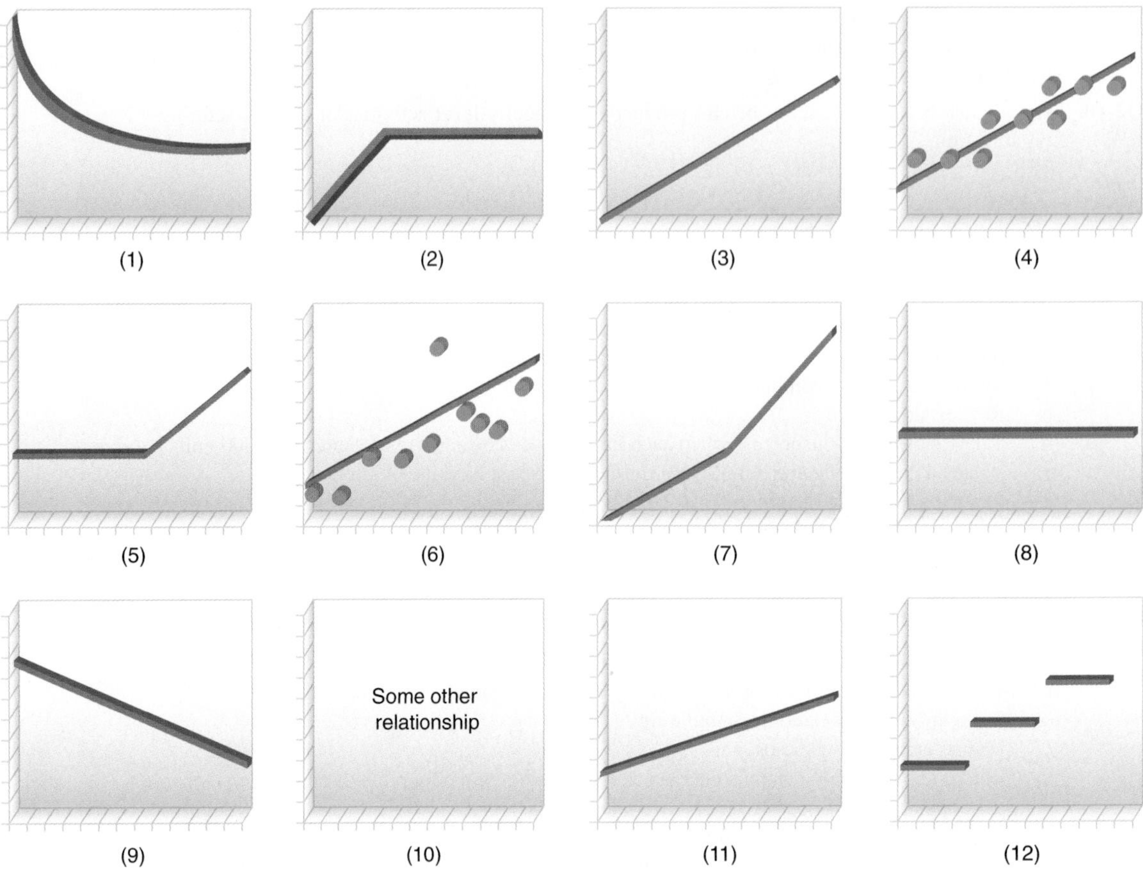

M2-14. Classifying Cost Behavior (LO1)

For each of the graphs displayed at the top of page 49, select the most appropriate cost behavior pattern where the lines represent the cost behavior pattern, the vertical axis represents total costs, the horizontal axis represents total volume, and the dots represent actual costs. Each pattern may be used more than once.

a. A cellular telephone bill when a flat fee is charged for the first 200 minutes of use per month and additional use costs $0.45 per minute
b. Total selling and administrative costs
c. Total labor costs when employees are paid per unit produced
d. Total overtime premium paid production employees
e. Average total cost per unit
f. Salaries of supervisors when each one can supervise a maximum of 10 employees
g. Total idle time costs when employees are paid for a minimum 40-hour week
h. Materials costs per unit
i. Total sales commissions
j. Electric power consumption in a restaurant
k. Total costs when high volumes of production require the use of overtime and obsolete equipment
l. A good linear approximation of actual costs
m. A linear cost estimation valid only within the relevant range

EXERCISES

E2-15. Computing Average Unit Costs (LO2)

The total monthly operating costs of Chili To Go are:

$10,000 + $0.40X

where

X = servings of chili

Required

a. Determine the average cost per serving at each of the following monthly volumes: 100; 1,000; 5,000; and 10,000
b. Determine the monthly volume at which the average cost per serving is $0.60.

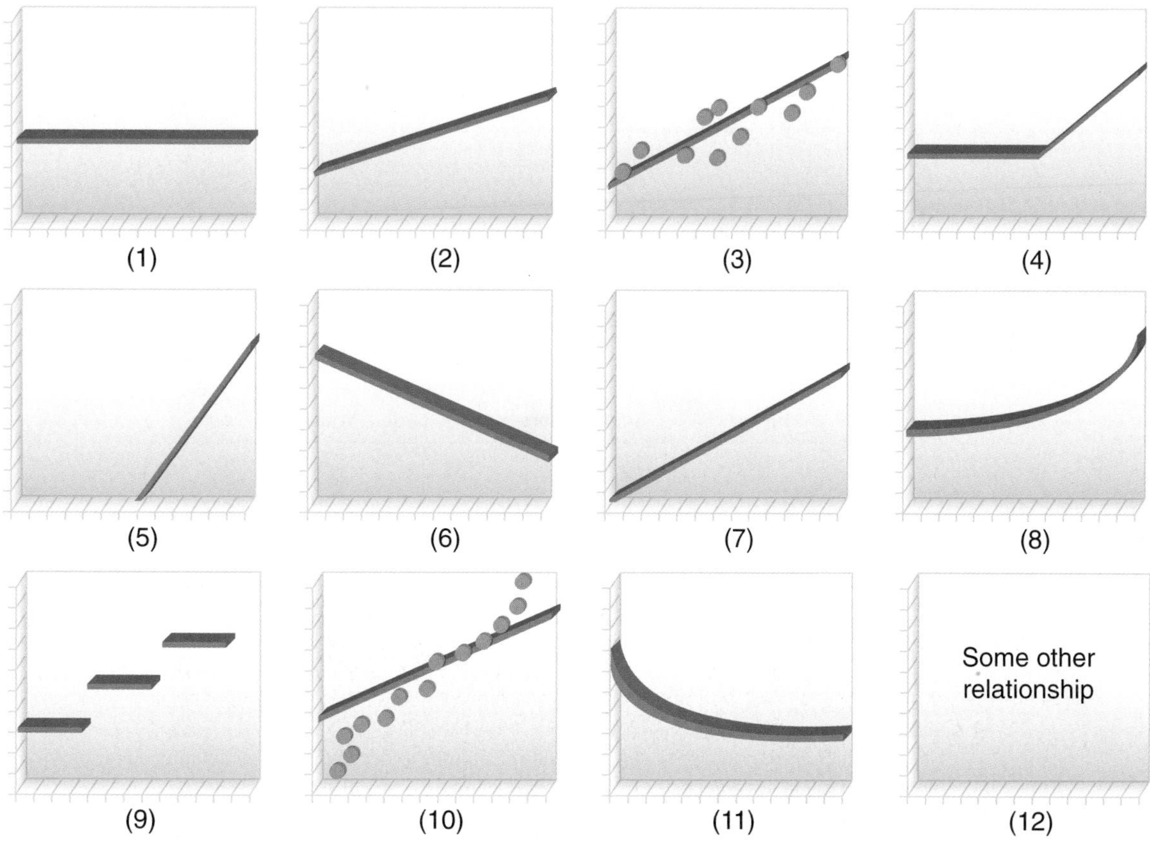

E2-16. Automatic versus Manual Processing (LO2)

Photo Station Company operates a printing service for customers with digital cameras. The current service, which requires employees to download photos from customer cameras, has monthly operating costs of $5,000 plus $0.20 per photo printed. Management is evaluating the desirability of acquiring a machine that will allow customers to download and make prints without employee assistance. If the machine is acquired, the monthly fixed costs will increase to $10,000 and the variable costs of printing a photo will decline to $0.04 per photo.

Required

a. Determine the total costs of printing 20,000 and 50,000 photos per month:
   1. With the current employee-assisted process.
   2. With the proposed customer self-service process.

b. Determine the monthly volume at which the proposed process becomes preferable to the current process.

E2-17. Automatic versus Manual Processing (LO2)

Mid-Town Copy Service processes 1,800,000 photocopies per month at its mid-town service center. Approximately 50 percent of the photocopies require collating. Collating is currently performed by high school and college students who are paid $8 per hour. Each student collates an average of 5,000 copies per hour. Management is contemplating the lease of an automatic collating machine that has a monthly capacity of 5,000,000 photocopies, with lease and operating costs totaling $1,550, plus $0.05 per 1,000 units collated.

Required

a. Determine the total costs of collating 500,000 and 1,500,000 per month:
   1. With student help.
   2. With the collating machine.

b. Determine the monthly volume at which the automatic process becomes preferable to the manual process.

c. Should Mid-Town Copy lease the automatic collating machine at this time?

E2-18. High-Low Cost Estimation (LO2)

DHL (DHL)

Assume the local DHL delivery service hub has the following information available about fleet miles and operating costs:

Year	Miles	Operating Costs
2006	556,000	$177,000
2007	684,000	209,000

Required

Use the high-low method to develop a cost-estimating equation for total annual operating costs.

E2-19. Scatter Diagrams and High-Low Cost Estimation (LO2, 3)

LensCrafters

Assume the local LensCrafters has the following information on the number of sales orders received and order-processing costs.

Month	Sales Orders	Order-Processing Costs
1	3,000	$40,000
2	1,500	28,000
3	4,000	65,000
4	2,800	39,000
5	2,300	32,000
6	1,000	20,000
7	2,000	30,000

Required

a. Use information from the high- and low-volume months to develop a cost-estimating equation for monthly order-processing costs.

b. Plot the data on a scatter diagram. Using the information from representative high- and low- volume months, develop a cost-estimating equation for monthly production costs.

c. What factors might have caused the difference in the equations developed for requirements (a) and (b)?

E2-20. Scatter Diagrams and High-Low Cost Estimation (LO2, 3)

From April 1 through October 31, Santa Cruz County Highway Department hires temporary employees to mow and clean the right of way along county roads. The County Road Commissioner has asked you to help her in determining the variable labor cost of mowing and cleaning a mile of road. The following information is available regarding current year operations:

Month	Miles Mowed and Cleaned	Labor Costs
April	350	$7,500
May	300	7,000
June	400	8,500
July	250	5,000
August	375	8,000
September	200	4,500
October	100	4,300

Required

a. Use the information from the high- and low-volume months to develop a cost-estimating equation for monthly labor costs.

b. Plot the data on a scatter diagram. Using the information from representative high- and low-volume months, use the high-low method to develop a cost-estimating equation for monthly labor costs.

c. What factors might have caused the difference in the equations developed for requirements (a) and (b)?

d. Adjust the equation developed in requirement (b) to incorporate the effect of an anticipated 7 percent increase in wages.

E2-21 Cost Behavior Analysis in a Restaurant: High-Low Cost Estimation (LO2)

Assume a Papa John's restaurant has the following information available regarding costs at representative levels of monthly sales: Papa John's (PZZA)

	Monthly sales in units		
	5,000	8,000	10,000
Cost of food sold	$10,000	$16,000	$20,000
Wages and fringe benefits	4,250	4,400	4,500
Fees paid delivery help.	1,250	2,000	2,500
Rent on building	1,200	1,200	1,200
Depreciation on equipment	600	600	600
Utilities	500	560	600
Supplies (soap, floor wax, etc.)	150	180	200
Administrative costs.	1,300	1,300	1,300
Total	$19,250	$26,240	$30,900

Required

a. Identify each cost as being variable, fixed, or mixed.

b. Use the high-low method to develop a schedule identifying the amount of each cost that is fixed per month or variable per unit. Total the amounts under each category to develop an equation for total monthly costs.

c. Predict total costs for a monthly sales volume of 9,500 units.

E2-22. Developing an Equation from Average Costs (LO2)

The America Dog and Cat Hotel is a pet hotel located in Las Vegas. Assume that in March, when dog-days (occupancy) were at an annual low of 500, the average cost per dog-day was $21. In July, when dog-days were at a capacity level of 4,000, the average cost per dog-day was $7.

Required

a. Develop an equation for monthly operating costs.

b. Determine the average cost per dog-day at an annual volume of 24,000 dog-days.

E2-23. Selecting an Independent Variable: Scatter Diagrams (LO2, 3)

Valley Production Company produces backpacks that are sold to sporting goods stores throughout the Rocky Mountains. Presented is information on production costs and inventory changes for five recent months:

	January	February	March	April	May
Finished goods inventory in units:					
Beginning	30,000	40,000	50,000	30,000	60,000
Manufactured	60,000	90,000	80,000	90,000	100,000
Available	90,000	130,000	130,000	120,000	160,000
Sold	(50,000)	(80,000)	(100,000)	(60,000)	(120,000)
Ending	40,000	50,000	30,000	60,000	40,000
Manufacturing costs. . .	$300,000	$500,000	$450,000	$450,000	$550,000

Required

a. With the aid of scatter diagrams, determine whether units sold or units manufactured is a better predictor of manufacturing costs.

b. Prepare an explanation for your answer to requirement (a).

c. Which independent variable, units sold or units manufactured, should be a better predictor of selling costs? Why?

E2-24. Selecting a Basis for Predicting Shipping Expenses (Requires Computer Spreadsheet*) (LO2, 3)
Pitt Company assembles and sells computer boards in western Pennsylvania. In an effort to improve the planning and control of shipping expenses, management is trying to determine which of three variables—units shipped, weight shipped, or sales value of units shipped—has the closest relationship with shipping expenses. The following information is available:

Month	Units Shipped	Weight Shipped (lbs.)	Sales Value of Units Shipped	Shipping Expenses
May.	3,000	6,200	$100,000	$ 5,000
June	5,000	8,000	110,000	7,000
July.	4,000	8,100	80,000	6,000
August	7,000	10,000	114,000	10,000
September	6,000	7,000	140,000	8,000
October	4,500	8,000	160,000	7,600

Required

a. With the aid of a spreadsheet program, determine whether units shipped, weight shipped, or sales value of units shipped has the closest relationship with shipping expenses.

b. Using the independent variable that appears to have the closest relationship to shipping expenses, develop a cost-estimating equation for total monthly shipping expenses.

c. Use the equation developed in requirement (b) to predict total shipping expenses in a month when 5,000 units, weighing 7,000 lbs., with a total sales value of $114,000 are shipped.

PROBLEMS

P2-25. High-Low and Scatter Diagrams with Implications for Regression (LO2, 3)
Glaze Donut Shop produces and sells donuts at each of its restaurants. Presented is monthly cost and sales information for one of Glaze's restaurants.

Month	Sales (Dozens)	Total Costs
January.	8,000	$24,000
February	6,500	22,000
March	4,500	17,000
April	2,000	16,000
May.	5,500	18,000
June	6,000	19,500

Required

a. Using the high-low method, develop a cost-estimating equation for the donut shop.

b. 1. Plot the equation developed in requirement (a).

2. Using the same graph, develop a scatter diagram of all observations for the donut shop. Select representative high and low values and draw a second cost-estimating equation.

c. Which is a better predictor of future costs? Why?

d. If you decided to develop a cost-estimating equation using least squares regression analysis, should you include all the observations? Why or why not?

e. Mention two reasons that the least-squares regression is superior to the high-low and scatter diagram methods of cost estimation.

P2-26. Multiple Cost Drivers (LO4)
Scottsdale Ltd. manufactures a variety of high-volume and low-volume products to customer demand. Presented is information on 2009 manufacturing overhead and activity cost drivers.

---

* This exercise and several subsequent assignments require the use of a computer spreadsheet such as Excel® to solve. This assignment assumes previous knowledge of computer spreadsheets.

Level	Total Cost	Units of Cost Driver
Unit	$500,000	20,000 machine hours
Batch	100,000	1,000 customer orders
Product	200,000	50 products

Product X1 required 2,000 machine hours to fill 10 customer orders for a total of 8,000 units.

Required

a. Assuming all manufacturing overhead is estimated and predicted on the basis of machine hours, determine the predicted total overhead costs to produce the 8,000 units of product X1.

b. Assuming manufacturing overhead is estimated and predicted using separate rates for machine hours, customer orders, and products (a multiple-level cost hierarchy), determine the predicted total overhead costs to produce the 8,000 units of product X1.

c. Calculate the error in predicting manufacturing overhead using machine hours versus using multiple cost drivers. Indicate whether the use of only machine hours results in overpredicting or underpredicting the costs to produce 8,000 units of product X1.

d. Determine the error in the prediction of X1 batch-level costs resulting from the use of only machine hours. Indicate whether the use of only machine hours results in overpredicting or underpredicting the batch-level costs of product X1.

e. Determine the error in the prediction of X1 product-level costs resulting from the use of only machine hours. Indicate whether the use of only machine hours results in overpredicting or underpredicting the product-level costs of product X1.

P2-27. Unit- and Batch-Level Cost Drivers (LO4)

KC, a fast-food restaurant, serves fried chicken, fried fish, and French fries. The managers have estimated the costs of a batch of fried chicken for KC's all-you-can-eat Friday Fried Fiesta. Each batch must be 100 pieces. The chicken is precut by the chain headquarters and sent to the stores in 10-piece bags. Each bag costs $3. Preparing a batch of 100 pieces of chicken with KC's special coating takes one employee two hours. The current wage rate is $8 per hour. Another cost driver is the cost of putting fresh oil into the fryers. New oil, costing $5, is used for each batch.

Required

a. Determine the cost of preparing one batch of 100 pieces.

b. If management projects that it will sell 300 pieces of fried chicken, determine the total batch and unit costs.

c. If management estimates the sales to be 350 pieces, determine the total costs.

d. How much will the batch costs increase if the government raises the minimum wage to $10 per hour?

e. If management decided to reduce the number of pieces in a batch to 50, determine the cost of preparing 350 pieces. Assume that the batch would take half as long to prepare, and management wants to replace the oil after 50 pieces are cooked.

f. Refer to your solutions to requirements (c) and (e). Would management be wise to reduce the batch size to 50?

CASES

C2-28. Negative Fixed Costs (LO3)

"This is crazy!" exclaimed the production supervisor as he reviewed the work of his new assistant. "You and that computer are telling me that my fixed costs are negative! Tell me, how did you get these negative fixed costs, and what am I supposed to do with them?"

Required

Explain to the supervisor the meaning of the negative "fixed costs" and what can be done with them.

C2-29. Significance of High R-Squared (LO3)

Oliver Morris had always been suspicious of "newfangled mathematical stuff," and the most recent suggestion of his new assistant merely confirmed his belief that schools are putting a lot of useless junk in students' heads. It seems that after an extensive analysis of historical data, the assistant suggested that the number of pounds of scrap was the best basis for predicting manufacturing overhead. In response to Mr. Morris's rage, the slightly intimidated assistant indicated that of the 35 equations he tried, pounds of scrap had the highest coefficient of determination with manufacturing overhead.

Required

Comment on Morris's reaction. Is it justified? Is it likely that the number of pounds of scrap is a good basis for predicting manufacturing overhead? Is it a feasible basis for predicting manufacturing overhead?

C2-30. Estimating Machine Repair Costs (LO3)

In an attempt to determine the best basis for predicting machine repair costs, the production supervisor accumulated daily information on these costs and production over a one-month period. Applying simple regression analysis to the data, she obtained the following estimating equation:

$$Y = \$800 - \$2.601X$$

where

$$Y = \text{total daily machine repair costs}$$
$$X = \text{daily production in units}$$

Because of the negative relationship between repair costs and production, she was somewhat skeptical of the results, even though the R-squared was a respectable 0.765.

Required

a. What is the most likely explanation of the negative variable costs?

b. Suggest an alternative procedure for estimating machine repair costs that might prove more useful.

C2-31. Ethical Problem Uncovered by Cost Estimation (LO3)

Phoenix Management Company owns and provides management services for several shopping centers. After five years with the company, Mike Moyer was recently promoted to the position of manager of X-Town, an 18-store mall on the outskirts of a downtown area. When he accepted the assignment, Mike was told that he would hold the position for only a couple of years because X-Town would likely be torn down to make way for a new sports stadium. Mike was also told that if he did well in this assignment, he would be in line for heading one of the company's new 200-store operations that were currently in the planning stage.

While reviewing X-Town's financial records for the past few years, Mike observed that last year's oil consumption was up by 8 percent, even though the number of heating degree days was down by 4 percent. Somewhat curious, Mike uncovered the following information:

- X-Town is heated by forced-air oil heat. The furnace is five years old and has been well maintained.
- Fuel oil is kept in four 5,000-gallon underground oil tanks. The oil tanks were installed 25 years ago.
- Replacing the tanks would cost $80,000. If pollution was found, cleanup costs could go as high as $2,000,000, depending on how much oil had leaked into the ground and how far it had spread.
- Replacing the tanks would add more congestion to X-Town's parking situation.

Required

What should Mike do? Explain.

C2-32. Activity Cost Drivers and Cost Estimation (LO3, 4)

Blue Ridge Ice Cream Company produces ten varieties of ice cream in large vats, several thousand gallons at a time. The ice cream is distributed to several categories of customers. Some ice cream is packaged in large containers and sold to college and university food services. Some is packaged in half-gallon or small containers and sold through wholesale distributors to grocery stores. Finally, some is packaged in a variety of individual servings and sold directly to the public from trucks owned and operated by Blue Ridge. Management has always assumed that costs fluctuated with the volume of ice cream, and cost-estimating equations have been based on the following cost function:

Estimated costs = Fixed costs + Variable costs per gallon × Production in gallons

Lately, however, this equation has not been a very accurate predictor of total costs. At the same time, management has noticed that the volumes and varieties of ice cream sold through the three distinct distribution channels have fluctuated from month to month.

Required

a. What *relevant* major assumption is inherent in the cost-estimating equation currently used by Blue Ridge?

b. Why might Blue Ridge wish to develop a cost-estimating equation that recognizes the hierarchy of activity costs? Explain.

c. Develop the general form of a more accurate cost-estimating equation for Blue Ridge. Clearly label and explain all elements of the equation, and provide specific examples of costs for each element.

C2-33. Multiple Regression Analysis for a Special Decision (Requires Computer Spreadsheet) (LO2, 3)
For billing purposes, Central City Health Clinic classifies its services into one of four major procedures, X1 through X4. A local business has proposed that Central City provide health services to its employees and their families at the following set rates per procedure:

X1	$ 45
X2	90
X3	60
X4	105

Because these rates are significantly below the current rates charged for these services, management has asked for detailed cost information on each procedure. The following information is available for the most recent 12 months.

		Number of Procedures			
Month	**Total Cost**	**X1**	**X2**	**X3**	**X4**
1	$23,000	30	100	205	75
2	25,000	38	120	180	90
3	27,000	50	80	140	150
4	19,000	20	90	120	100
5	20,000	67	50	160	80
6	27,000	90	75	210	105
7	25,500	20	110	190	110
8	21,500	15	120	175	80
9	26,000	60	85	125	140
10	22,000	20	90	100	140
11	22,800	20	70	150	130
12	26,500	72	60	200	120

Required

a. Use multiple regression analysis to determine the unit cost of each procedure. How much variation in monthly cost is explained by your cost-estimating equation?

b. Evaluate the rates proposed by the local business. Assuming Central City has excess capacity and no employees of the local business currently patronize the clinic, what are your recommendations regarding the proposal?

c. Evaluate the rates proposed by the local business. Assuming Central City is operating at capacity and would have to turn current customers away if it agrees to provide health services to the local business, what are your recommendations regarding the proposal?

C2-34. Cost Estimation, Interpretation, and Analysis (Requires Computer Spreadsheet) (LO2, 3)
Carolina Table Company produces two styles of tables, dining room and kitchen. Presented is monthly information on production volume and manufacturing costs:

Period	Total Manufacturing Costs	Total Tables Produced	Dining Room Tables Produced	Kitchen Tables Produced
June 2007.	$31,100	250	50	200
July.	33,925	205	105	100
August	40,420	285	105	180
September	26,495	210	40	170
October	28,080	175	75	100
November.	35,050	210	110	100
December.	35,245	245	90	155
January 2008	31,550	250	50	200
February	31,490	220	70	150
March	29,650	180	80	100
April	65,200	315	180	135
May.	39,955	280	105	175
June	34,695	255	75	180
July.	36,920	235	110	125
August	30,815	195	85	110
September	40,290	260	120	140
October	35,805	250	90	160
November.	38,400	270	100	170
December.	25,100	165	60	105

Required

a. Use the high-low method to develop a cost-estimating equation for total manufacturing costs. Interpret the meaning of the "fixed" costs and comment on the results.

b. Use the chart feature of a spreadsheet to develop a scatter graph of total manufacturing costs and total units produced. Use the graph to identify any unusual observations.

c. Excluding any unusual observations, use the high-low method to develop a cost-estimating equation for total manufacturing costs. Comment on the results, comparing them with the results in requirement (a).

d. Use simple regression analysis to develop a cost-estimating equation for total manufacturing costs. What advantages does simple regression analysis have in comparison with the high-low method of cost estimation? Why must analysts carefully evaluate the data used in simple regression analysis?

e. A customer has offered to purchase 50 dining room tables for $180 per table. Management has asked your advice regarding the desirability of accepting the offer. What advice do you have for management? Additional analysis is required.

C2-35. Simple and Multiple Regression (Requires Computer Spreadsheet) **(LO2, 3)**

Wanda Sable is employed by a mail-order distributor and reconditions used tuner/amplifiers, tape decks, and compact disk (CD) players. Wanda is paid $12 per hour, plus an extra $6 per hour for work in excess of 40 hours per week. The distributor just announced plans to outsource all reconditioning work. Because the distributor is pleased with the quality of Wanda's work, she has been asked to enter into a long-term contract to recondition used CD players at a rate of $30 per player, plus all parts. The distributor also offered to provide all necessary equipment at a rate of $200 per month. She has been informed that she should plan on reconditioning as many CD players as she can handle, up to a maximum of 20 CD players per week.

Wanda has room in her basement to set up a work area, but she is unsure of the economics of accepting the contract, as opposed to working for a local Radio Stuff store at $8 per hour. Data related to the time spent and the number of units of each type of electronic equipment Wanda has reconditioned in recent weeks is as follows:

Week	Tuner Amplifiers	Tape Decks	Compact Disk (CD) Players	Total Units	Total Hours
1	4	5	5	14	40
2	0	7	6	13	42
3	4	3	7	14	40
4	0	2	12	14	46
5	11	6	4	21	48
6	5	8	3	16	44
7	5	8	3	16	44
8	5	6	5	16	43
9	2	6	10	18	53
10	8	4	6	18	46
Total				160	446

Required

Assuming she wants to work an average of 40 hours per week, what should Wanda do?

Chapter 3

Cost-Volume-Profit Analysis and Planning

LEARNING OBJECTIVES

LO1 Identify the uses and limitations of traditional cost-volume-profit analysis. (p. 60)

LO2 Prepare and contrast contribution and functional income statements. (p. 63)

LO3 Apply cost-volume-profit analysis to find a break-even point and for preliminary profit planning. (p. 65)

LO4 Analyze the profitability and sales mix of a multiple-product firm. (p. 71)

LO5 Apply operating leverage ratio to assess opportunities for profit and the risks of loss. (p. 74)

COST STRUCTURE AND FIRM PROFITABILITY

Throughout the first decade of the 21st century, the profits of many established businesses were rocked by soaring energy costs and increased competition facilitated by innovation and technology. While many new businesses, taking advantage of new technologies and innovations, prospered, many established firms with high fixed costs struggled to maintain their position in their marketplace. The profitability challenges faced by **AMR Corporation** and **Blockbuster, Inc.** and the financial success of **Netflix** highlight the impact cost structure has on a firm's profitability.

So far in the 21st century, the profits of AMR Corporation's two major subsidiaries, **American Airlines** and **American Eagle Airlines**, have been battered by fuel costs, which increased from $0.781/gallon in 2000 to $3.310/gallon in 2008. Caught off guard, AMR reported losses through the mid-2000s, but returned to profitability in 2006 and 2007 by significantly reducing their fleet of aircraft (a facility-level cost), dropping unprofitable routes, reducing in-flight service such as complimentary meals, increasing their passenger load factor to more than 80 percent, and, where possible in the face of competition from discount carriers such as **Southwest Airlines**, increasing ticket prices.

The rivalry between Blockbuster and Netflix is another example of the impact cost structure and innovation have on businesses. Established in the 1980s, Blockbuster, Inc. initially rented and sold VHS video tapes through a network of stores it owned or franchised. At one time, there were more than 8,000 Blockbuster stores worldwide. Technological innovations including the digitization of video and the dramatic increase in the use of

Courtesy of Netflix

the Internet provided an opportunity for a new competitor, Netflix, to offer DVD rentals through the Internet. By using the Internet to market and distribute videos to customers, Netflix was able to avoid the fixed costs that result from having physical stores. In addition, the Internet makes it possible for customers to select movies from the comfort of their own home without having to drive to a store. Given the convenience, competitive price, and overall positive customer experience, it's no wonder that Netflix has enjoyed considerable growth in a very short period of time (fewer than 1 million subscribers in 2002 to more than 6 million in 2007). Netflix's growth comes at the expense of Blockbuster, which is burdened with high facility-level costs.

To reduce fixed costs, Blockbuster closed many retail outlets and implemented a service similar to Netflix's with online ordering and mail delivery/return of DVDs. In addition, Blockbuster offered customers the option of in-store pickup/return. Meanwhile, Netflix, using what its management describes as a "scalable, low-cost business model," opened more than 40 distribution centers providing one-day delivery to most of its customers. Raising the competitive bar, Netflix provided subscribers PC video streaming at no additional cost in 2007 and in 2008 contracted with LG Electronics to develop a device allowing Netflix subscribers to stream movies directly to their TVs.

High fixed costs can yield huge profits in the right circumstances. Yet, the recent experiences of such firms as AMR and Blockbuster illustrate that fixed cost structures have some inherent risks. Periods of rapid change often favor more nimble organizations that are not burdened with fixed costs resulting from past decisions. The relationships among cost structures, potential volumes, and opportunities for profit provide a conceptual basis for profitability analysis and planning, which is the focus of this chapter.

Sources: Susan Carey and Melanie Trottman, "Airlines Face New Reckoning As Fuel Costs Take Big Bite, *The Wall Street Journal,* March 20, 2008, pp. A1 & A15; Cliff Edwards, "Netflix's Breakout Move," *Business Week Online*, January 3, 2008, p.2.; Doug DesJardibs, "Blockbuster's Recent Moves Shifts Focus to Digital Business," *Retailing Today*, March 19, 2007, p. 4; annual reposts and press releases available at www.americanairlines.com, www.blockbuster.com, www.netflix.com.

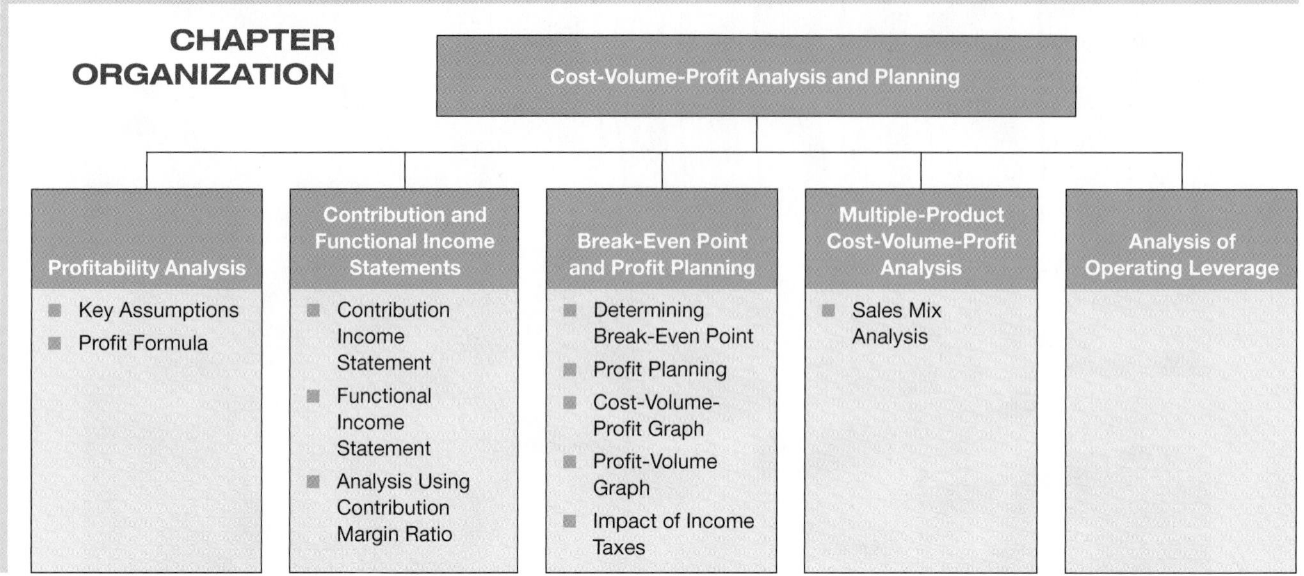

This chapter introduces basic approaches to profitability analysis and planning. We consider single-product, multiple-product, and service organizations; income taxes, sales mix, and the effects of cost structure on the relation between profit potential and the risk of loss.

PROFITABILITY ANALYSIS

LO1 Identify the uses and limitations of traditional cost-volume-profit analysis.

Profitability analysis involves examining the relationships among revenues, costs, and profits. Performing profitability analysis requires an understanding of selling prices and the behavior of activity cost drivers. Profitability analysis is widely used in the economic evaluation of existing or proposed products or services. Typically, it is performed before decisions are finalized in the operating budget for a future period.

Cost-volume-profit (CVP) analysis is a technique used to examine the relationships among the total volume of an independent variable, total costs, total revenues, and profits for a time period (typically a quarter or year). With CVP analysis, volume refers to a single activity cost driver, such as unit sales, that is assumed to correlate with changes in revenues, costs, and profits.

Cost-volume-profit analysis is useful in the early stages of planning because it provides an easily understood framework for discussing planning issues and organizing relevant data. CVP analysis is widely used by for-profit as well as not-for-profit organizations. It is equally applicable to service, merchandising, and manufacturing firms.

In for-profit organizations, CVP analysis is used to answer such questions as these: How many photocopies must the local Kinko's produce to earn a profit of $80,000? At what dollar sales volume will Burger King's total revenues and total costs be equal? What profit will General Electric earn at an annual sales volume of $60 billion? What will happen to the profit of Red Lobster if there is a 20 percent increase in the cost of food and a 10 percent increase in the selling price of meals? The Research Insight box on the following page indicates the importance of the concepts discussed in this and other chapters to the success of new businesses.

In not-for-profit organizations, CVP analysis is used to establish service levels, plan fund-raising activities, and determine funding requirements. How many meals can the downtown Salvation Army serve with an annual budget of $600,000? How many tickets must be sold for the benefit concert to raise $20,000? Given the current cost structure, current tuition rates, and projected enrollments, how much money must Cornell University raise from other sources?

Key Assumptions

CVP analysis is subject to a number of assumptions. Although these assumptions do not negate the usefulness of CVP models, especially for a single product or service, they do suggest the need for further analysis before plans are finalized. Among the more important assumptions are:

1. *All costs are classified as fixed or variable*. This assumption is most reasonable when analyzing the profitability of a specific event (such as a concert) or the profitability of an organization that produces a single product or service on a continuous basis.
2. *The total cost function is linear within the relevant range*. This assumption is often valid within a relevant range of normal operations, but over the entire range of possible activity, changes in efficiency are likely to result in a nonlinear cost function.
3. *The total revenue function is linear within the relevant range*. Unit selling prices are assumed constant over the range of possible volumes. This implies a purely competitive market for final products or services. In some economic models in which demand responds to price changes, the revenue function is nonlinear. In these situations, the linear approximation is accurate only within a limited range of activity.
4. *The analysis is for a single product, or the sales mix of multiple products is constant*. The **sales mix** refers to the relative portion of unit or dollar sales derived from each product or service. If products have different selling prices and costs, changes in the mix affect CVP model results.
5. *There is only one cost driver: unit or sales dollar volume*. In a complex organization it is seldom possible to represent the multitude of factors that drive cost with a single cost driver.

When applied to a single product (such as pounds of potato chips), service (such as the number of pages printed), or event (such as the number of tickets sold to a banquet), it is reasonable to assume the single independent variable is the cost driver. The total costs associated with the single product, service, or event during a specific time period are often determined by this single activity cost driver.

Although cost-volume-profit analysis is often used to understand the overall operations of an organization or business segment, accuracy decreases as the scope of operations being analyzed increases.

RESEARCH INSIGHT **Careless Financial Management Is a Primary Cause of Business Failure**

New small businesses, with fewer than 20 employees, have less than a twenty percent probability of surviving five years, with the highest failure rate occurring during the first year. Studies of business failure and testimony offered at the Securities and Exchange Commission's Government-Business Forum suggests that a leading cause of small businesses failures is the lack of knowledge about accounting, especially management accounting and internal control, by the owners and managers. "The antidote to small business failure," according to Samuel Bornstein writing in *Community Banker*, "is knowledge and understanding of practical accounting and its analytic tools and techniques, which provide the business owner indications of where the business has been, where it is, and where it is going."[1]

Profit Formula

The profit associated with a product, service, or event is equal to the difference between total revenues and total costs as follows:

$$\pi = R - Y$$

where

$$\pi = \text{Profit}$$
$$R = \text{Total revenues}$$
$$Y = \text{Total costs}$$

The revenues are a function of the unit sales volume and the unit selling price, while total costs for a time period are a function of the fixed costs per period and the unit variable costs as follows:

$$R = pX$$
$$Y = a + bX$$

[1] Samuel Bornstein, "Fighting Failure," *Community Banker*, May 2007, pp. 38–42.

where

$$\begin{aligned} p &= \text{Unit selling price} \\ a &= \text{Fixed costs} \\ b &= \text{Unit variable costs} \\ X &= \text{Unit sales} \end{aligned}$$

The equation for profit can then be expanded to include the above details of the total revenue and total cost equations as follows:

$$\pi = pX - (a + bX)$$

Using information on the selling price, fixed costs per period, and variable costs per unit, this formula is used to predict profit at any specified activity level.

To illustrate, assume that Benchmark Paper Company's only product is high-quality photocopy paper that it manufactures and sells to wholesale distributors at $8.00 per carton. Applying inventory minimization techniques, Benchmark does not maintain inventories of raw materials or finished goods. Instead, newly purchased raw materials are delivered directly to the factory, and finished goods are loaded directly onto trucks for shipment. Benchmark's variable and fixed costs follow.

1. **Direct materials** refer to the cost of the primary raw materials converted into finished goods. Because the consumption of raw materials increases as the quantity of goods produced increases, *direct materials represents a variable cost*. Benchmark's raw materials consist primarily of paper purchased in large rolls and packing supplies such as boxes. Benchmark also treats the costs of purchasing, receiving, and inspecting raw materials as part of the cost of direct materials. All together, these costs are $1.00 per carton of finished product.
2. **Direct labor** refers to wages earned by production employees for the time they spend working on the conversion of raw materials into finished goods. Based on Benchmark's manufacturing procedures, *direct labor represents a variable cost*. These costs are $0.25 per carton.
3. **Variable manufacturing overhead** includes all other variable costs associated with converting raw materials into finished goods. Benchmark's variable manufacturing overhead costs include the costs of lubricants for cutting and packaging machines, electricity to operate these machines, and the cost to move materials between receiving and shipping docks and the cutting and packaging machines. These costs are $1.25 per carton.
4. **Variable selling and administrative costs** include all variable costs other than those directly associated with converting raw materials into finished goods. At Benchmark, these costs include sales commissions, transportation of finished goods to wholesale distributors, and the cost of processing the receipt and disbursement of cash. These costs are $0.50 per carton.
5. **Fixed manufacturing overhead** includes all fixed costs associated with converting raw materials into finished goods. Benchmark's fixed manufacturing costs include the depreciation, property taxes, and insurance on buildings and machines used for manufacturing, the salaries of manufacturing supervisors, and the fixed portion of electricity used to light the factory. These costs are $5,000.00 per month.
6. **Fixed selling and administrative costs** include all fixed costs other than those directly associated with converting raw materials into finished goods. These costs include the salaries of Benchmark's president and many other staff personnel such as accounting and marketing. Also included are depreciation, property taxes, insurance on facilities used for administrative purposes, and any related utilities costs. These costs are $10,000.00 per month.

Benchmark's variable and fixed costs are summarized here.

Variable Costs per Carton			Fixed Costs per Month	
Manufacturing			Manufacturing overhead	$ 5,000.00
Direct materials.	$1.00		Selling and administrative	10,000.00
Direct labor	0.25		Total	$15,000.00
Manufacturing overhead. . .	1.25	$2.50		
Selling and administrative . . .		0.50		
Total		$3.00		

The cost estimation techniques discussed in Chapter 2 can be used to determine many detailed costs. Least-squares regression, for example, might be used to determine the variable and monthly fixed amount of electricity used in manufacturing. Benchmark manufactures and sells a single product on a continuous basis with all sales to distributors under standing contracts. Therefore, it is reasonable to assume that in the short run, Benchmark's total monthly costs respond to a single cost driver, cartons sold. Combining all this information, Benchmark's profit equation is:

$$\textbf{Profit} = \$8.00X - (\$15{,}000.00 + \$3.00X)$$

where

$$X = \textbf{cartons sold}$$

Using this equation, Benchmark's profit at a volume of 5,400 units is $12,000.00, computed as ($8.00 × 5,400) − [$15,000.00 + ($3.00 × 5,400)].

CONTRIBUTION AND FUNCTIONAL INCOME STATEMENTS

Contribution Income Statement

LO2 Prepare and contrast contribution and functional income statements.

To provide more detailed information on anticipated or actual financial results at a particular sales volume, a contribution income statement is often prepared. Benchmark's contribution income statement for a volume of 5,400 units is in Exhibit 3.1. In a **contribution income statement**, costs are classified according to behavior as variable or fixed, and the **contribution margin** (the difference between total revenues and total variable costs) that goes toward covering fixed costs and providing a profit is emphasized.

EXHIBIT 3.1 Contribution Income Statement

BENCHMARK PAPER COMPANY
Contribution Income Statement
For a Monthly Volume of 5,400 Cartons

Sales (5,400 × $8.00)		$43,200
Less variable costs		
Direct materials (5,400 × $1.00)	$ 5,400	
Direct labor (5,400 × $0.25)	1,350	
Manufacturing overhead (5,400 × $1.25)	6,750	
Selling and administrative (5,400 × $0.50)	2,700	(16,200)
Contribution margin		27,000
Less fixed costs		
Manufacturing overhead	5,000	
Selling and administrative	10,000	(15,000)
Profit		$12,000

Functional Income Statement

Contrast the contribution income statement in Exhibit 3.1 with the income statement in Exhibit 3.2 (next page). This statement is called a **functional income statement** because costs are classified according to function (rather than behavior), such as manufacturing, selling, and administrative. This is the type of income statement typically included in corporate annual reports.

EXHIBIT 3.2 Functional Income Statement

BENCHMARK PAPER COMPANY
Functional Income Statement
For a Monthly Volume of 5,400 Cartons

Sales (5,400 × $8.00)		$43,200
Less cost of goods sold		
Direct materials (5,400 × $1.00)	$ 5,400	
Direct labor (5,400 × $0.25)	1,350	
Variable manufacturing overhead (5,400 × $1.25)	6,750	
Fixed manufacturing overhead	5,000	(18,500)
Gross margin		24,700
Less other expenses		
Variable selling and administrative (5,400 × $0.50)	2,700	
Fixed selling and administrative	10,000	(12,700)
Profit		$12,000

A problem with a functional income statement is the difficulty of relating it to the profit formula in which costs are classified according to behavior rather than function. The relationship between sales volume, costs, and profits is not readily apparent in a functional income statement. Consequently, we emphasize contribution income statements because they provide better information to internal decision makers.

Analysis Using Contribution Margin Ratio

While the contribution income statement (shown in Exhibit 3.1) presents information on total sales revenue, total variable costs, and so forth, it is sometimes useful to present information on a per-unit or portion of sales basis.

	Total	Per Unit	Ratio to Sales
Sales (5,400 units)	$43,200	$8	1.000
Variable costs	(16,200)	(3)	(0.375)
Contribution margin	27,000	$5	0.625
Fixed costs	(15,000)		
Profit	$12,000		

The per-unit information assists in short-range planning. The **unit contribution margin** is the difference between the unit selling price and the unit variable costs. It is the amount, $5.00 in this case, that each unit contributes toward covering fixed costs and earning a profit.

The contribution margin is widely used in **sensitivity analysis** (the study of the responsiveness of a model to changes in one or more of its independent variables). Benchmark's income statement is an economic model of the firm, and the unit contribution margin indicates how sensitive Benchmark's income model is to changes in unit sales. If, for example, sales increase by 100 cartons per month, the increase in profit is readily determined by multiplying the 100-carton increase in sales by the $5 unit contribution margin as follows:

100 (carton sales increase) × $5 (unit contribution margin) = $500 (profit increase)

There is no increase in fixed costs, so the new profit level becomes $12,500 ($12,000 + $500) per month.

When expressed as a ratio to sales, the contribution margin is identified as the **contribution margin ratio**. It is the portion of each dollar of sales revenue contributed toward covering fixed costs and earning a profit. In the abbreviated income statement above, the portion of each dollar of sales revenue contributed toward covering fixed costs and earning a profit is \$0.625 (\$27,000 ÷ \$43,200). This is Benchmark's contribution margin ratio. If sales revenue increases by \$800 per month, the increase in profits is computed as follows:

\$800 (sales increase) × 0.625 (contribution margin ratio) = \$500 (profit increase)

The contribution margin ratio is especially useful in situations involving several products or when unit sales information is not available.

BREAK-EVEN POINT AND PROFIT PLANNING

LO3 Apply cost-volume-profit analysis to find a break-even point and for preliminary profit planning.

The **break-even point** occurs at the unit or dollar sales volume when total revenues equal total costs. The break-even point is of great interest to management. Until break-even sales are reached, the product, service, event, or business segment of interest operates at a loss. Beyond this point, increasing levels of profits are achieved. Also, management often wants to know the **margin of safety**, the amount by which actual or planned sales exceed the break-even point. Other questions of interest include the probability of exceeding the break-even sales volume and the effect of some proposed change on the break-even point.

Determining Break-Even Point

In determining the break-even point, the equation for total revenues is set equal to the equation for total costs and then solved for the break-even unit sales volume. Using the general equations for total revenues and total costs, the following results are obtained. Setting total revenues equal to total costs:

$$\textbf{Total revenues} = \textbf{Total costs}$$
$$pX = a + bX$$

Solving for the break-even sales volume:

$$pX - bX = a$$
$$(p - b)X = a$$
$$X = a/(p - b)$$

In words:

$$\textbf{Break-even unit sales volume} = \frac{\textbf{Fixed costs}}{\textbf{Selling price per unit} - \textbf{Variable costs per unit}}$$

Because the denominator is the unit contribution margin, the break-even point is also computed by dividing fixed costs by the unit contribution margin:

$$\textbf{Break-even unit sales volume} = \frac{\textbf{Fixed costs}}{\textbf{Unit contribution margin}}$$

With a \$5 unit contribution margin and fixed costs of \$15,000 per month, Benchmark's break-even point is 3,000 units per month (\$15,000 ÷ \$5). Stated another way, at a \$5 per-unit contribution margin, 3,000 units of contribution are required to cover \$15,000 of fixed costs. With a break-even point of 3,000 units, the monthly margin of safety and expected profit for a sales volume of 5,400 units are 2,400 units (5,400 expected unit sales − 3,000 break-even sales) and \$12,000 (2,400 unit margin of safety × \$5 unit contribution margin), respectively.

The break-even point concept is applicable to a wide variety of business and personal planning situations. The following Research Insight box illustrates how a personal financial planner might use break-even point concepts to assist a client making a retirement decision.

RESEARCH INSIGHT **Determining the Cash Break-Even Point for Delaying Retirement**

According to the Institute of Certified Financial Planners (ICFP), financial planning is the process of meeting life goals through the proper management of finances. Life goals can include buying a home, saving for a child's education, or planning for retirement. Among the many personal financial planning decisions related to retirement in the United States is the question of when to file for Social Security benefits.

Social Security retirement benefits are a function of years worked, contributions to the Social Security System, and the age at which the recipient files for Social Security retirement benefits. People born in 1960 and later are currently entitled to full retirement benefits if they start receiving benefits at age 67. They may, however, file for reduced benefits starting at age 62. Someone with an average annual income of $100,000 contemplating retirement at age 62 might ask: (1) how large is the reduction in benefits and (2) what is the break-even age at which the benefits from delaying retirement until age 67 equals the cumulative benefits from retiring at age 62?

An individual with the analytic skills obtained from a managerial accounting course can readily determine the answers to these questions after consulting the Social Security web site www.ssa.gov. Others might consult a personal financial planner.

(1) Assuming retirement at age 67, a person born in 1960 or later with an average annual income of $100,000 is entitled to monthly Social Security retirement benefits of $2,265. If that person started receiving benefits at age 62 their monthly benefits are reduced by 30 percent (www.ssa.gov/retirement/1960), or $679 ($2,265 × 0.30), to $1,586.

(2) With retirement at age 62, the early retiree would receive total benefits of $95,160 ($1,586 × 12 months × 5 years) by age 67, the normal retirement age. Treating this as a fixed amount to be recovered by the subsequent incremental monthly benefits of $679 from delaying the receipt of monthly benefits to age 67, the break-even age is computed as follows:

Months beyond age 67 = $95,160/$679 = 140 months or 11 2/3 years.

Hence, the break-even age is 78 2/3 years (67 years + 11 2/3 years).

Note that this analysis does not consider any return on the $95,160 that might be earned by investing the benefits received during early retirement. Such returns would increase the break-even age. Nor does it consider the lost wages that could have been earned between age 62 and age 67. [2]

Profit Planning

Establishing profit objectives is an important part of planning in for-profit organizations. Profit objectives are stated in many ways. They can be set as a percentage of last year's profits, as a percentage of total assets at the start of the current year, or as a percentage of owners' equity. They might be based on a profit trend, or they might be expressed as a percentage of sales. The economic outlook for the firm's products as well as anticipated changes in products, costs, and technology are also considered in establishing profit objectives.

Before incorporating profit plans into a detailed budget, it is useful to obtain some preliminary information on the feasibility of those plans. Cost-volume-profit analysis is one way of doing this. By manipulating cost-volume-profit relationships, management can determine the sales volume corresponding to a desired profit. Management might then evaluate the feasibility of this sales volume. If the profit plans are feasible, a complete budget might be developed for this activity level. The required sales volume might be infeasible because of market conditions or because the required volume exceeds production or service capacity, in which case management must lower its profit objective or consider other ways of achieving it. Alternatively, the required sales volume might be less than management believes the firm is capable of selling, in which case management might raise its profit objective.

Assume that Benchmark's management desires to know the unit sales volume required to achieve a monthly profit of $18,000. Using the profit formula, the required unit sales volume is determined by setting profits equal to $18,000 and solving for X, the unit sales volume.

[2] www.cfp.net, www.ssa.gov, and www.ssa.gov/retirement/1960.

$$\text{Profit} = \text{Total revenues} - \text{Total costs}$$
$$\$18{,}000 = \$8X - (\$15{,}000 + \$3X)$$

Solving for *X*

$$\$8X - \$3X = \$15{,}000 + \$18{,}000$$
$$X = (\$15{,}000 + \$18{,}000) \div \$5$$
$$= 6{,}600 \text{ units}$$

The total contribution must cover the desired profit as well as the fixed costs. Hence, the target sales volume required to achieve a desired profit is computed as the fixed costs plus the desired profit, all divided by the unit contribution margin.

$$\text{Target unit sales volume} = \frac{\text{Fixed costs} + \text{Desired profit}}{\text{Unit contribution margin}}$$

The Business Insight box below considers CVP analysis for **Hewlett-Packard**, a large manufacturer whose strategic position for personal computers focuses on cost leadership.

BUSINESS INSIGHT **HP's High-Volume, Low-Price Break-Even Point**

"The wealthiest 1 billion people in the world are pretty well served by IT companies," says HP's director of its e-inclusion program. "We're targeting the next 4 billion." The goal of e-inclusion is for HP to be the leader in satisfying a demand for simple and economical computer products for technology-excluded regions of the world. HP already derives 60 percent of its sales overseas, and it plans to build on these beachheads to develop what may be the greatest marketing frontier of the coming decades. With worldwide operations and a low selling price, the HP strategy combines high fixed costs and a low contribution margin, leading to a high break-even point. While the final payoff is unclear, one HP official observed, "You don't get a harvest until you start planting."[3]

Cost-Volume-Profit Graph

A **cost-volume-profit graph** illustrates the relationships among activity volume, total revenues, total costs, and profits. Its usefulness comes from highlighting the break-even point and depicting revenue, cost, and profit relationships over a range of activity. This representation allows management to view the relative amount of important variables at any graphed volume. Benchmark's monthly CVP graph is in Exhibit 3.3. Total revenues and total costs are measured on the vertical axis, with unit sales measured on the horizontal axis. Separate lines are drawn for total variable costs, total costs, and total revenues. The vertical distance between the total revenue and the total cost lines depicts the amount of profit or loss at a given volume. Losses occur when total revenues are less than total costs; profits occur when total revenues exceed total costs.

The total contribution margin is shown by the difference between the total revenue and the total variable cost lines. Observe that as unit sales increase, the contribution margin first goes to cover the fixed costs. Beyond the break-even point, any additional contribution margin provides a profit.

Profit-Volume Graph

In cost-volume-profit graphs, profits are represented by the difference between total revenues and total costs. When management is primarily interested in the impact of changes in sales volume on profits and less interested in the related revenues and costs, a **profit-volume graph** is sometimes used. A profit-volume graph illustrates the relationship between volume and profits; it does not show revenues and costs. Profits are read directly from a profit-volume graph, rather than being computed as the difference between total revenues and total costs. Profit-volume graphs are developed by plotting either unit sales or total revenues on the horizontal axis.

[3] Pete Engardio and Geri Smith, "Hewlett-Packard," *Business Week*, August 27, 2001, p. 137.

EXHIBIT 3.3 Cost-Volume-Profit Graph*

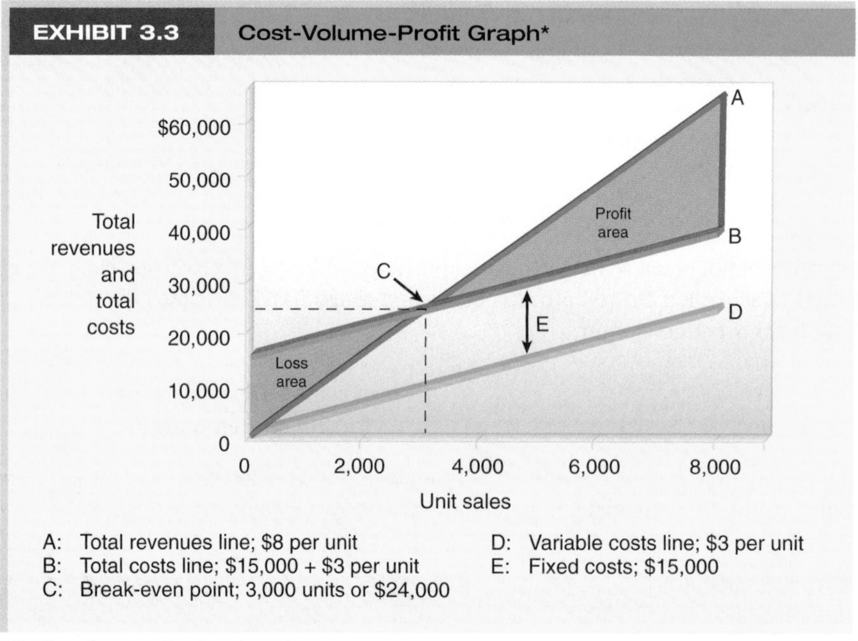

A: Total revenues line; $8 per unit
B: Total costs line; $15,000 + $3 per unit
C: Break-even point; 3,000 units or $24,000
D: Variable costs line; $3 per unit
E: Fixed costs; $15,000

*The three lines are developed as follows:

1. Total variable costs line, D, is drawn between the origin and total variable costs at an arbitrary sales volume. At 8,000 units, total variable costs are $24,000.
2. Total revenues line, A, is drawn through the origin and a point representing total revenues at some arbitrary sales volume. At 8,000 units, Benchmark's total revenues are $64,000.
3. Total cost line, B, is computed by layering fixed costs, $15,000 in this case, on top of total variable costs. This gives a vertical axis intercept of $15,000 and total costs of $39,000 at 8,000 units.

Benchmark's monthly profit-volume graph, is presented in Exhibit 3.4. Profit or loss is measured on the vertical axis, and volume (total revenues) is measured on the horizontal axis, which intersects the vertical axis at zero profit. A single line, representing total profit, is drawn intersecting the vertical axis at zero sales volume with a loss equal to the fixed costs. The profit line crosses the horizontal axis at the break-even sales volume. The profit or loss at any volume is depicted by the vertical difference between the profit line and the horizontal axis. The slope of the profit line is determined by the contribution margin. The greater the contribution margin ratio or the unit contribution margin, the steeper the slope of the profit line.

EXHIBIT 3.4 Profit-Volume Graph*

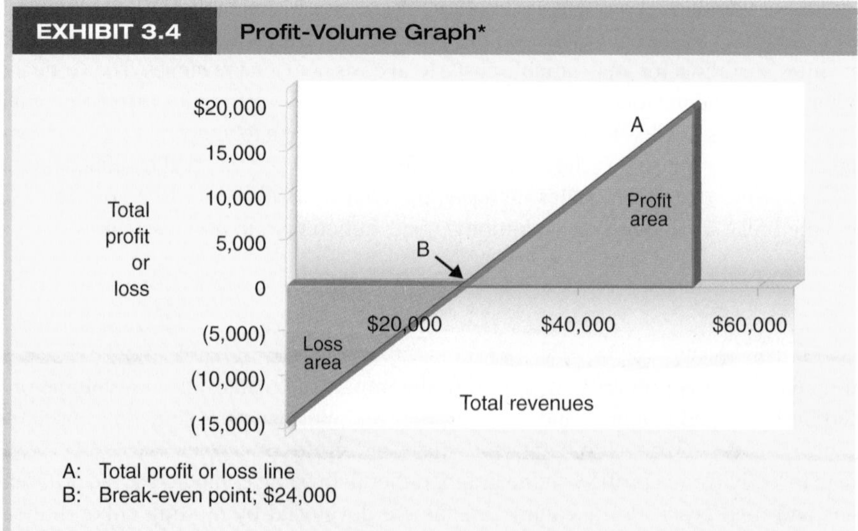

A: Total profit or loss line
B: Break-even point; $24,000

*The profit line is drawn by determining and plotting profit or loss at two different volumes and then drawing a straight line through the plotted values. Perhaps the easiest values to select are the loss at a volume of zero (with a loss equal to the fixed costs) and the volume at which the profit line crosses the horizontal axis (this is the break-even volume).

Impact of Income Taxes

Income taxes are imposed on individuals and for-profit organizations by government agencies. The amount of an individual's or organization's income tax is determined by laws that specify the calculation of taxable income (the income subject to tax) and the calculation of the amount of tax on taxable income. Income taxes are computed as a percentage of taxable income, with increases in taxable income usually subject to progressively higher tax rates. The laws governing the computation of taxable income differ in many ways from the accounting principles that guide the computation of accounting income. Consequently, taxable income and accounting income are seldom the same.

In the early stages of profit planning, income taxes are sometimes incorporated in CVP models by assuming that taxable income and accounting income are identical and that the tax rate is constant. Although these assumptions are seldom true, they are useful for assisting management in developing an early prediction of the sales volume required to earn a desired after-tax profit. Once management has developed a general plan, this early prediction should be refined with the advice of tax experts.

Assuming taxes are imposed at a constant rate per dollar of before-tax profit, income taxes are computed as before-tax profit multipled by the tax rate. After-tax profit is equal to before-tax profit minus income taxes.

$$\textbf{After-tax profit} = \textbf{Before-tax profit} - (\textbf{Before-tax profit} \times \textbf{Tax rate})$$

After-tax profit can also be expressed as before-tax profit times 1 minus the tax rate.

$$\textbf{After-tax profit} = \textbf{Before-tax profit} \times (1 - \textbf{Tax rate})$$

This formula can be rearranged to isolate before-tax profit as follows:

$$\textbf{Before-tax profit} = \frac{\textbf{After-tax profit}}{(1 - \textbf{Tax rate})}$$

Since all costs and revenues in the profit formula are expressed on a before-tax basis, the most straightforward way of determining the unit sales volume required to earn a desired after-tax profit is to:

1. Determine the required before-tax profit.
2. Substitute the required before-tax profit into the profit formula.
3. Solve for the required unit sales volume.

To illustrate, assume that Benchmark is subject to a 40 percent tax rate and that management desires to earn an after-tax profit of $18,000 for November 2009. The required before-tax profit is $30,000 [$18,000 ÷ (1 − 0.40)], and the unit sales volume required to earn this profit is 9,000 units [($15,000 + $30,000) ÷ $5].

Income taxes increase the sales volume required to earn a desired after-tax profit. A 40 percent tax rate increased the sales volume required for Benchmark to earn a profit of $18,000 from 6,600 to 9,000 units. These amounts are verified in Exhibit 3.5.

Another way to remember the computation of before-tax profit is shown on the right side of Exhibit 3.5. The before-tax profit represents 100 percent of the pie, with 40 percent going to income taxes and 60 percent remaining after taxes. Working back from the remaining 60 percent ($18,000), we can determine the 100 percent (before-tax profit) by dividing after-tax profit by 0.60.

EXHIBIT 3.5 Contribution Income Statement with Income Taxes

BENCHMARK PAPER COMPANY
Contribution Income Statement
Planned for the Month of November 2009

Sales (9,000 × $8.00)		$72,000	
Less variable costs			
Direct materials (9,000 × $1.00)	$ 9,000		
Direct labor (9,000 × $0.25)	2,250		
Manufacturing overhead (9,000 × $1.25)	11,250		
Selling and administrative (9,000 × $0.50)	4,500	(27,000)	
Contribution margin		45,000	
Less fixed costs			
Manufacturing overhead	5,000		
Selling and administrative	10,000	(15,000)	
Before-tax profit		30,000	100%
Income taxes ($30,000 × 0.40)		(12,000)	(40)%
After-tax profit		$18,000	60%

MID-CHAPTER REVIEW

Memorabilia Cup Company produces keepsake 16-ounce beverage containers for educational institutions. Memorabilia sells the cups for $40 per box of 50 containers. Variable and fixed costs follow:

Variable Costs per Box			Fixed Costs per Month	
Manufacturing			Manufacturing overhead	$15,000
Direct materials.	$15		Selling and administrative	10,000
Direct labor	3		Total	$25,000
Manufacturing overhead. . .	10	$28		
Selling and administrative . . .		2		
Total		$30		

In September 2009, Memorabilia produced and sold 3,000 boxes of beverage containers.

Required

a. Prepare a contribution income statement for September 2009.

b. Prepare a cost-volume-profit graph with unit sales as the independent variable. Label the revenue line, total costs line, fixed costs line, loss area, profit area, and break-even point. The recommended scale for the horizontal axis is 0 to 5,000 units, and the recommended scale for the vertical axis is $0 to $200,000.

c. Determine Memorabilia's unit contribution margin and contribution margin ratio.

d. Determine Memorabilia's monthly break-even point in units.

e. Determine the monthly dollar sales required for a monthly profit of $5,000 (ignoring taxes).

f. Assuming Memorabilia is subject to a 40 percent income tax, determine the monthly unit sales required to produce a monthly after-tax profit of $4,500.

Solution

a.

MEMORABILIA CUP COMPANY
Contribution Income Statement
For the Month of September 2009

Sales (3,000 × $40)		$120,000
Less variable costs		
Direct materials (3,000 × $15)	$45,000	
Direct labor (3,000 × $3).	9,000	
Manufacturing overhead (3,000 × $10)	30,000	
Selling and administrative (3,000 × $2)	6,000	(90,000)
Contribution margin		30,000
Less fixed costs		
Manufacturing overhead.	15,000	
Selling and administrative.	10,000	(25,000)
Profit.		$ 5,000

b.

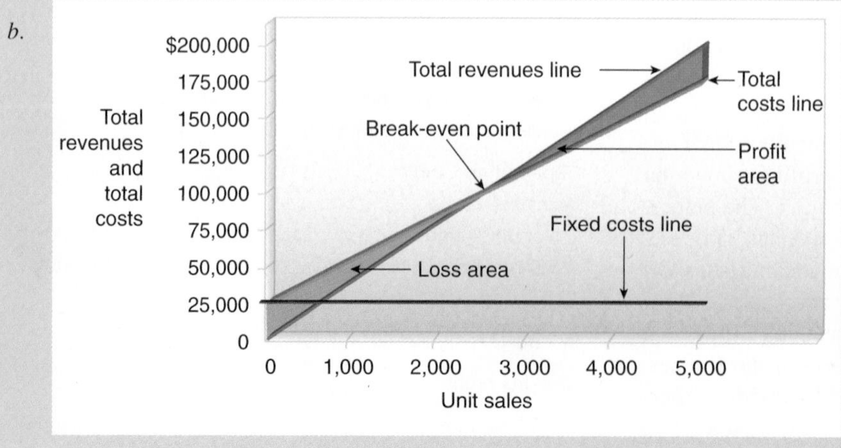

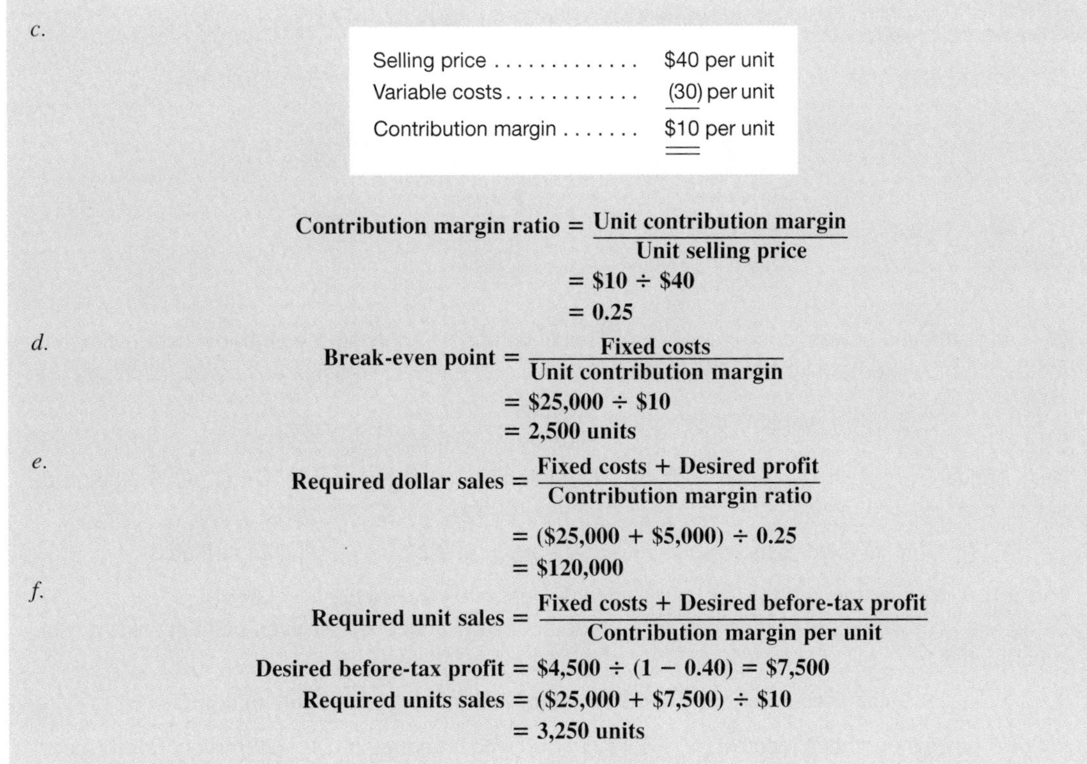

c.

Selling price	\$40 per unit
Variable costs.	(30) per unit
Contribution margin	\$10 per unit

$$\text{Contribution margin ratio} = \frac{\text{Unit contribution margin}}{\text{Unit selling price}}$$
$$= \$10 \div \$40$$
$$= 0.25$$

d.

$$\text{Break-even point} = \frac{\text{Fixed costs}}{\text{Unit contribution margin}}$$
$$= \$25{,}000 \div \$10$$
$$= 2{,}500 \text{ units}$$

e.

$$\text{Required dollar sales} = \frac{\text{Fixed costs + Desired profit}}{\text{Contribution margin ratio}}$$
$$= (\$25{,}000 + \$5{,}000) \div 0.25$$
$$= \$120{,}000$$

f.

$$\text{Required unit sales} = \frac{\text{Fixed costs + Desired before-tax profit}}{\text{Contribution margin per unit}}$$
$$\text{Desired before-tax profit} = \$4{,}500 \div (1 - 0.40) = \$7{,}500$$
$$\text{Required units sales} = (\$25{,}000 + \$7{,}500) \div \$10$$
$$= 3{,}250 \text{ units}$$

MULTIPLE-PRODUCT COST-VOLUME-PROFIT ANALYSIS

LO4 Analyze the profitability and sales mix of a multiple-product firm.

Unit cost information is not always available or appropriate when analyzing cost-volume-profit relationships of multiple-product firms. Assuming the sales mix is constant, the contribution margin ratio (the portion of each sales dollar contributed toward covering fixed costs and earning a profit) can be used to determine the break-even dollar sales volume or the dollar sales volume required to achieve a desired profit. Treating a dollar of sales revenue as a unit, the break-even point in dollars is computed as fixed costs divided by the contribution margin ratio (the number of cents from each dollar of revenue contributed to covering fixed costs and providing a profit).

$$\textbf{Dollar break-even point} = \frac{\textbf{Fixed costs}}{\textbf{Contribution margin ratio}}$$

If unit selling price and cost information were not available, Benchmark's dollar break-even point could be computed as \$24,000 (\$15,000 ÷ 0.625).

Corresponding computations can be made to find the dollar sales volume required to achieve a desired profit as follows.

$$\textbf{Target dollar sales volume} = \frac{\textbf{Fixed costs + Desired profit}}{\textbf{Contribution margin ratio}}$$

To achieve a desired profit of \$12,000, Benchmark needs sales of \$43,200 [(\$15,000 + \$12,000) ÷ 0.625].

These relationships can be graphed by placing sales dollars, rather than unit sales, on the horizontal axis. The slope of the variable and total cost lines, identified as the **variable cost ratio**, presents variable costs as a portion of sales revenue. It indicates the number of cents from each sales dollar required to pay variable costs. The Business Insight box on the following page demonstrates how CVP information can be developed from the published financial statements of a multiple-product firm.

BUSINESS INSIGHT **CVP Analysis Using Financial Statements**

Condensed data from Lowes's 2005 and 2006 income statements ($ millions) follow:

	2006	2005
Revenues	$43,243	$36,464
Operating Expenses	(38,589)	(32,768)
Operating Income	$ 4,654	$ 3,696

We can determine Lowes' cost-volume-profit relationships by applying the high-low cost estimation method. First, we determine variable costs as a portion of each sales dollar as follows ($ million):

$$\text{Variable cost ratio} = \frac{\$38{,}589 - \$32{,}768}{\$43{,}243 - \$36{,}464} = 0.8587$$

Next, annual fixed costs are determined by subtracting the variable costs for either period (the product of revenues and the variable cost ratio) from the corresponding total costs.

Annual fixed costs = $38,589 − ($43,243 × 0.8587) = $1,456.236 million

The contribution margin ratio (1 minus the variable cost ratio) is 0.1413 (1 − 0.8587).
Using fixed cost and contribution margin ratio data, Lowes' annual break-even point in sales dollars is computed.

Break-Even Point = $1,456.236 million/0.1413 = $10,305.987 million

In 2007, Lowes' operating income was $5,152 million with revenues of $46,927 million. For this level of revenue, the model developed from 2006 and 2007 data predicts an operating profit of $5,174.55 million ($46,927 million − [($46,927 million × 0.8587) + 1,456.236 million]). In this case, because of Lowes' stable cost structure, the model error is less than one-half of one percent.

Sales Mix Analysis

Sales mix refers to the relative portion of unit or dollar sales that are derived from each product. One of the limiting assumptions of the basic cost-volume-profit model is that the analysis is for a single product or the sales mix is constant. When the sales mix is constant, managers of multiple-product organizations can use the average unit contribution margin, or the average contribution margin ratio, to determine the break-even point or the sales volume required for a desired profit. Often, however, management is interested in the effect of a change in the sales mix rather than a change in the sales volume at a constant mix. In this situation, it is necessary to determine either the average unit contribution margin or the average contribution margin ratio for each alternative mix.

Unit Sales Analysis

Assume the Eagle Card Company sells two kinds of greeting cards, regular and deluxe. At a 1:1 (one-to-one) unit sales mix in which Eagle sells one box of regular cards for every box of deluxe cards, the following revenue and cost information is available:

	Regular Box	Deluxe Box	Average Box*
Unit selling price.	$4	$12	$8
Unit variable costs	(3)	(3)	(3)
Unit contribution margin.	$1	$ 9	$5
Fixed costs per month			$15,000

*At a 1:1 sales mix, the average unit contribution margin is $5[{($1 × 1 unit) + ($9 × 1 unit)} ÷ 2 units].

At a 1:1 mix, Eagle's current monthly break-even sales volume is 3,000 units ($15,000 ÷ $5), consisting of 1,500 boxes of regular cards and 1,500 boxes of deluxe cards. The top line in Exhibit 3.6 represents the current sales mix. Management wants to know the break-even sales volume if the unit sales mix became 3:1; that is, on average, a sale of 4 units contains 3 regular units and 1 deluxe unit. With no changes in the selling prices or variable costs of individual products, the average contribution margin becomes $3[{($1 × 3 units) + ($9 × 1 unit)} ÷ 4 units], and the revised break-even sales volume is 5,000 units ($15,000 ÷ $3). The revised break-even sales volume includes 3,750 boxes of regular cards [5,000 × $\frac{3}{4}$] and 1,250 boxes of deluxe cards [5,000 × $\frac{1}{4}$].

EXHIBIT 3.6 Sales Mix Analysis: Unit Sales Approach

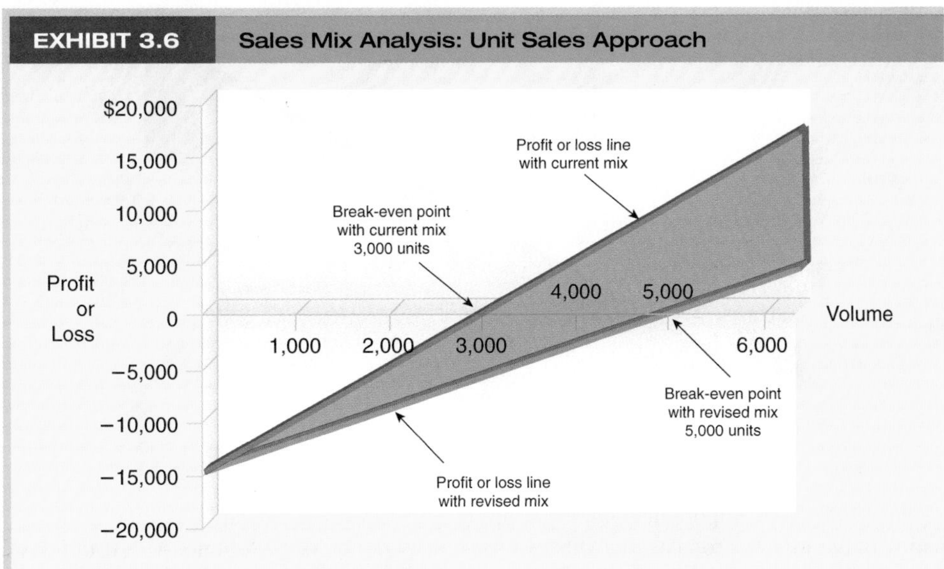

The bottom line in Exhibit 3.6 represents the revised sales mix. Because a greater portion of the revised mix consists of lower contribution margin regular cards, the shift in the mix increases the break-even point.

Sales Dollar Analysis

The preceding analysis focused on units and the unit contribution margin. An alternative approach focuses on sales dollars and the contribution margin ratio. Following this approach, the sales mix is expressed in terms of sales dollars.

Eagle's current sales dollars are 25 percent from regular cards and 75 percent from deluxe cards. The following display indicates the contribution margin ratios at the current sales mix and monthly volume of 5,400 units.

	Regular	Deluxe	Total
Unit sales	2,700	2,700	
Selling price	$4.00	$12.00	
Sales	$10,800	$32,400	$43,200
Variable costs	8,100	8,100	16,200
Contribution margin	$ 2,700	$24,300	$27,000
Contribution margin ratio	0.25	0.75	0.625

With monthly fixed costs of $15,000, Eagle's current break-even sales volume is $24,000 ($15,000 ÷ 0.625), consisting of $6,000 from regular cards ($24,000 × 0.25) and $18,000 from Deluxe cards ($24,000 × 0.75). The top line in Exhibit 3.7 illustrates the current sales mix.

Management wants to know the break-even sales volume if the unit sales mix became 70 percent regular and 30 percent deluxe. With no changes in the selling prices or variable costs of individual products, the contribution margin ratio becomes 0.40 [(0.25 × 0.70) + (0.75 × 0.30)], and the revised break-even sales volume is \$37,500 (\$15,000 ÷ 0.40). The revised break-even sales volume includes \$26,250 from regular cards (\$37,500 × 0.70) and \$11,250 from deluxe cards (37,500 × 0.30).

The bottom line in Exhibit 3.7 represents the revised sales mix. Because a greater portion of the revised mix consists of lower contribution ratio regular cards, the shift in the mix increases the break-even point.

EXHIBIT 3.7 Sales Mix Analysis: Sales Dollar Approach

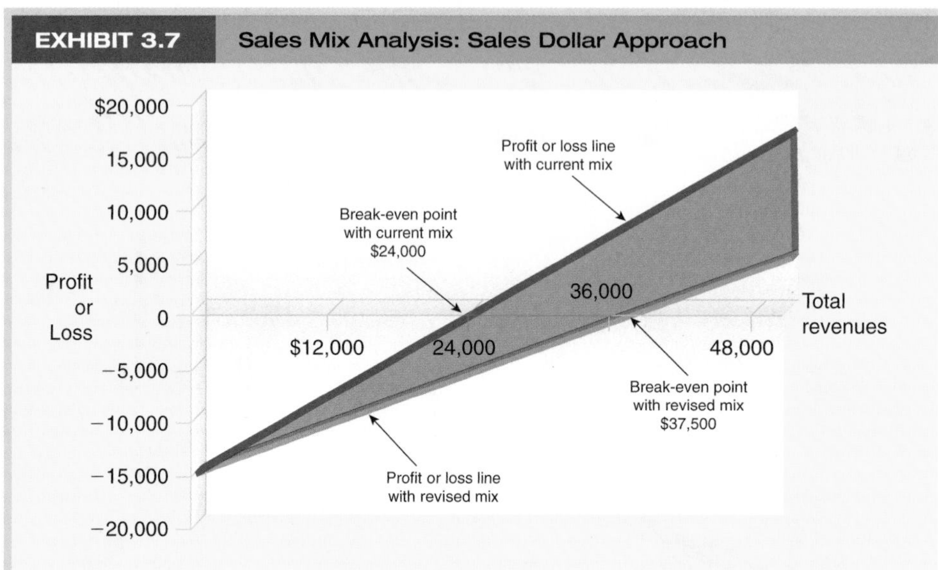

Sales mix analysis is important in multiple-product or service organizations. Management is just as concerned with the mix of products as with the total unit or dollar sales volume. A shift in the sales mix can have a significant impact on the bottom line. Profits may decline, even when sales increase, if the mix shifts toward products or services with lower unit margins. Conversely, profits may increase, even when sales decline, if the mix shifts toward products or services with higher unit margins. Other things being equal, managers of for-profit organizations strive to increase sales of high-margin products or services.

ANALYSIS OF OPERATING LEVERAGE

LO5 Apply operating leverage ratio to assess opportunities for profit and the risks of loss.

Operating leverage refers to the extent that an organization's costs are fixed. The **operating leverage ratio** is computed as the contribution margin divided by before-tax profit as follows.

$$\textbf{Operating leverage ratio} = \frac{\textbf{Contribution margin}}{\textbf{Before-tax profit}}$$

The rationale underlying this computation is that as fixed costs are substituted for variable costs, the contribution margin as a percentage of income before taxes increases. Hence, a high degree of operating leverage signals the existence of a high portion of fixed costs. As noted in Chapter 1, the shift from labor-based to automated activities has resulted in a decrease in variable costs and an increase in fixed costs, producing an increase in operating leverage.

Operating leverage is a measure of risk and opportunity. Other things being equal, the higher the degree of operating leverage, the greater the opportunity for profit with increases in sales. Conversely, a higher degree of operating leverage also magnifies the risk of large losses with a decrease in sales.

	Operating Leverage	
	High	**Low**
Profit opportunity with sales increase	High	Low
Risk of loss with sales decrease	High	Low

In addition to indicating the relative amount of fixed costs in the overall cost structure of a company, the operating leverage ratio can be used to measure the expected change in net income resulting from a change in sales. The operating leverage ratio multiplied times the percentage change in sales equals the percentage change in income before taxes. For example, if Benchmark Paper Company currently has an operating leverage ratio of 4.0, a change in sales of 12.5 percent will result in a 50 percent change in income before taxes; whereas, High-Fixed Paper Company, which has an operating leverage ratio of 5.2 will have an increase in sales of 65%.

	Current		Projected	
	Benchmark	**High-Fixed**	**Benchmark**	**High-Fixed**
Unit selling price	$ 8.00	$ 8.00	$ 8.00	$ 8.00
Unit variable costs	(3.00)	(1.50)	(3.00)	(1.50)
Unit contribution margin	5.00	6.50	5.00	6.50
Unit sales	× 4,000	× 4,000	× 4,500	× 4,500
Contribution margin	20,000	26,000	22,500	29,250
Fixed costs	(15,000)	(21,000)	(15,000)	(21,000)
Before-tax profit	$ 5,000	$ 5,000	$ 7,500	$ 8,250
Contribution margin	$20,000	$26,000		
Before-tax profit	÷ 5,000	÷ 5,000		
Operating leverage ratio	4.0	5.2		
Percent increase in sales			12.5%	12.5%
Percent increase in income before sales			50%	65%

Although both companies have identical before-tax profits at a sales volume of 4,000 units, High-Fixed has a higher degree of operating leverage and its profits vary more with changes in sales volume.

If sales are projected to increase by 12.5 percent, from 4,000 to 4,500 units, the percentage of increase in each firm's profits is computed as the percent change in sales multiplied by the degree of operating leverage.

	Benchmark	**High-Fixed**
Increase in sales	12.5%	12.5%
Degree of operating leverage	× 4.0	× 5.2
Increase in profits	50.0%	65.0%

As noted in the following Business Insight box, operating leverage was an important consideration in the proposed merger of XM and Sirius radio.

Management is interested in measures of operating leverage to determine how sensitive profits are to changes in sales. Risk-averse managers strive to maintain a lower operating leverage, even if this results in some loss of profits. One way to reduce operating leverage is to use more direct labor and less automated equipment. Another way is to contract outside organizations to perform tasks that could be done internally. This approach to reducing operating leverage is further considered in Chapter 4, where we examine the external acquisition of goods and services. While operating leverage is a useful analytic tool, long-run success comes from keeping the overall level of costs down, while providing customers with the products or services they want at competitive prices.

BUSINESS INSIGHT **Operating Leverage Makes XM- Sirius Merger Attractive**

Together, Sirius Satellite Radio and XM Satellite Radio had 17.3 million subscribers and annual revenues of $2,062.1 million in 2007. Yet, primarily because of high fixed costs, they also had a combined net loss of $1,247.7 million. Writing in **Money** magazine, Pablo Galarza reported that because of high operating leverage analysts believed that both firms could be highly profitable as independent entities once they reached the break-even point, ". . . since it doesn't really cost more to broadcast to 50 million than it does to one million." Analysts determined that above break-even, 80 percent of incremental revenues would become profit.

High fixed costs, high operating leverage, and lack or profitability were are among the considerations leading to a 2007 announcement of a merger agreement between XM Satellite Radio and Sirius Satellite Radio. The press release issued at the time of the announcement noted that the merger, "will enhance the long-term financial success of satellite radio by allowing the combined company to better manage its costs through sales and marketing and subscriber acquisition efficiencies, satellite fleet efficiencies, combined R&D, and other benefits from economies of scale."[4]

MANAGERIAL DECISION **You are the Division Manager**

As manager of a division responsible for both production and sales of products and, hence, division profits, you are looking for ways to leverage the profits of your division to a higher level. You are considering changing your cost structure to include more fixed costs and less variable costs by automating some of the production activities currently performed by people. What are some of the considerations that you should keep in mind as you ponder this decision? [Answer, p. 81]

CHAPTER-END REVIEW

Joe's Brews is a new shop in Cambridge village shopping center that sells high-end teas and coffees. Recently, they have added smoothie drinks to their product line. Below are sales and cost data for the company:

	Coffee	Tea	Smoothie
Sales price per (12 oz.) serving	$1.35	$1.25	$1.95
Variable cost per serving	0.60	0.45	0.75
Fixed costs per month $8,000			

Currently the company sells each month an average of 6,000 servings of coffee, 3,750 servings of tea, and 2,250 servings of smoothies.

Required:

a. Calculate the current before-tax profit, contribution margin ratio, and sales mix based on sales dollars.

b. Using a sales dollar analysis, calculate the monthly break-even point assuming the sales mix does not change.

c. Calculate Joe's operating leverage ratio. If sales increase by 20 percent, by how much will before-tax income be expected to change? If sales decrease by 20 percent, by how much will before-tax income be expected to change?

---

[4] Pable Galarza, "Flying Off the Shelves," *Money*, February 2005, p. 56.; Rick Boucher, "Why the XM-Sirius Merger Makes Sense, *Business Week Online*, November 16, 2007, p.4.; 2007 annual reports and press releases available at www.sirius.com and www.XMradio.com

Solution

a.

	Coffee	Tea	Smoothies	Total
Monthly unit sales	6,000	3,750	2,250	
Selling price	$1.35	$1.25	$1.95	
Sales	$8,100.00	$4,687.50	$4,387.50	$17,175.00
Variable cost	3,600.00	1,687.50	1,687.50	6,975.00
Contribution margin	$4,500.00	$3,000.00	$2,700.00	10,200.00
Fixed cost				8,000.00
Before-tax profit				$ 2,200.00
Contribution margin (CM) ratio	0.5556	0.640	0.6154	0.5939
Current sales mix (based on sales dollars)	47.16%	27.29%	25.55%	

b.

Break-even = Fixed costs/Total contribution margin ratio
= $8,000/0.5939
= $13,470

Proof:			Sales		C/M Ratio		
Coffee:	$13,470 × 47.16%	=	$ 6,352.45	×	0.5556	=	$3,529.42
Tea:	$13,470 × 27.29%	=	3,675.96	×	0.640	=	2,352.62*
Smoothies:	$13,470 × 25.55%	=	3,441.59	×	0.6154	=	2,117.96*
			$13,470.00				
Total contribution margin							8,000.00
Fixed costs							8,000.00
Before-tax profit							–0–

*Amounts adjusted to correct for minor rounding error.

c. Joe's Brews has an operating leverage of 4.636, calculated as a contribution margin of $10,200 divided by before-tax profit of $2,200. Therefore, if sales dollars increase by 20% to $20,610, before-tax profit should increase by 4.636 times 20%, or 92.72%, to $4,240. Because of the leverage caused by fixed costs, a 20% increase in sales results in a 92.72% increase in before-tax profit. Conversely, a 20% decrease in sales would result in a 92.72% decrease in before-tax profits to $160.

Proof:	20% Sales Increase	20% Sales Decrease
Sales	$20,610	$13,740
CM %	× 0.5939	× 0.5939
Total CM	12,240	8,160
Fixed costs	8,000	8,000
Before-tax profit	$ 4,240	$ 160

Current before-tax profit of $2,200 × (1 + .9272) = $4,240
Current before-tax profit of $2,200 × (1 − .9272) = $160

APPENDIX 3A: Profitability Analysis with Unit and Nonunit Cost Drivers

A major limitation of cost-volume-profit analysis and the related contribution income statement is the exclusive use of unit-level activity cost drivers. Even when multiple products are considered, the CVP approach either restates volume in terms of an average unit or in terms of a dollar of sales volume. Additionally, CVP analysis does not consider other categories of cost drivers.

We now expand profitability analysis to incorporate nonunit cost drivers. While the addition of multiple levels of cost drivers makes it difficult to develop graphical relationships (illustrating the impact of cost driver changes on revenues, costs, and profits), it is possible to modify the traditional contribution income statement to incorporate a hierarchy of cost drivers. The expanded framework is not only more accurate, but it encourages management to ask important questions concerning costs and profitability.

Multi-Level Contribution Income Statement

To illustrate the use of profitability analysis with unit and nonunit cost drivers, consider General Distribution, a multiple-product merchandising organization with the following cost hierarchy:

Unit-level activities	
Cost of goods sold	$0.80 per sales dollar
Order-level activities	
Cost of processing order	$20 per order
Customer-level activities	
Mail, phone, sales visits, recordkeeping, etc.	$200 per customer per year
Facility-level costs	
Depreciation, manager salaries, insurance, etc.	$120,000 per year

Assume that General Distribution, which is subject to a 40 percent income tax rate, has the following plans for the year 2009:

Sales	$3,000,000
Number of sales orders	3,200
Number of customers	400

While General Distribution's plans could be summarized in a functional income statement, we have previously considered the limitations of such statements for management. Contribution income statements are preferred because they correspond to the cost classification scheme used in CVP analysis. In this case, General Distribution's cost structure (unit level, order level, customer level, and facility level) does not correspond to the classification scheme used in traditional contribution income statements (variable and fixed). The problem occurs because traditional contribution income statements consider only unit-level cost drivers. When a larger set of unit and nonunit cost drivers is used for cost analysis, an expanded contribution income statement should be used for profitability analysis.

A multi-level contribution income statement for General Distribution is presented in Exhibit 3.8. Costs are separated using a cost hierarchy and there are several contribution margins, one for each level of costs that responds to a short-run change in activity. In the case of General Distribution, the contribution margins are at the unit level, order level, and customer level. Because the facility-level costs do not vary with short-run variations in activity, the final customer-level contribution goes to cover facility-level costs and to provide for a profit. If a company had a different activity cost hierarchy, it would use a different set of contribution margins.

A number of additional questions of interest to management can be formulated and answered using the multi-level hierarchy. Consider the following examples:

- Holding the number of sales orders and customers constant, what is the break-even dollar sales volume? The answer is found by treating all other costs as fixed and dividing the total nonunit-level costs by the contribution margin ratio. Here the contribution margin ratio indicates how many cents of each sales dollar is available for profits and costs above the unit level.

$$\textbf{Unit-level break-even point in dollars with no changes in other costs} = \frac{\textbf{Current order-level costs} + \textbf{Current customer-level costs} + \textbf{Facility-level costs}}{\textbf{Contribution margin ratio}}$$

$$= (\$64{,}000 + \$80{,}000 + \$120{,}000) \div (1 - 0.80)$$
$$= \$1{,}320{,}000$$

EXHIBIT 3.8 Multi-Level Contribution Income Statement with Taxes

General Distribution
Multi-Level Contribution Income Statement
For Year 2009

Sales	$3,000,000
Less unit-level costs	
Cost of goods sold ($3,000,000 × 0.80)	(2,400,000)
Unit-level contribution margin	600,000
Less order-level costs	
Cost of processing order (3,200 orders × $20)	(64,000)
Order-level contribution margin	536,000
Less customer-level costs	
Mail, phone, sales visits, recordkeeping, etc. (400 customers × $200)	(80,000)
Customer-level contribution margin	456,000
Less facility-level costs	
Depreciation, manager salaries, insurance, etc.	(120,000)
Before-tax profit	336,000
Income taxes ($336,000 × 0.40)	(134,400)
After-tax profit	$ 201,600

- What order size is required to break even on an individual order? Answering this question might help management to evaluate the desirability of establishing a minimum order size. To break even, each order must have a unit-level contribution equal to the order-level costs. Any additional contribution is used to cover customer- and facility-level costs and provide for a profit.

$$\textbf{Break-even order size} = \$20 \div (1 - 0.80)$$
$$= \$100$$

- What sales volume is required to break even on an average customer? Answering this question might help management to evaluate the desirability of retaining certain customers. Based on the preceding information, an average customer places 8 orders per year (3,200 orders ÷ 400 customers). With costs of $20 per order and $200 per customer, the sales to an average customer must generate an annual contribution of $360 [($20 × 8) + $200]. Hence, the break-even level for an average customer is $1,800 [$360 ÷ (1 − 0.80)]. Management might consider discontinuing relations with customers with annual purchases of less than this amount. Alternatively, they might inquire as to whether such customers could be served in a less costly manner.

The concepts of multi-level break-even analysis and profitability analysis are finding increasing use as companies such as Federal Express, US West, and Bank of America strive to identify profitable and unprofitable customers. At FedEx, customers are sometimes rated as "the good, the bad, and the ugly." FedEx strives to retain the "good" profitable customers, turn the "bad" into profitable customers, and ignore the "ugly" who seem unlikely to become profitable. The following Business Insight box also advises managers to think in terms of customer profitability rather than in terms of sales volume.

BUSINESS INSIGHT Think Customer Value Not Sales Volume

Marketing consultant and trainer Tom Reilly cautions against the exuberance that often accompanies a salesperson's announcement that he or she just landed a big account. According to Reilly, even if the sale results in celebration because sales quotas are met or exceeded, the sale might not be a good deal. "What happens when the big one is a low-margin sale? What if your cost of serving this customer is unusually high? How about the transactions cost of serving this customer? How much of your selling time will be consumed following up on this sale?"

Reilly cautions that high-volume customers such as Wal-Mart understand the lure of the big sale and strive to leverage volume to cut contribution margins to the bone. "You don't take volume to the bank—you take profit."[5]

[5] Tom Reilly, "Think Value, Not Volume," *Industrial Distribution*, April 2007, p. 23.

Variations in Multi-Level Contribution Income Statement

Classification schemes should be designed to fit the organization and user needs. In Chapter 2, when analyzing the costs of a manufacturing company, we used a manufacturing cost hierarchy. While formatting issues can seem mundane and routine, format is important because the way information is presented encourages certain types of questions while discouraging others. Hence, management accountants must inquire as to user needs before developing management accounting reports, just as users of management accounting information should be knowledgeable enough to request appropriate information and know whether the information they are receiving is the information they need. With computers to reduce computational drudgery and to provide a wealth of available data, the most important issues involve identifying the important questions and presenting information to address those questions.

In the case of General Distribution, we used a customer cost hierarchy with information presented in a single column. A multiple-column format is also useful for presenting and analyzing information. Assume that General Distribution's managment believes that the differences between the government and private sector markets are such that these markets could be better served with separate marketing activities. They would have two market segments, one for the government sector and one for the private sector, giving the following cost hierarchy:

1. Unit-level activities
2. Order-level activities
3. Customer-level activities
4. Market segment activities
5. Facility-level activities

One possible way of presenting General Distribution's 2010 multi-level income statement with two market segments is shown in Exhibit 3.9. The details underlying the development of this statement are not presented. In developing the statement, we assume the mix of units sold, their cost structure, and the costs of processing an order are unchanged. Finally, we present new market segment costs and assume that the addition of the segments allows for some reduction in previous facility-level costs.

EXHIBIT 3.9 Multi-Level Contribution Income Statement with Segments and Taxes

General Distribution
Multi-Level Contribution Income Statement
For Year 2010

	Government Segment	Private Segment	Total
Sales	$1,500,000	$2,000,000	$3,500,000
Less unit-level costs			
Cost of goods sold (0.80)	(1,200,000)	(1,600,000)	(2,800,000)
Unit-level contribution margin	300,000	400,000	700,000
Less order-level costs			
Cost of processing order (1,000 × $20; 3,000 × $20)	(20,000)	(60,000)	(80,000)
Order-level contribution margin	280,000	340,000	620,000
Less customer-level costs			
Mail, phone, sales visits, recordkeeping, etc. (150 × $200, 300 × $200)	(30,000)	(60,000)	(90,000)
Customer-level contribution margin	250,000	280,000	530,000
Less market segment-level costs	(80,000)	(20,000)	(100,000)
Market segment-level contribution	$ 170,000	$ 260,000	430,000
Less facility-level costs			
Depreciation, manager salaries, insurance, etc.			(90,000)
Before-tax profit			340,000
Income taxes ($340,000 × 0.40)			(136,000)
After-tax profit			$ 204,000

The information in the total column is all that is required for a multi-level contribution income statement. The information in the two detailed columns for the government and private segments can, however, prove useful in analyzing the profitability of each. Observe that the facility-level costs, incurred for the benefit of both segments, are not assigned to specific segments. Depending on the nature of the goods sold, it may be possible to further analyze the profitability of each product (or type of product) sold in each market segment. The profitability analysis of business segments is more closely examined in Chapter 11.

GUIDANCE ANSWER

MANAGERIAL DECISION **You are the Division Manager**

Fixed costs represent a two-edged sword. When a company is growing its sales, fixed costs cause profits to grow faster than sales; however, if a company should experience declining sales, the rate of reduction in profits is greater than the rate of reduction in sales. When sales decline, variable costs decline proportionately, while fixed costs continue. For this reason, when a company faces serious declines that are expected to continue, one of the first steps its top management should consider is reducing capacity in order to reduce fixed costs. The automobile companies in the U.S. have been employing this technique in recent years to try to offset the effect of sales lost to importers.

DISCUSSION QUESTIONS

Q3-1. What is cost-volume-profit analysis and when is it particularly useful?

Q3-2. Identify the important assumptions that underlie cost-volume-profit analysis.

Q3-3. When is it most reasonable to use a single independent variable in cost-volume-profit analysis?

Q3-4. Distinguish between a contribution and a functional income statement.

Q3-5. What is the unit contribution margin? How is it used in computing the unit break-even point?

Q3-6. What is the contribution margin ratio and when is it most useful?

Q3-7. How is the break-even equation modified to take into account the sales required to earn a desired profit?

Q3-8. How does a profit-volume graph differ from a cost-volume-profit graph? When is a profit-volume graph most likely to be used?

Q3-9. What impact do income taxes have on the sales volume required to earn a desired after-tax profit?

Q3-10. How are profit opportunities and the risk of losses affected by operating leverage?

MINI EXERCISES

M3-11. Profitability Analysis (LO3)

Assume a local Cost Cutters provides cuts, perms, and hairstyling services. Annual fixed costs are $120,000, and variable costs are 40 percent of sales revenue. Last year's revenues totaled $240,000.

Required

a. Determine its break-even point in sales dollars.

b. Determine last year's margin of safety in sales dollars.

c. Determine the sales volume required for an annual profit of $70,000.

M3-12. Cost-Volume-Profit Graph: Identification and Sensitivity Analysis (LO3)

A typical cost-volume-profit graph is presented below.

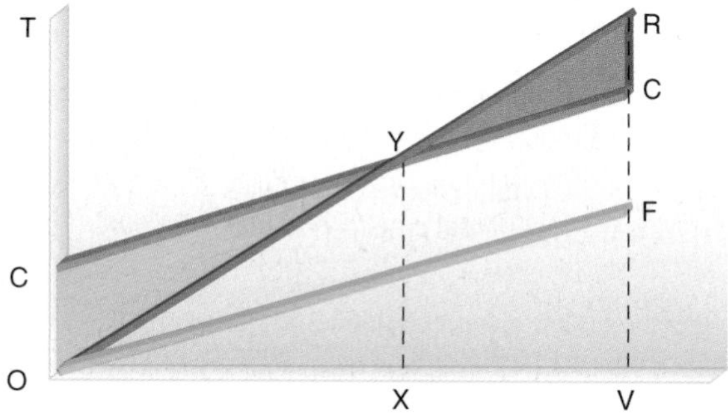

Required

a. Identify each of the following:
1. Line OF
2. Line OR
3. Line CC
4. The difference between lines OF and OV
5. The difference between lines CC and OF
6. The difference between lines CC and OV
7. The difference between lines OR and OF
8. Point X
9. Area CYO
10. Area RCY

b. Indicate the effect of each of the following independent events on lines CC, OR, and the break-even point:
1. A decrease in fixed costs
2. An increase in unit selling price
3. An increase in the variable costs per unit
4. An increase in fixed costs and a decrease in the unit selling price
5. A decrease in fixed costs and a decrease in the unit variable costs

M3-13. Profit-Volume Graph: Identification and Sensitivity Analysis (LO3)

A typical profit-volume graph follows.

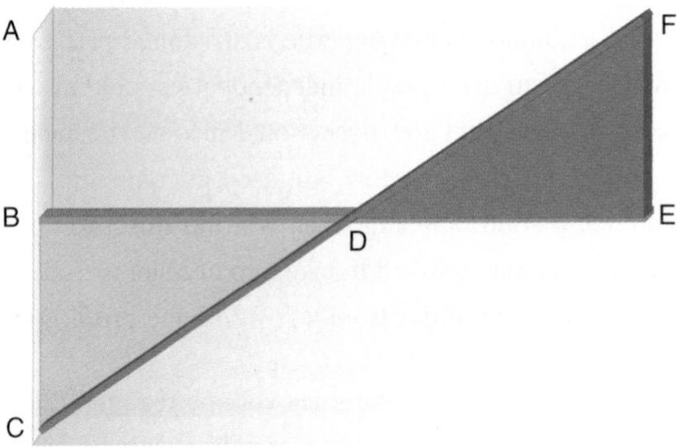

Required

a. Identify each of the following:
1. Area *BDC*
2. Area *DEF*
3. Point *D*
4. Line *AC*
5. Line *BC*
6. Line *EF*

b. Indicate the effect of each of the following on line *CF* and the break-even point:
1. An increase in the unit selling price
2. An increase in the variable costs per unit
3. A decrease in fixed costs
4. An increase in fixed costs and a decrease in the unit selling price
5. A decrease in fixed costs and an increase in the variable costs per unit

M3-14. Preparing Cost-Volume-Profit and Profit-Volume Graphs (LO3)

Papa John's Pizza (PZZA)

Assume a Papa John's Pizza shop has the following monthly revenue and cost functions:

Total revenues = $12.00X
Total costs = $18,000 + $3.00X

Required

a. Prepare a graph (similar to that in Exhibit 3.3) illustrating Papa John's cost-volume-profit relationships. The vertical axis should range from $0 to $72,000, in increments of $12,000. The horizontal axis should range from 0 units to 6,000 units, in increments of 2,000 units.

b. Prepare a graph (similar to that in Exhibit 3.4) illustrating Papa John's profit-volume relationships. The horizontal axis should range from 0 units to 6,000 units, in increments of 2,000 units.

c. When is it most appropriate to use a profit-volume graph?

M3-15. Preparing Cost-Volume-Profit and Profit-Volume Graphs (LO3)

Big Dog Company is a hot dog concession business operating at five baseball stadiums. It sells hot dogs, with all the fixings, for $5.00 each. Variable costs are $4.50 per hot dog, and fixed operating costs are $250,000 per year.

Required

a. Determine the annual break-even point in hot dogs.

b. Prepare a cost-volume-profit graph for the company. Use a format that emphasizes the contribution margin. The vertical axis should vary between $0 and $5,000,000 in increments of $1,000,000. The horizontal axis should vary between 0 hot dogs and 1,000,000 hot dogs, in increments of 250,000 hot dogs. Label the graph in thousands.

c. Prepare a profit-volume graph for the company. The vertical axis should vary between $(350,000) and $350,000 in increments of $50,000. The horizontal axis should vary as described in requirement (b). Label the graph in thousands.

d. Evaluate the profit-volume graph. In what ways is it superior and in what ways is it inferior to the traditional cost-volume-profit graph?

M3-16. Multiple Product Break-Even Analysis (LO4)

Presented is information for Stafford Company's three products.

	A	B	C
Unit selling price	$5	$7	$6
Unit variable costs	(4)	(5)	(3)
Unit contribution margin	$1	$2	$3

With monthly fixed costs of $112,500, the company sells two units of A for each unit of B and three units of B for each unit of C.

Required

Determine the unit sales of product A at the monthly break-even point.

EXERCISES

E3-17. Contribution Income Statement and Cost-Volume-Profit Graph (LO2, 3)

Manitoba Company produces a product that is sold for $50 per unit. The company produced and sold 6,000 units during May 2008. There were no beginning or ending inventories. Variable and fixed costs follow.

Variable Costs per Unit			Fixed Costs per Month	
Manufacturing:			Manufacturing overhead	$40,000
Direct materials	$ 5		Selling and administrative	20,000
Direct labor	10		Total	$60,000
Factory overhead	10	$25		
Selling and administrative		5		
Total		$30		

Required

a. Prepare a contribution income statement for May.

b. Prepare a cost-volume-profit graph. Label the horizontal axis in units with a maximum value of 10,000. Label the vertical axis in dollars with a maximum value of $400,000. Draw a vertical line on the graph for the current (6,000) unit sales level, and label total variable costs, total fixed costs, and total profits at 6,000 units.

E3-18. Contribution Margin Concepts (LO3, 4)
The following information is taken from the 2008 records of Navajo Art Shop.

	Fixed	Variable	Total
Sales.			$750,000
Costs			
Goods sold		$300,000	
Labor.	$160,000	60,000	
Supplies	2,000	5,000	
Utilities	12,000	13,000	
Rent	24,000	—	
Advertising	6,000	24,500	
Miscellaneous. . .	6,000	10,000	
Total costs.	$210,000	$412,500	(622,500)
Net income.			$127,500

Required

a. Determine the annual break-even dollar sales volume.
b. Determine the current margin of safety in dollars.
c. Prepare a cost-volume-profit graph for the art shop. Label both axes in dollars with maximum values of $1,000,000. Draw a vertical line on the graph for the current ($750,000) sales level, and label total variable costs, total fixed costs, and total profits at $750,000 sales.
d. What is the annual break-even dollar sales volume if management makes a decision that increases fixed costs by $35,000?

E3-19. Multiple Product Planning with Taxes (LO3, 4)
In the year 2008, Wiggins Processing Company had the following contribution income statement:

WIGGINS PROCESSING COMPANY Contribution Income Statement For the Year 2008		
Sales.		$1,000,000
Variable costs		
Cost of goods sold	$420,000	
Selling and administrative.	200,000	(620,000)
Contribution margin		380,000
Fixed costs		
Factory overhead	205,000	
Selling and administrative.	80,000	(285,000)
Before-tax profit		95,000
Income taxes (36%)		(34,200)
After-tax profit		$ 60,800

Required

a. Determine the annual break-even point in sales dollars.
b. Determine the annual margin of safety in sales dollars.
c. What is the break-even point in sales dollars if management makes a decision that increases fixed costs by $57,000?
d. With the current cost structure, including fixed costs of $285,000, what dollar sales volume is required to provide an after-tax net income of $200,000?
e. Prepare an abbreviated contribution income statement to verify that the solution to requirement (d) will provide the desired after-tax income.

E3-20. Not-for-Profit Applications (LO3)

Determine the solution to each of the following independent cases:

a. Hillside College has annual fixed operating costs of $12,500,000 and variable operating costs of $1,000 per student. Tuition is $8,000 per student for the coming academic year, with a projected enrollment of 1,500 students. Expected revenues from endowments and federal and state grants total $250,000. Determine the amount the college must obtain from other sources.

b. The Hillside College Student Association is planning a fall concert. Expected costs (renting a hall, hiring a band, etc.) are $30,000. Assuming 3,000 people attend the concert, determine the break-even price per ticket. How much will the association lose if this price is charged and only 2,700 tickets are sold?

c. City Hospital has a contract with the city to provide indigent health care on an outpatient basis for $25 per visit. The patient will pay $5 of this amount, with the city paying the balance ($20). Determine the amount the city will pay if the hospital has 10,000 patient visits.

d. A civic organization is engaged in a fund-raising program. On Civic Sunday, it will sell newspapers at $1.25 each. The organization will pay $0.75 for each newspaper. Costs of the necessary permits, signs, and so forth are $500. Determine the amount the organization will raise if it sells 5,000 newspapers.

e. Christmas for the Needy is a civic organization that provides Christmas presents to disadvantaged children. The annual costs of this activity are $5,000, plus $10 per present. Determine the number of presents the organization can provide with $20,000.

E3-21. Alternative Production Procedures and Operating Leverage (LO3, 5)

Paper Mate

Assume Paper Mate is planning to introduce a new executive pen that can be manufactured using either a capital-intensive method or a labor-intensive method. The predicted manufacturing costs for each method are as follows:

	Capital Intensive	Labor Intensive
Direct materials per unit	$ 5.00	$ 6.00
Direct labor per unit	$ 5.00	$12.00
Variable manufacturing overhead per unit	$ 4.00	$ 2.00
Fixed manufacturing overhead per year	$2,440,000.00	$700,000.00

Paper Mate's market research department has recommended an introductory unit sales price of $30. The incremental selling costs are predicted to be $500,000 per year, plus $2 per unit sold.

Required

a. Determine the annual break-even point in units if Paper Mate uses the:
   1. Capital-intensive manufacturing method.
   2. Labor-intensive manufacturing method.

b. Determine the annual unit volume at which Paper Mate is indifferent between the two manufacturing methods.

c. Management wants to know more about the effect of each alternative on operating leverage.
   1. Explain operating leverage and the relationship between operating leverage and the volatility of earnings.
   2. Compute operating leverage for each alternative at a volume of 250,000 units.
   3. Which alternative has the higher operating leverage? Why?

E3-22. Contribution Income Statement and Operating Leverage (LO3, 5)

Florida Berry Basket harvests early-season strawberries for shipment throughout the eastern United States in March. The strawberry farm is maintained by a permanent staff of 10 employees and seasonal workers who pick and pack the strawberries. The strawberries are sold in crates containing 100 individually packaged one-quart containers. Affixed to each one-quart container is the distinctive Florida Berry Basket logo inviting buyers to "Enjoy the berry best strawberries in the world!" The selling price is $90 per crate, variable costs are $80 per crate, and fixed costs are $275,000 per year. In the year 2008, Florida Berry Basket sold 45,000 crates.

Required

a. Prepare a contribution income statement for the year ended December 31, 2008.

b. Determine the company's 2008 operating leverage.

c. Calculate the percentage change in profits if sales decrease by 10 percent.

d. Management is considering the purchase of several berry-picking machines. This will increase annual fixed costs to $375,000 and reduce variable costs to $77.50 per crate. Calculate the effect of this acquisition on operating leverage and explain any change.

E3-23. Multiple Product Break-Even Analysis (LO4)
Yuma Tax Service prepares tax returns for low- to middle-income taxpayers. Its service operates January 2 through April 15 at a counter in a local department store. All jobs are classified into one of three categories: standard, multiform, and complex. Following is information for last year. Also, last year, the fixed cost of rent, utilities, and so forth were $45,000.

	Standard	Multiform	Complex
Billing rate.	$50	$125	$250
Average variable costs.	(30)	(75)	(150)
Average contribution margin	$20	$50	$100
Number of returns prepared.	1,750	500	250

Required

a. Determine Yuma's break-even dollar sales volume.
b. Determine Yuma's margin of safety in sales dollars.
c. Prepare a profit-volume graph for Yuma's Tax Service.

E3-24. Cost-Volume-Profit Relations: Missing Data (LO3)
Following are data from 4 separate companies.

	Case 1	Case 2	Case 3	Case 4
Unit sales	1,000	800	?	?
Sales revenue.	$20,000	?	?	$60,000
Variable cost per unit	$10	$1	$12	?
Contribution margin	?	$800	?	?
Fixed costs.	$8,000	?	$80,000	?
Net income.	?	$400	?	?
Unit contribution margin.	?	?	?	$15
Break-even point (units)	?	?	4,000	2,000
Margin of safety (units).	?	?	300	1,000

Required
Supply the missing data in each independent case.

E3-25. Cost-Volume-Profit Relations: Missing Data (LO3)
Following are data from 4 separate companies.

	Case A	Case B	Case C	Case D
Sales revenue.	$100,000	$80,000	?	?
Contribution margin	$40,000	?	$20,000	?
Fixed costs.	$30,000	?	?	?
Net income.	?	$5,000	$10,000	?
Variable cost ratio.	?	0.50	?	0.20
Contribution margin ratio	?	?	0.40	?
Break-even point (dollars)	?	?	?	$25,000
Margin of safety (dollars)	?	?	?	$20,000

Required
Supply the missing data in each independent case.

E3-26.[A] Customer-Level Planning
7-Eleven operates a number of convenience stores worldwide. Assume that an analysis of operating costs, customer sales, and customer patronage reveals the following: 7-Eleven

Fixed costs per store	$80,000.00/year
Variable cost ratio	0.80
Average sale per customer visit	$15.00
Average customer visits per week	1.75
Customers as portion of city population	0.04

Required
Determine the city population required for a single 7-Eleven to earn an annual profit of $40,000.

E3-27.[A] Multiple-Level Break-Even Analysis
Nielsen Associates provides marketing services for a number of small manufacturing firms. Nielsen receives a commission of 10 percent of sales. Operating costs are as follows:

Unit-level costs	$0.02 per sales dollar
Sales-level costs	$200 per sales order
Customer-level costs	$1,000 per customer per year
Facility-level costs	$60,000 per year

Required
a. Determine the minimum order size in sales dollars for Nielsen to break even on an order.
b. Assuming an average customer places four orders per year, determine the minimum annual sales required to break even on a customer.
c. What is the average order size in (b)?
d. Assuming Nielsen currently serves 100 customers, with each placing an average of four orders per year, determine the minimum annual sales required to break even.
e. What is the average order size in (d)?
f. Explain the differences in the answers to (a), (c), and (e).

PROBLEMS

P3-28. Profit Planning with Taxes (LO3)
Chandler Manufacturing Company produces a product that it sells for $35 per unit. Last year, the company manufactured and sold 20,000 units to obtain an after-tax profit of $54,000. Variable and fixed costs follow.

Variable Costs per Unit		Fixed Costs per Year	
Manufacturing	$18	Manufacturing	$ 80,000
Selling and administrative	7	Selling and administrative	30,000
Total	$25	Total	$110,000

Required
a. Determine the tax rate the company paid last year.
b. What unit sales volume is required to provide an after-tax profit of $90,000?
c. If the company reduces the unit variable cost by $2.50 and increases fixed manufacturing costs by $20,000, what unit sales volume is required to provide an after-tax profit of $90,000?
d. What assumptions are made about taxable income and tax rates in requirements (a) through (c)?

P3-29. High-Low Cost Estimation and Profit Planning (LO3, 4)

Comparative 2007 and 2008 income statements for Dakota Products Inc. follow:

DAKOTA PRODUCTS INC. Comparative Income Statements For Years Ending December 31, 2007 and 2008	2007	2008
Unit sales	5,000	8,000
Sales revenue	$65,000	$104,000
Expenses	(70,000)	(85,000)
Profit (loss)	$ (5,000)	$ 19,000

Required

a. Determine the break-even point in units.

b. Determine the unit sales volume required to earn a profit of $10,000.

P3-30. CVP Analysis and Special Decisions (LO3, 4)

Sweet Grove Citrus Company buys a variety of citrus fruit from growers and then processes the fruit into a product line of fresh fruit, juices, and fruit flavorings. The most recent year's sales revenue was $4,200,000. Variable costs were 60 percent of sales and fixed costs totaled $1,300,000. Sweet Grove is evaluating two alternatives designed to enhance profitability.

- One staff member has proposed that Sweet Grove purchase more automated processing equipment. This strategy would increase fixed costs by $300,000 but decrease variable costs to 54 percent of sales.
- Another staff member has suggested that Sweet Grove rely more on outsourcing for fruit processing. This would reduce fixed costs by $300,000 but increase variable costs to 65 percent of sales.

Required

a. What is the current break-even point in sales dollars?

b. Assuming an income tax rate of 34 percent, what dollar sales volume is currently required to obtain an after-tax profit of $500,000?

c. In the absence of income taxes, at what sales volume will both alternatives (automation and outsourcing) provide the same profit?

d. Briefly describe one strength and one weakness of both the automation and the outsourcing alternatives.

P3-31. Break-Even Analysis in a Not-for-Profit Organization (LO3)

Melford Hospital operates a general hospital but rents space to separately owned entities rendering specialized services such as pediatrics and psychiatry. Melford charges each separate entity for patients' services (meals and laundry) and for administrative services (billings and collections). Space and bed rentals are fixed charges for the year, based on bed capacity rented to each entity. Melford charged the following costs to Pediatrics for the year ended June 30, 2009:

	Patient Services (Variable)	Bed Capacity (Fixed)
Dietary	$ 600,000	
Janitorial		$ 70,000
Laundry	300,000	
Laboratory	450,000	
Pharmacy	350,000	
Repairs and maintenance		30,000
General and administrative		1,300,000
Rent		1,500,000
Billings and collections	300,000	
Total	$2,000,000	$2,900,000

In addition to these charges from Melford Hospital, Pediatrics incurred the following personnel costs:

	Annual Salaries*
Supervising nurses.	$100,000
Nurses	200,000
Assistants.	180,000
Total	$480,000

*These salaries are fixed within the ranges of annual patient-days considered in this problem.

During the year ended June 30, 2009, Pediatrics charged each patient $300 per day, had a capacity of 60 beds, and had revenues of $6,000,000 for 365 days. Pediatrics operated at 100 percent capacity on 90 days during this period. It is estimated that during these 90 days, the demand exceeded 80 beds. Melford has 20 additional beds available for rent for the year ending June 30, 2010. This additional rental would proportionately increase Pediatrics' annual fixed charges based on bed capacity.

Required

a. Calculate the minimum number of patient-days required for Pediatrics to break even for the year ending June 30, 2010, if the additional beds are not rented. Patient demand is unknown, but assume that revenue per patient-day, cost per patient-day, cost per bed, and salary rates for the year ending June 30, 2010, remain the same as for the year ended June 30, 2009.

b. Assume Pediatrics rents the extra 20-bed capacity from Melford. Determine the net increase or decrease in earnings by preparing a schedule of increases in revenues and costs for the year ending June 30, 2010. Assume that patient demand, revenue per patient-day, cost per patient-day, cost per bed, and salary rates remain the same as for the year ended June 30, 2009.

(CPA adapted)

P3-32. Cost-Volume-Profit Analysis of Alternative Products (LO3)

Siberian Ski Company recently expanded its manufacturing capacity to allow production of up to 15,000 pairs of the Mountaineering or the Touring models of cross-country skis. The sales department assures management that it can sell between 9,000 and 13,000 of either product this year. Because the models are very similar, Siberian Ski will produce only one of the two models. The Accounting Department compiled the following information:

	Model	
	Mountaineering	Touring
Selling price per unit.	$88.00	$80.00
Variable costs per unit	$52.80	$52.80

Fixed costs will total $369,600 if the Mountaineering model is produced but only $316,800 if the Touring model is produced. Siberian Ski Company is subject to a 40 percent income tax rate.

Required

a. Determine the contribution margin ratio of the Touring model.

b. If Siberian Ski Company desires an after-tax profit of $24,000, how many pairs of Touring model skis will the company have to sell? (Round answer to the nearest unit.)

c. Determine the unit sales volume at which Siberian Ski Company would make the same before-tax profit or loss regardless of the ski model it decides to produce. Also determine the resulting before-tax profit or loss.

d. Determine the dollar sales volume at which Siberian Ski Company would make the same before-tax profit or loss regardless of the ski model it decides to produce. Also determine the resulting before-tax profit or loss. (*Hint:* Work with contribution margin ratios.)

e. What action should Siberian Ski Company take if the annual sales of either model were guaranteed to be at least 12,000 pairs? Why?

f. Determine how much the unit variable costs of the Touring model would have to change before both models would have the same break-even point in units. (Round calculations to the nearest cent.)

g. Determine the new unit break-even point of the Touring model if its variable costs per unit decrease by 10 percent and its fixed costs increase by 10 percent. (Round answer to nearest unit.)

(CMA adapted)

P3-33. CVP Analysis Using Published Financial Statements (LO3, 4)

Choice Hotels International

Choice Hotels International franchises more than 5,300 hotels in the United States and more than 40 countries. Hotel brands include Comfort Inns, Comfort Suites, Quality Inn, Sleep Inn, Clarion, Econo Lodge, and Roadway Inn. Condensed data in thousands of dollars from Choice Hotels 2006 and 2005 financial statements follow.

	2006	2005
Revenues	$544,662	$477,399
Operating Expenses	(378,037)	(334,649)
Operating Income	$166,625	$142,750

Required

a. Develop a cost-estimating equation for Choice Hotels' annual operating expenses.
b. Determine Choice Hotels' annual break-even point.
c. What assumptions are required to use these equations?

P3-34.[A] Multiple-Product Profitability Analysis, Multiple-Level Profitability Analysis

University Bookstore sells new college textbooks at the publishers' suggested retail prices. It then pays the publishers an amount equal to 75 percent of the suggested retail price. The store's other variable costs average 5 percent of sales revenue and annual fixed costs amount to $300,000.

Required

a. Determine the bookstore's annual break-even point in sales dollars.
b. Assuming an average textbook has a suggested retail price of $60, determine the bookstore's annual break-even point in units.
c. University Bookstore is planning to add used book sales to its operations. A typical used book costs the store 25 percent of the suggested retail price of a new book. The bookstore plans to sell used books for 75 percent of the suggested retail price of a new book. What is the effect on bookstore profitability of shifting sales toward more used and fewer new textbooks?
d. College Publishing produces and sells new textbooks to college and university bookstores. Typical project-level costs total $260,000 for a new textbook. Production and distribution costs amount to 20 percent of the net amount the publisher receives from the bookstores. Textbook authors are paid a royalty of 15 percent of the net amount received from the bookstores. Determine the dollar sales volume required for College Publishing to break even on a new textbook.
e. For a project with predicted sales of 15,000 new books at $60 each, determine:
1. The bookstores' contribution.
2. The publisher's contribution.
3. The author's royalties.

P3-35. Multiple-Product Profitability Analysis (LO3, 4)

Hearth Manufacturing Company produces two models of wood-burning stoves, Cozy Kitchen and All-House. Presented is sales information for the year 2009.

	Cozy Kitchen	All-House	Total
Units manufactured and sold	1,000	1,500	2,500
Sales revenue	$300,000	$750,000	$1,050,000
Variable costs	(200,000)	(450,000)	(650,000)
Contribution margin	$100,000	$300,000	400,000
Fixed costs			(240,000)
Before-tax profit			160,000
Income taxes (40 percent)			(64,000)
After-tax profit			$ 96,000

Required

a. Determine the current break-even point in sales dollars.

b. With the current product mix and break-even point, determine the average unit contribution margin and unit sales.

c. Sales representatives believe that the total sales will increase to 3,000 units, with the sales mix likely shifting to 80 percent Cozy Kitchen and 20 percent All-House over the next few years. Evaluate the desirability of this projection.

P3-36. Multiple-Product Break-Even Analysis (LO3, 4)

Currently, Corner Lunch Counter sells only Super Burgers for $2.50 each. During a typical month, the Counter reports a profit of $9,000 with sales of $50,000 and fixed costs of $21,000. Management is considering the introduction of a new Super Chicken Sandwich that will sell for $3 and have variable costs of $1.80. The addition of the Super Chicken Sandwich will require hiring additional personnel and renting additional equipment. These actions will increase monthly fixed costs by $7,760.

In the short run, management predicts that Super Chicken sales will average 10,000 sandwiches per month. However, almost all short-run sales of Super Chickens will come from regular customers who switch from Super Burgers to Super Chickens. Consequently, management predicts monthly sales of Super Burgers will decline by 10,000 units to $25,000. In the long run, management predicts that Super Chicken sales will increase to 15,000 sandwiches per month and that Super Burger sales will increase to 30,000 burgers per month.

Required

a. Determine each of the following:
1. The current monthly break-even point in sales dollars.
2. The short-run monthly profit and break-even point in sales dollars subsequent to the introduction of Super Chickens.
3. The long-run monthly profit and break-even point in sales dollars subsequent to the introduction of Super Chickens.

b. Based on your analysis, what are your recommendations?

P3-37.[A] Multi-Level Profitability Analysis

AccuMeter manufactures and sells its only product (Z1) in lot sizes of 500 units. Because of this approach, lot (batch)-level costs are regarded as variable for CVP analysis. Presented is sales and cost information for the year 2009:

Sales revenue (50,000 units at $40)	$2,000,000
Direct materials (50,000 units at $10)	500,000
Processing (50,000 units at $15)	750,000
Setup (100 lots at $2,000)	200,000
Batch movement (100 lots at $400)	40,000
Order filling (100 lots at $200)	20,000
Fixed factory overhead	800,000
Fixed selling and administrative	300,000

Required

a. Prepare a traditional contribution income statement in good form.

b. Prepare a multi-level contribution income statement in good form. (*Hint:* First determine the appropriate cost hierarchy.)

c. What is the current contribution per lot (batch) of 500 units?

d. Management is contemplating introducing a limited number of specialty products. One product would sell for $60 per unit and have direct materials costs of $12 per unit. All other costs and all production and sales procedures will remain unchanged. What lot (batch) size is required for a contribution of $700 per lot?

CASES

C3-38. Ethics and Pressure to Improve Profit Plans (LO1)

Art Conroy is the assistant controller of New City Muffler, Inc., a subsidiary of New City Automotive, which manufactures tailpipes, mufflers, and catalytic converters at several plants throughout North America. Because of pressure for lower selling prices, New City Muffler has had disappointing financial performance in recent years. Indeed, Conroy is aware of rumblings from corporate headquarters threatening to close the plant.

One of Conroy's responsibilities is to present the plant's financial plans for the coming year to the corporate officers and board of directors. In preparing for the presentation, Conroy was intrigued to note that the focal point of the budget presentation was a profit-volume graph projecting an increase in profits and a reduction in the break-even point.

Curious as to how the improvement would be accomplished, Conroy ultimately spoke with Paula Mitchell, the plant manager. Mitchell indicated that a planned increase in productivity would reduce variable costs and increase the contribution margin ratio.

When asked how the productivity increase would be accomplished, Mitchell made a vague reference to increasing the speed of the assembly line. Conroy commented that speeding up the assembly line could lead to labor problems because the speed of the line was set by union contract. Mitchell responded that she was afraid that if the speedup were opened to negotiation, the union would make a big "stink" that could result in the plant being closed. She indicated that the speedup was the "only way to save the plant, our jobs, and the jobs of all plant employees." Besides, she did not believe employees would notice a 2 or 3 percent increase in speed. Mitchell concluded the meeting observing, "You need to emphasize the results we will accomplish next year, not the details of how we will accomplish those results. Top management does not want to be bored with details. If we accomplish what we propose in the budget, we will be in for a big bonus."

Required

What advice do you have for Art Conroy?

C3-39. CVP Analysis with Changing Cost Structure (LO1, 3, 5)

Homestead Telephone was formed in the 1940s to bring telephone services to remote areas of the U.S. Midwest. The early equipment was quite primitive by today's standards. All calls were handled manually by operators, and all customers were on party lines. By the 1970s, however, all customers were on private lines, and mechanical switching devices handled routine local and long distance calls. Operators remained available for directory assistance, credit card calls, and emergencies. In the 1990s Homestead Telephone added local Internet connections as an optional service to its regular customers. It also established an optional cellular service, identified as the Home Ranger.

Required

a. Using a unit-level analysis, develop a graph with two lines, representing Homestead Telephone's cost structure (1) in the 1940s and (2) in the late 1990s. Be sure to label the axes and lines.

b. With sales revenue as the independent variable, what is the likely impact of the changed cost structure on Homestead Telephone's (1) contribution margin percent and (2) break-even point?

c. Discuss how the change in cost structure affected Homestead's operating leverage and how this affects profitability under rising or falling sales scenarios.

C3-40. Cost Estimation and CVP Analysis (LO2, 3, 4)

Presented are the 2008 and 2009 functional income statements of Regional Distribution, Inc.:

REGIONAL DISTRIBUTION, INC.
Functional Income Statements
For Years Ending December 31, 2008 and 2009

	2008		2009	
Sales.		$5,520,000		$5,000,000
Expenses				
Cost of goods sold	$4,140,000		$3,750,000	
Shipping	215,400		200,000	
Sales order processing. . . .	52,500		50,000	
Customer relations	120,000		100,000	
Depreciation	80,000		80,000	
Administrative.	250,000	(4,857,900)	250,000	(4,430,000)
Before-tax profit		662,100		570,000
Income taxes (40%)		(264,840)		(228,000)
After-tax profit		$ 397,260		$ 342,000

Required

a. Determine Regional Distribution's break-even point in sales dollars.
b. What dollar sales volume is required to earn an after-tax profit of $480,000?
c. Assuming budgeted 2010 sales of $6,000,000, prepare a 2010 contribution income statement.
d. Discuss the reliability of the calculations in requirements *a-c*, including the limitations of the CVP model and how they affect the reliability of the model.

Chapter 4

Relevant Costs and Benefits for Decision Making

LEARNING OBJECTIVES

LO1 Distinguish between relevant and irrelevant revenues and costs. (p. 96)

LO2 Analyze relevant costs and indicate how they differ under alternative decision scenarios. (p. 99)

LO3 Apply differential analysis to decision scenarios, including whether to change plans; to accept a special order; to make, buy, or outsource; and to sell or further process a product. (p. 102)

LO4 Allocate limited resources for purposes of maximizing short-run profit. (p. 109)

COSTS AND BENEFITS OF OUTSOURCING

Contracting with other firms to obtain necessary goods and services—a process called *outsourcing*—emerged as a key management strategy during the nineties. Managers hope to benefit from outsourcing by taking advantage of specialization, focusing more attention on core activities, decreasing costs, and increasing flexibility. **The Boeing Company's** design and manufacture of its new generation of passenger aircraft, the Boeing 787 Dreamliner®, represents one of the most extensive examples of outsourcing ever undertaken by a major company. Not only does it represent a radically new design for commercial aircraft, with extensive utilization of carbon-fiber instead of aluminum, it is the first jet in Boeing's history designed and built largely by other companies. Boeing enlisted 43 supplier partners from many countries, including Japan, Korea, Australia, France, Sweden, Italy, and Canada, to finalize the design at 135 sites around the world. Eleven partners have built 3 million square feet of manufacturing facilities to bring this new aircraft to market. The plan was to save about $10 billion of the cost of developing the plane by having parts suppliers from around the world design and build major sections that would be assembled at Boeing's Seattle factory.

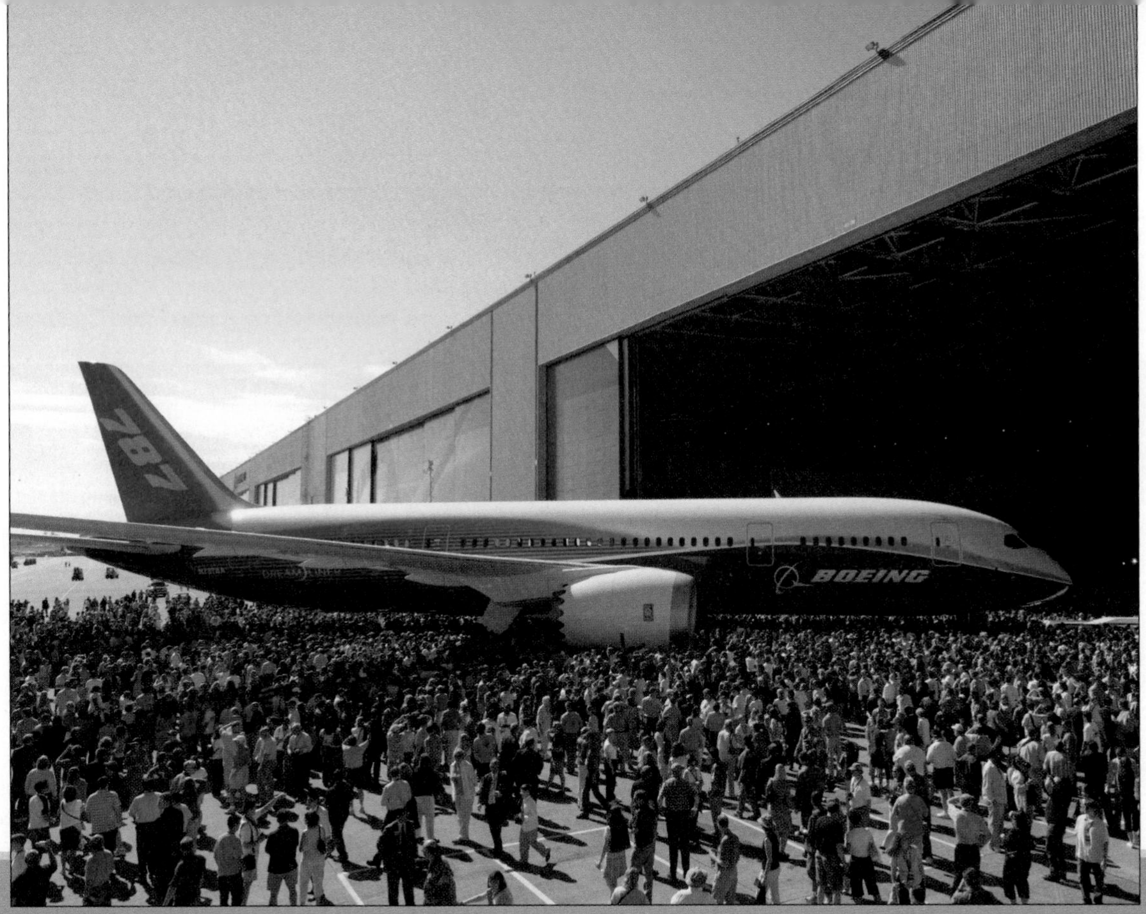

Courtesy of Boeing

The Wall Street Journal reported in late 2007 that, "outsourcing so much responsibility [by Boeing] has turned out to be far more difficult than anticipated. The supplier problems ranged from language barriers to snafus that erupted when some contractors themselves outsourced chunks of work. . . . The missteps underscore the hazards and limits of outsourcing."

Despite the problems of bringing the 787 to market, Boeing and its supplier partners still, "believe that this new method of developing planes is the model for future projects. Once the production line is running smoothly, they argue, it will be more efficient and profitable than existing construction methods."

Outsourcing, or the decision to buy products or services from an external source, rather than making them internally, is but one setting where relevant cost analysis is employed. This chapter will look further at outsourcing, as well as several other types of decisions for applying relevant cost analysis.

Source: *The Wall Street Journal* and The Boeing Company (www.boeing.com)[1]

[1] J. Lynn Lunsford, "Jet Blues: Boeing Scrambles to Repair Problems With New Plane—Layers of Outsourcing Slow 787 Production; 'Hostage to Suppliers'," *The Wall Street Journal*, December 7, 2007, p. A1.

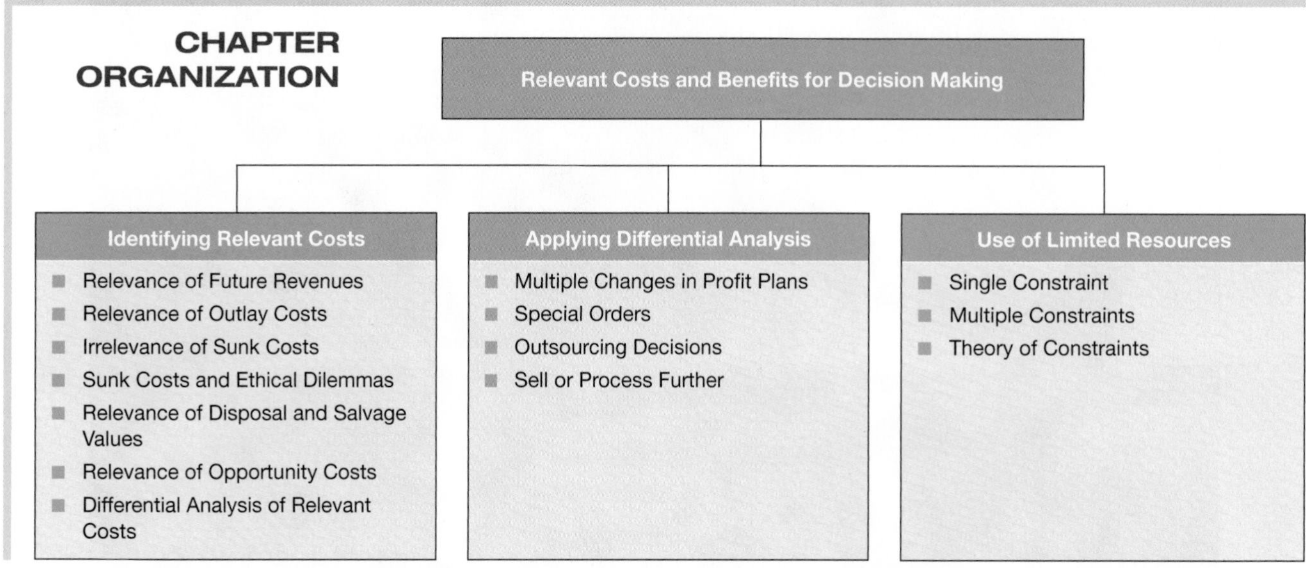

CHAPTER ORGANIZATION
Relevant Costs and Benefits for Decision Making
Identifying Relevant Costs
Relevance of Future Revenues
Relevance of Outlay Costs
Irrelevance of Sunk Costs
Sunk Costs and Ethical Dilemmas
Relevance of Disposal and Salvage Values
Relevance of Opportunity Costs
Differential Analysis of Relevant Costs
Applying Differential Analysis
Multiple Changes in Profit Plans
Special Orders
Outsourcing Decisions
Sell or Process Further
Use of Limited Resources
Single Constraint
Multiple Constraints
Theory of Constraints

The purpose of this chapter is to examine approaches to identifying and analyzing revenue and cost information for specific decisions, such as the decision to outsource. Our emphasis is on identifying **relevant costs** (future costs that differ among competing decision alternatives) and distinguishing relevant costs from **irrelevant costs** that do not differ among competing decision alternatives. We consider a number of frequently encountered decisions: to make multiple changes in profit plans, to accept or reject a special order, to acquire a component or service internally or externally, to sell a product or process it further, and how to best use limited capacity. These decision situations are not exhaustive; they only illustrate relevant cost concepts. Once we understand these concepts, we can apply them to a variety of decision scenarios.

Although our focus in this chapter is on profit maximization, decisions should not be based solely on this criterion, especially maximizing profit in the short run. Managers must consider the implications decisions have on long-run profit, as well as legal, ethical, social, and other nonquantitative factors. These factors can lead management to select a course of action other than that selected by financial information alone.

IDENTIFYING RELEVANT COSTS

LO1 Distinguish between relevant and irrelevant revenues and costs.

For a specific decision, the key to relevent cost analysis is first to identify the relevant costs (and revenues) and then to organize them in a manner that clearly indicates how they differ under each alternative. Consider the following equipment replacement decision.

Elektra, Inc. is a small start-up company that supplies high-quality components to manufacturers of wi-fi and bluetooth devices. One of its components used in wireless headsets is forecasted to sell 10,000 units during the coming year at a price of $20 per unit. Each of Elektra's components is manufactured with separate machines in a shared plant.

Headset Component Costs:	
Direct materials	$3.00 per unit
Conversion	5.00 per unit
Selling and distribution	1.00 per unit
Inspection and adjustment	$500 per batch (1,000 units)
Depreciation on machines	$15,000 per year
Machine maintenance	$200 per month
Advertising	$5,000 per year
Common Costs:	
Administrative salaries	$65,000 per year
Building operations	23,000 per year
Building rent	24,000 per year

The machine used in the manufacture of headset components is two years old and has a remaining useful life of four years. Its purchase price was $90,000 (new), and it has an estimated salvage value of zero dollars at the end of its useful life. Its current book value (original cost less accumulated depreciation) is $60,000, but its current disposal value is only $35,000.

Management is evaluating the desirability of replacing the machine with a new machine. The new machine costs $80,000, has a useful life of four years, and a predicted salvage value of zero dollars at the end of its useful life. Although the new machine has the same production capacity as the old machine, its predicted operating costs are lower because it consumes less electricity. Further, because of a computer control system, the new machine allows production of twice as many units between inspections and adjustments, and the cost of inspections and adjustments is lower. The new machine requires only annual, rather than monthly, overhauls. Hence, machine maintenance costs are lower. Costs for the new machine are predicted as follows:

Conversion costs	$4.00 per unit
Inspection and adjustment.	$300 per batch (2,000 units)
Machine maintenance	$200 per year

All other costs and all revenues remain unchanged.

The decision alternatives are to keep the old machine or to replace it with a new machine. An analysis of how costs and revenues differ under each alternative assists management in making the best choice. The first objective of this chapter is to study the distinction between relevant and irrelevant items. After evaluating the relevance of each item, we develop an analysis of relevant costs.

Relevance of Future Revenues

Revenues, which are inflows of resources from the sale of goods and services, are relevant if they differ between alternatives. In this example, revenues are not relevant because they are identical under each alternative. They would be relevant if the new machine had greater capacity or if management intended to change the selling price should it acquire the new machine. (The $35,000 disposal value of the old machine is an inflow. However, *revenues* refer to resources from the sale of goods and services to customers in the normal course of business. We include the sale of the old machine under disposal and salvage values.)

The keep-or-replace decision facing Elektra's management might be called a **cost reduction proposal** because it is based on the assumption that the organization is committed to an activity and that management desires to minimize the cost of activities. Here, the two alternatives are either to continue operating with the old machine or to replace it with a new machine.

Although this approach is appropriate for many activities, managers of for-profit organizations should remember that they have another alternative—discontinue operations. To simplify the analysis, managers normally do not consider the alternative to discontinue when operations appear to be profitable. However, if there is any doubt about an operation's profitability, this alternative should be considered. Because revenues change if an operation is discontinued, revenues are relevant whenever this alternative is considered.

Relevance of Outlay Costs

Outlay costs are costs that require future expenditures of cash or other resources. Outlay costs that differ under the decision alternatives are relevant; outlay costs that do not differ are irrelevant. Elektra's relevant and irrelevant outlay costs for the equipment replacement decision follow.

Relevant Outlay Costs	Irrelevant Outlay Costs
Conversion Costs	Direct Materials
Inspection and Adjustment Costs	Selling and Distributon
Cost of New Machine	Advertising
Machine Maintenance	Common Outlay Costs

Irrelevance of Sunk Costs

Sunk costs result from past decisions that cannot be changed. Suppose we purchased a car for $15,000 five years ago. Today we must decide whether to purchase another car or have major maintenance performed on our current car. In making this decision, the purchase price of our current car is a sunk cost.

Although the relevance of outlay costs is determined by the decision scenario, sunk costs are never relevant. The cost of the old machine is a sunk cost, not a future cost. This cost and the related depreciation result from the past decision to acquire the old machine. Even though all the outlay costs discussed earlier would be relevant to a decision to continue or discontinue operations, the sunk cost of the old machine is not relevant even to this decision.

If management elects to keep the old machine, its book value will be depreciated over its remaining useful life of four years. However, if management elects to replace the old machine, its book value is written off when it is replaced. Even if management elects to discontinue operations, the book value of the old machine must be written off.

Sunk Costs Can Cause Ethical Dilemmas

Although the book value of the old machine has no economic significance, the accounting treatment of past costs may make it psychologically difficult for managers to regard them as irrelevant. If management replaces the old machine, a $25,000 accounting loss is recorded in the year of replacement:

Book value	$60,000
Disposal value	(35,000)
Loss on disposal	$25,000

The possibility of recording an accounting loss can create an ethical dilemma for managers. Although an action may be desirable from the long-run viewpoint of the organization, in the short run, choosing the action may result in an accounting loss. Fearing the loss will lead superiors to question her judgment, a manager might prefer to use the old machine (with lower total profits over the four-year period) as opposed to replacing it and being forced to record a loss on disposal. Although this action may avoid raising troublesome questions in the near term, the cumulative effect of many decisions of this nature is harmful to the organization's long-run economic health.

From an economic viewpoint, the analysis should focus on future costs and revenues that differ. The decision should not be influenced by sunk costs. Although there is no easy solution to this behavioral and ethical problem, managers and management accountants should be aware of its potential impact.

MANAGERIAL DECISION **You are the Vice President of Manufacturing**

You recently made the decision to purchase a very expensive machine for your manufacturing plant that used technology that was well established over several years. The purchase of this machine was a major decision supported by the Chief Financial Officer, based solely on your recommendation. Shortly after making the purchase, you were attending a trade convention where you learned of new technology that is now available that essentially renders obsolete the machine you recently purchased. You feel that it may be best for the company to acquire the new technology since most of your competitors will be using it soon; however, you feel that this cannot be done now that you have recently purchased the new machine. What should you do? [Answer, p. 114]

Relevance of Disposal and Salvage Values

Elektra, Inc.'s revenues (inflows of resources from operations) from the sale of headset components were discussed earlier. The sale of fixed assets is also a source of resources. Because the sale of fixed assets is a nonoperating item, cash inflows obtained from these sales are discussed separately.

The disposal value of the old machine is a relevant cash inflow. It is obtained only if the replacement alternative is selected. Any salvage value available at the end of the useful life of either machine is also relevant. A loss on disposal can have a favorable tax impact if the loss can be offset against taxable gains or taxable income. In this case, although the book value of the old asset remains irrelevant, the expected tax reduction is relevant.

Relevance of Opportunity Costs

When making a decision between alternative courses of action, accepting one alternative results in rejecting the other alternative(s). Any benefit foregone as a result of rejecting one opportunity in favor of another opportunity is described as an **opportunity cost** of the accepted alternative. For example, if you are employed at a salary of $40,000 per year and you have the opportunity to continue to work or the opportunity to go back to school full-time for two years to earn a graduate degree, the cost of getting the degree includes not only all the outlay costs for tuition, books, and so forth, it also includes the salary foregone (or opportunity cost) of $40,000 per year. So, if your tuition and other outlay costs are going to be $25,000 per year for two years, the cost of earning the degree will be $50,000 of outlay costs and $80,000 of opportunity costs, for a total cost of earning the degree of $130,000. Opportunity costs are always relevant in making decisions among competing alternatives.

The following is a summary of all the relevant and irrelevant costs discussed in this section.

Relevant Costs		Irrelevant Costs	
Future costs that differ among competing alternatives		Future costs that do not differ among competing alternatives	
Opportunity Costs	**Relevant Outlay Costs**	**Irrelevant Outlay Costs**	**Sunk Costs**
Net benefits foregone of rejected alternatives	Future costs requiring future expenditures that differ	Future costs requiring future expenditures that do not differ	Historical costs resulting from past decisions

DIFFERENTIAL ANALYSIS OF RELEVANT COSTS

LO2 Analyze relevant costs and indicate how they differ under alternative decision scenarios.

Differential cost analysis is an approach to the analysis of relevant costs that focuses on the costs that differ under alternative actions. A differential analysis of relevant costs for Elektra Inc.'s equipment replacement decision is in Exhibit 4.1. Replacement provides a net advantage of $17,800 over the life of both machines.

An alternative analysis to that presented in Exhibit 4.1 is to present all revenues and costs (relevant and irrelevant) for each alternative in separate columns, such that the bottom line of the analysis is the total profit or loss for each alternative. This method is preferred if the goal is to determine the total profitability of each alternative. If the goal is to determine which of the two alternatives is most profitable, then a differential analysis is preferred.

Assuming the organization is committed to providing a particular product or service, a differential analysis of relevant costs (as shown in Exhibit 4.1) is preferred to a complete analysis of all costs and revenues for a number of reasons:

- A differential analysis focuses on only those items that differ, providing a clearer picture of the impact of the decision. Management is less apt to be confused by this analysis than by one that combines relevant and irrelevant items.
- A differential analysis contains fewer items, making it easier and quicker to prepare.
- A differential analysis can help to simplify complex situations (such as those encountered by multiple-product or multiple-plant firms), when it is difficult to develop complete firmwide statements to analyze all decision alternatives.

EXHIBIT 4.1 Differential Analysis of Relevant Costs

	Differential Analysis of Four-Year Totals			
	(1) Replace with New Machine		(2) Keep Old Machine	(1) − (2) Difference (effect of replacement on income)
Conversion:				
Old Machine (10,000 units × \$5 × 4 years)			\$200,000	
New Machine (10,000 units × \$4 × 4 years)	\$160,000			\$40,000
Inspection and adjustment:				
Old Machine (10* setups × \$500 × 4 years)			20,000	
New Machine (5** setups × \$300 × 4 years)	6,000			14,000
Machine maintenance:				
Old Machine (\$200 per month × 12 months × 4 years) . .			9,600	
New Machine (\$200 per month × 4 years)	800			8,800
Disposal of Old Machine	(35,000)			35,000
Cost of New Machine	80,000			(80,000)
Total costs	\$211,800		\$229,600	\$17,800
Advantage of replacement		\$17,800		

*Old Machine: 10,000 units ÷ 1,000 units per batch

**New Machine: 10,000 units ÷ 2,000 units per batch

Before preparing a differential analysis, it is always desirable to reassess the organization's commitment to a product or service. This helps avoid "throwing good money after bad." If Elektra, Inc. currently had large annual losses, acquiring the new machine would merely reduce total losses over the next four years by \$17,800. In this case, discontinuing operations (a third alternative) should also be considered.

MID-CHAPTER REVIEW

Tigertec Company manufactures golf clubs using a traditional process involving significant hand tooling and finishing. A European machine company has proposed to sell Tigertec a new highly automated machine that would reduce significantly the labor cost of producing its golf clubs. The cost of the machine is \$1,000,000, and would have an expected life of 5 years, at the end of which it would have a residual value of \$100,000. It has an estimated operating cost of \$10,000 per month. The direct labor cost savings per club from using the machine is estimated to be \$5 per club. In addition, one monthly salaried manufacturing manager, whose salary is \$6,000 per month would no longer be needed. The Vice President of Manufacturing earns \$10,000 per month. Also, the new machine would free up about 5,000 square feet of space from the displaced workers. Tigertec's building is held under a 10-year lease that has eight years remaining. The current lease cost is \$1 per square foot per month. Tigertec may be able to use the space for other purposes, and it has received an offer to rent it to a nearby related company for \$3,500 per month.

Required:

a. Identify all of the costs described above as either "relevant" or "irrelevant" to the decision to acquire the new machine.

b. Assuming the new machine would be used to produce an average of 5,000 clubs per month, prepare a differential analysis of the relevant costs of buying the machine and using it for the next five years, versus continuing to use hand labor.

c. In addition to the quantitative analysis in requirement b., what qualitative considerations are important for making the right decision?

Solution

a.

Relevant costs:	Irrelevant costs:
Cost of machine	Building lease cost
Residual value of machine	Vice President's salary
Operating cost of machine	
Direct labor savings	
Cost of manager	
Opportunity cost of renting released space	

b.

	(1) Purchase Machine	(2) Use Labor	(1) − (2) Difference (in total cost of purchasing machine)
Cost of new machine	$1,000,000		$1,000,000
Residual value of machine	(100,000)		(100,000)
Operating cost of machine ($10,000 × 60 months)	600,000		600,000
Cost of direct laborers (5,000 clubs × $5 × 60 months)		$1,500,000	(1,500,000)
Cost of one manager ($6,000 × 60 months)		360,000	(360,000)
Rental value of freed up space ($3,500 × 60 months)		210,000	(210,000)
Total costs	$1,500,000	$2,070,000	$ (570,000)
Advantage of purchasing machine	$570,000		

c. Even though the new machine would save an estimated cost of $570,000 over the next five years, there are several qualitative questions that should be answered, including the following:

- Will the new machine provide the same quality product as the current workers?
- How important is it to have a cost structure that includes variable labor costs versus more fixed machine costs? If a business decline should occur, variable costs are often easier to eliminate than fixed costs.
- What is the expected effect on worker morale and community image of eliminating a significant number of jobs in the plant?
- How important is it for the sales staff to be able to promote the product as primarily handmade, versus machine made?

APPLYING DIFFERENTIAL ANALYSIS

Differential analysis is used to provide information for a variety of planning and decision-making situations. This section illustrates some of the more frequently encountered applications of differential analysis. To focus on differential analysis concepts, we will use a simple example involving the production of one product on a continuous basis with all output sold to distributors. From the viewpoint of our single-product firm, all costs can be classified as either (1) costs that vary with units produced and sold or (2) costs that are fixed in the short run.

Multiple Changes in Profit Plans

LO3 Apply differential analysis to decision scenarios, including whether to change plans; to accept a special order; to make, buy, or outsource; and to sell or further process a product.

Mind Trek, Limited, located in Dublin, Ireland, manufactures an electronic game sold to distributors for €22 per unit (the Euro, represented by the symbol €, is the basic unit of currency in the Republic of Ireland, which is a member of the European Union). Variable costs per unit and fixed costs per month follow:

Variable Costs per Unit		Fixed Costs per Month	
Direct materials	€ 5	Manufacturing overhead	€30,000
Direct labor	3	Selling and administrative	15,000
Manufacturing overhead	2	Total	€45,000
Selling	2		
Total	€12		

The unit contribution margin (UCM) is €10 (€22 selling price − €12 variable costs). Mind Trek's contribution income statement for April 2009 is presented in Exhibit 4.2. The April 2009 operations are typical. Monthly production and sales average 5,000 units, and monthly profits average €5,000.

Management wants to know the effect that each of the following three mutually exclusive alternatives would have on monthly profits.

1. Increasing the monthly advertising budget by €4,000, which should result in a 1,000-unit increase in monthly sales.
2. Increasing the selling price by €3, which should result in a 2,000-unit decrease in monthly sales.
3. Decreasing the selling price by €2, which should result in a 2,000-unit increase in monthly sales. However, because of capacity constraints, the last 1,000 units would be produced during overtime with the direct labor costs increasing by €1 per unit.

It is possible to develop contribution income statements for each alternative and then determine the profit impact of the proposed change by comparing the new income with the current income. A more direct approach is to use differential analysis and focus on only those items that differ under each alternative.

Alternative 1	
Profit increase from increased sales (1,000 additional unit sales × €10 UCM)	€10,000
Profit decrease from increased advertising expenditures	(4,000)
Increase in monthly profit	€ 6,000

Alternative 2	
Profit decrease from reduced sales given no changes in prices or costs (2,000 lost unit sales × €10 UCM)	€(20,000)
Profit increase from increased selling price [(5,000 current unit sales − 2,000 lost unit sales) × €3 increase in unit selling price and UCM]	9,000
Decrease in monthly profit	€(11,000)

Alternative 3	
Profit increase from increased sales given no changes in prices or costs (2,000 increased unit sales × €10 UCM)	€20,000
Profit decrease from reduced selling price of all units [(5,000 current unit sales + 2,000 additional unit sales) × €2 decrease in unit selling price and UCM]	(14,000)
Profit decrease from increased direct labor costs of the last 1,000 units (1,000 units × €1 increase in unit labor costs and decrease in UCM)	(1,000)
Increase in monthly profit	€ 5,000

Alternative 2 is undesirable because it would result in a decrease in monthly profit. Because Alternative 1 results in a larger increase in monthly profit, it is preferred to Alternative 3.

Special Orders

Assume an Australian distributor offered to place a special, one-time order for 1,000 units at a reduced price of €12 per unit. The Australian distributor will contract for a shipping company to handle all packing and transportation. Mind Trek has sufficient production capacity to produce the additional units without reducing sales to its regular distributors. Management desires to know the profit impact of accepting the order. The following analysis focuses on those costs and revenues that will differ if the order is accepted.

Increase in revenues (1,000 units × €12)		€12,000
Increase in costs		
Direct materials (1,000 units × €5)	€5,000	
Direct labor (1,000 units × €3)	3,000	
Variable manufacturing overhead (1,000 units × €2)	2,000	(10,000)
Increase in profits		€ 2,000

Accepting the special order will result in a profit increase of €2,000.

If management were unaware of relevant cost concepts, it might be tempted to compare the special order price to average unit cost information developed from accounting reports. Based on Mind Trek's April 2009 contribution income statement in Exhibit 4.2, the average cost of all manufacturing, selling, and administrative expenses was €21 per unit as follows.

Variable costs	€ 60,000
Fixed costs	45,000
Total costs	€105,000
Unit production and sales	÷ 5,000
Average unit cost	€ 21

EXHIBIT 4.2 Contribution Income Statement

MIND TREK, LIMITED
Contribution Income Statement
For the Month of April 2009

Sales (5,000 units × €22)		€110,000
Less variable costs		
Direct materials (5,000 units × €5)	€25,000	
Direct labor (5,000 units × €3)	15,000	
Manufacturing overhead (5,000 units × €2)	10,000	
Selling and administrative (5,000 units × €2)	10,000	(60,000)
Contribution margin		50,000
Less fixed costs		
Manufacturing overhead	30,000	
Selling and administrative	15,000	(45,000)
Profit		€ 5,000

Comparing the special order price of €12 per unit to the average unit cost of €21, management might conclude the order would result in a loss of €9 per unit.

It is apparent that the €21 figure encompasses variable costs of €12 per unit (including irrelevant selling and administrative costs of €2 per unit) and irrelevant fixed costs of €45,000 spread over 5,000 units. But remember, management may not have detailed cost information. To obtain appropriate information for decision-making purposes, management must ask its accounting staff for the specific information needed. Different configurations of cost information are provided for different purposes. In the absence of special instructions, the accounting staff might not supply relevant cost information.

Importance of Time Span and Opportunity Costs

The special order is a one-time order for 1,000 units that will use current excess capacity. Because no special setups or equipment are required to produce the order, it is appropriate to consider only variable costs in computing the order's profitability.

But what if the Australian distributor wanted Mind Trek to sign a multiyear contract to provide 1,000 units per month at €12 each? Under these circumstances, management would be well advised to reject the contract because there is a high probability that cost increases would make the order unprofitable in later years. At the very least, management should insist that a cost escalation clause be added to the purchase agreement, specifying that the selling price would increase to cover any cost increases and detailing the cost computation.

Of more concern is the variable nature of all long-run costs. Given adequate time, management must replace fixed assets and may adjust both the number of machines as well as the size of machines used in the manufacturing process. Accordingly, *in the long run, all costs (including costs classified as fixed in a given period) are relevant.* To remain in business in the long run, Mind Trek must replace equipment, pay property taxes, pay administrative salaries, and so forth. Consequently, management should consider *all costs* (fixed and variable, manufacturing and nonmanufacturing) in evaluating a long-term contract.

Full costs include all costs, regardless of their behavior pattern or activity level. The average full cost per unit is sometimes used to approximate long-run variable costs. If accepting a long-term contract increases the monthly production and sales volume to 6,000 units, the average full cost per unit will be €19.5.

Direct materials	€ 5.0
Direct labor	3.0
Variable manufacturing overhead	2.0
Variable selling and administrative	2.0
Fixed manufacturing overhead (€30,000/6,000 units)	5.0
Fixed selling and administrative (€15,000/6,000 units)	2.5
Average full cost per unit	€19.5

If the Australian distributor agrees to pay separately all variable selling and administrative expenses associated with the contract, the estimated long-run variable costs are €17.5 per unit (€19.5 − €2). Many managers would say this is the minimum acceptable selling price, especially if the order extends over a long period of time.

Because Mind Trek has excess productive capacity, no opportunity cost is associated with accepting the Australian distributor's one-time order. There is no alternative use of the productive capacity in the short run, so there is no opportunity cost.

But what if Mind Trek were operating at capacity? In that case, accepting the special order would require reducing regular sales (assume overtime production is not possible). With an alternative use of the production capacity, an opportunity cost is associated with its use to fill the special order.

Each unit sold to the Australian distributor could otherwise generate a €10 contribution from regular customers. Accepting the special order would cause Mind Trek to incur an opportunity cost of €10,000 for the contribution margin lost from foregoing sales to regular customers.

Lost sales to regular customers (units)	1,000
Regular unit contribution margin	× €10
Opportunity cost of accepting special order	€10,000

Because this opportunity cost exceeds the €2,000 contribution derived from the special order, management should reject the special order. Accepting the order will reduce profits by €8,000 (€2,000 contribution − €10,000 opportunity cost).

Qualitative Considerations

Although an analysis of cost and revenue information may indicate that a special order is profitable in the short run, management might still reject the order because of qualitative considerations. Any concerns regarding the order's impact on regular customers might lead management to reject the order even if there is excess capacity. If the order involves a special low price, regular customers might demand a similar price reduction and threaten to take their business elsewhere. Alternatively, management might accept the special order while operating at capacity if they believed there were long-term benefits associated with penetrating a new market. Legal factors must also be considered if the special order is from a buyer who competes with regular customers.

Outsourcing Decisions (Make or Buy)

One of the most common applications of relevant cost analysis involves the make-or-buy decision. Virtually any service, product, or component that can be produced or manufactured internally can also be acquired from an external source. The procurement of services, products or components from an external source is call **outsourcing**. For example, the management of the bookstore at your college or university is likely outsourced to Barnes and Noble or Follett, and the dining facilities may be outsourced to Marriott or ARA. Similarly, Dell and HP actually manufacture very few of the components of their computers. Instead the manufacture of components is outsourced to other firms such as Intel for computer chips and Seagate for storage devices. Virtually all computer manufacturers, with the exception of Apple, outsource their operating systems to Microsoft.

Any time you call a customer support call center, the representative reached is likely to be working in a different country. A growing number of companies even outsource employees from employee leasing companies. In the past 25 years, outsourcing of goods and services has expanded exponentially with the emergence of well-trained, low-cost labor forces in China and India and other parts of the world. Although reducing costs may be the most common reason for outsourcing, there are many reasons for outsourcing, as discussed in the Research Insight below.

RESEARCH INSIGHT **Benefits of Outsourcing**

The Outsourcing Institute cited the following primary reasons for outsourcing from a recent survey of 1,410 companies:[2]

Primary Reason for Outsourcing	Percent of Respondents
Reduce and control operating costs	17
Improve company focus	16
Gain access to world-class capabilities	12
Free resources for other purposes	12
Resources not available internally	8
Take advantage of offshore capabilities	6
Reduce time to market	6

The survey also cited the following primary factors in selecting outsourcing vendors:

Price	21
Commitment to quality	16
Flexible contract terms	12
Reputation	11
Scope of resources	9
Additional value-added capability	7
Location	6
Existing relationship	6
Cultural match	6

As the above discussion reveals, the decision to outsource rather than to produce a service or product internally involves a vast array of qualitative issues. The quantitative issues surrounding the outsourcing

[2] "8th Annual Outsourcing Index: Money Matters," Outsourcing Essentials, Vol. 3, No. 4, Winter 2005.

(or make-or-buy) decision are often less challenging. To illustrate, we continue the Mind Trek example. Suppose a Canadian manufacturer offers a one-year contract to supply Mind Trek with an electronic component at a cost denominated in Euros at 2 Euros per unit. Mind Trek is now faced with the decision to continue to make the electronic component internally or outsource the component from the Canadian company. An analysis of the materials and operations required to manufacture the component internally reveals that if Mind Trek accepts the offer, it will be able to reduce the following:

- Materials costs by 10 percent per unit.
- Direct labor and variable factory overhead costs by 20 percent per unit.
- Fixed manufacturing overhead by €20,000 per year.

A differential analysis of Mind Trek's make or buy decision is presented in Exhibit 4.3. Continuing to make the component has a net advantage of €10,000.

EXHIBIT 4.3 **Differential Analysis of Make or Buy Decision**

	(1) Cost to Make		(2) Cost to Buy	(1) – (2) Difference (income effect of buying)
Cost to buy (€2 × 60,000* units)			€120,000	€(120,000)
Cost to make				
Direct materials (€5 × 0.10 × 60,000 units)	€ 30,000			30,000
Direct labor (€3 × 0.20 × 60,000 units)	36,000			36,000
Variable manufacturing overhead (€2 × 0.20 × 60,000 units)	24,000			24,000
Fixed manufacturing overhead	20,000			20,000
Total	€110,000		€120,000	€ (10,000)
Advantage of making		€10,000		

*5,000 units per month × 12 months

But what if the space currently used to manufacture the electronic component can be rented to a third party for €40,000 per year? In this case, the production capacity has an alternative use, and the net cash flow from this alternative use is an opportunity cost of making the component. Treating the rent Mind Trek will not receive if it continues to make the component as an opportunity cost, the analysis in Exhibit 4.4 indicates that buying now has a net advantage of €30,000.

EXHIBIT 4.4 **Differential Analysis of Make or Buy Decision with Opportunity to Rent Facilities**

	(1) Cost to Make		(2) Cost to Buy	(1) – (2) Difference (income effect of buying)
Cost to buy (€2 × 60,000* units)			€120,000	€(120,000)
Cost to make				
Direct materials (€5 × 0.10 × 60,000 units)	€ 30,000			30,000
Direct labor (€3 × 0.20 × 60,000 units)	36,000			36,000
Variable manufacturing overhead (€2 × 0.20 × 60,000 units)	24,000			24,000
Fixed manufacturing overhead	20,000			20,000
Opportunity cost of lost rent income	40,000			40,000
Total	€150,000		€120,000	€ 30,000
Advantage of buying		€30,000		

*5,000 units per month × 12 months

Even if outsourcing appears financially advantageous in the short run, management should not decide to outsource before considering a variety of qualitative factors. Is the outside supplier interested in developing a long-term relationship or merely attempting to use some temporarily idle capacity? If so, what will happen at the end of the contract period? What impact would a decision to outsource have on the morale of Mind Trek's employees? Will Mind Trek have to rehire laid-off employees after the contract expires? Will the outside supplier meet delivery schedules? Does the supplied part meet Mind Trek's quality standards? Will it continue to meet them? Organizations often manufacture products or provide services they can obtain elsewhere in order to control quality, to have an assured supply source, to avoid dealing with a potential competitor, or to maintain a core competency. Some of these issues are discussed in the Business Insight below within the context of outsourcing by a governmental organization.

BUSINESS INSIGHT **Using Cost Analysis to Decide Whether to Outsource Public Services**

A report published by the **Governmental Financial Officers Association** (GFOA) alerted governmental finance officers to the possible financial benefits and costs of outsourcing. It posed the question: "How can a government know whether outsourcing a given service will result in a cost savings or a cost increase?" and it responded by demonstrating how to perform a cost analysis. The report further emphasized the importance of using a differential perspective, and cautioned governmental financial analysts about the potential mistakes of treating sunk costs as relevant and opportunity costs as irrelevant.

Significantly, the GFOA report emphasized the importance of including a multi-year period in the analysis, but it also suggested using discounted cash flows to ensure that the appropriate weight is given to future costs and benefits. It proposed a four-step model: (1) Define the service, making sure that the service considered for outsourcing is comparable to the service currently being provided internally—an apples-to-apples comparison, (2) Calculate the in-house costs that would be avoided by outsourcing the service, including "those costs that are either eliminated immediately or eliminated after a brief transition period," (3) Calculate the cost of outsourcing, including the contractor's bid price, the contract administration costs, the transition costs, less any new revenues generated from outsourcing, and (4) Calculate the difference between the costs saved by outsourcing and the costs incurred. After the model is completed, sensitivity analysis should be conducted to test the sensitivity of the final result to changes in the underlying assumptions. To address the uncertainly inherent in the analysis, it was suggested that it may be advisable to require the cost savings from outsourcing to exceed the cost of providing the service in-house by a certain margin—for example, the State of Texas and the Federal Government use a 10 percent threshold.

Finally, the report highlighted the importance of considering the many nonfinancial costs and benefits that are difficult to quantify, such as differences in quality of service, underutilization of facilities, labor and equipment used during the transition period, and the potential impact on the government's ability to carry out policy goals. On the positive side, it noted that outsourcing may help transfer liability and other risks to outside contractors.[3]

Sell or Process Further

When a product is salable at various stages of completion, management must determine the product's most advantageous selling point. As each stage is completed, management must determine whether to sell the product then or to process it further. For example, petroleum companies have to determine how much crude oil to refine as diesel fuel and how much to process further as gasoline. We consider two types of sell or process further decisions: (1) for a single product and (2) for joint products.

Single Product Decisions

Assume that Scandinavian Furniture, Inc. manufactures modular wood furniture from precut and shaped wood. Although all units are salable before they are sanded and painted, Scandinavian Furniture, Inc. sands and paints all units before they are sold. Management wishes to know if this is the optimal selling point.

[3] R. Gregory Michel, *"Make or Buy? Using Cost Analysis to Decide Whether to Outsource Public Services"*, *Government Finance Review*, Vol. 20, Issue 4, p. 15.

A complete listing of unit costs and revenues for the alternative selling points follows for a low-end stereo cabinet:

	Per Cabinet			
	Sell after Assembly		Sell after Painting	Difference (income effect of painting)
Selling price	$40		$75	$35
Assembly costs	(25)		(25)	
Sanding and painting costs			(12)	(12)
Contribution margin	$15		$38	$23
Advantage of painting		$23		

The sanding and painting operation has an additional contribution of $23 per unit. The stereo cabinets should be sold after they are painted.

The assembly costs are the same under both alternatives. This illustrates that *all costs incurred prior to the decision point are irrelevant*. Given the existence of an assembled chair, the decision alternatives are to sell it now or to process it further. A differential analysis for the decision to sell or process further should include only revenues and the incremental costs of further processing as follows.

Increase in revenues		
Sell after painting	$75	
Sell after assembly	(40)	$35
Additional costs of sanding and painting		(12)
Advantage of sanding and painting		$23

The identical solution is obtained if the selling price without further processing is treated as an opportunity cost as follows.

Revenues after painting		$75
Additional costs of sanding and painting	$12	
Opportunity cost of not selling after assembly	40	(52)
Advantage of sanding and painting		$23

By processing a chair further, Scandinavian Furniture has foregone the opportunity to receive $40 from its sale. Since the chair is already made, this $40 is the net cash inflow from the most desirable alternative; it is the opportunity cost of painting.

Joint Product Decisions

Two or more products simultaneously produced by a single process from a common set of inputs are called **joint products**. Joint products are often found in basic industries that process natural raw materials such as dairy, chemical, meat, petroleum, and wood products. In the petroleum industry, crude oil is refined into fuel oil, gasoline, kerosene, lubricating oil, and other products.

The point in the process where the joint products become separately identifiable is called the **split-off point**. Materials and conversion costs incurred prior to the split-off point are called **joint costs**. For external reporting purposes, a number of techniques are used to allocate joint costs among joint products. We do not discuss these techniques here (interested students should consult a cost accounting textbook), except to note that none of the methods provide information useful for determining what to do with a joint product once it is produced. Because joint costs are incurred prior to the decision point, they are sunk costs. Consequently, *joint costs are irrelevant to a decision to sell a joint product or to* *process it further*. The only relevant factors are the alternative costs and revenues subsequent to the split-off point.

USE OF LIMITED RESOURCES

LO4 Allocate limited resources for purposes of maximizing short-run profit.

All of us have experienced time as a limiting or constraining resource. With two exams the day after tomorrow and a paper due next week, our problem is how to allocate limited study time. The solution depends on our objectives, our current status (grades, knowledge, skill levels, and so forth), and available time. Given this information, we devise a work plan to best meet our objectives.

Managers must also decide how to best use limited resources to accomplish organizational goals. A supermarket may lose sales because limited shelf space prevents stocking all available brands of soft drinks. A manufacturer may lose sales because limited machine hours or labor hours prevent filling all orders. Managers of for-profit organizations will likely find the problems of capacity constraints less troublesome than the problems of excess capacity; nonetheless, these problems are real. Ultimately, the problem often boils down to a product-mix decision, in which we must decide the mix of products or services we are going to offer our customers with the limited resources available to us.

If the limited resource is not a core business activity, it may be appropriate to outsource additional units of the limited resource externally. For example, many organizations have a small legal staff to handle routine activities; if the internal staff becomes fully committed, the organization seeks outside legal counsel. The external acquisition of such resources was discussed previously.

The long-run solution to the problem of limited resources to perform core activities may be to expand capacity. However, this is usually not feasible in the short run. Economic models suggest that another solution is to reduce demand by increasing the price. Again, this may not be desirable. A hotel, for example, may want to maintain competitive prices. A manufacturer might want to maintain a long-run price to retain customer goodwill to avoid attracting competitors, or to prevent accusations of "price gouging."

Single Constraint

The allocation of limited resources should be made only after a careful consideration of many qualitative factors. The following rule provides a useful starting point in making short-run decisions of how to best use limited resources: *To achieve short-run profit maximization, a for-profit organization should allocate limited resources in a manner that maximizes the contribution per unit of the limited resource.* The application of this rule is illustrated in the following example.

Luxury Auto Care Company offers three different service packages (A, B, and C) to its customers. These packages vary from a complete detailing of the automobile (wash, wax, carpet shampoo, etc.) to a simple hand wash. A limitation of 120 labor hours per week prevents Luxury from meeting the demand for its services. Information for the three service packages is as follows:

	A	B	C
Unit selling price	$100	$80	$50
Unit variable costs	(60)	(35)	(25)
Unit contribution margin	$ 40	$45	$25
Hours per unit	4	3	1

Package A has the highest selling price and Package B has the highest unit contribution margin. Package C is shown here to have the highest contribution per hour.

	A	B	C
Unit contribution margin	$40	$45	$25
Hours per unit	÷ 4	÷ 3	÷ 1
Contribution per hour	$10	$15	$25

Following the rule of maximizing the contribution per unit of a constraining factor, Luxury should use its limited labor hours to sell Package C. As shown in the following analysis, any other plan would result in lower profits:

	A Highest Selling Price per Unit	B Highest Contribution per Unit	C Highest Contribution per Constraining Factor
Hours available	120	120	120
Hours per unit	÷ 4	÷ 3	÷ 1
Weekly production in units	30	40	120
Unit contribution margin	× $40	× $45	× $25
Total weekly contribution margin	$1,200	$1,800	$3,000

Despite this analysis, management may decide on a product mix that includes some units of A or B or both to satisfy the requests of some "good" customers or to offer a full product line. However, such decisions sacrifice short-run profits.

Multiple Constraints

Continuing our illustration, assume the weekly demand for C is only 90 units although the company is capable of producing 120 units of C each week. In this case, the limited labor resource should first be used to satisfy the demand for Package C, with any remaining capacity going to produce Package B, which has the next highest contribution per unit of constraining factor. This allocation provides a total weekly contribution of $2,700 as follows.

Available hours	120
Required for C (90 units × 1 hour)	(90)
Hours available for B	30
Labor hours per unit	÷ 3
Production of B in units	10
Unit contribution margin of B	× $45
Contribution from B	$ 450
Contribution from C ($25 per unit × 90 units)	2,250
Total weekly contribution margin	$2,700

When an organization has alternative uses for several limited resources, the optimal use of those resources cannot be determined using the rule for short-run profit maximization. In these situations, techniques such as linear programming can be used to assist in determining the optimal mix of products or services.

Theory of Constraints

The **theory of constraints** states that every process has a bottleneck (constraining resource) and that production cannot take place faster than it is processed through that bottleneck. The goal of the theory of constraints is to maximize **throughput** (defined as sales revenue minus direct materials costs) in a constrained environment.[4] The theory has several implications for management.

[4] *The Goal,* by Eliyah M. Goldratt and Jeff Cox, presents the concepts underlying the theory of constraints in the form of a novel.

- Management should identify the bottleneck. This is often difficult when several different products are produced in a facility containing many different production activities. One approach is to walk around and observe where inventory is building up in front of workstations. The bottleneck will likely have the largest piles of work that have been waiting for the longest time.
- Management should schedule production to maximize the efficient use of the bottleneck resource. Efficiently using the bottleneck resource might necessitate inspecting all units before they reach the bottleneck rather than after the units are completed. The bottleneck resource is too valuable to waste on units that may already be defective.
- Management should schedule production to avoid a buildup of inventory. Reducing inventory lowers the cost of inventory investments and the cost of carrying inventory. It also assists in improving quality by making it easier to identify quality problems that might otherwise be hidden in large piles of inventory. Reducing inventory will require a change in the attitude of managers who like to see machines and people constantly working. To avoid a buildup of inventory in front of the bottleneck, it may be necessary for people and equipment to remain idle until the bottleneck resource calls for additional input.
- Management should work to eliminate the bottleneck, perhaps by increasing the capacity of the bottleneck resource, redesigning products so they can be produced with less use of the bottleneck resource, rescheduling production procedures to substitute nonbottleneck resources, or outsourcing work performed by bottleneck resources.

The theory of constraints has implications for management accounting performance reports. Keeping people and equipment working on production full-time is often a goal of management. To support this goal, management accounting performance reports have traditionally highlighted underutilization as an unfavorable variance (see Chapter 10). This has encouraged managers to have people and equipment producing inventory, even if the inventory is not needed or cannot be further processed because of bottlenecks. The theory of constraints suggests that it is better to have nonbottleneck resources idle than it is to have them fully utilized. To support the theory of constraints, performance reports should:

- Measure the utilization of bottleneck resources
- Measure factory throughput
- Not encourage the full utilization of nonbottleneck resources
- Discourage the buildup of excess inventory

While the theory of constraints is *similar* to our general rule for how to best use limited resources, it emphasizes throughput (selling price minus direct materials) rather than contribution (selling price minus variable costs) in allocating the limited resource. The exclusion of direct labor and variable manufacturing overhead yields larger unit margins, and it may affect resource allocations based on throughput rankings. The result will likely be a reduction in profits from those that could be achieved using our general rule for how to allocate limited resources.

Limitations of Decision Analysis Models

Analytical models, such as the relevant cost analysis model and applications presented in this chapter, are very useful in organizing information for purposes of determining the economics of a decision. However, it is important always to keep in mind that models do not make decisions—managers make decisions. The results of analytical models are an essential and necessary starting point in many decisions, but often there are other factors that weigh heavily on a decision that may cause the manager to go against the most economical alternative. There may be human resource, marketing, cultural, logistical, technological, or other factors that outweigh the analytics of a decision situation. It is in these situations where managers demonstrate leadership, problem-solving, and executive skill and potential, or the lack thereof.

BUSINESS INSIGHT **Delta Airline Adopts Theory of Constraints for Technical Operations**[5]

Recently coming out of bankruptcy, Delta Airline's management has focused on improving customer service, improving on-time performance, and making operations more efficient. Its Technical Operations (TechOps) division, which is responsible for the maintenance of Delta's fleet of airplanes, as well as providing third-party maintenance for other airlines, has been at the forefront of the emphasis on improving efficiency.

TechOps has shown a willingness to embrace change, especially when it delivers greater efficiency. The work management tool that TechOps currently uses is "theory of constraints." The intent is to identify and deal with the primary constraint preventing it from achieving its goal in order to better manage the maintenance process. Delta sees the theory of constraints as an ongoing improvement process that conjures three questions: What to change? What to change to? And how to cause the change?

"We're rolling the theory of constraints out into several of our work areas," said John Laughter, Delta TechOps' vice president of maintenance operations. "We rolled it out in 2006 in our engine shop; it starts in the support shops and then it will make its way into the engine assembly area."

"We are already beginning to see the benefits," he added, "as much as a 20 percent improvement on certain engine lines."

CHAPTER-END REVIEW

ColorTek Company produces color cartridges for inkjet printers. The cartridges are sold to mail-order distributors for $4.80 each. Manufacturing and other costs are as follows:

Variable Costs per Unit		Fixed Costs per Month	
Direct materials	$2.00	Factory overhead	$15,000
Direct labor	0.20	Selling and administrative	5,000
Factory overhead	0.25	Total	$20,000
Distribution	0.05		
Total	$2.50		

The variable distribution costs are for transportation to mail-order distributors. The current monthly production and sales volume is 15,000. Monthly capacity is 20,000 units.

Required

Determine the effect of the following independent situations on monthly profits.

a. A $1.50 increase in the unit selling price should result in an 1,800 unit decrease in monthly sales.

b. A $1.80 decrease in the unit selling price should result in a 6,000 unit increase in monthly sales. However, because of capacity constraints, the last 1,000 units would be produced during overtime, when the direct labor costs increase by 50 percent.

c. A Russian distributor has proposed to place a special, one-time order for 4,000 units next month at a reduced price of $4.00 per unit. The distributor would pay all transportation costs. There would be additional fixed selling and administrative costs of $500.00

d. An Austrian distributor has proposed to place a special, one-time order for 8,000 units at a special price of $4.00 per unit. The distributor would pay all transportation costs. There would be additional fixed selling and administrative costs of $500.00. Assume overtime production is not possible.

e. A Mexican manufacturer has offered a one-year contract to supply ink for the cartridges at a cost of $1.00 per unit. If ColorTek accepts the offer, it will be able to reduce variable manufacturing costs by 40 percent and rent some currently used space for $1,000.00 per month.

[5] David Jensen, *"Delta TechOps Rejuvenated ,"* *Aviation Maintenance*, April 15, 2007, Vol. 26; Issue 4.

f. The cartridges are currently unpackaged; that is, they are sold in bulk. Individual packaging would increase costs by $0.10 per unit. However, the units could then be sold for $5.05.

Solution

Unit selling price	$4.80
Unit variable costs	(2.50)
Unit contribution margin	$2.30

a.

Profit decrease from reduced sales given no changes in prices or costs (1,800 units × $2.30)	$ (4,140)
Profit increase from increase in selling price [(15,000 units − 1,800 units) × $1.50]	19,800
Increase in monthly profit	$15,660

b.

Profit increase from increased sales given no changes in prices or costs (6,000 units × $2.30)	$13,800
Profit decrease from reduced selling price of all units [(15,000 units + 6,000 units) × $1.80]	(37,800)
Profit decrease from increased direct labor costs for the last 1,000 units [1,000 units × ($0.20 × 0.50)]	(100)
Decrease in monthly profit	$(24,100)

c.

Increase in revenues (4,000 units × $4.00)		$16,000
Increase in costs		
Direct materials (4,000 units × $2.00)	$ 8,000	
Direct labor (4,000 units × $0.20)	800	
Factory overhead (4,000 units × $0.25)	1,000	
Selling and administrative	500	(10,300)
Increase in profits		$ 5,700

d.

Increase in revenues (8,000 units × $4.00)		$32,000
Increase in costs		
Direct materials (8,000 units × $2.00)	$16,000	
Direct labor (8,000 units × $0.20)	1,600	
Factory overhead (8,000 units × $0.25)	2,000	
Selling and administrative	500	
Opportunity cost of lost regular sales [(15,000 units + 8,000 units − 20,000 unit capacity) × $2.30]	6,900	(27,000)
Increase in profits		$ 5,000

e.

	Cost to Make		Cost to Buy	Difference (income effect of buying)
Cost to buy (15,000 units × $1.00)			$15,000	$(15,000)
Cost to make				
Direct materials (15,000 units × $2.00 × 0.40)	$12,000			12,000
Direct labor (15,000 units × $0.20 × 0.40)	1,200			1,200
Factory overhead (15,000 units × $0.25 × 0.40)	1,500			1,500
Opportunity cost	1,000			1,000
Totals	$15,700		$15,000	$ 700
Advantage of buying		$700		

f.

Increase in revenues		
Package individually (15,000 units × $5.05)	$75,750	
Sell in bulk (15,000 units × $4.80)	(72,000)	$3,750
Additional packaging costs (15,000 units × $0.10)		(1,500)
Advantage of individual packaging		$2,250

GUIDANCE ANSWER

MANAGERIAL DECISION **You are the Vice President of Manufacturing**

This is a decision that has both economic and ethical dimensions. Economically, the cost of the old machine is a sunk cost, since the expenditure for it has already been made. If it can be sold to another company to recover part of the initial cost, that amount would be relevant to the decision regarding the new technology. However, you should ignore the cost of the recently purchased machine and consider only the outlay costs that will differ between keeping the recently purchased machine and purchasing the new technology, plus any opportunity costs that may be involved with disposing of the existing machine and acquiring the new machine. From an ethical standpoint, managers are often hesitant to recommend an action that reflects poorly on their past decisions. The temptation is to try to justify the past decision. If you have evaluated all of the relevant costs and have considered all of the qualitative issues associated with upgrading the machine, these should be the basis for making your recommendation, not what it will do to your reputation with your superiors.

DISCUSSION QUESTIONS

Q4-1. Distinguish between relevant and irrelevant costs.

Q4-2. In evaluating a cost reduction proposal, what three alternatives are available to management?

Q4-3. When are outlay costs relevant and when are they irrelevant?

Q4-4. When are product-level activity costs relevant and when are they irrelevant?

Q4-5. Why is a differential analysis of relevant items preferred to a detailed listing of all costs and revenues associated with each alternative?

Q4-6. How can cost predictions be made when the acquisition of new equipment results in a technological change?

Q4-7. When are opportunity costs relevant to the evaluation of a special order?

Q4-8. Identify some important qualitative considerations in evaluating a decision to make or buy a part.

Q4-9. In a decision to sell or to process further, of what relevance are costs incurred prior to the decision point? Explain your answer.

Q4-10. How should limited resources be used to achieve short-run profit maximization?

Q4-11. What should performance reports do in support of the theory of constraints?

MINI EXERCISES

M4-12. Relevant Cost Terms: Matching (LO1)

A company that produces three products, M, N, and O, is evaluating a proposal that will result in doubling the production of N and discontinuing the production of O. The facilities currently used to produce O will be devoted to the production of N. Furthermore, additional machinery will be acquired to produce N. The production of M will not be affected. All products have a positive contribution margin.

Required

Presented below are a number of phrases related to the proposal followed by a list of cost terms. For each phrase, select the most appropriate cost term. Each term is used only once.

Phrases

1. Increased revenues from the sale of N
2. Increased variable costs of N
3. Property taxes on the new machinery
4. Revenues from the sale of M
5. Cost of the equipment used to produce O
6. Contribution margin of O
7. Variable costs of M
8. Company president's salary

Cost terms

a. Opportunity cost
b. Sunk cost
c. Irrelevant variable outlay cost
d. Irrelevant fixed outlay cost
e. Relevant variable outlay cost
f. Relevant fixed outlay cost
g. Relevant revenues
h. Irrelevant revenues

M4-13. Relevant Cost Terms: Matching (LO1)

A company that produces and sells 4,000 units per month, with the capacity to produce 5,000 units per month, is evaluating a one-time, special order for 2,000 units from a large chain store. Accepting the order will increase variable manufacturing costs and certain fixed selling and administrative costs. It will also require the company to forego the sale of 1,000 units to regular customers.

Required

Presented below are a number of statements related to the proposal followed by a list of cost terms. For each statement, select the most appropriate cost term. Each term is used only once.

Statements

1. Cost of existing equipment used to produce special order
2. Lost contribution margin from foregone sales to regular customers
3. Increased revenues from special order
4. Variable cost of 4,000 units sold to regular customers
5. Increase in fixed selling and administrative expenses
6. Revenues from 4,000 units sold to regular customers
7. Salary paid to current supervisor who oversees manufacture of special order
8. Increased variable costs of special order

Cost terms

a. Irrelevant variable outlay cost
b. Irrelevant fixed outlay cost
c. Sunk cost
d. Relevant variable outlay cost

e. Relevant fixed outlay cost
f. Opportunity cost
g. Relevant revenues
h. Irrelevant revenues

M4-14. Identifying Relevant Costs and Revenues (LO1)

The village of Twin Falls operates a power plant on the west side of a river that flows through town. The village uses some of this generated electricity to operate a water treatment plant and sells the excess electricity to a local utility. The village council is evaluating two alternative proposals:

- *Proposal 1* calls for replacing the generators used in the plant with more efficient generators that will produce more electricity and have lower operating costs. The salvage value of the old generators is higher than their removal cost.
- *Proposal 2* calls for raising the level of the dam to retain more water for generating power and increasing the force of water flowing through the dam. This will significantly increase the amount of electricity generated by the plant. Operating costs will not be affected.

Required

Presented are a number of cost and revenue items. Indicate in the appropriate columns whether each item is relevant or irrelevant to proposals 1 and 2.

	Proposal 1	Proposal 2
1. Cost of new fire engine		
2. Cost of old generators		
3. Cost of new generators		
4. Operating cost of old generators		
5. Operating cost of new generators		
6. Mayor's salary		
7. Depreciation on old generators		
8. Salvage value of old generators		
9. Removal cost of old generators		
10. Cost of raising dam		
11. Maintenance costs of water plant		
12. Revenues from sale of electricity		

M4-15. Classifying Relevant and Irrelevant Items (LO1)

The law firm of Taylor, Taylor, and Tower has been asked to represent a local client. All legal proceedings will be held out of town in Washington, D.C.

Required

The law firm's accountant has asked you to help determine the incremental cost of accepting this client. Classify each of the following items on the basis of their relationship to this engagement. Items may have multiple classifications.

	Relevant costs		Irrelevant costs	
	Opportunity	Outlay	Outlay	Sunk
1. The case will require three attorneys to stay four nights in a Washington hotel. The predicted hotel bill is $2,400.				
2. Taylor, Taylor, and Tower's professional staff is paid $2,000 per day for out-of-town assignments.				
3. Last year, depreciation on Taylor, Taylor, and Tower's office was $12,000.				
4. Round-trip transportation to Washington is expected to cost $250 per person.				
5. The firm has recently accepted an engagement that will require partners to spend two weeks in Atlanta. The predicted out-of-pocket costs of this trip are $8,500.				
6. The firm has a maintenance contract on its computer equipment that will cost $2,200 next year.				

(continued)

	Relevant costs		Irrelevant costs	
	Opportunity	Outlay	Outlay	Sunk
7. If the firm accepts the client and sends attorneys to Washington, it will have to decline a conflicting engagement in Hilton Head that would have provided a net cash inflow of $15,000.				
8. The firm's variable overhead is $80 per client hour.				
9. The firm pays $250 per year for Mr. Tower's subscription to a law journal.				
10. Last year the firm paid $3,500 to increase the insulation in its building.				

M4-16. Relevant Costs for Equipment Replacement Decision (LO1, 2, 3)

Health Scan, Inc. paid $50,000 for X-ray equipment four years ago. The equipment was expected to have a useful life of 10 years from the date of acquisition with annual operating costs of $40,000. Technological advances have made the machine purchased four years ago obsolete with a zero salvage value. An improved X-ray device incorporating the new technology is available at an initial cost of $55,000 and annual operating costs of $26,000. The new machine is expected to last only six years before it, too, is obsolete. Asked to analyze the financial aspects of replacing the obsolete but still functional machine, Health Scan's accountant prepared the following analysis. After looking over these numbers, the Center's manager rejected the proposal.

Six-year savings [($40,000 − $26,000) × 6]	$84,000
Cost of new machine	(55,000)
Undepreciated cost of old machine	(30,000)
Advantage (disadvantage) of replacement	$ (1,000)

Required

Perform an analysis of relevant costs to determine whether the manager made the correct decision.

M4-17. Special Order (LO1, 2, 3)

Tobitzu TV produces wall mounts for flat panel television sets. The forecasted income statement for 2009 is as follows:

TOBITZU TV Budgeted Income Statement For the Year 2009	
Sales ($44 per unit)	$4,400,000
Cost of good sold ($32 per unit)	(3,200,000)
Gross profit	1,200,000
Selling expenses ($3 per unit)	(300,000)
Net income	$ 900,000

Additional Information

(1) Of the production costs and selling expenses, $800,000 and $100,000, respectively, are fixed. (2) Tobitzu TV received a special order from a hospital supply company offering to buy 12,500 wall mounts for $30. If it accepts the order, there will be no additional selling expenses, and there is currently sufficient excess capacity to fill the order. The company's sales manager argues for rejecting the order because "we are not in the business of paying $32 to make a product to sell for $30."

Required

Do you think the company should accept the special order? Should the decision be based only on the profitability of the sale, or are there other issues that Tobitzu should consider? Explain?

M4-18. Sell or Process Further (LO1, 2, 3)

Great Lakes Boat Company manufactures sailboat hulls at a cost of $4,200 per unit. The hulls are sold to boatyards for $5,000. The company is evaluating the desirability of adding masts, sails, and rigging to the hulls prior to sale at an additional cost of $1,500. The completed sailboats could then be sold for $6,000 each.

Required

Determine whether the company should sell sailboat hulls or process them further into complete sailboats. Assume sales volume will not be affected.

EXERCISES

E4-19. Special Order (LO1, 2, 3)

Healthy Foods Farms grows organic vegetables and sells them to local restaurants after processing. The firm's leading product is Salad-in-a-Bag, which is a mixture of organic green salad ingredients prepared and ready to serve. The company sells a large bag to restaurants for $20. It calculates the variable cost per bag at $16 (including $1.50 for local delivery). The average cost per bag is $17.50. Because the vegetables are perishable and Healthy Foods Farms is experiencing a large crop, the firm has extra capacity. A representative of a restaurant association in another city has offered to buy fresh salad stock from the company to augment its regular supply during an upcoming international festival. The restaurant association wants to buy 2,500 bags during the next month for $18 per bag. Delivery to restaurants in the other city will cost the company $2 per bag. It can meet most of the order with excess capacity but would sacrifice 400 bags of regular sales to fill this special order. Please assist Healthy Foods Farms' management by answering the following questions.

Required

a. Using differential analysis, what is the impact on profits of accepting this special order?

b. What nonquantitative issues should management consider before making a final decision?

c. How would the analysis change if the special order were for 2,500 bags per month for the next five years?

E4-20. Special Order (LO1, 2, 3)

Nature's Garden, a new restaurant situated on a busy highway in Pomona, California, specializes in a chef's salad selling for $7. Daily fixed costs are $1,500, and variable costs are $4 per meal. With a capacity of 800 meals per day, the restaurant serves an average of 750 meals each day.

Required

a. Determine the current average cost per meal.

b. A busload of 40 Girl Scouts stops on its way home from the San Bernardino National Forest. The leader offers to bring them in if the scouts can all be served a meal for a total of $180. The owner refuses, saying he would lose $1.50 per meal if he accepted this offer. How do you think the owner arrived at the $1.50 figure? Comment on the owner's reasoning.

c. A local businessman on a break overhears the conversation with the leader and offers the owner a one-year contract to feed 300 of the businessman's employees one meal each day at a special price of $4.50 per meal. Should the restaurant owner accept this offer? Why or why not?

E4-21. Special Order: High-Low Cost Estimation (LO1, 2, 3)

SafeRide, Inc. produces air bag systems that it sells to North American automobile manufacturers. Although the company has a capacity of 300,000 units per year, it is currently producing at an annual rate of 180,000 units. SafeRide, Inc. has received an order from a German manufacturer to purchase 60,000 units at $9.00 each. Budgeted costs for 180,000 and 240,000 units are as follows:

	180,000 Units	240,000 Units
Manufacturing costs		
Direct materials	$ 450,000	$ 600,000
Direct labor	315,000	420,000
Factory overhead	1,215,000	1,260,000
Total	1,980,000	2,280,000
Selling and administrative	765,000	780,000
Total	$2,745,000	$3,060,000
Costs per unit		
Manufacturing	$11.00	$ 9.50
Selling and administrative	4.25	3.25
Total	$15.25	$12.75

Sales to North American manufacturers are priced at $20 per unit, but the sales manager believes the company should aggressively seek the German business even if it results in a loss of $3.75 per unit. She believes obtaining this order would open up several new markets for the company's product. The general manager commented that the company cannot tighten its belt to absorb the $225,000 loss ($3.75 × 60,000) it would incur if the order is accepted.

Required

a. Determine the financial implications of accepting the order.

b. How would your analysis differ if the company were operating at capacity? Determine the advantage or disadvantage of accepting the order under full-capacity circumstances.

E4-22. Outsourcing (Make-or-Buy) Decision (LO1, 2, 3)

Hewlett-Packard (HPQ)

Sanmina-SCI (SANM)

Assume a division of Hewlett-Packard currently makes 10,000 circuit boards per year used in producing diagnostic electronic instruments at a cost of $32 per board, consisting of variable costs per unit of $24 and fixed costs per unit of $8. Further assume Sanmina-SCI offers to sell Hewlett-Packard the 10,000 circuit boards for $32 each. If Hewlett-Packard accepts this offer, the facilities currently used to make the boards could be rented to one of Hewlett-Packard's suppliers for $25,000 per year. In addition, $5 per unit of the fixed overhead applied to the circuit boards would be totally eliminated.

Required

Should HP outsource this component from Samina-SCI? Support your answer with relevant cost calculations.

E4-23. Outsourcing (Make-or-Buy) Decision (LO1, 2, 3)

Mountain Air Limited manufactures a line of room air purifiers. Management is currently evaluating the possible production of an air purifier for automobiles. Based on an annual volume of 10,000 units, the predicted cost per unit of an auto air purifier follows.

Direct materials	$ 8.00
Direct labor	1.50
Factory overhead	7.00
Total	$16.50

These cost predictions include $50,000 in facility-level fixed factory overhead averaged over 10,000 units.

One of the component parts of the auto air purifier is a battery-operated electric motor. Although the company does not currently manufacture these motors, the preceding cost predictions are based on the assumption that it will assemble such a motor. Mini Motor Company has offered to supply an assembled battery-operated motor at a cost of $5.00 per unit, with a minimum annual order of 5,000 units. If Mountain Air accepts this offer, it will be able to reduce the variable labor and variable overhead costs of the auto air purifier by 50 percent. The electric motor's components will cost $2.00 if Mountain Air assembles the motors.

Required

a. Determine whether Mountain Air should continue to make the electric motor or outsource it from Mini Motor Company.

b. If it could otherwise rent the motor-assembly space for $20,000 per year, should it make or outsource this component?

c. What additional factors should it consider in deciding whether to make or outsource the electric motors?

E4-24. Make or Buy (LO1, 2, 3)

Rashad Rahavy, M.D., is a general practitioner whose offices are located in the South Falls Professional Building. In the past, Dr. Rahavy has operated his practice with a nurse, a receptionist/secretary, and a part-time bookkeeper. Dr. Rahavy, like many small-town physicians, has billed his patients and their insurance companies from his own office. The part-time bookkeeper, who works 10 hours per week, is employed exclusively for this purpose.

North Falls Physician's Service Center has offered to take over all of Dr. Rahavy's billings and collections for an annual fee of $10,000. If Dr. Rahavy accepts this offer, he will no longer need the bookkeeper. The bookkeeper's wages and fringe benefits amount to $12 per hour, and the bookkeeper works 50 weeks per year. With all the billings and collections done elsewhere, Dr. Rahavy will have two additional hours available per week to see patients. He sees an average of three patients per hour at an average fee of $30 per visit. Dr. Rahavy's practice is expanding, and new patients often have to wait several weeks for an appointment. He has resisted expanding his office hours or working more than 50 weeks per year. Finally, if Dr. Rahavy signs on with the center, he will no longer need to rent a records storage facility for $100 per month.

Required

a. Conduct a relevant cost analysis to determine if it is profitable to outsource the bookkeeping.

b. Assuming it is profitable, what are some of the pros and cons of outsourcing this service?

E4-25. Sell or Process Further (LO1, 2, 3)

Port Allen Chemical Company processes raw material D into joint products E and F. Raw material D costs $5 per liter. It costs $100 to convert 100 liters of D into 60 liters of E and 40 liters of F. Product F can be sold immediately for $5 per liter or processed further into Product G at an additional cost of $4 per liter. Product G can then be sold for $12 per liter.

Required

Determine whether Product F should be sold or processed further into Product G.

E4-26. Limited Resources (LO4)

Tempe Manufacturing Company, Ltd., produces three products: X, Y, and Z. A limitation of 200 labor hours per week prevents the company from meeting the sales demand for these products. Product information is as follows:

	X	Y	Z
Unit selling price	$160	$100	$210
Unit variable costs	(100)	(50)	(180)
Unit contribution margin	$ 60	$ 50	$ 30
Labor hours per unit	4	2	4

Required

a. Determine the weekly contribution from each product when total labor hours are allocated to the product with the highest
1. Unit selling price.
2. Unit contribution margin.
3. Contribution per labor hour.

(*Hint:* Each situation is independent of the others.)

b. What generalization can be made regarding the allocation of limited resources to achieve short-run profit maximization?

c. Determine the opportunity cost the company will incur if management requires the weekly production of 10 units of Z.

d. Give reasons why it might not be advisable to allocate resources in the most economical way in some situations.

E4-27. Limited Resources (LO4)

Olga Peña, a regional sales representative for WIFI Computer Supply Company, has been working more than 80 hours per week calling on a total of 140 regular customers each month. Because of family and health considerations, she has decided to spend no more than 40 hours per week (160 per month) with customers. Unfortunately, this cutback will require Olga to turn away some of her regular customers or, at least, serve them less frequently than once a month. Olga has developed the following information to assist her in determining how to best allocate time:

	Customer Classification		
	Large Business	Small Business	Individual
Number of customers	10	50	80
Average monthly sales per customer	$2,000	$1,000	$500
Commission percentage	5%	8%	10%
Hours per customer per monthly visit	4.0	2.0	2.5

Required

a. Develop a monthly plan that indicates the number of customers Olga should call on in each classification to maximize her monthly sales commissions.

b. Determine the monthly commissions Olga will earn if she implements this plan.

c. Give one or two reasons why Olga might want to keep one or more customers that are not in the most profitable categories.

PROBLEMS

P4-28. Multiple Changes in Profit Plans (LO1, 2, 3)

In an attempt to improve profit performance, Jacobson Company's management is considering a number of alternative actions. An April 2009 contribution income statement for Jacobson Company follows.

JACOBSON COMPANY
Contribution Income Statement
For Month of April 2009

Sales (10,000 units × $40)		$400,000
Less variable costs		
Direct materials (10,000 units × $5)	$ 50,000	
Direct labor (10,000 units × $14)	140,000	
Variable factory overhead (10,000 units × $6)	60,000	
Selling and administrative (10,000 units × $5)	50,000	(300,000)
Contribution margin (10,000 units × $10)		100,000
Less fixed costs		
Factory overhead	50,000	
Selling and administrative	60,000	(110,000)
Net income (loss)		$ (10,000)

Required

Determine the effect of each of the following independent situations on monthly profit.

a. Purchasing automated assembly equipment, which should reduce direct labor costs by $6 per unit and increase variable overhead costs by $2 per unit and fixed factory overhead by $22,000 per month.

b. Reducing the selling price by $5 per unit. This should increase the monthly sales by 5,000 units. At this higher volume, additional equipment and salaried personnel would be required. This will increase fixed factory overhead by $3,000 per month and fixed selling and administrative costs by $2,500 per month.

c. Buying rather than manufacturing a component of Jacobson's final product. This will increase direct materials costs by $15 per unit. However, direct labor will decline $4 per unit, variable factory overhead will decline $1 per unit, and fixed factory overhead will decline $10,000 per month.

d. Increasing the unit selling price by $3 per unit. This action should result in a 1,000-unit decrease in monthly sales.

e. Combining alternatives (a) and (d).

P4-29. Multiple Changes in Profit Plans: Multiple Products (LO1, 2, 3)

Information on Guadalupe Ltd.'s three products follows:

	A	B	C
Unit sales per month	900	1,400	900
Selling price per unit	$ 5.00	$7.50	$4.00
Variable costs per unit	(5.20)	(6.00)	(2.00)
Unit contribution margin	$(0.20)	$1.50	$2.00

Required

Determine the effect each of the following situations would have on monthly profits. Each situation should be evaluated independently of all others.

a. Product A is discontinued.

b. Product A is discontinued, and the subsequent loss of customers causes sales of Product B to decline by 100 units.

c. The selling price of A is increased to $5.50 with a sales decrease of 200 units.

d. The price of Product B is increased to $8.00 with a resulting sales decrease of 200 units. However, some of these customers shift to Product A; sales of Product A increase by 100 units.

e. Product A is discontinued, and the plant in which A was produced is used to produce D, a new product. Product D has a unit contribution margin of $0.30. Monthly sales of Product D are predicted to be 700 units.

f. The selling price of Product C is increased to $5.00, and the selling price of Product B is decreased to $7.00. Sales of C decline by 200 units, while sales of B increase by 300 units.

P4-30. Relevant Costs and Differential Analysis (LO1, 2)

Coastal Community Bank paid $50,000 for a check-sorting machine in January 2005. The machine had an estimated life of 10 years and annual operating costs of $40,000, excluding depreciation. Although management is pleased with the machine, recent technological advances have made it obsolete. Consequently, as of January 2009, the machine has a book value of $30,000, a remaining operating life of 6 years, and a salvage value of $0.

The manager of operations is evaluating a proposal to acquire a new optical scanning and sorting machine. The new machine would cost $90,000 and reduce annual operating costs to $20,000, excluding depreciation. Because of expected technological improvements, the manager believes the new machine will have an economic life of 6 years and no salvage value at the end of that life. Prior to signing the papers authorizing the acquisition of the new machine, the president of the Coastal Community Bank prepared the following analysis:

Six-year savings [($40,000 – $20,000) × 6 years]	$120,000
Cost of new machine	(90,000)
Loss on disposal of old machine	(30,000)
Advantage (disadvantage) of replacement	$ 0

After looking at these numbers, he rejected the proposal and commented that he was "tired of looking at marginal projects. This bank is in business to make a profit, not to break even. If you want to break even, go work for the government."

Required

a. Evaluate the president's analysis.

b. Prepare a differential analysis of six-year totals for the old and the new machines.

c. Speculate on some limitations of the model or other issues that might be a factor in making a final decision.

P4-31. Special Order (LO1, 2, 3)

Thousand Islands Company produces a variety of electric scooters. Management follows a pricing policy of manufacturing cost plus 60 percent. In response to a request from Northern Cycles, LLC, the following price has been developed for an order of 300 scooters (the smallest scooter Thousand Islands produces):

Manufacturing costs	
Direct materials	$10,000
Direct labor	12,000
Factory overhead	18,000
Total	40,000
Markup (60%)	24,000
Selling price	$64,000

Mr. Bass, the president of Northern Cycles, rejected this price and offered to purchase the 300 scooters at a price of $44,000. The following additional information is available:

- Thousand Islands has sufficient excess capacity to produce the scooters.
- Factory overhead is applied on the basis of direct labor dollars.

- Budgeted factory overhead is $400,000 for the current year. Of this amount, $100,000 is fixed. Of the $18,000 of factory overhead assigned to the Northern Cycles, only $13,500 is driven by the special order; $4,500 is a fixed cost.
- Selling and administrative expenses are budgeted as follows:

Fixed.	$90,000 per year
Variable. . . .	$20 per unit manufactured and sold

Required

a. The president of Thousand Islands wants to know if he should allow Mr. Bass to have the scooters for $44,000. Determine the effect on profits of accepting Mr. Bass's offer.

b. Briefly explain why certain costs should be omitted from the analysis in requirement (a).

c. Assume Thousand Islands is operating at capacity and could sell the 300 scooters at its regular markup.
1. Determine the opportunity cost of accepting Mr. Bass's offer.
2. Determine the effect on profits of accepting Mr. Bass's offer.

d. What other factors should Thousand Islands consider before deciding to accept the special order?

P4-32. Special Order (LO1, 2, 3)

Every Halloween, Glacier Ice Cream Shop offers a trick-or-treat package of 20 coupons for $3. The coupons are redeemable by children 12 years or under, for a single-scoop cone, with a limit of one coupon per child per visit. Coupon sales average 500 books per year. The printing costs are $60. A single-scoop cone of Glacier ice cream normally sells for $0.60. The variable costs of a single-scoop cone are $0.40.

Required

a. Determine the loss if all coupons are redeemed without any other effect on sales.

b. Assume all coupons will not be redeemed. With regular sales unaffected, determine the coupon redemption rate at which Glacier will break even on the offer.

c. Assuming regular sales are not affected and one additional single-scoop cone is sold at the regular price each time a coupon is redeemed, determine the coupon redemption rate at which Glacier will break even on the offer.

d. Determine the profit or loss incurred on the offer if the coupon redemption rate is 60 percent and:
1. One-fourth of the redeemed coupons have no effect on sales.
2. One-fourth of the redeemed coupons result in additional sales of two single-scoop cones.
3. One-fourth of the redeemed coupons result in additional sales of three single-scoop cones.
4. One-fourth of the redeemed coupons come out of regular sales of single-scoop cones.

P4-33. Applications of Differential Analysis (LO1, 2, 3)

Low Country Vision Company manufactures high-end sunglasses that it sells to mail-order distributors for $40. Manufacturing and other costs follow:

Variable Costs per Unit		Fixed Costs per Month	
Direct materials	$ 8	Factory overhead	$20,000
Direct labor.	7	Selling and administrative . . .	10,000
Factory overhead	2	Total	$30,000
Distribution.	3		
Total	$20		

The variable distribution costs are for transportation to mail-order distributors. The current monthly production and sales volume is 5,000 units. Monthly capacity is 6,000 units.

Required

Determine the effect of each of the following independent situations on monthly profits.

a. A $2.00 increase in the unit selling price should result in a 1,000-unit decrease in monthly sales.

b. A 15% decrease in the unit selling price should result in a 2,000-unit increase in monthly sales. However, because of capacity constraints, the last 1,000 units would be produced during overtime with the direct labor costs increasing by 60 percent.

c. A British distributor has proposed to place a special, one-time order for 1,000 units at a reduced price of $35 per unit. The distributor would pay all transportation costs. There would be additional fixed selling and administrative costs of $1,000.

d. A Dutch distributor has proposed to place a special, one-time order for 2,500 units at a special price of $35 per unit. The distributor would pay all transportation costs. There would be additional fixed selling and administrative costs of $1,500. Assume overtime production is not possible.

e. Low Country provides a designer case for each pair of sunglasses that it manufactures. A Canadian manufacturer has offered a one-year contract to supply the cases at a cost of $5 per unit. If Low Country accepts the offer, it will be able to reduce variable manufacturing costs by 10%, reduce fixed costs by $1,500, and rent out some freed-up space for $2,000 per month.

f. The glasses also come with four different color inserts that allow the user to change the appearance of the glasses to match her or his clothing. Making the glasses in only one color without the color inserts would reduce the cost by $5, but Low Country believes the selling price would only have to decrease to $33.

P4-34. Applications of Differential Analysis (LO1, 2, 3)

Bushwhack Expeditions offers guided back-country hiking/camping trips in British Columbia. Bushwhack provides a guide and all necessary food and equipment at a fee of $50 per person per day. Bushwhack currently provides an average of 600 guide-days per month in June, July, August, and September. Based on available equipment and staff, maximum capacity is 800 guide-days per month. Monthly variable and fixed operating costs (valued in Canadian dollars) are as follows:

Variable Costs per Guide-Day		Fixed Costs per Month	
Food	$ 5	Equipment rental	$ 5,000
Guide salary	25	Administration	5,000
Supplies	2	Advertising	2,000
Insurance	8	Total	$12,000
Total	$40		

Required

Determine the effect of each of the following situations on monthly profits. Each situation is to be evaluated independently of all others.

a. A $12 increase in the daily fee should result in a 200-unit decrease in monthly sales.

b. A $5 decrease in the daily fee should result in a 300-unit increase in monthly sales. However, because of capacity constraints, the last 100 guide-days would be provided by subcontracting to another firm at a cost of $46 per guide-day.

c. A French tour agency has proposed to place a special, one-time order for 80 guide-days at a reduced fee of $45 per guide-day. The agency would pay all insurance costs. There would be additional fixed administrative costs of $200.

d. An Italian tour agency has proposed to place a special, one-time order for 300 guide-days next month at a special fee of $45 per guide-day. The agency would pay all insurance costs. There would be additional fixed administrative costs of $200. Assume additional capacity beyond 800 guide-days is not available.

e. An Alberta outdoor supply company has offered to supply all necessary food and camping equipment at $7.50 per guide-day. This eliminates the current food costs and reduces the monthly equipment rental costs to $1,500.

f. Clients must currently carry a backpack and assist in camp activities such as cooking. Bushwhack is considering the addition of mules to carry all food and equipment and the hiring of college students to perform camp activities such as cooking. This will increase variable costs by $10 per guide-day and fixed costs by $1,200 per month. However, 600 full-service guide-days per month could now be sold at $75 each.

P4-35. Continue or Discontinue (LO1, 2)

Peachtree Eye Clinic primarily performs three medical procedures: cataract removal, corneal implants, and laser keratotomy. At the end of the first quarter of this year, Dr. Hartsfield, president of Peachtree, expressed grave concern about the cataract sector because it had reported a loss of $10,000. He rationalized that "since the cataract market is losing $10,000, and the overall practice is making $40,000, if we eliminate the cataract market, our total profits will increase to $50,000."

Required

a. Is the president's analysis correct?

b. Will total profits increase if the cataract section is dropped?

c. Is it possible total profits will decline?

CASES

C4-36. Assessing the Impact of an Incentive Plan[6] (LO1, 2, 3)

Overview

Ladbrecks is a major department store with fifty retail outlets. The company's stores compete with outlets run by companies such as Nordstrom, Macys, Marshall Fields, Bloomingdales and Saks Fifth Avenue. During the early nineties the company decided that providing excellent customer service was the key ingredient for success in the retail industry. Therefore, during the mid 1990s the company implemented an incentive plan for its sales associates in twenty of its stores. Your job is to assess the financial impact of the plan and to provide a recommendation to management to continue or discontinue the plan based on your findings.

Incentives in Retail

The past decade has evidenced a concerted effort by many firms to empower and motivate employees to improve performance. A recent New York Times article reported that more and more firms are offering bonus plans to hourly workers. An Ernst and Young survey of the retail industry indicates that virtually all department stores currently offer incentive programs such as straight commissions, base salary plus commission, and quota bonus programs. Although these programs can add to payroll costs, the survey respondents indicated that they believe these plans have contributed to major improvements in customer service.

Company's Background

Ladbrecks was founded by members of the Ladbreck family in the 1880s. The first store opened under the name Ladbreck Dry Goods. Growth was fueled through acquisitions as the industry consolidated during the 1960s. Over this hundred-year period, sales associates were paid a fixed hourly wage. Raises were based on seniority. Sales associates were expected to be neat and courteous to customers. The advent of specialty stores and the stated intention of an upscale west coast retailer to begin opening stores in the Midwest concerned Ladbreck's management. Building on its history of excellence in customer service, the company initiated its performance-based incentive plan to support its stated firm-wide strategy of "customer emphasis" with "employee empowerment." Management expected it to result in further enhancement of customer service and, consequently, in an increase in sales generated at its stores.

Incentive Plan

The plan was implemented in stores sequentially as company managers intended to examine and evaluate the plan's impact on sales and profitability. Initially, the firm selected one store from a group of similar stores in the same general area to begin the implementation. By the end of 1994, ten stores had implemented the plan. In 1995, ten more stores implemented the plan, bringing the total to 20 out of a total of 50.

The performance-based incentive plan is best described as a bonus program. At the time of the plan's implementation, sales associates received little in the form of annual merit increases, and promotions were rare. The bonus payment became the only significant reward for high performance. Each week sales associates are paid a base hourly rate times hours worked. In addition, under the plan sales associates could increase their compensation by receiving a bonus at the end of each quarter. The contract provides sales-force personnel with a cash bonus only if the actual quarterly sales generated by the employee exceed a quarterly sales goal. Individualized pre-specified sales goals were established for each employee based only on the individual's base hourly rate, hours worked and a multiplier (multiplier = 1/bonus rate). The bonus is computed as a fixed percentage of the excess sales (actual sales minus a pre-specified sales goal) by the employee in a quarter (see exhibit one).

Employee's Bonus	=	**.08**	×	**(Employee's actual sales for quarter − employee's targeted sales for quarter)**		
Where employee's targeted sales for quarter	=	**Employee's hourly wage**	×	**Hours worked in quarter**	×	**12.5**

Senior managers regarded the incentive plan as a major change for the firm and its sales force. Management expected that the new incentive scheme would motivate many changes in employee behavior that would enhance customer service. Sales associates were now expected to build a client base to generate repeat sales. Actions consistent with this approach include developing and updating customer address lists (including details of their needs and preferences), writing thank you notes and contacting customers about upcoming sales and new merchandise that matched their preferences.

[6] Written to illustrate the use of relevant costs and revenues for decision making. This example is based on an actual company's experience with implementing an incentive plan. The company name and the financial numbers and key ratios have been altered.

Consultant's Task

Management decided to call you in to provide an independent assessment. While the company thought that sales had increased with the plan's implementation, the human resource department did not know exactly how to quantify the plan's impact on sales and expenses. It suspected that employee salaries, cost of goods sold, and inventory carrying costs, as well as sales, may have changed due to the plan's implementation. You, therefore, requested information on these financial variables.

Sales Analysis: Because each of the twenty stores implemented the plan at different dates, and store sales fluctuated greatly with the seasons and the economy, you could not simply plot store sales. Instead, for each of the twenty stores, you picked another Ladbreck store as a control and computed for 48 months the following series of monthly sales[7]:

$$\text{Percent Change in Sales} = \begin{array}{c}[(\text{Plan Store Sales in Month t} \div \text{Plan Store Sales in Month t-24}) - \\ (\text{Control Store Sales in Month t/ Control Store Sales in Month t-24})] \times 100\end{array}$$

The plan's implementation was denoted as month 25, so you had 24 months prior to the plan and 24 months after the plan. Averages were then taken for the twenty stores. If the control procedure worked then you expected that the first 24 months of the series would fluctuate around zero. The actual results are reported in Figure 1 below. Month 25 is denoted as the rollout month, the month the incentive plan began.

Expense Analysis: You then plotted wage expense/sales, cost of goods sold/sales, and inventory turnover for the twenty stores for the 24 months preceding the plan and the first 24 months after plan implementation. After pulling out seasonal effects these monthly series are presented in figures 2, 3 and 4. If the plan has no impact on these expenses then you would expect no dramatic change in the series around month 25.

Figure 2 plots (wage expense in month t/sales in month t)
Figure 3 plots (cost of goods sold in month t/sales in month t)
Figure 4 plots annual turnover computed as (12 × cost of goods sold in month t/inventory at beginning of month t)

For example, if monthly cost of sales is $100 and the annual inventory turnover ratio is 4, it suggests a monthly turnover of 0.333 with the firm holding $300 in monthly inventory. (Note that a monthly inventory turnover of .333 implies an annual turnover of 4 (from 12 × 0.333).

Financial Report for Store: A typical annual income statement for a pre-plan Ladbreck store before fixed charges, taxes and incidentals looks as follows.

	Total	Percent
Sales	10,000,000	100
Cost of Goods Sold	6,300,000	63
Gross Profit	3,700,000	37
Employee salaries	800,000	8
Profit before fixed charges	2,900,000	29

A store also has substantial charges for rent, management salaries, insurance, etc. but they are fixed with respect to the incentive plan.

Required:

a. Suppose the goal of the firm is to now provide superior customer service by having the sales consultant identify and sell to the specific needs of the customer. What does this goal suggest about a change in managerial accounting and control systems?
b. Provide an estimate of the impact of the incentive plan on sales.
c. Did the sales impact occur all at once, or did it occur gradually?
d. What is the impact of the incentive plan on wage expense as a percent of sales?
e. What is the impact of the incentive plan on cost of good sold as a percent of sales?
f. What is the impact of incentive plan on inventory turnover (turnover = cost of goods sold ÷ inventory)? [If sales go up then stores are selling more goods; therefore, more goods need to be on the floor or those goods on floor need to turn over faster].

[7] For instance, assume sales for plan store were $2,200 this January and $2,000 two Januarys ago. Also assume that sales in the control store were $4,400 this January and $4,000 two Januarys ago. Percent change = 2,200/2,000 − 4,400/4,000 = 0.

g. What is the additional dollar amount of inventory that must be held?

h. Using the information on sales and expenses for a typical store, provide an analysis of the additional store profit contributed by the plan. Assume that it costs 12% a year to carry the added inventory.

i. Look at Exhibit One which provides a partial listing of employee pay for one small department within a store. Which "type" of employee is receiving the bonus.

j. Should the company keep the plan? Explain your estimate of the financial impact of the plan and also incorporate any nonfinancial information you feel is relevant in justifying your decision.

EXHIBIT 1

Wages by subset of employees in Ladbreck's fashion department.

Name	Years of Service	Hourly Wage Rate	Hours Worked in Quarter	Regular Pay	Actual Sales for Quarter	Bonus	Total Pay Quarter
BOB MARLEY	2	4.00	400	1,600	25,000	400	2,000
JIMI HENDRIX	16	7.50	440	3,300	41,000	0	3,300
MILLIE SMALL	24	9.99	440	4,396	40,000	0	4,396
AL GREEN	11	6.00	400	2,400	36,000	480	2,880
BOB DYLAN	4	5.00	400	2,000	30,000	400	2,400
JANUS JOPLIN	10	6.00	400	2,400	30,000	0	2,400
WILSON PICKETT	16	7.50	440	3,300	50,000	700	4,000
BRUCE SPRINGSTEEN	23	9.99	440	4,396	30,000	0	4,396
MICHIGAN & SMILEY	13	7.00	400	2,800	38,000	240	3,040
RICHIE FURAY	22	9.90	400	3,960	30,000	0	3,960
JOHN LENNON	5	5.00	400	2,000	34,000	720	2,720
JULIO IGLESIAS	4	5.00	480	2,400	46,000	1,280	3,680
TOMMY PETTY	11	6.00	400	2,400	36,000	480	2,880
JOAN BAEZ	21	9.90	400	3,960	40,000	0	3,960
BB KING	8	6.00	400	2,400	38,000	640	3,040
GLADYS KNIGHT	14	8.00	480	3,840	46,000	0	3,840
NEIL YOUNG	15	8.00	480	3,840	36,000	0	3,840
BO DIDDLEY	4	5.00	400	2,000	30,000	400	2,400

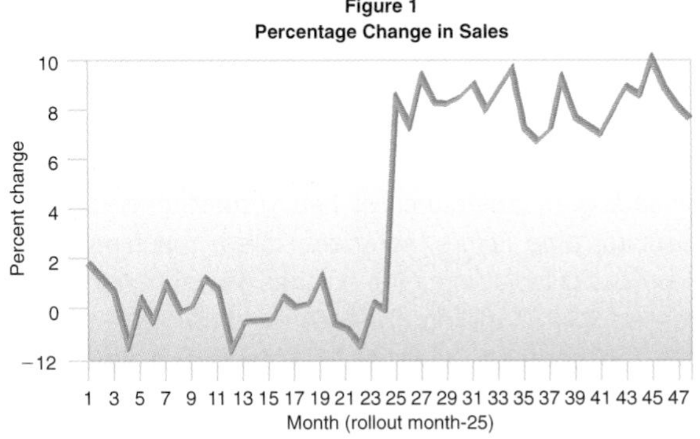

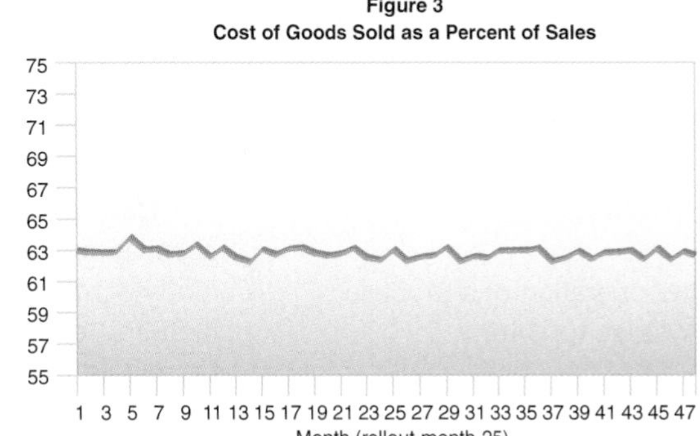

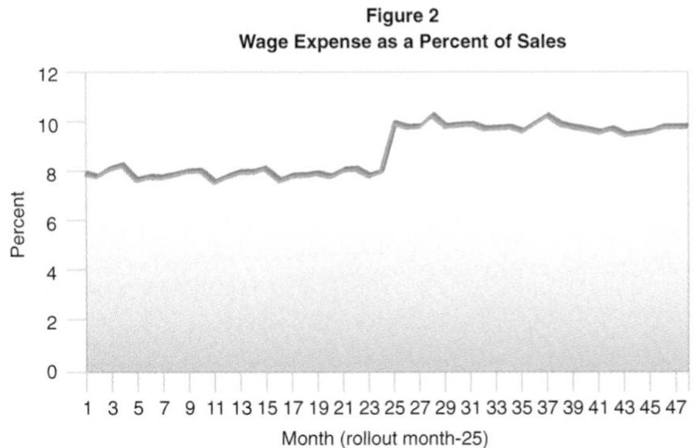

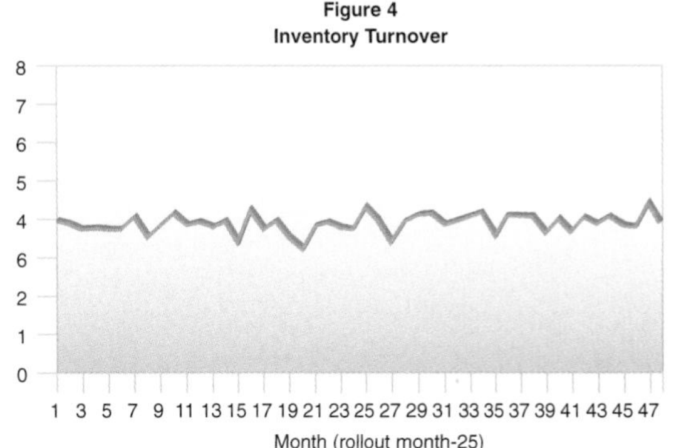

Chapter 5

Product Costing: Job and Process Operations

LEARNING OBJECTIVES

LO1 Describe inventory requirements and measurement issues for service, merchandising, and manufacturing organizations. (p. 130)

LO2 Explain the framework of inventory costing for financial reporting. (p. 131)

LO3 Describe the production environment as it relates to product costing systems. (p. 136)

LO4 Explain the operation of a job costing system. (p. 137)

LO5 Explain the operation of a process costing system. (p. 148)

COST COMPETITION AND COMPANY SUCCESS

Financial reporting is the process of preparing a firm's financial statements—income statement, balance sheet, and statement of cash flows—in accordance with generally accepted accounting principles (GAAP). GAAP requires that companies producing products measure the cost of products sold and the cost of ending inventory for each period. Caterpillar, Whirlpool Corporation, and Hershey Company present very different environments in which both the cost of products sold and ending inventory costs must be determined.

Caterpillar is a leading manufacturer of heavy moving equipment such as articulated trucks, pipe layers, scrapers, forest machines, and motor graders. Other products include marine engines and generator sets. In 2006 Caterpillar earned $3,537 million on revenues of $41,517 million. To remain competitive the company pursues "radical improvements in safety, quality, velocity, and costs."

Whirlpool Corporation is a global manufacturer of home appliances, including clothes washers and dryers, refrigerators, freezers, dishwashers, ranges, room air conditioners and microwaves. Whirlpool brands include Amana, Kitchen Aid, Maytag, Jenn-Air, and Whirlpool. According to management, lean manufacturing, operational excellence and continuous improvement are important elements of the company's success. In 2006 Maytag earned $433 million on sales of $15,420 million.

Courtesy of Whirlpool Corporation

The **Hershey Company** is the largest North American manufacturer of chocolate and sugar confectionery products. Hershey brands include Hershey's, Reese's, Hershey's Kisses, and Ice Breakers. With 2006 sales of $4,944 million, Hershey reported earnings of $559 million. Looking ahead, management sees higher costs for energy and raw materials and major challenges in controlling costs.

These three firms represent very different cost measurement environments. The volumes and products range from several hundred million units of an inexpensive commodity to thousands of highly customized, very expensive items. Although the specific accounting techniques and approaches differ for these three firms, the intent of these accounting efforts is the same. That is, each product costing system must accumulate and assign the costs of the direct and indirect activities involved in manufacturing its products.

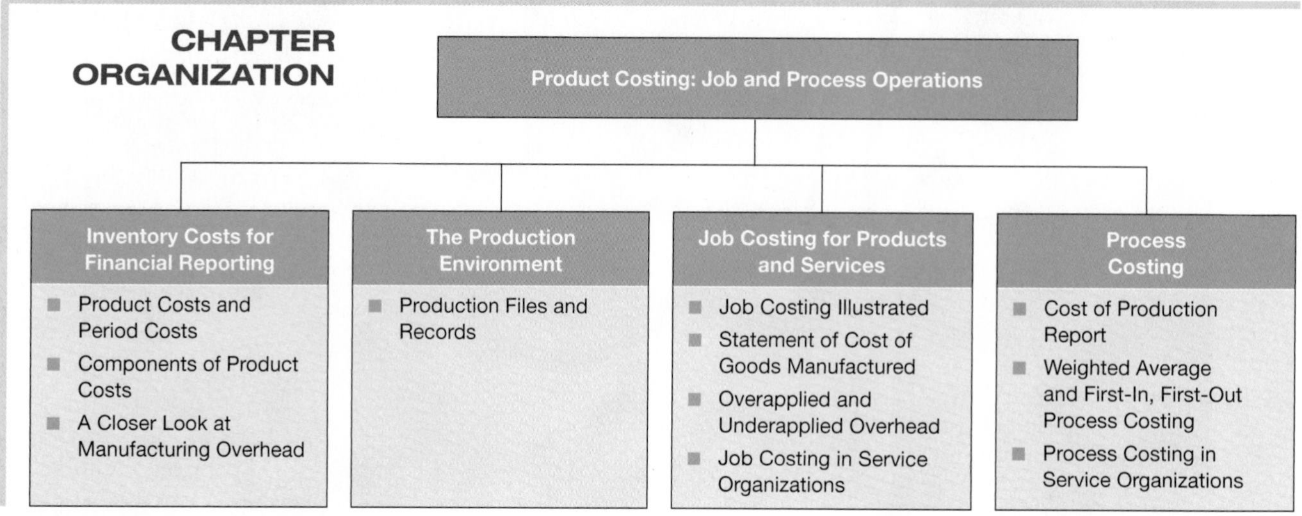

This chapter provides an overview of product costing systems and a framework for understanding costs in a production environment. It also examines aspects of the production environment that can affect product costing systems and discusses costing issues related to the production of physical products versus the production of services.

INVENTORY COSTS IN VARIOUS ORGANIZATIONS

LO1 Describe inventory requirements and measurement issues for service, merchandising, and manufacturing organizations.

Organizations can be classified as service, merchandising, or manufacturing. **Service organizations** perform work for others. Included in this category are Bank of America, Supercuts hair salons, Shriners Children's Hospitals, Cracker Barrel restaurants, United Artists movie theaters, Consolidated Edison electric utility, the City of New York, CSX Railroad, and Delta Air Lines. **Merchandising organizations** buy and sell goods and include companies such as Safeway grocery stores, L. L. Bean, Ace Hardware, and Wal-Mart. **Manufacturing organizations** process raw materials into finished products for sale to others and include General Motors, Birmingham Steel, and Georgia Pacific.

In general, service organizations have a low percentage of their total assets invested in inventory, which usually consists only of the supplies needed to facilitate their operations. In contrast, merchandising organizations usually have a high percentage of their total assets invested in inventory. Their largest inventory investment is merchandise purchased for resale, but they also have supplies inventories.

Manufacturing organizations, like merchandisers, often have a high percentage of their total assets invested in inventories. However, rather than just one major inventory category, manufacturing organizations typically have three: raw materials, work-in-process, and finished goods. **Raw materials inventories** contain the physical ingredients and components that will be converted by machines and/or human labor into a finished product. **Work-in-process inventories** are the partially completed goods that are in the process of being converted into a finished product. **Finished goods inventories** are the completely manufactured products held for sale to customers. In 2006, U.S. Steel reported the following inventories:

Raw materials	$ 560 million
Semi-finished products	597 million
Finished products	368 million
Supplies and sundry items	79 million
Total	$1,604 million

Manufacturing organizations also have supplies inventories used to facilitate production (see the U.S. Steel inventories, shown above) and selling and administrative activities. Exhibit 5.1 illustrates the flow of inventory costs in service, merchandising, and manufacturing organizations. In all three types of organizations, the financial accounting system initially records costs of inventories as assets; when they are eventually consumed or sold, inventory costs are recorded as expenses.

The formalized inventory costing systems in use today were developed to provide accountants with the necessary information for preparing company financial statements. Before the balance sheet and income statement could be prepared, accountants needed to know both the cost of inventory at the end of the year and the cost of inventory sold during the year.

Product cost information is crucial to business success. Managers use it to evaluate product profitability (since price minus cost equals profit) and organizational performance (since lower costs mean higher profit and higher profit means a better performance). It also affects the product mix as managers strive to replace low-profit products with high-profit products. Unreliable cost information can lead to disastrous results such as noncompetitive pricing of goods and services, wrong conclusions about performance, and bad decisions regarding product mix.

EXHIBIT 5.1 Inventory Costs in Various Organizations

Organization	Asset	Expense
Service	Supplies Inventory →	Supplies Expense
Merchandising	Merchandise Inventory →	Cost of Goods Sold
	Supplies Inventory →	Supplies Expense
Manufacturing	Raw Materials Inventory → Work-in-Process Inventory → Finished Goods Inventory →	Cost of Goods Sold
	Manufacturing Supplies Inventory → (Work-in-Process Inventory)	
	Office Supplies Inventory →	Office Supplies Expense

Although first developed in manufacturing organizations, costing systems are becoming increasingly important to service organizations. Whereas the term *product* was once used only to indicate a physical product, it has taken on a much broader meaning to include both physical products and services. In many cases, it is now difficult to determine whether a company is primarily a producer of goods or services. Is McDonald's producing food products or providing a service?

All organizations need information about the cost of their goods and services. Besides being used for preparing external financial reports, this information aids in good decision making on a day-to-day basis that ultimately leads to a strong and progressively improving balance sheet and income statement. The profit motive and the need to produce favorable financial statements are closely linked with the need for managers to have reliable and timely cost information. Throughout the book we discuss various costing systems, pointing out strengths and weaknesses of these systems in meeting management's information needs.

INVENTORY COSTS FOR FINANCIAL REPORTING

LO2 Explain the framework of inventory costing for financial reporting.

Financial reporting makes an important distinction between the cost of *producing* products and the cost of all other activities such as selling and administration. In general, inventory values for financial reporting purposes include only the costs of producing products. Costs related to *selling* inventories (such as marketing, distribution, customer service, and so forth) are all important for managerial decision-making purposes, but they are specifically excluded from product costs in the corporate financial statements.

Product Costs and Period Costs

For financial reporting, all costs incurred in the *manufacturing* of products are called **product costs**; these costs are carried in the accounts as an asset (inventory) until the product is sold, at which time they are recognized as an expense (cost of goods sold). Product costs include the costs of raw materials, plant employee salaries and wages, and all other *manufacturing* costs incurred to transform raw materials into finished products. Expired costs (other than those related to manufacturing inventory) are called **period costs** and are recognized as expenses when incurred. Period costs include the president's salary, sales commissions, advertising costs, and all other *nonmanufacturing* costs. Product and period costs are illustrated in Exhibit 5.2.

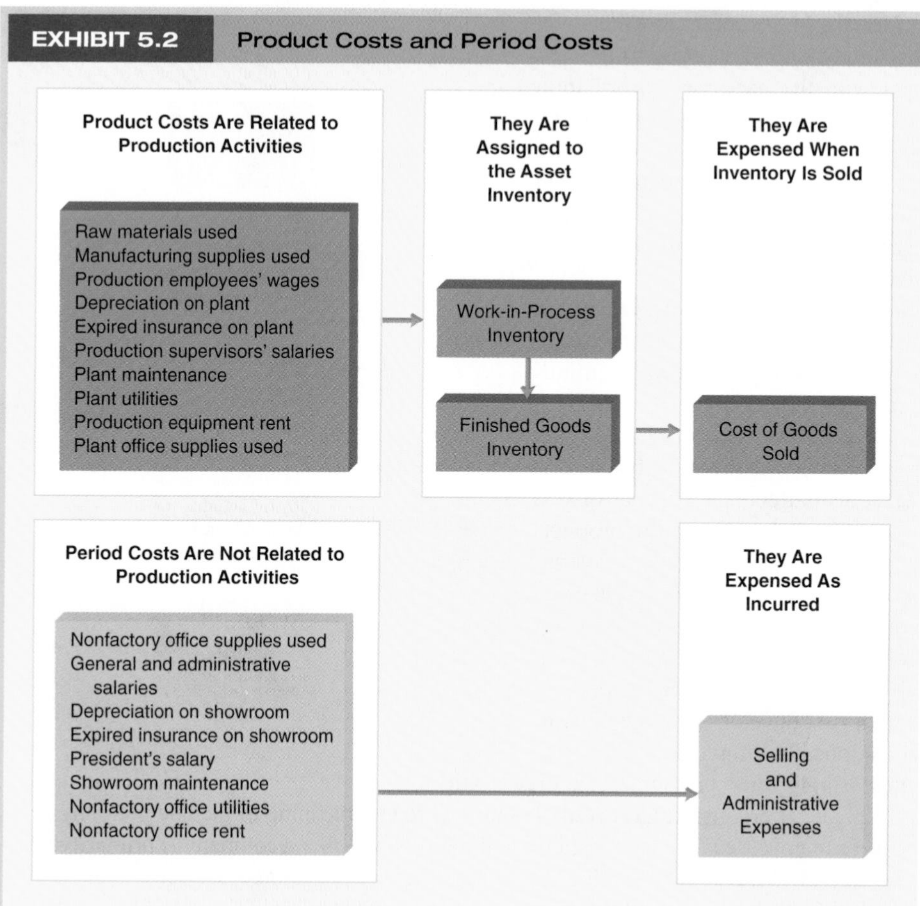

Costs such as research and development, marketing, distribution, and customer service are important for strategic analyses; however, since these costs are not incurred in the production process, they are not product costs for *financial reporting purposes*. For *internal managerial purposes*, accountants and managers often use the term *product costing* to embrace all costs incurred in connection with a product or service throughout the value chain.

To summarize, in the *product cost* versus *period cost* framework of *financial reporting*, costs are classified based on whether or not they are related to the production process. If they are related to the production process, they are product costs; otherwise, they are period costs. In this framework, costs that seem very similar may be treated quite differently. For example, note in Exhibit 5.2 that the expired cost of insurance on the *plant* is a *product cost*, but the expired cost of insurance on the *showroom* is a *period cost*. The reason is that the plant is used in production, but the showroom is not. This method of accounting for inventory that assigns all production costs to inventory is sometimes referred to as the **absorption cost** (or **full absorption cost**) method because all production costs are said to be fully absorbed into the cost of the product.

Three Components of Product Costs

The manufacture of even a simple product, such as a small wooden table, requires three basic ingredients: materials (wood), labor (the skill of a worker) and production facilities (a building to work in, a saw, and other tools). Corresponding to these three basic ingredients of any product are three basic categories of product costs: direct materials, direct labor, and manufacturing overhead.

Direct materials are the costs of the primary raw materials that are converted into finished goods. Examples of primary raw materials include iron ore to a steel mill, coiled aluminum to a manufacturer of aluminum siding, cow's milk to a dairy, logs to a sawmill, and lumber to a builder. The finished product of one firm may be the raw materials of another firm down the value chain. For example, rolled steel is a finished product of U.S. Steel, but it is the raw material of the Maytag Company for the manufacture of washers and dryers. **Direct labor** consists of wages earned by *production employees for the time they actually spend working on a product,* and **manufacturing overhead** includes all manufacturing costs other than direct materials and direct labor. (Manufacturing overhead is also called *factory overhead, burden, manufacturing burden,* and just *overhead.* Merchandising organizations occasionally refer to administrative costs as *overhead.*) **Conversion cost** consists of the combined costs of direct labor and manufacturing overhead incurred to convert raw materials into finished goods.

Examples of manufacturing overhead are manufacturing supplies, depreciation on manufacturing buildings and equipment, and the costs of plant taxes, insurance, maintenance, security, and utilities. Also included are production supervisors' salaries and all other manufacturing-related labor costs for employees who do not work directly on the product (such as maintenance, security, and janitorial personnel).

Just as raw materials, labor, and production facilities are combined to produce a finished product, direct materials costs, direct labor costs, and manufacturing overhead costs are accumulated to obtain the total cost of goods produced. Exhibit 5.3 illustrates that these product costs are accumulated in the general ledger in Work-in-Process Inventory (or just Work-in-Process) as production takes place and then are transferred to Finished Goods Inventory when production is completed. Product costs are finally assigned to Cost of Goods Sold when the finished goods are sold. (Account titles are capitalized to make it easier to determine when reference is being made to a physical item, such as work-in-process inventory, or to the account, Work-in-Process Inventory, in which costs assigned to the work-in-process inventory are accumulated.)

EXHIBIT 5.3 Three Product Cost Components

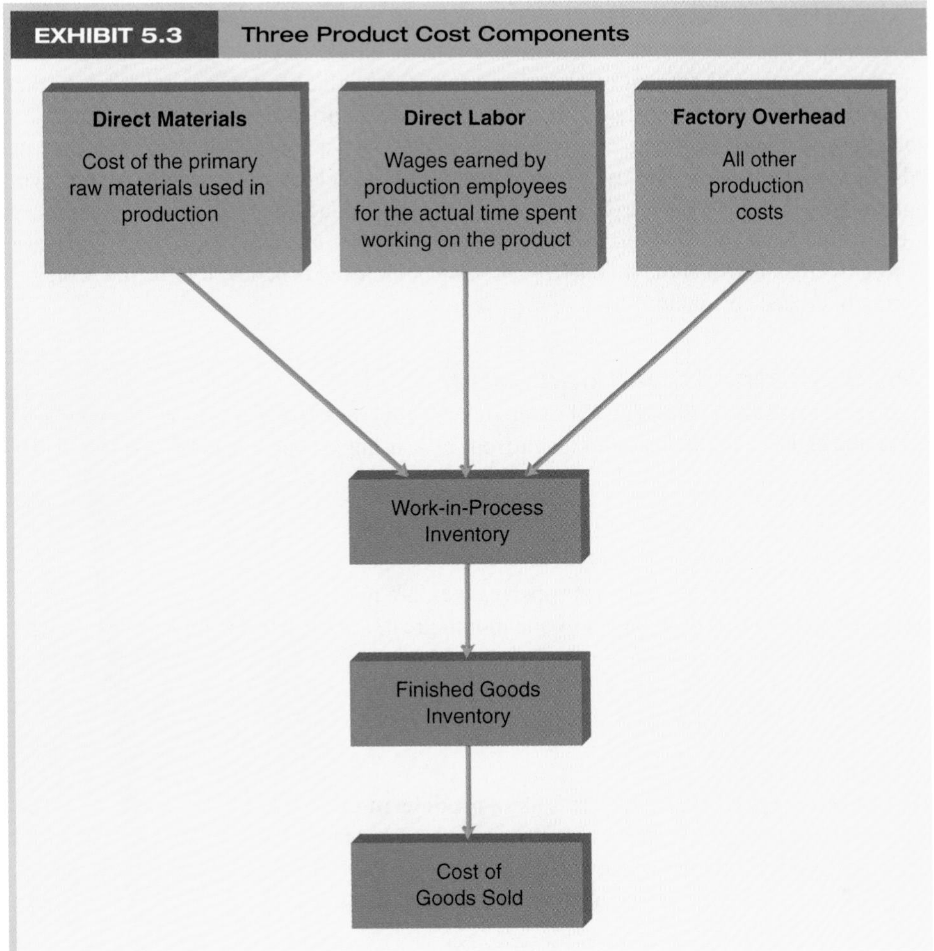

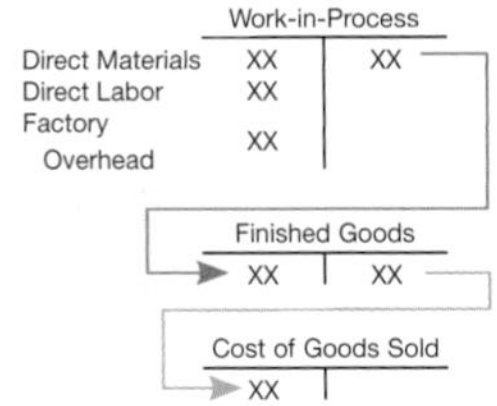

A Closer Look at Manufacturing Overhead

Possibly the biggest challenge in measuring the cost of a product is determining the amount of overhead incurred to produce it. Direct materials cost is driven by the number of raw materials units used; hence, its cost is simply the number of units of raw materials used multiplied by the related cost per unit. Direct labor cost is driven by the number of directly traceable labor hours worked on the product; so its cost is the number of direct labor hours used times the appropriate rate per hour. But what about manufacturing overhead? Manufacturing overhead often consists of dozens of different cost elements, potentially with many different cost drivers. Electricity cost is based on kilowatt-hours and water cost on gallons used; depreciation is usually measured in years of service and insurance in premium dollars per thousand dollars of coverage; and supervisors' salaries are a fixed amount per month.

Historically, accountants have believed that, even when possible, it is not cost effective to try to separately measure the cost incurred for each manufacturing overhead item to produce a unit of finished product. Instead of identifying separate cost drivers for each individual cost component in manufacturing overhead, all overhead costs for a department or plant are frequently placed in a cost pool and a single unit-level cost driver is used to assign (or apply) overhead to products.

If a company produced only one product, it would be simple to assign (or apply) overhead to the units produced because it would merely involve dividing total manufacturing overhead cost incurred by the number of units produced to get a cost per unit. For example, if total manufacturing overhead costs were $100,000 for a period when 20,000 units of product were produced, the overhead cost assigned to each unit would be $5.

Selecting a Basis (or Cost Driver) for Assigning Overhead

When multiple products are manufactured in the same facilities, using a simple average of manufacturing overhead cost per unit seldom provides a good estimate of the overhead costs incurred to produce each product. Units requiring extensive manufacturing activity will have too little cost assigned to them, while others requiring only a small amount of manufacturing effort will absorb too much cost. In these cases, units of production is not an appropriate cost driver for manufacturing overhead.

To solve this allocation problem, an overhead application base (or cost driver) other than number of units produced is usually used. The overhead application base selected is typically a unit-level activity that is common to all products but varies in quantity for each product, depending on the amount of manufacturing effort that went into making the product. For example, *machine hours* may be used to assign manufacturing overhead costs if the *number of machine hours used* is believed to be the primary cause of manufacturing overhead cost incurred.

Using Predetermined Overhead Rates

Although some organizations assign actual manufacturing overhead to products at the end of each period (normally a month), three problems often result from measuring product cost using "actual" manufacturing overhead costs:

1. Actual manufacturing overhead cost may not be known until days or weeks after the end of the period, delaying the calculation of unit product cost.
2. Some costs that are seasonal, such as property taxes, are not incurred each period, thus making the actual cost of a product produced in one month greater than that of another, even though nonseasonal costs may have been identical for both months.
3. When there is a significant amount of fixed manufacturing overhead, the costs assigned to each unit of product will vary from period to period, depending on the overall volume of activity for the period.

To overcome these problems, most firms use a **predetermined manufacturing overhead rate** to assign manufacturing overhead costs to products. A predetermined rate is established at the start of each year by dividing the *predicted overhead costs for the year* by the *predicted volume of activity in the overhead base* for the year. A predetermined manufacturing overhead rate based on direct labor hours is computed as follows:

$$\text{Predetermined manufacturing overhead rate per direct labor hour} = \frac{\text{Predicted total manufacturing overhead cost for the year}}{\text{Predicted total direct labor hours for the year}}$$

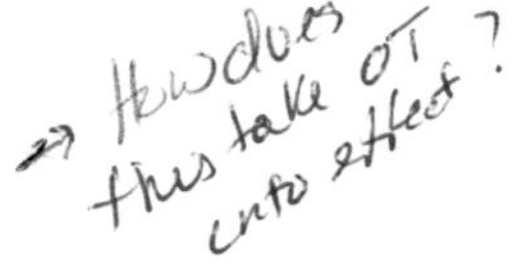

If management believed machine hours had a greater influence on the consumption of overhead, the denominator would change to predicted machine hours.

Using a predetermined manufacturing overhead rate based on direct labor hours, we compute the assignment of overhead to Work-in-Process Inventory as follows:

$$\text{Manufacturing overhead assigned to Work-in-Process Inventory} = \text{Actual direct labor hours} \times \text{Predetermined manufacturing overhead rate per direct labor hour}$$

To illustrate, late in 2008, Harmon Manufacturing Company predicted a 2009 activity level of 25,000 direct labor hours with manufacturing overhead totaling $187,500. Using this information, its 2009 predetermined overhead rate per direct labor hour was computed as follows:

$$\text{Predetermined overhead rate} = \frac{\$187{,}500}{25{,}000 \text{ direct labor hours}}$$
$$= \$7.50 \text{ per direct labor hour}$$

If 2,000 direct labor hours were used in September 2009, the applied overhead for September would be $15,000, as shown here:

$$2{,}000 \times \$7.50 = \$15{,}000$$

When a predetermined rate is used, monthly variations between actual and applied manufacturing overhead are expected because of the seasonality in costs and the variations in monthly activity. Hence, in some months overhead will be "overapplied" as applied overhead exceeds actual overhead; in other months overhead will be "underapplied" as actual overhead exceeds applied overhead. If the beginning-of-the-year estimates are accurate for annual overhead costs and annual activity in the application base, monthly over- and underapplied amounts during the year should offset each other by the end of the period. During the year, the cumulative balance should be monitored to identify an excessive over- or underapplied balance and to determine whether the estimate of the overhead rate should be revised before year-end. Later in this chapter, we consider methods for accounting for any over- or underapplied manufacturing overhead balance that may exist at the end of the year.

Changing Cost Structures Affect the Basis of Overhead Application

By using a single overhead rate, we assume that overhead costs are primarily caused by a single cost driver. Historically, a single plantwide overhead application rate based on direct labor hours was widely used when direct labor was the predominant cost factor in production and manufacturing overhead costs were driven by the utilization of direct labor.

Technological progress has caused changes in the factors of manufacturing costs, resulting in major shifts in costs in many industries from direct labor to manufacturing overhead. An example of this shift is the worldwide automobile industry where firms such as **General Motors**, **Toyota**, and **Daimler** have spent billions of dollars on robotics and other technologies, thereby reducing direct labor in the production process. In many cases, these technological changes mean that direct labor hours are no longer an appropriate basis for assigning manufacturing costs to products. In others, these changes mean there is no longer a single cost driver that is appropriate for assigning manufacturing overhead to products.

Although some companies continue to use a single (actual or predetermined) manufacturing overhead rate because it is convenient, many companies no longer use this approach. Instead, they have adopted multiple overhead rates based on either major departments or activities within the organization. One method for using multiple overhead rates is activity-based costing, discussed in Chapter 6.

THE PRODUCTION ENVIRONMENT

LO3 Describe the production environment as it relates to product costing systems.

Production personnel need to know the specific products to produce on specific machines on a daily or even hourly basis. The detailed scheduling of products on machines is performed by production scheduling personnel. Exactly how production is scheduled depends on whether process manufacturing or job production is used and whether production is in response to a specific customer sales order or for the company's inventory in anticipation of future sales.

In **process manufacturing**, production of identical units is on a *continuous* basis; a production facility may be devoted exclusively to one product or to a set of closely related products. Companies where you would likely find a process manufacturing environment include Exxon Mobil and Bowater Incorporated (which makes rolled paper for the printing of daily newspapers such as the *Chicago Tribune*). Process manufacturing is discussed later in this chapter.

In **job production**, also called **job order production**, products are manufactured in single units or in batches of identical units. Of course, the products included in different jobs may vary considerably. Examples of single-unit jobs are found at Hallco Builders, a builder of custom-designed homes; Metric Constructors Inc., which builds skyscrapers; and Riverwood International, which designs, produces, and installs packaging systems for food processors. Examples of multiple-unit jobs are found at Hartmarx, a clothing manufacturer; Steelcase Furniture Company, a large producer of office furnishings; and Intermet Corporation, a foundry company that makes parts for the automobile industry.

In a job production environment, when a customer's order is received, the marketing department forwards the order to production scheduling, where employees determine when and how the product is to be produced. Important scheduling considerations include the overall workload, raw materials availability, specific equipment or labor requirements, and the delivery date(s) of the finished product.

Important staff groups involved in production planning and control include engineering, scheduling, expediting, quality control, and accounting. Engineering is primarily concerned with determining how a product should be produced. Based on an engineering analysis and cost data, engineering personnel develop manufacturing specifications for each product. These manufacturing specifications are often summarized in two important documents: a bill of materials and an operations list. Each product's **bill of materials** specifies the kinds and quantities of raw materials required for one unit of product. The **operations list** (sometimes called an **activities list**) specifies the manufacturing operations and related times required for one unit or batch of product. The operations list should also include information on any machine setup time, movements between work areas, and other scheduled activities, such as quality inspections.

Scheduling personnel prepare a production order for each job. The **production order** contains a job's unique identification number and specifies such details as the quantity to be produced, raw materials requirements, manufacturing operations and other activities to be performed, and perhaps even the time when each manufacturing operation should be performed. In preparing a production order, scheduling personnel use the product's bill of materials and operations list to determine the materials, operations, and manufacturing times required for the job.

A **job cost sheet** is a document used to accumulate the costs for a specific job. The job cost sheet serves as the basic record for recording actual progress on the job. As production takes place, the materials, labor, and machine resources utilized are recorded on the job cost sheet along with the related costs. When a job is completed, the final cost of the job is determined by totalling the costs on the job cost sheet. See the following Business Insight box for a discussion of a new software product that supports job costing in the construction industry.

BUSINESS INSIGHT **Software for Job Costing**

A challenge of maintaining job cost systems with detailed cost sheets is capturing cost data in a timely manner. Job costing systems software is now available for the construction industry that enables job managers to automatically update and calculate job costs, projected job costs and profits, percentage of completion, and other information vital to completing jobs on budget. Integrated functionality in enterprise systems allows job cost software to articulate with software for purchasing, inventory management, billing, accounts receivable, and collections. To provide greater timeliness, software developers have even created linked programs for employees to record time worked on individual jobs from the job site.[1]

[1] Lori Widmer, "Job Costing Tracks All Jobs in Detail," *National Public Accountant*, April/May 2007, p. 55; Lori Widmer, "Advanced Job Costing Provides Management Tools," *National Public Accountant*, April/May 2007, p.54; www.construction-software.com.

Production Files and Records

Certain files in the cost system (typically in a computer database) provide the necessary detail for amounts maintained in total in the general ledger. For example, the raw materials inventory file contains separate records for each type of raw materials, indicating increases, decreases, and the available balance for both units and costs. Every time there is a change in the Raw Materials Inventory general ledger account, there must be an equal change in one or more individual inventory records. Therefore, at any given time, the total of the balances in the raw materials inventory file for all raw materials inventory items should equal the balance in the Raw Materials Inventory general ledger account. Because of this relationship between the raw materials inventory file and Raw Materials Inventory in the general ledger, Raw Materials Inventory is called a *control account* and the raw materials file of detailed records is called a *subsidiary ledger.* Other general ledger accounts related to the product cost system that have subsidiary files are Work-in-Process, Finished Goods Inventory, and Cost of Goods Sold.

Other records required to operate a job cost system include production orders, job cost sheets, materials requisition forms, and work tickets. Production orders and job cost sheets were previously discussed. The production order serves as authorization for production supervisors to obtain materials from the storeroom and to issue work orders to production employees, and the job cost sheet accumulates the cost of the job.

A **materials requisition form** indicates the type and quantity of each raw material issued to the factory. This form is used to record the transfer of responsibility for materials and to record materials changes on raw materials and job cost sheet records. The materials requisition form has a place to record the job number; the job cost sheet has a place to record the requisition number. If a question arises regarding the issuance of materials, the requisition number and job number provide a trail for tracing the destination and the source of the materials. The materials requisition form also identifies the materials warehouse employee who issued the materials and the production employee who received them.

A **work ticket** is used to record the time a job spends in a specific manufacturing operation. Each manufacturing operation performed on a job is documented by a work ticket. The completed work tickets for a job should correspond to the operations specified on the job production order. Time information on the work tickets is used by production scheduling or expediting personnel to determine whether the job is on schedule, and to assign costs to the job.

A production operation can involve a single employee, a group of employees, a machine, or even heating, cooling, or aging processes. When the operation involves a single employee, the rate recorded on the work ticket is simply the employee's wage rate. When it involves a group of employees, the rate is composed of the wage rates of all employees in the group. When the work involves a machine operation, the rate includes a charge for machine time, as well as the time of any machine operators. Other operations, such as heating, cooling, or aging, will also have a rate for each unit of time.

JOB COSTING FOR PRODUCTS AND SERVICES

LO4 Explain the operation of a job costing system.

Exhibit 5.4 shows how inventory costs in a manufacturing organization flow in a logical pattern through the financial accounting system. Pay particular attention to the major inventory accounts (Raw Materials, Work-in-Process, and Finished Goods Inventory), Manufacturing Overhead, and the flow of costs through the inventory accounts. Each of the numbered items, representing a cost flow affecting an inventory account or Manufacturing Overhead, is explained here:

1. The costs of purchased raw materials and manufacturing supplies are recorded in Raw Materials and Manufacturing Supplies, respectively. An increase in Accounts Payable typically offsets these increases.
2. As primary raw materials are requisitioned to the factory, direct materials costs are transferred from Raw Materials to Work-in-Process.
3. Direct labor costs are assigned to Work-in-Process on the basis of the time devoted to processing raw materials. Indirect labor costs associated with production employees are initially assigned to Manufacturing Overhead.

4.–6. Other production related costs are also assigned to Manufacturing Overhead. Other Payables represents the incurrence of a variety of costs such as repairs and maintenance, utilities, and property taxes.

EXHIBIT 5.4 Basic Production Cost Flows

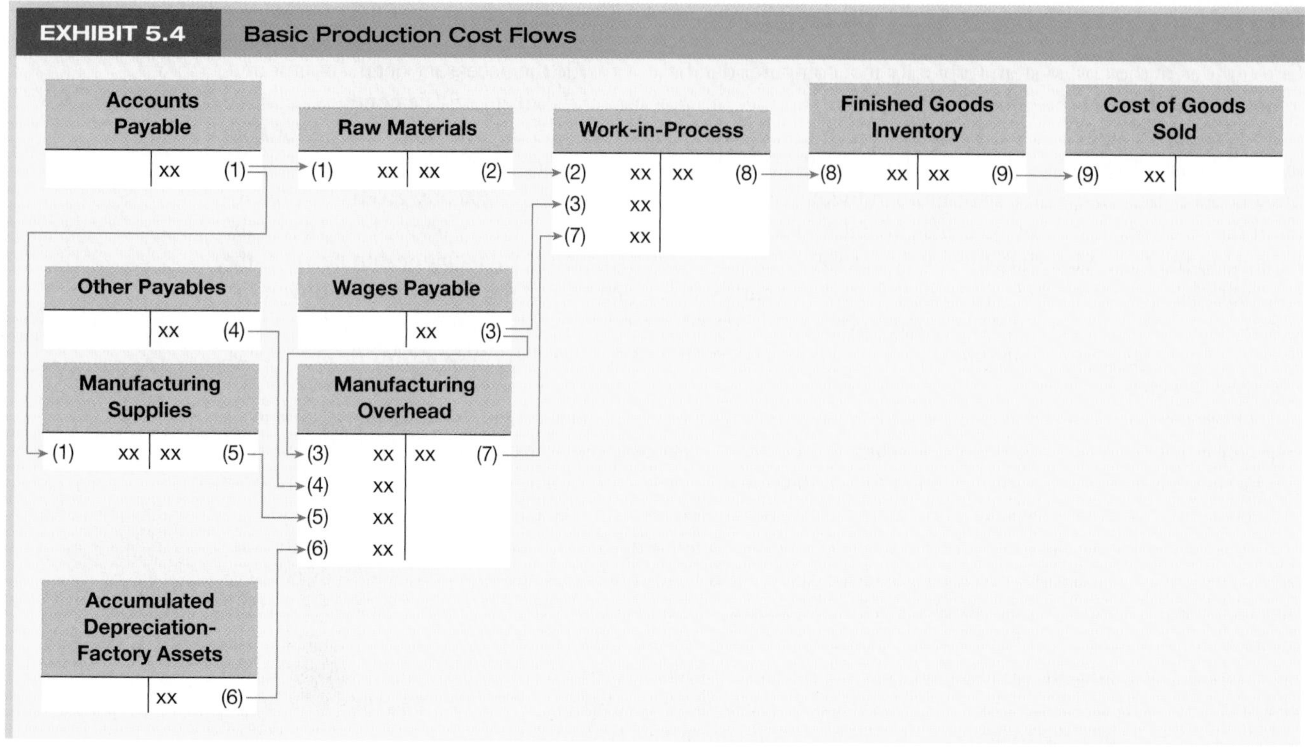

7. Costs assigned to Manufacturing Overhead are periodically reassigned (applied) to Work-in-Process, preferably with the use of a predetermined overhead rate such as direct labor hours, machine hours, or some other cost assignment base.
8. When products are completed, their accumulated product costs are totaled on a job cost sheet and transferred from Work-in-Process to Finished Goods Inventory.
9. When the completed products are sold, their costs are transferred from Finished Goods Inventory to Cost of Goods Sold.

Job Costing Illustrated

Even though data can be processed using manual or computerized systems, data processing procedures are best illustrated within the context of a paper-based manual system. Outdoor Rainwear custom manufactures waterproof parkas for retail under store labels. Because variations in styles cause differences in costs, detailed records are kept concerning the costs assigned to specific jobs. Raw materials consist of Gore-Tex fabric, liner fabric, and zippers.

Total inventory on August 1, 2009, included Raw Materials, $71,000; Work-in-Process, $109,900; and Finished Goods, $75,000. In addition there were manufacturing supplies of $1,600, consisting of various items such as thread, needles, sheers, and machine lubricant. The August 1 balance in Manufacturing Overhead was $0.

Raw Materials			
Description	Quantity	Unit Cost	Total Cost
Gore-Tex fabric	3,000 square yards	$20	$60,000
Liner	2,000 square yards	3	6,000
Zippers	1,000 units	5	5,000
Total			$71,000

Manufacturing Supplies	
Item	**Total Cost**
Various.	$1,600

Work-in-Process	
Job	**Total Cost**
425	$ 58,600
426	51,300
Total	$109,900

Finished Goods Inventory	
Job	**Total Cost**
424	$75,000

To illustrate manufacturing cost flows in a job cost system, "T" accounts are presented in the margin for the cost system transactions for Outdoor Rainwear, for August 2009. Each cost assignment is supported by documented information that is recorded in subsidiary cost system records. The manufacturing cost transactions for Outdoor Rainwear for August 2009 are discussed here.

1. Raw materials and manufacturing supplies are purchased on account. The vendor's invoice totals $31,000, including $1,000 of manufacturing supplies and $30,000 of raw materials. The cost of the raw materials must be assigned to specific raw materials inventory records:

Gore-Tex fabric.	850 square yards	×	$20	=	$17,000
Liner	2,000 square yards	×	$3	=	6,000
Zippers	1,400 units	×	$5	=	7,000
Total					$30,000

Raw Materials Inventory		
Beg. Bal.	71,000	
(1)	30,000	

Manufacturing Supplies		
Beg. Bal.	1,600	
(1)	1,000	

Accounts Payable		
	31,000	(1)

2. Materials needed to complete Jobs 425 and 426 are requisitioned. Two new jobs, 427 and 428, were also started and direct materials were requisitioned for them. A total of $54,300 of raw materials was requisitioned:

	Job 425	Job 426	Job 427	Job 428	Total
Gore-Tex fabric.					
975 sq. yds. × $20			$19,500		$19,500
955 sq. yds. × $20				$19,100	19,100
Liner					
500 sq. yds. × $3			1,500		1,500
1,100 sq. yds. × $3				3,300	3,300
Zippers					
960 units × $5	$4,800				4,800
720 units × $5		$3,600			3,600
500 × $5			2,500		2,500
Total	$4,800	$3,600	$23,500	$22,400	$54,300

Work-in-Process Inventory		
Beg. Bal.	109,900	
(2)	54,300	

Raw Materials Inventory			
Beg. Bal.	71,000	54,300	(2)
(1)	30,000		

Work-in-Process Inventory	
Beg. Bal. 109,900	
(2) 54,300	
(3) 34,450	

Manufacturing Overhead	
Beg. Bal. -0-	
(3) 7,200	

Wages Payable	
	41,650 (3)

3. The August payroll liability was $41,650, including $34,450 for direct labor and $7,200 for indirect labor. Direct labor was assigned to the jobs as follows:

	Job 425	Job 426	Job 427	Job 428	Total
Labor hours	600	900	1,000	945	
Labor rate..........................	× $10	× $10	× $10	× $10	
Total	$6,000	$9,000	$10,000	$9,450	$34,450

Note: The $7,200 of indirect labor costs is assigned to products as part of applied overhead.

Manufacturing Overhead	
Beg. Bal. -0-	
(3) 7,200	
(4) 950	
(5) 2,400	
(6) 3,230	

Manufacturing Supplies	
Beg. Bal. 1,600	950 (4)
(1) 1,000	

Accumulated Depreciation	
	2,400 (5)

Other Payables	
	3,230 (6)

4.-6. In addition to indirect labor, Outdoor Rainwear incurred the following manufacturing overhead costs:

Manufacturing Supplies	$ 950
Accumulated Depreciation—Factory Assets	2,400
Miscellaneous (Other Payables)..................................	3,230

7. Manufacturing overhead is applied to jobs using a predetermined rate of $4 per direct labor hour. Assignments to individual jobs are as follows:

Work-in-Process Inventory	
Beg. Bal. 109,900	
(2) 54,300	
(3) 34,450	
(7) 13,780	

Manufacturing Overhead	
Beg. Bal. -0-	13,780 (7)
(3) 7,200	
(4) 950	
(5) 2,400	
(6) 3,230	

	Job 425	Job 426	Job 427	Job 428	Total
Labor hours	600	900	1,000	945	
Labor rate..........................	× $4	× $4	× $4	× $4	
Total	$2,400	$3,600	$4,000	$3,780	$13,780

8. Jobs 425, 426, and 427 are completed with the following costs:

Finished Goods Inventory	
Beg. Bal. 75,000	
(8) 176,800	

Work-in-Process Inventory	
Beg. Bal. 109,900	176,800 (8)
(2) 54,300	
(3) 34,450	
(7) 13,780	

	Job 425	Job 426	Job 427	Total
Beginning balance	$58,600	$51,300	$ 0	$109,900
Current costs:				
Direct materials (entry 2)	4,800	3,600	23,500	31,900
Direct labor (entry 3).........................	6,000	9,000	10,000	25,000
Applied overhead (entry 7).....................	2,400	3,600	4,000	10,000
Total	$71,800	$67,500	$37,500	$176,800

Additional analysis for the completed jobs indicates the following:

	Job 425	Job 426	Job 427
Total cost of job	$71,800	$67,500	$37,500
Units in job..	÷ 1,200	÷ 900	÷ 500
Unit cost...	$ 59.83	$ 75.00	$ 75.00

9. Jobs 424, 425, and 426 are delivered to customers for a sales price of $400,000. Determining the costs transferred from Finished Goods Inventory to Cost of Goods Sold requires summing the total cost of jobs sold.

Cost of Goods Sold	
(9) 214,300	

Finished Goods Inventory	
Beg. Bal. 75,000	214,300 (9)
(8) 176,800	

Job 424	$ 75,000
Job 425	71,800
Job 426	67,500
Total	$214,300

At this point we can determine the gross profit on the completed jobs:

Sales	$400,000
Cost of goods sold	(214,300)
Gross profit	$185,700

If inventory were produced in anticipation of future sales rather than in response to specific customer orders, it is likely that not all units in a job would be sold at the same time. In this case, the unit cost information is used to determine the amount transferred from Finished Goods Inventory to Cost of Goods Sold.

Exhibit 5.5 shows the cost system records supporting the ending balances in the major inventory accounts and Cost of Goods Sold. Note the importance of the job cost sheets for determining cost transfers affecting Work-in-Process and Finished Goods Inventory. The job cost sheets are also used in determining the ending balances of these accounts.

Outdoor Rainwear's product costing system is probably adequate for determining the cost for each job for purposes of valuing ending inventories and cost of goods sold in its external financial statements. It recognizes the differences in materials costs by carefully tracking each type of material as a separate cost pool. Because all direct labor employees are paid the same rate, it is necessary to maintain only one labor cost pool. Although there are three distinct operations in making parkas (cutting, sewing, and finishing), the various styles of parkas likely require the same proportionate times on each operation. Hence, with only one plantwide manufacturing overhead cost pool applied on the basis of direct labor hours, individual product costs are reasonably accurate.

Although the Outdoor Rainwear's costing system may be adequate for inventory costing for financial statement purposes, the data it routinely generates do not provide management with information required for many management decisions. To evaluate product or customer profitability, management needs additional information concerning marketing, distributing, selling, and customer service costs, which are not included in the product cost system. Also, the cost system does not provide information for decisions concerning individual operations, such as cutting. A comparison of budgeted and planned cutting hours may be useful in evaluating the cutting operation. The system also does not provide the detailed information required for special decisions such as subcontracting cutting operations rather than performing them internally. To answer these questions, Outdoor Rainwear's accountants should perform a special cost study to obtain activity-cost information (see Chapter 6). In spite of these limitations, this system may be adequate for the purposes it was designed. Management probably will continue to operate the system if the costs of improving and modifying the cost system exceed the perceived benefits. The Business Insight box that follows provides an example of how advances in technology are influencing costing models in the commercial printing industry.

BUSINESS INSIGHT **Weaknesses in the Job Cost Business Model**

The printing industry has long been one of the classic examples of job cost accounting. One can readily visualize the large envelope on which is printed the job cost sheet, which follows each printing job through the various processes. The time and materials records are placed in the envelope, and at the completion of the job, all costs are added and then a markup is applied to determine what the customer should pay for the job. The job cost envelope represents the cost accounting system. The problem with a job-focused business model is that it tends to overlook the efficiency of the processes that go into completing the job. Statistical print production management (SPPM) is a process model that offers improved decision support as well as better harmonization with general ledger costs. It recognizes that any activity consuming time or materials in the print process that does not result in value-added product in the hands of a customer is a loss. Changeovers, stops, trashed materials, waiting, and idle time are misuse and nonuse; they are process loss that must not be hidden away in job envelopes. They must be openly measured and managed. As a supplement to traditional job costing, SPPM is providing valuable decision support information for managers in an increasingly competitive industry.[2]

[2] Roger V. Dickeson, "Goodbye Job Cost Accountancy," *Printing Impressions*, January 2001, pp. 67–68.

EXHIBIT 5.5 General Ledger Accounts and Subsidiary Records for Inventory Categories and Cost of Goods Sold

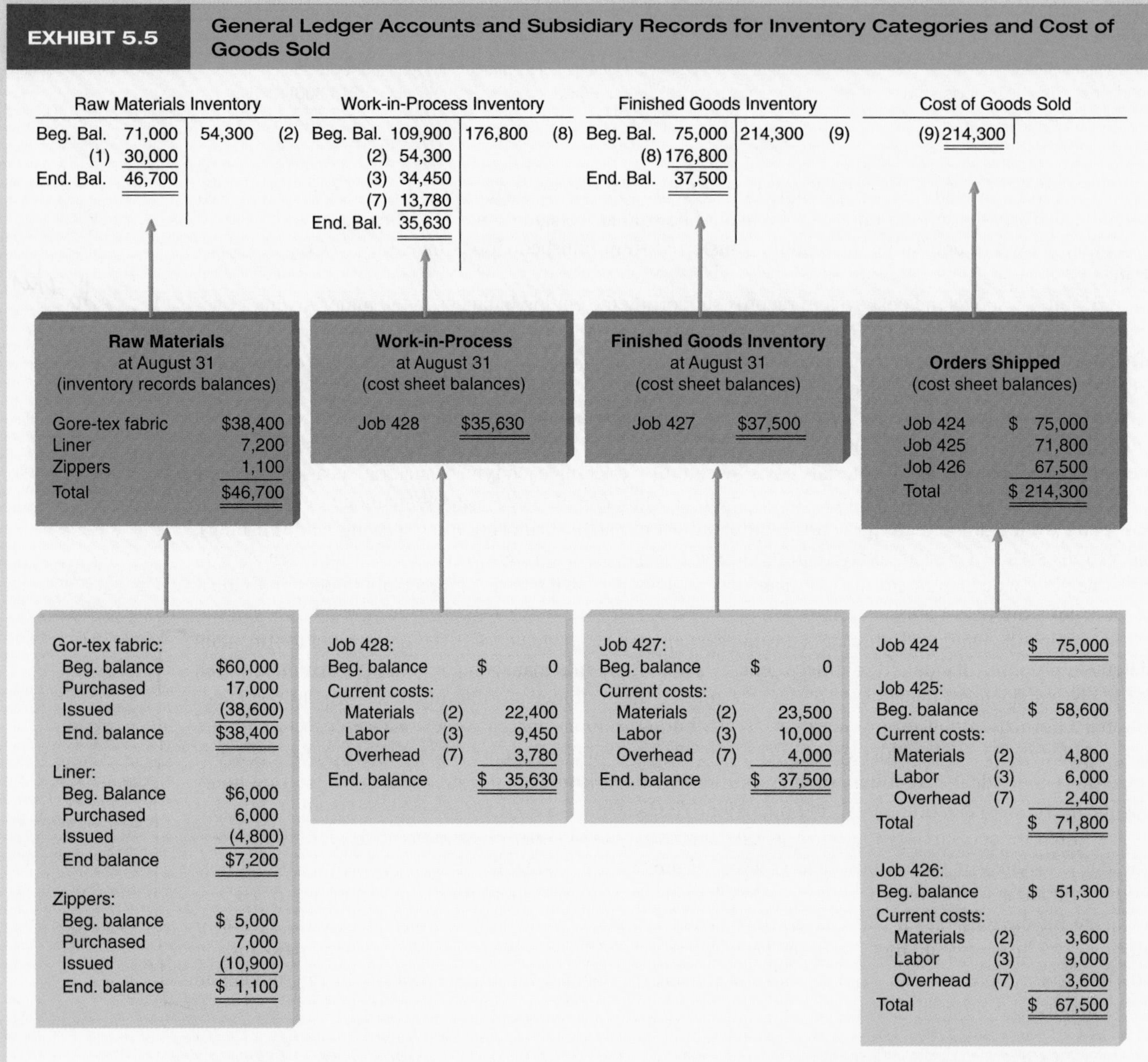

Statement of Cost of Goods Manufactured

The income statement for a merchandising organization, which purchases products ready to sell, normally includes the following calculation of cost of goods sold:

Sales		$X,XXX
Less cost of goods sold		
Beginning inventory	$X,XXX	
Plus purchases	X,XXX	
Goods available for sale	X,XXX	
Less ending inventory	(X,XXX)	
Cost of goods sold		(X,XXX)
Gross profit		X,XXX
Less selling and administrative expenses		(X,XXX)
Net income		$X,XXX

Manufacturing organizations modify only one line of this income statement format, changing Purchases to Cost of goods manufactured. Since a manufacturer acquires finished goods from the factory, its cost of goods manufactured is the total cost transferred from Work-in-Process to Finished Goods Inventory during the period.

For internal reporting purposes, most companies prepare a separate **statement of cost of goods manufactured**, which summarizes the cost of goods completed and transferred into Finished Goods Inventory during the period. A statement of cost of goods manufactured and an income statement for Outdoor Rainwear, are presented in Exhibit 5.6 for August 2009.

EXHIBIT 5.6 Statement of Cost of Goods Manufactured and Income Statement

OUTDOOR RAINWEAR
Statement of Cost of Goods Manufactured
For Month Ending August 31, 2009

Current manufacturing costs			
Cost of materials placed in production			
Raw materials, 8/1/09	$71,000		
Purchases	30,000		
Total available	101,000		
Raw materials, 8/31/09	(46,700)	$ 54,300	
Direct labor		34,450	
Manufacturing overhead		13,780	$102,530
Work-in-process, 8/1/09			109,900
Total costs in process			212,430
Work-in-process, 8/31/09			(35,630)
Cost of goods manufactured			$176,800

OUTDOOR RAINWEAR
Income Statement
For Month Ending August 31, 2009

Sales		$400,000
Cost of goods sold		
Finished goods inventory, 8/1/09	$ 75,000	
Cost of goods manufactured	176,800	
Total goods available for sale	251,800	
Finished goods inventory, 8/31/09	(37,500)	214,300
Gross profit		185,700
Selling and administrative expenses*		(90,000)
Net income		$ 95,700

*Selling and administrative expenses for Outdoor Rainwear are assumed to be $90,000.

Overapplied and Underapplied Overhead

In the Outdoor Rainwear example, assume that the predetermined manufacturing overhead rate of $4 per direct labor hour was based on predicted manufacturing overhead for the year of $100,000 and predicted direct labor hours of 25,000. Assume further that it was determined that the company actually incurred $100,000 in manufacturing overhead during the year and that actual direct labor hours for the year were 25,000, resulting in applied overhead of $100,000 (25,000 hours × $4). The activity in Manufacturing Overhead is summarized as follows:

Manufacturing Overhead	
Beginning balance	$ 0
Actual overhead	100,000
Total	100,000
Applied overhead	(100,000)
Ending balance	$ 0

With identical amounts of actual and applied overhead, the ending balance in Manufacturing Overhead is zero. However, if either the actual overhead cost or the actual level of the production activity base differed from its predicted value, there would be a balance in Manufacturing Overhead representing overapplied or underapplied overhead.

Assume, for example, that the prediction of 25,000 direct labor hours was correct but that actual overhead cost was $105,000. In this case, Manufacturing Overhead shows a $5,000 positive balance, representing underapplied manufacturing overhead:

Manufacturing Overhead	
Beginning balance	$ 0
Actual overhead	105,000
Total	105,000
Applied overhead	(100,000)
Ending balance	$ 5,000*

*Underapplied; actual exceeds applied.

If actual manufacturing overhead were only $98,000, Manufacturing Overhead would be overapplied and show a $2,000 negative balance.

If the *prediction* of total manufacturing overhead cost is not accurate, there will be an underapplied or overapplied balance in Manufacturing Overhead at the end of the year. A similar result occurs when the *predicted* activity level used in computing the predetermined rate differs from the actual activity level. It is not uncommon for such differences to occur. Predictions are exactly that—predictions.

Month-to-month balances in Manufacturing Overhead are usually allowed to accumulate during the year. In the absence of evidence to the contrary, it is assumed that such differences result from seasonal variations in production or costs or both. However, any year-end balance in Manufacturing Overhead must be eliminated.

Theoretically, the disposition of any year-end balance in Manufacturing Overhead should be accomplished in a manner that adjusts every account to what its balance would have been if an actual, rather than a predetermined, overhead rate had been used. This involves adjusting the ending balances in Work-in-Process, Finished Goods Inventory, and Cost of Goods Sold. Procedures to do this are examined in cost accounting textbooks.

In most situations, the simple procedure of treating the remaining overhead as an adjustment to Cost of Goods Sold is adequate. Unless there are large ending balances in inventories and a large year-end balance in Manufacturing Overhead, this simple procedure produces acceptable results. Underapplied overhead indicates that the assigned costs are less than the actual costs, understating Cost of Goods Sold. Hence, disposing of an underapplied balance in Manufacturing Overhead increases the balance in Cost of Goods Sold.

Manufacturing Overhead		
Beginning balance	$ 0	
Actual overhead	105,000	
Total	105,000	
Applied overhead	(100,000)	
Ending balance	$ 5,000*	← Increase Cost of Goods Sold

*Underapplied; actual exceeds applied.

Conversely, overapplied overhead indicates that the assigned costs are more than the actual costs, overstating Cost of Goods Sold. Hence, disposing of an overapplied balance in Manufacturing Overhead decreases Cost of Goods Sold.

Job Costing in Service Organizations

Service costing, the assignment of costs to services performed, uses job costing concepts to determine the cost of filling customer service orders in organizations such as automobile repair shops, charter airlines, CPA firms, hospitals, and law firms. Many of these organizations bill clients on the basis of resources consumed. Consequently, they maintain detailed records for billing purposes. On the invoice sent to the client, the organization itemizes any materials consumed on the job at a selling price per unit, the labor hours worked on the job at a billing rate per hour, and the time special facilities were used at a billing rate per unit of time. Employees with different capabilities and experience often have different billing rates. In a CPA firm, for example, a partner or a senior manager has a higher billing rate than a staff accountant.

The prices and rates must be high enough to cover costs not assigned to specific jobs and to provide for a profit. To evaluate the contribution to common costs and profit from a job, a comparison must be made between the price charged the customer and the actual cost of the job. This is easily done when the actual cost of resources itemized on the customer's invoice is presented on a job cost sheet. A CPA firm, for example, should accumulate the actual hardware and software costs of an accounting system installed for a client, along with the actual wages earned by employees while working on the job and any related travel costs. Comparing the total of these costs with the price charged, the client indicates the total contribution of the job to common costs and profit.

Although service organizations may identify costs with individual jobs for management accounting purposes, there is considerable variation in the way job cost information is presented in financial statements. Some organizations report the cost of jobs completed in their income statements using an account such as Cost of Services Provided. They use procedures similar to those outlined in Exhibit 5.6; the only major change involves replacing Cost of Goods Sold with Cost of Services Provided.

BUSINESS INSIGHT **Service Contractors Learn Poor Cost Measurement Can Really Hurt**

Many service contractors bill on the basis of materials plus labor and a markup on labor. But what is the appropriate markup on labor? Twenty percent? Fifty percent? Seventy-five percent? If the employee's wage rate is $20 and the markup is one-hundred percent, the hourly charge, excluding materials, is $40. According to heating, ventilation, air conditioning (HVAC) consultant Bill Ligon, what contractors don't know about overhead costs can really hurt.

The Mechanical Service Contractors of America conducted a study of the total direct and indirect costs per labor hour and hourly billing rates. In addition to the obvious direct cost of the employee's wage rate, they considered the costs of: vacation pay, holiday pay, sick pay, non-billable time, benefits such as pension and health, payroll taxes such as Social Security and workers' compensation, and non-labor costs such as truck expense (lease, gas/oil, maintenance), communication equipment and charges, uniforms, and tools. By region of the U.S. they determined the average total non-materials costs varied between $47.22 per hour in the Southeast and $63.13 in the Southwest, marking it apparent that a one-hundred percent markup on an hourly wage rate of $20 would really hurt.[3]

More often, however, service organizations do not formally establish detailed procedures to trace the flow of service costs. Instead, service job costs are left in their original cost categories such as materials expense, salaries and wages expense, travel expense, and so forth. Because all service costs are typically regarded as expenses rather than product costs, either procedure is acceptable for financial reporting. Regardless of the formal treatment of service costs in financial accounting records and statements, the managers of a well-run service organization have a need for information regarding job cost and contribution. The previous Business Insight considers the importance of accurate cost estimation by service contractors.

---

[3] John R. Hall," MSCA Examines Salaries, Costs," *Air Conditioning Heating & Refrigeration News*, January 27, 2003, p.8; Bill Ligon, "What You Don't Know Can Really Hurt," *Air Conditioning Heating & Refrigeration News*, October 9, 2006, p.46.

All preceding examples of service costing involve situations in which the order is filled in response to a specific customer request. Job order costing can also be used to determine the cost of making services available even when the names of specific customers are not known in advance and the service is being provided on a speculative basis. A regularly scheduled airline flight, for example, could be regarded as a job. Management is interested in knowing the cost of the job in order to determine its profitability. This is but another example of the versatility of job order costing.

MANAGERIAL DECISION **You are the Chief Financial Officer**

You have asked the accounting staff to provide you with cost information on each of the products manufactured by your company so you can conduct profitability analysis on each product. Accounting provided you with the costs that are used in the company's external financial statements. What additional information are you going to need before you can conduct a complete profitability analysis? [Answer p. 159]

MID-CHAPTER REVIEW

Tri-Star Printing Company prints sales fliers for retail and mail-order companies. Production costs are accounted for using a job cost system. At the beginning of June 2009, raw materials inventories totaled $7,000; manufacturing supplies amounted to $800; two jobs were in process—Job 225 with assigned costs of $13,750, and Job 226 with assigned costs of $1,800—and there were no finished goods inventories. There was no underapplied or overapplied manufacturing overhead on June 1. The following information summarized June manufacturing activities:

- Purchased raw materials costing $40,000 on account.
- Purchased manufacturing supplies costing $9,000 on account.
- Requisitioned materials needed to complete Job 226. Started two new jobs, 227 and 228, and requisitioned direct materials for them as follows:

Job 226	$ 2,600
Job 227	18,000
Job 228	14,400
Total	$35,000

- Incurred June salaries and wages as follows:

Job 225 (500 hours × $10 per hour)	$ 5,000
Job 226 (1,500 hours × $10 per hour)	15,000
Job 227 (2,050 hours × $10 per hour)	20,500
Job 228 (800 hours × $10 per hour)	8,000
Total direct labor	48,500
Indirect labor	5,000
Total	$53,500

- Used manufacturing supplies costing $5,500.
- Recognized depreciation on factory fixed assets of $5,000.
- Incurred miscellaneous factory overhead cost of $10,750 on account.
- Applied factory overhead at the rate of $5 per direct labor hour.
- Completed Jobs 225, 226, and 227.
- Delivered Jobs 225 and 226 to customers.

Required

a. Prepare "T" accounts showing the flow of costs through the Work-in-Process, Finished Goods, and Cost of Goods Sold accounts.

b. Show the job cost details to support the June 30, 2009, balances in Work-in-Process, Finished Goods and Cost of Goods Sold.

c. Prepare a statement of cost of goods manufactured for June 2009.

Solution

a.

Work-in-Process			
Balance, June 1, 2009	15,550	96,900	Cost of Goods Manufactured in June
Direct materials	35,000		
Direct labor	48,500		
Applied overhead	24,250		
Balance, June 30, 2009	26,400		

Finished Goods Inventory			
Balance, June 1, 2009	–0–	48,150	Cost of jobs sold in June
Cost of goods manufactured in June	96,900		
Balance, June 30, 2009	48,750		

Cost of Goods Sold		
Cost of jobs sold in June 2009	48,150	

b. Job in Work-in-Process at June 30, 2009:

	Job 228
Direct materials	$14,400
Direct labor	8,000
Applied overhead (800 × $5)	4,000
Total	$26,400

Job in Finished Goods at June 30, 2009:

	Job 227
Direct materials	$18,000
Direct labor	20,500
Applied overhead (2,050 × $5)	10,250
Total	$48,750

Jobs sold in June 2009:

	Job 225	Job 226	Total
Costs assigned from prior period	$13,750	$ 1,800	$15,550
June Costs: Direct materials	–0–	2,600	2,600
Direct labor	5,000	15,000	20,000
Applied overhead (500 & 1,500 × $5)	2,500	7,500	10,000
Total	$21,250	$26,900	$48,150

c. Statement of cost of goods manufactured for June 2009.

TRI-STAR PRINTING COMPANY
Statement of Cost of Goods Manufactured
For Month Ending June 30, 2009

Current manufacturing costs			
Cost of materials placed in production			
Raw materials, 6/1/09	$ 7,000		
Purchases	40,000		
Total available	47,000		
Raw materials, 6/30/09	(12,000)	$35,000	
Direct labor		48,500	
Manufacturing overhead applied		24,250	$107,750
Work-in-process, 6/1/09			15,550
Total costs in process			123,300
Work-in-process, 6/30/09			(26,400)
Cost of goods manufactured			$ 96,900

PROCESS COSTING

LO5 Explain the operation of a process costing system.

A job costing system works well when products are made one at a time (building houses) or in batches of identical items (making blue jeans). However, if products are produced in a continuous manufacturing environment, where production does not have a distinct beginning and ending (refining fossil fuels such as gasoline or diesel), companies usually use a process costing system.

In job costing, the unit cost is the total cost of the "job" divided by the units produced in the job. Costs are accumulated for each job on a job cost sheet, and those costs remain in Work-in-Process until the job is completed, regardless of how long the job is in progress. A multiple-unit job is not considered completed until all units in the job are finished. The cost is not determined until the job is completed, which will not necessarily coincide with the end of an accounting period. Large jobs (such as construction projects) and jobs started near the end of the period frequently overlap two or more accounting periods.

In process costing, the cost of a single unit is equal to the total product costs assigned to a "process" or "department" during the accounting period (frequently a month) divided by the number of units produced. Since goods in the beginning and ending work-in-process inventory are only partially processed during the period, it is necessary to determine the total production for the period in terms of the equivalent number of completed units. For example, if 300 units were started and completed through 40 percent of the process during the period, then the equivalent of 120 fully completed units (300 units × 0.40) were produced. The average cost per unit is computed as total product costs divided by the number of equivalent units produced.

A good example of a process costing environment involving continuous production is the soft drink bottling process. At Coca-Cola's bottling facility in Atlanta, more than 2,000 twelve-ounce cans of Coca-Cola are produced per minute in a continuous process. The process adds the ingredients (concentrate syrup, water, sweetener, and the carbonation agent) at various points in the process and blends the ingredients in the can. At the end of the process, the cans are automatically wrapped in either 6-pack or 12-pack sizes. For another example, see the following Business Insight box for a discussion of the process costing environment at a large Japanese chemicals producer.

In a job cost system, job cost sheets are used to collect cost information for each and every job. In a process costing system, cost accumulation requires fewer records because each department's production is treated as the only job worked on during the period. In a department that has just one manufacturing process, process costing is particularly straightforward because the Work-in-Process account is, in effect, the departmental cost record. If a department has more than one manufacturing process, separate records should be maintained for each process.

BUSINESS INSIGHT **Process Costing in a Japanese Dyestuffs Plant**

Nippon Kayaku is a large industrial company in Japan that produces a wide range of products, including industrial explosives, pharmaceuticals, agrochemicals, sophisticated products (resins, flame retardants, etc.) and dyestuffs. Nippon Kayaku's dyestuff division produces dyes that are particularly targeted to the polyester and cotton-blended textiles market.

The Fukuyama plant manufactures about 600 products for the sophisticated products and dyestuffs divisions, some of which are produced in continuous processes and others in batches. The costing system accumulates costs separately for the more than 1,000 processes, and product costs are determined for a particular product merely by adding the unit costs of the processes used to make that product. For example, the cost of the dyestuff product, Kayaset, consists of the costs of five processes: condensation, filtration, drying, grinding, and packaging. Nippon Kayaku uses these product costs for inventory valuation purposes and for managerial decision-making purposes.[4]

Cost of Production Report

To illustrate process costing procedures, consider Micro Systems Co., which manufactures memory chips for microcomputers in a one-step process using sophisticated machinery. Each finished unit requires one unit of raw materials added at the beginning of the manufacturing process. The production and cost data for the month of July 2009 for Micro Systems are as follows:

July Production Data	
Units in process, beginning of period (75% converted)	4,000
Units started	36,000
Completed and transferred to finished goods	35,000
Units in process, end of period (20% converted)	5,000

July Cost Data		
Beginning work-in-process		
Materials costs		$ 16,000
Conversion costs		9,000
Total		$ 25,000
Current manufacturing costs		
Direct materials (36,000 × $4)		$144,000
Conversion costs		
Direct labor	$62,200	
Manufacturing overhead applied	46,700	108,900
Total		$252,900

Developing a cost of production report is a useful way of organizing and accounting for costs in a process costing environment. A **cost of production report**, which summarizes unit and cost data for each department or process for each period, consists of the following sections:

- Summary of units in process.
- Equivalent units.
- Total cost to be accounted for and cost per equivalent unit.
- Accounting for total costs.

[4] www.nipponkayaku.co.jp/english/

The cost of production report for Micro Systems Co. is shown in Exhibit 5.7, and its four sections are discussed below.

EXHIBIT 5.7 Cost of Production Report for Process Costing

MICRO SYSTEMS CO.
Cost of Production Report
For the Month Ending July 31, 2009

Summary of units in process	
Beginning	4,000
Units started	36,000
In process	40,000
Completed	(35,000)
Ending	5,000

Equivalent units in process	**Materials**	**Conversion**
Units completed	35,000	35,000
Plus equivalent units in ending inventory	5,000	1,000*
Equivalent units in process	40,000	36,000

Total cost to be accounted for and cost per equivalent unit in process	**Materials**	**Conversion**	**Total**
Beginning work-in-process	$ 16,000	$ 9,000	$ 25,000
Current cost	144,000	108,900**	252,900
Total cost in process	$160,000	$117,900	$277,900
Equivalent units in process	÷ 40,000	÷ 36,000	
Cost per equivalent unit in process	$ 4.00	$ 3.275	$ 7.275
Accounting for total costs			
Transferred out (35,000 × $7.275)			$254,625
Ending work-in-process			
Materials (5,000 × $4.00)		$20,000	
Conversion (1,000 × $3.275)		3,275	23,275
Total cost accounted for			$277,900

*5,000 units, 20% converted

**Includes direct labor of $62,200 and applied manufacturing overhead of $46,700

Summary of Units in Process

This section of the cost of production report provides a summary of all units in the department during the period—both from an input and an output perspective—regardless of their stage of completion. From an input perspective, total units in process during the period consisted of the following:

- Units in process at the beginning of the period, plus
- Units started during the period.

From an output perspective, these units in process during the period were either

- Completed and transferred out of the department, or
- Still on hand at the end of the period.

In the summary of units in process, all units are treated as the same, regardless of the amount of processing that took place on them during the period. The objective here is to account for all discrete units of product in process at any time during the period. In the summary of units in process in Exhibit 5.7, 40,000 individual units were in process, including 4,000 partially completed units in the beginning inventory and 36,000 new units started during the month. During the period, 35,000 units were completed, and the remaining 5,000 were still in process at the end of the month.

Equivalent Units in Process

This section of the report translates the number of units in process during the period into equivalent completed units of production. The term **equivalent completed units** refers to the number of completed units that is equal, in terms of production effort, to a given number of partially completed units. For example, 80 units for which 50 percent of the expected total processing cost has been incurred is the equivalent of 40 completed units (80 × 0.50).

Frequently, direct materials costs are incurred largely, if not entirely, at the beginning of the process, whereas direct labor and manufacturing overhead costs are added throughout the production process. If direct labor and manufacturing costs are added to the process simultaneously, it is common to treat them jointly as conversion costs. Micro Systems Co. adds all materials at the beginning of the process; all conversion costs are added evenly throughout the process. Therefore, separate computations are made for equivalent units of materials and equivalent units of conversion. Although the department worked on 40,000 units during the period, the total number of equivalent units in process with respect to conversion costs was only 36,000 units, consisting of 35,000 finished units plus 1,000 equivalent units in ending inventory (5,000 units 20 percent converted). Because all materials are added at the start of the process, 40,000 equivalent units (35,000 finished and 5,000 in process) were in process with respect to materials costs.

Total Cost to Be Accounted for and Cost per Equivalent Unit in Process

This section of the report summarizes total costs in Work-in-Process during the period and calculates the cost per equivalent unit for materials, conversion, and in total. Total cost consists of the beginning Work-in-Process balance (if any) plus current costs incurred. For Micro Systems, the total cost to be accounted for during July was $277,900, consisting of $25,000 in Work-in-Process at the beginning of the period plus current costs of $252,900 incurred in July. Exhibit 5.7 shows these amounts broken down between materials costs and conversion costs.

To compute cost per equivalent unit, divide total cost in process by the equivalent units in process. This is done separately for materials cost and conversion cost. The total cost per equivalent unit is the sum of the unit costs for materials and conversion. Because the number of equivalent units in process was different for materials and conversion, it is not possible to get the total cost per unit by dividing total costs of $277,900 by some equivalent unit amount.

Accounting for Total Costs

This section shows the disposition of the total costs in process during the period divided between units completed (and sent to finished goods) and units still in process at the end of the period. As noted in the previous section, total cost in process is $277,900 and each equivalent unit in process has $4.00 of materials cost and $3.275 of conversion costs for a total of $7.275.

The first step in assigning total costs is to calculate the cost of units transferred out by multiplying the units completed during the period by the total cost per unit (35,000 units × $7.275). This assigns $254,625 of the total cost to units transferred out, leaving $23,275 ($277,900 − $254,625) to be assigned to ending Work-in-Process. To verify that $23,275 is the correct amount of cost remaining in ending Work-in-Process, the materials and conversion costs in ending Work-in-Process are calculated separately. Recall that the 5,000 units in process at the end of the period are 100 percent completed with materials costs, but only 20 percent completed with conversion costs. Therefore, in ending Work-in-Process, the materials cost component is $20,000 (5,000 × 1.00 × $4.00), the conversion cost component is $3,275 (5,000 × 0.20 × $3.275), and the total cost of ending Work-in-Process is $23,275 ($20,000 + $3,275).

The cost of production report summarizes manufacturing costs assigned to Work-in-Process during the period and provides information for determining the transfer of costs from Work-in-Process to Finished Goods Inventory. The supporting documents are similar to those previously illustrated for job costing, except that the single cost of production report replaces all the job cost sheets that flow through a department or process. The flow of costs through Work-in-Process is as follows:

Work-in-Process		
Beginning balance		$ 25,000
Current manufacturing costs		
Direct materials	$144,000	
Direct labor	62,200	
Applied overhead	46,700	252,900
Total		277,900
Cost of goods manufactured		(254,625)
Ending balance		$ 23,275

The reduction in Work-in-Process for the units completed during the period is determined in the cost of production report (see Exhibit 5.7). This amount is transferred to Finished Goods Inventory. The $23,275 ending balance in Work-in-Process is also determined in the cost of production report as the amount assigned to units in ending Work-in-Process.

Weighted Average and First-In, First-Out Process Costing

Because the costs of materials, labor, and overhead are constantly changing, unit costs are seldom exactly the same from period to period. Hence, if a unit is manufactured partially in one period and partially in the following period, its actual cost is seldom equal to the unit cost of units produced in either period.

In the cost of production report in Exhibit 5.7, we made no attempt to account separately for the completed units that came from beginning inventory and those that were started during the current period. The method illustrated in Exhibit 5.7 is called the **weighted average method**, and it simply spreads the combined beginning inventory cost and current manufacturing costs (for materials, labor, and overhead) over the units completed and those in ending inventory on an average basis. For example, the total cost in process for conversion ($117,900) included both beginning inventory cost and current costs; the 36,000 equivalent units in process for conversion included both units from beginning inventory and units started during the current period. Hence, the average cost per unit of $3.275 (or $117,900 ÷ 36,000) is a weighted average cost of the partially completed units in beginning inventory (prior period costs) and units started during the current period. It is not a precise cost per unit for the current period's production activity but an average cost that includes the cost of partially completed units in beginning inventory carried over from the previous period.

An alternative, more precise process costing method is the **first-in, first-out (FIFO) method**. It accounts for unit costs of beginning inventory units separately from those started during the current period. Under this method, the first costs incurred each period are assumed to have been used to complete the unfinished units carried over from the previous period. Hence, the cost of the beginning inventory is partially based on the prior period's unit costs and partially based on the current period's unit costs.

If unit costs are changing from period to period and beginning inventories are large in relation to total production for the period, the FIFO method is more accurate. However, with the current trend toward smaller inventories, the additional effort and cost of the FIFO method may not be justified. Detailed coverage of the FIFO method is included in cost accounting textbooks.

Process Costing in Service Organizations

There are many applications of process costing for service organizations. Process costing in service organizations is similar to that in manufacturing organizations, the primary purpose being to assign costs to cost objectives. Generally, the use of process costing techniques for service organizations is easier than for manufacturing organizations because the raw materials element is not necessary. The applications for the labor and overhead costs are similar, if not identical, to those of a manufacturing firm.

Process costing for services is similar to job costing for batches in that an average cost for similar or identical services is determined. There are important differences, though, between batch and process costing. In a batch environment, a discrete group of services is identified, but in a process environment, services are performed on a continuous basis. Batch costing accumulates the cost for a specific group of services as the batch moves through the various activities that make up the service. Process service costing measures the average cost of identical or similar services performed each period (each month) in a department. An example of batch service costing is determining the cost of registering a student at your college during the fall term registration period; an example of process service costing is determining the cost each month of processing a check by a bank. If continuously performed services involved multiple processes, the total cost of the service would be the sum of the costs for each process.

After it is determined that process costing would be appropriate for a service activity, the actual decision to use it is generally contingent on two important factors about the items being evaluated. First, is average cost per unit acceptable as an input item to the decision process? For some activities, the answer is obvious. For instance, tracking the actual cost of processing each check through a bank would probably not be as useful as determining the average cost of processing checks for a given period; therefore, average cost is acceptable. For other activities, the answer is more difficult to determine. Should the decision model include average cost per patient-day or actual cost per individual patient?

The second issue relates to the benefits versus the costs of the resulting information. Normally, it is easier to track and record the cost of an activity or process than it is to track and record the cost of each individual item in the activity. Often actual cost tracking is impossible for practical reasons (the actual cost of processing a check through a banking system, for example). Although process costing will not work in every situation, it has many applications in service organizations. As illustrated in this text, there are many possibilities for applying either job or process costing to activities in service organizations.

CHAPTER-END REVIEW

Magnetic Media, Inc. manufactures data disks that are used in the computer industry. Since there is little product differentiation between Magnetic's products, it uses a process costing system to determine inventory costs. Production and manufacturing cost data for 2009 are as follows:

Production data (units)	
Units in process, beginning of period (60% converted).	3,000,000
Units started.	27,000,000
Completed and transferred to finished goods	25,000,000
Units in process, end of period (30% converted).	5,000,000

Manufacturing costs	
Work-in-Process, beginning of period (materials, $468,000; conversion, $252,000)	$ 720,000
Current manufacturing costs:	
Raw materials transferred to processing	6,132,000
Direct labor for the period.	1,550,000
Overhead applied for the period.	3,498,000

Required:

Prepare a cost of production report for Magnetic Media, Inc. for 2009.

Solution

MAGNETIC MEDIA, INC.
Cost of Production Report
For the Year 2009

Summary of units in process:			
Beginning	3,000,000		
Units started	27,000,000		
In process	30,000,000		
Completed	−25,000,000		
Ending	5,000,000		
Equivalent units in process:	**Materials**	**Conversion**	
Units completed	25,000,000	25,000,000	
Plus equivalent units in ending inventory	5,000,000	1,500,000	
Equivalent units in process	30,000,000	26,500,000	
Total costs to be accounted for and cost per equivalent unit in process:	**Materials**	**Conversion**	**Total**
Work-in-Process, beginning	$ 468,000	$ 252,000	$ 720,000
Current cost	6,132,000	5,048,000	11,180,000
Total cost in process	$ 6,600,000	$ 5,300,000	$11,900,000
Equivalent units in process	÷ 30,000,000	÷26,500,000	
Cost per equivalent unit in process	$0.22	$0.20	$0.42
Accounting for total costs:			
Transferred out (25,000,000 × $0.42)			$10,500,000
Work-in-Process, ending:			
Materials (5,000,000 × $0.22)		$ 1,100,000	
Conversion (1,500,000 × $0.20)		300,000	1,400,000
Total cost accounted for			$11,900,000

APPENDIX 5A: Absorption and Variable Costing

Product costing for inventory valuation is the link between financial and managerial accounting. Product costing systems determine the cost-based valuation of the manufactured inventories used in making key financial accounting measurements (cost of goods sold and income on the income statement as well as inventory and total assets on the balance sheet). They also provide vital information to managers for setting prices, controlling costs, and evaluating management performance. The influence of financial accounting on product costing systems is apparent in the design of traditional job order and process costing systems. These systems reflect the requirement of financial accounting (i.e., generally accepted accounting principles) that all manufacturing costs be included in inventory valuations for external financial reporting purposes. In these systems, all other costs incurred, such as selling, general, and administrative costs, are treated as expenses of the period.

Basic Concepts

A debate exists over how to treat fixed manufacturing overhead costs in the valuation of inventory. The debate centers around whether fixed costs such as depreciation on manufacturing equipment should be considered an *inventoriable product cost* and treated as an asset cost until the inventory is sold, or as a *period cost* and recorded immediately as an operating expense. **Absorption costing** (also called **full costing**) treats fixed manufacturing overhead as a product cost, whereas **variable costing** (also called **direct costing**) treats it as a period cost. Therefore, fixed manufacturing overhead is recorded initially as an asset (inventory) under absorption costing but as an operating expense under variable costing.

Fixed manufacturing costs:

Absorption costing treats **fixed manufacturing costs** as **product costs.**

Variable costing treats **fixed manufacturing costs** as **period costs.**

Since fixed product costs are eventually recorded as expenses under both variable and absorption costing by the time the inventory is sold, why does it matter whether fixed overhead is treated as a product cost or a period cost? It matters because the way it is treated affects the measurement of income for a particular period and the valuation assigned to inventory on the balance sheet at the end of the period. Because absorption costing presents fixed factory overhead as a cost per unit rather than a total cost per period, management's perceptions of cost behavior, and decisions based on perceptions of cost behavior, may also be affected.

Inventory Valuations

To illustrate the difference in inventory valuations between absorption and variable costing, consider the following cost data for Nutech Company at a monthly volume of 4,000 units:

Direct materials	$ 5 per unit
Direct labor	2 per unit
Variable manufacturing overhead	3 per unit
Total variable cost	$ 10 per unit
Fixed manufacturing overhead	$8,000 per month

To determine the unit cost of inventory using absorption costing, an average fixed overhead cost per unit is calculated by dividing the monthly fixed manufacturing overhead by the monthly volume. Even though fixed manufacturing overhead is not a variable cost, under absorption costing it is applied to inventory on a per-unit basis, the same as variable costs. At a monthly volume of 4,000 units, Nutech's total inventory cost per unit, is $10 under variable costing, and $12 under absorption costing.

The $2 difference in total unit cost is attributed to the treatment of fixed overhead of $8,000 divided by 4,000 units. The difference in the total inventory valuation on the balance sheet between absorption and variable costing is the number of units in ending inventory times $2. So if 1,000 units are on hand at the end of the month, they are valued at $12,000 if absorption costing is used but at only $10,000 with variable costing.

Income Under Absorption and Variable Costing

The income statement formats used for variable and absorption costing are not the same. One benefit of variable costing is that it separates costs into variable and fixed costs, making it possible to present the income statement in a contribution format. As illustrated in Chapter 3, in a contribution income statement, variable costs are subtracted from revenues to compute contribution margin; fixed costs are then subtracted from contribution margin to calculate profit, also called net income or earnings.

When absorption costing is used, the income statement is usually formatted using the functional format, which classifies costs based on cost function, such as manufacturing, selling, or administrative. The functional income statement, used for financial reporting, subtracts manufacturing costs (represented by cost of goods sold) from revenues to calculate gross profit; selling and administrative costs are then subtracted from gross profit to calculate profit or income.

The contribution format provides information for determining the contribution margin ratio, which is calculated as total contribution margin divided by total sales. It also provides the total amount of fixed costs. These are the primary items of data needed to determine the break-even point and to conduct other cost-volume-profit analysis (see Chapter 3).

Not only is the income statement format different for absorption and variable costing methods, but also as illustrated in the following examples for Nutech Company, the amount of income reported on the income statement might not be the same because of the difference in the treatment of fixed manufacturing overhead. The following additional information is necessary for the Nutech Company examples:

Selling price	$30 per unit
Variable selling and administrative expenses. . .	$3 per unit
Fixed selling and administrative expenses.	$10,000 per month

Production Equals Sales

Nutech has no inventory on June 1, 2009. Production and sales for the third quarter of 2009 are:

Month	Production	Sales
June	3,200 units	3,200 units
July.	4,000 units	3,500 units
August	4,000 units	4,500 units
Third quarter.	11,200 units	11,200 units

Production and sales both total 11,200 units for the third quarter. A summary of unit production, sales, and inventory levels is presented in Exhibit 5.8 A. Using previously presented cost and a selling price of $30 per unit, monthly contribution (variable costing) and functional (absorption costing) income statements are presented in Exhibit 5.8 parts B and C. An analysis of fixed manufacturing overhead with absorption costing is presented in part D.

In June, with 3,200 units produced and sold all $8,000 of fixed manufacturing overhead is deducted as a period cost under variable costing and expensed as part of the cost of goods sold under absorption costing. No costs were assigned to ending inventory under either method.

Production Exceeds Sales

July production of 4,000 units exceeded sales of 3,500 units by 500 units. The ending inventory under variable costing consisted of only the variable cost of production, $5,000 (500 × $10). The entire $8,000 of fixed manufacturing overhead is deducted as a period cost.

Under absorption costing, in addition to the variable cost of production, a portion of the fixed manufacturing overhead is assigned to the ending inventory. As shown in the July column of Exhibit 5.8 D, absorption costing assigns $1,000 of the month's fixed manufacturing overhead to the July ending inventory and $7,000 to the cost of goods sold. Consequently, under absorption costing the July ending inventory is $1,000 higher, the July expenses are $1,000 lower, and the July net income is $1,000 higher than under variable costing.

Sales Exceed Production

In August just the opposite of July's situation occurred: sales of 4,500 units exceeded production of 4,000 units by 500 units. The additional units came from the July production. Under variable costing all current manufacturing costs are expensed either as the variable cost of goods sold or as part of the fixed expense. Additionally, the August variable cost of goods sold includes variable costs assigned the July ending inventory.

Under absorption costing all current manufacturing costs are expensed as part of the cost of goods sold. Additionally, the cost of goods sold includes the variable and fixed costs assigned the July ending inventory. The inclusion of the July fixed costs caused absorption costing net income to be $1,000 lower than the corresponding variable costing amount.

The above relationships between absorption and variable costing are summarized in Exhibit 5.9.

EXHIBIT 5.8 Contribution (Variable Costing) and Functional (Absorption Costing) Income Statements with Variations in Production and Sales

	June (Production equals sales)	July (Production exceeds sales)	August (Sales exceed production)
A. NuTech Company: Summary of Unit Inventory Changes			
Beginning inventory	0	0	500
Production	3,200	4,000	4,000
Total available	3,200	4,000	4,500
Sales	(3,200)	(3,500)	(4,500)
Ending inventory	0	500	0
B. Contribution (Variable Costing) Income Statements			
Sales ($30/unit)	$96,000	$105,000	$135,000
Less variable expenses:			
Cost of goods sold ($10/unit)	$32,000	$ 35,000	$ 45,000
Selling & admin. ($3/unit)	9,600	10,500	13,500
Total	(41,600)	(45,500)	(58,500)
Contribution margin	54,400	59,500	76,500
Less fixed expenses			
Manufacturing overhead	8,000	8,000	8,000
Selling & admin.	10,000	10,000	10,000
Total	(18,000)	(18,000)	(18,000)
Net income	$36,400	$ 41,500	$ 58,500
C. Functional (Absorption Costing) Income Statements			
Sales ($30/unit)	$96,000	$105,000	$135,000
Cost of goods sold (Part D.)	(40,000)	(42,000)	(54,000)
Gross profit	56,000	63,000	81,000
Selling & admin. expenses			
Variable ($3/unit)	9,600	10,500	13,500
Fixed	10,000	10,000	10,000
Total	(19,600)	(20,500)	(23,500)
Net income	$36,400	$ 42,500	$ 57,500
D. Analysis of Fixed Manufacturing Overhead under Absorption Costing			
Fixed manufacturing overhead	$ 8,000	$ 8,000	$ 8,000
Units produced	÷ 3,200	÷ 4,000	÷ 4,000
Absorption fixed cost per unit*	$ 2.50	$ 2.00	$ 2.00
Units in ending inventory	× 0	× 500	× 0
Fixed costs in ending inv.	$ 0	$ 1,000	$ 0
Fixed cost of goods sold:			
From beginning inventory	$ 0	$ 0	$ 1,000
June (3,200 units × $2.50)	8,000		
July (3,500 units × $2.00)		7,000	
August (4,000 × $2.00)			8,000
Total fixed	8,000	7,000	9,000
Variable cost of goods sold	32,000	35,000	45,000
Absorption cost of goods sold	$40,000	$ 42,000	$ 54,000

* To simplify the illustration, the example does not use a predetermined overhead rate. If a predetermined overhead rate were used, an increase or decrease in the balance of Manufacturing Overhead is treated as an adjustment to ending inventory.

EXHIBIT 5.9 Comparative Effects of Absorption and Variable Costing

Relationship between period production and sales	Effect on inventory costs	Effect on operating income	Explanation
Production = Sales	No change in inventory costs.	Absorption costing income = Variable costing income	All current fixed manufacturing costs are expensed under both absorption and variable costing.
Production > Sales	Absorption costing ending inventory increases more than variable costing inventory.	Absorption costing income > Variable costing income	Under absorption costing some current fixed manufacturing costs are assigned to ending inventory. Under variable costing all current fixed manufacturing costs are expensed.
Sales > Production	Absorption costing ending inventory declines more than variable costing inventory.	Absorption costing income < Variable costing income	Under absorption costing fixed manufacturing costs previously assigned to ending inventory are expenses along with current fixed manufacturing costs. Under variable costing only current fixed manufacturing costs are expensed.

Exhibits 5.8 and 5.9 reveal several important relationships between absorption costing net income and variable costing net income, as well as the way net income responds to changes in sales and production under both methods.

For each period, the income differences between absorption and variable costing can be explained by analyzing the change in inventoried fixed manufacturing overhead under absorption costing net income. In general, the following relationship exists:

$$\begin{array}{c} \textbf{Variable} \\ \textbf{costing} \\ \textbf{net income} \end{array} + \begin{array}{c} \textbf{Increase (or minus decrease)} \\ \textbf{in inventoried fixed} \\ \textbf{manufacturing overhead} \end{array} = \begin{array}{c} \textbf{Absorption} \\ \textbf{costing} \\ \textbf{net income} \end{array}$$

Using Nutech's July information, the equation is as follows:

$$\$41{,}500 + (500 \times \$2.00) = \$42{,}500$$

For any given time period, regardless of length, if total units produced equals total units sold, net income is the same for absorption costing and variable costing, all other things being equal. Under absorption costing, all fixed manufacturing overhead is released as a product cost through cost of goods sold when inventory is sold. Under variable costing, all fixed manufacturing overhead is reported as a period cost and expensed in the period incurred. Consequently, over the life of a product, the income differences within periods are offset since they occur only because of the timing of the release of fixed manufacturing overhead to the income statement.

Evaluating Alternatives to Inventory Valuation

The issue in the variable costing debate is whether or not fixed manufacturing costs add value to products. Proponents of variable costing argue that these costs do not add value to a product. They believe that fixed costs are incurred to provide the capacity to produce during a given period, and these costs expire with the passage of time regardless of whether the related capacity was used. Variable manufacturing costs, on the other hand, are incurred only if production takes place. Consequently, these costs are properly assignable to the units produced.

Proponents of variable costing also argue that inventories have value only to the extent that they avoid the necessity of incurring costs in the future. Having inventory available for sale avoids the necessity of incurring some future variable costs, but the availability of finished goods inventory does not avoid the incurrence of future fixed manufacturing costs. Proponents conclude that inventories should be valued at their variable manufacturing cost, and fixed manufacturing costs should be expensed as incurred.

Opponents of variable costing argue that fixed manufacturing costs are incurred for only one purpose, namely, to manufacture the product. Because they are incurred to manufacture the product, they should be assigned to the product. It is also argued that in the long run all costs are variable. Consequently, by omitting fixed costs, variable costing understates long-run variable costs and misleads decision makers into underestimating true production costs.

On a pragmatic level, the central arguments for variable costing center around the fact that use of variable costing facilitates the development of contribution income statements and cost-volume-profit analysis. With costs accumulated on an absorption costing basis, contribution income statements are difficult to develop, and cost-volume-profit analysis becomes very complicated unless production and sales are equal.

Proponents of activity-based costing typically do not favor variable costing because ABC is based on the assumption that, in the long run, all costs are variable and that fixed costs should be assigned to products or services to represent long-run variable costs. Hence, inventory valuation using an ABC approach will tend to be closer to absorption costing values than variable costing values.

As modern manufacturing techniques have led to major reductions in inventory levels (see the following Research Insight) in many companies, the significance of the debate over absorption versus variable costing has declined. If a company has no inventories, all its costs are deducted as expenses (either as operating expenses or cost of goods sold expense) during the current period whether it uses absorption or variable costing. Hence, from an income determination standpoint, it does not matter in such cases whether fixed costs are considered a product or period cost.

RESEARCH INSIGHT **Inventory Levels and Company Financial Performance**

Professors Chen, Frank, and Wu examined inventory trends and related financial performance of American companies over a 20-year period and found that the average yearly rate of inventory reduction was two percent per year. Looking closer, they identified significant differences in the reductions of various types of inventories, with raw materials inventories declining three percent per year, work-in-process inventory declining by about six percent per year and finished goods inventory not declining at all.

They concluded "A firm that deals effectively with its suppliers will have low raw-materials inventories. A firm that has efficient internal operations will have low work-in-process inventories." They also observed that the type of supply chain management and information sharing required for reductions in finished goods inventory is more difficult to implement, suggesting further room for improvement.

As for profitability, "Firms with abnormally high inventories have abnormally poor long-term stock returns. Firms with slightly lower than average inventories have good stock returns, but firms with the lowest inventories have only ordinary returns."[5]

GUIDANCE ANSWER

MANAGERIAL DECISION **You are the Chief Financial Officer**

Inventory costs that are provided for financial statement purposes for external stockholders and lenders are required by generally accepted accounting principles to include only the manufacturing costs of the product for direct materials, direct labor, and factory overhead. To conduct a complete profitability analysis, the CFO will need to gather data for all other costs that relate to the marketing, sales, and distribution of each product, as well as any costs related to providing service to customers who buy the products.

DISCUSSION QUESTIONS

Q5-1. Distinguish among service, merchandising, and manufacturing organizations on the basis of the importance and complexity of inventory cost measurement.

Q5-2. Distinguish between product costing and service costing.

Q5-3. When is depreciation a product cost? When is depreciation a period cost?

Q5-4. What are the three major product cost elements?

Q5-5. How are predetermined overhead rates developed? Why are they widely used?

Q5-6. Briefly distinguish between process manufacturing and job order production. Provide examples of products typically produced under each system.

Q5-7. Briefly describe the role of engineering personnel and production scheduling personnel in the production planning process.

Q5-8. Identify the primary records involved in the operation of a job cost system.

Q5-9. Describe the flow of costs through the accounting system of a labor-intensive manufacturing organization.

Q5-10. Identify two reasons that a service organization should maintain detailed job cost information.

[5] Source: Chen, Hong; Murray Z. Frank; and Owen Q. Wu, "What Actually Happened to the Inventories of American Companies Between 1981 and 2000?", *Management Science*, Vol. 51, No. 7, July 2005, pp. 1015-1031.

Q5-11. What are the four major elements of a cost of production report?

Q5-12. What are equivalent completed units?

Q5-13. Under what conditions will equivalent units in process be different for materials and conversion costs?

MINI EXERCISES

M5-14. Classification of Product and Period Costs (LO2)

Classify the following costs incurred by a manufacturer of golf clubs as product costs or period costs. Also classify the product costs as direct materials or conversion costs.

a. Depreciation on computer in president's office
b. Salaries of legal staff
c. Graphite shafts
d. Plant security department
e. Electricity for the corporate office
f. Rubber grips
g. Golf club heads
h. Wages paid assembly line maintenance workers
i. Salary of corporate controller
j. Subsidy of plant cafeteria
k. Wages paid assembly line production workers
l. National sales meeting in Orlando
m. Overtime premium paid assembly line workers
n. Advertising on national television
o. Depreciation on assembly line

M5-15. Developing and Using a Predetermined Overhead Rate (LO2)

Milliken & Company

Assume that the following predictions were made for 2009 for one of the plants of Milliken & Company:

Total manufacturing overhead for the year.	$40,000,000
Total machine hours for the year	2,000,000

Actual results for February 2009 were as follows:

Manufacturing overhead	$5,520,000
Machine hours	310,000

Required

a. Determine the 2009 predetermined overhead rate per machine hour.
b. Using the predetermined overhead rate per machine hour, determine the manufacturing overhead applied to Work-in-Process during February.
c. As of February 1, actual overhead was underapplied by $400,000. Determine the cumulative amount of any overapplied or underapplied overhead at the end of February.

M5-16. Job Order Costing and Process Costing Applications (LO4, 5)

For each of the following manufacturing situations, indicate whether job order or process costing is more appropriate and why.

a. Peanut butter manufacturer
b. Chemical plant that produces household cleaners
c. Shoe manufacturer
d. Modular home builder
e. Company that makes windshields for automobile manufacturers

M5-17. Job Order Costing and Process Costing Applications (LO4, 5)

For each of the following situations, indicate whether job order or process costing is more appropriate and why.

a. Building contractor for residential dwellings
b. Manufacturer of nylon yarn that sells to fabric-making textile companies
c. Clothing manufacturer that makes suits in several different fabrics, colors, styles, and sizes
d. Hosiery mill that manufactures a one-size-fits-all product

e. Vehicle battery manufacturer that has just received an order for 400,000 identical batteries to be delivered as completed over the next 12 months

M5-18. Process Costing (LO5)

Tempe Manufacturing Company makes a single product that is produced on a continuous basis in one department. All materials are added at the beginning of production. The total cost per equivalent unit in process in March 2009 was $4.60, consisting of $3.00 for materials and $1.60 for conversion. During the month, 8,500 units of product were transferred to finished goods inventory; on March 31, 3,500 units were in process, 10 percent converted. The company uses weighted average costing.

Required

a. Determine the cost of goods transferred to finished goods inventory.
b. Determine the cost of the ending work-in-process inventory.
c. What was the total cost of the beginning work-in-process inventory plus the current manufacturing costs?

M5-19.[A] Absorption and Variable Costing; Inventory Valuation

Intel, Inc., has a highly automated assembly line that uses very little direct labor. Therefore, direct labor is part of variable overhead. For October, assume that it incurred the following unit costs:

Direct materials	$200
Variable overhead.......	180
Fixed overhead.........	60

The 100 units of beginning inventory for October had an absorption costing value of $38,000 and a variable costing value of $32,000. For October, assume that Intel produced 500 units and sold 540 units.

Required

Compute the amount of ending inventory under both absorption and variable costing if the FIFO inventory method was used.

M5-20.[A] Absorption and Variable Costing; Cost of Goods Sold

Use data from Mini Exercise 5-19.[A]

Required

Compute the Cost of Goods Sold using both the variable and absorption costing methods.

EXERCISES

E5-21. Analyzing Activity in Inventory Accounts (LO2, 4)

Selected data concerning operations of Cascade Manufacturing Company for the past fiscal year follow:

Raw materials used	$300,000
Total manufacturing costs charged to production during the year (includes raw materials, direct labor, and manufacturing overhead applied at a rate of 60 percent of direct labor costs)	681,000
Cost of goods available for sale..................................	826,000
Selling and general expenses.....................................	30,000

	Inventories	
	Beginning	Ending
Raw materials.............	$70,000	$ 80,000
Work-in-process..........	85,000	30,000
Finished goods...........	90,000	110,000

Required

Determine each of the following:

a. Cost of raw materials purchased

b. Direct labor costs charged to production
c. Cost of goods manufactured
d. Cost of goods sold

E5-22. Statement of Cost of Goods Manufactured and Income Statement (LO4)
Information from the records of the Jackson Hole Manufacturing Company for August 2010 follows:

Sales	$205,000
Selling and administrative expenses	83,000
Purchases of raw materials	25,000
Direct labor	15,000
Manufacturing overhead	32,000

	Inventories	
	August 1	August 31
Raw materials	$ 7,000	$ 5,000
Work-in-process	14,000	11,000
Finished goods	15,000	19,000

Required
Prepare a statement of cost of goods manufactured and an income statement for August 2010.

E5-23. Statement of Cost of Goods Manufactured from Percent Relationships (LO4)
Information about NuWay Products Company for the year ending December 31, 2010, follows:

- Sales equal $450,000.
- Direct materials used total $64,000.
- Manufacturing overhead is 150 percent of direct labor dollars.
- The beginning inventory of finished goods is 20 percent of the cost of goods sold.
- The ending inventory of finished goods is twice the beginning inventory.
- The gross profit is 20 percent of sales.
- There is no beginning or ending work-in-process.

Required
Prepare a statement of cost of goods manufactured for 2010. (*Hint:* Prepare an analysis of changes in Finished Goods Inventory.)

E5-24. Developing and Using a Predetermined Overhead Rate: High-Low Cost Estimation (LO2)
For years, Daytona Parts Company has used an actual plantwide overhead rate and based its prices on cost plus a markup of 25 percent. Recently the marketing manager, Jan Arton, and the production manager, Sue Yount, confronted the controller with a common problem. The marketing manager expressed a concern that Daytona's prices seem to vary widely throughout the year. According to Arton, "It seems irrational to charge higher prices when business is bad and lower prices when business is good. While we get a lot of business during high-volume months because we charge less than our competitors, it is a waste of time to even call on customers during low-volume months because we are raising prices while our competitors are lowering them." Yount also believed that it was "folly to be so pushed that we have to pay overtime in some months and then lay employees off in others." She commented, "While there are natural variations in customer demand, the accounting system seems to amplify this variation."

Required

a. Evaluate the arguments presented by Arton and Yount. What suggestions do you have for improving the accounting and pricing procedures?
b. Assume that the Daytona Parts Company had the following total manufacturing overhead costs and direct labor hours in 2007 and 2008:

	2007	2008
Total manufacturing overhead	$200,000	$237,500
Direct labor hours	20,000	27,500

Use the high-low method to develop a cost estimating equation for total manufacturing overhead.
c. Develop a predetermined rate for 2009, assuming 25,000 direct labor hours are budgeted for 2009.

d. Assume that the actual level of activity in 2009 was 30,000 direct labor hours and that the total 2009 manufacturing overhead was $250,000. Determine the underapplied or overapplied manufacturing overhead at the end of 2009.

e. Describe two ways of handling any underapplied or overapplied manufacturing overhead at the end of the year.

E5-25. Manufacturing Cost Flows with Machine Hours Allocation (LO4)

On November 1, Robotics Manufacturing Company's beginning balances in manufacturing accounts and finished goods inventory were as follows:

Raw Materials.	$ 9,000
Manufacturing Supplies	500
Work-in-Process.	5,000
Manufacturing Overhead	0
Finished Goods	25,000

During November, Robotics Manufacturing completed the following manufacturing transactions:

1. Purchased raw materials costing $58,000 and manufacturing supplies costing $3,000 on account.
2. Requisitioned raw materials costing $40,000 to the factory.
3. Incurred direct labor costs of $27,000 and indirect labor costs of $4,800.
4. Used manufacturing supplies costing $3,000.
5. Recorded manufacturing depreciation of $15,000.
6. Miscellaneous payables for manufacturing overhead totaled $3,600.
7. Applied manufacturing overhead, based on 2,250 machine hours, at a predetermined rate of $10 per machine hour.
8. Completed jobs costing $85,000.
9. Finished goods costing $96,000 were sold.

Required

a Prepare "T" accounts showing the flow of costs through all manufacturing accounts, Finished Goods Inventory, and Cost of Goods Sold.

b. Calculate the balances at the end of November for Work-in-Process Inventory and Finished Goods Inventory.

E5-26. Service Cost Flows (LO4)

Viva Marketing, Ltd., produces television advertisements for businesses that are marketing products in the western provinces of Canada. To achieve cost control, Viva Marketing uses a job cost system similar to that found in a manufacturing organization. It uses some different account titles:

Account	Replaces
Videos-in-Process	Work-in-Process
Video Supplies Inventory	Manufacturing Supplies Inventory
Cost of Videos Completed	Cost of Goods Sold
Accumulated Depreciation, Studio Assets	Accumulated Depreciation, Factory Assets
Studio Overhead	Manufacturing Overhead

Viva Marketing does not maintain Raw Materials or Finished Goods Inventory accounts. Materials, such as props needed for videos, are purchased as needed from outside sources and charged directly to Videos-in-Process and the appropriate job. Videos are delivered directly to clients upon completion. The October 1, balances were as follows:

Video Supplies	$ 300	
Videos-in-Process	1,000	
Studio Overhead	250	underapplied

During October, Viva Marketing completed the following production transactions:

1. Purchased video supplies costing $1,475 on account.
2. Purchased materials for specific jobs costing $27,000 on account.
3. Incurred direct labor costs of $65,000 and indirect labor costs of $3,200.
4. Used production supplies costing $850.

5. Recorded studio depreciation of $3,000.
6. Incurred miscellaneous payables for studio overhead of $1,800.
7. Applied studio overhead at a predetermined rate of $18 per studio hour, with 480 studio hours.
8. Completed jobs costing $100,000 and delivered them directly to clients.

Required

a. Prepare "T" accounts showing the flow of costs through all service accounts and Cost of Videos Completed.

b. Calculate the cost incurred as of the end of October for the incomplete jobs still in process.

E5-27. Cost of Production Report: No Beginning Inventories (LO5)

Oregon Paper Company produces newsprint paper through a special recycling process using scrap paper products. Production and cost data for October 2009, the first month of operations for the company's new Portland plant, follow:

Units of product started in process during October	90,000 tons
Units completed and transferred to finished goods	75,000 tons
Machine hours operated	10,000
Direct materials costs incurred	$486,000
Direct labor costs incurred	$190,530

Raw materials are added at the beginning of the process for each unit of product produced, and labor and manufacturing overhead are added evenly throughout the manufacturing process. Manufacturing overhead is applied to Work-in-Process at the rate of $24 per machine hour. Units in process at the end of the period were 65 percent converted.

Required

Prepare a cost of production report for Oregon Paper Company for October.

E5-28. Cost of Production Report: No Beginning Inventories (LO5)

Quality Paving Products Company manufactures asphalt paving materials for highway construction through a one-step process in which all materials are added at the beginning of the process. During October 2009, the company accumulated the following data in its process costing system:

Production data	
Work-in-process, 10/1/09	0 tons
Raw materials transferred to processing	25,000 tons
Work-in-process, 10/31/09 (75% converted)	5,000 tons
Cost data	
Raw materials transferred to processing	$625,000
Conversion costs	
Direct labor cost incurred	$38,000
Manufacturing overhead applied	?

Manufacturing overhead is applied at the rate of $2 per equivalent unit (ton) processed.

Required

Prepare a cost of production report for October 2009.

E5-29.[A] Absorption and Variable Costing Comparisons: Production Equals Sales

Assume that Heinz manufactures and sells 15,000 cases of catsup each quarter. The following data are available for the third quarter of 2009.

Total fixed manufacturing overhead	$30,000
Fixed selling and administrative expenses	10,000
Sales price per case	30
Direct materials per case	12
Direct labor per case	6
Variable manufacturing overhead per case	3

Required

a. Compute the cost per case under both absorption costing and variable costing.

b. Compute net income under both absorption costing and variable costing.
c. Reconcile any differences in income. Explain.

E5-30.[A] Absorption and Variable Costing Income Statements: Production Exceeds Sales
Glendale Company sells its product at a unit price of $12.00. Unit manufacturing costs are direct materials, $2.00; direct labor, $3.00; and variable manufacturing overhead, $1.50. Total fixed manufacturing costs are $20,000 per year. Selling and administrative expenses are $1.00 per unit variable and $10,000 per year fixed. Though 25,000 units were produced during 2009, only 22,000 units were sold. There was no beginning inventory.

Required
a. Prepare a functional income statement using absorption costing.
b. Prepare a contribution income statement using variable costing.

E5-31.[A] Absorption and Variable Costing Comparisons: Sales Exceed Production
Eskew Development purchases, develops, and sells commercial building sites. As the sites are sold, they are cleared at an average cost of $2,500 per site. Storm drains and driveways are also installed at an average cost of $4,000 per site. Selling costs are 10 percent of sales price. Administrative costs are $425,000 per year. During 2009, the company bought 1,000 acres of land for $5,000,000 and divided it into 200 sites of equal size. The average selling price per site was $80,000 during 2009 when 50 sites were sold. During 2010, the company purchased and developed another 1,000 acres, divided into 200 sites. Sales totaled 300 sites in 2010 at an average price of $80,000.

Required
a. Prepare 2009 and 2010 functional income statements using absorption costing.
b. Prepare 2009 and 2010 contribution income statements using variable costing.

PROBLEMS

P5-32. Cost of Goods Manufactured and Income Statement (LO4)
Following is information from the records of the Calgary Company for July 2009.

Purchases	
Raw materials	$ 80,000
Manufacturing supplies	3,500
Office supplies	1,200
Sales	425,700
Administrative salaries	12,000
Direct labor	117,500
Production employees' fringe benefits*	4,000
Sales commissions	50,000
Production supervisors' salaries	7,200
Plant depreciation	14,000
Office depreciation	20,000
Plant maintenance	10,000
Plant utilities	35,000
Office utilities	8,000
Office maintenance	2,000
Production equipment rent	6,000
Office equipment rent	1,300

*Classified as manufacturing overhead

Inventories	July 1	July 31
Raw materials	$17,000	$25,000
Manufacturing supplies	1,500	3,000
Office supplies	600	1,000
Work-in-process	51,000	40,000
Finished goods	35,000	27,100

Required

Prepare a statement of cost of goods manufactured and an income statement. Actual overhead costs are assigned to products.

P5-33. Cost of Goods Manufactured and Income Statement with Predetermined Overhead and Labor Cost Classifications (LO2, 4)

Callaway Golf Company (ELY)

Assume information pertaining to Callaway Golf Company for April 2009 follows.

Sales	$200,000
Purchases	
Raw materials	37,000
Manufacturing supplies	800
Office supplies	500
Salaries (including fringe benefits)	
Administrative	6,000
Production supervisors	3,600
Sales	15,000
Depreciation	
Plant and machinery	8,000
Office and office equipment	4,000
Utilities	
Plant	5,250
Office	890

Inventories	April 1	April 30
Raw materials	$3,000	$3,500
Manufacturing supplies	1,000	1,100
Office supplies	900	800
Work-in-process	2,000	2,300
Finished goods	8,000	9,000

Additional information follows:

- Manufacturing overhead is applied to products at 85 percent of direct labor dollars.
- Employee base wages are $12 per hour.
- Employee fringe benefits amount to 40 percent of the base wage rate. They are classified as manufacturing overhead.
- During April, production employees worked 5,600 hours, including 4,800 regular hours and 200 overtime hours spent working on products. There were 600 indirect labor hours.
- Employees are paid a 50 percent overtime premium. Any overtime premium is treated as manufacturing overhead.

Required

a. Prepare a statement of cost of goods manufactured and an income statement for April.
b. Determine underapplied or overapplied overhead for April.
c. Recompute direct labor and actual manufacturing overhead assuming employee fringe benefits for direct labor hours are classified as direct labor.

P5-34. Actual and Predetermined Overhead Rates (LO2, 4)

Allison's Engines, which builds high performance auto engines for race cars, started operations on January 1, 2009. During the month, the following events occurred:

- Materials costing $6,500 were purchased on account.
- Direct materials costing $3,000 were placed in process.
- A total of 380 direct labor hours was charged to individual jobs at a rate of $15 per hour.
- Overhead costs for the month of January were as follows:

Depreciation on building and equipment	$ 500
Indirect labor	1,500
Utilities	600
Property taxes on building	650
Insurance on building	550

- On January 31, only one job (A06) was in process with materials costs of $600, direct labor charges of $450 for 30 direct labor hours, and applied overhead.
- The building and equipment were purchased before operations began and the insurance was prepaid. All other costs will be paid during the following month.

Note: Predetermined overhead rates are used throughout the chapter. An alternative is to accumulate actual overhead costs for the period in Manufacturing Overhead, and apply actual costs at the close of the period to all jobs in process during the period.

Required

a. Assuming Allison's Engines assigned actual monthly overhead costs to jobs on the basis of actual monthly direct labor hours, prepare an analysis of Work-in-Process for the month of January.

b. Assuming Allison's Engines uses a predetermined overhead rate of $10.50 per direct labor hour, prepare an analysis of Work-in-Process for the month of January. Describe the appropriate treatment of any overapplied or underapplied overhead for the month of January.

c. Review the overhead items and classify each as fixed or variable in relation to direct labor hours. Next, predict the actual overhead rates for months when 200 and 1,000 direct labor hours are used. Assuming jobs similar to A06 were in process at the end of each month, determine the costs assigned to these jobs. (*Hint:* Determine a variable overhead rate.)

d. Why do you suppose predetermined overhead rates are preferred to actual overhead rates?

P5-35. Job Costing with Predetermined Overhead Rate (LO2, 4)

Herman Miller, Inc.
(MLHR)

Herman Miller, Inc. manufactures desks, chairs, file cabinets, and similar office products in batches for inventory stock. Assume that Herman Miller's production costs are accounted for using a job cost system. At the beginning of April 2009, raw materials inventories totaled $8,500,000, manufacturing supplies amounted to $1,200,000 and finished goods inventories totaled $6,000,000. Two jobs were in process: Job 522 with assigned costs of $5,640,000 and Job 523 with assigned costs of $2,400,000. The following information summarizes April manufacturing activities:

- Purchased raw materials costing $25,000,000 on account.
- Purchased manufacturing supplies costing $3,000,000 on account.
- Requisitioned materials needed to complete Job 523. Started two new jobs, 524 and 525, and requisitioned direct materials for them.

Direct materials	
Job 523	$ 3,000,000
Job 524	12,900,000
Job 525	9,600,000
Total	$25,500,000

- Recorded April salaries and wages as follows:

Direct labor	
Job 522 (300,000 hours × $12 per hour)	$ 3,600,000
Job 523 (800,000 hours × $12 per hour)	9,600,000
Job 524 (1,200,000 hours × $12 per hour)	14,400,000
Job 525 (1,000,000 hours × $12 per hour)	12,000,000
Total direct labor	39,600,000
Indirect labor	6,400,000
Total	$46,000,000

- Used manufacturing supplies costing $2,250,000.
- Recognized depreciation on factory fixed assets of $4,000,000.
- Incurred miscellaneous manufacturing overhead costs of $5,500,000 on account.
- Applied manufacturing overhead at the rate of $6 per direct labor hour.
- Completed Jobs 522, 523, and 524.

Required

Prepare a complete analysis of all activity in Work-in-Process. Be sure to show the beginning and ending balances, all increases and decreases, and label each item. Provide support information on decreases with job cost sheets.

P5-36. Job Costing with Predetermined Overhead Rate (LO2, 4)

TruCut Mower Company manufactures a variety of gasoline-powered mowers for discount hardware and department stores. TruCut uses a job cost system and treats each customer's order as a separate job. The primary mower components (motors, chassis, and wheels) are purchased from three different suppliers under long-term contracts that call for the direct delivery of raw materials to the production floor as needed. When a customer's order is received, a raw materials purchase order is electronically placed with suppliers. The purchase order specifies the scheduled date that production is to begin as the delivery date for motors and chassis; the scheduled date production is to be completed is specified as the delivery date for the wheels. As a consequence, there are no raw materials inventories; raw materials are charged directly to Work-in-Process upon receipt. Upon completion, goods are shipped directly to customers rather than transferred to finished goods inventory. At the beginning of July 2009, TruCut had the following work-in-process inventories:

Job 365	$20,000
Job 366	16,500
Job 367	15,000
Job 368	9,000
Total	$60,500

During July, the following activities took place:

- Started Jobs 369, 370, and 371.
- Ordered and received the following raw materials for specified jobs:

Job	Motors	Chassis	Wheels	Total
366	$ 0	$ 0	$ 800	$ 800
367	0	0	1,200	1,200
368	0	0	1,600	1,600
369	12,000	4,000	1,000	17,000
370	9,000	3,500	900	13,400
371	8,500	3,800	0	12,300
Total	$29,500	$11,300	$5,500	$46,300

- Incurred July manufacturing payroll:

Direct labor	
Job 365.	$ 500
Job 366.	3,200
Job 367.	3,400
Job 368.	4,160
Job 369.	1,300
Job 370.	2,620
Job 371.	2,000
Total	17,180
Indirect labor	3,436
Total	$20,616

- Incurred additional manufacturing overhead costs for July:

Manufacturing supplies purchased on account and used.	$ 2,800
Depreciation on factory fixed assets	6,000
Miscellaneous payables.	5,100
Total	$13,900

- Applied manufacturing overhead using a predetermined rate based on predicted annual overhead of $190,000 and predicted annual direct labor of $200,000.
- Completed and shipped Jobs 365 through 370.

Required

Prepare a complete analysis of all activity in Work-in-Process. Be sure to show the beginning and ending balances, all increases and decreases, and label each item. Provide support information on decreases with job cost sheets.

P5-37. Weighted Average Process Costing (LO5)

Minot Processing Company manufactures one product on a continuous basis in two departments, Processing and Finishing. All materials are added at the beginning of work on the product in the Processing Department. During December 2009, the following events occurred in the Processing Department:

Units started	16,000 units
Units completed and transferred to Finishing Department	15,000 units

Costs assigned to processing	
Raw materials (one unit of raw materials for each unit of product started)	$142,900
Manufacturing supplies used	18,000
Direct labor costs incurred	51,000
Supervisors' salaries	12,000
Other production labor costs	14,000
Depreciation on equipment	6,000
Other production costs	18,000

Additional information follows:

- Minot uses weighted average costing and applies manufacturing overhead to Work-in-Process at the rate of 100 percent of direct labor cost.
- Ending inventory in the Processing Department consists of 3,000 units that are one-third converted.
- Beginning inventory contained 2,000 units, one-half converted, with a cost of $27,300 ($17,300 for materials and $10,000 for conversion).

Required

a. Prepare a cost of production report for the Processing Department for December.
b. Prepare an analysis of all changes in Work-in-Process.

P5-38. Weighted Average Process Costing (LO5)

Assume that JIF, which is part of J.M. Smucker Company, processes its only product, 12-ounce jars of peanut butter, in a single process and uses weighted average process costing to account for inventory costs. All materials are added at the beginning of production. The following inventory, production, and cost data are provided for June 2009:

JIF
J.M. Smucker Company (SJM)

Production data	
Beginning inventory (25% converted)	210,000 units
Units started	650,000 units
Ending inventory (50% converted)	180,000 units

Manufacturing costs	
Beginning inventory in process:	
Materials cost	$146,000
Conversion cost	88,000
Raw materials cost added at beginning of process	739,800
Direct labor cost incurred	410,000
Manufacturing overhead applied	333,600

Required

a. Prepare a cost of production report for June.
b. Prepare a statement of cost of goods manufactured for June.

P5-39. Weighted Average Process Costing with Error Correction (LO5)

Blue Sky Manufacturing Company began operations on December 31, 2010. At December 31, 2010, a new accounting intern was assigned the task of calculating and costing ending inventories.

The intern estimated that the ending work-in-process inventory was 40 percent complete as to both materials and conversion, resulting in 2,000 equivalent units of materials and conversion. The ending work-in-process was then valued at $80,000, including $40,000 for materials and $40,000 for conversion. A subsequent review of the intern's work revealed that although the materials portion of the ending inventory was correctly estimated to be 40 percent complete, the units in ending inventory, on average, were only 20 percent complete as to conversion.

Required:

a. Determine the number of units in the ending inventory.
b. How many equivalent units of conversion were in the ending inventory?
c. What cost per unit did the intern calculate for conversion?
d. Assuming 9,000 units were completed during the month of December, determine the correct cost per equivalent unit. *Hint:* Find the total conversion costs in process.
e. Determine the corrected cost of the ending inventory.
f. By how much was the cost of goods manufactured misstated as a result of the intern's error? Indicate whether the cost of goods manufactured was overstated or understated.

P5-40.[A] Absorption and Variable Costing Comparisons

Never Quit Shoe Company is concerned with changing to the variable costing method of inventory valuation for making internal decisions. Functional income statements using absorption costing for January and February follow.

NEVER QUIT SHOE COMPANY
Functional (Absorption Costing) Income Statements
For January and February 2009

	January	February
Sales (8,000 units)	$160,000	$160,000
Cost of goods sold	(99,200)	(108,800)
Gross profit	60,800	51,200
Selling and administrative expenses	(30,000)	(30,000)
Net income	$ 30,800	$ 21,200

Production data follow.

Production units	10,000	6,000
Variable costs per unit	$10	$10
Fixed overhead costs	$24,000	$24,000

The preceding selling and administrative expenses include variable costs of $1 per unit sold.

Required

a. Compute the absorption cost per unit manufactured in January and February.
b. Explain why the net income for January was higher than the net income for February when the same number of units was sold in each month.
c. Prepare contribution income statements for both months using variable costing.
d. Reconcile the absorption costing and variable costing net income figures for each month. (Start with variable costing net income.)

P5-41.[A] Absorption and Variable Costing Comparisons

Peachtree Company manufactures peach jam. Because of bad weather, its peach crop was small. The following data have been gathered for the summer quarter of 2009:

Beginning inventory (cases)	0
Cases produced	10,000
Cases sold	9,400
Sales price per case	$60
Direct materials per case	$8
Direct labor per case	$9
Variable manufacturing overhead per case	$3
Total fixed manufacturing overhead	$400,000
Variable selling and administrative cost per case	$2
Fixed selling and administrative cost	$48,000

Required

a. Prepare a functional income statement for the quarter using absorption costing.
b. Prepare a contribution income statement for the quarter using variable costing.
c. What is the value of ending inventory under absorption costing?
d. What is the value of ending inventory under variable costing?
e. Explain the difference in ending inventory under absorption costing and variable costing.

P5-42.[A] Variable and Absorption Costing with High-Low Cost Estimation and CVP Analysis Including Taxes

Presented are the Charger Company's functional income statements for January and February of 2010.

CHARGER COMPANY Functional (Absorption Costing) Income Statements For the Months of January and February 2010	January	February
Production and sales	40,000	50,000
Sales Revenue	$1,000,000	$1,250,000
Cost of goods manufactured and sold	(525,000)	(625,000)
Gross profit	475,000	625,000
General and administrative expenses	(235,000)	(235,000)
Net income before taxes	240,000	390,000
Income taxes at 0.40	(96,000)	(156,000)
Net income after taxes	$ 144,000	$ 234,000

Required:

a. Using the high-low method, develop a cost estimating equation for total monthly manufacturing costs.
b. Determine Charger Company's monthly break-even point.
c. Determine the unit sales required to earn a monthly after-tax income of $150,000.
d. Prepare a January 2010 contribution income statement using variable costing.
e. If the January 2010 net income amounts differ using absorption and variable costing, explain why. If they are identical, explain why.

CASES

C5-43. Cost Data for Financial Reporting and Special Order Decisions (LO2, 4)

Friendly Greeting Card Company produces a full range of greeting cards sold through pharmacies and department stores. Each card is designed by independent artists. A production master is then prepared for each design. The production master has an indefinite life. Product designs for popular cards are deemed to be valuable assets. If a card sells well, many batches of the design will be manufactured over a period of years. Hence, Friendly Greeting maintains an inventory of production masters so that cards may be periodically reissued. Cards are produced in batches that may vary by increments of 1,000 units. An average batch consists of 10,000 cards. Producing a batch requires placing the production master on the printing press, setting the press for the appropriate paper size, and making other adjustments for colors and so forth. Following are facility-, product-, batch-, and unit-level cost information:

Product design and production master per new card	$ 1,500.00
Batch setup (typically per 10,000 cards)	150.00
Materials per 1,000 cards	100.00
Conversion per 1,000 cards	80.00
Shipping	
Per batch	20.00
Per card	0.01
Selling and administrative	
Companywide	200,000.00
Per product design marketed	500.00

Information from previous year:

Product designs and masters prepared for new cards	90
Product designs marketed	120
Batches manufactured	500
Cards manufactured and sold	5,000,000

Required

You may need to review materials in Chapters 2 and 3 to complete the requirements.

a. Describe how you would determine the cost of goods sold and the value of any ending inventory for financial reporting purposes. (No computations are required.)

b. You have just received an inquiry from Mall-Mart department stores to develop and manufacture 20 special designs for sale exclusively in Mall-Mart stores. The cards would be sold for $1.50 each, and Mall-Mart would pay Friendly Greeting $0.30 per card. The initial order is for 20,000 cards of each design. If the cards sell well, Mall-Mart plans to place additional orders for these and other designs. Because of the preestablished sales relationship, no marketing costs would be associated with the cards sold to Mall-Mart. How would you evaluate the desirability of the Mall-Mart proposal?

c. Explain any differences between the costs considered in your answer to requirement (a) and the costs considered in your answer to requirement (b).

C5-44. Continue or Discontinue: Plantwide Overhead with Labor- and Machine-Intensive Operations (LO2, 4)

When Dart Products started operation five years ago, its only product was a radar detector known as the Bear Detector. The production system was simple, with Bear Detectors manually assembled from purchased components. With no ending work-in-process inventories, unit costs were calculated once a month by dividing current manufacturing costs by units produced.

Last year, Dart Products began to manufacture a second product, code-named the Lion Tamer. The production of Lion Tamers involves both machine-intensive fabrication and manual assembly. The introduction of the second product necessitated a change in the firm's simple accounting system. Dart Products now separately assigns direct material and direct labor costs to each product using information contained on materials requisitions and work tickets. Manufacturing overhead is accumulated in a single cost pool and assigned on the basis of direct labor hours, which is common to both products. Following are last year's financial results by product:

	Bear Detector		Lion Tamer	
Sales				
Units		5,000		2,000
Dollars		$ 500,000		$ 300,000
Cost of goods sold				
Direct materials	$110,000		$65,000	
Direct labor	150,000		45,000	
Applied overhead	270,000		81,000	
Total		(530,000)		(191,000)
Gross profit		$ (30,000)		$ 109,000

Management is concerned about the mixed nature of last year's financial performance. It appears that the Lion Tamer is a roaring success. The only competition, the Nittney Company, has been selling a competing product for considerably more than Dart's Lion Tamer; this company is in financial difficulty and is likely to file for bankruptcy. The management of Dart Products attributes the Lion Tamer's success to excellent production management. Management is concerned, however, about the future of the Bear Detector and is likely to discontinue that product unless its profitability can be improved. You have been asked to help with this decision and have obtained the following information:

- The labor rate is $15 per hour.
- Dart has two separate production operations, fabrication and assembly. Bear Detectors undergo only assembly operations and require 2.0 assembly hours per unit. Lion Tamers undergo both fabrication and assembly and require 1.0 fabrication hour and 0.5 assembly hour per unit.

- The annual Fabricating Department overhead cost function is:

\$200,000 + \$5 (labor hours)

- The annual Assembly Department overhead cost function is:

\$20,000 + \$11 (labor hours)

Required

You may need to review materials in Chapters 2 through 4 to complete this case. Evaluate the profitability of Dart's two products and make any recommendations you believe appropriate.

C 5-45.[A] Absorption Costing and Performance Evaluation

On July 2, 2009 Go Go Incorporated acquired 90 percent of the outstanding stock of Medioker Industries in exchange for 2,000 shares of its own stock. Go Go Incorporated has a reputation as a "high flier" company that commands a high price-to-earnings ratio because its management team works wonders in improving the performance of ailing companies.

At the time of the acquisition, Medioker was producing and selling at an annual rate of 100,000 units per year. This is in line with the firm's average annual activity. Fifty thousand units were produced during the first half of 2009.

Immediately after the acquisition Go Go installed its own management team and increased production to practical capacity. One-hundred thousand units were produced during the second half of 2009.

At the end of the year, the new management declared another dramatic turnaround and a \$500,000 cash dividend when the following set of income statements were issued:

MEDIOKER INDUSTRIES
Income Statement
For the first and second half-years of 2009

	First	Second	Total
Sales	\$1,500,000	\$1,500,000	\$3,000,000
Cost of goods sold*	(1,200,000)	(700,000)	(1,900,000)
Gross profit	300,000	800,000	1,100,000
Selling and administrative expenses	(200,000)	(400,000)	(600,000)
Net income	\$ 100,000	\$ 400,000	\$ 500,000

* Absorption costing with any under-absorbed or over-absorbed overhead written off as an adjustment to cost of goods sold. Medioker applies manufacturing overhead using a predetermined overhead rate based on annual production of 100,000 units.

Required:

As the only representative of the minority interest on the board of directors, evaluate the performance of the new management team.

Chapter 6

Activity-Based Costing, Customer Profitability, and Activity-Based Management

LEARNING OBJECTIVES

LO1 Explain the changes in the modern production environment that have affected cost structures. (p. 176)

LO2 Understand the concept of activity-based costing (ABC) and how it is applied. (p. 177)

LO3 Explain the difference between traditional plantwide and departmental overhead methods and ABC. (p. 185)

LO4 Describe the implementation of an activity-based costing system. (p. 190)

LO5 Explain customer profitability analysis based on ABC. (p. 191)

LO6 Explain the difference between ABC and activity-based management. (p. 193)

UNDERSTANDING COSTS EQUALS UNDERSTANDING THE BUSINESS

Effective management of costs is a hallmark of sound management, and indirect costs (commonly referred to as overhead) are the most challenging costs to measure and to manage. Direct costs, including direct materials and direct labor, can be readily traced to a job, product[1], or other unit of work. Indirect costs, which are typically incurred for the benefit of several different products or cost objectives, are not as easily traced to specific units or projects. The problem of managing indirect costs (which includes both production overhead and general administrative overhead costs) has become a major concern of managers because this broad category of costs has grown from what was an overall average of about 10 percent of total sales several decades ago to about 35 percent of total sales today. Unfortunately, cost systems did not always reflect the growing significance of these costs.

Many companies that once thrived have failed, arguably, because they did not manage indirect costs effectively. You might say they failed because they did not fully understand their business or their business model. If the true cost of producing and selling products is more than the revenues generated by those products, the business producing and selling those products will not succeed in the long-term. We maintain that many companies persist in following that type of unsuccessful business model

[1] Throughout this chapter, the term "product" should be interpreted to encompass both tangible products sold by a manufacturer, wholesaler, or retailer, as well as services sold by those companies, and services sold by professional or other service providers.

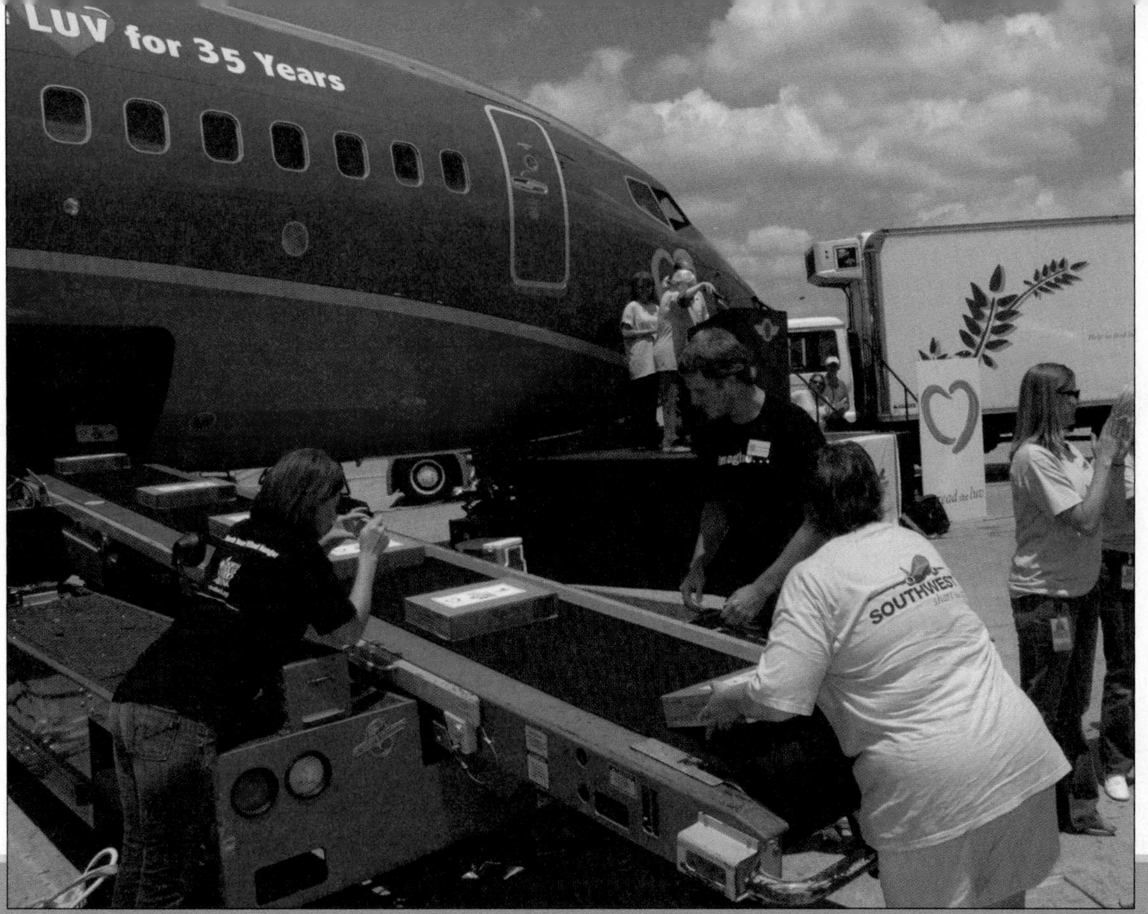

Courtesy of Southwest Airlines

for some or all of their products or customers because they *really* don't know their true costs and, hence, they *really* don't understand their business.

As competition from home and abroad puts increasing pressure on companies to price products more competitively, the importance of cost management becomes increasingly crucial. Two classic examples of the profit squeeze are the airline industry and the auto industry. **Eastern Airlines**, **TWA,** and other air carriers failed primarily because of mounting losses from price competition and lack of good cost management. The recent financial woes of **General Motors** and **Ford** can be traced to similar circumstances.

Fortunately, today many companies have found that the culprit responsible for poor decisions concerning products offerings and product pricing originate with the cost systems used to measure the cost of products, especially the systems used to assign indirect costs to products. In recent years, indirect cost assignment systems have improved significantly, and companies like **Chrysler** and **Southwest Airlines** have benefited greatly from improved cost management systems.

This chapter will introduce and discuss *activity-based costing* (ABC), which is possibly the most important breakthrough of this generation in the realm of cost measurement and cost management. We will define and discuss the concept of activity-based costing, compare it with traditional costing systems, and demonstrate how it can be applied to customer profitability analysis. Finally, we will introduce the notion of activity-based management, which uses activity-based costing information to better manage processes and activities within an organization.

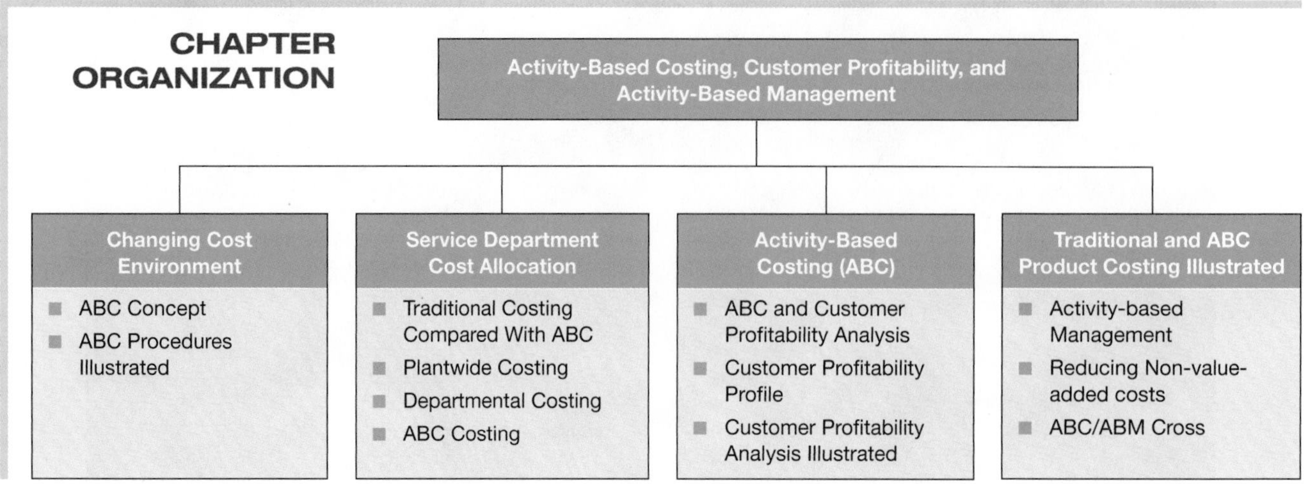

CHANGING COST ENVIRONMENT

LO1 Explain the changes in the modern production environment that have affected cost structures.

As technology has advanced and competition has intensified over the last century, there has been a fundamental shift in manufacturing organizations from labor-intensive to automated assembly techniques. These changes have influenced the activities performed to meet customer needs and, consequently, the costs of producing goods and services.

At the beginning of the twentieth century, products had long life cycles, production procedures were relatively straightforward, production was labor based, and only a limited number of related products were produced in a single plant. It was said of the Model T Ford that "you could have any color you wanted, as long as it was black." The largest cost elements of most manufactured goods were the cost of raw materials and the wages paid to production employees. Manufacturing overhead was a relatively small portion of the overall cost of manufacturing products.

The twentieth century saw an accelerating shift from traditional labor-based activities to production procedures requiring large investments in automated equipment. In the past, production employees used equipment to assist them in performing their jobs. Now employees spend considerable time scheduling, setting up, maintaining, and moving materials to and from equipment. They spend relatively little time on actual production. The equipment does the work, and the employees keep it running efficiently. Increased complexity of production procedures and an increase in the variety of products produced in a single facility have also caused a shift toward more support personnel and fewer production employees. The result is a significant increase in manufacturing overhead as a percentage of total product cost. This change in the typical production cost structure over the past century is illustrated in Exhibit 6.1.

EXHIBIT 6.1 Changing Production Cost Structures

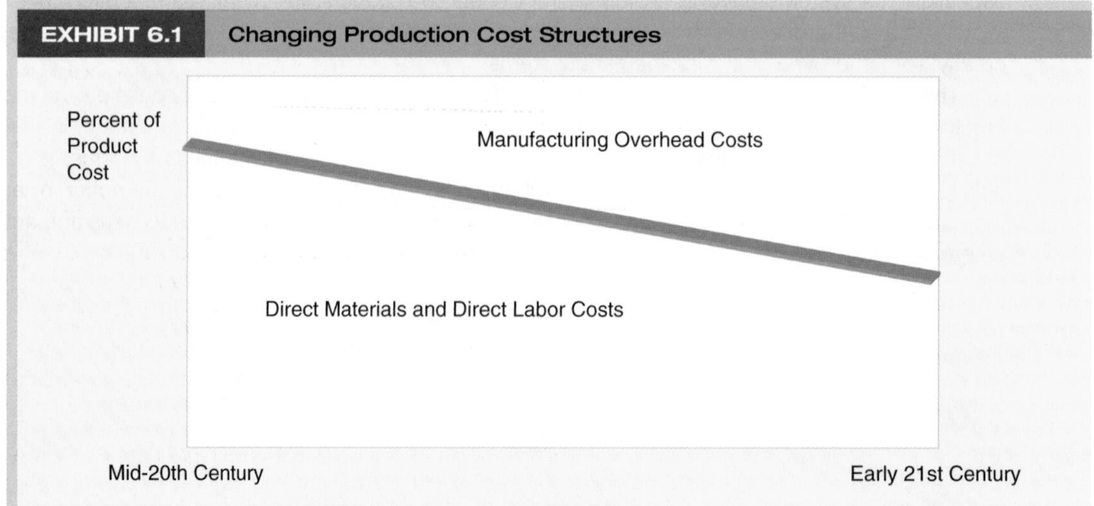

In the "low-tech," labor-intensive manufacturing environment, factors related to direct labor were often the primary drivers of manufacturing overhead costs; however, in today's "high-tech" automated environment there are many other factors that drive manufacturing overhead costs, and the specific set of cost drivers differs from organization to organization.

The previous chapter on product costing illustrated a simplified traditional system for allocating manufacturing overhead to products using a single, volume-based cost driver, such as direct labor hours. The following section introduces activity-based costing (ABC), which recognizes the multiple activities that drive manufacturing overhead costs in today's production environment.

ACTIVITY-BASED COSTING

LO2 Understand the concept of activity-based costing (ABC) and how it is applied.

The manufacturing overhead cost pool has been referred to as a "blob" of common costs. The constant growth of costs classified as overhead has forced us to search for increasingly detailed methods to analyze these costs. If overhead costs are low in comparison with other costs and if factories produce few products in large production runs, the use of an overhead rate based on direct labor hours or machine hours may be adequate. However, as the amount of overhead costs continues to grow, as manufacturing facilities produce a wider variety of products, and as competition intensifies, the inadequacies of a single overhead rate based on a single cost driver such as direct labor hours become evident.

Fortunately, advances in information technology and the declining costs of computerized information systems have facilitated the development and maintenance of increasingly detailed databases. These and other factors (such as declining inventory levels that make product costing less significant for financial reporting) gave rise to the emergence and development of activity-based costing during the 1980s and 1990s.

Activity-based costing involves determining the cost of activities and tracing their costs to cost objectives on the basis of the cost objective's utilization of units of activity.

The concepts underlying ABC can be summarized in the following two statements and illustrations:

1. Activities performed to fill customer needs consume resources that cost money.

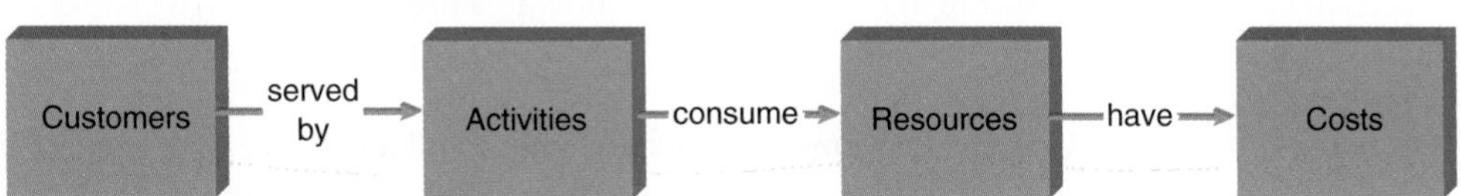

2. The cost of resources consumed by activities should be assigned to cost objectives on the basis of the units of activity consumed by the cost objective.

*Based on units of activity utilized by the cost objective.

The cost objective is typically a product or service provided to a customer. Depending on the information needs of decision makers, the cost objective might be the customer.

To summarize, activity-based costing is a system of analysis that identifies and measures the cost of key activities, and then traces these activity costs to products or other cost objectives based on the quantity of activity consumed by the cost objectives. ABC is based on the premise that activities drive costs and that costs should be assigned to products (or other cost objectives) in proportion to the volume of activities they consume. Although activity cost analysis is most often associated with product costing, it offers many benefits for controlling and managing costs, as we will see later in this chapter. As the following Research Insight box explains, ABC was actually used first to improve cost management before it was used for product costing.

ABC Product Costing Model

Traditional costing considers the cost of a product to be its direct costs for materials and labor plus some allocated portion of factory overhead, using overhead rates typically based on direct labor or machine hours. Activity-based costing is based on the notion that companies incur costs because of

RESEARCH INSIGHT **The History of ABC**

ABC came to the forefront in the 1980s and 1990s; however, it was beginning to evolve as early as the 1960s when **General Electric's** (GE) finance and accounting staff attempted to improve the usefulness of accounting information in controlling ever-increasing indirect costs. The GE staff noted that indirect costs were often the result of "upstream" decisions, such as engineering design and change orders, which were made long before the costs were actually incurred. Frequently, the engineering department was not informed of the consequences their actions had on the other parts of the organization.[2]

The second phase of the development of ABC was accomplished by business consultants, professors, and manufacturing companies during the 1970s and early 1980s. By generating more accurate cost and profitability measures for the various products offered by companies, these consultants and professors hoped to improve product cost information used in pricing and product mix decisions. ABC has since been extended to assess customer profitability.

In the late 1980s and 1990s, ABC was being promoted by many of the leading consulting firms, and it almost became a fad, much as TQM and JIT had become before it. Consequently, many companies that jumped on the ABC bandwagon early in its life, later determined that it was not for them. Most of the companies that abandoned ABC, probably adopted it initially for the wrong reasons.

Knowledge of the historical development of activity-based costing is important in order to clearly understand what ABC analysis was intended to accomplish, as well as what it was not intended to accomplish.

the activities they conduct in pursuit of their goals and objectives. For example, various activities take place to produce a particular product, such as setting up, maintaining, or monitoring the machines to make the product, physically moving raw materials and work in process, and so forth. Each of these activities has a cost; therefore, the total cost of producing a product using ABC is the sum of the direct materials and direct labor costs of that product, plus the cost of other activities conducted to produce that product.

The general two-stage ABC product cost model is illustrated in Exhibit 6.2. The first stage includes the assignment of manufacturing overhead resource costs, such as indirect labor, depreciation, and utilities, to activity cost pools for the key activities identified. Typical activity cost pools in a manufacturing environment include pools for machine setup, material movement, and engineering. The second stage assigns those activity cost pools to products.

Notice in Exhibit 6.2 that direct product costs, such as direct materials and direct labor, are directly assigned to products and are excluded from the activity cost pools. Only indirect product costs (manufacturing overhead) are assigned to products via activity cost pools.

Probably the most critical step in ABC is identifying cost drivers. The activity cost driver for a particular cost (or cost pool) is the characteristic selected for measuring the quantity of the activity for a particular period of time. For example, if an activity cost pool is established for machine setup, it is necessary to select some basis for measuring the quantity of machine setup activity associated with the costs in the pool. The quantity of setup activity could be measured by the number of different times machines are set up to produce a different product, the amount of time used in completing machine setups, the number of staff working on setups, or some other measure. It is critical that the activity measure used has a logical causal relationship to the costs in the pool and that the quantity of the activity is highly correlated with the amount of cost in the pool. Statistical methods, such as regression analysis and correlation analysis, can be very useful in selecting activity cost drivers.

Once the total cost in the activity pool and the activity cost driver have been determined, the cost per unit of activity is calculated as the total cost divided by the total amount of activity. For example, if total costs assigned to the setup activity pool in July were $100,000 and 200 setups were completed in July, the cost per setup for the month would be $500. If during July machines were set up 10 times to make product JX2, the total setup cost that would be assigned to product JX2 would be $5,000 ($500 × 10).

[2] Latshaw, Craig A. Cortese-Danile, Teresa M., Activity-based costing: usage and pitfalls," *Review of Business*, Winter, 2002

EXHIBIT 6.2 Two-Stage Activity-Based Costing Model

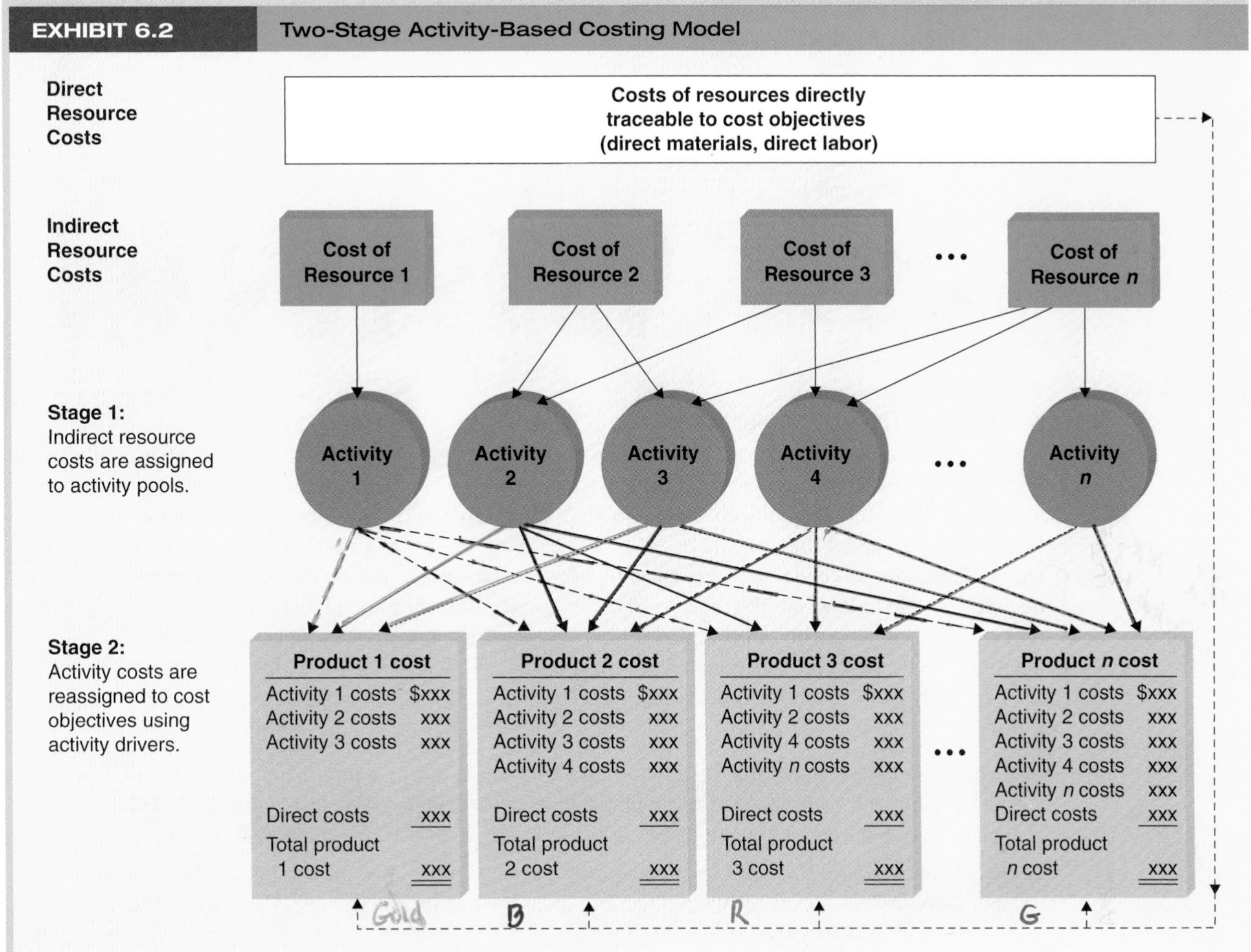

Activity-Based Costing Illustrated

Operationalizing the two-stage model requires the following:

1. Identifying activities.
2. Assigning costs to activities.
3. Determining the basis (activity cost driver) for assigning the cost of activities to cost objectives.
4. Determining the cost per unit of activity.
5. Reassigning costs from the activity to the cost objective on the basis of the cost objective's volume of consumption of activities.

Identifying Activities

To simplify the illustration of ABC concepts, the example below for Seattle Metal Crafters involves two processes: (1) inbound logistics and (2) operations in a manufacturing organization. We assume that the purpose is to determine the total cost and profitability of jobs completed. The mid-chapter review problem continues the example with the addition of activity costs for outbound logistics, marketing and sales, and service. The following example combined with the review problem illustrates the use of activity-based costing across an organization's entire internal value chain.

Seattle Metal Crafters produces custom products in response to customer job orders. Inbound logistics are handled by the Purchasing Department, whose primary activities include placing the purchase orders for raw materials used in specific jobs and receiving the raw materials. Operations are handled in the Machining and Finishing departments. The Machining Department activities include setup, performed once for each job, and conversion, which is a function of the time (work) required to complete machine operations on the job. Conversion activities are performed automatically by machines once the machines have been set up. In the Finishing Department, the metal parts are polished by hand and packed. Seattle's inbound logistics and operations activities are summarized as follows:

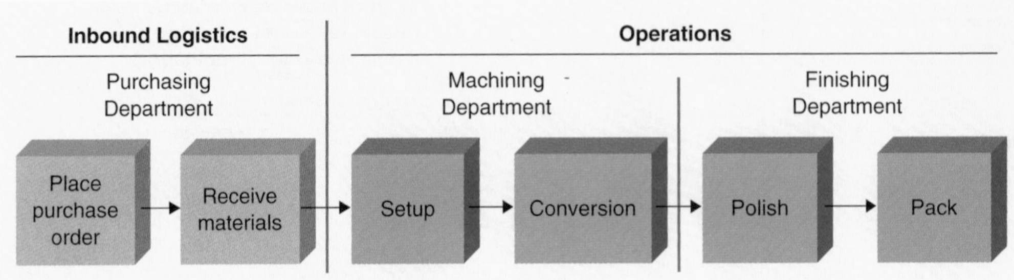

Assigning Costs to Activities

Because accounting systems are typically designed to assign costs to departments, additional analysis is required to determine the cost of activities performed in each department. The assignment of costs to activities may be based on objective data, perhaps from job descriptions or engineering time studies. Cost assignments are just as likely to be based on subjective estimates obtained from interviews and questionnaires. The costs and benefits of increasingly accurate cost assignments must be considered. Although it may be possible to have employees keep detailed logs of how they spend their time, keeping such a log is time-consuming and costly. Consequently, in assigning costs to activities, the analyst will often settle for approximately correct information.

An analysis of available records and interviews with Purchasing Department personnel reveals the following:

- The total costs of operating the Purchasing Department during a month amount to $45,000 (when the department is operating at its practical capacity of 200 purchase orders for $800,000 of direct materials). Salaries and wages of $33,000 and other costs of $12,000 are included in the $45,000.
- Three purchasing agents are involved in contacting suppliers and processing purchase orders. Each purchase order receives identical attention, regardless of its dollar value. Purchasing agents earn an average of $4,000 per month.
- Five receiving employees are involved in unloading, unpacking, and inspecting incoming goods. During interviews, the receiving employees indicated that approximately 20 percent of their time is spent verifying the specific requirements for each order and 80 percent of their time is spent on factors related to the dollar amount of each order. Receiving employees are paid $3,000 per month.
- The department supervisor indicated that his time is equally divided among each of the eight purchasing agents and receiving room employees. The supervisor is paid $6,000 per month.
- Other costs of the Purchasing Department are related to space. Ignoring the space of the supervisor's office, the purchase order-processing activity uses approximately 15 percent of the department's space, and the receiving area uses the remaining 85 percent.

Monthly costs of the Purchasing Department's two primary activities are as follows:

	Placing Purchase Orders	Receiving Materials	Total Costs
Salaries			
Purchasing agents ($4,000 × 3 agents)	$12,000		
Receiving room employees ($3,000 × 5 employees)		$15,000	
Supervisor			
($6,000 × 0.375 time with purchasing agents)	2,250		
($6,000 × 0.625 time with receiving employees)		3,750	
Other costs			
($12,000 × 0.15 purchasing space)	1,800		
($12,000 × 0.85 receiving space)		10,200	
Total	$16,050	$28,950	$45,000

Seattle's accounting system showed that the total resource costs incurred in the Purchasing Department, consisting of salaries and other costs, was $45,000. The above tabulation shows how the activities of the Department consumed these costs: the activity of placing purchase orders consumed $16,050, and the activity of receiving materials consumed $28,950.

Determining the Cost Driver for Assigning Cost of Activities to Cost Objectives

The cost driver identified for assigning activity costs to cost objectives can be determined from direct observation, from interviews, from questionnaires, from statistical analysis, and from logical analysis. Interviews with Seattle's purchasing agents reveal that the number of purchase orders is the best basis for assigning the costs of the activity *placing purchase orders*.

Interviews with receiving employees further reveal that the *receiving materials* activity has two important subactivities: (1) verifying the purchase order and (2) unloading, unpacking, and inspecting. It is determined that the number of purchase orders is the best basis for assigning the costs of the activity *verifying purchase orders* and that the dollar amount of purchase orders is the best basis for assigning the costs of the activity *unloading/unpacking/inspecting*.

Reanalyzing the Purchasing Department costs, we now have three major activities with the following activity costs:

	Placing Purchase Orders	Verifying Purchase Orders	Unloading/ Unpacking/ Inspecting	Total Costs
Salaries				
Purchasing agent ($4,000 × 3 agents)	$12,000			
Receiving room employees				
($3,000 × 5 employees × 0.20 verifying time)		$3,000		
($3,000 × 5 employees × 0.80 unloading/unpacking/inspecting time)			$12,000	
Supervisor				
($6,000 × 0.375 time with purchasing agents)	2,250			
($6,000 × 0.625 time with receiving employees × 0.20 verifying time)		750		
($6,000 × 0.625 time with receiving employees × 0.80 unloading/unpacking/inspecting time)			3,000	
Other costs*				
($12,000 × 0.15 purchasing space)	1,800			
($12,000 × 0.85 receiving space)			10,200	
Total	$16,050	$3,750	$25,200	$45,000

Because the purchase order is verified before the delivery trucks are unloaded, the space devoted to this activity is assumed to be insignificant.

The number of purchase orders processed is the cost driver used for assigning the cost of two activities, "placing purchase orders" and "verifying purchase orders." To minimize computations, when the costing purpose is to determine the cost of a product or service, some analysts recommend combining activities that have the same basis of cost assignment. However, if the purpose of the analysis is to improve the process, it is better to separately track activities and costs, even if two or more activities have the same cost driver.

Determining the Cost per Unit of Activity

After the cost of activities and the activity cost drivers have been identified, the determination of the cost per unit of cost driver is straightforward:

Cost per unit of activity cost driver = Cost of activity ÷ Units of cost driver

For Seattle Metal Fabricators, the cost per unit of activity follows:

	Placing Purchase Orders	Verifying Purchase Orders	Unloading/ Unpacking/ Inspecting
Total cost of activity	$16,050	$3,750	$ 25,200
Units of cost driver	÷ 200 orders	÷ 200 orders	÷$800,000 dollar value
Cost per unit of activity	$ 80.25 per order	$18.75 per order	0.0315 per dollar

Assigning Activity Costs to Cost Objectives

Once the cost per unit of activity is found, the activity costs are assigned to the cost objectives based on the number of units of activity performed for the cost objective. Seattle's management wishes to know the total costs of each job. The cost of direct materials is an important element of the final cost of each job. Assume that Job 102 requires two purchase orders for direct materials, in the amounts of $5,000 and $3,500, respectively.

An activity-based cost system treats these two purchases as cost objectives, assigning costs as follows:

	Purchase Order 1	Purchase Order 2	Total
Direct materials costs	$5,000.00	$3,500.00	$8,500.00
Activity costs			
Placing purchase order	80.25	80.25	160.50
Verifying purchase order	18.75	18.75	37.50
Unloading/unpacking/inspecting			
($5,000 × 0.0315)	157.50		
($3,500 × 0.0315)		110.25	267.75
Total	256.50	209.25	465.75
Total costs assigned to cost objective	$5,256.50	$3,709.25	$8,965.75

The relationships between the Purchasing Department, the three activities performed in the department, and the purchase orders are illustrated below.

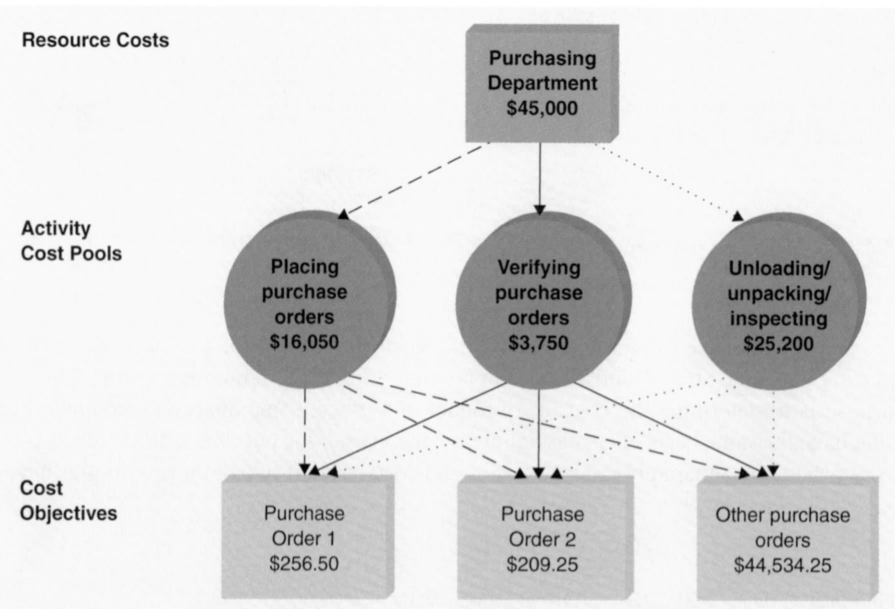

Continuing with the Seattle Metal Crafters example, assume that procedures similar to those discussed for the Purchasing Department activities were used to determine the following activity costs in the Machining and Finishing departments:

Machining Department	
Setup	$250 per job
Conversion	100 per machine hour
Finishing Department	
Polish	50 per labor hour
Pack	5 per kilogram

If Job 102 requires 35 machine hours in the Machining Department and 20 labor hours in the Finishing Department and has a final weight of 450 kilograms, the costs assigned to this cost objective for operations processes total $7,000 as follows.

Activity costs	Job 102
Machining Department	
Setup	$ 250
Conversion ($100 × 35 machine hours)	3,500
Finishing Department	
Polish ($50 × 20 labor hours)	1,000
Pack ($5 × 450 kilograms)	2,250
Total costs assigned to cost objective	$7,000

The relationships among the Machining and Finishing departments, the four activities performed, and Job 102 are illustrated by the following diagram:

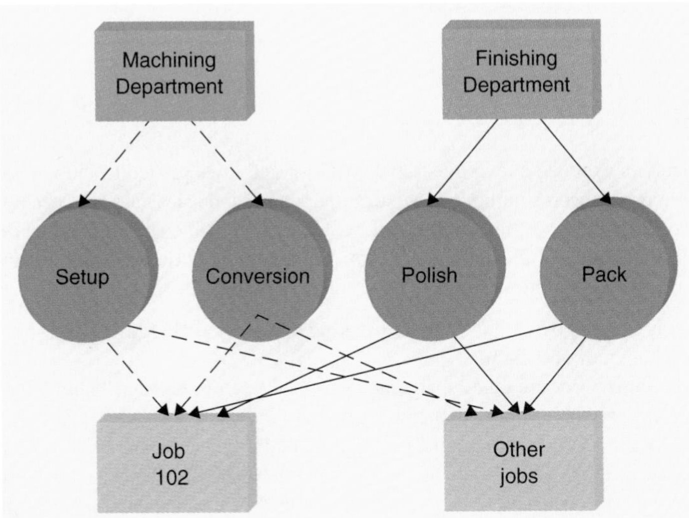

The costs assigned to Job 102 through the end of inbound logistics and operations total $15,965.75.

Direct materials		
Order 1	$5,000.00	
Order 2	3,500.00	$ 8,500.00
Inbound logistics		
Placing purchase order	160.50	
Verifying purchase order	37.50	
Unloading/unpacking/inspecting	267.75	465.75
Operations		
Setup	250.00	
Conversion	3,500.00	
Polish	1,000.00	
Pack	2,250.00	7,000.00
Total costs assigned to Job 102		$15,965.75

The Seattle Metal Crafters illustration is a classic example of ABC in a manufacturing environment. Although the early examples of ABC were all manufacturing related, it has since been applied successfully to service, not-for-profit, and governmental organizations. Any organization that incurs costs to produce desired outputs is potentially a candidate for ABC. The Business Insight box that follows, as well as many of the assignments at the end of this chapter, deal with ABC in a non-manufacturing setting.

BUSINESS INSIGHT **Blue Cross and Blue Shield of Florida Ensures Adequate Product Pricing with Activity-Based Management**

One of the leading ABC consulting and systems firms in the world is SAS, which provides services across all industries. One of their clients, Blue Cross and Blue Shield of Florida, offered the following views on their experience with ABC.[3]

"In the mid-1990s, we knew we must understand the cost of our products to help us determine pricing as well as analyze profitability," explains Lee Boardman, Director of Accounting for Blue Cross and Blue Shield of Florida's Diversified Business Sector. "We also wanted to gain efficiencies and, in general, get a better handle on our costs. With ABC, we're accomplishing that."

The Diversified Business Sector offers ancillary products that complement health insurance—such as life insurance, disability insurance, dental insurance, workers' compensation and long-term care. Some are sold at fixed prices, although benefits may be paid far beyond the date sold. Consequently, having access to precise cost information is crucial to ensuring that products are priced accurately.

"Our challenge was to maintain product profitability and support effective product management in a highly competitive market," he explains. "Therefore, we needed a good understanding of the activity cost of providing our products and services."

MID-CHAPTER REVIEW

The Seattle Metal Crafters example above illustrated ABC for activities related to inbound logistics and operations. This review problem concerns outbound logistics, marketing and sales, and service. When combined with the previous example, we have completed an illustration of activity-based costing across an organization's entire internal value chain. An analysis of the activities, costs, and measures of activity cost drivers for each of these processes provided the following information:

- Outbound logistics is handled by an independent trucking service that charges $10 per pickup, $10 per delivery, and $0.50 per kilogram of weight.
- Marketing and sales employees are paid an annual salary and no commission. Their primary activities relate to maintaining customer relationships, assisting customers in developing specifications and taking orders, and providing subsequent service. The annual costs of maintaining a customer are $1,000 per customer. Each visit to develop specifications, take an order, or provide subsequent service costs an average of $175.
- Seattle Metal Crafters does not have a separate service staff. Marketing and sales employees perform all service activities.

Job 102 was produced in response to an order from Orleans Company. Developing the order specifications and taking the order for Job 102 required three site visits to Orleans' headquarters. The order contains parts for delivery to two separate facilities operated by Orleans. Subsequent to delivery, Seattle representatives made one visit to an Orleans facility to offer technical advice. The final selling price of Job 102 was $20,000.

Required

a. Using appropriate measures of activity, assign all remaining activity costs that can be specifically identified with Job 102.

b. Identify any costs that are not specifically related to Job 102.

c. Determine the profitability of Job 102 by developing a statement that shows sales revenue and summarizes costs in each of five generic processes.

[3] http://www.sas.com/success/bcbsfla_abm.html

d. Assuming Job 102 is the only order received this year from the Orleans Company, determine the current-year profitability of the relationship with the Orleans Company.

Solution to Review Problem

a.

Additional costs of Job 102:		
Outbound logistics		
Pickup ($10 × 1 pickup)	$ 10.00	
Deliveries ($10 × 2 deliveries)	20.00	
Weight ($0.50 × 450 kilograms)	225.00	$255.00
Marketing and sales		
Site visit ($175 × 3 visits)		525.00
Service		
Site visit ($175 × 1 visit)		175.00
Total remaining costs assigned to Job 102		$955.00

b. The annual costs of maintaining customer relations are not specifically driven by Job 102.

c.

Profitability of Job 102:		
Selling price		$20,000.00
Costs		
Direct materials	$8,500.00	
Inbound logistics	465.75	
Operations	7,000.00	
Outbound logistics	255.00	
Marketing and sales	525.00	
Service	175.00	(16,920.75)
Profit		$ 3,079.25

d.

Profitability of relationship with Orleans Company:	
Profit on Job 102	$3,079.25
Annual costs to maintain customer	(1,000.00)
Profitability of customer	$2,079.25

TRADITIONAL PRODUCT COSTING AND ABC COMPARED

LO3 Explain the difference between traditional plantwide and departmental overhead methods and ABC.

Recall that Outdoor Rainwear in Chapter 5 recognized manufacturing overhead using a plantwide manufacturing overhead rate of $4 per direct labor hour. It was assumed that each hour of labor worked on product caused $4 of manufacturing overhead to be incurred. In that case, all manufacturing costs were assumed to be driven by one factor, direct labor hours. As discussed at the beginning of this chapter, such an assumption is often not appropriate with modern methods of producing goods (or services) where manufacturing overhead is related to a diverse set of activities and cost drivers.

Applying Overhead with a Plantwide Rate

To illustrate, assume that VitaDrink, Inc. produces two beverages fortified with vitamins and minerals, VitaVeg and VitaFruit. VitaDrink has been facing intense competition from other health beverage producers in the vegetable drink market, and it is considering shifting its strategy entirely to the fruit drink market.

Each product is worked on in two departments, Mixing and Bottling. Both Mixing and Bottling operations are highly automated; therefore, the most common element of both products is machine hours in both Mixing and Bottling. The products are produced in large 1,000-gallon batches. VitaVeg requires 3 machine hours per batch and VitaFruit requires 2 machine hours per batch. For July, a total of 232 batches of VitaVeg and VitaFruit were produced, with total manufacturing overhead of $187,000 and 1,496 total machine hours, or $125 per machine hour. Assigning $125 to each machine hour used is the simplest method of assigning manufacturing overhead to the products and, as the tabulation below shows, results in a total cost per batch of $610 for VitaVeg and $400 for VitaFruit after adding the direct materials and direct labor costs.

	Unit Costs	
	VitaVeg	VitaFruit
Direct materials	$125	$120
Direct labor	110	30
Manufacturing overhead		
Vegetable: 3 machine hours × $125	375	
Fruit: 2 machine hours × $125		250
Total unit cost	$610	$400

A plantwide overhead allocation method is often used in situations where companies produce only one product in a plant, or where multiple products are very similar in regard to the use of activities, such as machine or labor hours, that drive most of the overhead costs. If multiple products are produced that consume varying levels of activities in multiple production departments, departmental overhead allocation rates will produce a more accurate allocation of overhead costs to the various products.

Applying Overhead with Department Rates

For VitaDrink to establish overhead allocation rates for the two production departments, it is necessary first to assign the $187,000 of total overhead costs for the plant to the two production departments, some of which is directly assignable to the departments. For example, the departmental supervisors' salaries could be directly assignable to the departments. Other manufacturing overhead costs, such as support costs for maintenance, payroll, and so forth, are allocated to the production departments. After these allocations, the total costs assigned to the departments were $59,100 for Mixing and $127,900 for Bottling.

The next step in the product costing process is to assign the departmental costs to the products. Assume that the manufacturing process at VitaDrink is labor intensive in Mixing and machine intensive in Bottling and that manufacturing overhead is applied to products as follows:

Department	Manufacturing Overhead Application Base
Mixing	Direct labor hours
Bottling	Machine hours

During the month of July, 500 direct labor hours were worked in Mixing, and Bottling used 800 machine hours. The department manufacturing overhead rates based on actual costs for July, and the total product costs using departmental overhead rates, are calculated in the following tables:

Overhead costs per unit for July	VitaVeg	VitaFruit
Total department manufacturing overhead (direct department costs plus allocated costs)	$59,100	$127,900
Quantity of overhead application base		
Direct labor hours	÷ 500	
Machine hours		÷ 800
Department manufacturing overhead rates	$118.20	$159.875
	Per direct labor hour	Per machine hour

Total costs per unit for July using department rates	Unit Costs per Batch	
	VitaVeg	**VitaFruit**
Direct materials	$125	$120
Direct labor	110	30
Manufacturing overhead		
Mixing: 1 labor hr. × $118.20	118*	
0.67 labor hrs. × $118.20		79*
Bottling: 1 machine hr. × $159.875	160*	
1.42 machine hrs. × $159.875		227*
Total costs	$513	$456

*Rounded

Allocating factory overhead costs based on department rates (rather than on a plantwide rate of $125 per machine hour) causes a shift in costs from VitaVeg to VitaFruit because VitaVeg's overhead activity is incurred evenly in both Mixing and Bottling (1.00 hour each) while VitaFruit incurs more of its overhead activity in Bottling (1.42 hours versus 0.67 hour).

The per-unit costs with multiple allocations are substantially different from the per-unit costs when using plantwide rates and, in fact, show the cost of VitaVeg to be slightly below a competitor's bid of $525 that was offered to one of VitaDrink's customers. Based on the plantwide rate, the cost of $610 for VitaVeg was higher than the competitor's price.

By creating separate manufacturing overhead cost allocation pools, allocation bases, and overhead application rates for Mixing and Bottling, it is possible to recognize overhead cost differences in various products based on differences in Mixing Department labor hours used and Bottling Department machine hours used for each product. In most multiproduct manufacturing environments, this approach represents a cost system improvement over using a single, plantwide overhead rate, and it reduces the likelihood of cost cross-subsidization, which occurs when one product is assigned too much cost as a result of another being assigned too little cost. While department overhead rates may improve product costing results for many organizations, and in fact may be satisfactory, this method does not attempt to reflect the actual activities used in producing the different product.

Applying Overhead with Activity-Based Costing

An even more precise method of measuring the cost of products than plantwide or departmental rates is the activity-based costing method. As stated earlier, activity-based costing involves determining the cost of activities associated with a particular cost objective. ABC for product costing identifies and measures the cost of activities used to produce the various products and sums the cost of those activities to determine the cost of the products.

For VitaDrink, Mixing and Bottling have overhead costs of $59,100 and $127,900, respectively. The overhead rates for each department were determined in the last section as $118.20 and $159.875, respectively, per relevant hour of use. The easiest way to assign these costs to products is by using one base and one rate for all products going through a given process (e.g., mixing). However, different products typically use different amounts of resources from a given process and using the same base and overhead rate for all may distort the cost for some or all products.

Overhead costs in the Mixing and Bottling departments consisted of two types of costs: direct department costs and allocated costs from other support departments. Direct department overhead costs are costs that are incurred directly by the department such indirect labor, indirect materials, depreciation on equipment, supervisory wages, and so forth. Allocated support costs are costs allocated from other departments (specifically, engineering, support services, and building and grounds) that provide services to both Mixing and Bottling. VitaDrink's accountants determined that the *direct* department overhead costs in Mixing were driven primarily by labor hours, whereas *direct* department overhead costs in Bottling were driven primarily by machine hours. It was also determined that each component of engineering, support services, and building and grounds represents a separate activity cost pool and that these costs should be assigned to the products based on specific cost drivers.

The following is a detailed analysis of overhead cost data for July's operations:

Overhead Activity	Total Activity Cost	Activity Cost Driver (number of)	Quantity of Activity	Unit Activity Rates
Direct departmental overhead costs				
Mixing	$ 40,000	Labor hours	500	$ 80.00
Bottling	90,000	Machine hours	800	112.50
Common overhead costs				
Support Services				
Receiving	14,000	Purchase orders	100	140.00
Inventory control	13,000	Units produced	632	20.57*
Engineering Resources				
Production setup	12,000	Production runs	20	600.00
Engineering and testing	8,000	Machine hours	800	10.00
Building and Grounds				
Maintenance, machines	4,000	Machine hours	800	5.00
Depreciation, machines	6,000	Units produced	632	9.49*
Total	$187,000			

*Rounded

The amounts of activity attributed to VitaVeg and VitaFruit and the factory overhead cost per unit based on ABC costs are as follows:

	VitaVeg		VitaFruit	
Activity (cost per unit of driver activity)	Quantity of Activity	Cost of Activity	Quantity of Activity	Cost of Activity
Mixing ($80.00 per labor hour)	232	$18,560	268	$ 21,440
Bottling ($112.50 per machine hour)	174	19,575	626	70,425
Receiving ($140.00 per order)	40	5,600	60	8,400
Inventory control ($20.57 per unit produced)	232	4,772*	400	8,228
Production setup ($600.00 per run)	5	3,000	15	9,000
Engineering and testing ($10.00 per machine hour)	174	1,740	626	6,260
Maintenance, machines ($5.00 per machine hour)	174	870	626	3,130
Depreciation, machines ($9.49 per unit produced)	232	2,202*	400	3,796
Total factory overhead product cost		$56,319		$130,679
Units produced		÷ 232		÷ 400
Factory overhead cost per unit of product*		$ 243*		$327*
Direct materials cost per unit of product		125		120
Direct labor cost per unit of product		110		30
Total unit product cost using ABC		$ 478		$ 477

*Rounded

ABC costing of VitaDrink's products presents a very different cost picture from plantwide or departmental costing. The following table summarizes the total product costs for VitaDrink's two products using the three different overhead cost assignment methods:

	VitaVeg	VitaFruit
Plantwide overhead rate.	$610	$400
Departmental overhead rates.	513	456
ABC	478	477

ABC product costing reveals a dramatically different cost picture. Using either a plantwide overhead rate or departmental rates, the VitaVeg drink is bearing more than its share of total overhead costs. Using either of these methods could lead the company into the very damaging strategy of abandoning the vegetable drink market. With an actual per-batch cost of $478, rather than $513 or $610, the company clearly has significant latitude to compete on price with other companies in this market and remain profitable. Obviously, the effect of adopting ABC is not always as significant as it was for VitaDrink in this example. However, even with less dramatic differences among the various cost methods, inaccurate costing can affect management's assessment of product profitability and its decisions regarding which products to continue to produce and which products to discontinue. Flawed product costing information can cause management mistakenly to decide to keep products that are losing money, while discontinuing products that are profitable. Using a plantwide overhead allocation method could have led VitaDrink Management to shift its emphasis from the vegetable to the fruit drink market, a decision that could have been devastating to the company.

MANAGERIAL DECISION **You are the Controller**

You have heard about companies that have adopted ABC and experienced significant differences in product costs compared with previous cost calculations using traditional costing methods. Consequently, you were surprised when your newly implemented ABC system provided product costs that were almost identical to those from the old costing system. You are, therefore, thinking about abandoning the ABC system, since it is quite costly to maintain. Should you abandon your ABC system?
[Answer, p. 199]

Limitations of ABC Illustration

Several limitations of the VitaDrink illustration should be mentioned. For the sake of simplicity, the example was limited to manufacturing cost considerations. A complete analysis would also require considerations of nonmanufacturing costs, such as marketing, distribution, and customer service, before a final determination of product profitability could be made. Finally, in calculating the activity cost per unit of activity, it is necessary to decide how to measure the total quantity of activity. For example, for VitaDrink, the receiving cost per purchase order was calculated as $140.00 based on the actual quantity of 100 purchase orders for the period. Alternatively, the receiving cost could have been calculated based on **practical capacity**, which is the maximum possible volume of activity, while allowing for normal downtime for repairs and maintenance. If the plant has a practical capacity to prepare 140 purchase orders per period, the cost per purchase order based on the practical capacity is $100 per purchase order, or $14,000 ÷ 140. Using this overhead rate in costing product, only $10,000 would have been assigned to the two products, which required only 100 purchase orders, and the remaining $4,000 for the 40 purchase orders of excess (or idle) capacity not used would be written off as an operating expense of the period as underapplied overhead. Practical capacity is generally regarded as better than actual capacity for calculating activity costs because it does not hide the cost of idle capacity within product costs, and it gives a truer cost of the activities used to produce the product.

Comparing Traditional and Activity-Based Costing

Procedurally, ABC is not a new method for assigning costs to cost objectives. Traditional costing systems have used a two-stage allocation model (similar to the ABC model) to assign costs to cost pools (such as departments) and subsequently assign those cost pools to products using an allocation base. In most traditional costing systems, overhead is assigned to one or more cost pools based on departments and functional characteristics (such as labor-related, machine-related, and space-related costs) and then reassigned to products using a general allocation base such as direct labor hours or machine hours. ABC is different in that it divides the overall manufacturing processes into activities. ABC accumulates costs in cost pools for the major activities and then assigns the costs of these activities to products or other cost objectives that benefit from these activities. *Conceptually,* ABC is different because of the way it views the operations of the company; *procedurally,* it uses a methodology that has been around for a long time.

The challenge in using ABC is specifying the model; that is, determining how many activity pools should be established for a given cost measurement purpose, which costs should be assigned to each activity pool, and the appropriate activity driver for each pool. Specifying the model also includes determining the resource cost drivers for assigning indirect resource costs to the various activity cost pools.

ABC IMPLEMENTATION ISSUES

LO4 Describe the implementation of an activity-based costing system.

The distortion in product costs for VitaDrink from using traditional cost systems based on plantwide or departmental rates, while hypothetical, is not uncommon. Studies have shown that distortions of this type occur regularly in traditional systems in which a significant variation exists in the volume and complexity of products and services produced.[4] Traditional systems tend to overcost high-volume, low-complexity products, and they tend to undercost low-volume, high-complexity products. These studies indicate that the typical amount of overcosting is up to 200 percent for high-volume products with low complexity and that the typical undercosting can be more than 1,000 percent for low-volume, highly complex products. In companies with a large number of different products, traditional costing can show that most products are profitable. After changing to ABC, however, these companies might find that 10 to 15 percent of the products are profitable while the remainder are unprofitable. Adopting ABC often leads to increased profits merely by changing the product mix to minimize the number of unprofitable products.

Most companies initially do not abandon their traditional cost system and move to a system that uses ABC for management and financial reporting purposes because financial statements must withstand the scrutiny of auditors and tax authorities. This scrutiny typically implies more demands on the cost accounting system for consistency, objectivity, and uniformity than required when the system is used only for management purposes. In addition, ABC systems must be built facility by facility rather than being embedded in a software program that can be used by all facilities within the company.[5] Often companies maintain traditional costing for external reporting purposes and ABC for pricing and other internal decision-making purposes.

Once an ABC system has been developed for a production facility, including an activities list (sometimes called an activities dictionary), identification of activity cost drivers, and calculation of cost per unit of driver activity, the activity costs of a current or proposed product can be readily determined. In ABC, as illustrated for VitaDrink, manufacturing a product is viewed simply as the combination of activities selected to make it; therefore, the activity cost of a product or service is the sum of the costs of those activities. This approach to viewing a product enables management to evaluate the importance of each of the activities consumed in making a product. Possibly some activities can be eliminated or a lower cost activity substituted for a more costly one without reducing the quality or performance of the product. The Coca-Cola Company used ABC to determine that it was less costly—and thus, more profitable—to deliver soft drink concentrate to some fountain drink retailers (such as fast-food restaurants) in nonreturnable, disposable containers rather than in returnable stainless steel containers, which had been standard in the industry for many years.

Although an ABC system may be complex, it merely mirrors the complexity of an organization's design, manufacturing, and distribution systems. If a firm's products are diverse and its production and distribution procedures complex, the ABC system will also be complex; however, if its products are homogeneous and its production environment relatively simple, its ABC system should also be relatively simple. Even in highly complex manufacturing environments, ABC systems usually have no more than 10 to 20 cost pools. Many ABC experts in practice have observed that creating a large number of activity cost pools for a given costing application normally does not significantly improve cost accuracy above that of a smaller number of cost pools. As with any information system design, the costs of developing and maintaining the system must not exceed its benefits; hence, although adding more activity cost pools may result in some small amount of increased accuracy, it may be so small as not to be cost effective.

---

[4] Gary Cokins, Alan Stratton, and Jack Helbling, An ABC Manager's Primer (Montvale, NJ: Institute of Management Accountants, 1993).

[5] Robert S. Kaplan and Robin Cooper, *Cost and Effect* (Boston: Harvard Business School Press, 1998), p. 105.

ABC is not just a product costing system used to provide data for external financial reports. If that were its only use, its cost of implementation would seldom be justifiable. ABC's primary benefit is that it provides more accurate cost data for internal decision-making purposes. Companies that sell virtually everything they produce obviously have little or no inventories. Consequently, they do not need a product costing system for external reporting purposes because all manufacturing costs are expensed as cost of goods sold each period. However, even these companies need a good cost system for evaluating product profitability, tracking changes in costs over time, and benchmarking against their competitors.

In addition to using ABC for product costing purposes, other important uses for ABC have also been found. One of the most useful applications for ABC is in evaluating customer costs and distribution channel costs. Other applications include costing administrative functions such as processing accounts receivable or accounts payable; costing the process of hiring and training employees; and costing such menial tasks as processing a letter or copying a document. Any process, function, or activity performed in an organization, whether it is related to production, marketing and sales, finance and accounting, human resources, or even research and development, is a candidate for ABC analysis. In short, almost any cost objective that has more than an insignificant amount of indirect costs can be more effectively measured using ABC.

ABC AND CUSTOMER PROFITABILITY ANALYSIS

LO5 Explain customer profitability analysis based on ABC.

One of the most beneficial applications of activity-based costing is in the analysis of the profitability of customers. Companies that have a large number of diverse customers also usually have widely varied profits from serving those customers. Many companies never attempt to calculate the profit earned from individual customers. They merely assume that if they are selling products above their costs, and that overall the company is earning a profit, then each of the customers must be profitable. Unfortunately, the cost incurred to sell goods and services, and to provide service, to individual customers is not usually proportionate with the gross profits generated by those sales. Customers with high sales volume are not necessarily the most profitable. Profitability of individual customers depends on whether the gross profits from sales to those customers exceed the customer-specific costs of serving those customers. Some customers are simply more costly than others, and some may even be unprofitable, and the unprofitable customers are eating away at the total profits of the company. In an ideal world, only profitable customers would be retained, and unprofitable customers would be either converted to a profitable status or they would be dropped as customers.

Customer Profitability Profile

If a company knows the amount of profits (or losses) generated by each of its customers, a customer profitability profile can be prepared similar to the one illustrated in Exhibit 6.3.

EXHIBIT 6.3 Customer Profitability Profile Graph

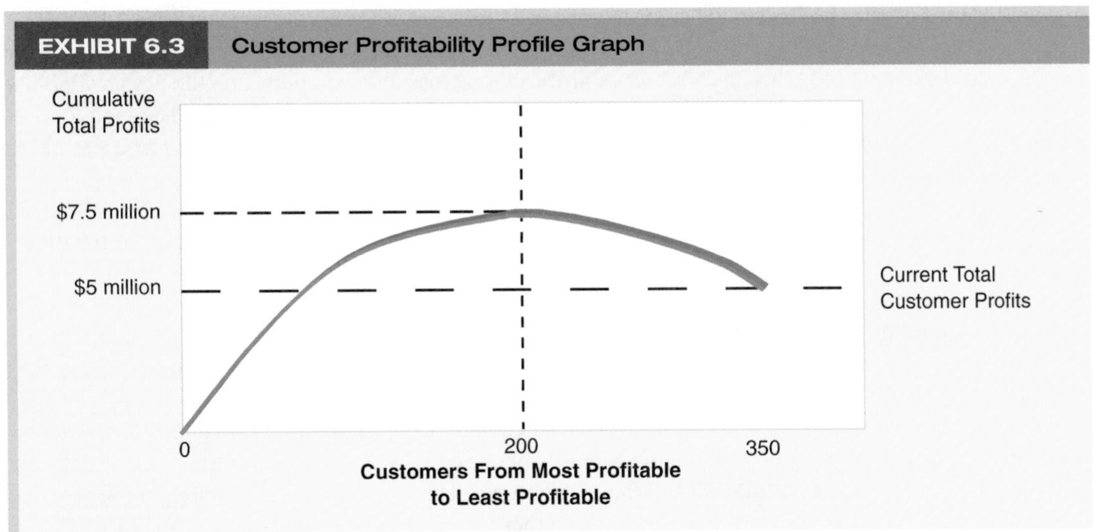

This hypothetical company has 350 customers and has current total profits of $5 million, but only 200 of its customers are profitable. Cumulative profits reach $7.5 million when the 200th customer is added to the graph, but the 201st through the 350th customers cause cumulative profits to decline to $5 million because they are unprofitable. Once a company has profitability data on each of its customers (or categories of customers), only then can it proceed to try to convert them to profitability, or seek to terminate the relationship with those customers. Just as we saw that ABC provided a model for producing more accurate product cost data, ABC is also a valuable tool for generating customer profitability data.

ABC Customer Profitability Analysis Illustrated

Pure Water Company is a "green" company located in the Midwest that manufactures and sells all-natural compounds for purifying water distributed through large public water systems. Rod James, the CEO and founder of Pure Water, personally developed the compounds using natural materials obtained from remote regions of the world. He knows that he has a product that is far superior to the traditional processes based on synthetic chemicals that have been used for generations to purify water. After five years in business, Pure Water has built a solid and growing customer base, but it has to invest significant time and expense servicing customers, especially those who have recently embraced its approach to water purification. Some customers require a lot of "hand-holding" with frequent visits and telephone calls, and they tend to purchase frequently in small amounts, often requiring repackaging. Other customers require little attention and support, and many of them purchase in large amounts once a year.

Although the company is making money, there is concern that profits could be higher if sales and other customer-related costs could be decreased. Pure Water's accountant, Mary West, has decided to conduct a customer profitability analysis using activity-based costing. As a first step, she determined that there were five primary activities related to serving customers: visits of customers by sales representatives, remote contacts (phone, email, fax), processing and shipping of customer orders, repackaging, and billing and collection. After extensive analysis, including numerous interviews and statistical analyses of activity and cost data, Mary determined the following cost drivers and cost per unit of activity for the five customer-related activities:

Activity	Activity Cost Driver	Cost per Unit of Driver Activity
Visits to customers	Visits	$800
Remote contacts	Number of contacts	75
Processing & shipping	Customer orders	450
Repackaging	Number of requests	250
Billing & Collection	Invoices	90

After collecting activity driver data on each of these activities for its major customers, the accounting group prepared the customer activity cost and profitability analysis presented in Exhibit 6.4 for its five largest customers (in terms of sales dollars) in the order of greatest to least profit for the most recent year.

Since Pure Water is selling only one product to all of its customers, and has the same pricing policy for all customers, there is a constant 40% gross profit ratio across all customers, and the net profitability of these customers is 11.6% of sales. However, all customers are not equally profitable. The high level of support required by Manhattan and Great Lakes resulted in a net customer loss from sales to Great Lakes and only a 6.8% customer profitability ratio for Manhattan.

Armed with the information in the customer activity cost and profitability analysis, Pure Water can take proactive steps to increase its overall profitability ratio. An obvious option would be to try to terminate its relationship with Great Lakes since the company is clearly losing money on that customer. If Great Lakes were terminated as a customer, and assuming that all of the activity costs associated with Great Lakes could be avoided by the termination, Pure Water's total sales would drop to $68,750, but its total profit would increase to $11,785, resulting in a profitability ratio on the remaining four customers of 17.1%.

A more proactive approach would be to work with Great Lakes and Manhattan that have high support requirements, such as repackaging, frequent visits, and phone contacts to try to lower the level of high-cost support activities without reducing sales to those customers. This could result in maintaining the current level of gross profit, but generating a significantly higher level of total net customer profitability.

EXHIBIT 6.4 Pure Water Company

Customer Activity Cost and Profitability Analysis	Seattle Water District	Manhattan Water Authority	Great Lakes Utility	Gulf Coast Utilities	Consolidated Water, Inc.	Total
Customer Activity Cost Analysis:						
Activity Cost Driver Data						
Visits to customers	3	5	4	1	1	
Remote contacts	5	7	8	2	3	
Processing & shipping	3	3	5	4	1	
Repackaging	0	2	3	0	0	
Billing & Collection	3	3	5	4	1	
Customer Activity Cost						
Visits to customers	$ 2,400	$ 4,000	$ 3,200	$ 800	$ 800	
Remote contacts	375	525	600	150	225	
Processing & shipping	1,350	1,350	2,250	1,800	450	
Repackaging	0	500	750	0	0	
Billing & Collection	270	270	450	360	90	
Total Activity Cost	$ 4,395	$ 6,645	$ 7,250	$ 3,110	$ 1,565	
Customer Profitability Analysis:						
Customer sales	$17,500	$20,000	$12,000	$15,000	$16,250	$80,750
Less cost of goods sold	10,500	12,000	7,200	9,000	9,750	48,450
Gross profit on sales	7,000	8,000	4,800	6,000	6,500	32,300
Less activity costs	4,395	6,645	7,250	3,110	1,565	22,965
Customer profitability	$ 2,605	$ 1,355	$ (2,450)	$2,890	$4,935	$ 9,335
Customer profitability ratio*	14.9%	6.8%	(20.4%)	19.3%	30.4%	11.6%

*Customer profitability ÷ Sales

Two caveats should be considered when using activity cost data to manage customer profitability. First, there may be justifiable reasons (such as having a new customer that requires a high level of early-stage support, trying to penetrate a new geographic market, or existing relationships with other more profitable customers) for keeping customers that have lower profitability, or even customers that are not profitable. If so, these customers should be managed intensely to attempt to reduce the activities devoted to their support. Another caveat is that eliminating a customer may not immediately translate into an immediate reduction of activity costs. Some activity costs may not have a variable cost behavior pattern, and eliminating customers may merely create excess capacity in the short term. Of course, as stated previously, activity-based costing views virtually all costs as variable in the longer term. As the following Business Insight box illustrates, despite these limitations, activity analysis of customer profitability analysis provides managers with valuable insights into the differences among customers that may otherwise not be apparent, and which can be used to enhance the overall performance of the organization.

ACTIVITY-BASED MANAGEMENT

LO6 Explain the difference between ABC and activity-based management.

Activity-based costing has been highly touted as a technique for improving the measurement of the cost and profitability of products, customers, and other cost objectives. In the early development of ABC, it was discovered that a by-product of accurately measuring the cost of cost objectives using ABC is that management invariably gains a much better understanding of the processes and activities that are used to create those cost objectives. Although ABC could be justified on the basis of its value as a tool in helping produce more accurate cost measurements for various cost objectives, its greatest potential value may be in its (originally unintended) by-products. The access to ABC data enables managers to engage in **activity-based management (ABM),** defined as the identification and selection of activities to maximize the value of the activities while minimizing their cost from the perspective of the final consumer. In other words,

BUSINESS INSIGHT **Managing the Drivers of Customer Profitability**

The Chartered Institute of Management Accountants in the United Kingdom, along with the American Institute of CPAs and the Society of Management Accountants of Canada jointly published a Management Accounting Guideline titled "Customer Profitability Analysis." The following summary of that Guideline was published recently in *Financial Management.*

"The goal of business is not to improve customer or employee satisfaction at any cost, but rather to manage these relationships and the drivers of customer profitability to improve corporate performance. In order to do this, the company should identify the most and least profitable elements of its total customer base (and those in between), and manage these relationships accordingly. Customer profitability analysis (CPA) is the first stage in this process. Meeting the challenge of understanding the concept of customer profitability and conducting CPA requires a clear understanding of the causes of both revenues and costs. Strategic cost management tools such as activity-based costing (ABC) facilitate this understanding. The two models rely on the identification, measurement and understanding of the drivers and causal relationships among employee satisfaction, customer satisfaction, customer profitability and corporate profitability. Only with the specification and measurement of these relationships can the costs and revenues related to improving corporate performance be managed properly."

Source: Liz Murby, "Customer Profitability," *Financial Management,* December 2007, p. 33.

ABM is concerned with how to efficiently and effectively manage activities and processes to provide value to the final consumer.

Defining processes and identifying key activities helps management better understand the business and to evaluate whether activities being performed add value to the customer. ABM focuses managerial attention on what is most important among the activities performed to create value for customers.

A helpful analogy in understanding what ABC can do for a company is to compare a company's operations with a large retail store, such as a Home Depot store. In a Home Depot store there is a clearly marked price on each of the tens of thousands of individual items that customers may decide whether or not to purchase. Similarly, every activity that takes place in any organization has a cost that can be determined and that management can use to make a judgment about the activity's value. In an ideal world, a manager could walk through the business and evaluate the cost of every activity being performed—maybe thousands of different activities—and then decide which ones are worth the cost and which ones are not adding value. Since generating ABC data has a cost, management must decide which ABC data are likely to be useful and cost beneficial.

Reducing Non-Value-Added Activities

One way to *start* improving processes is to classify each activity as value-added or non-value-added and then determine how to minimize non-value-added activities. A **value-added activity** adds value to a product or service from the viewpoint of the customer. A **non-value-added activity** does not add value to a product or service from the viewpoint of the customer.

Because non-value-added activities take time and require the use of costly resources, both continuous improvement and process reengineering seek to minimize non-value-added activities. As noted in Exhibit 6.5, the four classic examples of non-value-added activities within a manufacturing process are movement, waiting, setup, and inspection.

EXHIBIT 6.5 **Non-Value-Added Activities in a Manufacturing Process**

- Movement—time spent for transfer between workstations where value-added activities are performed.
- Waiting—time spent between value-added activities.
- Setup—time spent preparing to perform a value-added activity.
- Inspection—time spent verifying that a value-added activity was done correctly.

The movement of product between workstations in a factory or the movement of patient records between offices in a hospital increases costs without independently adding value. The movement merely facilitates adding value after the product has been delivered to the next work station. Many manufacturing organizations are rearranging the layout of equipment to minimize product movement. The introduction of the electronic filing of tax returns has allowed the **Internal Revenue Service** to eliminate some physical movement without rearranging workstations. Likewise, many colleges use electronic registration to minimize student movement.

Setup involves preparing to do work. Gathering your book, calculator, paper, and pencil prior to starting homework is an example of setup. Fifteen minutes spent trying to locate your calculator is a non-value-added activity. Keeping your calculator in the top drawer of your desk will reduce nonproductive setup time prior to doing homework.

Inspection involves determining whether goods or services meet quality standards. If processes can be established to ensure a job is done right the first time, every time, inspection can be eliminated.

Examining non-value-added activities for possible areas of waste is a useful starting point that may yield savings in time and money. It is seldom possible to eliminate all non-value-added activities because the way value-added activities are performed may impact the need for non-value-added activities, such as inspection. However, a change in a value-added activity that enhances product quality would reduce the need for inspection. In an ideal situation with 100 percent efficiency, we would not have to set up equipment, move goods, and so forth. In reality, these tasks are necessary even if they do not directly add to customer value.

Once the easy changes have been made, attention must be turned to the more difficult task of reducing the cost of value-added activities. In manufacturing organizations, engineers with an understanding of cost management concepts typically take the lead in efforts to improve value-added activities. Engineers at **Maytag**, for example, determined that manufacturing a washing machine agitator using a gas-assisted molding process reduced the time of this value-added activity by 38 percent, cut part weight by 12 percent, and increased product quality (measured as conformance to part specifications).[6] The following Business Insight box highlights some of the the benefits of ABC and ABM to Mercy Hospital as it sought to improve capital investment decisions.

BUSINESS INSIGHT **Using ABC to Justify Capital Equipment**

Mercy Hospital in Miami implemented an activity-based costing system in the radiology and laboratory departments in order to capture the "true cost" of the procedures they perform. The old financial performance systems had failed to properly evaluate major capital equipment expenditures because they relied on standard costs that included arbitrary cost allocations. These costs failed to recognize the activities and costs that supported the actual procedures performed on the equipment, and the arbitrary allocations tended to distort the actual costs of the procedures and tests. The problem was further exacerbated by the fact that the depreciation cost was being spread across all revenue centers through a broad-based allocation formula.

Mercy Hospital selected an off-the-shelf ABC system by ExactCost because most of the activities performed in radiology were predefined in the application and required minimal customization, which reduced implementation time. The Director of Radiology Services stated that "by using the ExactCost activity-based solution, we were able to determine the "true" cost of every radiographic procedure today and on an ongoing basis."

"Having an activity-based system gave us the ability to determine which activities could be eliminated or added, and which activities would change. We were also able to determine the cost of labor and supplies for the new scanner and, more important, the actual cost of depreciation for the new equipment and the facility that would house the new equipment."

Having an integrated activity-based system has provided Mercy with an ongoing level of detail that enhances daily operations, including budget preparation, capital equipment expenditures, procedural cost containment, and enhanced services.

Source: Kevin Gregory and Paul H. Monge, "Radiology ROI Case Study: Using Activity Based Methods to Justify Capital Equipment," *Imaging Economics*, December 1, 2007.

[6] Joseph Ogando, "Gas-Assisted Molding Proves Its Worth," *Plastics Technology*, July 1997, p. 29.

The ABC/ABM Cross

The following graphic illustrates two ways to look at the components of activity-based costing: the ABC/cost assignment view and the ABM/process management view. Because it has the shape of a cross, it is referred to as the *ABC Cross*.[7] More appropriately, it could be called the ABC/ABM cross.

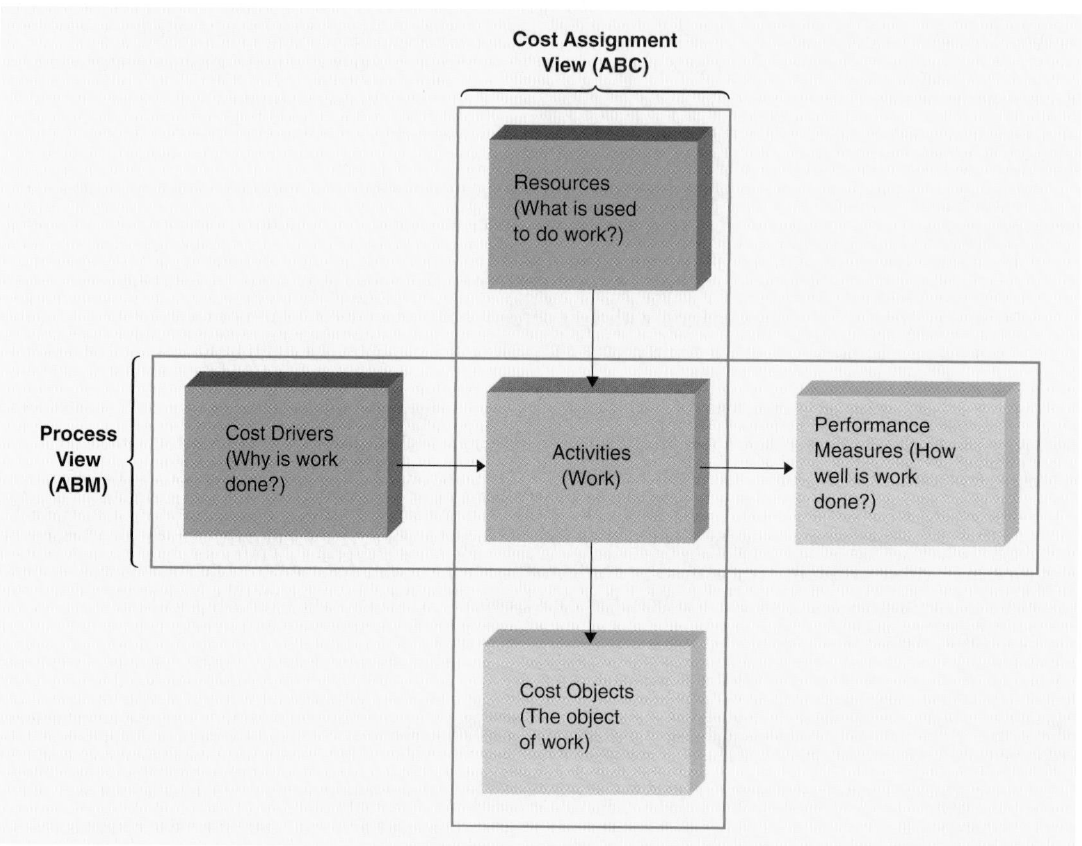

The vertical "costing" view of the ABC/ABM Cross focuses on the cost of individual activities that produce the various cost objects and how much activity cost was incurred to produce a given cost objective. The ABC view is primarily concerned with the accurate measurement of cost objectives, not with how effective or efficient the company was in producing the cost objective.

On the other hand, the horizontal "process" view of the ABC/ABM Cross analyzes and evaluates the cost of each activity as well as the individual elements of the cost of each activity. It is not enough to know that a unit of finished product cost $25 or that a machine setup used in producing a batch of product cost $400. If we believe $400 is too high a cost of a setup procedure, then we need to know what the cost components of setups are so we can decide whether to try to lower the cost or to redesign the process to produce a lower setup cost. When management knows the cost of an activity (value added or not), or better still, its detailed cost components, it can make a better informed decision on how to manage that activity. This clearly shifts the focus from the cost objects to processes and activities and how best to manage them, which is the essence of activity-based management.

Mission-Driven Processes and Activities

World-class organizations today are able to compete in the global marketplace on the dimensions of quality, cost, and service because they have a well-defined strategy aimed at achieving a higher-level organizational mission. An alternative to the value-added/non-value-added dichotomy for classifying activities

[7] The original ABC Cross concept was published in 1991 in *The CAM-I Glossary of Activity-Based Management*, edited by Norm Raffish and Peter B.B. Turney. Variations of the ABC Cross have been published in *An ABC Manager's Primer* by Gary Cokins, Alan Stratton, and Jack Helbling (Homewood, Illinois: Irwin Professional Publishing, 1993); and *Cost and Effect*, by Robert S. Kaplan and Robin Cooper (Boston: Harvard Business School Press, 1998).

is to evaluate their contribution to the achievement of the organization's mission. In this sense, mission-driven activities might be described as adding value, and non-mission-driven activities might be described as not adding value.

Activities associated with improving a company's quality programs (if its mission is to be the high-quality producer in the industry) are examples of mission-driven activities. At Maytag, for instance, the company's whole strategic image has been focused on producing the highest-quality appliances. Quality enhancement programs aimed at supporting this objective could be described as mission-driven activities.

As companies launch activity-based management programs, they usually find multiple criteria, or attributes, for evaluating their processes and activities. We have discussed two: value-added versus non-value-added and mission-driven versus non-mission driven. Other dimensions on which companies may evaluate their processes and activities include social responsibility, environmental effectiveness, total quality enhancement, and business process improvement. Identifying the activities that relate to each dimension and measuring their activity costs help management to assess how well it is performing on each of these dimensions. In addition, once activity costs have been generated for a company's key activities, these costs can be compared, or benchmarked, with comparable activity costs throughout the company, as well as with other companies, as a basis for evaluating performance.

CHAPTER-END REVIEW

Slack Corporation has the following predicted indirect costs and cost drivers for 2009 for the given activity cost pools:

	Fabrication Department	Finishing Department	Cost Driver
Maintenance	$ 20,000	$10,000	Machine hours
Materials handling	30,000	15,000	Material moves
Machine setups	70,000	5,000	Machine setups
Inspections	—	25,000	Inspection hours
	$120,000	$55,000	

The following activity predictions were also made for the year:

	Fabrication Department	Finishing Department
Machine hours	10,000	5,000
Materials moves	3,000	1,500
Machine setups	700	50
Inspection hours	—	1,000

It is assumed that the cost per unit of activity for a given activity does not vary between departments.

Slack's president, Charles Slack, is trying to evaluate the company's product mix strategy regarding two of its five product models, ZX300 and SL500. The company has been using a plantwide overhead rate based on machine hours but is considering switching to either department rates or activity-based rates. The production manager has provided the following data for the production of a batch of 100 units for each of these models:

	ZX300	SL500
Direct materials cost	$12,000	$18,000
Direct labor cost	$5,000	$4,000
Machine hours (Fabrication)	500	700
Machine hours (Finishing)	200	100
Materials moves	30	50
Machine setups	5	9
Inspection hours	30	60

Required

a. Determine the cost of one unit each of ZX300 and SL500, assuming a plantwide overhead rate is used based on total machine hours.

b. Determine the cost of one unit of ZX300 and SL500, assuming department overhead rates are used. Overhead is assigned based on machine hours in both departments.

c. Determine the cost of one unit of ZX300 and SL500, assuming activity-based overhead rates are used for maintenance, materials handling, machine setup, and inspection activities.

d. Comment on the results of these cost calculations.

Solution

a. **Plantwide overhead rate = Total manufacturing overhead ÷ Total machine hours**
= ($120,000 + $55,000) ÷ (10,000 + 5,000)
= $175,000 ÷ (15,000)
= $11.67 per machine hour

	ZX300	SL500
Product costs per unit		
Direct materials.	$12,000	$18,000
Direct labor	5,000	4,000
Manufacturing overhead		
700 machine hours × $11.67	8,169	
800 machine hours × $11.67		9,336
Total cost per batch	$25,169	$31,336
Number of units per batch	÷ 100	÷ 100
Cost per unit.	$251.69	$313.36

b. **Departmental overhead rates = Total departmental overhead ÷ Dept. allocation base**
Fabrication = $120,000 ÷ 10,000 machine hours
= $12 per machine hour
Finishing = $55,000 ÷ 5,000 machine hours
= $11 per machine hour

	ZX300	SL500
Product costs per unit		
Direct materials.	$12,000	$18,000
Direct labor	5,000	4,000
Manufacturing overhead		
Fabrication Department		
500 machine hours × $12.	6,000	
700 machine hours × $12.		8,400
Finishing Department		
200 machine hours × $11.	2,200	
100 machine hours × $11.		1,100
Total cost per batch	$25,200	$31,500
Number of units per batch	÷ 100	÷ 100
Cost per unit.	$252.00	$315.00

c. **Activity-based overhead rates = Activity cost pool ÷ Activity cost driver**
Maintenance = $30,000 ÷ 15,000 machine hours
= $2 per machine hour
Materials handling = $45,000 ÷ 4,500 materials moves
= $10 per materials move
Machine setups = $75,000 ÷ 750 setups
= $100 per machine setup
Inspections = $25,000 ÷ 1,000 inspection hours
= $25 per inspection hour

	ZX300	SL500
Product costs per unit		
Direct materials.	$12,000	$18,000
Direct labor	5,000	4,000
Manufacturing overhead		
Maintenance activity		
700 machine hours × $2.	1,400	
800 machine hours × $2.		1,600
Materials handling activity		
30 materials moves × $10.	300	
50 materials moves × $10.		500
Machine setups activity		
5 machine setups × $100.	500	
9 machine setups × $100.		900
Inspections activity		
30 inspection hours × $25	750	
60 inspection hours × $25		1,500
Total cost per batch	$19,950	$26,500
Number of units per batch	÷ 100	÷ 100
Cost per unit.	$199.50	$265.00

d. Following is a summary of product costs for ZX300 and SL500 assigning overhead costs based on a plantwide rate, department rates, and activity-based rates:

	ZX300	SL500
Plantwide rate.	$251.69	$313.36
Department rates	$252.00	$315.00
Activity rates.	$199.50	$265.00

Changing from a plantwide rate to department rates had little effect on unit costs because the department rates per machine hour are close to the plantwide rate per machine hour. Based on machine hours, both departments have similar cost structures.

When using activity rates, however, the cost of these two products drops dramatically because they use only a small portion (less than 2 percent) of the activities of setup (14 of 750) and materials moves (80 of 4,500). Neither a plantwide rate nor department rates recognize this fact, resulting in a large amount of cost cross-subsidization of other products by ZX300 and SL500 for these costs. Although this problem did not include cost analysis of the other three products, it shows that they are less profitable and that ZX300 and SL500 are much more profitable than management previously thought.

GUIDANCE ANSWER

MANAGERIAL DECISION You are the Controller

It probably is not the right decision to abandon the ABC system because there are many benefits to using ABC other than just calculating product costs. Indeed, in cases where companies produce multiple products that are fairly homogeneous in terms of the use of resources, ABC may not produce more accurate costs than traditional methods; however, there are many uses of ABC information beyond just calculating the cost of products. Having detailed information about activities and their costs can significantly improve the management of those activities. Identifying key activities and measuring their costs often causes companies to seek more efficient processes, possibly considering outsourcing activities that are currently performed internally, or even looking for ways to eliminate activities altogether. Activity cost information can also be used to identify best practices within an organization, or to benchmark internal activity costs with other organizations.

DISCUSSION QUESTIONS

Q6-1. Summarize the concepts underlying activity-based costing in two sentences.

Q6-2. What steps are required to implement the two-stage activity-based costing model?

Q6-3. Define activity cost pool, activity cost driver, and cost per unit of activity.

Q6-4. Name two possible activity cost drivers for each of the following activities: maintenance, materials movement, machine setup, inspection, materials purchases, and customer service.

Q6-5. What is the premise of activity-based costing for product costing purposes?

Q6-6. In what ways does ABC product costing differ from traditional product cost methods?

Q6-7. Explain why ABC often reveals existing product cost cross-subsidization problems.

Q6-8. How can ABC be used to improve customer profitability analysis?

Q6-9. Explain activity-based management and how it differs from activity-based costing.

Q6-10. Why should activity-based costs be based on practical capacity?

Q6-11. Explain the two perspectives illustrated by the ABC/ABM Cross.

Q6-12. Define and discuss the term *mission-driven activities.*

MINI EXERCISES

M6-13. Activities and Cost Drivers (LO2)

For each of the following activities, select the most appropriate cost driver. Each cost driver may be used only once.

Activity	Cost Driver
1. Pay vendors	*a.* Number of different kinds of raw materials
2. Evaluate vendors	*b.* Number of classes offered
3. Inspect raw materials	*c.* Number of tables
4. Plan for purchases of raw materials	*d.* Number of employees
5. Packaging	*e.* Number of operating hours
6. Supervision	*f.* Number of units of raw materials received
7. Employee training	*g.* Number of moves
8. Clean tables	*h.* Number of vendors
9. Machine maintenance	*i.* Number of checks issued
10. Move patients to and from surgery	*j.* Number of customer orders

M6-14. Developing a List of Activities for Baggage Handling at an Airport (LO2)

As part of a continuous improvement program, you have been asked to determine the activities involved in the baggage-handling process of a major airline at one of the airline's hubs. Prior to conducting observations and interviews, you decide that a list of possible activities would help you to better observe key activities and ask meaningful questions.

Required

For incoming aircraft only, develop a sequential list of baggage-handling activities. Your list should contain between 8 and 10 activities.

M6-15. Stage 1 ABC at a College: Assigning Costs to Activities (LO2)

An economics professor at State College devotes 65 percent of her time to teaching, 20 percent of her time to research and writing, and 15 percent of her time to service activities such as committee work and student advising. The professor teaches two semesters per year. During each semester, she teaches two sections of an introductory economics course (with a maximum enrollment of 70 students each) and one section of a graduate economics course (with a maximum enrollment of 30 students). Including course preparation, classroom instruction, and appointments with students, each course requires an equal amount of time. The economics professor is paid $117,000 per year.

Required

Determine the activity cost of instruction per student in both the introductory and the graduate economics courses.

M6-16. Stage 1 ABC for a Machine Shop: Assigning Costs to Activities (LO2)

As the chief engineer of a small fabrication shop, Brenda Tanner refers to herself as a "jack-of-all-trades." When an order for a new product comes in, Brenda must do the following:

1. Design the product to meet customer requirements.
2. Prepare a bill of materials (a list of materials required to produce the product).
3. Prepare an operations list (a sequential list of the steps involved in manufacturing the product).

Each time the foundry manufactures a batch of the product, Brenda must perform these activities:

1. Schedule the job.
2. Supervise the setup of machines that will work on the job.
3. Inspect the first unit produced to verify that it meets specifications.

Brenda supervises the production employees who perform the actual work on individual units of product. She is also responsible for employee training, ensuring that production facilities are in proper operating condition, and attending professional meetings. Brenda's estimates (in percent) of time spent on each of these activities last year are as follows:

Designing product	15%
Preparing bills of materials	5
Preparing operations lists	10
Scheduling jobs	18
Supervising setups	5
Inspecting first units	2
Supervising production	20
Training employees	15
Maintaining facility	7
Attending professional meetings	3
	100%

Required

Assuming Brenda Tanner's salary is $125,000 per year, determine the dollar amount of her salary assigned to unit-, batch-, product-, and facility-level activities. (You may need to review Chapter 2 before answering this question.)

M6-17. Stage 2 ABC for a Wholesale Company (LO2)

Information is presented for the activity costs of Cambridge Wholesale Company:

Activity	Cost per Unit of Activity Driver
Customer relations	$100.00 per customer per month
Selling	0.06 per sales dollar
Accounting	5.00 per order
Warehousing	0.50 per unit shipped
Packing	0.25 per unit shipped
Shipping	0.10 per pound shipped

The following information pertains to Cambridge Wholesale Company's activities in Vermont for the month of March 2009:

Number of orders	235
Sales revenue	$122,200
Cost of goods sold	$73,320
Number of customers	25
Units shipped	4,700
Pounds shipped	70,500

Required

Determine the profitability of sales in Vermont for March 2009.

M6-18. Stage 2 ABC for Manufacturing: Reassigning Costs to Cost Objectives (LO2)
Regal Products has developed the following activity cost information for its manufacturing activities:

Activity	Activity Cost
Machine setup	$60.00 per batch
Movement	15.00 per batch move
	0.10 per pound
Drilling.	3.00 per hole
Welding.	4.00 per inch
Shaping	25.00 per hour
Assembly	18.00 per hour
Inspection.	2.00 per unit

Filling an order for a batch of 50 fireplace inserts that weighed 150 pounds each required the following:

- Three batch moves
- Two sets of inspections
- Drilling five holes in each unit
- Completing 80 inches of welds on each unit
- Thirty minutes of shaping for each unit
- One hour of assembly per unit

Required
Determine the activity cost of converting the raw materials into 50 fireplace inserts.

M6-19. Two-Stage ABC for Manufacturing (LO2)
Columbus Foundry, a large manufacturer of heavy equipment components, has determined the following activity cost pools and cost driver levels for the year:

Activity Cost Pool	Activity Cost	Activity Cost Driver
Machine setup	$600,000	12,000 setup hours
Material handling	120,000	2,000 tons of materials
Machine operation	500,000	10,000 machine hours

The following data are for the production of single batches of two products, C23 Cams and U2 Shafts:

	C23 Cams	U2 Shafts
Units produced.	500	300
Machine hours	4	5
Direct labor hours.	200	400
Direct labor cost.	$5,000	$10,000
Direct materials cost.	$30,000	$20,000
Tons of materials	12.5	8
Setup hours	3	7

Required
Determine the unit costs of C23 Cams and U2 Shafts using ABC.

M6-20. Two-Stage ABC for Manufacturing (LO2)

Sherwin-Williams (SHW)

Assume Sherwin-Williams Company, a large paint manufacturer, has determined the following activity cost pools and cost driver levels for the latest period:

Activity Cost Pool	Activity Cost	Activity Cost Driver
Machine setup	$950,000	2,500 setup hours
Material handling	820,000	5,000 materials moves
Machine operation	200,000	20,000 machine hours

The following data are for the production of single batches of two products, Mirlite and Subdue:

	Mirlite	Subdue
Gallons produced.	50,000	30,000
Direct labor hours.	400	250
Machine hours	800	250
Direct labor cost.	$10,000	$7,500
Direct materials cost.	$350,000	$150,000
Setup hours	15	12
Material moves.	60	35

Required

Determine the batch and unit costs per gallon of Mirlite and Subdue using ABC.

M6-21. Customer Profitability Analysis (LO5)

Roland, Inc. provides residential painting services for three home building companies, Alpha, Beta, and Gamma, and it uses a job costing system for determining the costs for completing each job. The job cost system does not capture any cost incurred by Roland for return touchups and refinishes after the homeowner occupies the home. Roland paints each house on a square footage contract price, which includes painting as well as all refinishes and touchups required after the homes are occupied. Each year, Roland generates about one-third of its total revenues and gross profits from each of the three builders. Roland has observed that the builders, however, require substantially different levels of support following the completion of jobs. The following data have been gathered:

Support Activity	Driver	Cost per Driver Unit
Major refinishes	Hours on jobs	$ 60
Touchups	Number of visits	$100
Communication	Number of calls	$ 40

Builder	Major Refinishes	Touchups	Communication
Alpha	80	150	360
Beta	35	110	205
Gamma.	42	115	190

Required:

a. Assuming that each of the three customers produces gross profits of $100,000, calculate the profitability from each builder after taking into account the support activity required for each builder.

b. Comment on the usefulness of this type of analysis. What reasonable actions might Roland take as a result of this analysis.

EXERCISES

E6-22. Two-Stage ABC for Manufacturing (LO2)

Meridian Company has determined its activity cost pools and cost drivers to be the following:

Cost pools	
Setup	$ 56,000
Material handling	12,800
Machine operation.	240,000
Packing	60,000
Total indirect manufacturing costs.	$368,800
Cost drivers	
Setups	350
Material moves.	640
Machine hours	20,000
Packing orders.	1,200

One product made by Meridian, metal casements, used the following activities during the period to produce 500 units:

Setups	20
Material moves	80
Machine hours	1,900
Packing orders	150

Required

a. Calculate the cost per unit of activity for each activity cost pool.
b. Calculate the manufacturing overhead cost per metal casement manufactured during the period.
c. Comment on the adequacy of Meridian's costing system.

E6-23. Calculating Manufacturing Overhead Rates (LO3)
Goldratt Company, accumulated the following data for 2009:

Milling Department manufacturing overhead	$344,000
Finishing Department manufacturing overhead	$120,000
Machine hours used	
Milling Department	10,000 hours
Finishing Department	2,000 hours
Labor hours used	
Milling Department	1,000 hours
Finishing Department	1,000 hours

Required

a. Calculate the plantwide manufacturing overhead rate using machine hours as the allocation base.
b. Calculate the plantwide manufacturing overhead rate using direct labor hours as the allocation base.
c. Calculate department overhead rates using machine hours in Milling and direct labor hours in Finishing as the allocation bases.
d. Calculate department overhead rates using direct labor hours in Milling and machine hours in Finishing as the allocation bases.
e. Which of these allocation systems seems to be the most appropriate? Explain.

E6-24. Calculating Activity-Based Costing Overhead Rates (LO2, 3, 4)
Assume that manufacturing overhead for Goldratt Company in the previous exercise consisted of the following activities and costs:

Setup (1,000 setup hours)	$144,000
Production scheduling (400 batches)	60,000
Production engineering (60 change orders)	120,000
Supervision (2,000 direct labor hours)	56,000
Machine maintenance (12,000 machine hours)	84,000
Total activity costs	$464,000

The following additional data were provided for Job 845:

Direct materials costs	$7,000
Direct labor cost (5 Milling direct labor hours; 35 Finishing direct labor hours)	$1,000
Setup hours	5 hours
Production scheduling	1 batch
Machine hours used (25 Milling machine hours; 5 Finishing machine hours)	30 hours
Production engineering	3 change orders

Required

a. Calculate the cost per unit of activity driver for each activity cost category.
b. Calculate the cost of Job 845 using ABC to assign the overhead costs.
c. Calculate the cost of Job 845 using the plantwide overhead rate based on machine hours calculated in the previous exercise.
d. Calculate the cost of Job 845 using the departmental overhead rates calculated in the previous exercise.
e. What additional cost data will management need for Job 845 to adequately evaluate its price and profitability?

E6-25. Activity-Based Costing and Conventional Costs Compared (LO2, 3, 4)
Chef Grill Company manufactures two types of cooking grills: the Gas Cooker and the Charcoal Smoker. The Cooker is a premium product sold in upscale outdoor shops; the Smoker is sold in major discount stores. Following is information pertaining to the manufacturing costs for the current month.

	Gas Cooker	Charcoal Smoker
Units	1,000	5,000
Number of batches	50	10
Number of batch moves	80	20
Direct materials	$40,000	$100,000
Direct labor	$20,000	$25,000

Manufacturing overhead follows:

Activity	Cost	Cost Driver
Materials acquisition and inspection	$30,800	Amount of direct materials cost
Materials movement	16,200	Number of batch moves
Scheduling	36,000	Number of batches
	$83,000	

Required

a. Determine the total and per-unit costs of manufacturing the Gas Cooker and Charcoal Smoker for the month, assuming all manufacturing overhead is assigned on the basis of direct labor dollars.
b. Determine the total and per-unit costs of manufacturing the Gas Cooker and Charcoal Smoker for the month, assuming manufacturing overhead is assigned using activity-based costing.
c. Comment on the differences between the solutions to requirements (a) and (b). Which is more accurate? What errors might managers make if all manufacturing overhead costs are assigned on the basis of direct labor dollars?
d. Comment on the adequacy of the preceding data to meet management's needs.

E6-26. Traditional Product Costing versus Activity-Based Costing (LO2, 3, 4)
Assume that Panasonic Company has determined its estimated total manufacturing overhead cost for one of its plants to be $198,000, consisting of the following activity cost pools for the current month: Panasonic Company

Activity Centers	Activity Costs	Cost Drivers	Activity Level
Assembly setups	$ 45,000	Setup hours	1,500
Materials handling	15,000	Number of moves	300
Assembly	120,000	Assembly hours	12,000
Maintenance	18,000	Maintenance hours	1,200
Total	$198,000		

Total direct labor hours used during the month were 8,000. Panasonic produces many different electronic products, including the following two products produced during the current month:

	Model X301	Model Z205
Units produced	1,000	1,000
Direct materials costs	$15,000	$15,000
Direct labor costs	$12,500	$12,500
Direct labor hours	500	500
Setup hours	50	100
Materials moves	25	50
Assembly hours	800	800
Maintenance hours	10	40

Required

a. Calculate the total per-unit cost of each model using direct labor hours to assign manufacturing overhead to products.

b. Calculate the total per-unit cost of each model using activity-based costing to assign manufacturing overhead to products.

c. Comment on the accuracy of the two methods for determining product costs.

d. Discuss some of the strategic implications of your answers to the previous requirements.

E6-27. Traditional Product Costing versus Activity-Based Costing (LO2, 3, 4)

Outback Luggage, Inc., makes backpacks for large sporting goods chains that are sold under the customers' store brand names. The accounting department has identified the following overhead costs and cost drivers for next year:

Overhead Item	Expected Costs	Cost Driver	Maximum Quantity
Setup costs	$ 900,000	Number of setups	7,200
Ordering costs	240,000	Number of orders	60,000
Maintenance	1,200,000	Number of machine hours	96,000
Power	120,000	Number of kilowatt hours	600,000

Total predicted direct labor hours for next year is 60,000. The following data are for two recently completed jobs:

	Job 201	Job 202
Cost of direct materials	$13,500	$15,000
Cost of direct labor	$18,000	$71,250
Number of units completed	1,125	900
Number of direct labor hours	270	330
Number of setups	18	22
Number of orders	24	45
Number of machine hours	540	450
Number of kilowatt hours	270	360

Required

a. Determine the unit cost for each job using a traditional plantwide overhead rate based on direct labor hours.

b. Determine the unit cost for each job using ABC. (Round answers to two decimal places.)

c. As the manager of Outback, is there additional information that you would want to help you evaluate the pricing and profitability of Jobs 201 and 202?

d. Assuming the company has been using the method required in part a., how should management react to the findings in part b.

E6-28. Customer Profitability Analysis (LO5, 6)

Gonalong, Inc. has 10 customers that account for all of its $4,500,000 of net income. Its activity-based costing system is able to assign all costs, except for $650,000 of general administrative costs, to key activities incurred in connection with serving its customers. A customer profitability analysis based on activity costing produced the following customer profits and losses:

Customer #1	$346,000
#2	624,000
#3	(257,000)
#4	969,000
#5	1,040,000
#6	872,000
#7	628,000
#8	322,000
#9	(105,000)
#10	711,000
Total	$5,150,000

Required:

a. Prepare a customer profitability profile like the one in Exhibit 6.3.

b. If Gonalong were to notify customers 3 and 9 that it will no longer be able to provide them services in the future, will that increase company profits by $362,000? Why or why not?

c. What is the primary benefit of preparing a customer profitability analysis?

PROBLEMS

P6-29. Two-Stage ABC for Manufacturing with ABC Variances (LO2, 3, 4)

Marietta Manufacturing has developed the following activity cost pool information for its 2009 manufacturing activities:

	Budgeted Activity Cost	Activity Cost Driver at Practical Capacity
Purchasing and materials handling	$675,000	900,000 kilograms
Setup	700,000	1,120 setups
Machine operations	960,000	12,000 hours
First unit inspection	50,000	800 batches
Packaging	250,000	312,500 units

Actual 2009 production information is as follows:

	Standard Product A	Standard Product B	Specialty Products
Units	150,000	100,000	50,000
Batches	100	80	600
Setups*	300	160	900
Machine operations (hours)	6,000	3,000	2,000
Kilograms of raw materials	400,000	300,000	200,000
Direct materials costs	$900,000	$600,000	$800,000

*Some products require setups on two or more machines.

Required

a. Determine the unit cost of each product.

b. Explain why the unit cost of the specialty products is so much higher than the unit cost of Standard Product A or Standard Product B.

c. Determine the total idle capacity variance for 2009.

d. What arguments can be made in favor of basing activity costs on practical capacity rather than on actual activity?

P6-30. ABC—A Service Application (LO2, 3, 4)

Rest Haven is a senior living community that offers a full range of services including independent living, assisted living, and skilled nursing care. The assisted living division provides residential space, meals, and medical services (MS) to its residents. The current costing system adds the cost of all of these services (space, meals, and MS) and divides by total resident days to get a cost per resident day for each month. Recognizing that MS tends to vary significantly among the residents, Cumberland's accountant recommended that an ABC system be designed to calculate more accurately the cost of MS provided to residents. She decided that residents should be classified into four categories (A, B, C, D) based on the level of services received, with group A representing the lowest level of service and D representing the highest level of service. Two cost drivers being considered for measuring MS costs are number of assistance calls and number of assistant contacts. A contact is registered each time an assistance professional provides medical services or aid to a resident. The accountant has gathered the following data for the most recent annual period:

Resident Classification	Annual Resident Days	Annual Assistance Hours	Number of Assistance Contacts
A	8,760	15,000	60,000
B	6,570	20,000	52,000
C	4,380	22,500	52,000
D	2,190	32,500	52,000
	21,900	90,000	216,000

Other data:	
Total cost of medical services for the period	$2,500,000
Total cost of meals and residential space	$2,000,000

Required (round answers to the nearest dollar):

a. Determine the ABC cost of a resident day for each category of residents using assistance hours as the cost driver.

b. Determine the ABC cost of a resident day for each category of residents using assistance contacts as the cost driver.

c. Which cost driver do you think provides the more accurate measure of the cost per day for a Rest Haven resident?

P6-31. Activity-Based Costing Application (LO2, 3, 4)

Aristocrat Tableware manufactures quality place settings (knives, forks, spoons). Presented is information regarding predicted annual manufacturing overhead costs at capacity:

Activity Level	Predicted Cost	Cost Driver	Units of Driver at Capacity
Unit level			
Purchasing costs	$ 18,000	Direct materials cost	$1,000,000
Inspection	30,000	Units of final product	240,000
Batch level			
Setups	300,000	Number of setups	3,000
Moves	180,000	Number of moves	18,000
Scheduling	30,000	Number of jobs (batches)	500
Product level			
Maintain molds, bills of materials, & operations lists	20,000	Number of products	20
Facility level			
Depreciation	432,000	Unit processing steps	2,880,000*
Total	$1,010,000		

*Total units of final product times the average number of processing steps per product

In 2009 Aristocrat produced 12,000 units of the Plutocrat line in two jobs. Direct costs of these two jobs were materials costs of $33,000 and direct labor costs of $5,500. The following information is available regarding overhead activities:

Jobs (batches)	2
Units of final product	12,000
Direct materials	$33,000
Setups	24
Moves	72
Unit processing steps	144,000

Required

a. Determine the total and average unit manufacturing cost of the Plutocrat line during 2009 using activity-based costing.

b. Determine the maximum possible cost savings from producing the total annual requirements for the Plutocrat line in one job instead of two jobs. Mention at least one other factor that should be considered before a decision is made to do this.

c. Why is practical capacity rather than actual activity preferred as a basis for determining the activity costs of a product or service?

P6-32. ABC Costing for a Service Organization (LO2, 3, 4)

First Mortgage Company is a full-service residential mortgage company in the Baltimore area that operates in a very competitive market. The manager, Richard Sissom, is concerned about operating costs associated with processing mortgage applications and has decided to install an ABC costing system to help him get a handle on costs. Although labor hours seems to be the primary driver of the cost of processing a new mortgage, the labor cost for the different activities involved in processing new loans varies widely. The Accounting Department has provided the following data for the company's five major cost pools for 2009:

Activity Cost Pools		Activity Drivers	
Taking customer applications	$ 300,000	Time—assistant managers	12,000 hours
Conducting credit investigations	450,000	Time—credit managers	16,500 hours
Underwriting	500,000	Time—Underwriting Department	10,000 hours
Preparing loan packages	200,000	Time—Processing Department	10,000 hours
Closing loans	600,000	Time—Legal Department hours	6,000 hours
	$2,050,000		54,500 hours

During 2009, the company processed and issued 5,000 new mortgages, two of which are summarized here with regard to activities used to process the mortgages:

	Loan 5066	Loan 5429
Application processing hours	1.50	2.75
Credit investigating hours	4.00	3.00
Underwriting hours	2.50	4.75
Processing hours	3.50	3.00
Legal processing hours	1.50	1.50
Total hours	13.00	15.00

Required

a. Determine the cost per unit of activity for each activity cost pool.

b. Determine the cost of processing loans 5066 and 5429.

c. Determine the cost of preparing loans 5066 and 5429 assuming that an average cost per hour for all activities is used.

d. Compare and discuss your answers to requirements (*b*) and (*c*).

P6-33. Using Activity Cost Data: Value-Added and Non-Value-Added Activities (LO2, 3, 4, 6)
Mayville Inc. has developed the following activity cost data for its purchasing and manufacturing activities:

Activity	Activity Cost
Prepare purchase order and receiving report.	$20.00 per order
Unpack and inspect incoming goods	$0.50 per unit purchased
Raw materials inventory carrying cost	1% of invoice cost
Issue raw materials.	$14.00 per type of item/batch
Move to a workstation, inspection station, or to finished goods.	$1.50 per unit in batch
In-process inventory carrying cost*	$0.50 per unit in batch/day
Assembly/labor activities	$25.00 per hour
Perform quality inspection	$0.50 per inspection
Set up Machine A.	$50.00 per batch
Operate Machine A	$40.00 per hour
Set up Machine B.	$60.00 per batch
Operate Machine B	$42.00 per hour
Set up Machine C.	$55.00 per batch
Operate Machine C	$30.00 per hour

*Applicable to all units, regardless of whether they are being worked on or are awaiting work

Management is contemplating the production of a new product, G57, and desires to know the average annual unit cost at an annual production volume of 10,000 units (10 batches of 1,000 units). Purchasing, engineering, and production scheduling have developed the following information for an annual volume of 10,000 units:

Raw Material	Annual Requirements	Order Quantity	Orders per Year	Unit Price
D34.	20,000	5,000	4	$ 5.50
G77.	30,000	10,000	3	0.55
H65.	10,000	1,000	10	20.00

Production requirements per batch of 1,000 units are as follows:

Raw materials	
D34.	2,000 units
G77	3,000 units
H65	1,000 units
Machine activities	
A.	100 hours
B.	50 hours
C	50 hours
Labor	60 hours
Quality inspections.	2 per unit

All raw materials required for the batch will be issued at the start of production. The machines will be set up before production on the batch begins, and units will be moved directly from one operation to the next as each is ready. This will reduce work-in-process inventories as much as possible. Inspections take place at an inspection station containing sophisticated equipment. The average cycle time for a unit from start to finish is estimated to be three days.

Required

a. Use activity cost data to determine the total annual and average unit cost of product G57. Round computations to the nearest cent.

b. At a recent seminar, a discussion leader proposed these theories: all materials movement, inspection, and carrying activities are non-value-added and conversion costs related to materials movement, inspection, and carrying inventory are wasted, therefore management should strive to eliminate the activities that cause them. Break total conversion costs into the categories of value added and non-value added.

P6-34. Activity-Based Costing in a Service Organization (LO2, 3, 4, 6)

Mesa National Bank has ten automatic teller machines spread throughout the city maintained by the Automatic Teller Department. You have been assigned the task of determining the cost of operating each machine. Management will use the information you develop, along with other information pertaining to the volume and type of transactions at each machine, to evaluate the desirability of continuing to operate each machine and/or changing security arrangements for a particular machine.

The Automatic Teller Department consists of a total of six employees: a supervisor, a head cashier, two associate cashiers, and two maintenance personnel. The associate cashiers make between two and four daily trips to each machine to collect and replenish cash and to replenish supplies, deposit tickets, and so forth. Each machine contains a small computer that automatically summarizes and reports transactions to the head cashier. The head cashier reconciles the activities of the two associate cashiers to the computerized reports. The supervisor, who does not handle cash, reviews the reconciliation. When an automatic teller's computer, a customer, or a cashier reports a problem, the two maintenance employees and one cashier are dispatched immediately. The cashier removes all cash and transaction records, and the maintenance employees repair the machine.

Maintenance employees spend all of their time on maintenance-related activities. The associate cashiers spend approximately 50 percent of their time on maintenance-related activities and 50 percent on daily trips. The head cashier's time is divided, with 75 percent directly related to daily trips to each machine and 25 percent related to supervising cashiers on maintenance calls. The supervisor devotes 20 percent of the time to daily trips to each machine and 80 percent to the equal supervision of each employee. Cost information for a recent month follows:

Salaries	
Supervisor	$ 4,000
Head cashier	3,000
Other ($1,800 each)	7,200
Lease and operating costs	
Cashiers' service vehicle	1,200
Maintenance service vehicle	1,400
Office rent and utilities	2,300
Machine lease, space rent, and utilities ($1,500 each)	15,000
Total	$34,100

Related monthly activity information for this month follows:

Machine	Routine Trips	Maintenance Hours
1	30	5
2	90	17
3	60	15
4	60	30
5	120	15
6	30	10
7	90	25
8	120	5
9	60	20
10	60	18
Total	720	160

Additional information follows:

- The office is centrally located with about equal travel time to each machine.
- Maintenance hours include travel time.
- The cashiers' service vehicle is used exclusively for routine visits.
- The office space is divided equally between the supervisor and the head cashier.

Required

a. Determine the monthly operating costs of machines 7 and 8 when cost assignments are based on the number of machines.

b. Determine the activity cost of a routine trip and a maintenance hour for the month given. Round answers to the nearest cent.

c. Determine the operating costs assigned and reassigned to machines 7 and 8 when activity-based costing is used.

d. How can ABC cost information be used to improve the overall management of monthly operating costs?

P6-35. Product Costing: Plantwide Overhead versus Activity-Based Costing (LO3, 4)

Sconti, Inc., produces machine parts as a contract provider for a large manufacturing company. Sconti produces two particular parts, shafts and gears. The competition is keen among contract producers, and Sconti's top management realizes how vulnerable its market is to cost-cutting competitors. Hence, having a very accurate understanding of costs is important to Sconti's survival.

Sconti's president, Joe Disharoon, has observed that the company's current cost to produce shafts is \$21.24, and the current cost to produce gears is \$12.62. He indicated to the controller that he suspects some problems with the cost system because Sconti is suddenly experiencing extraordinary competition on shafts, but it seems to have a virtual corner on the gears market. He is even considering dropping the shaft line and converting the company to a one-product manufacturer of gears. He asked the controller to conduct a thorough cost study and to consider whether changes in the cost system are necessary. The controller collected the following data about the company's costs and various manufacturing activities for the most recent month:

	Shafts	Gears
Production units	50,000	10,000
Selling price	\$31.86	\$24
Overhead per unit (based on direct labor hours)	\$12.71	\$6.36
Materials and direct labor cost per unit	\$8.53	\$6.26
Number of production runs	10	20
Number of purchasing and receiving orders processed	40	100
Number of machine hours	12,500	6,000
Number of direct labor hours	25,000	2,500
Number of engineering hours	5,000	5,000
Number of material moves	50	40

The controller was able to summarize the company's total manufacturing overhead into the following pools:

Setup costs	\$ 24,000
Machine costs	175,000
Purchasing and receiving costs	210,000
Engineering costs	200,000
Materials handling costs	90,000
Total	\$699,000

Required

a. Calculate Sconti's current plantwide overhead rate based on direct labor hours.

b. Verify Sconti's calculation of overhead cost per unit of \$12.71 for shafts and \$6.36 for gears.

c. Calculate the manufacturing overhead cost per unit for shafts and gears using activity-based costing, assuming each of the five cost pools represents a separate activity pool. Use the most appropriate activity driver for assigning activity costs to the two products.

d. Comment on Sconti's current cost system and the reason the company is facing fierce competition for shafts but little competition for gears.

P6-36. Customer Profitability Analysis (LO2, 5, 6)

Avion, LTD, is a British aeronautics subcontract company that designs and manufactures electronic control systems for commercial airlines. The vast majority of all commercial aircraft are manufactured by Boeing in the U.S. and Airbus in Europe; however, there is a relatively small group of companies that manufacture narrow-body commercial jets. Assume for this exercise that Avion does contract work for the two major manufacturers plus three companies in the second tier.

Because competition is intense in the industry, Avion has always operated on a fairly thin gross profit margin; hence, it is crucial that it manage non-manufacturing overhead costs effectively in order to achieve an acceptable net profit margin. With declining profit margins in recent years, Avion's CEO has become concerned that the cost of obtaining contracts and maintaining relations with its five major customers may be getting out of hand. You have been hired to conduct a customer profitability analysis.

Avion's non-manufacturing overhead consists of \$3 million of general and administrative expense, including, among other expenses, the CEO's salary and bonus and the cost of operating the company's corporate jet. Selling and customer support expenses as recorded in the company's financial accounting system are also $3 million, including 5% sales commissions and $1,050,000 of additional costs.

The accounting staff determined that the $1,050,000 of additional selling and customer support expenses related to the following four activity cost pools:

Activity	Activity Cost Driver	Cost per Unit of Activity
1. Sales visits	Number of visit days	$1,200
2. Product adjustments	Number of adjustments	1,500
3. Phone and email contacts	Number of calls/contacts	150
4. Promotion and entertainment events	Number of events	1,500

Financial and activity data on the five customers follows (in millions):

			Quantity of Sales and Support Activity			
Customer	Sales	Gross Profit	Activity 1	Activity 2	Activity 3	Activity 4
#1	$17	$3.4	106	23	220	82
#2	12	2.4	130	36	354	66
#3	3	0.6	52	10	180	74
#4	4	0.8	34	6	138	18
#5	3	0.6	16	5	104	10
	$39	$7.8	338	80	996	250

In addition to the above, the sales staff used the corporate jet at a cost of $800 per hour for trips to customers as follows:

Customer #1	24 hours
Customer #2	36 hours
Customer #3	5 hours
Customer #4	0 hours
Customer #5	6 hours

Required:

a. Prepare a customer profitability analysis that shows the gross profits less all expenses that can reasonably be assigned to the five customers.

b. Now assume that the remaining general and administrative costs are assigned to the five customers based on relative sales dollars, calculate net profit for each customer.

c. Discuss the merits of the analysis in part a. versus part b.

CASES

C6-37. Designing an ABC System for a Country Club (LO2, 5, 6)

The Reserve Club is a traditional private golf and country club that has three different categories of memberships: golf, tennis & swimming, and social. Golf members have access to all amenities and programs in the Club, Tennis & Swimming members have access to all amenities and programs except use of the golf course, and Social members have access to only the social activities of the club, excluding golf, tennis, and swimming. All members have clubhouse privileges, including use of the bar and restaurant, which is operated by an outside contractor. During the past year, the average membership in each category, along with the number of club visits during the year, was

	Members	Visits
Golf	260	9,360
Tennis & Swimming	50	1,500
Social	120	2,160

Some members of the Club have been complaining that heavy users of the Club are not bearing their share of the costs through their membership fees. Dess Rosmond, General Manager of the Reserve Club, agrees that monthly fees paid by the various member groups should be based on the annual average amount of cost-related activities provided by the club for the three groups, and he intends to set fees on that basis for the coming year. The annual direct costs of operating the golf course, tennis courts, and swimming pool have been calculated by the Club's controller as follows:

Golf course	$900,000
Swimming pool	50,000
Tennis courts	25,000

The operation of the bar and restaurant and all related costs, including depreciation on the bar and restaurant facilities, are excluded from this analysis. In addition to the above costs, the Club incurs general overhead costs in the following amounts for the most recent (and typical) year:

General Ledger Overhead Accounts	Amounts
Indirect labor for the Club management staff (the general manager, assistant general manager, membership manager, and club controller)	$250,000
Utilities (other than those directly related to golf, swimming and tennis)	24,000
Website maintenance	2,000
Postage	5,000
Computers and information systems maintenance	7,500
Clubhouse maintenance & depreciation	30,000
Liability insurance	4,000
Security contract	12,000
	$334,500

Dess believes that the best way to assign most of the overhead costs to the three membership categories is with an activity-based system that recognizes four key activities that occur regularly in the club:

Recruiting and providing orientation for new members
Maintaining the membership roster and communicating with members
Planning, scheduling and managing Club events
Maintaining the financial records and reporting for the Club

Required:

a. Identify and explain which overhead costs can reasonably be assigned to one or more of the four key activities, and suggest a basis for making the assignment.

b. Identify a cost driver for each activity cost pool that would seem to be suitable for assigning the activity cost pool to the three membership categories.

c. Suggest a method for assigning any overhead costs to the three membership categories that cannot reasonably be assigned to activity pools.

d. Comment on the suitability of ABC to this cost assignment situation.

C6-38. Product Costing: Department versus Activity-Based Costing for Overhead **(LO2, 4, 6)**
Advertising Services Company (ASCO), a wholly owned subsidiary of Bell-of-the-South Tele-communications, Inc. (BOST), specializes in providing published and online advertising services for the business marketplace. The company monitors its costs based on the cost per column inch of published space printed in the advertising book ("The Peach Pages") and based on the cost per minute of telephone advertising time delivered on "The Peach Line," a computer-based, online advertising service. ASCO has one major competitor, Atlantatec, in the teleadvertising market; with increased competition, ASCO has seen a decline in sales of online advertising in recent years. ASCO's president, Andrea Remington, believes that predatory pricing by Atlantatec has caused the problem. The following is a recent conversation between Andrea and Jim Tate, director of marketing for ASCO.

Jim: I just received a call from one of our major customers concerning our advertising rates on "The Peach Line" who said that a sales rep from another firm (it had to be Atlantatec) had offered the same service at $1 per minute, which is $1.50 per minute less than our price.

Andrea: It's costing about $1.27 per minute to produce that product. I don't see how they can afford to sell it so cheaply. I'm not convinced that we should meet the price. Perhaps the better strategy is to emphasize producing and selling more published ads, which we're more experienced with and where our margins are high and we have virtually no competition.

Jim: You may be right. Based on a recent survey of our customers, I think we can raise the price significantly for published advertising and still not lose business.

Andrea: That sounds promising; however, before we make a major recommitment to publishing, let's explore other possible explanations. I want to know how our costs compare with our competitors. Maybe we could be more efficient and find a way to earn a good return on teleadvertising.

After this meeting, Andrea and Jim requested an investigation of production costs and comparative efficiency of producing published versus online advertising services. The controller, Joanna Turner, indicated that ASCO's efficiency was comparable to that of its competitors and prepared the following cost data:

	Published Advertising	Online Advertising
Estimated number of production units	200,000	10,000,000
Selling price	$200	$2.50
Direct product costs	$21,000,000	$5,000,000
Overhead allocation*	$9,800,000	$7,700,000
Overhead per unit	$49	$0.77
Direct costs per unit	$105	$0.50
Number of customers	180,000	25,000
Number of salesperson days	28,000	2,000
Number of art and design hours	35,000	5,000
Number of creative services subcontract hours	100,000	25,000
Number of customer service calls	72,000	8,000

*Based on direct labor costs

Upon examining the data, Andrea decided that she wanted to know more about the overhead costs since they were such a high proportion of total production costs. She was provided the following list of overhead costs and told that they were currently being assigned to products in proportion to direct labor costs.

Selling costs	$7,500,000
Visual and audio design costs	3,000,000
Creative services costs	5,000,000
Customer service costs	2,000,000

Required

Using the data provided by the controller, prepare analyses to help Andrea and Jim in making their decisions. (*Hint:* Prepare cost calculations for both product lines using ABC to see whether there is any significant difference in their unit costs). Should ASCO switch from the fast-growing, online advertising market back into the well-established published advertising market? Does the charge of predatory pricing seem valid? Why are customers likely to be willing to pay a higher price to get published services? Do traditional costing and activity-based costing lead to the same conclusions?

C6-39. ABC/ABM Discussion Questions (LO4, 6)

The following questions relate to activity-based costing and activity-based management.

a. Suppose that Dell Computer has been using a traditional costing system but has decided to adopt ABC with the expectation that it would produce more accurate product cost calculations. To management's surprise, the new ABC costs were not significantly different from the old product costs using traditional costing methods. Does this mean that Dell does not stand to benefit from using ABC and should abandon it if it is less costly to use the old costing methods? Discuss.

b. IT Corporation is a hypothetical company that makes only one product, a high-speed computer processor chip sold only to one customer, an Asian laptop computer manufacturer. IT has a single plant that is highly automated with the latest production technology. Is IT a candidate for using an ABC system? Would an ABC system be expected to produce different unit product cost calculations than a traditional system? What are the possible benefits of using ABC at IT other than possible improvements in the accuracy of cost data?

c. Assume that Dell Computer's ABC system includes two activity pools (product warranty costs and procurement costs) that have the same cost driver (number of parts). Is there any advantage to maintaining separate cost pools for these two activities, or should they be combined into a single cost pool since they have the same cost driver?

d. Even though ABC usually assigns direct costs associated with a particular cost objective directly to the cost objective, are there situations in which it might be advantageous from an ABM perspective to assign some direct costs to an activity pool and then reassign them to the cost objective? Is it possible that in some contexts, ABC and ABM perspectives may conflict with each other?

C6-40. Unit-Level and Multiple-Level Cost Assignments with Decision Implications (LO2, 3, 4, 6)
CarryAll Company[8] produces briefcases from leather, fabric, and synthetic materials in a single production department. The basic product is a standard briefcase made from leather and lined with fabric. CarryAll has a good reputation in the market because the standard briefcase is a high-quality item that has been produced for many years.

Last year, the company decided to expand its product line and produce specialty briefcases for special orders. These briefcases differ from the standard in that they vary in size, contain both leather and synthetic materials, and are imprinted with the buyer's logo (the standard briefcase is simply imprinted with the CarryAll name in small letters). The decision to use some synthetic materials in the briefcase was made to hold down the materials cost. To reduce the labor costs per unit, most of the cutting and stitching on the specialty briefcases is done by automated machines, which are used to a much lesser degree in the production of the standard briefcases. Because of these changes in the design and production of the specialty briefcases, CarryAll management believed that they would cost less to produce than the standard briefcases. However, because they are specialty items, they were priced slightly higher; standards are priced at $30 and specialty briefcases at $32.

After reviewing last month's results of operations, CarryAll's president became concerned about the profitability of the two product lines because the standard briefcase showed a loss while the specialty briefcase showed a greater profit margin than expected. The president is wondering whether the company should drop the standard briefcase and focus entirely on specialty items. Units and cost data for last month's operations as reported to the president are as follows:

	Standard	Specialty
Units produced	10,000	2,500
Direct materials		
Leather (1 sq. yd. × $15.00; ½ sq. yd. × $15.00)	$15.00	$ 7.50
Fabric (1 sq. yd. × $5.00; 1 sq. yd. × $5.00)	5.00	5.00
Synthetic		5.00
Total materials	20.00	17.50
Direct labor (½ hr. × $12.00, ¼ hr. × $12.00)	6.00	3.00
Manufacturing overhead (½ hr. × $8.98; ¼ hr. × $8.98)	4.49	2.25
Cost per unit	$30.49	$22.75

Factory overhead is applied on the basis of direct labor hours. The rate of $8.98 per direct labor hour was calculated by dividing the total overhead ($50,500) by the direct labor hours (5,625). As shown in the table, the cost of a standard briefcase is $0.49 higher than its $30 sales price; the specialty briefcase has a cost of only $22.75, for a gross profit per unit of $9.25. The problem with these costs is that they do not accurately reflect the activities involved in manufacturing each product. Determining the costs using ABC should provide better product costing data to help gauge the actual profitability of each product line.

The manufacturing overhead costs must be analyzed to determine the activities driving the costs. Assume that the following costs and cost drivers have been identified:

- The Purchasing Department's cost is $6,000. The major activity driving these costs is the number of purchase orders processed. During the month, the Purchasing Department prepared the following number of purchase orders for the materials indicated:

Leather	20
Fabric	30
Synthetic material	50

- The cost of receiving and inspecting materials is $7,500. These costs are driven by the number of deliveries. During the month, the following number of deliveries were made:

[8] The CarryAll Company case, prepared by Professors Harold Roth and Imogene Posey, was originally published in the *Management Accounting Campus Report*.

Leather	30
Fabric	40
Synthetic material	80

- Production line setup cost is $10,000. Setup activities involve changing the machines to produce the different types of briefcases. Each setup for production of the standard briefcases requires one hour; each setup for specialty briefcases requires two hours. Standard briefcases are produced in batches of 200, and specialty briefcases are produced in batches of 25. During the last month, there were 50 setups for the standard item and 100 setups for the specialty item.
- The cost of inspecting finished goods is $8,000. All briefcases are inspected to ensure that quality standards are met. However, the final inspection of standard briefcases takes very little time because the employees identify and correct quality problems as they do the hand cutting and stitching. A survey of the personnel responsible for inspecting the final products showed that 150 hours were spent on standard briefcases and 250 hours on specialty briefcases during the month.
- Equipment-related costs are $6,000. Equipment-related costs include repairs, depreciation, and utilities. Management has determined that a logical basis for assigning these costs to products is machine hours. A standard briefcase requires 1/2 hour of machine time, and a specialty briefcase requires two hours. Thus, during the last month, 5,000 hours of machine time relate to the standard line and 5,000 hours relate to the specialty line.
- Plant-related costs are $13,000. These costs include property taxes, insurance, administration, and others. For the purpose of determining average unit costs, they are to be assigned to products using machine hours.

Required

a. Using activity-based costing concepts, what overhead costs should be assigned to the two products?
b. What is the unit cost of each product using activity-based costing concepts?
c. Reevaluate the president's concern about the profitability of the two product lines.
d. Discuss the merits of activity-based management as it relates to CarryAll's ABC cost system.

Chapter 7

Additional Topics in Product Costing

LEARNING OBJECTIVES

LO1 Differentiate between product and service department costs and direct and indirect department costs. (p. 220)

LO2 Describe the allocation of service department costs under the direct, step, and linear algebra methods. (p. 220)

LO3 Understand lean production and just-in-time inventory management. (p. 229)

LO4 Explain how lean production and just-in-time affect performance evaluation and recordkeeping. (p. 232)

LO5 Discuss performance reporting in a lean production environment. (p. 234)

The challenge of product costing, which we have explored in the previous two chapters, is how to trace and assign the costs of production to a company's various products. Determining how much it costs to make a product can be very simple and straightforward for a company that makes only one product; however, as product lines become more extensive and processes more complex, the costing system becomes more complex. The product cost system is essentially a reflection of a company's product strategy and production processes.

The development of highly complex product lines, processes, and cost systems is illustrated by the automobile industry in the post World War II era. What began as a simple business plan with Ford Motor Company producing a single model automobile in one color in the 1920s and 1930s evolved into an explosion of diversity and choice in automobile brands. General Motors had five major divisions, each offering multiple models with an almost unlimited combination of options; Ford and Chrysler were forced to follow a similar strategy just to keep from losing ground to GM. In the last half of the 20th century, the number of different automobile brands expanded exponentially, and product cost systems at the "Big Three" U.S. auto manufacturers evolved in complexity to keep up with this rapidly expanding product diversity.

At the same time the automobile industry was developing in the U.S., a small struggling Japanese automobile company, founded by Kiichiro

Courtesy of JAM Images

Toyoda in the 1930s, and later renamed **Toyota Motor Corporation**, was establishing itself as a leading Japanese auto manufacturer. Toyoda's colleague and chief production manager, Taiichi Ohno, soon began developing a production philosophy, which came to be known as the Toyota Production System. Ironically, Ohno's inspiration for his system originated with a tour of a Ford Motor plant in the U.S. and the belief that the methods that U.S. grocery supermarkets used to manage their inventories could be applied to an automobile plant. Over the past two decades, the Toyota system arguably has had more influence on production methods worldwide than any other single influence or person. *Business Week* magazine described Toyota's influence in the following manner: " . . . Toyota didn't just revolutionize car making – but pretty much global manufacturing as well.[1]

In the early 1980s Toyota's Chairman came to the U.S. to study the U.S. automobile industry and concluded that to be successful in the international markets, especially the U.S., it could not simply copy the U.S. industry, but had to produce superior automobiles, and do it with creativity, resourcefulness, wisdom, and hard work. Twenty-five years later, in the first quarter of 2007, Toyota became the World's largest automobile manufacturer by selling 2.35 million cars worldwide, compared with GM's 2.26 million for the same period.[2]

This chapter discusses two major topics in cost management: (1) service department cost allocations, which are likely to be found in an organization like GM with its many divisions and departments, and (2) the lean production/just-in-time approach to managing production and product costs, first introduced by the Toyota Company.

---

[1] Brian Bremner, "Toyota: A Carmaker Wired to Win," *Business Week*, April 24, 2007, as presented at http://www.businessweek.com/globalbiz/content/apr2007/gb20070424_480904.htm)

[2] Ronal M. Becker, "Lean Manufacturing and the Toyota Production System," Society of Automotive Engineers International (SAE), as presented at http://www.sae.org/topics/leanjun01.htm

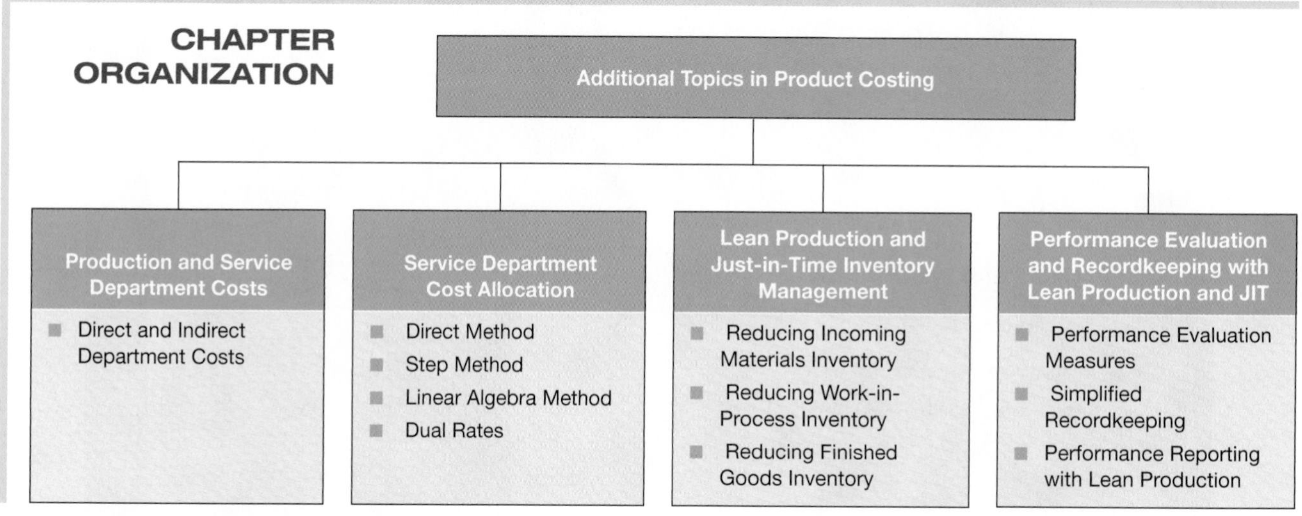

PRODUCTION AND SERVICE DEPARTMENT COSTS

LO1 Differentiate between product and service department costs and direct and indirect department costs.

In Chapter 5, we discussed two basic methods (job order costing and process costing) for accumulating, measuring and recording the costs of producing goods. In Chapter 6, we discussed both traditional and activity-based methods for assigning indirect costs to products. We now look in more detail at another aspect of assigning indirect costs.

In addition to *production* departments that actually perform work on a product, many companies have production *support* departments, such as payroll, human resources, security, and facilities, that provide support services for all of the production departments, and sometimes even for each other. These departments are typically called **service departments**. The cost of producing products, therefore, includes the costs incurred within production departments, as well as the cost of services received from service departments.

A **direct department cost** is a cost assigned directly to a department (production or service) when it is incurred. For a production department, direct department costs include both *direct* product costs (direct materials and direct labor) as well as *indirect* product costs (such as indirect labor and indirect materials) incurred directly in the department. An **indirect department cost** is a cost assigned to a department as a result of an indirect allocation, or reassignment, from another department, such as a service department.

The product costing system must include a policy for assigning to products the cost of services received from service departments. For companies that use a plantwide overhead rate, the costs of all service departments are added to the indirect product costs incurred within all of the producing departments to get total plantwide manufacturing overhead, which is then assigned to products using a single overhead rate based on a common factor such as direct labor hours. For companies that use departmental overhead rates, service department costs are allocated to the production departments that utilize their services, and the allocated service department costs are added to the indirect costs incurred within the department to arrive at total departmental overhead and allocation rates. Also, as illustrated in Chapter 6, service department costs may also be assigned to products using activity-based costing.

SERVICE DEPARTMENT COST ALLOCATION

LO2 Describe the allocation of service department costs under the direct, step, and linear algebra methods.

As discussed above, service departments (maintenance, administration, security, etc.) provide a wide range of support functions, primarily for one or more production departments. These departments, which are considered essential elements in the overall manufacturing process, do not work directly on the "product" but provide auxiliary support to the producing departments. In addition to providing support for the various producing departments, some service departments also provide services to *other service departments*. For example, the payroll and personnel departments may provide services to all departments, and maintenance may provide services to the producing departments as well as to the medical center and food services. Services provided by one service department to other service departments are called **interdepartment services**.

To illustrate service department cost allocations, consider the Manufacturing Division of Krown Drink Company, which has two producing departments, three service departments, and two products. The service departments and their respective service functions and cost allocation bases are as follows:

Department	Service Functions	Allocation Base
Support Services	Receiving and inventory control	Total amount of department capital investment
Engineering Resources	Production setup and engineering and testing	Number of employees
Building and Grounds	Machinery maintenance and depreciation	Amount of square footage occupied

Difficulty in choosing an allocation base for service department costs is not uncommon. For example, Krown Drink may have readily determined the appropriate allocation bases for the Engineering Resources and the Building and Grounds Departments but may have found the choice for Support Services to be less clear. Perhaps after conducting correlation studies, the most equitable base for allocating Support Services costs to other departments was determined to be total capital investment in the departments because they included expensive computer-tracking equipment, both manual and automated forklifts, and other material-moving equipment. The following Business Insight box discusses how computer software helps companies to track and allocate telephone service costs in a large organization.

Direct department costs and allocation base information used to illustrate Krown Drink's July service department cost allocations are summarized as follows:

	Direct Department Costs	Number of Employees		Amount of Square Footage Occupied		Total Amount of Department Capital Investment	
Service departments							
Support Services	$ 27,000	15	15%	4,000	8%	—	—
Engineering Resources.	20,000	—	—	2,000	4	$ 45,000	8%
Building and Grounds.	10,000	5	5	—	—	50,000	9
Producing departments							
Mixing	40,000*	24	24	11,000	22	180,000	33
Bottling	90,000*	56	56	33,000	66	270,000	50
	$187,000	100	100%	50,000	100%	$545,000	100%

*Direct department overhead

The preceding information omitted the amount of capital investment in the Support Services Department, the number of employees in the Engineering Resources Department, and the amount of square footage used by the Building and Grounds Department. These data were omitted because a department normally does not allocate costs to itself; it allocates costs only to the departments it serves. The three methods commonly used for service department cost allocations—direct, step, and linear algebra—are discussed next.

Direct Method

The **direct method** allocates all service department costs based only on the amount of services provided to the producing departments. Exhibit 7.1 shows the flow of costs using the direct method. All arrows depicting the cost flows extend directly from service departments to producing departments; there are no cost allocations between the service departments.

BUSINESS INSIGHT **Computer Software Aids Telephone Service Cost Allocation**

In a large organization, a service as basic as telephone usage can represent a substantial cost and, hence, a significant cost allocation challenge. All departments, both production and service, are users of telephone services, including installing and repairing new lines and providing ongoing monthly service. Many companies have thousands of telephones in service for which costs have to be allocated to the various departments.

A Canadian software company, Digital Fairway, is a leading developer of software that helps organizations centralize and automate the management of their telecommunications infrastructure. Most companies still manage the allocations of these costs manually using spreadsheets. "Keeping track of cost center assignments and cost allocations for communication services in a spreadsheet are time consuming and error prone tasks," says Digital Fairway CEO Joe Warnement. Digital's Provergent software product enables enterprises to associate a communications service and its cost to a general ledger code within the telecommunications electronics system, allowing the service costs to be accurately allocated to the cost center consuming that service. The ability to associate a unique service or circuit identifier to both the cost and a general ledger code enables enterprises to gain a more accurate view into the telecoms services being consumed by different parts of the organization.

Source: "Digital Fairway's Provergent Enables Enterprises to Accurately Allocate Corporate Telecom Costs," *Market Wire*, September 4, 2007.

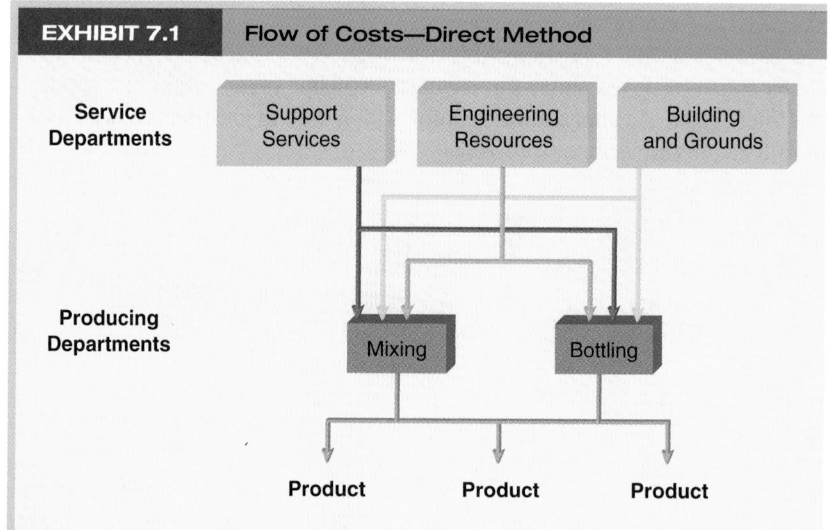

Exhibit 7.2 shows the service department cost allocations for the direct method. Notice the allocation base used to allocate Engineering Resources costs; only the employees in the producing departments are considered in computing the allocation percentages—24 in Mixing and 56 in Bottling, for a total of 80 employees in the allocation base. Thirty percent (24 ÷ 80) of the producing department employees work in Mixing; therefore, 30 percent of Engineering Resources costs are allocated to Mixing. Applying the same reasoning, 70 percent of Engineering Resources costs are allocated to Bottling. Similar logic is followed in computing the cost allocations for Building and Grounds and Support Services.

The cost allocation summary at the bottom of Exhibit 7.2 shows that all service department costs have been allocated, decreasing the service department costs to zero and increasing the producing department overhead balances by the amounts of the respective allocations. Also, total costs are not affected by the allocations; the total of $187,000 was merely redistributed so that all costs are reassigned to the producing departments. Total department overhead costs of the producing departments after allocation of service costs are $59,300 for Mixing and $127,700 for Bottling.

The advantage of the direct method of allocating service department costs is that it is easy and convenient to use (see the Business Insight that follows). Its primary disadvantage is that it does not recognize the costs for interdepartment services provided by one service department to another. Instead, any costs incurred to provide services to other service departments are passed directly to the producing departments.

EXHIBIT 7.2 Service Department Cost Allocations—Direct Method

	Total	Mixing	Bottling
Support Services Department			
Allocation base (capital investment)	$450,000	$180,000	$270,000
Percent of total base	100%	40%	60%
Cost allocations	$ 27,000	$ 10,800	$ 16,200
Engineering Resources Department			
Allocation base (number of employees)	80	24	56
Percent of total base	100%	30%	70%
Cost allocations	$ 20,000	$ 6,000	$ 14,000
Building and Grounds Department			
Allocation base (square footage occupied)	44,000	11,000	33,000
Percent of total base	100%	25%	75%
Cost allocations	$ 10,000	$ 2,500	$ 7,500

Cost Allocation Summary

	Support Services	Engineering Resources	Building and Grounds	Mixing	Bottling	Total
Department cost before allocations	$27,000	$20,000	$10,000	$40,000	$ 90,000	$187,000
Cost allocations						
Support Services	(27,000)			10,800	16,200	—
Engineering Resources		(20,000)		6,000	14,000	—
Building and Grounds			(10,000)	2,500	7,500	—
Department costs after allocations	$ 0	$ 0	$ 0	$59,300	$127,700	$187,000

The step method improves on the allocation procedure by redirecting some of the costs to other service departments before they are finally allocated to the production departments.

BUSINESS INSIGHT Cost Allocations for College Services

Service department cost allocation using the direct method is applied at many colleges. The producing departments of a college are its academic departments and professional schools; its support service departments are those such as student services (which includes housing, dining, and student life activities), facilities management (which is responsible for the physical campus), academic support (such as libraries and computer centers), and administration (such as the president's office, fund-raising activities, and the legal department). Commonly used bases for allocating these service department costs are the number of students for student services and academic support, square footage of space occupied for facilities management, and total revenues for administration.

The allocation of these support service costs are often major budget line items in the operating budgets for deans and department heads. These costs greatly affect the amount of money left for direct operating needs such as faculty salaries, research support, and professional development. It is important that the cost allocation method be perceived as fair and appropriate by those whose budgets are charged with these allocated costs. Using the direct allocation method is appropriate in allocating some college service costs, such as student services; it would probably not be appropriate in allocating others, such as computer services, which are used by both academic departments and other service departments.

Step Method

The **step method** gives partial recognition of interdepartmental services by using a methodology that allocates the service department costs *sequentially* both to the remaining service departments and the

chronological order of events.

producing departments. Any indirect costs allocated to a service department in this process are added to that department's direct costs to determine the total costs for allocation to the remaining departments. All service department costs will be assigned to the production departments and ultimately to the products.

To illustrate the problem that can result from using the direct method, assume that Ramso Company has two service departments, S1 and S2, and two producing departments, P1 and P2, that provide services as follows:

	Receiver of Services			
Provider of Services......	S1	S2	P1	P2
S1..............	0%	0%	70%	30%
S2..............	50%	0%	25%	25%

If the direct method is used to allocate service department costs to the producing departments, S2 total costs will be allocated equally to the producing departments because they use the same amount of S2 services (25 percent each). Is this an equitable allocation of S2 costs? S2 actually provides half of its services to the other service department (S1), which, in turn, provides the majority of its services to P1. Assume that S2 has total direct department costs of $100,000. If the direct method is used to allocate service department costs, the entire $100,000 will be divided equally among the two producing departments, each being allocated $50,000, with no allocation to S1.

	S1	S2	P1	P2
Direct allocation of S2 to P1 and P2	$0	$(100,000)	$50,000	$50,000

Consider the following alternative allocation of the $100,000 of S2 costs that takes into account inter-department services. First, 25 percent, or $25,000, is allocated to each of the producing departments, and 50 percent, or $50,000, is allocated to S1. Next, the $50,000 allocated to S1 from S2 is reallocated to the producing departments in proportion to the amount of services provided to them by S1: 70 percent and 30 percent, respectively. In this scenario, the $100,000 of S2 costs is ultimately allocated $60,000 to P1 and $40,000 to P2 as follows:

	S1	S2	P1	P2
Step 1:				
Allocate S2 costs to S1, P1, and P2....	$50,000	$(100,000)	$25,000	$25,000
Step 2:				
Reallocate S1 costs to P1 and P2	(50,000)	0	35,000	15,000
Total allocation of S2 costs via step method	$ 0	$ 0	$60,000	$40,000

This calculation shows only the ultimate allocation of S2 costs. Of course, any S1 direct department costs would also have to be allocated to P1 and P2 on a 70:30 basis. If interdepartmental services are ignored, P1 is allocated only $50,000 of S2 costs; by considering interdepartmental services, P1 is allocated $60,000. Certainly, a more accurate measure of both the direct and indirect services received by P1 from S2 is $60,000, not $50,000.

As long as all producing departments use approximately the same percentage of services of each service department, the direct method provides a reasonably accurate cost assignment. In this example, the percentages of services used by the producing departments were quite different: 70 percent and 30 percent for S1, and 50 percent and 50 percent for S2. In such situations, the direct method can result in significantly different allocations.

The step method is illustrated graphically in Exhibit 7.3 for the Krown Drink Company. Notice the sequence of the allocations: Engineering Resources, Support Services, and Building and Grounds.

When using the step method, the sequence of allocation is typically based on the relative percentage of services provided to other service departments, with the largest provider of interdepartmental services allocated first and the smallest provider of interdepartmental services allocated last. For Krown Drink, Engineering Resources is allocated first because, of the three service departments, it provides the largest percentage (20 percent) of its services to other service departments: 15 percent to Support Services and 5 percent to Building and Grounds (see previous cost allocation data). Building and Grounds is allocated last because it provides the least amount (12 percent) of its services to other service departments: 8 percent to Support Services and 4 percent to Engineering Resources. The service department cost allocations for Krown Drink using the step method are shown in Exhibit 7.4.

EXHIBIT 7.3 Flow of Costs—Step Method

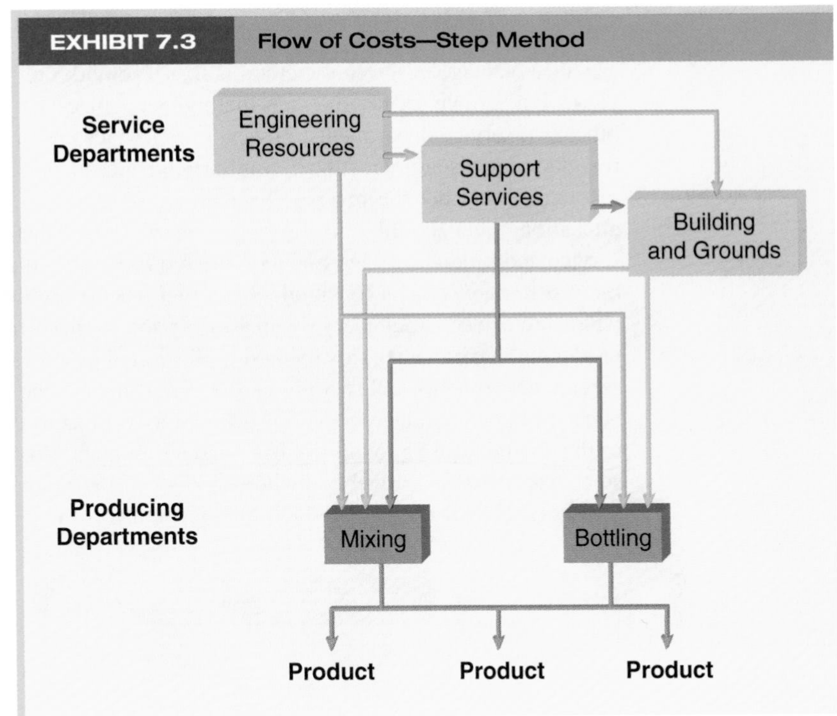

EXHIBIT 7.4 Service Department Cost Allocations—Step Method

	Total	Support Services	Building and Grounds	Mixing	Bottling
Engineering Resources Department					
Allocation base (number of employees)	100	15	5	24	56
Percent of total base.	100%	15%	5%	24%	56%
Cost allocations	$20,000	$3,000	$1,000	$4,800	$11,200
Support Services Department					
Allocation base (capital investment).	$500,000		$50,000	$180,000	$270,000
Percent of total base.	100%		10%	36%	54%
Cost allocations	$30,000		$3,000	$10,800	$16,200
Building and Grounds Department					
Allocation base (square footage occupied) .	44,000			11,000	33,000
Percent of total base.	100%			25%	75%
Cost allocations	$14,000			$3,500	$10,500

Cost Allocation Summary

	Engineering Resources	Support Services	Building and Grounds	Mixing	Bottling	Total
Department costs before allocations	$ 20,000	$ 27,000	$ 10,000	$40,000	$ 90,000	$187,000
Cost allocations						
Engineering Resources	(20,000)	3,000	1,000	4,800	11,200	—
Support Services.		(30,000)	3,000	10,800	16,200	—
Building and Grounds			(14,000)	3,500	10,500	—
Department costs after allocations.	$ 0	$ 0	$ 0	$59,100	$127,900	$187,000

Linear Algebra (Reciprocal) Method

The disadvantage of the step method is that it provides only partial recognition of interdepartmental services. For Krown Drink, the step method recognizes Engineering Resources services provided to the other two service departments; however, no services received by Engineering Resources from the other two departments are recognized. Similarly, services from Support Services to Building and Grounds are recognized, but not the reverse. To achieve the most mathematically accurate service department cost allocation, there should be full recognition of services between service departments as well as between service and producing departments. This requires using the linear algebra method, sometimes called the *reciprocal method.* The **linear algebra (reciprocal) method** uses a series of linear algebraic equations, which are solved simultaneously, to allocate service department costs both interdepartmentally and to the producing departments. This method is illustrated graphically in Exhibit 7.5 for a company that has two service departments and two producing departments. The cost allocation arrows run from each service department to the other service department as well as to the producing departments. Further discussion of this method can be found in Cost Accounting texts. Whether a company should use the direct method, step method, or linear algebra method depends on the extensiveness of interdepartmental services and how evenly services are used by the producing departments.

EXHIBIT 7.5 Flow of Costs—Linear Algebra Method

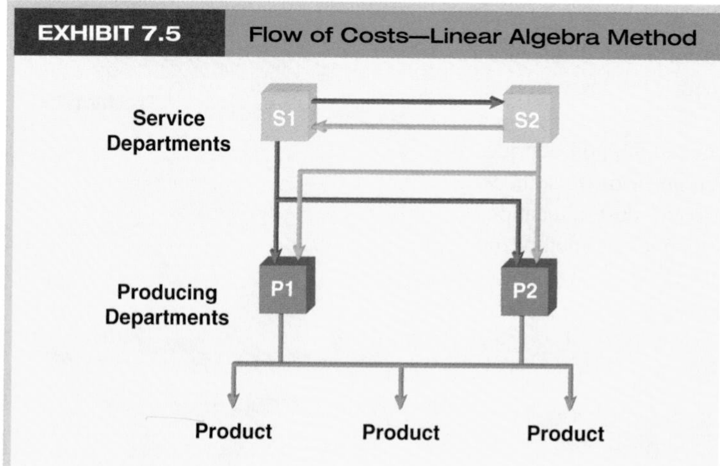

MANAGERIAL DECISION **You are the Controller**

As the person responsible for the product costing system, you are trying to decide which method is best to use in allocating service department costs to the producing departments and to the products. Some of the service departments provide services only to producing departments; whereas, others provide services to both producing and service departments. You would like to use the method that provides reliable cost measurements, but without creating more costs than the benefits derived. Which method do you recommend? [Answer, p. 236]

Dual Rates

When pooling costs for subsequent reassignment or allocation, it can be useful to provide separate pools for fixed costs and variable costs. This will result in cost allocations that more accurately reflect the factors that drive costs. The capacity provided most often drives fixed costs, whereas some type of actual activity usually drives variable costs. Dual rates involve establishing separate bases for allocating fixed and variable costs. Dual rates may be used for one or all service departments, depending on the size and nature of the costs in each service department. They may also be used in conjunction with the direct, step, or linear algebra methods.

It is important to remember the relationship between capacity and cost when selecting the allocation method. Total variable costs change as activity changes. Fixed costs, however, are the same whether the activity is at or below capacity. Fixed costs should usually be allocated based on the relative capacity provided the benefiting department, while variable costs should be allocated on the basis of actual usage. The allocation methods and bases also may be different for variable and fixed costs.

Fixed costs based on capacity provided eliminates the possibility that the amount of the cost allocation to one department is affected by the level of services utilized by other departments. When fixed service department costs are allocated based on the capacity provided to the user department, managers of the user departments are charged for that capacity whether they use it or not, and their use of services has no effect on the amount of costs allocated to other departments. A benefit of this allocation system is that it reduces the temptation for managers to avoid or delay services to minimize fixed cost allocations to their departments. Dual rates are examined in more detail in most cost accounting texts.

MID-CHAPTER REVIEW

The Apparel Store, LTD is organized into four departments: Women's Apparel, Men's Apparel, Administrative Services, and Facilities Services. The first two departments are the primary producing departments; the last two departments provide services to the producing departments as well as to each other. Top management has decided that, for internal reporting purposes, the cost of service department operations should be allocated to the producing departments. Administrative Services costs are allocated on the basis of the number of employees, and Facilities Services costs are allocated based on the amount of square footage of floor space occupied. Data pertaining to the cost allocations for February 2009 are as follows:

Department	Direct Department Cost	Number of Employees	Square Footage Occupied
Women's Apparel	$ 60,000	15	15,000
Men's Apparel.	50,000	9	7,500
Administrative Services	18,000	3	2,500
Facilities	12,000	2	1,000
Total	$140,000	29	26,000

Required

a. Determine the amount of service department costs to be allocated to the producing departments under both the *direct method* and the *step method* of service department cost allocation.

b. Discuss the *linear algebra method* of service department cost allocation, explaining circumstances when it should be considered over the direct and step methods.

c. Should The Apparel Store consider using the linear algebra method?

Solution

Service Department Cost Allocation

a. *Direct Method*

	Total	Women's	Men's
Administrative Services Department			
Allocation base (number of employees)	24	15	9
Percent of total base.	100%	62.5%	37.5%
Cost allocation	$18,000	$11,250	$6,750
Facilities Services Department			
Allocation base (square footage)	22,500	15,000	7,500
Percent of total base.	100%	66.7%	33.3%
Cost allocation	$12,000	$ 8,000	$4,000

Cost Allocation Summary

	Administrative	Facilities	Women's	Men's	Total
Departmental costs before allocation	$18,000	$12,000	$60,000	$50,000	$140,000
Cost allocations					
Administrative	(18,000)	—	11,250	6,750	0
Facilities	—	(12,000)	8,000	4,000	0
Departmental costs after allocation	$ 0	$ 0	$79,250	$60,750	$140,000

Step Method

Allocation Sequence

	Administrative	Facilities
Allocation base	Number of employees	Amount of square footage
Total base for other service and producing departments (a)	26	25,000
Total base for other service departments (b)	2	2,500
Percent of total services provided to other service departments (b ÷ a)	7.7%	10.0%
Order of allocation	Second	First

Step Allocations

	Total	Administrative	Women's	Men's
Facilities Services Department				
Allocation base (square footage)	25,000	2,500	15,000	7,500
Percent of total base	100%	10%	60%	30%
Cost allocation	$12,000	$1,200	$ 7,200	$3,600
Administrative Services Department				
Allocation base (number of employees)	24	—	15	9
Percent of total base	100%	—	62.5%	37.5%
Cost allocation ($18,000 + $1,200)	$19,200	—	$12,000	$7,200

Cost Allocation Summary

	Facilities	Administrative	Women's	Men's	Total
Departmental costs before allocation	$12,000	$18,000	$60,000	$50,000	$140,000
Cost allocations					
Facilities	(12,000)	1,200	7,200	3,600	0
Administrative	—	(19,200)	12,000	7,200	0
Departmental costs after allocations	$ 0	$ 0	$79,200	$60,800	$140,000

b. Another service department cost allocation method is the *linear algebra method.* This method simultaneously allocates service department costs both to other service departments and to the producing departments. It has an advantage over the *step method* in that it fully recognizes interdepartmental services.

c. If The Apparel Store wants the most precise allocation of service department costs to the producing departments, considering both direct services and indirect services, it must use the linear algebra method of service department allocation. As indicated in the Allocation sequence section of the step method in (a), Facilities provides 10 percent of its services to Administrative, and Administrative provides 7.7 percent of its services to Facilities. The step method recognized the Facilities services provided to Administrative, but it did not recognize the Administrative services provided to Facilities.

In this case, the producing departments are using approximately the same proportion of services from each of the service departments (60.0 percent to 62.5 percent for the Women's Department and 30.0 percent to 37.5 percent for the Men's Department). Hence, using a more precise measure of cost allocation is not likely to produce significantly different results, especially since the interdepartmental services are so close (7.7 percent versus 10.0 percent). Just as the step method allocation results were quite close to the direct method results, the linear method results would likely be quite close to both the direct and step method results. Use of the linear algebra method is not recommended in this case. On the basis of simplicity and convenience, the direct method is probably the best method for The Apparel Store to use.

LEAN PRODUCTION AND JUST-IN-TIME INVENTORY MANAGEMENT

LO3 Understand lean production and just-in-time inventory management.

Previously, our discussions about inventories have centered around how to measure the cost of products. A related issue is how to manage the production process and physical inventory levels. Cost accounting textbooks, as well as operations management textbooks, usually discuss models that have been used for decades to determine the economic order quantities for products given the particular level of inventory a company wants to maintain. Although these models are still relevant in many situations, managing the production process and inventory levels has changed dramatically for companies that have adopted a value chain approach to management. No longer do most managers consider only their company's strategies, goals, and objectives in deciding the characteristics and quantities of inventory that should be acquired or produced and maintained.

A value chain approach to inventory management requires that managers consider their suppliers' and customers' strategies, goals, and objectives as well if they hope to compete successfully in a global marketplace. Computer technology has affected the way inventories are manufactured and handled (using robotics, fully computerized manufacturing and product handling systems, bar code identification systems, etc.), and it is changing the way companies relate to other parties in the value chain. It has spawned worldwide use of alternative inventory production and management techniques and processes including just-in-time (JIT) inventory management and lean production methods.

Just-in-time (JIT) inventory management is a comprehensive inventory management philosophy that emerged in the 1970s that stresses policies, procedures, and attitudes by managers and other workers that result in the efficient production of high-quality goods while maintaining the minimum level of inventories. JIT is often described simply as an inventory model that maintains only the level of inventories required to meet current production and sales requirements, but it is, in reality, much more than that. The key elements of the JIT philosophy, which has come to be known as the "lean production" philosophy, include increased coordination throughout the value chain, reduced inventory, reduced production times, increased product quality, and increased employee involvement and empowerment.

In sum, JIT/lean production is a system aimed at reducing or eliminating waste, increasing cost efficiency, and securing a competitive advantage. Accordingly, it emphasizes a nimble production process with small lot sizes, short setup and changeover times, effective and efficient quality controls, a minimum number of bottlenecks and backups, and maximum efficiency of people. See the following Business Insight for background on the development of lean production.

BUSINESS INSIGHT **The History of Lean Production**

Although the lean concept was developed by Toyota based primarily on mass production processes first developed by Henry Ford, the term "lean production" was coined by MIT research scientists in their book, *The Machine that Changed the World*, published in 1990. In this landmark study of the automobile industry, Jim Womack, Dan Jones, and Daniel Roos explain lean production to the world for the first time, and discuss its profound implications for society. The book is self-described as a report of "the largest and most thorough study ever undertaken in any industry: the MIT five-million-dollar, five-year, fourteen-country International Motor Vehicle Program's study of the worldwide auto industry."

Since the publication of *The Machine that Changed the World*, Womack and Jones have gone on to study, promote, and document the development of lean production around the world. To gain additional insights into lean issues, see the websites of two organizations founded and headed by Womack and Jones, the Lean Enterprise Institute and the Lean Enterprise Academy. Their websites are, respectively, www.lean.org and www.leanuk.org. For an informative overview of the State of Lean in 2007 see http://www.lean.org/Community/Registered/ArticleDocuments/Lean%20Yearbook%202007.pdf

Source: www.lean.org

Survey research has documented the cost cutting and other benefits of lean production, as shown in the following Research Insight.

RESEARCH INSIGHT **Survey Documents Benefits of Lean Production Strategy**

Although cutting costs was rated the top benefit in a recent lean production survey conducted by the Lean Enterprise Institute (LEI) and completed by nearly 2,500 businesspeople, James Womack, Ph.D., the founder of LEI, warned that companies are missing the full growth potential of lean management.

A whopping 46.1 percent of the managers and executives rated "reduced cost" as the biggest benefit of implementing lean management concepts, more than all other benefits combined, according to the opinion survey conducted by LEI. Respondents rated the other top three benefits as increased customer satisfaction (16.3 percent), reduced inventory (7.5 percent), and increased product quality (6.4 percent).

"When I look back over the past 10 years, I'm gratified that most products cost less and work better," said Womack, Ph.D., who launched LEI in 1997. "And I'm equally gratified that lean management works in every company, industry, and country where it is seriously tried."

"But the biggest benefit of lean is that it frees resources by using less human effort, less space, less capital, and less time to make a given amount of products and services and to make them with fewer defects to precise customer desires, compared with traditional management," Womack continued. "By freeing resources, lean management turns waste into available capacity. The biggest benefits come when management uses this capacity to grow the business, whether it is a service or manufacturing enterprise."

Source: *Business Wire,* Aug 15, 2007

Reducing Incoming Materials Inventory

The JIT/lean approach to reducing incoming materials includes these elements:

1. Developing long-term relationships with a limited number of vendors.
2. Selecting vendors on the basis of service and material quality, as well as price.
3. Establishing procedures for key employees to order materials for current needs directly from approved vendors.
4. Accepting vendor deliveries directly to the shop floor, and only as needed.

When fully implemented, these steps minimize or eliminate many materials inventories. Sufficient materials would be on hand to meet only immediate needs, and the materials inventories in the manufacturing setting are located on the shop floor.

To achieve this reduction, it is apparent that vendors and buyers must work as a team and that key employees must be involved in decision making. The goal of the JIT approach to purchasing is not to shift materials carrying costs to vendors. A close, long-term working relationship between purchasers and vendors should be beneficial to both. Purchasers' scheduling information is provided to vendors so that vendors also can reduce inventories and minimize costs. Vendors are therefore able to manufacture small batches frequently, rather than manufacturing large batches infrequently. Further, vendors are more confident of future sales.

Reducing Work-in-Process Inventory

Reducing the total time required to complete a process, or the **cycle time**, is the key to reducing work-in-process inventories and is central to a lean production approach. In a manufacturing organization, cycle time is composed of the time needed for setup, processing, movement, waiting, and inspection. **Setup time** is the time required to prepare equipment to produce a specific product, or to change from producing one product to another product. **Processing time** is the time spent working on units. **Movement time** is the time units spend moving between work or inspection stations. **Waiting time** is the time units spend in temporary storage waiting to be processed, moved, or inspected. **Inspection time** is the amount of time it takes units to be inspected. Of the five elements of cycle time, only processing time adds value to the product. Efforts to reduce cycle time are appropriate for both continuous and batch production.

Devising means of reducing setup times will directly reduce the cycle time for batch production and thus reduce setup costs. Setup times can also be reduced by shifting from batch to continuous production whenever practical. Rearranging the shop floor to eliminate unnecessary movements of materials can help reduce movement time for both continuous and batch production.

Many companies have created **quality circles**, which are groups of employees involved in production who have the authority, within certain parameters, to address and resolve quality problems as they occur, without seeking management approval. Giving employees more authority and responsibility for quality, including the right to stop production whenever quality problems are noted, can reduce the need for separate inspection time.

Waiting time can be reduced by moving from a materials push to a materials pull approach to production. Under a traditional **materials push system**, employees work to reduce the pile of inventory building up at their workstations. Workers at each station remove materials from an in-process storage area, complete their operation, and place the output in another in-process storage area. Hence, they *push* the work to the next workstation. The emphasis is on production efficiency at each station. In a push system, one of the functions of work-in-process inventory is to help make workstations independent of each other. Inventories are large enough to allow for variations in processing speeds, for discarding defective units without interrupting production, and for machine downtime.

Under a **materials pull system** (often called a **Kanban system**), employees at each station work to provide inventory for the next workstation only as needed. (*Kanban*, the Japanese word for *card*, is a system created in Japan that originally used cards to indicate that a department needed additional components.) The building of excess inventories is strictly prohibited. When the number of units in inventory reaches a specified limit, work at the station stops until workers at a subsequent station pull a unit from the in-process storage area. Hence, the *pull* of inventory by a subsequent station authorizes production to continue.

A pull, or Kanban, system's low inventory levels require a team effort. To avoid idle time, processing speeds must be balanced and equipment must be kept in good repair. Quality problems are identified immediately, and the low inventory levels require immediate correction of quality problems. To make a pull system work, management must accept the notion that it is better to have employees idle than to have them building excess inventory. A pull system also requires careful planning by management and active participation in decision making by employees. A lean production process involves minimizing cycle time, eliminating waste, producing inventory only as needed, and ensuring the highest level of quality and efficiency. To achieve these results on a continuing basis, there is a strong emphasis on continuous improvement programs (See Chapter 8). The following Business Insight discusses the use of a type of JIT, called Just-in-Sequence, used by Mercedes in making its Smart Car.

Reducing Finished Goods Inventory

Finished goods inventory can be reduced by reducing cycle time and by better predicting customer demand for finished units. Lowering cycle times reduces the need for speculative inventories. If finished goods

BUSINESS INSIGHT **Mercedes Benz Produces Smart Car Using Just-in-Sequence Production**

In early 2008, Mercedes Benz delivered the first units of its newly redesigned "Smart Car" automobile in the United States after ten years of success with this tiny vehicle in Europe and around the world. This two-person vehicle that sells for under $12,000 is designed to occupy less space in crowded cities and operate at a higher level of fuel efficiency than virtually any other car, and it is produced with an emphasis on environmental sustainability and the latest in production technology.

The plant where the Smart ForTwo is produced is called "Smartville" and is touted in the Smart Car product brochure as ". . . one of the most modern factories on the planet . . . . where the environmental aspects have been thoroughly thought out." The production system is described as one where "many components are produced on the premises of system partners. This reduces transport costs, packaging material and enables just-in-sequence production: all parts are delivered in the exact order in which they are required."

Source: "The 2008 Smart For Two" marketing brochure, Smart USA Distributor LLC, Bloomfield Hills, MI.

can be replenished quickly, the need diminishes for large inventory levels to satisfy customer needs and to provide for unanticipated fluctuations in customer orders. Anticipating customers' demand for goods can be improved by adopting a value chain approach to inventory management by which the manufacturer or supplier is working as a partner with its customers to meet their inventory needs. This frequently involves having online computer access to customers' inventory levels on a real-time basis and being able to synchronize changes in production with changes in customers' inventory levels as they occur.

Sharing this type of information obviously requires an enormous amount of mutual trust between a manufacturer or supplier and its customers, but it is becoming increasingly common among world-class organizations. An example of this type of vendor-customer relationship is the relationship between Procter & Gamble, one of the world's largest consumer products companies, and its largest customer, Wal-Mart. By having access to Wal-Mart's computer inventory system, Procter & Gamble is better able to determine and fill Wal-Mart's specific needs for products, such as disposable diapers.

PERFORMANCE EVALUATION AND RECORDKEEPING WITH LEAN PRODUCTION AND JIT

LO4 Explain how lean production and just-in-time affect performance evaluation and recordkeeping.

Movement toward a JIT/lean production philosophy requires changes in performance evaluation procedures and offers opportunities for significant reductions in recordkeeping costs. These changes are discussed in this section.

Performance Evaluation

JIT regards inventory as something to be eliminated. Hence, in a manufacturing organization, inventories are kept as small as possible. Under the JIT ideal, inventories do not exist because vendors deliver raw materials in small batches directly to the shop floor. JIT also strives to minimize, or eliminate, work-in-process inventory by minimizing the non-processing elements of cycle time and by having processing times as short as possible. Ideally, setup, waiting, movement, and inspection times do not exist.

Dysfunctional Effects of Traditional Performance Measures

A potential conflict exists between the goals of JIT and lean production and those of traditional performance measures applied at the level of the department or cost center. Although lean production emphasizes overall efficiency, many traditional performance measures emphasize local (departmental) cost savings and local (departmental) efficiency. Consider the following traditional performance measures for a purchasing agent and a departmental production supervisor:

- To achieve quantity discounts and favorable prices, a purchasing agent might order excess inventory, thereby increasing subsequent storage, obsolescence, and handling costs.
- To obtain a low price, a purchasing agent might order from a supplier whose goods have not been certified as meeting quality specifications, thereby causing subsequent inspection, rework, and spoilage costs, and perhaps, dissatisfied customers further down the value chain.
- To avoid having idle employees and equipment, a supervisor might refuse to halt production to determine the cause of a quality problem, thereby increasing inspection, rework, and spoilage costs.
- To obtain low fixed costs per unit under absorption costing, a supervisor might produce in excess of current needs (preferably in long production runs), thereby causing subsequent increases in storage, obsolescence, and handling costs.

Performance Measures Under Lean Production and JIT

In accordance with the goal of eliminating inventory and reducing cycle time to processing time, JIT supportive performance measures emphasize inventory turnover, cycle time, and **cycle efficiency** (the ratio of value-added to non-value-added manufacturing activities).

When applied to a specific item of raw materials or finished goods, **inventory turnover** is computed as the annual demand in units divided by the average inventory in units:

$$\text{Inventory turnover} = \frac{\text{Annual demand in units}}{\text{Average inventory in units}}$$

Progress toward the goal of reducing inventory is measured by comparing successive inventory turnover ratios. Generally, the higher the inventory turnover, the better.

When stated in dollars, inventory turnover can be used as a measure of the organization's overall success in reducing inventory, or in increasing sales in relation to inventories. This financial measure can be derived directly from a firm's financial statements.

$$\text{Inventory turnover} = \frac{\text{Cost of goods sold}}{\text{Average inventory (in dollars)}}$$

Another ratio often used to monitor the effectiveness of inventory levels is gross margin return on inventory investment (GMROI), calculated as follows:

$$\text{GMROI} = \frac{\text{Gross margin}}{\text{Average inventory}}$$

Cycle time is a measure of the total time required to produce one unit of a product:

$$\text{Cycle time} = \text{Setup time} + \text{Processing time} + \text{Movement time} + \text{Waiting time} + \text{Inspection time}$$

Under ideal circumstances, cycle time would consist of only processing time, and processing time would be as low as possible. Only processing time adds value to the product; hence, the time required for all other activities should be driven toward zero. The use of flexible manufacturing systems, properly sequencing jobs, and properly placing tools will minimize setup time. If the shop floor is optimally arranged, workers pass products directly from one workstation to the next. If production is optimally scheduled, inventory will not wait in temporary storage between workstations. If raw materials are of high quality and products are manufactured so that they always conform to specifications, separate inspection activities are not needed.

Cycle efficiency is computed as the ratio of processing time to total cycle time:

$$\text{Cycle efficiency} = \frac{\text{Processing time}}{\text{Cycle time}}$$

The highest cycle efficiency possible is always sought. If all non-value-added activities are eliminated, this ratio equals one.

Simplified Recordkeeping

Lean Production and JIT enable significant reductions in the number of accounting transactions required for purchasing and production activities. This results in cost savings for bookkeeping activities and in shifting accounting resources from detailed bookkeeping to the development of more useful activity cost data.

Purchasing

In a traditional accounting system, every purchase results in the generation of several documents. Additional documents are prepared for the issuance of raw materials to the factory. JIT, on the other hand, attempts to minimize inventory levels and stresses long-term relationships with a limited number of vendors who have demonstrated their ability to provide quality raw materials on a timely basis, as well as at a competitive price. Under a JIT inventory system, a company often has standing purchase orders for specified materials from specified vendors at specified prices. Production personnel are authorized to requisition materials directly from authorized vendors, who deliver limited quantities of materials as needed directly to the shop floor. Production personnel verify receipt of the raw materials. Periodically, each vendor sends an invoice for several shipments, which the company acknowledges and pays.

Product Costing

Another advantage of a lean production system is that it reduces the amount of detailed bookkeeping required for financial accounting purposes. If ending inventories are nonexistent, or so small that the costs assigned to them are insignificant in comparison with the costs assigned to Cost of Goods Sold, it makes little sense to track product costs through several inventory accounts. Instead of using a traditional product cost accounting system (as illustrated in Chapter 5), firms that have implemented JIT often use what is sometimes referred to as a backflush approach to accounting for product costs.

Under **backflush costing**, all costs of direct materials, direct labor, and manufacturing overhead are assigned as incurred to Cost of Goods Sold. If there are no inventories on hand at the end of the period, no additional steps are required. However, if there are inventories on hand at year-end, costs are backed out of Cost of Goods Sold and assigned to the appropriate inventory accounts. For a complete discussion of backflush costing, refer to a cost accounting text.

Also under a JIT inventory approach, many of the distinctions and arguments regarding absorption versus variable costing are moot. If the quantity of inventory is insignificant, it matters little whether inventory cost includes only variable manufacturing costs or both variable and fixed manufacturing costs. Whether absorption or variable costing is used, the total cost assigned to inventory on the balance sheet will be small, and the income reported on the income statement is likely to be about the same amount.

Performance Reporting With Lean Production

LO5 Discuss performance reporting in a lean production environment.

As we discussed in previous chapters, traditional product costing systems go to great lengths to calculate the materials, labor, and manufacturing overhead cost per unit for each unit produced. Overhead is typically assigned to inventory using a predetermined overhead rate based on an assumed volume-based driver such as direct labor hours or machine hours. If actual production is less than budgeted production, there will be underapplied overhead, which is usually written off as an expense of the period. To avoid this expense, managers are often motivated to overproduce product in order to ensure that all overhead is allocated to product. Also, by budgeting a large amount of produced units, fixed overhead cost is spread over more units, resulting in a lower cost per unit. Such overproduction is equivalent to a cardinal sin in a lean production company.

As we will see in Chapter 10, many companies also adopt standard cost systems where they account for product cost components on both an actual and budgeted cost basis, with variances between actual cost and standard (or allowed) costs reported on the internal performance reports as increased expenses if they are unfavorable and as a reduction of expenses if they are favorable. In such cases, managers are motivated to maximize favorable variances and minimize or eliminate unfavorable variances. Such systems of reporting often lead managers to actions that are contrary to the lean production philosophy.

Consider the example of a company using traditional costing and performance reporting that had the income statement shown in Exhibit 7.6 for one of its groups of products.

EXHIBIT 7.6 Traditional Performance Report with Standard Costs

	Current Period		Prior Period	
Net sales	$1,400	100%	$1,000	100%
Less cost of goods sold (based on standard costs)	−770	55%	−540	54%
Gross margin (based on standard costs)	630	45%	460	46%
Materials variance	(80)	(5.7%)	(30)	(3%)
Labor variance	(54)	(3.9%)	(40)	(4%)
Overhead variance	(50)	(3.6%)	(35)	(3.5%)
Gross margin (actual)	$ 446	31.9%	$ 355	35.5%

This performance report provides limited insight into what happened during the period that caused the gross margin percentage to drop by seven percentage points from 35.5% to 31.9%, even though net sales increased by 40%. About all we can determine is that the standard cost of goods sold increased by 1% of sales from 54% to 55%, and the unfavorable materials variance increased from 3% to 5.7% of sales. Now, see how the same performance might appear under a lean production reporting approach, as shown in Exhibit 7.7.

EXHIBIT 7.7 Lean Production Performance Report

	Current Year	Prior Year	Percent Change
Net Sales	$1,400	$1,000	40%
Less cost of goods sold:			
Materials cost	600	350	71.4%
Wages	140	120	16.7%
Employee benefits	120	60	100%
Services & Supplies	25	26	(3.8%)
Equipment depreciation	20	18	11.1%
Scrap	26	40	(35%)
Total processing costs	331	264	25.4%
Building depreciation	3	3	—
Building services	20	28	(28.6%)
Total occupancy costs	23	31	(25.8%)
Total cost of goods sold	954	645	47.9%
Gross margin	$ 446	$355	25.6%

This performance report provides a much clearer picture of why the company's gross margin increased by only 25.6%, even though there was a 40% increase in sales. Immediately, we can see that the percentage increases in materials cost and employee benefits were each substantially higher than the rate of increase in sales. All other cost categories had percentage decreases, or increases proportionately less than the increase in sales. This report clearly shows areas of improvement during the year as well as areas for needed improvement in the future. In a lean environment, managers are not seeking to perform well against an artificial standard; instead, the goal is constant improvement in cost efficiency and quality.

discuss w/ Steve!

These reports assume a pure JIT system where there were no significant amounts in inventories at the end of the period. If that were not the case, it would be necessary to make an adjustment to total cost of goods sold for the increase or decrease in inventory during the period in the lean production report.

In a lean production environment, costs are typically collected for each **value stream**. A value stream consists of the production processes for similar products. For example, a company like Hewlett Packard that produces multiple types and models of computers and printers may have two value streams, one for computers and another for printers. By identifying value streams as the primary cost objectives, more costs are directly traceable to the cost objectives, resulting in fewer cost allocations. You might recall that we said in an earlier chapter that a company that produces only one product does not have to make any cost allocations for product costing purposes, because the cost per unit is equal to total cost for the period divided by units produced in the period. Each value stream in a lean company not only has lean processes; it also has a lean accounting system because most costs should be directly traceable to one of the value streams. For indirect costs that cannot be traced directly to the value streams, cost assignments would need to be made using either a volume-based or activity-based method, as illustrated in Chapter 6.

CHAPTER-END REVIEW

The Champion Golf Company is trying to decide which automated production line to use to produce its new Pro XII golf balls. The two best systems under consideration have the following estimated performance characteristics, based on minutes per 1,000 balls produced:

	System A	System B
Setup time	25	10
Movement time from start to finish	10	14
Waiting time	3	16
Inspection time	5	7
Processing time	40	30
Total time in minutes	83	77

Required

a. Determine the cycle time per batch for each system.
b. Determine the cycle efficiency for each system.
c. Which system do you recommend and why?
d. Assuming Champion is a "lean" manufacturer, what improvements in the selected system is it likely to pursue.

Solution

a. Cycle time is the total time required to produce one batch, including both value-added and non-value-added activities: System A = 83 System B = 77
b. The cycle efficiency is the percent of total time used in value-added activities. In this case, only the processing time is adding value to the product. Cycle efficiency: System A = 40/83 = 0.48 System B = 30/77 = 0.39
c. In selecting between A and B, the system with the highest efficiency would not likely be chosen because it has the longest total cycle time. Assuming both systems produce products of equal quality and characteristics, B is appealing because it requires one-fourth less processing time than A and offers greater opportunity for continuous improvement.
d. In a lean environment management and all employees involved will be seeking ways to reduce the cycle time while maintaining a high-quality product. For B, the most likely opportunity for significant reduction is to reduce the large amount of movement and waiting time. If these components of total cycle time can be reduced, B becomes even more attractive.

GUIDANCE ANSWER

MANAGERIAL DECISION **You are the Controller**

Designing any information processing system is a matter of weighing benefits with the costs of designing and operating the system. The same is true for a cost allocation system. Also, you have to decide how the cost information will be used. If it is used only for external financial reporting purposes, a high degree of precision may not be necessary. However, if it is used to determine the most profitable product mix, it may be crucial to have the most precise cost information. For the service departments that provide only services to producing departments and that receive no services from other service departments, a direct allocation method might be adequate. For departments that provide and/or receive interdepartmental services, you should consider using either a step or linear algebra approach to assigning costs. Whether you use a direct, step or linear algebra approach, you will have to decide whether to assign the costs using a single volume-based cost driver (such as square footage or number of employees) or using multiple cost drivers that reflect the actual activities performed. In most cases, the ABC approach will give a higher level of precision, but at considerably greater cost.

DISCUSSION QUESTIONS

Q7-1. Distinguish between the following sets of terms:

a. Direct product costs and indirect product costs.

b. Direct department costs and indirect department costs.

Q7-2. Define the terms direct cost and indirect cost.

Q7-3. Differentiate between cost assignment and cost allocation.

Q7-4. Explain how a cost item can be both a direct cost and an indirect cost.

Q7-5. What is the primary advantage of separately allocating fixed and variable indirect costs?

Q7-6 Define interdepartmental services.

Q7-7. To what extent are interdepartmental services recognized under the direct, step, and linear algebra methods of service department cost allocation?

Q7-8. Is it feasible to assign interdepartmental services to production departments using ABC?

Q7-9. Explain the concept of just-in-time inventory management.

Q7-10. What are the major elements of lean production?

Q7-11. What is the relationship between JIT and the lean production concept?

Q7-12. What role did Toyota have in the development of the lean production concept?

Q7-13. What elements of the JIT approach contribute to reducing materials inventories?

Q7-14. Define and identify the elements of cycle time. Which of these elements adds value to the product?

Q7-15. Explain briefly how JIT/lean production benefits organizations that take a value-chain approach to management.

Q7-16. Explain how traditional performance evaluation systems using standard costs conflict with the lean production concept.

MINI EXERCISES

M7-17. Allocating Service Department Costs: Allocation Basis Alternatives (LO2)

Korning Glassworks has two producing departments, P1 and P2, and one service department, S1. Estimated direct overhead costs per month are as follows:

P1	$100,000
P2	200,000
S1	66,000

Other data follow:

	P1	P2
Number of employees	75	25
Production capacity (units).	50,000	30,000
Space occupied (square feet).	2,500	7,500
Five-year average percent of S1's service output used	65%	35%

Required

a. For each of the following allocation bases, determine the total estimated overhead cost for P1 and P2 after allocating S1 cost to the producing departments.

1. Number of employees
2. Production capacity in units
3. Space occupied
4. Five-year average percentage of S1 services used
5. Estimated direct overhead costs. (Round your answer to the nearest dollar.)

b. For each of the five allocation bases, explain the circumstances (including examples) under which each allocation base might be most appropriately used to allocate service department cost in a manufacturing plant such as Korning Glassworks. Also, discuss the advantages and disadvantages that might result from using each of the allocation bases.

M7-18. Indirect Cost Allocation: Direct Method (LO2)

Sprint Manufacturing Company has two production departments, Melting and Molding. Direct general plant management and plant security costs benefit both production departments. Sprint allocates general plant management costs on the basis of the number of production employees and plant security costs on the basis of space occupied by the production departments. In November, the following overhead costs were recorded:

Melting Department direct overhead	$150,000
Molding Department direct overhead.	300,000
General plant management	100,000
Plant security	35,000

Other pertinent data follow:

	Melting	Molding
Number of employees	25	45
Space occupied (square feet).	10,000	40,000
Machine hours	10,000	2,000
Direct labor hours.	4,000	20,000

Required

a. Prepare a schedule allocating general plant management costs and plant security costs to the Melting and Molding Departments.

b. Determine the total departmental overhead costs for the Melting and Molding Departments.

c. Assuming the Melting Department uses machine hours and the Molding Department uses direct labor hours to apply overhead to production, calculate the overhead rate for each production department.

M7-19. Interdepartment Services: Direct Method (LO2)

Tucson Manufacturing Company has five operating departments, two of which are producing departments (P1 and P2) and three of which are service departments (S1, S2, and S3). All costs of the service departments are allocated to the producing departments. The following table shows the distribution of services from the service departments.

Services provided from	Services Provided to				
	S1	S2	S3	P1	P2
S1	—	5%	25%	50%	20%
S2	10%	—	5	45	40
S3	15	5	—	20	60

The direct operating costs of the service departments are as follows:

S1	$42,000
S2	85,000
S3	19,000

Required

Using the direct method, prepare a schedule allocating the service department costs to the producing departments.

M7-20. Inventory Ratio Calculations (LO3, 4)

Delroi, Inc. provided the following data for 2008 and 2009:

Inventory	
December 31, 2007	$200,200
December 31, 2008	190,400
December 31, 2009	182,500
Cost of goods sold	
2008	$654,000
2009	724,000
Gross margin	
2008	$340,000
2009	410,000

Required

(round all calculations to two decimal places)

a. Calculate the inventory turnover ratio for 2008 and 2009.

b. Calculate the gross margin return on inventory investment for 2008 and 2009.

c. Comment on Delroi's progress toward becoming a more lean company.

M7-21. Inventory Ratio Calculations (LO3, 4)

McMahan, LTD. provided the following data for 2008 and 2009:

Inventory	
December 31, 2007	$176,000
December 31, 2008	185,000
December 31, 2009	194,000
Cost of goods sold	
2008	$546,000
2009	589,000
Gross margin	
2008	$256,000
2009	287,000

Required

(round all calculations to two decimal places)

a. Calculate the inventory turnover ratio for 2008 and 2009.

b. Calculate the gross margin return on inventory investment for 2008 and 2009.

c. Comment on McMahan's progress toward becoming a more lean company.

M7-22. Evaluating Production Options (LO4)

Jonas Manufacturing operates a small facility with several different flexible production cells that are used in making a variety of extruded material products. A potential customer has requested a quote for making 10,000 plastic components. Jonas is committed to lean production and is considering using one of two production cells for the job. Data (in hours) for the two cells is provided below.

	Cell1	Cell 2
Setup time	8.5	6.2
Total movement time	.6	.8
Waiting time	1.3	.8
Inspection time	.5	.5
Processing time	12.5	16.6
Total time	23.4	24.9

Required

a. Which of the above items are included in the calculation of total cycle time?

b. Which of the above items would be considered to be non-value added?

c. Calculate the cycle efficiency of the two options.

d. Which cell do you recommend for this job?

e. If Jonas is truly committed to a lean production, what additional actions might it take to make the job more profitable?

EXERCISES

E7-23. Interdepartment Services: Step Method (LO2)

Refer to the data in Mini-Exercise M7-19. Using the step method, prepare a schedule for Tucson Manufacturing Company allocating the service department costs to the producing departments. (Round calculations to the nearest dollar.)

E7-24. Interdepartment Services: Step Method (LO2)

O'Brian's Department Stores allocates the costs of the Personnel and Payroll departments to three retail sales departments, Housewares, Clothing, and Furniture. In addition to providing services to the operating departments, Personnel and Payroll provide services to each other. O'Brian's allocates Personnel Department costs on the basis of the number of employees and Payroll Department costs on the basis of gross payroll. Cost and allocation information for June is as follows:

	Personnel	Payroll	Housewares	Clothing	Furniture
Direct department cost.	$6,900	$3,200	$12,200	$20,000	$15,750
Number of employees	5	3	8	15	4
Gross payroll	$6,000	$3,300	$11,200	$17,400	$8,100

Required

a. Determine the percentage of total Personnel Department services that was provided to the Payroll Department.

b. Determine the percentage of total Payroll Department services that was provided to the Personnel Department.

c. Prepare a schedule showing Personnel Department and Payroll Department cost allocations to the operating departments, assuming O'Brian's uses the step method. (Round calculations to the nearest dollar.)

E7-25. Product Costing in a JIT/Lean Environment (LO3, 4)

Doll Computer manufactures laptop computers under its own brand, but acquires all the components from outside vendors. No computers are assembled until the order is received online from customers, so there is no finished goods inventory. When an order is received, the bill of materials required to fill the order is prepared automatically and sent electronically to the various vendors. All components are received from vendors within three days and the completed order is shipped to the customer immediately when completed, usually on the same day the components are received from vendors. The number of units in process at the end of any day is negligible.

The following data are provided for the most recent month of operations:

Actual components costs incurred	$905,000
Actual conversion costs incurred.	$192,000
Units in process, beginning of month	-0-
Units started in process during the month.	5,000
Units in process, end of month	-0-

Required

a. Assuming Doll uses traditional cost accounting procedures:
   1. How much cost was charged to Work-in-Process during the month?
   2. How much cost was charged to cost of goods sold during the month?

b. Assuming Doll is a lean production company and uses backflush costing method:
   1. How much cost was charged to Work-in-Process during the month?
   2. How much cost was charged to cost of goods sold during the month?

E7-26. Performance Reporting With Lean Production (LO3, 4, 5)

Hi-Standard Company prepared the following performance report for the month of March 2009:

	2009
Net sales.	$350,000
Less cost of goods sold (based on standard costs)	(178,000)
Gross margin (based on standard costs)	172,000
Materials variance	(5,000)
Labor variance	3,000
Manufacturing overhead variance	2,000
Gross margin (actual)	$172,000

Hi-Standard's general ledger included the following:

Materials purchases	$51,000
Wages expense	61,000
Services & supplies	14,000
Equipment depreciation	20,000
Building depreciation	18,000
Building services	11,000
Scrap	3,000

Inventories at the end of the month were negligible.

Required

a. Prepare a revised performance report that would be more appropriate if Hi-Standard were following a lean production strategy.

b. What additional information would be useful for evaluating Hi-Standard's performance for March.

c. What are some of the potential pitfalls associated with reporting variances such as those presented in Hi-Standard's original performance report for March.

E7-27. Inventory Management Metrics (LO4)

Large retailers like The Home Depot and Wal-Mart typically use gross margin ratio (gross margin ÷ sales), inventory turnover (sometimes referred to as inventory turns), and gross margin return on investment (GM-ROI) to evaluate how well inventory has been managed. The goal is to maximize profits while minimizing the investment in inventory. Below are data for four scenarios, a base scenario (# 1) followed by three modifications (#s 2, 3, & 4) to the base scenario.

	Scenario 1	Scenario 2	Scenario 3	Scenario 4
Sales	$10,000	$20,000	$12,000	$10,000
Cost of goods sold	6,000	12,000	6,000	6,000
Gross profit	$ 4,000	$ 8,000	$ 6,000	$ 4,000
Average inventory	$ 6,000	$ 6,000	$ 6,000	$ 5,000

Required

a. For each scenario calculate the gross margin percent, the inventory turnover, and GMROI.

b. For Scenarios 2 though 4, explain what change occurred relative to Scenario 1 to cause GMROI to change. For example, was the change in GMROI caused by a change in inventory turns, a change in gross margin percent, or by reducing inventory levels.

c. What general conclusions can be made from the above calculations and observations regarding the factors that influence GMROI.

PROBLEMS

P7-28. Selecting Cost Allocation Bases and Direct Method Allocations (LO2)

Ohio Company has three producing departments (P1, P2, and P3) for which direct department costs are accumulated. In January, the following indirect costs of operation were incurred.

Plant manager's salary and office expense	$ 9,600
Plant security	2,400
Plant nurse's salary and office expense.........	3,000
Plant depreciation	4,000
Machine maintenance	4,800
Plant cafeteria cost subsidy..................	2,400
	$26,200

The following additional data have been collected for the three producing departments:

	P1	P2	P3
Number of employees	10	15	5
Space occupied (square feet).......	2,000	5,000	3,000
Direct labor hours...............	1,600	4,000	750
Machine hours	4,800	8,000	3,200
Number of nurse office visits	20	45	10

Required

a. Group the indirect cost items into cost pools based on the nature of the costs and their common basis for allocation. Identify the most appropriate allocation basis for each cost pool and determine the total January costs in the pool. (*Hint:* A cost pool may consist of one or more cost items.)

b. Allocate the cost pools directly to the three producing departments using the allocation bases selected in requirement (a).

c. How much indirect cost would be allocated to each producing department if Ohio Company were using a plantwide rate based on direct labor hours? Based on machine hours?

d. Comment on the benefits of allocating costs in pools compared with using a plantwide rate.

P7-29. Evaluating Allocation Bases and Direct Method Allocations (LO2)

Cheyenne Company has two service departments, Maintenance and Cafeteria, that serve two producing departments, Mixing and Packaging. The following data have been collected for these departments for the current year:

	Cafeteria	Maintenance	Mixing	Packaging
Direct department costs	$176,000	$112,000	$465,000	$295,000
Number of employees			50	30
Number of meals served			9,000	7,000
Number of maintenance hours used			800	600
Number of maintenance orders			180	170

Required

a. Using the direct method, allocate the service department costs under the following independent assumptions:

1. Cafeteria costs are allocated based on the number of employees, and Maintenance costs are allocated based on the number of maintenance hours used.
2. Cafeteria costs are allocated based on the number of meals served, and Maintenance costs are allocated based on the number of maintenance orders.

b. Comment on the reasonableness of the bases used in the calculations in requirement (a). What considerations should determine which bases to use for allocating Cafeteria and Maintenance costs?

P7-30. Cost Reimbursement and Step Allocation Method (LO2)

Community Clinic is a not-for-profit outpatient facility that provides medical services to both fee-paying patients and low-income government-supported patients. Reimbursement from the government is based on total actual costs of services provided, including both direct costs of patient services and indirect operating costs. Patient services are provided through two producing departments, Medical Services and Ancillary Services (includes X-ray, therapy, etc.). In addition to the direct costs of these departments, the clinic incurs indirect costs in two service departments, Administration and Facilities. Administration costs are allocated based on the number of full-time employees, and Facilities costs are allocated based on space occupied. Costs and related data for the current month are as follows:

	Administration	Facilities	Medical Services	Ancillary Services
Direct costs	$18,000	$6,000	$121,400	$37,200
Number of employees	5	4	12	8
Amount of space occupied (square feet)	1,500	—	8,000	2,000
Number of patient visits	—	—	4,000	1,500

Required

a. Using the step method, prepare a schedule allocating the common service department costs to the producing departments.

b. Determine the amount to be reimbursed from the government for each low-income patient visit.

P7-31. Budgeted Service Department Cost Allocation: Pricing a New Product (LO2)

Trimco Products Company is adding a new diet food concentrate called Body Trim to its line of bodybuilding and exercise products. A plant is being built for manufacturing the new product. Management has decided to price the new product based on a 100 percent markup on total manufacturing costs. A direct cost budget for the new plant projects that direct department costs of $2,100,000 will be incurred in producing an expected normal output of 700,000 pounds of finished product. In addition, indirect costs for Administration and Technical Support will be shared by Body Trim with the two exercise products divisions, Commercial Products and Retail Products. Budgeted annual data to be used in making the allocations are summarized here.

	Administration	Technical Support	Commercial Products	Retail Products	Body Trim
Number of employees	5	5	50	30	20
Amount of technical support time (hours)	500	—	1,500	1,250	750

Direct costs are budgeted at $135,000 for the Administration Department and $240,000 for the Technical Support Department.

Required

a. Using the step method, determine the total direct and indirect costs of Body Trim.

b. Determine the selling price per pound of Body Trim. (Round calculations to the nearest cent.)

P7-32. Allocation and Responsibility Accounting (LO2)

Assume that Timberland Company uses a responsibility accounting system for evaluating its managers, and that abbreviated performance reports for the company's three divisions for the month of March are as presented on the following page (amounts in thousands).

Timberland Company (TBL)

	Total	East	Central	West
Income	$165,000	$60,000	$75,000	$30,000
Less allocated costs:				
Computer Services	(66,000)	(22,000)	(22,000)	(22,000)
Personnel	(72,000)	(28,000)	(32,000)	(12,000)
Division income	$ 27,000	$10,000	$21,000	$ (4,000)

The West Division manager is very disturbed over his performance report and recent rumors that his division may be closed because of its failure to report a profit in recent periods. He believes that the reported profit figures do not fairly present operating results because his division is being unfairly burdened with service department costs. He is particularly concerned over the amount of Computer Services costs charged to his division. He believes that it is inequitable for his division to be charged with one-third of the total cost when it is using only 20 percent of the services. He believes that the Personnel Department's use of the Computer Services Department should also be considered in the cost allocations. Cost allocations were based on the following distributions of service provided:

		Services Receiver			
Services Provider	Personnel	Computer Services	East	Central	West
Computer Services	40%	—	20%	20%	20%
Personnel	—	10%	35	40	15

Required

a. What method is the company using to allocate Personnel and Computer Services costs?

b. Recompute the cost allocations using the step method. (Round calculations to the nearest dollar.)

c. Revise the performance reports to reflect the cost allocations computed in requirement (b).

d. Comment on the complaint of the West Division's manager.

P7-33. Allocating Service Department Costs: Direct and Step Methods; Department and Plantwide Overhead Rates (LO2)

Pennington Group

Assume that Pennington Group, a manufacturer of fine casual outdoor furniture, allocates Human Resources Department costs to the producing departments (Cutting and Welding) based on number of employees; Facilities Department costs are allocated based on the amount of square footage occupied. Direct department costs, labor hours, and square footage data for the four departments for October are as follows:

	Human Resources	Facilities	Cutting	Welding
Direct department overhead costs	$60,000	$120,000	$800,000	$350,000
Number of employees	5	5	35	60
Number of direct labor hours	—	—	8,000	10,000
Amount of square footage	10,000	3,000	100,000	50,000

Assume that two jobs, A1 and A2, were completed during October and that each job had direct materials costs of $1,200. Job A1 used 80 direct labor hours in the Cutting Department and 20 direct labor hours in the Welding Department. Job A2 used 20 direct labor hours in the Cutting Department and 80 direct labor hours in the Welding Department. The direct labor rate is $50 in both departments.

Required

a. Find the cost of each job using a plantwide rate based on direct labor hours.

b. Find the cost of each job using department rates with *direct* service department cost allocation.

c. Find the cost of each job using department rates with *step* service department cost allocation.

d. Explain the differences in the costs computed in requirements (a)–(c) for each job. Which costing method is better for product pricing and profitability analysis?

P7-34. JIT/Lean Production and Product Costing (LO4)

Presented is information pertaining to the standard or budgeted unit cost of a product manufactured in a JIT/Lean Production environment at Simko Systems Inc.:

Direct materials	$15
Conversion	10
Total	$25

All materials are added at the start of the production process. All raw materials purchases and conversion costs are directly assigned to Cost of Goods Sold. At the end of the period, costs are backed out and assigned to Raw Materials in Process (only for materials still in the plant) and Finished Goods Inventory (for materials and conversion costs). Costs assigned to inventories are based on the standard or budgeted cost multiplied by the number of units in inventory. Conversion costs are assigned to inventories only for fully converted units. Since inventory levels tend to be small in this JIT environment, partially completed units are assigned no conversion costs. Simko had no beginning inventories on August 1, 2009. During the month, it incurred the following manufacturing-related costs:

Purchase of raw materials on account	$300,000
Factory wages	125,000
Factory supervision salaries	30,000
Utilities bill for month	17,000
Factory supplies purchased	15,000
Depreciation	9,500

The end-of-month inventory included raw materials in process of 600 units and finished goods of 400 units. One hundred units of raw materials were zero percent converted; the other 500 units averaged 60 percent converted.

Required

a. Calculate the total cost charged to Cost of Goods Sold during August.

b. Calculate the balances in Raw Materials in Process, Finished Goods Inventory, and Cost of Goods Sold at the end of August.

c. Assuming that August is a typical month, is it likely that using the company's shortcut backflush accounting procedures will produce misleading financial statements? Explain.

P7-35. Benefits of Implementing a Just-in-Time Inventory System (LO4)

Car Parts Inc. distributes replacement parts for various automobile models, competing primarily with the dealers for the major automobile manufacturers. The key to Car Parts' success is having parts in stock when independent mechanics come to one of its retail stores. The firm's controller has become concerned about the escalating costs of maintaining large inventories at each store location. At the beginning of 2009, she decided to test a modified just-in-time inventory system in the Canton, Ohio, store that significantly reduced the number of parts for each inventory item stocked. After one year of experience with the JIT system, the controller assessed the benefits of using JIT and gathered the following data for the Canton store:

- Average inventory declined from $800,000 to $200,000.
- Annual insurance costs declined from $60,000 to $15,000.
- As a result of reduced inventory levels, a 5,000-square-foot warehouse that had been leased for $10,000 per year to store parts was not used at all during the year. Car Parts was able to sublet the space for the year for $2.50 per square foot.
- The employee who staffed the parts warehouse was reassigned to help coordinate the JIT inventory system. His $30,000 salary was charged to the fixed portion of indirect manufacturing costs.
- With the reduction in inventory levels, increases in overnight shipping costs were required to meet customer demands on a timely basis. The estimated overnight shipping premium paid was $5 per part on a total of 5,000 parts. It was also estimated that sales of 3,000 parts were lost due to stockouts.
- In the past, Car Parts store in Canton has had an annual expense of about $30,000 for obsolete inventories. With the implementation of JIT, the current year's expense was only $5,000.
- Car Parts has a cost of capital rate of 15 percent for investments in inventory.

Before deciding to implement the JIT inventory system, the budgeted income statement for the Canton, Ohio, store for 2009 had been projected as follows:

Sales (300,000 parts)		$6,600,000
Cost of goods sold		
Variable manufacturing costs	$2,850,000	
Fixed manufacturing costs	1,200,000	(4,050,000)
Gross profit		2,550,000
Selling and administrative expenses		
Variable	750,000	
Fixed	550,000	(1,300,000)
Operating income		1,250,000
Interest expense		(160,000)
Income before taxes		$1,090,000

Required

a. Calculate the savings (loss) before taxes for Car Parts' Canton, Ohio, store related to implementing the JIT inventory system.

b. What factors other than financial considerations should Car Parts consider before deciding whether to implement the JIT inventory system throughout its entire retail organization?

P7-36. Just-in-Time Performance Evaluation (LO5)

To control operations, JVC Company makes extensive and exclusive use of financial performance reports for each department. Although all departments have been reporting favorable cost variances in most periods, management is perplexed by the firm's low overall return on investment. You have been asked to look into the matter. Believing the purchasing department is typical of the company's operations, you obtained the following information concerning the purchases of parts for a product it started producing in 2004:

Year	Purchase Price Variance	Quantity Used (units)	Average Inventory (units)
2004	$ 1,000 F	20,000	5,000
2005	10,000 F	30,000	7,500
2006	12,000 F	30,000	10,000
2007	20,000 U	25,000	6,250
2008	8,000 F	36,000	9,000
2009	9,500 F	29,000	7,250

Required

a. Compute the inventory turnover for each year. What conclusions can be drawn from a yearly comparison of the purchase price variance and the inventory turnover?

b. Identify problems likely to be caused by evaluating purchasing only on the basis of the purchase price variance.

c. Offer whatever recommendations you believe appropriate.

P7-37. Dual Allocation of Shared Services (LO2)

Greenwood Corporation is part owner in three major hotels in the Boston area. To create cost efficiencies Greenwood runs a centralized reservation system (CRS) for the three hotels. The reservation center has the following monthly cost structure: $120,000 in fixed costs and $3 in variable cost per room sold. The following information is available for the three hotels:

Property #	Rooms	Rooms Sold
1	400	9,600
2	800	16,800
3	1200	21,600

Required:

a. Allocate the reservation center costs to the hotels assuming that all costs are allocated based on number of rooms sold.

b. Allocate the reservation center costs to the hotels assuming that fixed costs are allocated based on capacity provided and variable costs are allocated based on rooms sold.

c. Comment on the advantages and disadvantages of the two methods in parts a. and b.

P7-38. Dual Allocation Approach and Charging for Services (LO2)

The Maintenance Department of Management Suites Hotel has fixed costs of $400,000 a year. It also incurs $20 in out-of-pocket expenses for every hour of work. During the year the Rooms Department used 20,000 maintenance hours. The Food and Beverage (F&B) Department used 5,000 maintenance hours. When the Maintenance Department was established the Rooms and F&B departments estimated they would need 20,000 and 12,000 maintenance hours, respectively. It turns out F&B cut back on maintenance hours used to insure it would meet its budget.

Required:

a. Calculate the amount of Maintenance Department costs to allocate to Rooms and F&B based entirely on actual usage.

b. Calculate the amount of Maintenance Department costs to allocate to Rooms and F&B using a dual allocation approach where fixed cost is allocated based on estimated capacity needed and variable cost is allocated based on actual usage.

c. Which of the two methods applied in parts a. and b. is most fair to the two departments?

d. Assume that the maintenance department allocates costs to the producing departments using a user charge. What amount would you suggest for the user charge? Is it a good idea to use a user charge for allocating costs?

CASES

C7-39. Cost Allocation and Performance Evaluation (LO1)

The Village Branch of First Bank is managed by Ron Short, who has full responsibility for the bank's operations. The Village Branch is treated as a profit center within the company's responsibility accounting system; according to rumors throughout the company, if The Village Branch does not become more profitable, it is likely to be closed. Ron is upset with the corporate accounting department because of the number of different indirect costs that are allocated to his branch each period. He believes that many of these costs provide no direct benefits to his branch and that they are not relevant to an evaluation of his performance or that of The Village Branch. An income statement for The Village Branch for February follows:

Branch revenues		$450,000
Direct branch costs		(345,000)
Branch margin		105,000
Allocated costs		
Computer operations	$14,500	
Personnel	15,000	
Payroll	23,800	
Maintenance	6,000	
Accounting	5,200	
Legal and audit	4,200	
Transportation	9,000	
Administrative overhead	22,000	(99,700)
Branch net income		$ 5,300

An investigation of Mr. Short's complaint by the controller's office provided the following additional information:

- Computer operations costs are billed based on actual CPU and computer connection time used by the branch.
- Personnel and payroll costs, primarily fixed, are allocated to the various operating departments based on the number of employees in each division.
- Maintenance costs are charged to the operating departments based on the standard hours actually worked in each department plus the actual cost of materials and supplies used.
- Accounting costs are allocated based on the number of transactions processed by the computer for each branch.
- Legal and audit costs are allocated based on the total revenues of the operating departments. The Village Branch has been involved in only one lawsuit, which was about five years ago. Mr. Short receives a copy of the company audit report each year but seldom reads it.
- Transportation costs consist primarily of the costs of operating the company helicopter and the company airplane. The helicopter is used to deliver checks to the local clearing center and for local executive transportation; the airplane is used primarily for executive travel out of town. Transportation costs are allocated to the operating departments based on revenues. Mr. Short has never flown in the corporate airplane.
- Administrative overhead consists of all other administrative costs including home office salaries and office expenses. These costs are allocated to the operating departments based on revenues. Mr. Short seldom sees anyone from the home office.

Required

a. Evaluate each cost allocation to determine whether it seems appropriate to allocate it to the operating divisions. Also evaluate the basis on which each cost is allocated to the operating departments.

b. Prepare a revised income statement for The Village Branch based on your evaluations in requirement (a).

c. Do you agree with Mr. Short's complaint? How do the cost allocations affect the decision to continue or discontinue The Village Branch?

C7-40. Materials Push and Materials Pull Systems (LO3, 4)

Media Storage Inc. produces three models of hard disk drives for personal computers. Each model is produced on a separate assembly line. Production consists of several operations in separate work centers. Because of a high demand for Media's products, management is most interested in high-production volume and operating efficiency. Each work center is evaluated on the basis of its operating efficiency. To avoid idle time caused by defective units, variations in machine times, and machine breakdowns, significant inventories are maintained between each workstation.

At a recent administrative committee meeting, the director of research announced that the firm's engineers have made a dramatic breakthrough in designing a low-cost, read/write optical storage device. Media Storage's president is very enthusiastic, and the vice president of marketing wishes to add an assembly line for optical storage devices as soon as possible. The equipment necessary to manufacture the new product can be purchased and installed in less than 60 days. Unfortunately, all available plant space is currently devoted to the production of hard disk drives, and expansion is not possible at the current plant location. It appears that adding the new product will require dropping a current product, relocating the entire operation, or manufacturing the optical storage devices at a separate location.

The vice president of marketing is opposed to dropping a current product. The vice president of finance is opposed to relocating the entire operation because of financing requirements and the associated financial risks. The vice president of production is opposed to splitting up production activities because of the loss of control and the added costs for various types of overhead.

Required

Explain how switching to a materials pull (Kanban) system can help solve Media Storage's space problems while improving quality and cycle time. Describe how a materials pull system works and the changes required in management attitude toward inventory and efficiency to make it work.

C7-41. Product Costing Using Activity-Based Costing and Just-in-Time: A Value Chain Approach **(LO3, 4)**

Wearwell Carpet Company is a small residential carpet manufacturer started by Don Stegall, a longtime engineer and manager in the carpet industry. Stegall began Wearwell in the early 1990s after learning about ABC, JIT, total quality management, and several other manufacturing concepts being used successfully in Japan and other parts of the world. Although it was a small company, he believed that with his many years of experience and by applying these advanced techniques, Wearwell could very quickly become a world-class competitor.

Stegall buys dyed carpet yarns for Wearwell from three different major yarn manufacturers with which he has done business for many years. He chose these companies because of their reputation for producing high-quality products and their state-of-the art research and development departments. He has arranged for two carpet manufacturing companies to produce (tuft) all of his carpets on a contractual basis. Both companies have their own brands, but they also do contract work for other companies. For each manufacturer, Stegall had to agree to use the full output of one manufacturing production line at least one day per month. Each production line was dedicated to producing only one style of carpet, but each manufacturer had production lines capable of running each type of carpet that Wearwell sold.

Stegall signed a contract with a large transport company (CTC), which specializes in carpet-related shipping, to pick up and deliver yarn from the yarn plants to the tufting mills. This company will then deliver the finished product from the tufting mills to Wearwell's ten customers, which are carpet retailers in the ten largest residential building markets in the country. These retailers pay the shipping charges to have the carpets delivered to them. Wearwell maintains a small sales staff (which also doubles as a customer service staff) to deal with the retailers and occasionally with the end customers on quality problems that arise.

Wearwell started selling only one line of carpet, a medium-grade plush, but as new carpet styles were developed, it added two additional lines, a medium-grade berber carpet and a medium-grade textured carpet. Three colors are offered in each carpet style. By selling only medium grades with limited color choices, Stegall felt that he would reach a very large segment of the carpet market without having to deal with a large number of different products. As textured (trackless) carpets have become more popular, sales of plush have diminished substantially.

Required

a. Describe the value chain for Wearwell Carpet Company, and identify the parties who compose this value chain.

b. Identify and discuss the cost categories that would be included in the cost of the product for financial reporting purposes.

c. Identify and discuss the cost categories that would be included in the cost of the product for pricing and other management purposes.

d. Discuss some of the challenges that Stegall will have trying to apply JIT to regulate the levels of control at Wearwell. Suggest changes that might be necessary to make JIT work.

e. Does Wearwell seem to be an appropriate setting for implementing ABC? If so, what are likely to be the most important activities and related cost drivers?

C7-42. JIT/Lean Production Performance Evaluation (LO3, 4, 5)

The vice president of manufacturing is perplexed. When the new southside plant began operations, it appeared to live up to the expectations of top management. The plant was modern, well lighted, and spacious. Cost variances were favorable, customers were highly satisfied with quality and service, and the plant reported large segment contributions to common costs and profits despite high start-up costs and early period depreciation.

Just three years later, the southside plant seems to be declining into crisis management. Although most cost variances, especially those dealing with cost center efficiency, remain favorable, the plant's segment contribution is declining, and customers are complaining about poor quality and slow delivery. Several customers have suggested that if the firm cannot correct its quality and delivery problems, they will take their business elsewhere. The shop floor is a mess with work-in-process inventory piled everywhere. Production employees complain of difficulty in locating jobs to be worked on, and scheduling personnel have recently requested a larger computer to help track work in process. The vice president said she does not know where to begin to determine how to solve the plant's problems. She commented, "What is really weird is that we all work so hard. Our facilities are the best in the business, and I know our employees are dedicated, well trained, and hardworking. They do exactly what we ask, and we have never had any labor problems. It just seems like the harder we work, the worse our problems become."

Required

Suggest the nature of the southside plant's problems and recommend how the vice president might begin to determine how to solve the plant's problems.

Chapter 8

Pricing and Other Product Management Decisions

LEARNING OBJECTIVES

LO1 Explain the importance of the value chain in managing products and identify the key components of an organization's internal and external value chain. (p. 252)

LO2 Distinguish between economic and cost-based approaches to pricing. (p. 256)

LO3 Explain target costing and its acceptance in highly competitive industries. (p. 261)

LO4 Describe the relation between target costing and continuous improvement costing. (p. 266)

LO5 Explain how benchmarking enhances quality management, continuous improvement, and process reengineering. (p. 267)

GREEN CARS: MANAGING COSTS AND PRICES

Strong competition exists among Japanese, U.S., and European automakers to develop the next generation of cars—the "green cars" that cut pollution and boost fuel economy. Rising international tensions and spiraling oil prices (topping $100 per barrel for the first time in early 2008) have added intensity to the race for new technologies to power automobiles. The technological, production, and marketing challenges, however, are substantial. Competing technologies include hydrogen fuel cells and hybrid-powered formats.

Honda and **Toyota** favor hybrid car technology that combines gasoline and electric power. **Ford**, **General Motors**, and **Daimler** favor hydrogen fuel cells that combine hydrogen and oxygen to make electricity and water. Despite competing technological approaches, all of these firms share an important strategic management goal—convincing customers to buy a green car. To achieve this goal, firms must price these cars competitively and create reasonable alternatives for potential customers who are satisfied with a regular car.

To succeed in this emerging market, automakers rely on important management accounting tools, such as target costing and continuous improvement (Kaizen) costing, to achieve a competitive price that is also profitable. Two hybrid cars, the Honda *Insight* and Toyota *Prius*, both had initial price tags of around $20,000 and initial yearly target sales between 4,000 and 12,000 units. During development, Toyota relied on continuous improvement to achieve the cost savings necessary to make the *Prius* profitable. The firm established this price to be competitive with its popular

Courtesy of Getty Images

Corolla model. Toyota has now added the hybrid to its luxury Lexus brand, and the Detroit auto manufacturers have followed suit.

For manufacturers using hydrogen fuel cell technology, the goal is a $20,000 hydrogen fuel cell vehicle before 2010. Managers on these projects count on increased fuel cell performance, reductions in size, and changes in materials to lower the cost of this power source.

Ford and Daimler transferred their hydrogen fuel cell research and development to **Ballard Power Systems** of Canada—a world leader in hydrogen fuel cell technology. In return, both Ford and Daimler hold substantial ownership stakes in Ballard. Ballard's mandate from the automakers is clear: Develop a fuel cell automobile propulsion system that has the right size, weight, range, and cost attributes to be commercially successful. Mercedes buses in Australia, and UPS package delivery vehicles in the U.S., are now being tested with hydrogen fuel cells.

Within this emerging market for green cars as well as other emerging and existing markets, strategic cost management tools are increasingly important for managers involved in the development, manufacture, and marketing of products and services. Companies that are successful in introducing new products, as well as managing existing products, invariably have a focus on the value chain for all of their products.[1]

---

[1] Jeffrey Ball, "Ballard Power Expands Fuel-Cell Drive as Ford, DaimlerChrysler Boost Stakes, *The Wall Street Journal (Interactive Edition)*, October 3, 2001; Terril Ye Jones, "Whose Car Is Greener?" *Forbes*, October 18, 1999, p. 60; Keith Naughton, "Can You Have Green Cars Without Red Ink?" *Business Week*, December 29, 1997, p. 50; Keith Naughton, "Detroit's Impossible Dream," *Business Week*, March 2, 1998, pp. 66 & 68; Emily Thornton, Keith Naughton, and David Woodruff, "Toyota's Green Machine," *Business Week*, December 15, 1997, pp. 108–110; David Woodruff and William C. Symonds, "The Hottest Thing in 'Green' Wheels," *Business Week*, April 28, 1997, p. 42.

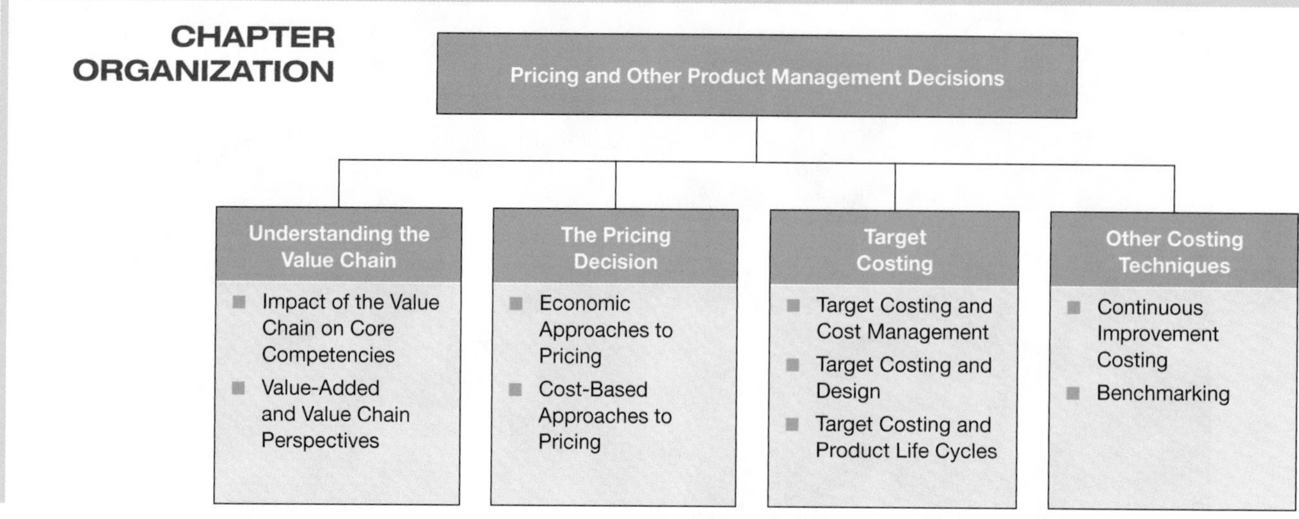

Strategic cost management techniques, such as *target costing* and *continuous improvement costing*, represent important concepts for product management professionals involved in the development, manufacture, and marketing of products and services. Virtually all such techniques are grounded in the notion of managing the value chain. This chapter examines pricing, the interrelation between price and cost, and the role of benchmarking in meeting customer needs at the lowest possible price.

We begin with a discussion of the value chain, followed by an overview of the pricing model economists use to explain price equilibrium. Given the limitations of this long-run equilibrium model for determining price of a product or service, we consider the widely used cost-plus approach to identifying initial prices. We then examine how intense competition (such as that for the green car market) has inverted the cost-plus pricing model into one that starts with an acceptable market price and subtracts a desired profit to determine a target cost. We also consider *life cycle costs* from the perspectives of both the seller, who increasingly plans for all costs before production begins, and the buyer, who regards subsequent operating, maintenance, repair, and disposal costs as important as price. Finally, we consider how *benchmarking* can assist in improving competitiveness and profitability.

UNDERSTANDING THE VALUE CHAIN

LO1 Explain the importance of the value chain in managing products and identify the key components of an organization's internal and external value chain.

The **value chain** for a product or service is the set of value-producing activities that stretches from basic raw materials to the final consumer. Each product or service has a distinct value chain, and all entities along the value chain depend on the final customer's perception of the value and cost of a product or service. It is the final customer who ultimately pays all costs and provides all profits to all organizations along the entire value chain. Consequently, *the goal of every organization is to maximize the value, while minimizing the cost, of a product or service to final customers.*

The value chain provides a viewpoint that encompasses all activities performed to deliver products and services to final customers. Depending on the needs of management, value chains are developed at varying levels of detail. Analyzing a value chain from the perspective of the final consumer requires working backward from the end product or service to the basic raw materials entering into the product or service. Analyzing a value chain from the viewpoint of an organization that is in the middle of a value chain requires working forward (downstream) to the final consumer and backward (upstream) to the source of raw materials. The paper industry provides a convenient context for illustrating the value chain concept.

Exhibit 8.1 presents the value chain for the paperboard cartons used to package beverages, such as Coca-Cola, Pepsi, or Evían products. The value chain is presented at three levels, with each successive level containing additional details. The first level depicts the various business entities in the value chain:

- Timber producers grow the pulp wood (usually pine) used as the basic input into paper products. Some large paper companies, such as Boise Cascade and Georgia Pacific, harvest much of their pulp wood from timberlands that they manage. Other companies, including Riverwood

EXHIBIT 8.1 Value Chain for a Beverage-Packaging Product

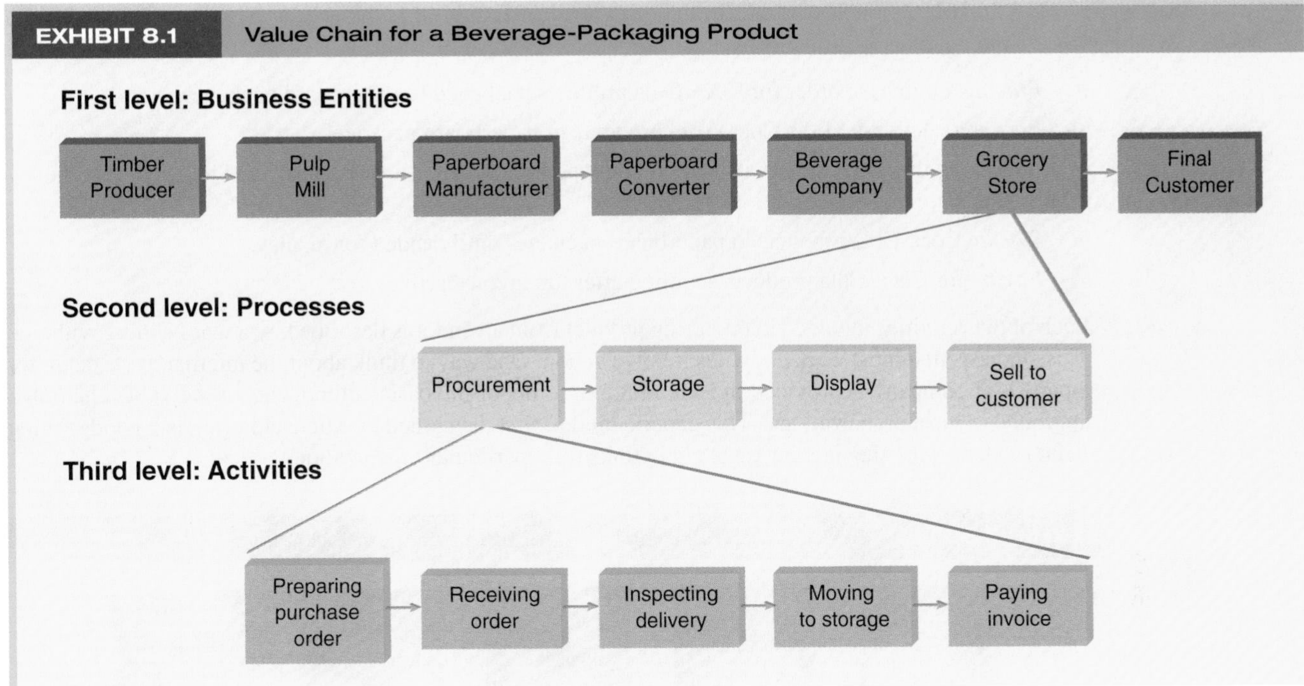

International, which is a leading producer of paperboard for the beverage industry, do not manage their own timberlands, but purchase pulp for their mills on the open market through pulp intermediaries.

- Pulp mills produce the kraft (unbleached) paper used to produce the paperboard. Some of the smaller paperboard manufacturers purchase the kraft paper product from pulp mills; Riverwood International, however, owns its own paper mills that produce paper for its paperboard production facilities.
- Paperboard manufacturers perform a laminating process of coating paperboard material used to produce beverage packages. The paperboard consists of two layers of paper product plus three layers of coating that gives the top surface a high gloss finish that is water resistent and suitable for multicolor printing. Riverwood International is a manufacturer of paperboard for the beverage industry that is marketed under the name of Aqua-Kote.
- The paperboard converter uses manufactured paperboard to print and produce the completed beverage packaging product, such as the cartons used to package the Diet Coca-Cola 12-pack.
- Beverage distributors, such as Coca-Cola Enterprises and Anheuser-Busch, purchase the completed paperboard packages from Riverwood International to package their many different brands in various package sizes and shapes.
- Grocery and convenience stores, such as Safeway and 7-Eleven, display and sell beverages packaged in the paperboard containers.
- The final customer purchases beverages packaged in paperboard packages and uses the packages to carry the beverages and to store them until consumed. The packages not only perform a transport and storage function but also serve as an advertising medium for the beverage company. The beverage company's advertising on the paperboard packages is intended to entice customers to purchase the beverage company's product and to help create a sense of satisfaction for the customer.

To better understand how business entities within the chain add value and incur costs, management might further refine the value chain into **processes**, collections of related activities intended to achieve a common purpose. The second level in Exhibit 8.1 represents major processes concerning the procurement and sale of Coca-Cola products by a grocery store. To simplify our illustration, we show only the processes for the grocery store related to the purchase and sale of Coca-Cola products packaged in paperboard packages. These processes include procuring Coca-Cola products from the bottling company, storing and displaying the product, and selling the product to the final consumer.

An **activity** is a unit of work. In the third level of Exhibit 8.1, the grocery store process to procure Coca-Cola products is further broken up into the following activities:

- *Placing* a purchase order for Coca-Cola products packaged in paperboard packages.
- *Receiving* delivery of the Coca-Cola products in paperboard packages.
- *Inspecting* the delivery to make sure it corresponds with the purchase order and to verify that the products are in good condition.
- *Storing* Coca-Cola products in paperboard packages until needed for display.
- *Paying* for Coca-Cola products acquired after the invoice arrives.

Each of the activities involved in procuring product from a vendor is described by a word ending with *ing*. This suggests that most work activities involve action. One way to think about the internal value chain for a particular company is provided in Exhibit 8.2 in terms of the basic components of the value chain that are found in most organizations. This generic model, first developed by Michael Porter, is a good starting point in identifying the internal value chain links for a particular organization.

EXHIBIT 8.2 Generic Internal Processes of the Internal Value Chain

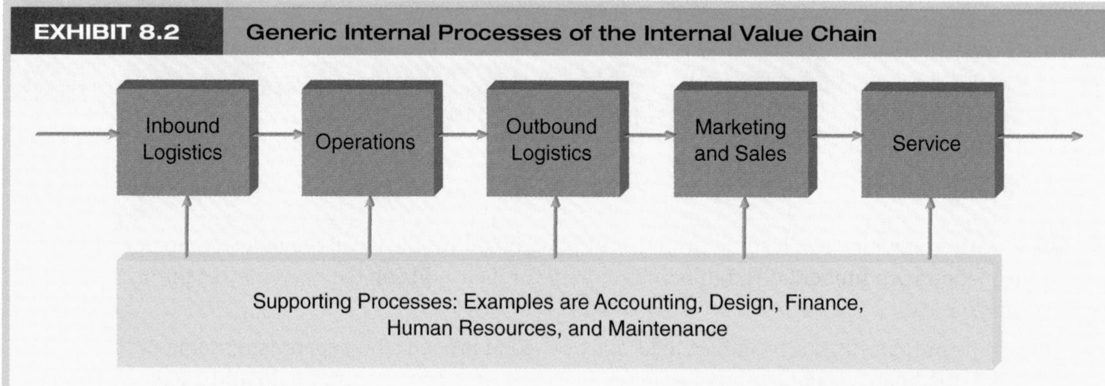

Usefulness of a Value Chain Perspective

The goal of maximizing final customer value while minimizing final customer cost leads organizations to examine *internal* and *external links* in the value chain rather than the departments, processes, or activities independently. From a value chain perspective, it is total cost across the entire value chain, not the cost of individual businesses, departments, processes, or activities that is most important.

Value Chain Perspective Fosters Supplier-Buyer Partnerships

In the past, relationships between suppliers and buyers were often adversarial. Contact between suppliers and buyers was solely through the selling and purchasing departments. Suppliers attempted merely to meet purchasing contract specifications at the lowest possible cost. Buyers encouraged competition among suppliers with the primary—and often single—goal of obtaining the lowest purchase price.

As discussed in Chapter 7 with JIT and lean production, exploiting cost reduction and value-enhancing opportunities in the value chain has led many buyers and suppliers to view each other as partners rather than as adversaries. Buyers have reduced the number of suppliers they deal with, often developing long-term partnerships with a single supplier. Once they establish mutual trust, both proceed to share detailed information on internal operations and help each other solve problems. Partners work closely to examine mutual opportunities by studying their common value chain. Supplier engineers might determine that a minor relaxation in buyer specifications would significantly reduce supplier manufacturing costs with only minor increases in subsequent buyer processing costs. Working together, they determine how best to modify processes to reduce overall costs and share increased profits.

Companies such as Hewlett-Packard and Boeing involve suppliers in design, development, and manufacturing decisions. Motorola has even developed a survey asking suppliers to assess Motorola as a buyer. Among other questions, the survey asks sellers to evaluate Motorola's performance in helping suppliers to identify major cost drivers and to increase their profitability. These questions represent the concerns of a partner rather than those of an adversary. The following Business Insight box describes how Dell has molded partnerships with upstream suppliers and downstream customers into what company founder Michael Dell identifies as "virtual integration."

BUSINESS INSIGHT **Internet Driven Virtual Value Chain at Dell**

When Dell Inc. first began using the Internet to expand its business, the company had three basic objectives: to make it easier to do business with Dell, to reduce the cost of doing business with Dell, and to enhance their customer relationships. By 1999, Dell was selling more than $35 million per day over the Internet, and by 2006 its annual sales exceeded $57 billion. "But for Dell, online commerce was only the beginning," writes Michael Dell, the Founder & CEO of Dell Computer Corporation. "Because we viewed the Internet as a central part of our IT strategy, we started to view the ownership of information differently, too. Rather than closely guarding our information databases, which took us years to develop, we used Internet browsers to essentially give that same information to our customers and suppliers—bringing them literally inside our business. This became the key to what I call a virtually integrated organization—an organization linked not by physical assets, but by information. By using the Internet to speed information between companies, essentially eliminating inter-company boundaries, it would be possible to achieve precision and speed-to-market for products and services in ways not dreamed possible before. It would be the ultimate business system for a digital economy."[2]

On a smaller scale, the grocery store in Exhibit 8.1 should examine its external links. It may be willing to pay more for Coca-Cola products if the distributors cooperate to help reduce costs such as the following:

- Making more frequent deliveries in small lots would reduce storage costs.
- Being responsible for maintaining and changing the product displays would relieve store workers of these tasks.
- Streamlining ordering and payment procedures would reduce bookkeeping costs.

If partnership arrangements with upstream suppliers enable the grocery store to reduce its total costs, the store can enhance or maintain its competitive position by reducing prices charged to its consumers. Remember that competitors are also striving to reduce costs and enhance their competitive position. Hence, failing to strive for improvements will likely result in reduced sales and profits.

Value Chain Perspective Fosters Focus on Core Competencies

Using value chain concepts, relationships with suppliers often begin to represent an extended family, allowing companies to focus on core competencies; this capability provides a distinct competitive advantage. In addition, a new breed of contract manufacturers, such as Solectron Corporation and Sanmina-SCI have emerged in recent years. These organizations manufacture products for other companies, ranging from Hewlett-Packard printers to Xerox photocopy machines, with such close partnership arrangements that they behave like a single company. This allows Hewlett-Packard and Xerox to focus on marketing and product development while Solectron and SCI Systems focus on efficient, low-cost manufacturing.

Interestingly, because their facilities are available to all innovators with the necessary financing, the emergence of contract manufacturers may speed innovation. Michael Dell attributes much of Dell's rapid growth and profitability to virtual integration with suppliers (see Business Insight box above). **Virtual integration** is the use of information technology and partnership concepts to allow two or more entities along a value chain to act as if they were a single economic entity.

Value-Added and Value Chain Perspectives

The value chain perspective is often contrasted with a value-added perspective. Under a value-added perspective, decision makers consider only the cost of resources to their organization and the selling price of products or services to their immediate customers. Using a value-added perspective, the goal is to maximize the value added (the difference between the selling price and costs) by the organization. To do

[2] *Direct from Dell*, Michael Dell with Catherine Fredman, Harper Collins Publishers, 1999. Also, see http://money.cnn.com/magazines/fortune/fortune500/2007/full_list/index.html

this, the value-added perspective focuses primarily on internal activities and costs. Under a value chain perspective, the goal is to maximize value and minimize cost to final customers, often by developing linkages or partnerships with suppliers and customers.

Although initial efforts to enhance competitiveness might start with a value-added perspective, it is important to expand to a value chain perspective. World-class competitors utilize both a value-added and a value chain perspective. These firms always keep the final customer in mind and recognize that the profitability of each entity in the value chain depends on the overall value and cost of the products and services delivered to final customers.

The value-added perspective is the foundation of the make or buy (outsourcing) decision considered in Chapter 4. The key differences between the partnering decisions considered here and the make or buy decision in Chapter 4 concern time frame, perspective, and attitude. The make or buy decision is a stand-alone decision, often in the short run, that does not view vendors and customers as partners. In contrast, characteristics of the value chain perspective are as follows:

- Comprehensive.
- Focused on the final customers.
- Strategic.
- Basis for partnerships between vendors and customers.

Enhancing or maintaining a competitive position requires an understanding of the entire system used to develop and deliver value to final customers, including interactions among organizations along the value chain. All organizations in the value chain are in business together and should work together as partners rather than as adversaries.

THE PRICING DECISION

LO2 Distinguish between economic and cost-based approaches to pricing.

Pricing products and services is one of the most important and complex decisions facing management. Pricing decisions directly affect the salability of individual products or services, as well as the profitability, and even the survival, of the organization. Many economists have spent their entire careers examining the foundations of pricing. To respond to the needs of pricing hundreds or thousands of individual items, managers have developed pricing guidelines that are typically based on costs. More recently, global competition has turned cost-based approaches upside down. Managers of world-class organizations increasingly start with a price that customers are willing to pay and then determine allowable costs.

Economic Approaches to Pricing

In economic models, the firm has a profit-maximizing goal and known cost and revenue functions. Typically, increases in sales quantity require reductions in selling prices, causing **marginal revenue** (the varying increment in total revenue derived from the sale of an additional unit) to decline as sales increase. Increases in production cause an increase in **marginal cost** (the varying increment in total cost required to produce and sell an additional unit of product). In economic models, profits are maximized at the sales volume at which marginal revenues equal marginal costs. Firms continue to produce as long as the marginal revenue derived from the sale of each additional unit exceeds the marginal cost of producing that unit.

Economic models provide a useful framework for considering pricing decisions. The ideal price is the one that will lead customers to purchase all units a firm can provide up to the point at which the last unit has a marginal cost exactly equal to its marginal revenue.

Despite their conceptual merit, economic models are seldom used for day-to-day pricing decisions. Perfect information and an indefinite time period are required to achieve equilibrium prices at which marginal revenues equal marginal costs. In the short run, most for-profit organizations attempt to achieve a target profit rather than a maximum profit. One reason for this is an inability to determine the single set of actions that will lead to profit maximization. Furthermore, managers are more apt to strive to satisfy a number of goals (such as profits for investors, job security for themselves and their employees, and being a "good" corporate citizen) than to strive for the maximization of a single profit goal. In any case, to maximize profits, a company's management would have to know the cost and revenue functions of every product the firm sells. For most firms, this information cannot be developed at a reasonable cost.

Cost-Based Approaches to Pricing

Although cost is not the only consideration in pricing, it has traditionally been the most important for several reasons.

- *Cost data are available.* When hundreds or thousands of different prices must be set in a short time, cost could be the only feasible basis for product pricing.
- *Cost-based prices are defensible.* Managers threatened by legal action or public scrutiny feel secure using cost-based prices. They can argue that prices are set in a manner that provides a "fair" profit.
- *Revenues must exceed costs if the firm is to remain in business.* In the long run, the selling price must exceed the full cost of each unit.

Cost-based pricing is illustrated in Exhibit 8.3. The process begins with market research to determine customer wants. If the product requires components to be designed and produced by vendors, the process of obtaining prices can be time consuming. When some costs, such as those fixed costs at the facility level, are not assigned to specific products, a markup is added to cover these costs. An additional markup is added to achieve a desired profit. The selling price is then set as the sum of the assigned costs, the markup to cover unassigned costs, and the markup to achieve the desired profit.

The proposed selling price should be evaluated with regard to competitive information and what customers are willing to pay. If the price is acceptable, the product or service is produced. If the price is too high, the product might be redesigned, manufacturing procedures might be changed, and different types of materials might be considered until either an acceptable price is achieved or it is determined that the product cannot be produced at an acceptable price. The following Business Insight box discusses cost-based pricing as a strategy for physician practice groups.

EXHIBIT 8.3 Cost-Based Pricing for a New Product

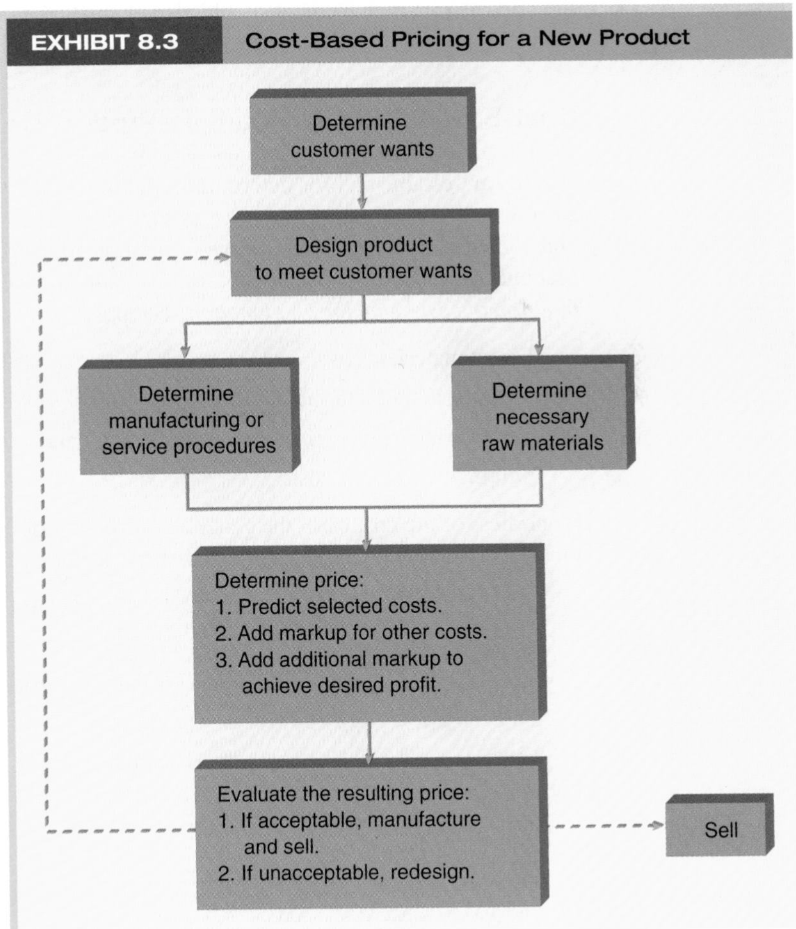

Cost-Based Pricing in Single-Product Companies

Implementing cost-based pricing in a single-product company is straightforward if everything is known but the selling price. In this case, all known data are entered into the profit formula, which is then solved for the variable price. Assume that Bright Rug Cleaners' annual fixed facility-level costs are $200,000 and the unit cost of cleaning a rug is $10. Management desires to achieve an annual profit of $30,000 at an annual volume of 10,000 rugs. To simplify the example, assume that management charges the same price regardless of the type, size, or shape of the rug. Using the profit formula, the cost-based price is determined to be $33:

Profit = Total revenues − Total costs

$30,000 = (Price × 10,000 rugs) − ($200,000 + [$10 × 10,000 rugs])

Solving for the price:

(Price × 10,000) = $300,000 + $30,000

Price = $330,000 ÷ 10,000

= $33

BUSINESS INSIGHT **Cost-based Pricing Advocated for Medical Groups**

Physician practice groups are constantly negotiating with insurers over appropriate pricing of services, often without regard for the costs incurred in providing the services. One healthcare consultant has argued that hospitals and healthcare systems should consider pursuing pricing strategies that take into account the true costs of operating a primary-care-based physician group. Cost-based pricing strategies will allow organizations with underperforming physician groups to reach break-even positions on their group practice investments. The cost-based pricing approach is most effective if used as the first step—preparation—in the contract negotiation process. In the second step—education—the approach is one of leveraging the information learned and educating payers regarding the true cost of providing high-quality physician services to a payer's patient population. Initially, payers are likely to resist a move toward cost-based pricing. However, an employed physician group that has prepared the necessary documentation and information should be able to support its case that it has efficient operations and appropriate overhead levels.[3]

A price of $33 to clean a rug will allow Bright to achieve its desired profit. However, before setting the price at $33, management should also evaluate the competitive situation and consider what customers are willing to pay for this service.

Cost-Based Pricing in Multiple-Product Companies

In multiple-product companies, desired profits are determined for the entire company, and standard procedures are established for determining the initial selling price of each product. These procedures typically specify the initial selling price as the costs assigned to products or services plus a markup to cover unassigned costs and provide for the desired profit. Depending on the sophistication of the organization's accounting system, possible cost bases in a manufacturing organization include markups based on a *combination of cost behavior and function*. The possible cost bases include:

- Direct materials costs.
- Variable manufacturing costs.
- Total variable costs (manufacturing, selling, and administrative).
- Full manufacturing costs.

Regardless of the cost base, the general approach to developing a markup is to recognize that the markup must be large enough to provide for costs not included in the base plus the desired profit.

$$\textbf{Markup on cost base} = \frac{\textbf{Costs not included in the base + Desired profit}}{\textbf{Costs included in the base}}$$

First we illustrate a pricing decision with variable costs as the cost base; full manufacturing costs is the cost base in the second illustration.

1. When the markup is based on variable costs, it must be large enough to cover all fixed costs and the desired profit. Assume that the predicted annual variable and fixed costs for Magnum Enterprises are as follows:

Variable		Fixed	
Manufacturing	$600,000	Manufacturing.........	$300,000
Selling and administrative........	200,000	Selling and administrative	100,000
Total	$800,000	Total.................	$400,000

[3] Craig D Pederson, "Cost-based Pricing and the Underperforming Physician Group," *Healthcare Financial Management*, Oct 2005.

Furthermore, assume that Magnum Enterprises has total assets of $1,250,000; management believes that an annual return of 16 percent on total assets is appropriate in Magnum's industry. A 16 percent return translates into a desired annual profit of $200,000 ($1,250,000 × 0.16). Assuming all cost predictions are correct, obtaining a profit of $200,000 requires a 75 percent markup on variable costs:

$$\textbf{Markup on variable costs} = \frac{\$400{,}000 + \$200{,}000}{\$800{,}000}$$
$$= 0.75$$

If the predicted variable costs for Product A1 are $12 per unit, the initial selling price for Product A1 is $21:

$$\textbf{Initial selling price} = \$12 + (\$12 \times 0.75)$$
$$= \$21$$

2. When the markup is based on full manufacturing costs, it must be large enough to cover selling and administrative expenses and to provide for the desired profit. Again, it is necessary to determine the desired profit and predict all costs for the pricing period. The initial prices of individual products are then determined as their unit manufacturing costs plus the markup. For Magnum, the markup on manufacturing costs would be 55.6 percent:

$$\textbf{Markup on manufacturing costs} = \frac{\$300{,}000 + \$200{,}000}{\$900{,}000}$$
$$= 0.556$$

If the predicted manufacturing costs for Product B1 are $10, the initial selling price for Product B1 is $15.56:

$$\textbf{Initial selling price} = \$10 + (\$10 \times 0.556)$$
$$= \$15.56$$

Cost-Based Pricing for Special Orders

Many organizations use cost-based pricing to bid on unique projects. If the project requires dedicated assets, the acquisition of new fixed assets, or an investment in employee training, the desired profit on the special order or project should allow for an adequate return on the dedicated assets or additional investment.

Critique of Cost-Based Pricing

Cost-based pricing has four major drawbacks:

1. Cost-based pricing requires accurate cost assignments. If costs are not accurately assigned, some products could be priced too high, losing market share to competitors; other products could be priced too low, gaining market share but being less profitable than anticipated.
2. The higher the portion of unassigned costs, the greater is the likelihood of over- or under-pricing individual products.
3. Cost-based pricing assumes that goods or services are relatively scarce and, generally, customers who want a product or service are willing to pay the price.
4. In a competitive environment, cost-based approaches increase the time and cost of bringing new products to market.

Cost-based pricing became the dominant approach to pricing during an era when products were relatively long-lived and there was relatively little competition. Also, these systems tend to focus on organizational units such as departments, plants, or divisions and not on activities or cost drivers. While easy to implement, reflecting the need to recover costs and earn a return on investment, and easily justified, cost-based prices might not be competitive. Competition puts intense downward pressure on prices and removes slack from pricing formulas. There is little margin for error in pricing. In a highly competitive market, small variations in pricing make significant differences in success.

MID-CHAPTER REVIEW

Presented is the 2009 contribution income statement of Knox Company.

KNOX COMPANY
Contribution Income Statement
For Year Ended December 31, 2009

Sales (100,000 units at $12 per unit)		$1,200,000
Less variable costs		
Manufacturing.	$300,000	
Selling and administrative.	150,000	(450,000)
Contribution margin		750,000
Less fixed costs		
Manufacturing.	400,000	
Selling and administrative.	200,000	(600,000)
Net income.		$ 150,000

Knox has total assets of $2,000,000, and management desires an annual return of 10 percent on total assets.

Required

a. Determine the dollar amount by which Knox Company exceeded or fell short of the desired annual rate of return in 2009.

b. Given the current sales volume and cost structure, determine the unit selling price required to achieve an annual profit of $250,000.

c. Assume that management wants to state the selling price as a percentage of variable manufacturing costs. Given your answer to requirement (b) and the current sales volume and cost structure, determine the selling price as a percentage of variable manufacturing costs.

d. Restate your answer to requirement (c), dividing into two separate markup percentages:
1. The markup on variable manufacturing costs required to cover unassigned costs.
2. The additional markup on variable manufacturing costs required to achieve an annual profit of $250,000.

Solution

a.

Desired annual profit ($2,000,000 × 0.10)	$200,000
Actual profit	(150,000)
Amount actual profit fell short of achieving the desired return.	$ 50,000

b.

Predicted costs		
Variable	$450,000	
Fixed	600,000	$1,050,000
Desired profit		250,000
Required revenue		$1,300,000
Unit sales		÷ 100,000
Required unit selling price		$ 13

c.

Variable manufacturing costs per unit ($300,000/100,000 unit)	= $3
Selling price as a percent of variable manufacturing costs	= $13/3
	= 433⅓%
Markup as a percent of variable manufacturing costs ($10/$3)	= 333⅓.

d. Detail of markup on variable manufacturing costs:

1. Unassigned costs		
Variable selling and administrative	$150,000	
Fixed costs	600,000	$750,000
Variable manufacturing costs		÷300,000
Markup on variable manufacturing costs to cover unassigned costs		250%
2. Desired profit		$250,000
Variable manufacturing costs		÷300,000
Additional markup on variable manufacturing costs to achieve desired profit ($250,000)		83⅓%

TARGET COSTING

LO3 Explain target costing and its acceptance in highly competitive industries.

Economists argue that cost-based prices are not realistic, because in the real world prices are determined by the confluence of supply and demand. However, when a new product is introduced into the market for which there is no previously existing supply or demand, there has to be a starting point. As discussed above, cost has often been the baseline for determining initial selling prices. All too often, however, companies introduce new products into the market based on what the designers and engineers "think" the market wants (or based on inadequate market research), only to find out later that either the market does not want the product, or it is not willing to buy the new product at a price sufficient to cover its cost plus an acceptable profit to the producer. This often leads to costly redesign, or in many cases, complete abandonment of the product, typically resulting in substantial financial losses.

Toyota, which has pioneered many of the innovations in manufacturing systems discussed in Chapter 7, turned the notion of cost-based pricing around and came up with the idea of price-based costing, referred to as target costing. Toyota determined that before a new product is introduced into the market, it must be able to be produced at a cost that will make it profitable when sold at a price acceptable to customers. The acceptable selling price to the marketplace determines the acceptable cost of producing the product.

Target Costing Is Proactive for Cost Management

Target costing starts with determining what customers are willing to pay for a product or service and then subtracts a desired profit on sales to determine the allowable, or target, cost of the product or service. This target cost is then communicated to a cross-functional team of employees representing such diverse areas as marketing, product design, manufacturing, and management accounting. Reflecting value chain concepts and the notion of partnerships up and down the value chain, suppliers of raw materials and components are often included in the teams. The target costing team is assigned the task of designing a product that meets customer price, function, and quality requirements while providing a desired profit. Its job is not completed until the target cost is met, or a determination is made that the product or service cannot be profitably introduced under the current circumstances. See Exhibit 8.4 for an overview of target costing.

Although a formula can be used to determine a markup on cost, it is not possible to develop a formula indicating how to achieve a target cost. Hence, target costing is not a technique. It is more a philosophy or an approach to pricing and cost management. It takes a proactive approach to cost management, reflecting the belief that costs are best managed by decisions made during product development. This contrasts with the more passive cost-plus belief that costs result from design, procurement, and manufacture. Like the value chain, target costing helps orient employees toward the final customer and reinforces the notion that all departments within the organization and all organizations along the value chain must work together. Target costing also empowers employees who will be assigned the

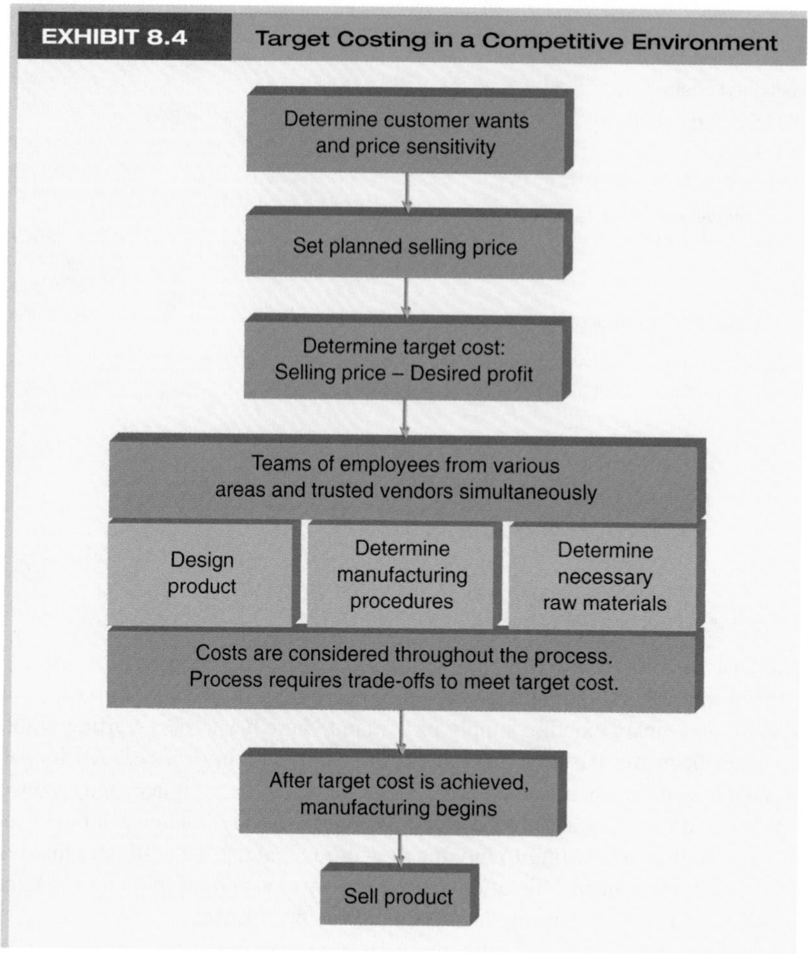
EXHIBIT 8.4
Target Costing in a Competitive Environment
Determine customer wants and price sensitivity
Set planned selling price
Determine target cost: Selling price – Desired profit
Teams of employees from various areas and trusted vendors simultaneously
Design product
Determine manufacturing procedures
Determine necessary raw materials
Costs are considered throughout the process. Process requires trade-offs to meet target cost.
After target cost is achieved, manufacturing begins
Sell product

responsibility for carrying out activities necessary to deliver a product or service with the authority to determine what activities will be selected. Like process mapping, it helps employees to better understand their role in serving the customer. The following Business Insight box explains one company's approach to implementing target costing.

BUSINESS INSIGHT **Target Costing and New Product Development**

A personal homecare products company (name withheld by authors) in the Southwest has adopted target costing as a key element in the introduction of new products. This consumer products company also uses a proprietary product development control system, called Stage Gate®, which provides an operational roadmap for driving new product-development projects from idea to launch by dividing the process into a series of stages (activities) and gates (decision points). A gate precedes each stage where a decision is made whether or not to proceed to the next stage. At each gate, or decision point, a senior leader decides to go, kill, hold, or recycle the project. Target costing concepts are applied at each gate, requiring financial analysis to determine whether a business case can be made to support the new product introduction. This process requires a hard cost target for each new product that must be achieved in order to move forward with the project. Otherwise, the senior leader kills the product or places it on hold until the cost target is met.[4]

[4] Gopalakrishnan, Samuels, and Swenson, "Target Costing at a Consumer Products Company," *Strategic Finance*, December 2007.

Target Costing Encourages Design for Production

In the absence of a target costing approach, design engineers are apt to focus on incorporating leading-edge technology and the maximum number of features in a product. Target costing keeps the customer's function, quality, and price requirements in the forefront at all times. If customers do not want leading-edge technology (which could be expensive and untested) and several product features, they will resist paying for them. Focusing on achieving a target cost keeps design engineers tuned in to the final customer.

Left on their own, design engineers might believe that their job ends when they design a product that meets the customer's functional requirements. The tendency is to simply pass on the design to manufacturing and let manufacturing determine how best to produce the product. Further down the line, if the product needs servicing, it becomes the service department's responsibility to determine how best to service the product. A target costing approach forces design engineers to explicitly consider the costs of manufacturing and servicing a product while it is being designed. This is known as **design for manufacture**.

Minor changes in design that do not affect the product's functioning can often produce dramatic savings in manufacturing and servicing costs. Examples of design for manufacture include the following:

- Using molded plastic parts to avoid assembling several small parts.
- Designing two parts that must be fit together so that joining them in the correct manner is obvious to assembly workers.
- Placing an access panel in the side of an appliance so service personnel can make repairs quickly.
- Using standard-size parts to reduce inventory requirements, to reduce the possibility of assembly personnel inserting the incorrect part, and to simplify the job of service personnel.
- Ensuring that tolerance requirements for parts that must fit together can be met with available equipment.
- Using manufacturing procedures that are common to other products.

The successful implementation of target costing requires employees from all involved disciplines to be familiar with costing concepts and the notions of value-added and non-value-added activities. When considering the manufacturing process, team members should minimize non-value-added activities such as movement, storage, inspection, and setup. They should also select the lowest-cost value-added activities that do the job properly.

Target Costing Reduces Time to Introduce Products

By designing a product to meet a target cost (rather than evaluating the marketability of a product at a cost-plus price and having to recycle the design through several departments), target costing reduces the time required to introduce new products. Involving vendors in target costing design teams makes the vendors aware of the necessity of meeting a target cost. This facilitates the concurrent engineering of components to be produced outside the organization and reduces the time required to obtain components.

Target Costing Requires Cost Information

Implementing target costing requires detailed information on the cost of alternative activities. This information allows decision makers to select design and manufacturing alternatives that best meet function and price requirements. Tables that contain detailed databases of cost information for various manufacturing variables are occasionally used in designing products and selecting processes to meet target costs.

Target Costing Requires Coordination

Limitations of target costing are employee and supplier attitudes and the many meetings required to coordinate product design and to select manufacturing processes. All people involved must have a basic understanding of the overall processes required to bring a product to market and an appreciation of the cost consequences of alternative actions. They must also respect, cooperate, and communicate with other team members and be willing to engage in a negotiation process involving trade-offs. Finally, they must understand that although the total time required to bring a new product to market can be reduced, the countless coordinating meetings could be quite intrusive on the individuals' otherwise orderly schedule. See Exhibit 8.5 for an evaluation of target costing.

EXHIBIT 8.5	Pros and Cons of Target Costing

Pros

- Takes proactive approach to cost management.
- Orients organization toward customer.
- Breaks down barriers between departments.
- Enhances employee awareness and empowerment.
- Fosters partnerships with suppliers.
- Minimizes non-value-added activities.
- Encourages selection of lowest-cost value-added activities.
- Reduces time to market.

Cons

- To be effective, requires the development of detailed cost data.
- Requires willingness to cooperate.
- Requires many meetings for coordination.

This aspect of the process is even more difficult when suppliers must be brought in as part of the coordination process. This concept is frequently referred to as **chained target costing** because the supply chain's support is critical for the product to be both competitively priced and delivered to the final customer in a timely manner. When multiple suppliers are required, the organization must obtain everyone's support or the process will probably not be successful due to gaps in the reliability of delivery, quality, and cost control. Each organization and unit must understand that if the product is not brought to market within the defined constraints, all will lose. They must make firm commitments for the project undertaken and to have faith that each participant will carry out whatever part of the supply chain it has promised to fulfill. An example of this process with suppliers of parts and components to Whirlpool Corporation is presented in the following Business Insight box. Coordination across the supply chain is vital in the overall process of continuous improvement as discussed later in this chapter.

BUSINESS INSIGHT **Quality Parts Yield Product Success**

Industry leaders in electric motor manufacturing are attempting to provide their customers, equipment manufacturers, with high efficiency and quieter motors at consistently lower costs as part of the supply chain. An example is Emerson Appliance Solutions, which has teamed with Whirlpool Corporation to develop a customized capacitor motor for the Sears' Kenmore, Kitchen Aid, and Whirlpool brand names. Says Emerson's Whirlpool account manager, "An approximate 20 percent motor energy savings was the result of efforts by engineering teams at both Whirlpool and Emerson that resulted in a smaller, more efficient motor-pump assembly."

Illustrating Emerson's commitment to Whirlpool, the company had three managers who coordinated components for washers, motors, and controls. These managers worked with Whirlpool to achieve its new product objective of emphasizing reduced sound and water consumption while delivering good wash performance. To further enhance the product, Emerson then worked with its supplier, AMP (going up the supply chain), for an improved connection method for the motors' magnet wires and lead wires. Each member of the supply chain was well aware of Whirlpool's concern about cost of the new product and made every effort to contain costs from development to production. As a result, the new product was within the target set by Whirlpool.[5]

Target Costing is Key for Products with Short Life Cycles

From a traditional marketing perspective, products with a relatively long life go through four distinct stages during their life cycle:

[5] Joe Jancsurak, "Value-Added Power," *Appliance Manufacturer Magazine*, February 26, 2001, http://www.ammagazine.com.

1. *Start-up.* Sales are low when a product is first introduced. Traditionally, initial selling prices are set high, and customers tend to be relatively affluent trendsetters.
2. *Growth.* Sales increase as the product gains acceptance. Traditionally, prices have remained high during this stage because of customer loyalty and the absence of competitive products.
3. *Maturity.* Sales level off as the product matures. Because of increased competition, pressure on prices is increasing; some price reductions could be necessary.
4. *Decline.* Sales decline as the product becomes obsolete. Significant price cuts could be required to sell remaining inventories.

Target costing is more important for products with a relatively short market life cycle. Products with a long life cycle present many opportunities to continuously improve design and manufacturing procedures that are not available when a product has a short life cycle. Hence, extra care must go into the initial planning for short-lived products. This is especially true when short product life cycles are combined with increased worldwide competition. It is important to introduce a product first and at a price that ensures rapid market penetration.

Target Costing Helps Manage Life Cycle Costs

An awareness of the impact of today's actions on tomorrow's costs underlies the notion of **life cycle costs**, which include all costs associated with a product or service ranging from those incurred with the initial conception through design, pre-production, production, and after-production support.

The lower line in Exhibit 8.6 illustrates the cumulative expenditure of funds over the life of a product. For low-technology products with relatively long product lives, decisions committing the organization to spend money are made at approximately the same time the money is spent. However, for high-technology products with relatively short product lives, most of the critical decisions affecting cost, such as product design and the selection of manufacturing procedures, are made before production begins. The top line in Exhibit 8.6 represents decisions committing the organization to expenditures for a product. It has been estimated that as much as 70% of the cost of the typical automobile, and 95% of the cost of high-technology products, is committed during the design stage.

EXHIBIT 8.6 Commitment and Expenditure for High-Technology Products with Relatively Short Product Lives

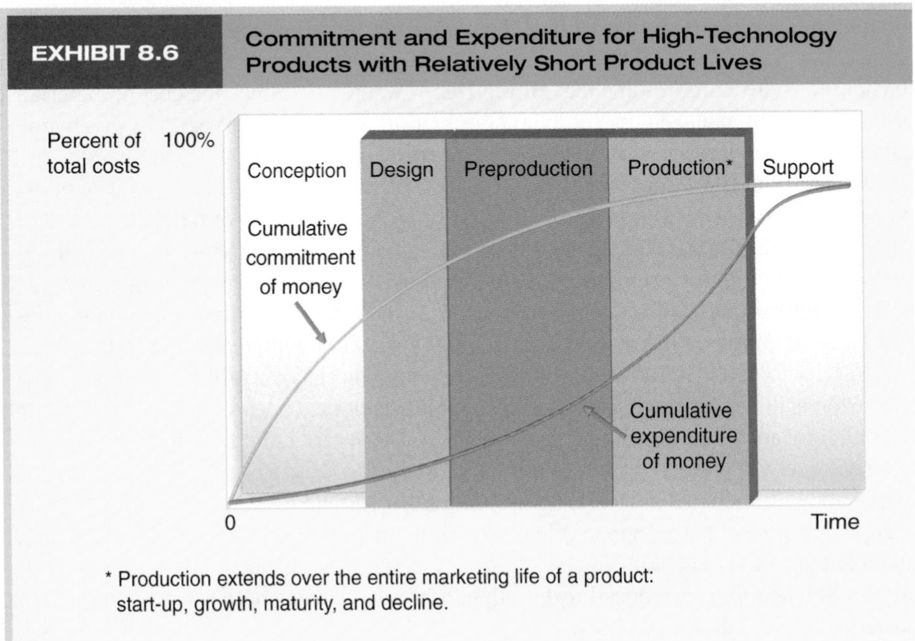

* Production extends over the entire marketing life of a product: start-up, growth, maturity, and decline.

Reflecting significant changes in vehicle production since the time of Henry Ford and the Model T, General Motors estimates that 70 percent of the cost of manufacturing truck transmissions is determined during design. Others estimate that up to 95 percent of the total costs associated with high-technology products are committed before the first unit is produced.

Life cycle cost concepts have also been usefully applied to low-technology issues, such as repair versus replace decisions. The New York State Throughway Authority uses life cycle concepts to determine the point at which it is more expensive to repair than to replace bridges.

MANAGERIAL DECISION **You are the Vice President of Product Development**

As head of new product development for your electronics company, you are concerned that so many of the ideas for new products coming from your research and development group are not succeeding in the market. Many recent attempts to take new products to market have failed, not because of technological deficiencies in the products, but because the market would not support the high prices for new products that were necessary to produce a satisfactory profit. What should you do to try to reverse this trend of new product failures? [Answer, p. 274]

CONTINUOUS IMPROVEMENT COSTING

LO4 Describe the relation between target costing and continuous improvement costing.

Continuous improvement (Kaizen) costing calls for establishing cost reduction targets for products or services that an organization is currently providing to customers. Developed in Japan, this approach to cost management is often referred to as *Kaizen costing*. *Kaizen* means "continuous improvement" in Japanese. Continuous improvement costing begins where target costing ends. Target costing takes a proactive approach to cost management during the conception, design, and preproduction stages of a product's life; continuous improvement costing takes a proactive approach to cost management during the production stage of a product's life:

Time			
Conception	Design	Preproduction	Production
	Target costing		Continuous improvement costing

Continuous improvement costing adds a specific target to be achieved during a time period to the target costing concept previously discussed. Basically, the mathematics of the concept is quite simple, but its implementation is difficult. Assume that Home Depot wanted to reduce the cost of materials handling in each of its stores, and management set a target reduction of 2 percent a year. If a given store had current annual materials handling costs of $100,000 and expected an increase the next year due to 10 percent growth, the budget for the next year would be $107,800 [($100,000 × 1.10) × 0.98]. The budget for next year based on growth is $110,000 less the continuous improvement factor of 0.02.

Like target costing, Kaizen costing should be viewed as a serious attempt to make processes more efficient, while maintaining or improving quality, thereby making the company more competitive and profitable. In Kaizen costing, cost reductions can be achieved both internally and externally through continuous redesign and improved internal processes, and by working with vendors to improve their designs and processes. Kaizen is a team effort involving everyone who has an influence on costs. As stated in Chapter 7, Kaizen is typically found in companies that have adopted a lean production philosophy.

Successful companies use continuous improvement costing to avoid complacency. Competitors are constantly striving to win market share through better quality or lower prices. Hewlett-Packard studied Epson to determine its strengths and weaknesses. Isuzu Motors takes competitors' products apart to determine a target cost it must beat. To fend off competition, prices and costs must be continuously reduced. To maintain its competitive position, Hewlett-Packard has reduced the list price of the basic inkjet printer from nearly $400 when first introduced to less than $50 today. This could not have been done without continuous reductions in costs.

The Daihatsu Motor Company sets Kaizen cost reduction targets for each cost element, including purchased parts per car, direct materials per car, labor hours per car, and office utilities. Performance reports developed at the end of each month compare targeted and actual cost reductions. If actual cost reductions are more than the targeted cost reductions, the results are favorable; if the actual cost reductions are less than the targeted cost reductions, the results are unfavorable.

Because cost reduction targets are set before it is known how they will be achieved, continuous improvement costing can be stressful to employees. To help reduce this stress at Daihatsu, a period of about three months following the introduction of a new product is allowed before organizational units are expected to meet target costs and Kaizen costing targets. A critical element in motivating employee cooperation and teamwork in aggressive cost management techniques, such as target and continuous improvement costing, is to avoid using performance reports to place blame for failure. The proper response to an unfavorable performance report must be an offer of assistance to correct the failure.

BENCHMARKING

LO5 Explain how benchmarking enhances quality management, continuous improvement, and process reengineering.

When Isuzu Motors takes a competitor's product apart to determine the competitor's manufacturing costs, or when Hewlett-Packard studies Epson to identify Epson's strengths and weaknesses, each company is engaging in *benchmarking*, a practice that has been around for centuries. In recent years, however, as globalization and increased competitiveness have forced businesses to more aggressively compete on the bases of cost, quality, and service, benchmarking has become more formalized and open. No longer regarded as spying, **benchmarking** is now a systematic approach to identifying the best practices to help an organization take action to improve performance.

The formalization of benchmarking is largely attributed to a book written in the 1980s by Robert Camp of Xerox. Since then, many managers have come to believe that benchmarking is a requirement for success. Although benchmarking can focus on anything of interest, it typically deals with target costs for a product, service, or operation, customer satisfaction, quality, inventory levels, inventory turnover, cycle time, and productivity. Benchmarking initially focused on studying competitors, but benchmarking efforts have changed dramatically in recent years to include competitors, as well as companies in very different industries. For example, a computer company like Dell may benchmark its order fulfillment processes against Amazon, or an electronics company like Sony may benchmark its inventory management processes against an apparel company like Gap.

In considering how to go about benchmarking, an organization must be careful because it must consider nonfinancial limitations. No single numerical measurement can completely describe the performance of a complex device such as a microprocessor or a television camera, but benchmarks can be useful tools for comparing different products, components, and systems. The only totally accurate way to measure the performance of a given product is to test it against other products while performing the exact same activity. The following Business Insight box describes how Intel Corporation makes benchmarks available with some information on how to use them.

BUSINESS INSIGHT **Intel Benchmarks Performance**

Intel Corporation divides its benchmarks into two types, component and system. *Component benchmarks* measure the performance of specific parts of a computer system, such as a microprocessor or hard disk drive. *System benchmarks* typically measure the performance of the entire computer system. The performance obtained will almost certainly vary from benchmark performance for a number of reasons. First, individual components must usually be tested in a complete computer system, and it is not always possible to eliminate the considerable effects that differences in system design and configuration have on benchmark results. For instance, vendors sell systems with a wide variety of disk capabilities and speeds, system memory, and video and graphics capabilities, all of which influence how the system components perform in actual use. Differences in software, including operating systems and compilers, also affect component and system performance. Finally, benchmark tests are typically written to be exemplary for only a certain type of computer application, which might or might not be similar to what is being compared.

A benchmark is, at most, only one type of information that an organization might use during the purchasing or manufacturing process. To get a true picture of the performance of a component or system being considered, the organization should consult industry sources, publicly available research reports, and even government publications of related information.[6]

[6] As described on the Intel website at http://www.intel.com/performance/resources/benchmark_limitations.htm

Benchmarking provides measurements that are useful in setting goals. It can lead to dramatic innovations, and it can help overcome resistance to change. When presented with a major cost reduction target, employees often believe they are being asked to do the impossible. Benchmarking can be a psychological tool that helps overcome resistance to change by showing how others have already met the target.

Although each organization has its own approach to benchmarking, the following six steps are typical:

1. Decide what to benchmark.
2. Plan the benchmark project.
3. Understand your own performance.
4. Study others.
5. Learn from the data.
6. Take action.

In recent years, professional organizations, such as the Institute of Management Accountants, have set up clearinghouses for benchmark information or have performed benchmarking studies of interest to members as have certain corporations such as Intel.

CHAPTER-END REVIEW

MBW, Inc. has been conducting early-stage research on hydrogen powered automobiles and is nearing the point where product development will soon begin. In order to determine the feasibility of the product, MBW has conducted marketing research that indicates that the price target for the product must be no more than $35,000 if it is to appeal to a large enough market segment to sell a minimum of 150,000 automobiles in the first year of production. The CFO has indicated that the new product must meet a 15% minimum profit margin requirement.

Required

a. Calculate the target cost per unit to produce the hydrogen powered automobile.
b. How would MBW go about determining whether the target cost can be achieved.
c. What should MBW do if the estimated cost to produce the product exceeds the target cost?

Solution

a.

Total revenue (150,000 × $35,000)	$5,250,000,000
Required profit margin (15%)	−787,500,000
Total cost	$4,462,500,000
Number of units	÷ 150,000
Target cost per unit	$ 29,750

b. A new product such as an automobile is an extremely complex product with hundreds, if not thousands, of different components, involving many different vendors. Once MBW has determined what product features potential customers want, its engineers must determine how best to provide those features, working with vendors and potential vendors. The idea is to determine how best to provide the final product that the customers want at a cost that will provide a reasonable profit to MBW and its vendors.

c. Teams of engineers, accountants, designers, etc. from MBW and its vendors should work together to try to achieve the target cost. If initial cost estimates are too high, they should explore every possibility, including redesign of the product, using components from existing products, developing new production systems, etc. to meet the target cost. If it is finally determined that the target cannot be reached, then management has to decide if it is willing to go forward with the product with a lower than desired initial profit margin. In some cases, managers will proceed with the idea that additional cost savings will be found (using Kaizen costing methods) after the product is in production.

APPENDIX 8A: Quality Costs

Life cycle costs were previously considered from the seller's perspective within the context of developing target costs. From the buyer's perspective, life cycle costs include the total costs associated with a product, such as a refrigerator, furnace, X-ray machine, or tractor, over its entire life. Sophisticated buyers look beyond acquisition cost to life cycle costs in making decisions. Major home appliances come with stickers estimating their annual operating costs, and new automobiles have stickers with information on fuel efficiency. The life cycle costs of a furnace include the purchase price, operating costs such as fuel, maintenance costs such as cleaning the burner, and repair costs such as replacing an exhaust fan. The preferred furnace is the one that provides the desired heat at the lowest life cycle cost.

Applying the life cycle cost concept, the total cost of materials to a manufacturing company includes much more than the purchase price. It also includes costs caused by potential and actual quality problems with materials. A concern that some materials are defective might require purchasing extra materials or inspecting materials. The use of defective materials could cause a manufacturer to incur costs for production downtime and rework. When life cycle costs are considered, purchasing decisions are less likely to be made solely on the basis of price. When the effect of quality on subsequent costs is considered, raw materials quality becomes just as important as price.

Quality, defined as conformance to customer expectations, is an important competitive factor.[7] Successful companies know that they must meet customers' quality and price expectations. In addition to being ethically questionable, reducing quality to achieve a target cost will not lead to long-run profits in today's highly competitive markets. Consistent product quality is a component in the success of companies such as **Federal Express**, **Ford**, **McDonald's**, **Toyota**, and **Intel**. **American Airlines** found that poor quality (in the form of late arrivals) cost it customer goodwill and millions of dollars a year in "lost" baggage and employee overtime.[8] In manufacturing, Intel found that quality leads to lower manufacturing costs, lower inventory levels, higher productivity, and increased profits. In repetitive activities, such as processing checks at a bank, an emphasis on "doing it right the first time" reduces the need for inspection and for rework.

Quality is an essential element of the JIT approach to inventory management. Purchasing high-quality materials reduces the need to inspect incoming materials, reduces the need for extra inventory, and facilitates the delivery of materials directly to the shop floor. As inventories are reduced, the presence of defective units becomes increasingly disruptive. Indeed, without buffer stocks, manufacturers might have to stop operations as soon as a defective unit is detected. While costly in the short run, these disruptions call attention to quality problems and encourage changes that prevent their recurrence. By eliminating the effort devoted to detecting and reworking or disposing of defective units, organizations are able to increase their productivity and profitability.

Productivity is the relationship between outputs and inputs:

$$\textbf{Productivity} = \textbf{Outputs} \div \textbf{Inputs}$$

Measurement of productivity requires a measure of output and of input. Partial measures of productivity are based on the relationship of units produced to a single input such as the number of employees, direct labor hours, or machine hours. Total measures of productivity convert all inputs into dollars (a common denominator) and restate outputs in terms of sales dollars.

Improvements in quality increase productivity by reducing the inputs required to obtain a given level of output. In turn, these improvements in productivity increase profits by lowering costs for the given level of output. If some of the cost savings are passed on to customers in the form of lower selling prices, an increase in sales volume could generate increased profits. Additionally, if an organization achieves a reputation for quality, it might be able to charge premium prices. The known quality of international brands, such as Coke and Pepsi, allow vendors to sell them at higher prices than they charge for local brands of soft drinks.

Quality of Design and Quality of Conformance

A key to improving quality is recognizing that quality is everyone's responsibility. The responsibility for quality starts with determining customer expectations and concludes with the delivery of products and services that conform to these expectations. The process of delivering a quality product or service can be broken into the following five steps:

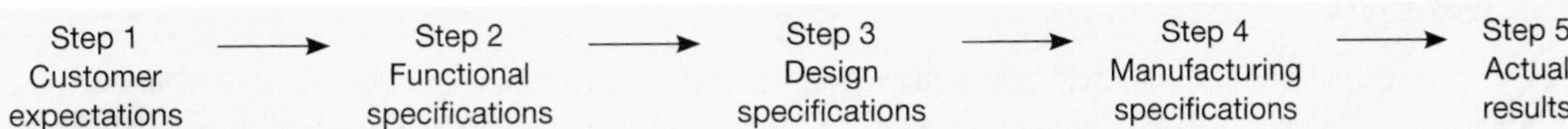

1. Quality starts with determining *customer expectations*. An agreement is necessary as to what customers expect and what the vendor will deliver. If customers at a McDonald's restaurant expect table service, lobster, and candlelight, they will be disappointed. If they expect fast, courteous service and low prices, they are likely to be satisfied.
2. The next step in delivering a quality product is to develop *functional specifications* for the product or service. These are explicit statements regarding the service or product capabilities, expressed in quantitative terms whenever possible. Functional specifications for a new automobile engine might include specifications for horsepower, fuel consumption, and emissions. Functional specifications at a hotel might refer to the types of services provided for guests, such as prompt room service.
3. The functional specifications then must be turned into *design specifications*. These are detailed statements regarding the physical characteristics of the product and engineering drawings illustrating those physical characteristics. At a **Holiday Inn** hotel, the number of towels to be left in each room is a design specification.

[7] Much of the material in this section is based on Wayne J. Morse, Harold P. Roth, and Kay M. Poston, *Measuring, Planning, and Controlling Quality Costs* (Montvale, NJ: National Association of Accountants, 1987).

[8] Wendy Zeller, "Coffee, Tea—And On-Time Arrival," *Business Week*, January 20, 1997, p. 30.

4. Detailed specifications of how a product will be manufactured to meet design specifications or how a service will be performed must also be developed. At a Wendy's fastfood restaurant, *manufacturing specifications* include the specified sequence of activities required to prepare a hamburger.
5. Finally, the *actual results* of a product or service are determined following its delivery in conformance with its design specifications.

For clarity, we have identified five distinct steps in delivering a quality product or service. In reality, these steps are often intermingled. As indicated in the discussion of target costing, teams of employees from various functional areas should work on Steps 1 through 4 concurrently. Many efforts to deliver quality products succeed or fail during the design stage. Quality problems and manufacturing costs increase when a complex design makes manufacture difficult. Warranty costs and buyers' life cycle costs increase when a design does not consider ease of service.

To develop standards for evaluating product quality, it is necessary to distinguish between quality of design and quality of conformance. **Quality of design** refers to the degree of conformance between customer expectations for a product or service and the design specifications of the product or service. **Quality of conformance** refers to the degree of conformance between a product and its design specifications. Conformance to customer expectations requires both the quality of design and the quality of conformance.

As shown in Exhibit 8.7, doing the right things wrong (high quality of design but poor quality of conformance) or the wrong things right (poor quality of design but high quality of conformance) results in failure. The only way to win customers is by doing the right things right.

EXHIBIT 8.7 Success Requires Quality of Design and Conformance

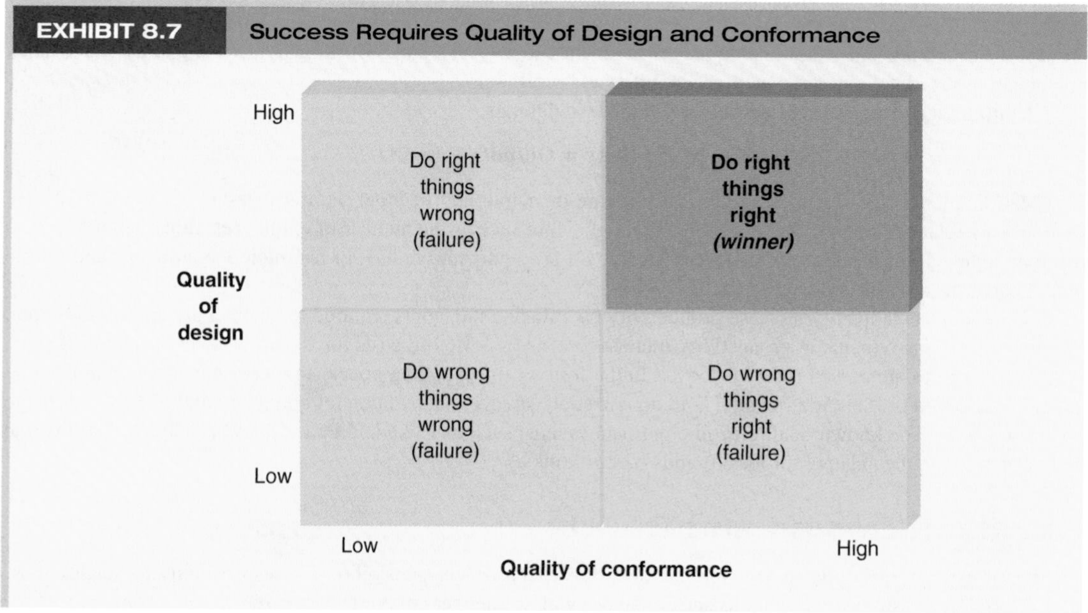

Types of Quality Costs

Many managers find financial information related to quality useful for determining the financial significance of quality problems, developing an overall strategy for improving quality, evaluating proposals to invest in quality improvement activities, and appraising the performance of quality improvement activities. The concepts of quality costs serve as the basis for these special-purpose accounting reports for management.

Quality costs are costs incurred because poor quality of conformance does (or could) exist. There are two basic types of quality costs, and each basic type is classified in two subcategories:

1. Quality costs *are incurred because of the possibility of poor conformance* between actual products or services and their design standards:
   a. **Prevention costs** are incurred to prevent nonconforming products from being produced or nonconforming services from being performed.
   b. **Appraisal costs** are incurred to identify nonconforming products or services before they are delivered to customers.
2. Quality costs *are incurred because of poor conformance* between actual products or services and their design standards:
   a. **Internal failure costs** occur when materials, components, products, or services are identified as defective before delivery to customers.
   b. **External failure costs** occur when nonconforming products or services are delivered to customers. For example, State Farm Insurance Company sued Ford Motor Company, claiming it paid millions of

dollars for fires caused by faulty ignition switches on Ford vehicles. Ford had previously recalled 8.7 million vehicles due to the faulty switch. State Farm estimated that 26 million more vehicles had the potentially faulty switch.[9]

Quality cost information is periodically summarized in a quality cost report, such as the one in Exhibit 8.8, which also presents examples of costs in each category. Quality cost information cuts across organizational boundaries and quality costs are related to specific activities. By associating costs with activities, activity based costing facilitates the development of quality cost information. To provide a benchmark (see later discussion in this chapter) for comparison between periods with different levels of activity, quality cost information is often restated as a percent of sales or total manufacturing costs.

Exhibit 8.8 reveals that external failure costs are very high in comparison with other quality costs. This indicates that quality problems are not being identified and corrected before goods are delivered to customers, a situation frequently encountered before the initiation of a quality improvement program. In this case, expenditures on appraisal and prevention might pay off handsomely with reductions in failure costs.

Quality cost information can be prepared for any time period or cost objective such as a machine, department, plant, division, company, product, or product line. Depending on management's information needs, quality cost reports can include fewer than four cost categories. They can even include subjective information such as an estimate of lost sales resulting from quality problems (an external failure cost). Some organizations have devised unique ways of turning the unrecorded opportunity cost of a lost future sale into a current out-of-pocket cost that is recorded. To avoid the cost of lost sales due to quality problems, the Ritz-Carlton Hotel Co. authorizes employees to spend up to $2,000 to correct the problem of a guest's grievance. The underlying philosophy is that guests, remembering the level of service and the extra effort taken to resolve problems, will return.

EXHIBIT 8.8 Quality Cost Report

BEST WATCH COMPANY
Quality Cost Report
For the Month Ended March 31

	Amount	Percent of Sales*
Prevention		
Design for manufacture	$ 0	
Quality planning	2,000	
Quality training	3,000	
Supplier verification	0	
Total prevention	5,000	0.25%
Appraisal		
Accuracy review of sales orders	0	
Depreciation of testing equipment	1,000	
Field inspection and testing	8,000	
In-process inspection and testing	0	
Total appraisal	9,000	0.46%
Internal failure		
Downtime due to quality problems	0	
Reinspection	400	
Retest	0	
Rework labor and overhead	10,000	
Scrap	1,600	
Total internal failure	12,000	0.61%
External failure		
Complaint adjustment	30,000	
Product recalls	60,000	
Returns and allowances	10,000	
Warranty repairs	50,000	
Warranty replacement	80,000	
Insurance for product liability	20,000	
Legal fees for product liability	0	
Total external failure	250,000	12.68%
Total quality costs	$276,000	14.00%

*Sales for the month total $1,972,208 (100%).

[9] "State Farm Sues Ford over Faulty Ignition Switch," *The Huntsville Times*, January 21, 1998.

Quality Cost Trend Analysis

A *trend analysis* illustrating the effect on quality costs of successfully implementing a quality improvement program is presented in Exhibit 8.9. The most immediate action management can take to prevent the delivery of poor-quality products is to implement a rigorous inspection program and identify defective goods before they are delivered. If the inspection program is successful, there should be a shift in quality costs as a percent of sales, with external failure costs declining and appraisal and internal failure costs increasing. At this stage in a quality improvement program, total known quality costs are likely to increase. The ultimate solution to quality problems is to increase efforts to prevent the occurrence of defects. In addition to reducing external and internal failure costs, a successful quality improvement program will make it possible to reduce appraisal costs when management is confident the job is done right the first time.

EXHIBIT 8.9 Quality Cost Trend Analysis of a Successful Quality Improvement Program

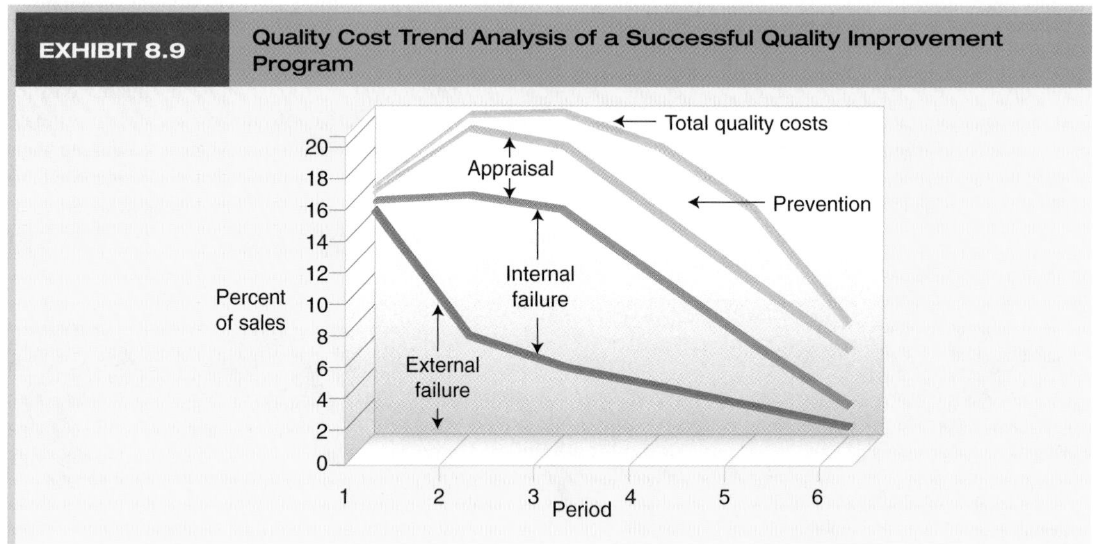

While the implementation of a quality improvement program could have a significant effect on the total amount and distribution of quality costs, it is unlikely that quality costs can be reduced to zero. Management must continue to invest in prevention as new products are introduced and production procedures are changed. Even if the goal of zero defects is reached, some prevention must be required to maintain this ideal state. Appraisal and internal failure costs are better than external failure costs, and prevention costs are preferred to appraisal or failure costs. Quality is not free, but it is less expensive than the alternative.

Exhibit 8.10 shows a hypothesized short-run relationship between the quality of conformance and quality costs. Assuming static conditions with a given technology and level of knowledge, the graph shows that total quality costs are high when quality is low. Total quality costs decline as expenditures for appraisal and prevention produce improvements in quality. As quality nears perfection, the incremental returns to additional efforts to improve quality decline to such an extent that total quality costs begin to rise.

While this hypothesized relationship is a useful way of thinking about quality costs in the short run, remember that these are *static* relationships applicable for a given technology and level of knowledge. Advances in technology or knowledge should have the effect of shifting the prevention and appraisal cost curve down and to the right, increasing the optimal level of quality. The search for quality improvements is never ending. Once a temporary optimal level of quality is achieved, management should strive for advances in technology and knowledge that will permit additional improvements. Competitors who continue to work toward quality improvements could achieve breakthroughs that improve quality, productivity, sales volume, and profitability.

International Organization for Standardization (ISO)

The ability to demonstrate a commitment to quality is becoming increasingly important for companies doing business in global markets. The opening of countries to external competition has a dramatic impact on how managers and employees of companies in those countries view customers and the need for quality.

ISO 9000 Certification for Quality Management

The International Organization for Standardization (ISO) has issued a series of standards for quality assurance systems. These standards, known as *ISO 9000 standards*, provide organizations with internationally recognized models for the design and operation of a quality management system. ISO certification means that an organization has documented

EXHIBIT 8.10 **Short-Run Analysis of the Economics of Quality***

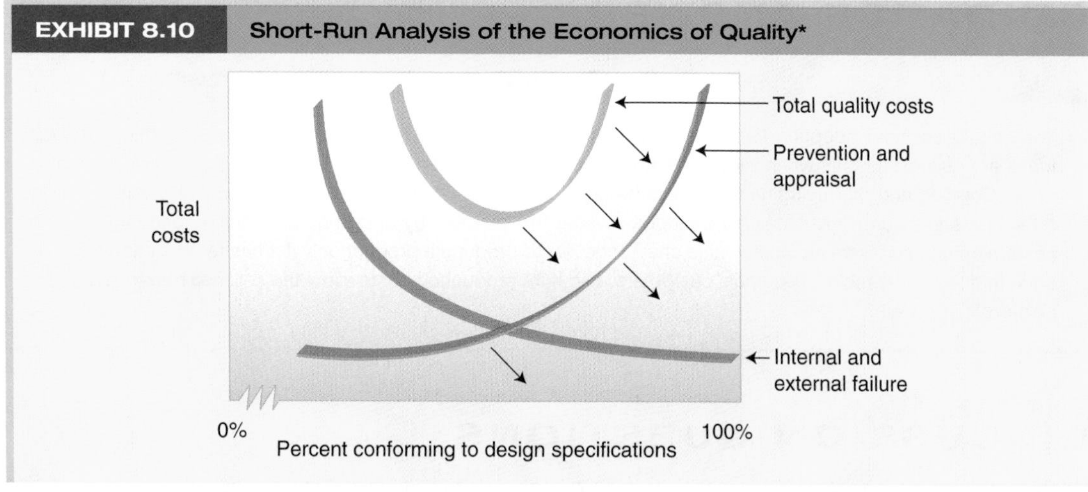

*Arrows represent the effect of technological breakthrough in prevention; they cause the prevention and appraisal cost curve to shift down and to the right. This, in turn, causes the total quality cost curve to shift down and to the right. The net result is an increase in the percent conforming that minimizes total quality costs.

the procedures used to ensure a quality product and that it follows them consistently. Meeting ISO 9000 standards beyond the first level requires an independent audit by an outside organization. ISO certification does not ensure that specific products or services meet customer expectations. Like developing a process map, the most important benefit of obtaining ISO 9000 certification often comes from forcing everyone involved in a process to carefully consider how their actions relate to each other and the purpose of the process. Once the current practice is documented, areas for improvement are easier to detect.

The European Union requires suppliers of certain products to have ISO 9000 certification. The North Atlantic Treaty Organization, the U.S. Department of Defense, and many U.S. companies, such as IBM and General Electric, also require suppliers to be ISO 9000 certified. Even when it is not a requirement, achieving ISO 9000 certification enables companies to differentiate themselves from competitors. Although initially intended for manufacturing operations, law firms, waste removal companies, and professional associations (such as the American Institute of Certified Public Accountants) have achieved ISO 9000 certification.

ISO 14000 Certification for Environmental Management

Few companies measure environmental costs, but awareness of the magnitude and decision usefulness of environmental cost information is increasing. Environmental costs have traditionally been pooled with other overhead items, causing them to be hidden. Placing environmental costs into broad overhead cost pools before assigning them to final cost objectives results in cross-subsidization, with environmental costs misassigned to products that are less environmentally hazardous.

As is the case for quality costs, the development of ABC makes it easier to evaluate environmental costs. One approach to organizing environmental cost information is to use a framework similar to that developed for quality costs:

- *Prevention*—efforts to reduce or prevent environmental hazards from occurring.
- *Appraisal*—inspection to determine whether an environmental problem exists.
- *Failure*—efforts to correct environmental problems.

The Internal Standards Organization issued a series of environmental management standards. Identified as ISO 14000 standards, they are similar to the ISO 9000 standards in that they focus on systems rather than specific results, they are flexible to meet an organization's specific situation, and they call for external certification. The standards are intended to help management communicate environmental information within and outside the company and to provide management the information to help assess the impact of business decisions on the environment.

Environmental costs, such as those associated with waste treatment, landfill, hazardous waste disposal, and environmental inspections, are important parts of the life cycle costs of many products. Previously, future costs, such as those associated with removing oil storage tanks and cleaning up any possible pollution, were seldom considered; however, financial accounting standards now require the present value of such costs to be included on the balance sheet, making it also easier to include them in life cycle cost analysis. Including environmental expenditures as part of a product's life cycle costs could reveal that a product with low acquisition costs but high environmental costs is less desirable than a product with a higher initial cost.

GUIDANCE ANSWER

MANAGERIAL DECISION **You are the Vice President of Product Development**

You should consider adopting target costing methods for new product development. Great product research ideas are successful only when they translate into products that can be produced and sold for an acceptable profit. Creating and producing new products before determining what the customer wants and is willing to pay often leads to failure. Target costing methods reverse this process by applying value chain concepts to bring customers and suppliers along the value chain together to produce a product only if it has features and a selling price that are acceptable to potential customers, and if its production costs allow the seller to make an acceptable profit.

DISCUSSION QUESTIONS

Q8-1. What are the relationships among an organization's value chain, processes, and activities?

Q8-2. What should be the goal of every organization along the value chain?

Q8-3. Distinguish between the value-added perspective and the value chain perspective.

Q8-4. Why are economic models seldom used for day-to-day pricing decisions?

Q8-5. Identify three reasons that cost-based approaches to pricing have traditionally been important.

Q8-6. Identify four drawbacks to cost-based pricing.

Q8-7. How does target costing differ from cost-based pricing?

Q8-8. Why is cost-based pricing more a technique, and target costing is more a philosophy? Which approach takes a more proactive approach to cost management?

Q8-9. Distinguish between the marketing life cycles of products incorporating advanced technology (such as household electronic equipment) and those using more traditional technology (such as household paper products). Why would life cycle costing be more important to a manufacturer of household electronic equipment than to a manufacturer of household paper products?

Q8-10. What is the relationship between target costing and continuous improvement (Kaizen) costing?

Q8-11. Distinguish between the seller's and the buyer's perspective of life cycle costs.

Q8-12. What advantage is derived from benchmarking against firms other than competitors?

MINI EXERCISES

M8-13. Developing a Value Chain from the Perspective of the Final Customer (LO1)
Prepare a value chain for bottled orange juice that was purchased for personal consumption at an on-campus cafeteria.

M8-14. Developing a Value Chain: Upstream and Downstream Entities (LO1)
Prepare a value chain for a firm that produces gasoline fuel. Clearly identify upstream and downstream entities in the value chain.

M8-15. Classifying Activities Using the Generic Internal Value Chain: Aluminum Cable Manufacturer (LO1)
Using the generic internal value chain shown in Exhibit 8.2, classify each of the following activities of an aluminum cable manufacturer as inbound logistics, operations, outbound logistics, marketing and sales, service, or support.

a. Advertising in a construction magazine
b. Inspecting incoming aluminum ingots
c. Placing bar codes on coils of finished products
d. Borrowing money to finance a buildup of inventory
e. Hiring new employees
f. Heating aluminum ingots
g. Drawing wire from aluminum ingots
h. Coiling wire
i. Visiting a customer to determine the cause of cable breakage
j. Filing tax returns

M8-16. Classifying Activities Using the Generic Internal Value Chain: Cable TV Company (LO1)

Using the generic internal value chain shown in Exhibit 8.2, classify each of the following activities of a cable television company as inbound logistics, operations, outbound logistics, marketing and sales, service, or support.

a. Installing cable in the apartment of a new customer
b. Repairing cable after a windstorm
c. Mailing brochures to prospective customers
d. Discussing a rate increase with members of a regulatory agency
e. Selling shares of stock in the company
f. Monitoring the quality of reception at the company's satellite downlink
g. Preparing financial statements
h. Visiting a customer to determine the cause of poor-quality television reception
i. Traveling to a conference to learn about technological changes affecting the industry
j. Inspecting television cables for wear

M8-17. Product Pricing: Single Product (LO2)

Sue Bee Honey is one of the largest processors of its product for the retail market. Assume that it processes honey at one large facility. Its annual fixed costs total \$8,000,000, of which \$3,000,000 is for administrative and selling efforts. Sales are anticipated to be 800,000 cases a year. Variable costs for processing are \$4 per case, and variable selling expenses are 24 percent of selling price. There are no variable administrative expenses. Sue Bee Honey

Required

If the company desires a profit of \$4,000,000, what is the selling price per case?

M8-18. Product Pricing: Single Product (LO2)

Assume that you plan to open a soft ice cream franchise in a resort community during the summer months. Fixed operating costs for the three-month period are projected to be \$5,250. Variable costs per serving include the cost of the ice cream and cone, \$0.25, and a franchise fee payable to Snowdrift Cooler, \$0.10. A market analysis prepared by Snowdrift Cooler indicates that summer sales in the resort community should total 24,000 units.

Required

Determine the price you should charge for each ice cream cone to achieve a \$7,000 profit for the three-month period.

M8-19.[A] Quality Costs: Service Emphasis

Categorize each of the following quality costs as prevention, appraisal, internal failure, or external failure.

a. Inspecting incoming supplies.
b. Following up on complaints by service department.
c. Training new employees.
d. Reconciling of agency contracts with billing statements.
e. Retraining staff members who are not current in area of expertise.
f. Maintaining toll-free telephone for client questions.
g. Redesigning reception area so clients have privacy during consultations.
h. Dismissing staff member found guilty of unethical acts regarding company matters.
i. Senior staff reviewing final report before giving it to client.

M8-20.[A] Quality Costs: Manufacturing Emphasis

Categorize each of the following quality costs as prevention, appraisal, internal failure, or external failure.

a. Disposal of spoiled work-in-process inventory.
b. Downtime due to quality problems.
c. Expediting of work to meet delivery schedule.
d. Field tests.
e. Internal audits of inventory.
f. Support of complaint department.
g. Opportunity cost of lost sales because of bad reputation for quality.
h. Product liability.
i. Quality circles.
j. Quality training.
k. Reinspection.
l. Revision of computer programs due to software errors.
m. Rework labor and overhead.
n. Scrap.

o. Supplier verification.
p. Technical support provided to vendors.
q. Testing and inspection of equipment.
r. Testing and inspection of purchased raw materials.
s. Utilities used by inspection area.
t. Warranty repairs.

EXERCISES

E8-21. Product Pricing: Single Product (LO2)

Presented is the 2009 contribution income statement of Colgate Products.

COLGATE PRODUCTS Contribution Income Statement For Year Ended December 31, 2009		
Sales (12,000 units)		$1,440,000
Less variable costs		
Cost of goods sold	$480,000	
Selling and administrative	132,000	(612,000)
Contribution margin		828,000
Less fixed costs		
Manufacturing overhead	520,000	
Selling and administrative	210,000	(730,000)
Net income		$ 98,000

During the coming year, Colgate expects an increase in variable manufacturing costs of $8 per unit and in fixed manufacturing costs of $48,000.

Required

a. If sales for 2010 remain at 12,000 units, what price should Colgate charge to obtain the same profit as last year?
b. Management believes that sales can be increased to 16,000 units if the selling price is lowered to $107. Is this action desirable?
c. After considering the expected increases in costs, what sales volume is needed to earn a profit of $98,000 with a unit selling price of $107?

E8-22. Cost-Based Pricing and Markups with Variable Costs (LO2)

Compu Services provides computerized inventory consulting. The office and computer expenses are $600,000 annually. The consulting hours available for the year total 20,000, and the average consulting hour has $30 of variable costs.

Required

a. If the company desires a profit of $80,000, what should it charge per hour?
b. What is the markup on variable costs if the desired profit is $120,000?
c. If the desired profit is $60,000, what is the markup on variable costs to cover (1) unassigned costs and (2) desired profit?

E8-23. Computing Markups (LO2)

The predicted 2009 costs for Osaka Motors are as follows:

Manufacturing Costs		Selling and Administrative Costs	
Variable	$100,000	Variable	$300,000
Fixed	220,000	Fixed	200,000

Average total assets for 2009 are predicted to be $6,000,000.

Required

a. If management desires a 12 percent rate of return on total assets, what are the markup percentages for total variable costs and for total manufacturing costs?

b. If the company desires a 10 percent rate of return on total assets, what is the markup percentage on total manufacturing costs for (1) unassigned costs and (2) desired profit?

E8-24. Product Pricing: Two Products (LO2)

Quality Data manufactures two products, CD-ROMs and zip disks, both on the same assembly lines and packaged 10 disks per pack. The predicted sales are 400,000 packs of CD-ROMs and 500,000 packs of zip disks. The predicted costs for the year 2009 are as follows:

	Variable Costs	Fixed Costs
Materials.	$200,000	$500,000
Other.	250,000	800,000

Each product uses 50 percent of the materials costs. Based on manufacturing time, 40 percent of the other costs are assigned to the CD-ROMs, and 60 percent of the other costs are assigned to the zip disks. The management of Quality Data desires an annual profit of $150,000.

Required

a. What price should Quality Data charge for each disk pack if management believes the zip disks sell for 20 percent more than the CD-ROMs?

b. What is the total profit per product using the selling prices determined in part *a*?

c. Based on your answer to requirement (b), how should the company evaluate the status of the two products?

E8-25. Benchmarking (LO5)

Your company is developing a new product for the computer printer industry. You have talked to several material vendors about being able to supply quality components for the new product. The product designers are satisfied with the company's ability to make the product in the current facilities. Numerous potential customers also have been surveyed, and most have indicated a willingness to buy the product if the price is competitive.

Required

What are some means of benchmarking the development and production of your new product?

E8-26. Target Costing (LO3)

Oregon Equipment Company wants to develop a new log-splitting machine for rural homeowners. Market research has determined that the company could sell 5,000 log-splitting machines per year at a retail price of $600 each. An independent catalog company would handle sales for an annual fee of $2,000 plus $50 per unit sold. The cost of the raw materials required to produce the log-splitting machines amounts to $80 per unit.

Required

If company management desires a return equal to 10 percent of the final selling price, what is the target unit cost?

E8-27.[A] Quality Costs Report: Manufacturing Firm C

CompTech had November sales totaling $4,200,000 and incurred the following quality-related costs:

Spoiled work-in-process inventory disposal	$23,000
Downtime due to quality problems	44,000
Field test of new computer.	84,000
Support of a customer complaint department.	22,000
Product liability insurance	8,000
Quality training	12,000
Reinspection.	3,000
Rework labor and overhead.	18,000
New vendor verification and facility inspections	28,000
Technical support provided to vendors	4,000
Equipment inspection.	33,000
Test and inspection of purchased parts.	42,000
Warranty repairs	15,000

Required

Prepare a quality cost report for November with appropriate classifications.

E8-28.[A] Quality Cost Report: Food Processor

Assume that Hormel Meat Packers incurred the following costs during July:

Livestock inspection at auction yard	$ 4,800
Livestock inspection upon delivery	6,000
Inspector training—finished products	2,000
Redesign of processing procedures and sequence	10,000
Inspection and testing of packing procedure	8,200
Product liability insurance	4,000
Product returns	7,400
Scrap disposal	6,600
Downtime due to spoiled products	12,000
Contract negotiations with large vendor	1,500
Rework labor due to processing errors	4,900

Sales for July totaled $4,000,000, and the company's return on investment is expected to be 15 percent for the year on an asset base of $10,000,000.

Required

Prepare a quality cost report for July with appropriate classifications.

PROBLEMS

P8-29. Product Pricing: Two Products (LO2)

Earthlink, Inc. (ELNK)

Earthlink, Inc., provides a variety of computer-related services to its clients. Two of the many services offered by each office are Web page design (WPD), and electronic interchange development (EID) services. Assume that each office is expected to earn a 20 percent return on the assets invested. Earthlink has invested $5 million in the Atlanta office since its opening. The annual costs for the coming year are expected to be as follows:

	Variable Costs	Fixed Costs
Consulting support	$600,000	$850,000
Sales and administration	100,000	950,000

The two services expend about equal costs per hour, and the predicted hours for the coming year are 50,000 for WPD and 30,000 for EID.

Required

a. If markup is based on variable costs, how much revenue must each service generate in the Atlanta office to provide the profit expected by corporate headquarters? What is the anticipated revenue per hour for each service?

b. If the markup is based on total costs, how much revenue must each service generate to provide the expected profit?

c. Explain why answers in requirements (a) and (b) are either the same or different.

d. Comment on the advantages and disadvantages of using a cost-based pricing model.

P8-30. Target Costing (LO3)

Redback Networks, Inc. (RBAK)

Redback Networks, Inc., provides networking services and related systems hardware to its customers. Assume that it is developing a new networking system that small businesses can use. To attract small business owners, Redback must keep the price low without giving up too many of the features of larger networking systems. A marketing research study conducted on the company's behalf found that the price range must be $25,000 to $30,000. Management has determined a target price to be $26,000. The company's minimum profit percentage of sales is normally 20 percent, but the company is willing to reduce it to 15 percent to get the new product on the market. The fixed costs for the first year are anticipated to be $14,000,000. If sales reach 1,200 installed networks, the company needs to know how much it can spend on variable costs, which are primarily related to installation.

Required

a. What is the amount of total cost allowed if the 15 percent profit target is allowed and the sales target is met? Show the amount for fixed and for variable costs.

b. What is the amount of total costs allowed if the 20 percent normal profit target is desired at the 1,200 sales target? Show the amount for fixed and for variable costs.

c. Discuss the advantages of using a target costing model versus using cost-based pricing.

P8-31. Continuous Improvement (Kaizen) Costing (LO4)

Matzumi manufactures cameras. At its Pacific plant, cost control has become a concern of management. The actual costs per unit for the years 2009 and 2010 were as follows:

	2009	2010
Direct materials		
Plastic case	$ 4.00	$ 3.90
Lens set	17.00	17.20
Electrical component set	6.00	5.40
Film track	11.00	10.00
Direct labor	32.00 (1.6 hours)	30.00 (1.5 hours)
Indirect manufacturing costs		
Variable	7.50	7.10
Fixed	2.00 (100,000 unit base)	1.90 (120,000 unit base)

The company manufactures all of the camera components except the lens sets, which it purchased from several vendors. The company has used target costing in the past but has not been able to meet the very competitive global pricing. Beginning in 2010, the company implemented a continuous improvement program that requires cost reduction targets.

Required

a. If continuous improvement (Kaizen) costing sets a first-year target of a 10 percent reduction of the 2009 base, how successful was the company in meeting 2010 per unit cost reduction targets? Support your answer with appropriate computations.

b. Evaluate and discuss Matzumi's use of Kaizen costing.

P8-32. Continuous Improvement (Kaizen) Costing (LO4)

General Electric (GE)

Assume that GE Capital, a division of General Electric, has been displeased with the costs of servicing its consumer loans. Assume that it has decided to implement a Kaizen-based cost improvement program. For 2009, GE Capital incurred the following costs:

Loan processing	$14,500,000
Customer relations	3,500,000
Printing, mailing, and postage	800,000

For the next two years, GE Capital expects an increase in consumer loans of 4 percent annually with related increases in costs.

Required

a. If the company has a continuous improvement of 1 percent each year, develop a budget for the next two years for the consumer loan department.

b. Identify some possible ways that GE Capital can achieve the Kaizen costing goal.

c. Discuss the potential benefits and limitations of GE's Kaizen costing model.

P8-33. Price Setting: Multiple Products (LO2)

Snap Tools Company's predicted 2009 variable and fixed costs are as follows:

	Variable Costs	Fixed Costs
Manufacturing	$400,000	$260,000
Selling and administrative	100,000	50,000
Total	$500,000	$310,000

Snap Tools produces a wide variety of small tools. Per-unit manufacturing cost information about one of these products, the Type-A Clamp, is as follows:

Direct materials	$ 8
Direct labor	7
Manufacturing overhead	
Variable	6
Fixed	6
Total manufacturing costs	$27

Variable selling and administrative costs for the Type-A Clamp is $3 per unit. Management has set a 2009 target profit of $150,000 on the sale of Type-A Clamps.

Required

a. Determine the markup percentage on variable costs required to earn the desired profit.
b. Use variable cost markup to determine a suggested selling price for the Type-A Clamp.
c. For the Type-A Clamp, break the markup on variable costs into separate parts for fixed costs and profit. Explain the significance of each part.
d. Determine the markup percentage on manufacturing costs required to earn the desired profit.
e. Use the manufacturing costs markup to determine a suggested selling price for the Type-A Clamp.
f. Evaluate the variable and the manufacturing cost approaches to determine the markup percentage.

P8-34. Price Setting: Multiple Products **(LO2)**
Chesapeake Tackle Company produces a wide variety of commercial fishing equipment. In the past, product managers set prices using their professional judgment. John Marlin, the new controller, believes this practice has led to the significant underpricing of some products (with lost profits) and the significant overpricing of other products (with lost sales volume). You have been asked to assist Marlin in developing a corporate approach to pricing. The output of your work should be a cost-based formula that can be used to develop initial selling prices for each product. Although product managers are allowed to adjust these prices to meet competition and to take advantage of market opportunities, they must explain such deviations in writing. The following 2009 cost information from the accounting records is available:

	Manufacturing Costs	Selling and Administrative Costs
Variable	$350,000	$ 50,000
Fixed	150,000	200,000

In 2009, Chesapeake reported earnings of $80,000. However, the controller believes that proper pricing should produce earnings of at least $120,000 on the same sales mix and unit volume. Accordingly, you are to use the preceding cost information and a target profit of $120,000 in developing a cost-based pricing formula. Selling and administrative expenses are not currently associated with individual products. However, you have obtained the following unit production cost information for the Tigershark Reel:

Variable manufacturing costs	$120
Fixed manufacturing costs	60
Total	$180

Required

a. Determine the standard markup percentage for each of the following cost bases. Round answers to three decimal places.
   1. Full costs, including fixed and variable manufacturing costs, and fixed and variable selling and administrative costs.
   2. Manufacturing costs plus variable selling and administrative costs.
   3. Manufacturing costs.
   4. Variable costs.
   5. Variable manufacturing costs.

b. Explain why the markup percentages become progressively larger from requirement (a), parts (1) through (5).

c. Determine the initial price of a Tigershark Reel using the manufacturing cost markup and the variable manufacturing cost markup.

d. Do you believe the controller's approach to product pricing is reasonable? Why or why not?

P8-35.[A] Predicting External Failure Costs[10]

Several years ago, Intel Corporation offered to replace any Pentium processor that had a "floating-point divide flaw" with an updated version of the Pentium processor. This offer came in response to pressure from computer manufacturers, the communications media, and the general public. Intel's management remained convinced, however, that the floating-point divide flaw was a minor issue that should not cause a problem for most users. Intel estimated that the replacement of each chip would cost about $200, including service fees. Intel sold a total of 5.3 million flawed Pentium chips before the problem was identified. The following information is available about the response rate to product recalls:

- The response rate in automobile recalls, where safety is an issue, averages 68 percent.
- Sears reports that the response rate to a recall of a toaster with a safety defect might be as high as 40 percent, but it would be much lower without a safety issue.
- An independent analyst predicted that 30 to 40 percent of the Pentium processors had been sold to companies and that half of them would not ask for replacements. The analyst also estimated that 90 percent of individual consumers would not ask for a replacement because the flaw does not affect the applications they run.

Required

Based on the preceding information, develop several alternative predictions of the external failure cost of replacing flawed Pentium processors. If you were to select one estimate, what would it be? Are there any other external failure costs that should be considered?

P8-36.[A] Preparing and Analyzing Quality Cost Reports

Assume that Black & Decker Company, concerned about competitive pressures, implemented a program in 2009 to reduce inventory levels, improve productivity, improve on-time delivery of goods to customers, and reduce customer complaints about quality. To help evaluate the success of these efforts, management requested a quality cost report for the year ended December 31, 2009. After a detailed review of the accounting records and several interviews with key personnel, you have developed the following data for 2009:

Sales	$5,100,000
Inspection of purchased raw materials	60,000
Inspection of finished goods	110,000
Rework	80,000
Disposal cost of spoiled goods	30,000
Reinspection of finished goods	12,000
Development of design-for-manufacture program	5,000
Out-of-warranty adjustments	50,000
Warranty adjustments	60,000
Returns and allowances	10,000
Indirect costs of inspection department	25,000
Development of quality control training programs	9,000
Downtime due to quality problems	210,000

Required

a. Prepare a quality control cost report with appropriate classifications.

b. Management is concerned about the success of the recently implemented program. The vice president of finance observed, "Although sales were essentially unchanged from 2008, profits declined. Furthermore, the decline in profits appears entirely due to increases in inspection, downtime, rework, and similar costs. Increases in these costs far exceeded the cost savings from lower customer complaints." Prepare a response to the concerns expressed by the vice president of finance.

P8-37.[A] Quality Cost Trend Analysis

The following information pertains to quality costs and total sales for Garrick Company for the years 2005 through 2009.

[10] Based on Jim Carlton, "Humble Pie: Intel to Replace Its Pentium Chips," The Wall Street Journal, December 21, 1994, pp. B1, B6

	2005	2006	2007	2008	2009
Prevention	$ 20,000	$ 40,000	$ 25,000	$ 10,000	$ 5,000
Appraisal	10,000	10,000	10,000	5,000	5,000
Internal failure	50,000	55,000	40,000	20,000	10,000
External failure	50,000	25,000	15,000	55,000	65,000
Sales	1,000,000	1,500,000	1,600,000	1,200,000	1,000,000

Required

a. Prepare a quality cost trend analysis graph based on total dollars of quality costs in each category.
b. Prepare a quality cost trend analysis graph based on quality costs as a percent of total sales.
c. Compare the graphs prepared for requirements (a) and (b). Which is more meaningful? Why?
d. Based on the graphs, can any conclusions be made about the company's quality control program?

P8-38.[A] **Activity-Cost Analysis: Quality Costs and Non-Value-Added Costs**
Maine Manufacturing has developed the following activity cost data for its purchasing and manufacturing activities:

Activity	Cost
Prepare purchase order and receive order	$ 36.00/order
Unpack and inspect incoming goods	0.50/unit purchased
Move in-process goods	2.50/unit in job
Hold in-process goods (no work being performed)	0.50/unit in job per day
Set up machine	60.00/machine per job
Operate machine A.	80.00/hour
Operate machine B	60.00/hour
Perform rework	150.00/hour
Inspect work in process or finished goods	1.50/unit
Pack and ship finished goods	5% of previous costs plus $25.00 per job

Maine produces only to fill customer orders. Because suppliers deliver on 24-hours' notice, it does not maintain raw materials inventories. Materials are purchased in the required quantities as needed, unpacked and inspected, and sent immediately to the shop floor. Finished goods are inspected, packed, and immediately shipped to customers. The following information is available for Job 91-Z24, which consisted of 20 units of a special machine part:

Activity		
Prepare purchase order 91-B34		
Material M1	100 units	$1,200 purchase price
Material J2	300 units	300 purchase price
Prepare purchase order 91-B35		
Material N6.	50 units	$ 800 purchase price
Move materials for job to Machine A		
Store at Machine A	1 day	
Set up Machine A		
Run Machine A.	4 hours	
Set up Machine B		
Move job to Machine B		
Run Machine B	12 hours	
Move job to inspection		
Inspect goods	20 units	
Move job to rework station		
Store at rework station.	2 days	
Perform rework	2.5 hours	
Move job to inspection		
Inspect reworked goods	6 units	
Move to packing and shipping		
Pack and ship finished goods		

Required

a. Use activity cost data to determine the total cost of Job 91-Z24. Round computations to the nearest cent.

b. Determine the quality costs associated with Job 91-Z24. Assume that 40 percent of the costs of unpacking and inspecting incoming goods are attributable to inspection.

c. Determine the cost of non-value-added activities associated with Job 91-Z24.

CASES

C8-39. Telephone Pole Rental Rates (LO2, LO3)

Most utility poles carry electric and telephone lines. In areas served by cable television, they also carry television cables. However, cable television companies rarely own any utility poles. Instead, they pay utility companies a rental fee for the use of each pole on a yearly basis. The determination of the rental fee is a source of frequent disagreement between the pole owners and the cable television companies. In one situation, pole owners were arguing for a $7 annual rental fee per pole; this was the standard rate the electric and telephone companies charged each other for the use of poles.

"We object to that," stated the representative of the cable television company. "With two users, the $7 fee represents a rental fee for one-half the pole. This fee is too high because we only use about six inches of each 40-foot pole."

"You are forgetting federal safety regulations," responded a representative of the electric company. "They specify certain distances between different types of lines on a utility pole. Television cables must be a minimum of 40 inches below power lines and 12 inches above telephone lines. If your cable is added to the pole, the total capacity is reduced because this space cannot be used for anything else. Besides, we have an investment in the poles; you don't. We should be entitled to a fair return on this investment. Furthermore, speaking of fair, your company should pay the same rental fee that the telephone company pays us and we pay them. We do not intend to change this fee."

In response, the cable television company representative made two points. First, any fee represents incremental income to the pole owners because the cable company would pay all costs of moving existing lines. Second, because the electric and telephone companies both strive to own the same number of poles in a service area, their pole rental fees cancel themselves. Hence, the fee they charge each other is not relevant.

Required

Evaluate the arguments presented by the cable television and electric company representatives. What factors should be considered in determining a pole rental fee?

C8-40. Target Costing (LO3)

The president of Himatzi Electronics was pleased with the company's newest product, the HE Versatile CVD. The product is portable and can be attached to a computer to play or record computer programs or sound, attached to an amplifier to play or record music, or attached to a television to play or record TV programs. It can even be attached to a camcorder to record videos directly on compact disks rather than on tape. It also can be used with a headset to play or record sound. The proud president announced that this unique and innovative product would be an important factor in reestablishing the North American consumer electronics industry.

Based on development costs and predictions of sales volume, manufacturing costs, and distribution costs, the cost-based price of the HE Versatile CVD was determined to be $380. Following a market-skimming strategy, management set the initial selling price at $450. The marketing plan was to reduce the selling price by $50 during each of the first two years of the product's life to obtain the highest contribution possible from each market segment.

The initial sales of the HE Versatile CVD were strong, and Himatzi Electronics found itself adding second and third production shifts. Although these shifts were expensive, at a selling price of $450, the product had ample contribution margin to remain highly profitable. The president was talking with the company's major investors about the desirability of obtaining financing for a major plant expansion when the bad news arrived. A foreign company had announced that it would shortly introduce a similar product that would incorporate new design features and sell for only $250. The president was shocked. "Why," she remarked, "it costs us $300 to put a complete unit in the hands of customers."

Required

How could the foreign competitor profitably sell a similar product for less than the manufacturing costs to Himatzi Electronics? What advice do you have for the president concerning the HE Versatile CVD? What advice would you have to help the company avoid similar problems in the future?

C8-41. Benchmarking (LO5)

Your company is developing a new product for the computer printer industry. You have talked to several material vendors about being able to supply quality components for the new product. The product designers are satisfied with the company's ability to make the product in the current facilities. Numerous potential customers also have been surveyed, and most have indicated a willingness to buy the product if the price is competitive.

Required

What are some means of benchmarking the development and production of your new product?

C8-42.[A] Electronic Scanning Errors

Law enforcement officials and the general public are concerned about errors in electronic checkout scanning systems. Consider the following:

- A survey by Vermont's attorney general found that local outlets of Ames Department Stores, Inc., and Macy's Department Stores had serious errors in their scanning systems.
- Michigan's attorney general announced the detection of errors in scanning systems at Sears and Wal-Mart stores.
- An official of the Morris County New Jersey Office of Weights and Measures found many mistakes at the checkout counter of a Bradlees, Inc., store.[11]

While authorities and retailers say the mistakes are the result of human error rather than fraud, experts believe electronic scanning errors (typically caused by the failure to update price data in computers) represent a serious problem. It most likely occurs when merchandise is placed on sale. Making the problem worse is the fact that electronic scanning allows stores to save money by not placing a price sticker on each item of merchandise. Some communities have responded to concerns about scanning errors by requiring local merchants to continue attaching stickers to each item so that customers can review their bill when they unpack their purchases.

Required

a. Identify some costs that merchants are likely to incur because of scanning errors.
b. Are these costs related to prevention, appraisal, internal failure, or external failure?
c. Mention several actions a merchant can take to reduce the costs identified in requirement (a). Classify the costs of each action as prevention, appraisal, internal failure, or external failure.

C8-43.[A] Costs of Defective Work

The production manager and the plant controller of Nampa Limited are disagreeing on the importance and extent of using quality cost reports as part of the normal monthly reporting operations of the Boise plant. The Boise operations are very materials intensive, with most per-unit costs being the actual cost of the materials used. Defective units require substantial replacement of most of the original materials.

The production manager argues that the cost of preparing the report (including major efforts to collect the data) exceeds the benefits to be received. He argues that other than the cost of rework of defective (nonquality) units, the other quality costs are negligible and the quality cost reports would not add anything to the decision model that he does not already know.

The controller disagrees with this assessment of quality cost reports and presents the production manager a list of possible categories that could be used to classify the cost of quality. However, knowing that the production manager is not receptive to more information on quality costs, the controller is planning to provide the manager a list of costs identified as the cost of nonquality work.

Required

Using the production manager's example of rework as a nonquality cost, assist the controller in developing a list of nonquality costs in addition to rework.

C8-44.[A] Ethics and Quality of Design

In a short period of time, high concentrations of carbon monoxide in the body can cause death. Over a long period, low concentrations can cause a variety of health problems. The U.S. Consumer Product Safety Commission, concerned about health problems resulting from carbon monoxide, encourages all homeowners to buy carbon monoxide detectors. The City of Chicago even passed an ordinance mandating the installation of carbon monoxide detectors.

In accordance with Commission guidelines, First Alert, a well-known manufacturer of smoke detectors, designed a carbon monoxide detector to warn when relatively low levels of carbon monoxide were present.

[11] Based on Catherine Yank and Willy Stern, "Maybe They Should Call Them Scammers," Business Week, January 16, 1995, pp. 32–33.

First Alert had sold more than 3 million detectors at about $45 each. Most other manufacturers set their detectors so that only life-threatening amounts of carbon monoxide would trigger an alarm. After nearly 10,000 false carbon monoxide alarms sounded within a 48-hour period, Chicago officials were so angry that they threatened to sue First Alert. Although the false alarms were blamed on an unusual temperature inversion that trapped auto exhausts and other pollutants near the ground, officials charged that the First Alert detectors were too sensitive. A fire department representative in another city noted that five of six false carbon monoxide alarms were caused by First Alert detectors.

Despite recommending an increase in the alarm threshold standard set by the Consumer Products Safety Commission, Underwriters Laboratories, Inc., indicated that First Alert detectors warranted its endorsement. First Alert endorsed Underwriters Laboratories' proposed standards although the Carbon Monoxide Safety and Health Association, a manufacturers' trade group, proposed a standard with an even higher alarm threshold.

Required

Discuss the issues management of First Alert faced in setting the design standards for its carbon monoxide detector. What arguments can be made in favor of setting relatively low alarm thresholds and in favor of setting relatively high alarm thresholds? Are any ethical issues involved in setting alarm standards? How should First Alert respond to the public relations problem caused by the "false" alarms?

Chapter 9

Operational Budgeting and Profit Planning

LEARNING OBJECTIVES

LO1 Discuss the importance of budgets. (p. 288)

LO2 Describe basic approaches to budgeting. (p. 289)

LO3 Explain the relations among elements of a master budget and develop a basic budget. (p. 293)

LO4 Explain and develop a basic manufacturing budget. (p. 301)

LO5 Describe the relationship between budget development and manager behavior. (p. 304)

THE FUTURE OF BUDGETING

Managers use budgeting to integrate the various components of the firm and provide insights into the appropriate scale of operations for future months or years. By linking marketing, operations, and financial information, an effective budget aids managers in their planning activities.

The sales forecast is a key starting point in the budget process. Managers estimate the volume of goods and/or services that customers will purchase. These volumes, in turn, drive the level of activities and resulting costs the firm will incur.

To effectively forecast sales, managers must evaluate leading economic indicators, potential changes in consumer preferences, and possible changes in competition. Macroeconomic variables such as income levels and interest rates provide basic information for sales forecasters. Many firms and industry segments rely on specialized economic indicators that signal upcoming activity levels. The volume of corrugated boxes is one such leading indicator.

During a recent economic expansion, corrugated box production increased 27 percent. Known commonly as cardboard boxes, these corrugated boxes lead expansionary times because manufacturers usually increase their box orders before expanding production. Although 1,500 firms make these boxes, four firms dominate the industry: **Smurfit-Stone** (with 20 percent market share), **Weyerhaeuser** (12 percent), **International Paper** (10 percent), and **Georgia Pacific** (9 percent). Industry associations track the volumes of corrugated boxes shipped by these firms, and managers monitor this leading indicator.

Courtesy of JAM Images

Over time, consumers' preferences change. As a result, some product volumes soar while others slide. One shift in consumer tastes concerned the relative demand for carbonated versus noncarbonated drinks. Consumers have shifted their interest from carbonated soda to noncarbonated juice drinks and water, and the latter market has grown 15 times faster than the traditional soda market. Industry estimates suggest that water and juice drinks will make up more than 50 percent of soft-drink growth in the next 5 years. At **7-Eleven** stores, two-thirds of the cooler space reserved for nonalcoholic drinks is devoted to noncarbonated juice and bottled water. This trend impacts the budgets of bottlers of all types within the industry.

The competitive environment can also change. As one example, many nonprofit charities and civic organizations rely on Christmas tree sales as a major fundraising activity. In recent years, retailers such as **Wal-Mart**, **Home Depot**, **Target**, and many supermarkets have added Christmas trees to their garden centers during the holiday season. These stores offer expanded shopping hours and prices that often beat the nonprofit organizations by $10–$15 per tree. Although nonprofit managers complain, retailers contend that nonprofits have a natural advantage because of the public's appreciation for their services.

Overall, budgets benefit managers by providing insight into the impact of the inevitable adjustments required as circumstances change. The budget, however, is no better than the quality of the sales forecast upon which the budget is built. Managerial accounting helps managers with the general relations within a budget and provides guidelines to assess the quality of the sales forecast.

Source: *The Wall Street Journal, 10-K Reports.*[1]

---

[1] Based on Kelly Greene, "Boy Scout Troops Face Stiff Competition from Big Retailers Selling Cheap Trees," *The Wall Street Journal* (Interactive Edition), December 19, 2000; Carol Hymowitz, "Managers Must Adjust Quickly in Changing Economic Environment," *The Wall Street Journal* (Interactive Edition) January 9, 2001; Betsy McKay, "Consumers' Appetite for Soda Is Going Flat," *The Wall Street Journal* (Interactive Edition), September 19, 2000; and Dan Morse, "Sales of Corrugated Boxes Offer One Measure of Economy's Health," *The Wall Street Journal* (Interactive Edition), February 12, 2001.

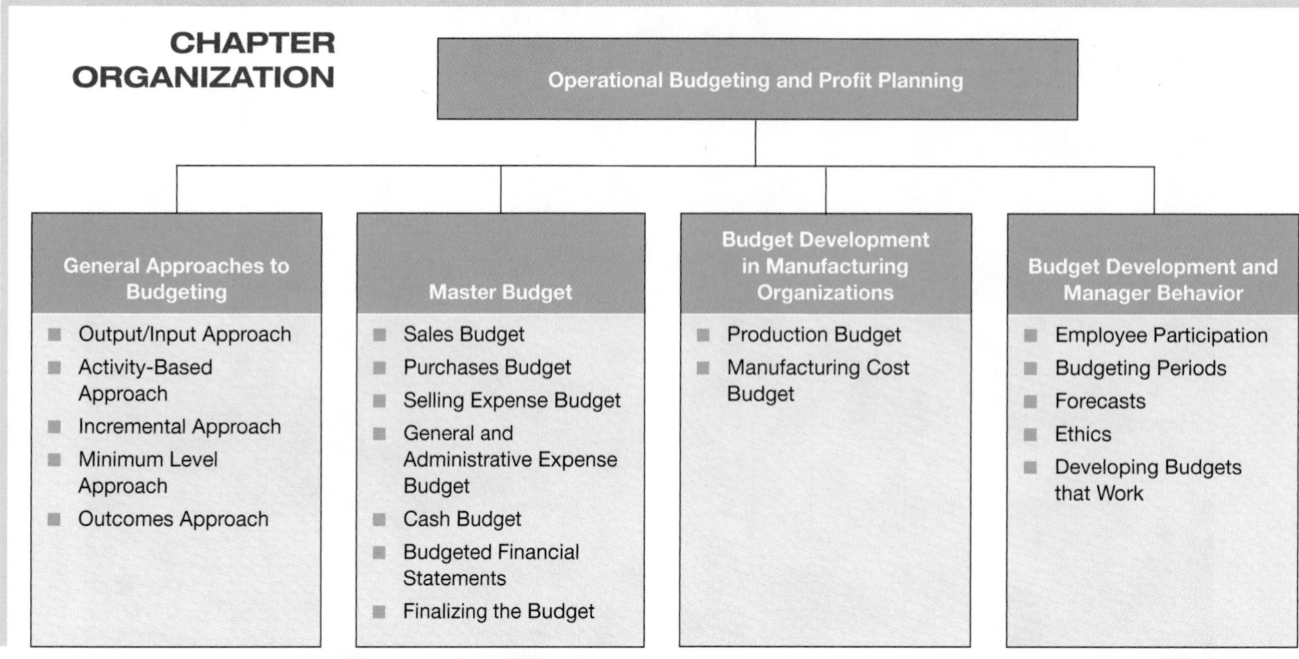

The process of projecting the operations of an organization and their financial impact into the future is called **budgeting**. A **budget** is a formal plan of action expressed in monetary terms. The purpose of this chapter is to examine the concepts, relationships, and procedures used in budgeting. Our emphasis is on **operating budgets**, which concern the development of detailed plans to guide operations throughout the budget period. We consider the reasons that organizations budget and alternative approaches to budget development. We also examine budget assembly and consider issues related to manager behavior and the budgeting process.

REASONS FOR BUDGETING

LO1 Discuss the importance of budgets.

Operating managers frequently regard budgeting as a time-consuming task that diverts attention from current problems. Indeed, the development of an effective budget is a difficult job. It is also a necessary one. Organizations that do not plan are likely to wander aimlessly and ultimately succumb to the swirl of current events. The formal development of a budget helps to ensure both success and survival. As discussed below, budgeting compels planning; it improves communications and coordination among organizational elements; it provides a guide to action; and it provides a basis of performance evaluation.

Formal budgeting procedures require people to think about the future. Without the discipline of formal planning procedures, busy operating managers would not find time to plan. Immediate needs would consume all available time. Formal budgeting procedures, with specified deadlines, force managers to plan for the future by making the completion of the budget another immediate need. Budgeting moves an organization from an informal "reactive" style to a formal "proactive" style of management. As a result, management and other employees spend less time solving unanticipated problems and more time on positive measures and preventative actions.

When operating responsibilities are divided, it is difficult to synchronize activities. Production must know what marketing intends to sell. Purchasing and personnel must know the factory's material and labor requirements. The treasurer must plan to ensure the availability of the cash to support receivables, inventories, and capital expenditures. Budgeting forces the managers of these diverse functions to communicate their plans and coordinate their activities. It helps ensure that plans are feasible (Can purchasing obtain adequate inventories to support projected sales?) and that they are synchronized (Will inventory be available in advance of an advertising campaign?). The final version of the budget emerges after an extensive (often lengthy) process of communication and coordination. As examined in the Research Insight that follows, recent advances in computer software allow organizations to better coordinate budget development.

RESEARCH INSIGHT **Data Warehousing Gives Managers Control**

A multi-user budgeting system provides shared access to a single database (data warehouse) through which all involved in the budgeting process can access common revenue and expense definitions, use similar layouts, use the same encoding and decoding structures, and share budget projections. This type of budgeting system allows the budget manager more control over the process while providing executives with better overviews. Characteristics of a good multi-user budgeting system include:

1. Support for changes to hierarchy so that different levels of budgets can be examined.
2. Shared access to common data warehouses.
3. Automatic mapping of imported data for use in multiple applications.
4. Numerous "what-if" functions.

This system is effective only if the data warehouse is well designed and managed. The design team for and management of a data warehouse should include the following technical personnel who are available to monitor and maintain the system:

1. Technical data warehouse designer (creates the database and maintains it).
2. Systems analyst/programmer (continually evaluates and creates new programs as needed).
3. End-user analyst (evaluates and monitors user needs).
4. Database administrator (creates physical database and monitors performance).
5. Technical support (maintains system integrity and reliability).

A successful data warehouse consists of a group of technologies that integrates the operational information of all budget centers into a single database. This allows managers access to the data and gives them the ability to generate budgets to their own specifications.[2]

Once the budget has been finalized, the various operating managers know what is expected of them, and they can set about doing it. If employees do not have a guide to action, their efforts could be wasted on unproductive or even counterproductive activities.

After employees accept the budget as a guide to action, they can be held responsible for their portion of the budget. When results do not agree with plans, managers attempt to determine the cause of the divergence. This information is then used to adjust operations or to modify plans. More generally, budgeting is an important part of **management by exception**, whereby management directs attention only to those activities not proceeding according to plan. Without the budget, management might spend an inordinate amount of time seeking explanation of past activities and not enough time planning future activities. The process of developing a budgeting system could produce unexpected benefits.

GENERAL APPROACHES TO BUDGETING

LO2 Describe basic approaches to budgeting.

Before an organization can develop operating budgets, management must decide which approaches to budget planning will be used for the various revenue and expenditure activities and organizational units. Widely used planning approaches to budgeting include the input/output, activity-based, incremental, and minimum level approaches.

Output/Input Approach

The **output/input approach** budgets physical inputs and costs as a function of planned unit-level activities. This approach is often used for service, merchandising, manufacturing, and distribution activities that have defined relationships between effort and accomplishment. If each unit produced requires 2 pounds of direct materials that cost \$5 each, and the planned production volume is 25 units, the budgeted inputs and costs for direct materials are 50 pounds (25 units × 2 pounds per unit) and \$250 (50 pounds × \$5 per pound).

[2] Guy Haddleton, "10 Rules for Selecting Budget Management Software," *Management Accounting*, January 1998, pp. 24, 26–27; and Marc Levine and Joel Siegel, "What the Accountant Must Know about Data Warehousing," *The CPA Journal*, January 2001, pp. 37, 39–42.

The budgeted inputs are a function of the planned outputs. The output/input approach starts with the planned outputs and works backward to budget the inputs. It is difficult to use this approach for costs that do not respond to changes in unit-level cost drivers.

Activity-Based Approach

The **activity-based approach** is a type of output/input method, but it reduces the distortions in the transformation through emphasis on the expected cost of the planned *activities* that will be consumed for a process, department, service, product, or other budget objective. Overhead costs are budgeted on the basis of the cost objective's anticipated consumption of activities, not based only on some broad-based cost driver such as direct labor hours or machine hours.

The amount of each activity cost driver used by each budget objective (for example, product or service) is determined and multiplied by the cost per unit of the activity cost driver. The result is an estimate of the costs of each product or service based on cost drivers such as assembly-line setup or inspections, as well as the traditional volume-based drivers such as direct labor hours or units of direct materials consumed. Activity-based budgeting predicts costs of budget objectives by adding all costs of the activity cost drivers that each product or service is budgeted to consume. In evaluating the proposed budget, management would focus their attention on identifying the optimal set of activities rather than just the output/input relationships.

Incremental Approach

The **incremental approach** budgets costs for a coming period as a dollar or percentage change from the amount budgeted for (or spent during) some previous period. This approach is often used when the relationships between inputs and outputs are weak or nonexistent. For example, it is difficult to establish a clear relationship between sales volume and advertising expenditures. Consequently, the budgeted amount of advertising for a future period is often based on the budgeted or actual advertising expenditures in a previous period. If budgeted advertising expenditures for 2008 were $200,000, the budgeted expenditures for 2009 would be some increment, say 5 percent, above $200,000. In evaluating the proposed 2009 budget, management would accept the $200,000 base and focus attention on justifying the increment.

The incremental approach is widely used in government and not-for-profit organizations. In seeking a budget appropriation, a manager using the incremental approach need only justify proposed expenditures in excess of the previous budget. The primary advantage of the incremental approach is that it simplifies the budget process by considering only the increments in the various budget items. A major disadvantage is that existing waste and inefficiencies could escalate year after year.

Minimum Level Approach

As the portion of non-variable costs increased for most companies throughout the twentieth century, an increasing portion of costs was budgeted using the less precise incremental approach. This lack of good budgetary control led to further increases in costs. Management attempted to better control costs by employing a number of variations on the incremental approach. The minimum level approach is representative of these attempts to control the growth of costs not responding to unit-level drivers.

Using the **minimum level approach**, an organization establishes a base amount for budget items and requires explanation or justification for any budgeted amount above the minimum (base). This base is usually significantly less than the base used in the incremental approach. It likely is the minimum amount necessary to keep a program or organizational unit viable. For example, the corporate director of product development would need some basic amount to avoid canceling ongoing projects. Additional increments might also be included, first to support the current level of product development and second to undertake desirable new projects.

Some organizations, especially units of government, employ a variation of the minimum level approach, identified as *zero-based budgeting*. Under **zero-based budgeting** every dollar of expenditure must be justified. The essence of zero-based budgeting is breaking an organizational unit's total budget into program packages with related costs. Management then ranks all program packages on the basis of the perceived benefits in relationship to their costs. Program packages are then funded for the budget period using this ranking. High-ranking packages are most likely to be funded and low-ranking packages are least likely to be funded.

Budgeting for objectives is a variation on the minimum level approach that combines elements of activity-based and zero-based budgeting with a need to live within fixed financial constraints. The Business Insight that follows examines the implementation of budgeting for objectives by the city management of Fort Collins, Colorado.

The minimum level approach improves on the incremental approach by questioning the necessity for costs included in the base of the incremental approach, but it is very time consuming. All three approaches are often used within the same organization. A pharmaceutical company might use the output/input or the activity-based approach to budget distribution expenditures, the incremental approach to budget administrative salaries, and the minimum level approach to budget research and development.

BUSINESS INSIGHT Fort Collins Budgets for Outcomes

When Daren Atteberry became city manager of Fort Collins, Colorado, he was faced with declining tax revenues and inflation in the cost of providing city services. Using an incremental approach to budgeting that focused on budget allocations to city departments, department budgets had been cut by six percent, services reduced, and employee compensation frozen for three years. Clearly it was time for a change.

Responding to the financial mess, city officials put away the budget axe and adopted "Budgeting for Objectives (BFO)." Instead of starting with the previous year's budget and justifying incremental changes, BFO starts by asking what results matter most to citizens. The Government Finance Officers Association outlines the steps in budgeting for objectives as follows:

1. Determine how much money is available.
2. Prioritize the results.
3. Allocate resources among high priority results.
4. Conduct analysis to determine what strategies, programs, and activities will best achieve the desired results.
5. Budget available dollars to the most significant programs and activities.
6. Set measures of annual progress, monitor, and close the feedback loop.
7. Check what actually happened.

This results-oriented approach considers processes and activities that cut across the city's departmentalized organization structure, resulting in changes in what is done and in how objectives are accomplished. Evaluating this new approach, Fort Collins Mayor Doug Hutchinson observed "Previous budget processes focused primarily on funding city departments, rather than on providing services to citizens. With BFO, council had an unprecedented level of involvement, setting the priorities and identifying the outcomes that matter most to our citizens."

Source: Camille Cates Barnett and Darin Atteberry, "Your Budget: From Axe to Aim," *Public Management*, May 2007, pp 6-12.

MID-CHAPTER REVIEW

To illustrate the various approaches to budgeting discussed above, assume that Alpha Company manufactures two products, Beta and Gamma. Last period, Alpha produced 18,000 units of Beta and 45,000 units of Gamma at a total unit cost of $38 for Beta and $32 for Gamma. During the current period, overall costs are expected to rise about 3.5 percent over the last period. Total estimated overhead costs of $408,500 for the next period include the cost of assembly-line setups, engineering and maintenance, and inspections. Total estimated assembly hours is 50,000 hours; therefore, the estimated overhead cost per assembly hour is $8.17. Other predicted data for the next period follow:

	Beta	Gamma
Direct materials (per unit)	$20.00	$14.50
Direct labor hours of assembly time (per unit)	0.5	0.8
Assembly labor cost (per hour)	$18	$18
Total estimated production (in units)	20,000	50,000
Total setup hours	1,000	1,500
Total engineering and maintenance hours	500	600
Total inspections	650	580
Setup cost (per setup hour)	$25	$25
Engineering and maintenance (per hour)	$35	$35
Inspection cost (per inspection)	$250	$250

Required

a. Calculate Alpha's budgeted cost per unit to produce Beta and Gamma during the next period, assuming it uses an output/input approach and budgets overhead cost based only on assembly hours.

b. Repeat a., assuming Alpha uses an activity-based approach and budgets overhead cost based on budgeted activity costs.

c. Repeat a., assuming Alpha uses an incremental approach for budgeting overhead cost.

d. Explain how the minimum level approach differs from the above methods.

Solution

a. Under the output/input approach, the output of units dictates the expected cost inputs. Here budgeted overhead costs are based on the number of budgeted assembly hours.

	Beta	Gamma
Direct materials (20,000 × $20)	$400,000	
(50,000 × $14.50)		$ 725,000
Direct assembly labor (20,000 × 0.5 × $18)	180,000	
(50,000 × 0.8 × $18)		720,000
Overhead (20,000 × 0.5 × $8.17)	81,700	
(50,000 × 0.8 × $8.17)		326,800
Total budgeted cost	$661,700	$1,771,800
Unit Cost	$33.085	$35.436

b. Under the activity-based approach, budgeted overhead costs are based on expected activities to produce the products, not only on assembly hours.

Direct materials (20,000 × $20)	$400,000	
(50,000 × $14.50)		$ 725,000
Direct assembly labor (20,000 × 0.5 × $18)	180,000	
(50,000 × 0.8 × $18)		720,000
Setup (1,000 hours × $25)	25,000	
(1,500 hours × $25)		37,500
Engineering and Maintenance (500 hours × $35)	17,500	
(600 hours × $35)		21,000
Inspections (650 inspections × $250)	162,500	
(580 inspections × $250)		145,000
Total budgeted cost	$785,000	$1,648,500
Unit cost	$39.25	$32.97

c. Under the incremental approach to budgeting, the cost per unit would be budgeted at last period's cost, plus an increment for expected additional costs in the current period. Based on last period's actual cost of $38 for Beta and $32 for Gamma, and using the 3.5 percent overall expected increase in costs, the current period's budgeted cost would be $39.33 for Beta and $33.12 for Gamma.

d. Under the minimum level approach, the company begins with either a zero or very low cost estimate, and then requires all additional costs beyond this minimum to be justified by the production managers. This approach forces managers to evaluate thoroughly all elements of cost each period.

MASTER BUDGET

LO3 Explain the relations among elements of a master budget and develop a basic budget.

The culmination of the budgeting process is the preparation of a master budget for the entire organization that considers all interrelationships among organization units. The **master budget** groups together all budgets and supporting schedules and coordinates all financial and operational activities, placing them into an organization-wide set of budgets for a given time period.

Because it explicitly considers organizational interrelationships, the master budget is more complex than budgets developed for products, services, organization units, or specific processes. The elements of the master budget depend on the nature of the business, its products or services, processes and organization, and management needs.

A major goal of developing a master budget is to ensure the smooth functioning of a business throughout the budget period and the organization's operating cycle. As shown in Exhibit 9.1, the operating cycle involves the conversion of cash into other assets, which are intended to produce revenues in excess of their costs. The cycle generally follows a path from cash, to inventories, to receivables (via sales or services), and back to cash. There are, of course, intermediate processes such as the purchase or manufacture of inventories, payments of accounts payable, and the collection of receivables. The master budget is merely a detailed model of the firm's operating cycle that includes all internal processes.

EXHIBIT 9.1 Operating Cycle of a Manufacturer or Merchandiser

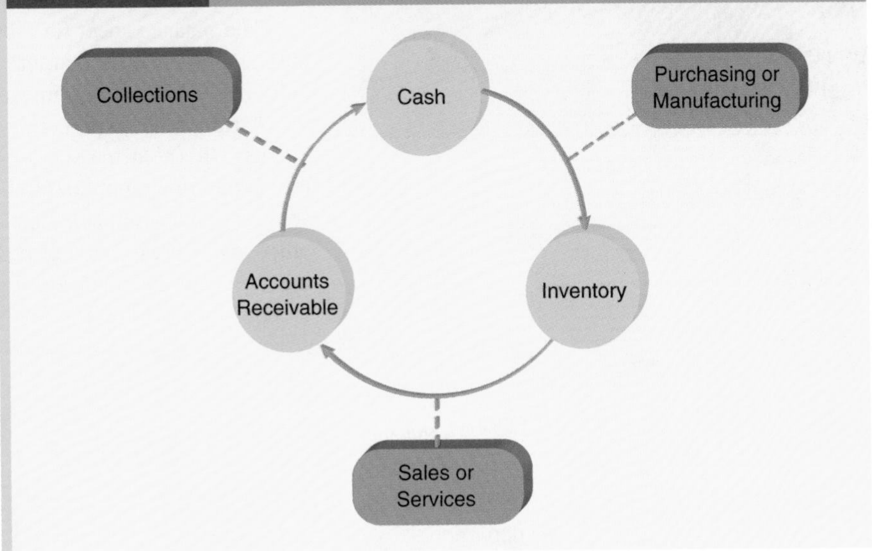

Most for-profit organizations begin the budgeting process with the development of the sales budget and conclude with the development of budgeted financial statements. Exhibit 9.2 depicts the annual budget assembly process in a retail merchandising organization. Most of the budget data flow from sales toward cash and then toward the budgeted financial statements.

To illustrate the procedures involved in budget assembly, a monthly budget for the second quarter of 2009 is developed for Blue Mountain Sports (BMS), a retail organization specializing in outdoor

EXHIBIT 9.2 Budget Assembly for a Merchandiser

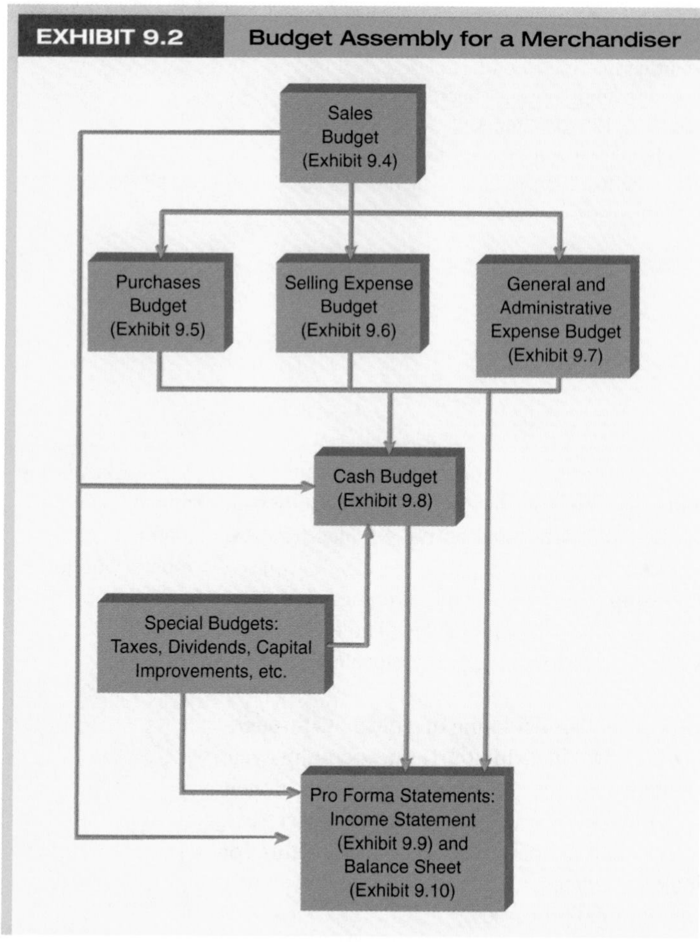

clothing and equipment. The assembly sequence follows the overview illustrated in Exhibit 9.2. Each element of the budget process in Exhibit 9.2 is illustrated in a separate exhibit. Because of the numerous elements in the budget process illustrated for BMS, you will find it useful to refer to Exhibit 9.2 often.

The activities of a business can be summarized under three broad categories: operating activities, financing activities, and investing activities. To simplify the illustration, assume that Blue Mountain Sports engaged in no investing activities during the budget period and that the only anticipated financing activity is short-term borrowing. Normal profit-related activities performed in conducting the daily affairs of an organization are called **operating activities**. The operating activities of Blue Mountain Sports include the following:

1. Purchasing inventory intended for sale.
2. Selling goods or services.
3. Purchasing and using goods and services classified as selling expenses.
4. Purchasing and using goods and services classified as general and administrative expenses.

In addition to preparing the budget for each operating activity, companies prepare a cash budget for cash receipts and disbursements related to their operating activities as well as for financing and investing activities. The importance of cash planning makes this budget a vital part of the total budget process. Management must, for example, be aware in advance of the need to borrow and have some idea when borrowed funds can be repaid.

EXHIBIT 9.3 Initial Balance Sheet

BLUE MOUNTAIN SPORTS
Balance Sheet
April 1, 2009

Assets			
Current assets			
Cash		$ 15,000	
Accounts receivable, net		59,200	
Merchandise Inventory		157,000	$231,200
Fixed assets			
Buildings and equipment	$460,000		
Less accumulated depreciation	(124,800)	335,200	
Land		60,000	395,200
Total assets			$626,400
Liabilities and Stockholders' Equity			
Current liabilities			
Accounts payable		$ 84,000	
Taxes payable*		35,000	$119,000
Stockholders' equity			
Capital stock		350,000	
Retained earnings		157,400	507,400
Total liabilities and stockholders' equity			$626,400

*Quarterly income taxes are paid within 30 days of the end of each quarter.

The balance sheet for April 1, 2009, the start of the second quarter, is presented in Exhibit 9.3. It contains information used as a starting point in preparing the various budgets. To reduce complexity, we use the output/input approach to budget variable costs and assume that the budgets for other costs were previously developed using the incremental approach. Budgets to be prepared include those for sales, purchases, selling expense, general and administrative expense, and cash.

Sales Budget

The **sales budget** includes a forecast of sales revenue, and it can also contain a forecast of unit sales and sales collections. Because sales drive almost all other activities in a for-profit organization, developing a sales budget is the starting point in the budgeting process. Managers use the best available information to accurately forecast future market conditions. These forecasts, when considered along with merchandise available, promotion and advertising plans, and expected pricing policies, should lead to the most dependable sales budget. The sales budget of BMS is in Exhibit 9.4.

EXHIBIT 9.4 Sales Budget

BLUE MOUNTAIN SPORTS
Sales Budget
For the Second Quarter Ending June 30, 2009

	April	May	June	Quarter Total	July
Sales	$190,000	$228,000	$250,000	$668,000	$309,000

The information in the sales budget along with predictions of the expected portion of cash sales and the timing of collections from credit sales are used to calculate cash receipts. In the event of a projected cash shortfall, management could consider ways to increase cash sales or to accelerate the collection of receipts from credit sales.

Purchases Budget

The **purchases budget** indicates the merchandise that must be acquired to meet sales needs and ending inventory requirements. It can be referred to as a *merchandise budget* if it contains only purchases of merchandise for sale. However, for a manufacturer it would include purchase of raw materials. The purchases budget, shown in Exhibit 9.5, includes only purchases of merchandise.

EXHIBIT 9.5 Purchases Budget

BLUE MOUNTAIN SPORTS
Purchases Budget
For the Second Quarter Ending June 30, 2009

	April	May	June	Quarter Total	July
Budgeted sales (Exhibit 9.4)	$190,000	$228,000	$250,000	$668,000	$309,000
Current cost of goods sold*	$114,000	$136,800	$150,000	$400,800	
Desired ending inventory**	168,400	175,000	192,700	192,700	
Total needs	282,400	311,800	342,700	593,500	
Less beginning inventory***	(157,000)	(168,400)	(175,000)	(157,000)	
Purchases	$125,400	$143,400	$167,700	$436,500	

*Cost of goods sold is 60 percent of selling price

**Fifty percent of inventory required for next month's budgeted sales plus base inventory of $100,000.
April: ($228,000 May sales x 0.60 cost x 0.50 desired ending inventory) + $100,000
May: ($250,000 June sales x 0.60 cost x 0.50 desired ending inventory) + $100,000
June :($309,000 July sales x 0.60 cost x 0.50 desired ending inventory) + $100,000

***Fifty percent of current month sales plus base inventory of $100,000. Note monthly beginning inventory. Same as previous month's ending inventory.

In reviewing BMS's purchases budget, note the following:

- Because BMS sells a wide variety of items, the purchases budget is expressed in terms of sales dollars, with the cost of merchandise averaging 60 percent of the selling price. Management also keeps detailed records for budgeting the number of units of items carried. An organization that only sold a small number of items might present the sales budget in units as well as dollars.

- Management desires to have 50 percent of the inventory needed to fill the following month's sales in stock at the end of the previous month.
- To provide for a possible delay in the receipt of inventory and to meet variations in customer demand, BMS maintains an additional base inventory of $100,000.
- The total inventory needs equal current sales plus desired ending inventory, including the base inventory.
- Budgeted purchases are computed as total inventory needs less the beginning inventory.

The information in the purchases budget and the information on expected timing of payments for purchases are used to budget cash disbursements for purchases. In the event of a projected cash shortfall, management can consider ways to delay the purchase of inventory or the payment for inventory purchases.

Selling Expense Budget

The **selling expense budget** presents the expenses the organization plans to incur in connection with sales and distribution. In the selling expense budget, Exhibit 9.6, the budgeted variable selling expenses are determined as a percentage of budgeted sales dollars. The budgeted fixed selling expenses are based on amounts obtained from the manager of the sales department. To simplify the presentation of the cash budget, assume BMS pays its selling expenses in the month they are incurred.

EXHIBIT 9.6 Selling Expense Budget

BLUE MOUNTAIN SPORTS
Selling Expense Budget
For the Second Quarter Ending June 30, 2009

	April	May	June	Quarter Total
Budgeted sales (Exhibit 9.4)	$190,000	$228,000	$250,000	$668,000
Variable selling expenses				
Setup/Display (1% sales)	$ 1,900	$ 2,280	$ 2,500	$ 6,680
Commissions (2% sales)	3,800	4,560	5,000	13,360
Miscellaneous (1% sales)	1,900	2,280	2,500	6,680
Total	7,600	9,120	10,000	26,720
Fixed selling expenses				
Advertising	2,250	2,250	2,250	6,750
Office	1,250	1,250	1,250	3,750
Miscellaneous	1,000	1,000	1,000	3,000
Total	4,500	4,500	4,500	13,500
Total selling expenses	$ 12,100	$ 13,620	$ 14,500	$ 40,220

General and Administrative Expense Budget

The **general and administrative expense budget** presents the expenses the organization plans to incur in connection with the general administration of the organization. Included are expenses for the accounting department, the computer center, and the president's office, for example. Blue Mountain's general and administrative expense budget is presented in Exhibit 9.7.

The depreciation of $2,000 per month is a noncash item and is not carried forward to the cash budget. No variable general and administrative costs are included because most expenditures categorized as general and administrative are related to top-management operations that do not vary with unit-level cost drivers. To simplify the presentation of the cash budget, assume that general and administrative expenses, except depreciation, are paid in the month they are incurred.

EXHIBIT 9.7 General and Administrative Expense Budget

BLUE MOUNTAIN SPORTS
General and Administrative Expense Budget
For the Second Quarter Ending June 30, 2009

	April	May	June	Quarter Total
General and administrative expenses				
Compensation	$25,000	$25,000	$25,000	$75,000
Insurance	2,000	2,000	2,000	6,000
Depreciation	2,000	2,000	2,000	6,000
Utilities	3,000	3,000	3,000	9,000
Miscellaneous	1,000	1,000	1,000	3,000
Total general and administrative expenses	$33,000	$33,000	$33,000	$99,000

Cash Budget

The **cash budget** summarizes all cash receipts and disbursements expected to occur during the budget period. Cash is critical to survival. Income is like food and cash is like water. Food is necessary to survive and prosper over time, but you can get along without food for a short period of time. You cannot survive very long without water. Hence, cash budgeting is very important, especially in a small business, such as the one considered in the following Business Insight.

BUSINESS INSIGHT Going Broke Getting Rich

Frank used his own cash plus some borrowed from his bank to start a business. In the first two years, Frank's company showed a small operating loss that he considered acceptable. In the third year, it showed a profit of more than $100,000. Frank thought this was great until the accountant told him that the company did not have enough cash to pay income taxes. Frank did not believe his accountant until the differences between income and cash flow were explained and the accountant showed him a cash flow statement for his business. Because income is not the same as cash inflow, cash budgets are critical to all businesses, especially small ones. Managers who do not understand cash flow can really have problems, even when profits are evident. Cash can be tied up in inventory purchased in anticipation of sales growth. When sales are on account, additional cash is tied up in receivables rather than being available to pay bills. Worse, the money Frank borrowed to start the business might come due just as the business starts to turn a profit. Managers must understand the operating cycle and relationship between income and cash flows. For Frank, a cash budget would show the cash generated by operations, the cash outflow needed for paying back his loan, and the amount of cash tied up in inventory and receivables.[3]

After it makes sales predictions, an organization uses information regarding credit terms, collections policy, and prior collection experience to develop a cash collections budget. Collections on sales normally include receipts from the current period's sales and collections from sales of prior periods. An allowance for bad debts, which reduces each period's collections, is also predicted. Other items often included are cash sales, sales discounts, allowances for volume discounts, and seasonal changes of sales prices and collections. BMS's cash budget is in Exhibit 9.8. Note the following important points:

- Management estimates that one-half of all sales are for cash and the other half are on the company's credit card. (When sales are on bank credit cards, the collection is immediate, less any bank user fee; however, charges using Blue Mountain's credit card are collected by the company from the customer.) Twenty-five percent of the credit card sales are collected in the month of sale, and 74

[3] Gary Gibbs, "Managing Cash Flow: A Constant Business Challenge," *Wichita Business Journal*, December 1997, pp. 8b–14b.

EXHIBIT 9.8 Cash Budget

BLUE MOUNTAIN SPORTS
Cash Budget
For the Second Quarter Ending June 30, 2009

	April	May	June	Quarter Total
Budgeted sales (Exhibit 9.4)	$190,000	$228,000	$250,000	$668,000
Cash balance, beginning	$ 15,000	$ 15,770	$ 44,850	$ 15,000
Collections on sales				
Cash sales (50% sales)	95,000	114,000	125,000	
Credit sales				
Current month (25% credit sales)	23,750	28,500	31,250	
Prior month (74% credit sales)	59,200*	70,300	84,360	
Total	177,950	212,800	240,610	631,360
Cash available for operations	192,950	228,570	285,460	646,360
Disbursements				
Purchases (Exhibit 9.5)				
Current month (20% purchases)	25,080	28,680	33,540	
Prior month (80% purchases)	84,000**	100,320	114,720	
Total	109,080	129.000	148,260	386,340
Selling expenses (Exhibit 9.7)	12,100	13,620	14,500	40,220
General & Administrative Expenses				
(Exhibit 9.7, excluding depreciation)	31,000	31,000	31,000	93,000
Taxes (Exhibit 9.3)	35,000			35,000
Total	(187,180)	(173,620)	(193,760)	(554,560)
Excess (deficiency) cash available over disbursements	5,770	54,950	91,700	91,800
Short-term financing***				
New loans	10,000			10,000
Repayments		(10,000)		(10,000)
Interest	—	(100)	—	(100)
Net cash from financing	10,000	(10,100)	—	(100)
Cash balance, ending	$ 15,770	$ 44,850	$ 91,700	$ 91,700

*April 1 accounts receivable.

**April 1 accounts payable.

***Loans are obtained in $1,000 increments at the start of the month to maintain a minimum balance of $15,000 at all times. Repayments are made at the end of the month, as soon as adequate cash is available. Interest of 12 percent per year (1 percent per month) is paid when the loan is repaid.

percent are collected in the following month. Bad debts are budgeted at 1 percent of credit sales. This resource flow is graphically illustrated as follows:

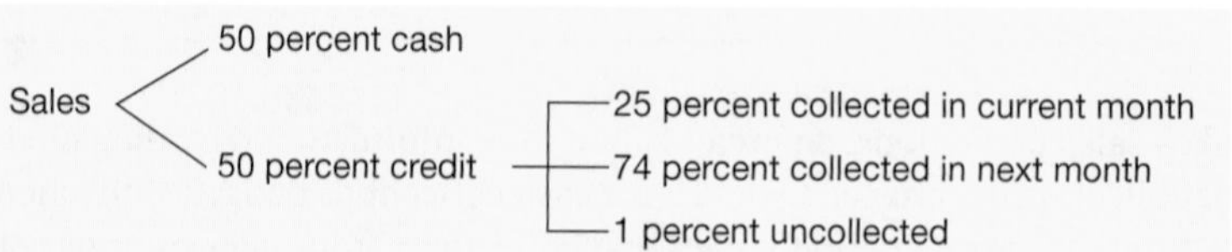

- Payments for purchases are made 20 percent in the month purchased and 80 percent in the next month.
- Information on cash expenditures for selling expenses and for general and administrative expenses is based on budgets for these items. The monthly cash expenditures for general and administrative expenses are $31,000 rather than $33,000. The $2,000 difference relates to depreciation, which does not require use of cash.
- Blue Mountain's accountant provided tax information. Income taxes are determined on the basis of predicted taxable income following IRS rules. Estimated tax payments are made during the month following the end of each quarter. Hence, the taxes payable on April 1 are paid during April.

- The cash budget shows cash operating deficiencies and surpluses expected to occur at the end of each month; this is used to plan for borrowing and loan payment.
- The cash maintenance policy for Blue Mountain specifies that a minimum balance of $15,000 is to be maintained.
- BMS has a line of credit with a bank, with any interest on borrowed funds computed at the simple interest rate of 12.0 percent per year, or 1.0 percent per month. All necessary borrowing is assumed to occur at the start of each month in increments of $1,000. Repayments are assumed to occur at the end of the month. Interest is paid when loans are repaid.
- The cash budget indicates Blue Mountain needs to borrow $10,000 in April. The $10,000 plus interest is repaid in May.

If Blue Mountain had any cash disbursements for dividends or capital expenditures they would be included in the cash budget. These items, along with information on income taxes, would be shown in special budgets.

Budgeted Financial Statements

The preparation of the master budget culminates in the preparation of budgeted financial statements. **Budgeted financial statements** are pro forma statements that reflect the "as-if" effects of the budgeted activities on the actual financial position of the organization. That is, the statements reflect the results of operations assuming all budget predictions are correct. Spreadsheets that permit the user to immediately determine the impact of any assumed changes facilitate developing budgeted financial statements. The budgeted income statement can follow the functional format traditionally used for financial accounting or the contribution format introduced in Chapter 3. In either case, the balance sheet amounts reflect the corresponding budgeted entries.

Exhibit 9.9 presents the budgeted income statement for the quarter ending June 30, 2009. If all predictions made in the operating budget are correct, BMS will produce a net income of $51,540 for the quarter. Almost every item on the budgeted income statement comes from one of the budget schedules.

EXHIBIT 9.9 Budgeted Income Statement

BLUE MOUNTAIN SPORTS
Budgeted Income Statement
For the Second Quarter Ending June 30, 2009

Sales (Exhibit 9.4)		$668,000
Cost of goods sold:*		
Beginning inventory (Exhibit 9.3)	$157,000	
Purchases (Exhibit 9.5)	436,500	
Cost of merchandise available	593,500	
Ending inventory (Exhibit 9.5)	(192,700)	(400,800)
Gross profit		267,200
Other expenses:		
Bad debt (1% of credit sales)**	3,340	
Selling (Exhibit 9.6)	40,220	
General and administrative (Exhibit 9.7)	99,000	(142,560)
Income from operations		124,640
Interest expense (Exhibit 9.8)		(100)
Net income from operations		124,540
Allowance for income taxes***		(73,000)
Net income		$ 51,540

*Also computed at sales x 0.6

**$668,000 x 0.5 credit sales x 0.01 bad debts

***Provided by accounting

The budgeted balance sheet, presented in Exhibit 9.10 shows Blue Mountain's financial position as of June 30, 2009, assuming that all budget predictions are correct. Sources of the budgeted balance sheet data are included as part of the exhibit.

EXHIBIT 9.10 Budgeted Balance Sheet

BLUE MOUNTAIN SPORTS Balance Sheet June 30, 2009			
Assets:			
Current assets			
Cash (Exhibit 9.8)		$ 91,700	
Accounts receivable, net*		92,500	
Merchandise inventory (Exhibit 9.5 and 9.9)		192,700	$376,900
Fixed assets			
Buildings and equipment (Exhibit 9.3)	$460,000		
Less accumulated depreciation (Exhibit 9.3 plus depreciation Exhibit 9.7)	(130,800)	329,200	
Land (Exhibit 9.3)		60,000	389,200
Total assets			$766,100
Liabilities and Stockholders' Equity			
Current liabilities			
Accounts payable**		$134,160	
Taxes payable (Exhibit 9.9)		73,000	$207,160
Stockholders' equity			
Capital stock (Exhibit 9.3)		350,000	
Retained earnings (Exhibit 9.3 plus net income Exhibit 9.9)		208,940	558,940
Total liabilities and stockholders' equity			$766,100

*June credit sales collected in July, $250,000 x 0.50 x 0.74.

**June purchases paid in July, $167,700 x 0.80.

Finalizing the Budget

After studying the BMS example, you might conclude that developing the master budget is a mechanical process. That is not the case. Understanding the basics of budget assembly is not the end; it is a tool to assist in efficient and effective budgeting. Before finalizing the budget, the following two questions must be addressed:

- Is the proposed budget feasible?
- Is the proposed budget acceptable?

To be feasible, the organization must be able to actually implement the proposed budget. Without the line of credit, Blue Mountain's budget is not feasible because the company would run out of cash sometime in April. Knowing this, management can take timely corrective action. Possible actions include obtaining equity financing, issuing long-term debt, reducing the amount of inventory on hand at the end of each quarter, or obtaining a line of credit. Other constraints that would make the budget infeasible include the availability of merchandise and, in the case of a manufacturing organization, production capacity.

Once management determines that the budget is feasible, they still need to determine if it is acceptable. To evaluate acceptability, management might consider various financial ratios, such as return on assets. They might compare the return provided by the proposed budget with past returns, industry averages, or some organizational goal.

BUDGET DEVELOPMENT IN MANUFACTURING ORGANIZATIONS

LO4 Explain and develop a basic manufacturing cost budget.

The importance of inventory in various organizations was introduced in Chapter 5 where Exhibit 5.1 (page 131) summarized inventory and related expense accounts for service, merchandising, and manufacturing organizations. Recall that service organizations usually have a low percentage of their assets invested in inventory, usually consisting of the supplies needed to facilitate operations. In contrast, merchandising organizations usually have a high percentage of their total assets invested in inventory, with the largest inventory investment in merchandise purchased for resale. The preceding illustration of the development of a master budget was for a merchandising organization.

Production Budget

Because manufacturing organizations convert raw materials into finished goods that are sold to customers, there are additional steps in developing their master budget. Contrast the assembly of a budget for a merchandiser in Exhibit 9.2 with the assembly of a budget for a manufacturer in Exhibit 9.11. The management of a manufacturing organization must determine the production volume required to support sales and finished goods ending inventory requirements (production budget). Then, based on available inventories or raw materials and the raw materials required for production, management develops a purchases budget.

EXHIBIT 9.11 Budget Assembly for a Manufacturer

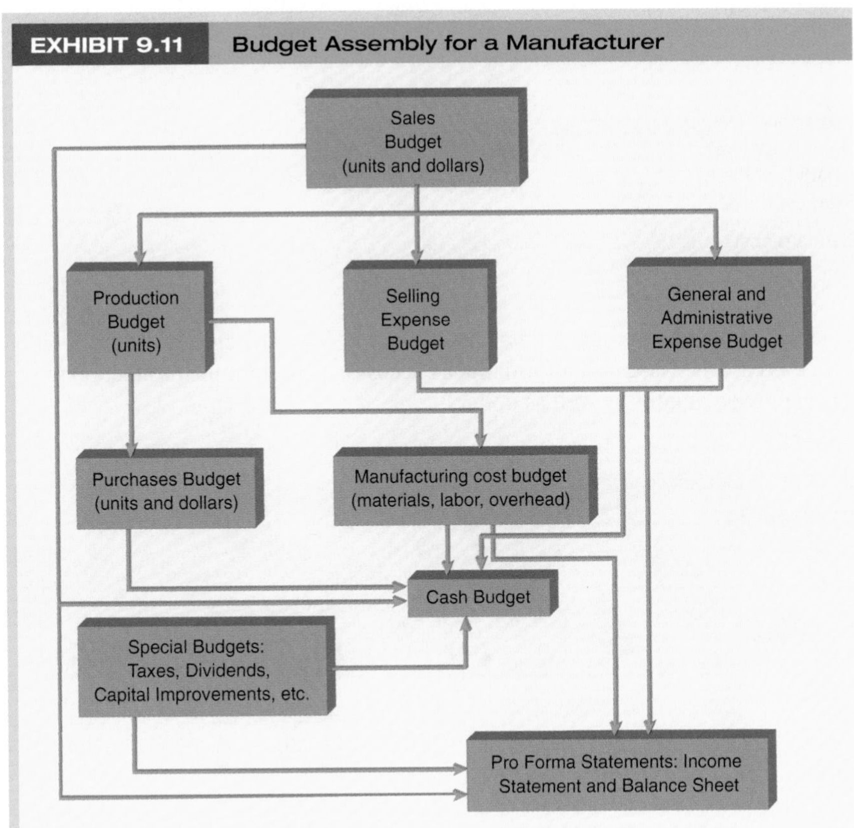

Manufacturing Cost Budget

In addition to a selling expense budget and a general and administrative expense budget, management needs also to develop a manufacturing cost budget, which is similar in design to a statement of cost of goods manufactured (see Exhibit 5.6, page 143) except that it is prepared in advance of production rather than after production. Reflecting these additional steps, the cash budget includes payments for direct labor and manufacturing overhead, based on information in the manufacturing cost budget, and payments for purchases of raw materials based on the purchases budget. Note cash disbursements are for materials purchased rather than materials used in production.

Continuing our Blue Mountain Sports example, assume that management is considering the option of manufacturing a high-quality backpack, tentatively named the "Trekpack" as an alternative to purchasing a similar item from an outside vendor. Unit variable and monthly fixed cost estimates associated with the manufacture of Trekpacks follow:

Unit costs:		
Direct materials:		
Fabric: 2 square years at $10 per yard	$20	
Hardware kits (buckles, straps, etc.)	5	$ 25
Direct labor 0.5 hours at $30 per hour		15
Variable overhead, per unit		8
Total variable costs per unit		$ 48
Fixed costs per month (rent, utilities, supervision)		$6,000

Because management anticipates an average monthly production volume of 500 Trekpacks, the average fixed cost per unit, a predetermined overhead rate, is $12 ($6,000/500).

For budgeting purposes, management uses a standard cost, a budget per unit of product, for valuing inventories and forecasting the cost of goods sold. The standard cost of a Trekpack is $60:

Direct materials	$25
Direct labor	15
Variable overhead	8
Fixed overhead	12
Standard cost	$60

Management, planning to introduce this new product in May, developed the sales budget shown in Exhibit 9.12. In this case, because unit information is necessary to determine production requirements, the sales budget is expressed in units as well as dollars.

EXHIBIT 9.12 Sales Budget

BLUE MOUNTAIN SPORTS
Sales Budget (Trekpacks)
For the Second Quarter Ending June 30, 2009

	April	May	June	Quarter Total	July
Sales - Units	0	400	500	900	600
Sales - Dollars ($100 each)	0	$40,000	$50,000	$90,000	$60,000

Introducing Trekpacks in May requires some April production. To meet the initial sales requirement for the start of each month, management desires end-of-month inventories equal to 40 percent of the following month's budgeted sales. The sales budget and ending inventory plans, along with information on beginning inventories, is used to develop the production budget in Exhibit 9.13.

The production budget, along with information on beginning inventories of raw materials and planned ending inventory levels (500 square yards of fabric and 200 kits) is then used to budget the purchases in Exhibit 9.14 for raw materials in units and dollars. The production budget, along with

EXHIBIT 9.13 Production Budget

BLUE MOUNTAIN SPORTS
Production Budget (Trekpacks)
For the Second Quarter Ending June 30, 2009

	April	May	June	Quarter Total
Budgeted Sales	0	400	500	900
Desired ending inventory				
40% following month sales	160	200	240	240
Total requirements	160	600	740	1,140
Less beginning inventory	0	(160)	(200)	0
Budgeted production	160	440	540	1,140

standard variable and predicted fixed cost information is also used to develop the manufacturing cost budget in Exhibit 9.15.

EXHIBIT 9.14 Purchase Budget

BLUE MOUNTAIN SPORTS
Purchases Budget
For the Second Quarter Ending June 30, 2009

	April	May	June	Quarter Total
Fabric:				
Current needs (2 yards per unit)	320	880	1,080	2,280
Desired ending inventory (500 yards)	500	500	500	500
Total requirements	820	1,380	1,580	2,780
Less beginning inventory	−0	−500	−500	−0
Fabric purchases in yards	820	880	1,080	2,780
Assembly kits:				
Current needs (1 per unit)	160	440	540	1,140
Desired ending inventory (200 kits)	200	200	200	200
Total requirements	360	640	740	1,340
Less beginning inventory	−0	−200	−200	−0
Kit purchases in units	360	440	540	1,340
Purchases (Dollars)				
Fabric at $10 per yard	$ 8,200	$ 8,800	$10,800	$27,800
Kits at $5 each	1,800	2,200	2,700	6,700
Total purchases in dollars	$10,000	$11,000	$13,500	$34,500

Because it does not require the introduction of new concepts, the cash budget and the pro-forma financial statements for Blue Mountain Sports with the manufacturing of Trekpacks are not presented. Keep in mind that the cash budget will include disbursements for purchases shown in Exhibit 9.14 and for direct labor, variable overhead, and fixed overhead shown in Exhibit 9.15. A pro-forma functional income statement using absorption costing will include the predicted cost of goods sold for Trekpacks at a $60 standard cost per unit. A contribution income statement using variable costing would include the cost of goods sold for Trekpacks at a $48 standard cost per unit with all fixed manufacturing costs expensed in the period incurred. Finally, the pro-forma balance sheet will include standard costs of any June raw

EXHIBIT 9.15 Manufacturing Cost Budget

BLUE MOUNTAIN SPORTS
Manufacturing Cost Budget
For the Second Quarter Ending June 30, 2009

	April	May	June	Quarter Total
Direct materials				
Fabric used in production (production × 2 yards × $10)	$ 3,200	$ 8,800	$10,800	$22,800
Kits used in production (production × 1 kit × $5)	800	2,200	2,700	5,700
Total	4,000	11,000	13,500	28,500
Direct labor (production × 1/2 hour × $30)	2,400	6,600	8,100	17,100
Manufacturing overhead				
Variable ($8 per unit)	1,280	3,520	4,320	9,120
Fixed	6,000	6,000	6,000	18,000
Total	7,280	9,520	10,320	27,120
Total manufacturing costs	$13,680	$27,120	$31,920	$72,720

materials (500 square yards at $10 per yard and 200 kits at $5 each), work in process (none), and finished goods. Any unpaid liabilities for purchases of raw materials, direct labor, and manufacturing overhead would also be shown under current liabilities. Note that completing the cash budget and the pro-forma statements requires information on the timing of payments for the purchases of raw materials, direct labor, and manufacturing overhead.

BUDGET DEVELOPMENT AND MANAGER BEHAVIOR

LO5 Describe the relationship between budget development and manager behavior.

Organizations are composed of individuals who perform a wide variety of activities in pursuit of the organization's goals. To accomplish these goals, management must recognize the effects that budgeting and performance evaluation methods have on the behavior of the organization's employees.

Employee Participation

Budgeting should be used to promote productive employee behavior directed toward meeting the organization's goals. While no two organizations use exactly the same budgeting procedures, two approaches to employee involvement in budgeting represent possible end points on a continuum. These approaches are sometimes referred to as *top-down* and *bottom-up* methods.

With a **top-down** or **imposed budget**, top management identifies the primary goals and objectives for the organization and communicates them to lower management levels. Because relatively few people are involved in top-down budgeting, an imposed budget saves time. It also minimizes the slack that managers at lower organizational levels are sometimes prone to build into their budgets. However, this nonparticipative approach to budgeting can have undesirable motivational consequences. Personnel who do not participate in budget preparation might lack a commitment to achieve their part of the budget.

With a **bottom-up** or **participative budget**, managers at all levels—and in some cases, even nonmanagers—are involved in budget preparation. Budget proposals originate at the lowest level of management possible and are then integrated into the proposals for the next level, and so on, until the proposals reach the top level of management, which completes the budget.

Participation helps ensure that important issues are considered and that employees understand the importance of their roles in meeting the organization's goals. It also provides opportunities for problem solving and fosters employee commitment to agreed-upon goals. Hence, budget predictions are likely to be more accurate, and the people responsible for the budget are more likely to strive to accomplish its objectives. These *self-imposed budgets* reinforce the concept of participative management and should strengthen the overall budgeting process.

BUSINESS INSIGHT **Budgetary Slack May Provide Flexibility for Innovation and Improve Control in Unstructured Environments**

When one of the authors became responsible for budgeting and financial control of a business school, department budgets were developed using the incremental approach. There were two major problems. First, there was inadequate information on the activities and programs financed by college funds. Second, department heads with budget authority frequently requested additional funds for special projects and overspent their budget, causing the college to dip into discretionary funds contributed by alumni and friends.

Practicing what is taught in this book, the author implemented different approaches to budgeting different costs. For example average salary increases were budgeted on an incremental basis, instructional supplies and photocopying were budgeted using the output/input approach, and various student and alumni events were budgeted per event using budgeting for objectives. Funds were then allocated to the budget of the department responsible for the activity or event. This approach demystified the budgeting process and allowed personnel to understand what was accomplished with college's funds.

The availability of dollars in regular budgets almost always expires at the end of the budget year, leading managers to spend all of their funds, and even a bit more. To provide flexibility for department managers to undertake new initiatives during the year, each department was provided an additional budget allocation, funded by college alumni and friends for unspecified discretionary items. If the manager spent more than the regular budget, the overspending would be taken from the allocated discretionary funds. If the manager spent less than the regular budget plus the allocated discretionary funds, the unspent discretionary funds were carried forward to the following year.

The availability of the discretionary funds reduced the tendency of managers to make special requests throughout the year. Interestingly, department managers saw the discretionary funds as a savings account that they were reluctant to spend without good reason. The result was a significant decline in overspending of the regular budget.

Participative approaches to budgeting have a few disadvantages. Because they require the involvement of many people, the preparation period is longer than that for an imposed budget. Another disadvantage is the tendency of some managers to intentionally understate revenues or overstate expenses to provide **budgetary slack**. A manager might do this to reduce his or her concern regarding unfavorable performance reviews or to make it easier to obtain favorable performance reviews. If a department consistently produces favorable variances (actual results versus budget) with little apparent effort, this might be a symptom of budgetary slack. On the other hand, as discussed in the preceding Business Insight, budgetary slack can produce favorable results under certain circumstances.

MANAGERIAL DECISION **You are the Chief Financial Officer**

As the CFO of a relatively new and fast-growing entrepreneurial enterprise, you and the other top managers have previously emphasized technical and marketing innovation and creativity over planning and budgeting. But now with growing competition and the maturing of the company's products, you recognized that a culture of better financial planning must be established if the company is to succeed in the long run. You feel that the financial staff have the best expertise and understanding of the business to prepare effective budgets, but you are concerned about the motivational effects of excluding the lower-level managers from the process and are seeking advice. [Answer, p. 313]

Budgeting Periods

Although most organizations use a one-year budget period, some organizations budget for shorter or longer periods. In addition to fixed-length budget periods, two other types of budget periods commonly used are life cycle budgeting and continuous budgeting.

When a fixed time period is not particularly relevant to planning, an organization can use **life cycle budgeting**, which involves developing a budget for a project's entire life. An ice cream vendor at the beach might develop a budget for the season. A general contractor might budget costs for the entire (multiple-year) time required to construct a building.

Under **continuous budgeting**, the budget (sometimes called a **rolling budget**) is based on a moving time frame. For example, an organization on a continuous four-quarter budget system adds a quarter to the budget at the end of each quarter of operations, thereby always maintaining a budget for four quarters into the future. Under this system, plans for a full year into the future are always available, whereas under a fixed annual budget, operating plans for a full year ahead are available only at the beginning of the budget year. Because managers are constantly involved in this type of budgeting, the budget process becomes an active and integral part of the management process. Managers are forced to be future oriented throughout the year rather than just once each year.

Forecasts

Budget preparation requires the development of a variety of forecasts. The sales forecast is based on a variety of interrelated factors such as historical trends, product innovation, general economic conditions, industry conditions, and the organization's strategic position for competing on the basis of price, product differentiation, or market niche. Many organizations first determine the industry forecast for a given product or service and then extract from it their sales estimations.

Although the sales forecast is primary to most organizations, there are many other forecasts of varying importance that must be made, including (a) the collection period for sales on account, (b) percent of uncollectable sales on account, (c) cost of materials, supplies, utilities, and so forth, (d) employee turnover, (e) time required to perform activities, (f) interest rates, and (g) development time for new products or services.

Ethics

Because most wrongful activities related to budgeting are unethical, rather than illegal, organizations often have difficulty dealing with them. However, when managers' actions cross the gray area between ethical and fraudulent behavior, organizations are not reluctant to dismiss employees or even pursue legal actions against them.[4]

Although most managers have a natural inclination to be conservative in developing their budgets, at some level the blatant padding or building slack into the budget becomes unethical. In an extreme case, it might even be considered theft if an inordinate level of budgetary slack creates favorable performance variances that lead to significant bonuses or other financial gain for the manager. Another form of falsifying budgets occurs when managers include expense categories in their budgets that are not needed in their operations and subsequently use the funds to pad other budget categories. The deliberate falsification of budgets is unethical behavior and is grounds for dismissal in most organizations.

Ethical issues might also arise in the reporting of performance results, which usually compares actual data with budgeted data. Examples of unethical reporting of actual performance data include misclassification of expenses, overstating revenues or understating expenses, postponing or accelerating the recording of activities at the end of the accounting period, or creating fictitious activities. The views of the former CEO of Phillips Petroleum on this type of behavior and the competitive environment from which it is often motivated are summarized in the following Business Insight.

Developing Budgets that Work

It is important for management to understand that budgets are not perfect. Mistakes in prediction and judgment are made, and unforeseen circumstances often develop, necessitating modification of the budget. Unless top management is willing to recognize that changes in the budget are needed, support for the budget at lower levels will quickly erode. If an organization is to receive maximum benefit from the budget process, support for the budget at the top management level, as well as at lower levels, must be maintained. Achieving this support could be the most difficult challenge facing an organization undertaking budgeting for the first time. Lower-level managers are not likely to respect the budget and the related performance reports if they perceive a lack of commitment by top management. Disregard for the budget by top management can quickly destroy the effectiveness of the budget throughout the organization.

---

[4] *Fraud Survey Results 1993*, (New York: KPMG Peat Marwick, 1993).

BUSINESS INSIGHT **The Heart of Every Decision**

The retired CEO of **Phillips Petroleum** stated, "What we are all called upon to do, whatever professional field we have chosen, is to make ethics the heart of every decision we make, from boardroom to the mailroom." He cites several examples of managers making the wrong decisions, one involving a budget-related situation. Specifically, a plant manager at a glass container plant, inflated the results of operations, not slightly, but by 33 percent over actual levels. When the plant manager confessed to his wrongdoings, he stated that the actual results were so unfavorable that he "was afraid the company would close the aging plant, throwing [him] and 300 employees out of work." The former CEO admitted, "It's a lot harder to resist temptation when honesty and integrity could mean the end of your job, your company, even your town." Still, he says that organizations must establish policies of operations that do not cause direct conflicts with managers' decisions, a concept he labeled "the moral dimension of competitiveness." An example is an executive order to a manager to cut costs but not to cut customer satisfaction. Organizations should provide guidelines and expectations of actions, not blatant orders for which the means and goals seem to conflict.[5]

Managers who follow the suggestions listed here are more likely to be successful in using budgets as a positive motivational tool for accomplishing organizational goals through people.

1. Emphasize the importance of budgeting as a planning device.
2. Encourage wide participation in budget preparation at all levels.
3. Demonstrate that the budget has the complete support of top management.
4. Recognize that the budget is alterable; modifications may be required if conditions change.
5. Use budget performance reports to identify poor performers *and* to recognize good performance.
6. Conduct budget training to provide managers information about the purposes of budgets and to dispel any erroneous misconceptions.

Properly used, an operating budget is an effective mechanism for motivating employees to higher levels of performance and productivity. Improperly developed and administered, budgets can foster feelings of animosity toward management and the budget process. Behavioral research has generally concluded that when employees participate in the preparation of budgets and believe that the budgets represent fair standards for evaluating their performance, they receive personal satisfaction from accomplishing the goals set in the budgets.

CHAPTER-END REVIEW 1: BUDGET FOR A MERCHANDISING ORGANIZATION

Stumphouse Cheese Company is a wholesale distributor of blue cheese and ice cream. The following information is available for April 2009.

Estimated sales	
Blue cheese	160,000 hoops at $10 each
Ice cream	240,000 gallons at $5 each

Estimated costs	
Blue cheese	$8 per hoop
Ice cream	$2 per gallon

	Beginning	Ending
Desired inventories		
Blue cheese	10,000	12,000
Ice cream	4,000	5,000

[5] C. J. Silas, "The Moral Dimension of Competitiveness," *Management Accounting*, December 1994, p. 72.

Financial information follows:

- Beginning cash balance is $400,000.
- Purchases of merchandise are paid 60 percent in the current month and 40 percent in the following month. Purchases totaled $1,800,000 in March and are estimated to be $2,000,000 in May.
- Employee wages, salaries, and commissions are paid for in the current month. Employee expenses for April totaled $156,000.
- Overhead expenses are paid in the next month. The accounts payable amount for these expenses from March is $80,000 and for May will be $90,000. April's overhead expenses total $80,000.
- Sales are on credit and are collected 70 percent in the current period and the remainder in the next period. March's sales were $3,000,000, and May's sales are estimated to be $3,200,000. Bad debts average 1 percent of sales.
- Selling and administrative expenses are paid monthly and total $450,000, including $40,000 of depreciation.
- All unit costs for April are the same as they were in March.

Required

Prepare the following for April:

a. Sales budget in dollars.
b. Purchases budget.
c. Cash budget.
d. Budgeted income statement.

Solution to Chapter-End Review 1

a.

STUMPHOUSE CHEESE COMPANY
Sales Budget
For Month of April 2009

	Units	Price	Sales
Blue cheese	160,000	$10	$1,600,000
Ice cream	240,000	5	1,200,000
Total			$2,800,000

b.

STUMPHOUSE CHEESE COMPANY
Purchases Budget
For Month of April 2009

	Blue Cheese	Ice Cream	Total
Units			
Sales needs	160,000	240,000	
Desired ending inventory	12,000	5,000	
Total	172,000	245,000	
Less beginning inventory	(10,000)	(4,000)	
Purchases	162,000	241,000	
Dollars			
Sales needs	$1,280,000	$480,000	
Desired ending inventory	96,000	10,000	
Total	1,376,000	490,000	
Less beginning inventory	(80,000)	(8,000)	
Purchases needed	$1,296,000	$482,000	$1,778,000

c.

STUMPHOUSE CHEESE COMPANY
Cash Budget
For Month of April 2009

Cash balance, beginning		$ 400,000
Collections on sales		
Current month's sales ($2,800,000 × 0.70)	$1,960,000	
Previous month's sales ($3,000,000 × 0.29)	870,000	2,830,000
Cash available from operations		3,230,000
Less budgeted disbursements		
March purchases ($1,800,000 × 0.40)	720,000	
April purchases ($1,778,000 × 0.60)	1,066,800	
Labor	156,000	
Overhead (March)	80,000	
Selling and administrative ($450,000 − $40,000 depreciation)	410,000	(2,432,800)
Cash balance, ending		$ 797,200

d.

STUMPHOUSE CHEESE COMPANY
Budgeted Income Statement
For Month of April 2009

Sales (sales budget)			$2,800,000
Allowance for bad debts			(28,000)
Net sales			2,772,000
Costs of merchandise sold			
Blue cheese (160,000 × $8)	$1,280,000		
Ice cream (240,000 × $2)	480,000	$1,760,000	
Wages and salaries	156,000		
Overhead	80,000		
Selling and administrative	450,000	686,000	(2,446,000)
Net income			$ 326,000

CHAPTER-END REVIEW 2: BUDGET FOR A MANUFACTURER

Handy Company manufactures and sells two industrial products in a single plant. The new manager wants to have quarterly budgets and has prepared the following information for the first quarter of 2009:

Budgeted sales		
Drills		60,000 at $100 each
Saws		40,000 at $125 each
Budgeted inventories		
	Beginning	**Ending**
Drills, finished	20,000 units	25,000 units
Saws, finished	8,000 units	10,000 units
Metal, direct materials	32,000 pounds	36,000 pounds
Plastic, direct materials	29,000 pounds	32,000 pounds
Handles, direct materials	6,000 each	7,000 each

continued

continued from previous page

Standard variable costs per unit

	Drills		Saws	
Direct materials				
Metal	5 pounds × $8.00	$40.00	4 pounds × $8.00	$32.00
Plastic	3 pounds × $5.00	15.00	3 pounds × $5.00	15.00
Handles	1 handle × $3.00	3.00		
Total		58.00		47.00
Direct labor.	2 labor hours × $12.00	24.00	3 labor hours × $16.00	48.00
Variable manufacturing Overhead	2 hours × $1.50	3.00	3 hours × $1.50	4.50
Total		$85.00		$99.50

Fixed factory overhead is $214,000 per quarter (including noncash expenditures of $156,000) and is allocated on total units produced. Financial information follows:

- Beginning cash balance is $1,800,000.
- Sales are on credit and are collected 50 percent in the current period and the remainder in the next period. Last quarter's sales were $8,400,000. There are no bad debts.
- Purchases of direct materials and labor costs are paid for in the quarter acquired.
- Manufacturing overhead expenses are paid in the quarter incurred.
- Selling and administrative expenses are all fixed and are paid in the quarter incurred. They are budgeted at $340,000 per quarter, including $90,000 of depreciation.

Required

For the first quarter of 2009, prepare the following:

a. Sales budget in dollars.
b. Production budget in units.
c. Purchases budget.
d. Manufacturing cost budget.
e. Cash budget.
f. Budgeted contribution income statement. (Hint: See Chapter 3.)

Solution Chapter-End Review 2

a.

HANDY COMPANY
Sales Budget
For First Quarter of 2009

	Units	Price	Sales
Drills	60,000	$100	$ 6,000,000
Saws.	40,000	125	5,000,000
Total			$11,000,000

b.

HANDY COMPANY
Production Budget
For First Quarter of 2009

	Drills	Saws
Budget sales.	60,000	40,000
Plus desired ending inventory	25,000	10,000
Total inventory requirements	85,000	50,000
Less beginning inventory	(20,000)	(8,000)
Budgeted production	65,000	42,000

c.

HANDY COMPANY
Purchases Budget
For First Quarter of 2009

	Drills	Saws	Total
Metal purchases			
Production units (production budget)	65,000	42,000	
Metal (pounds)	× 5	× 4	
Production needs (pounds)	325,000	168,000	493,000
Desired ending inventory (pounds)			36,000
Total metal needs (pounds)			529,000
Less beginning inventory (pounds)			(32,000)
Purchases needed (pounds)			497,000
Cost per pound			× $8
Total metal purchases			$3,976,000
Plastic purchases			
Production units (production budget)	65,000	42,000	107,000
Plastic (pounds)			× 3
Production needs (pounds)			321,000
Desired ending inventory (pounds)			32,000
Total plastic needs (pounds)			353,000
Less beginning inventory (pounds)			(29,000)
Purchases needed (pounds)			324,000
Cost per pound			× $5
Total plastic purchases			$1,620,000
Handle purchases			
Production units (production budget)	65,000		65,000
Handles			× 1
Production needs			65,000
Desired ending inventory			7,000
Total handle needs			72,000
Less beginning inventory			(6,000)
Purchases needed			66,000
Cost per handle			× $3
Total handle purchases			$198,000
Total purchases			
Metal			$3,976,000
Plastic			1,620,000
Handles			198,000
Total purchases			$5,794,000

d.

HANDY COMPANY
Manufacturing Cost Budget
For First Quarter of 2009

	Drills	Saws	Total
Direct materials			
Metal			
Production units (production budget)	65,000	42,000	
Metal per unit of product (pounds)	× 5	× 4	
Production needs for metal (pounds)	325,000	168,000	
Unit cost	× $8	× $8	
Cost of metal issued to production	$2,600,000	$1,344,000	$3,944,000

continued

continued from previous page

HANDY COMPANY
Manufacturing Cost Budget
For First Quarter of 2009

	Drills	Saws	Total
Plastic			
Production units (production budget)	65,000	42,000	
Plastic (pounds)	× 3	× 3	
Production needs for plastic (pounds)	195,000	126,000	
Unit cost	× $5	× $5	
Cost of plastic issued to production	$ 975,000	$ 630,000	1,605,000
Handles			
Production units (production budget)	65,000		
Handles	× 1		
Production needs for handles	65,000		
Unit cost	× $3		
Cost of handles issued to production	$ 195,000		195,000
Total			5,744,000
Direct labor			
Budgeted production	65,000	42,000	
Direct labor hours per unit	× 2	× 3	
Total direct labor hours	130,000	126,000	
Labor rate	× $12	× $16	
Labor expenditures	$1,560,000	$2,016,000	3,576,000
Variable factory overhead			
Direct labor hours	130,000	126,000	
Variable factory overhead rate	× $1.50	× $1.50	
Total variable overhead	$ 195,000	$ 189,000	384,000
Fixed factory overhead			214,000
Total			$9,918,000

e.

HANDY COMPANY
Cash Budget
For First Quarter of 2009

Cash balance, beginning		$ 1,800,000
Collections on sales		
Current quarter's sales ($11,000,000 × 0.50)	$5,500,000	
Previous quarter's sales ($8,400,000 × 0.50)	4,200,000	9,700,000
Cash available from operations		11,500,000
Less budgeted disbursements		
Materials (purchases budget)	5,794,000	
Labor (manufacturing cost budget)	3,576,000	
Manufacturing overhead (manufacturing cost budget) ($598,000 − 156,000)	442,000	
Selling and administrative ($340,000 − $90,000 depreciation)	250,000	(10,062,000)
Cash balance, ending		$ 1,438,000

f.

HANDY COMPANY Contribution Income Statement For First Quarter of 2009		
Sales (sales budget)		$11,000,000
Less variable costs of goods sold		
Drills (60,000 × $85.00)	$5,100,000	
Saws (40,000 × $99.50)	3,980,000	(9,080,000)
Gross profit		1,920,000
Less fixed costs		
Manufacturing overhead	214,000	
Selling and administrative expenses	340,000	(554,000)
Net income		$ 1,366,000

GUIDANCE ANSWER

MANAGERIAL DECISION **You are the Chief Financial Officer**

You seem to be leaning toward using a top-down approach to budgeting. While this method may produce an effective set of benchmarks for planning and evaluation, it does not maximize the benefits of budgeting. A key element in any effective budgeting system is that it must be embraced by the managers whose performance will be evaluated by it. If the budget is imposed from the top down, it is far less likely to be embraced by managers than if they have participated from the beginning of the budget development process. The most effective budgeting systems are those that are strongly embraced by managers at all levels, which is most readily achieved through a participative (bottom-up) approach.

DISCUSSION QUESTIONS

Q9-1. What are the primary phases in the planning and control cycle?

Q9-2. Does budgeting require formal or informal planning? What are some advantages of this style of management?

Q9-3. Identify the advantages and disadvantages of the incremental approach to budgeting.

Q9-4. Explain the minimum level approach to budgeting.

Q9-5. How does activity-based budgeting predict a cost objective's budget?

Q9-6. Explain the continuous improvement concept of budgeting.

Q9-7. Which budget brings together all other budgets? How is this accomplished?

Q9-8. What budgets are normally used to support the cash budget? What is the net result of cash budget preparations?

Q9-9. Define *budgeted financial statements.*

Q9-10. Identify the two budgets that are part of the master budget of a manufacturing organization but not part of the master budget of a merchandising organization.

Q9-11. Contrast the top-down and bottom-up approaches to budget preparation.

Q9-12. Is budgetary slack a desirable feature? Can it be prevented? Why or why not?

Q9-13. Why are annual budgets not always desirable? What are some alternative budget periods?

Q9-14. Explain how continuous budgeting works.

Q9-15. In addition to the sales forecast, what forecasts are used in budgeting?

Q9-16. Why should motivational considerations be a part of budget planning and utilization? List several ways to motivate employees with budgets.

MINI EXERCISES

M9-17. Department Budget Using Output/Input Approach (LO2)

The following data are from the general records of Department 16 for October.

- Each unit of product requires 6 direct labor hours, 20 liters of direct materials, and 1 container.
- Each unwasted liter of material processed requires $13 of manufacturing overhead.
- Average wages for direct laborers are $15 per hour.
- Direct materials currently cost $3 per liter.
- Containers cost $9 each.
- Direct material waste amounts to 10 percent of materials started in process.

Required

Prepare an October department budget for Department 16 if planned production is 2,000 units of output.

M9-18. Department Budget Using Incremental Approach (LO2)

Assume that the Assembly Department of Applied Materials' Texas plant prepares its budget using the incremental approach for both fixed and variable costs. For 2010 assume that the following costs were incurred for the production of 100,000 units.

Direct materials	$240,000
Direct labor	600,000
Supervision	90,000
Depreciation, equipment (straight line)	34,000
Variable overhead ($1.20 per unit)	120,000

Assume that each unit takes one-half hour to assemble.

Required

Prepare a budget for the Assembly Department that allows for a 4 percent inflation rate if the Texas plant sets a production level of 140,000 for 2011.

M9-19. Purchases Budget in Units and Dollars (LO3)

Budgeted sales of The Music Shop for the first six months of 2010 are as follows:

Month	Unit Sales	Month	Unit Sales
January	130,000	April	210,000
February	160,000	May	180,000
March	200,000	June	240,000

Beginning inventory for 2010 is 40,000 units. The budgeted inventory at the end of a month is 40 percent of units to be sold the following month. Purchase price per unit is $5.

Required

Prepare a purchases budget in units and dollars for each month, January through May.

M9-20. Cash Budget (LO3)

Wilson's Retail Company is planning a cash budget for the next three months. Estimated sales revenue is as follows:

Month	Sales Revenue	Month	Sales Revenue
January	$300,000	March	$200,000
February	225,000	April	175,000

All sales are on credit; 60 percent is collected during the month of sale, and 40 percent is collected during the next month. Cost of goods sold is 80 percent of sales. Payments for merchandise sold are made in the month following the month of sale. Operating expenses total $41,000 per month and are paid during the month incurred. The cash balance on February 1 is estimated to be $30,000.

Required

Prepare monthly cash budgets for February, March, and April.

M9-21 Production and Purchases Budgets in Units (LO4)
At the end of business on June 30, 2009, the Wooly Rug Company had 100,000 square yards of rugs and 400,000 pounds of raw materials on hand. Budgeted sales for the third quarter of 2009 are:

Month	Sales
July	200,000 sq. yards
August	180,000 sq. yards
September	150,000 sq. yards
October	160,000 sq. yards

The Wooly Rug Company wants to have sufficient square yards of finished product on hand at the end of each month to meet 40 percent of the following month's budgeted sales and sufficient pounds of raw materials to meet 30 percent of the following month's production requirements. Five pounds of raw materials are required to produce one square yard of carpeting.

Required
Prepare a production budget for the months of July, August, and September and a purchases budget in units for the months of July and August.

M9-22 Manufacturing Cost Budget (LO4)
Huntsville Products produces a product with the following standard costs:

Unit costs:		
Direct materials:		
Wood: 20 square feet at $3	$60	
Hardware kits (screws, etc)	2	$ 62
Direct labor 0.5 hours at $26 per hour		13
Variable overhead, per unit		5
Total variable costs per unit		$ 80
Fixed costs per month (rent, utilities, supervision)		$50,000

Management plans to produce 8,000 units in April 2010.

Required
Prepare a manufacturing cost budget for April 2010.

EXERCISES

E9-23. Activity-Based Budget (LO2)
Merrit Industries Inc. has the following budget information available for February:

Administration	$40,000
Advertising	$15,000
Assembly	½ hour per unit × $8
Direct materials	2 pounds per unit × $3
Inspection	$200 per batch of 1,000 units
Manufacturing overhead	$2 per unit
Manufactured units	20,000
Product development	$15,000
Sales units	20,000 units × $30
Setup cost	$10 per batch of 1,000 units

Required
Prepare a February activity-based budgeted income statement.

E9-24. Product and Department Budgets Using Activity-Based Approach (LO2)

The following data are from the general records of the Loading Department of Bowman Freight Company for November.

- Cleaning incoming trucks, 20 minutes.
- Obtaining and reviewing shipping documents for loading truck and instructing loaders, 30 minutes.
- Loading truck, 1 hour and 30 minutes.
- Cleaning shipping dock and storage area after each loading, 10 minutes.
- Employees perform both cleaning and loading tasks and are currently averaging $16 per hour in wages and benefits.
- The supervisor spends 10 percent of her time overseeing the cleaning activities; 60 percent overseeing various loading activities; and the remainder of her time making general plans and managing the department. Her current salary is $4,000 per month.
- Other overhead of the department amounts to $10,000 per month, 20 percent for cleaning and 80 percent for loading.

Required

Prepare an activities budget for cleaning and loading in the Loading Department for November, assuming 20 working days and the loading of an average of 14 trucks per day.

E9-25. Activity-Based Budgeting (LO2)

St. Mary's Hospital is preparing its budget for the coming year. It uses an activity-based approach for all costs except physician care. Its emergency room has three activity areas with cost drivers as follows:

1. *Reception*—paperwork of incoming patients. Cost driver is the number of forms completed.
2. *Treatment*—initial diagnosis and treatment of patients. Cost driver is the number of diagnoses treated.
3. *Cleaning*—general cleaning plus preparing treatment facilities for next patient. Cost driver is the number of people visiting emergency room (patients plus person(s) accompanying them).

Activity Area	Cost Driver Rates	Budgeted Amount of Cost Driver	
		Outpatients	Admitted Patients
Reception	$30	7,400 forms	5,500 forms
Treatment	90	7,000 diagnoses	4,400 diagnoses
Cleaning	12	6,400 people	2,400 people

Required

a. Prepare the total budgeted cost for each activity.

b. How might you adjust the budget approach if you found that outpatients were kept in the emergency room for one hour on average while admitted patients remained for two hours?

c. What advantage does an activity-based approach have over the hospital's former budgeting method of basing the next year's budget on the last year's actual amount plus a percentage increase?

E9-26. Sales Budget (LO3)

Summer Fun T-Shirt Shop has very seasonal sales. For 2009, management is trying to decide whether to establish a sales budget based on average sales or on sales estimated by quarter. The unit sales for 2009 are expected to be 10 percent higher than 2008 sales. Unit shirt sales by quarter for 2008 were as follows:

	Children's	Women's	Men's	Total
Winter quarter	200	200	100	500
Spring quarter	200	250	200	650
Summer quarter	400	300	200	900
Fall quarter	200	250	100	550
Total	1,000	1,000	600	2,600

Children's T-shirts sell for $5 each, women's sell for $9, and men's sell for $10.

Required

Assuming a 10 percent increase in sales, prepare a sales budget for each quarter of 2009 using the following:

a. Average quarterly sales. (*Hint:* Winter quarter children's shirts are 275 [1,000 × 1.10 ÷ 4].)

b. Actual quarterly sales. (*Hint:* Winter quarter children's shirts are 220 [200 × 1.10].)

c. Suggest advantages of each method.

E9-27. Sales Budget (LO3)

Assume that Datek, a leader in on-line stock trading, is preparing for a surge in growth with a new set of stock trading fees. The following information is available:

Category	Number of Shares	Current Fee	New Fee as of July	Revenue
A	0–10,000	$ 11	$ 10	$1,210,000
B	10,001–50,000	50	40	50,000
C	50,001 and above	200	150	20,000

With the new fees, Datek expects to take many big-volume traders from its competitors. Anticipated monthly growth is expected to be 10 percent, 20 percent, and 30 percent, respectively, for each category for the first three months after the new rates go into effect.

Required

a. What are the anticipated revenues per month for July and August?

b. Is the new fee structure satisfactory? Explain.

E9-28. Cash Budget (LO3)

Peruvian Tea Company began July with a cash balance of $145,000. A cash receipts and payments budget for each six-month period is prepared in advance. Sales have been estimated as follows:

Month	Sales Revenue	Month	Sales Revenue
May.	$120,000	September.	$ 80,000
June	140,000	October	100,000
July.	80,000	November	100,000
August	60,000	December	110,000

All sales are on credit with 75 percent collected during the month of sale, 20 percent collected during the next month, and 5 percent collected during the second month following the month of sale. Cost of goods sold averages 70 percent of sales revenue. Ending inventory is one-half of the next month's predicted cost of sales. The other half of the merchandise is acquired during the month of sale. All purchases are paid for in the month after purchase. Operating costs are estimated at $20,000 each month and are paid for during the month incurred.

Required

Prepare monthly cash budgets for the six months from July to December. (*Hint:* Prepare monthly purchases budgets for June through November.)

E9-29. Cash Receipts (LO3)

The sales budget for Perrier Inc. is forecasted as follows:

Month	Sales Revenue
May.	$120,000
June	160,000
July.	180,000
August	120,000

To prepare a cash budget, the company must determine the budgeted cash collections from sales. Historically, the following trend has been established regarding cash collection of sales:

- 60 percent in the month of sale.
- 20 percent in the month following sale.
- 15 percent in the second month following sale.
- 5 percent uncollectible.

The company gives a 2 percent cash discount for payments made by customers during the month of sale. The accounts receivable balance on April 30 is $24,000, of which $7,000 represents uncollected March sales and $17,000 represents uncollected April sales.

Required

Prepare a schedule of budgeted cash collections from sales for May, June, and July. Include a three-month summary of estimated cash collections.

E9-30. Cash Disbursements (LO3)

Montana Timber Company is in the process of preparing its budget for next year. Cost of goods sold has been estimated at 70 percent of sales. Lumber purchases and payments are to be made during the month preceding the month of sale. Wages are estimated at 15 percent of sales and are paid during the month of sale. Other operating costs amounting to 10 percent of sales are to be paid in the month following the month of sale. Additionally, a monthly lease payment of $12,000 is paid to BMI for computer services. Sales revenue is forecast as follows:

Month	Sales Revenue
February	$100,000
March	160,000
April	180,000
May.	210,000
June	180,000
July.	230,000

Required

Prepare a schedule of cash disbursements for April, May, and June.

E9-31. Cash Disbursements (LO3)

Assume that Waycross Manufacturing manages its cash flow from its home office. Waycross controls cash disbursements by category and month. In setting its budget for the next six months, beginning in July, it used the following managerial guidelines:

Category	Guidelines
Purchases.	Pay half in current and half in following month.
Payroll.	Pay 80 percent in current month and 20 percent in following month.
Loan payments. . .	Pay total amount due each month.

Predicted activity for selected months follow:

Category	May	June	July	August
Purchases.	$ 30,000	$ 44,000	$ 48,000	$ 50,000
Payroll.	100,000	110,000	120,000	100,000
Loan payments.	10,000	10,000	15,000	15,000

Required

Prepare a schedule showing cash disbursements by account for July and August.

E9-32. Budgeted Income Statement (LO3)

Pendleton Company, a merchandising company, is developing its master budget for 2010. The income statement for 2009 is as follows:

PENDLETON COMPANY Income Statement For Year Ending December 31, 2009	
Gross sales	$750,000
Less estimated uncollectible accounts	(7,500)
Net sales	742,500
Cost of goods sold	(430,000)
Gross profit	312,500
Operating expenses (including $25,000 depreciation)	(200,500)
Net income	$112,000

The following are management's goals and forecasts for 2010:

1. Selling prices will increase by 8 percent, and sales volume will increase by 5 percent.
2. The cost of merchandise will increase by 4 percent.
3. All operating expenses are fixed and are paid in the month incurred. Price increases for operating expenses will be 10 percent. The company uses straight-line depreciation.
4. The estimated uncollectibles are 1 percent of budgeted sales.

Required

Prepare a budgeted functional income statement for 2010.

E9-33. Budgeted Income Statement (LO3)

Dakota Mfg. is planning a budget for the next fiscal year. The estimate of sales revenue is $1,000,000 and of cost of goods sold is 70 percent of sales revenue. Depreciation on the office building and fixtures is budgeted at $50,000. Salaries and wages should amount to 15 percent of sales revenue. Advertising has been budgeted at $80,000, and utilities should amount to $25,000. Income tax is estimated at 40 percent of operating income.

Required

Prepare a budgeted income statement for the next fiscal year.

E9-34 Production and Purchases Budgets (LO4)

At the beginning of October, the Comfort Cushion Company had 2,400 cushions and 7,740 pounds of raw materials on hand. Budgeted sales for the next three months are:

Month	Sales
October	8,000 cushions
November	10,000 cushions
December	12,000 cushions

Comfort Cushion wants to have sufficient raw materials on hand at the end of each month to meet 25 percent of the following month's production requirements and sufficient cushions on hand at the end of each month to meet 30 percent of the following month's budgeted sales. Three pounds of raw materials, at a standard cost of $0.60 per pound, are required to produce each cushion.

Required:

a. Prepare a production budget for October and November.
b. Prepare a purchases budget in units and dollars for October.

E9-35. Production and Purchases Budgets (LO4)

Budgeted sales for the Avalanche Plow Company for the next several months are:

Month	Sales
September	4,500
October	6,000
November	9,000
December	9,400

At the beginning of September, 1,200 units of finished goods were in inventory. Plans are to have an inventory of finished goods equal to 40 percent of the following month's sales. Each unit of finished goods requires 200 pounds of raw materials at a cost of $10 per pound. Management wishes to maintain month-end inventories of raw materials equal to one-fourth of the following month's needs. Five hundred thousand pounds of raw materials were on hand at the start of September.

Required:

a. Prepare a production budget for September, October, and November.

b. Prepare a purchases budget in units and dollars for September and October.

PROBLEMS

P9-36. Cash Budget (LO3)

Cash budgeting for Carolina Apple, a merchandising firm, is performed on a quarterly basis. The company is planning its cash needs for the third quarter of 2009, and the following information is available to assist in preparing a cash budget. Budgeted income statements for July through October 2009 are as follows:

	July	August	September	October
Sales	$18,000	$24,000	$28,000	$36,000
Cost of goods sold	(10,000)	(14,000)	(16,000)	(20,000)
Gross profit	8,000	10,000	12,000	16,000
Less other expenses				
Selling	2,300	3,000	3,400	4,200
Administrative	2,600	3,000	3,200	3,600
Total	(4,900)	(6,000)	(6,600)	(7,800)
Net income	$ 3,100	$ 4,000	$ 5,400	$ 8,200

Additional information follows:

1. Other expenses, which are paid monthly, include $1,000 of depreciation per month.
2. Sales are 30 percent for cash and 70 percent on credit.
3. Credit sales are collected 20 percent in the month of sale, 70 percent one month after sale, and 10 percent two months after sale. May sales were $15,000, and June sales were $16,000.
4. Merchandise is paid for 50 percent in the month of purchase; the remaining 50 percent is paid in the following month. Accounts payable for merchandise at June 30 totaled $6,000.
5. The company maintains its ending inventory levels at 25 percent of the cost of goods to be sold in the following month. The inventory at June 30 is $2,500.
6. An equipment note of $5,000 per month is being paid through August.
7. The company must maintain a cash balance of at least $5,000 at the end of each month. The cash balance on June 30 is $5,100.
8. The company can borrow from its bank as needed. Borrowings and repayments must be in multiples of $100. All borrowings take place at the beginning of a month, and all repayments are made at the end of a month. When the principal is repaid, interest on the repayment is also paid. The interest rate is 12 percent per year.

Required

a. Prepare a monthly schedule of budgeted operating cash receipts for July, August, and September.

b. Prepare a monthly purchases budget and a schedule of budgeted cash payments for purchases for July, August, and September.

c. Prepare a monthly cash budget for July, August, and September. Show borrowings from the company's bank and repayments to the bank as needed to maintain the minimum cash balance.

P9-37. Cash Budget (LO3)

The Peoria Supply Company sells for $30 one product that it purchases for $20. Budgeted sales in total dollars for next year are $720,000. The sales information needed for preparing the July budget follows:

Month	Sales Revenue
May.	$30,000
June	42,000
July.	48,000
August	50,000

Account balances at July 1 include these:

Cash.	$20,000
Merchandise inventory.	16,000
Accounts receivable (sales)	23,000
Accounts payable (purchases).	15,000

The company pays for one-half of its purchases in the month of purchase and the remainder in the following month. End-of-month inventory must be 50 percent of the budgeted sales in units for the next month. A 2 percent cash discount on sales is allowed if payment is made during the month of sale. Experience indicates that 50 percent of the billings will be collected during the month of sale, 40 percent in the following month, 8 percent in the second following month, and 2 percent will be uncollectible. Total budgeted selling and administrative expenses (excluding bad debts) for the fiscal year are estimated at $186,000, of which one-half is fixed expense (inclusive of a $20,000 annual depreciation charge). Fixed expenses are incurred evenly during the year. The other selling and administrative expenses vary with sales. Expenses are paid during the month incurred.

Required

a. Prepare a schedule of estimated cash collections for July.

b. Prepare a schedule of estimated July cash payments for purchases. (Round calculations to the nearest dollar.)

c. Prepare schedules of July selling and administrative expenses, separately identifying those requiring cash disbursements.

d. Prepare a cash budget in summary form for July.

P9-38. Budgeting Purchases, Revenues, Expenses, and Cash in a Service Organization (LO3)

Round Lake Medical Center is located in a summer resort community. During the summer months the center operates an out-patient clinic for the treatment of minor injuries and illnesses. The clinic is administered as a separate department within the hospital. It has its own staff and maintains its own financial records. All patients requiring extensive or intensive care are referred to other hospital departments.

An analysis of past operating data for the out-patient clinic reveals the following:

- Staff: Seven full-time employees with total monthly salaries of $40,000. On a monthly basis, one additional staff member is hired for every 500 budgeted patient visits in excess of 3,000, at a cost of $4,000 per month.
- Facilities: Monthly facility costs, including depreciation of $2,000, total $9,000.
- Supplies: The supplies expense averages $10 per patient visit. The center maintains an end-of-month supplies inventory equal to ten percent of the predicted needs of the following month, with a minimum ending inventory of $3,000, which is also the desired inventory at the end of August.
- Additional variable patient costs, such as medications, are charged directly to the patient by the hospital pharmacy.
- Payments: All staff and maintenance expenses are paid in the month the cost is incurrent. Supplies are purchased at cost directly from the hospital with an immediate transfer of cash from the clinic cash account to the hospital cash account.

- Collections: The average bill for services rendered is $55. Of the total bills, 40 percent are paid in cash at the time the service is rendered, 10 percent are never paid, and the remaining 50 percent are covered by insurance. In the past, insurance companies have disallowed 20 percent of the claims filed and paid the balance two months after services are rendered.
- May 30 status: At the end of May, the clinic had $12,000 in cash and supplies costing $3,000.

Budgeted patient visits for next summer are as follows:

Month	Patient visits
June	2,000
July	3,500
August	4,000

Required:

For the Round Lake Out-patient Clinic:

a. Prepare a supplies purchases budget for June, July, and August, with a total column.
b. Prepare a revenue and expense budget for June, July, and August with a total column.
c. Prepare a cash budget for June, July and August with a total column. Hint: See requirement d.
d. Explain why you were unable to develop a feasible cash budget and make any appropriate recommendations for management's consideration.

P9-39. Developing a Master Budget for a Merchandising Organization (LO3)

Peyton Department Store prepares budgets quarterly. The following information is available for use in planning the second quarter budgets for 2010.

PEYTON DEPARTMENT STORE
Balance Sheet
March 31, 2010

Assets		Liabilities and Stockholders' Equity	
Cash	$ 3,000	Accounts payable	$26,000
Accounts receivable	25,000	Dividends payable	17,000
Inventory	30,000	Rent payable	2,000
Prepaid insurance	2,000	Stockholders' equity	40,000
Fixtures	25,000		
Total assets	$85,000	Total liabilities and equity	$85,000

Actual and forecasted sales for selected months in 2010 are as follows:

Month	Sales Revenue
January	$60,000
February	50,000
March	40,000
April	50,000
May	60,000
June	70,000
July	90,000
August	80,000

Monthly operating expenses are as follows:

Wages and salaries	$25,000
Depreciation	100
Utilities	1,000
Rent	2,000

Cash dividends of $17,000 are declared during the third month of each quarter and are paid during the first month of the following quarter. Operating expenses, except insurance, rent, and depreciation are paid as incurred. Rent is paid during the following month. The prepaid insurance is for five more months. Cost of goods sold is equal to 50 percent of sales. Ending inventories are sufficient for 120 percent of the next month's sales. Purchases during any given month are paid in full during the following month. All sales are on account, with 50 percent collected during the month of sale, 40 percent during the next month, and 10 percent during the month thereafter. Money can be borrowed and repaid in multiples of $1,000 at an interest rate of 12 percent per year. The company desires a minimum cash balance of $3,000 on the first of each month. At the time the principal is repaid, interest is paid on the portion of principal that is repaid. All borrowing is at the beginning of the month, and all repayment is at the end of the month. Money is never repaid at the end of the month it is borrowed.

Required

a. Prepare a purchases budget for each month of the second quarter ending June 30, 2010.
b. Prepare a cash receipts schedule for each month of the second quarter ending June 30, 2010. Do not include borrowings.
c. Prepare a cash disbursements schedule for each month of the second quarter ending June 30, 2010. Do not include repayments of borrowings.
d. Prepare a cash budget for each month of the second quarter ending June 30, 2010. Include budgeted borrowings and repayments.
e. Prepare an income statement for each month of the second quarter ending June 30, 2010.
f. Prepare a budgeted balance sheet as of June 30, 2010.

P9-40. Developing a Master Budget for a Manufacturing Organization (LO4)

Jacobs Incorporated manufactures a product with a selling price of $50 per unit. Units and monthly cost data follow:

Variable:	
Selling and administrative	$ 5 per unit sold
Direct materials	10 per unit manufactured
Direct labor	10 per unit manufactured
Variable manufacturing overhead	5 per unit manufactured
Fixed:	
Selling and administrative	$20,000 per month
Manufacturing (including depreciation of $10,000)	30,000 per month

Jacobs pays all bills in the month incurred. All sales are on account with 50 percent collected the month of sale and the balance collected the following month. There are no sales discounts or bad debts.

Jacobs desires to maintain an ending finished goods inventory equal to 20 percent of the following month's sales and a raw materials inventory equal to 10 percent of the following month's production. January 1, 2011, inventories are in line with these policies.

Actual unit sales for December and budgeted unit sales for January, February, and March of 2011 are as follows:

JACOBS INCORPORATED
Sales Budget
For the Months of January, February, and March 2011

Month	December	January	February	March
Sales - Units	6,250	5,000	10,000	8,000
Sales - Dollars	$312,500	$250,000	$500,000	$400,000

Additional information:

- The January 1 beginning cash is projected as $5,000.
- For the purpose of operational budgeting, units in the January 1 inventory of finished goods are valued at variable manufacturing cost.
- Each unit of finished product requires one unit of raw materials.
- Jacobs intends to pay a cash dividend of $10,000 in January

Required:

a. A production budget for January and February.
b. A purchases budget in units for January.
c. A manufacturing cost budget for January.
d. A cash budget for January.

e. A budgeted contribution income statement for January.

f. Management is concerned that their supplier of raw materials will have a strike. Determine the budget implications if management plans to increase the January end raw materials inventory to 100 percent of February's production needs. Offer any recommendations you believe appropriate.

P9-41. Developing a Master Budget for a Manufacturing Organization: Challenge Problem (LO4)
Banana Computer Accessories assembles a computer networking device from kits of imported components. You have been asked to develop a quarterly and annual operating budget and pro-forma income statements for 2010. You have obtained the following information:

Beginning-of-year balances				
Cash		$40,000.00		
Accounts receivable (previous quarter's sales)		$15,000.00		
Raw materials		300 kits		
Finished goods		400 units		
Accounts payable		$40,000.00		
Borrowed funds		$10,000.00		
Desired end-of-year inventory balances				
Raw materials		500 kits		
Finished goods		200 units		
Desired end-of-quarter balances				
Cash		$10,000.00		
Raw materials as a portion of the following quarter's production		0.2		
Finished goods as a portion of the following quarter's sales		0.15		
Manufacturing costs				
Standard cost per unit		Units	Unit price	Total
Raw materials		1 kit	$40.00	$40.00
Direct labor hours at rate		0.8 hour	$20.00	16.00
Variable overhead/labor hour		0.8 hour	$10.00	8.00
Total standard variable cost				$64.00
Fixed cost per quarter				
Cash		$40,000.00		
Depreciation		10,000.00		
Total		$50,000.00		
Selling and administrative costs				
Variable cost per unit		$5.00		
Fixed costs per quarter				
Cash		$20,000.00		
Depreciation		5,000.00		
Total		$25,000.00		
Interest rate per quarter		0.04		
Portion of sales collected				
Quarter of sale		0.75		
Subsequent quarter		0.24		
Bad debts		0.01		
Portion of purchases paid				
Quarter of purchase		0.75		
Subsequent quarter		0.25		
Unit selling price		$110.00		
Sales forecast				
Quarter	First	Second	Third	Fourth
Unit sales	2,400	1,500	2,000	3,100

Additional information

- All cash payments except purchases are made quarterly as incurred.
- All borrowings occur at the start of the quarter.

- All repayments on borrowings occur at the end of the quarter.
- All interest on borrowed funds is paid at the end of each quarter.
- Borrowings and repayments may be made in any amount.

Required:

a. A sales budget for each quarter and the year. Hint: Use of spreadsheet software strongly recommended for this problem.
b. A production budget for each quarter and the year.
c. A purchases budget for each quarter and the year.
d. A manufacturing cost budget for each quarter and the year.
e. A selling and administrative expense budget for each quarter and the year.
f. A cash budget for each quarter and the year.
g. A pro-forma contribution income statement for each quarter and the year.

CASES

C9-42. Behavioral Implications of Budgeting (LO5)

Andrea Rawls, controller of Data Scientific, believes that effective budgeting greatly assists in meeting the organization's goals and objectives. She argues that the budget serves as a blueprint for the operating activities during each reporting period, making it an important control device. She believes that sound management evaluations can be based on the comparisons of performance and budgetary schedules and that employees respond more favorably when they participate in the budgetary process. Jeff Cooke, treasurer of Data Scientific, agrees that budgeting is essential for overall organization success, but he argues that human resources are too valuable to spend much time planning and preparing the budgetary process. He thinks that the roles people play in budgetary preparation are not important in the final analysis of a budget's effectiveness.

Required

Contrast the participative versus imposed budgeting concepts and indicate how the ideas of Rawls and Cooke fit the two categories.

C9-43. Behavioral Considerations and Budgeting (LO5)

Scott Weidner, the controller in the Division of Social Services for the state, recognizes the importance of the budgetary process for planning, control, and motivation purposes. He believes that a properly implemented participative budgeting process for planning purposes and a management by exception reporting procedure based on that budget will motivate his subordinates to improve productivity within their particular departments. Based on this philosophy, Weidner has implemented the following budget procedures.

- An appropriation target figure is given to each department manager. This amount is the maximum funding that each department can expect to receive in the next fiscal year.
- Department managers develop their individual budgets within the following spending constraints as directed by the controller's staff.
    1. Expenditure requests cannot exceed the appropriation target.
    2. All fixed expenditures should be included in the budget; these should include items such as contracts and salaries at current levels.
    3. All government projects directed by higher authority should be included in the budget in their entirety.
- The controller consolidates the departmental budget requests from the various departments into one budget that is to be submitted for the entire division.
- Upon final budget approval by the legislature, the controller's staff allocates the appropriation to the various departments on instructions from the division manager. However, a specified percentage of each department's appropriation is held back in anticipation of potential budget cuts and special funding needs. The amount and use of this contingency fund are left to the discretion of the division manager.
- Each department is allowed to adjust its budget when necessary to operate within the reduced appropriation level. However, as stated in the original directive, specific projects authorized by higher authority must remain intact.
- The final budget is used as the basis of control for a management by exception form of reporting. Excessive expenditures by account for each department are highlighted on a monthly basis. Department managers are expected to account for all expenditures over budget. Fiscal responsibility is an important factor in the overall performance evaluation of department managers.

Weidner believes that his policy of allowing the department managers to participate in the budget process and then holding them accountable for their performance is essential, especially during these times of limited resources. He also believes that department managers will be positively motivated to increase the efficiency and effectiveness of their departments because they have provided input into the initial budgetary process and are required to justify any unfavorable performances.

Required

a. Explain the operational and behavioral benefits that generally are attributed to a participative budgeting process.

b. Identify deficiencies in Weidner's participative budgetary policy for planning and performance evaluation purposes. For each deficiency identified, recommend how the deficiency can be corrected.

(CMA Adapted)

C9-44. Budgetary Slack with Ethical Considerations (LO5)

Alene Adams was promoted to department manager of a production unit in Dallas Industries three years ago. She enjoys her job except for the evaluation measures that are based on the department's budget. After three years of consistently poor annual evaluations based on a set annual budget, she has decided to improve the evaluation situation. At a recent budget meeting of junior-level managers, the topic of budgetary slack was discussed as a means to maintain some consistency in budgeting matters. As a result of this meeting, Adams decided to take the following steps in preparing the upcoming year's budget:

1. Use the top quartile for all wage and salary categories.
2. Select the optimistic values for the estimated production ranges for the coming year. These are provided by the marketing department.
3. Use the average of the three months in the current year with poorest production efficiency as benchmarks of success for the coming year.
4. Base equipment charges (primarily depreciation) on replacement values furnished by the purchasing department.
5. Base other fixed costs on current cost plus an inflation rate estimated for the coming year.
6. Use the average of the ten newly hired employees' performance as a basis of labor efficiency for the coming year.

Required

a. For each item on Adams' list, explain whether it will create budgetary slack. Use numerical examples as necessary to illustrate.

b. Given the company's use of static budgets as one of the performance evaluation measures of its managers, can the managers justify the use of built-in budgetary slack?

c. What would you recommend as a means for Adams to improve the budgeting situation in the company? Provide some specific examples of how the budgeting process might be improved.

C9-45. Budgetary Slack with Ethical Considerations (LO5)

Norton Company, a manufacturer of infant furniture and carriages, is in the initial stages of preparing the annual budget for next year. Scott Ford recently joined Norton's accounting staff and is interested to learn as much as possible about the company's budgeting process. During a recent lunch with Marge Atkins, sales manager, and Pete Granger, production manager, Ford initiated the following conversation:

Ford: Since I'm new around here and am going to be involved with the preparation of the annual budget, I'd be interested to learn how the two of you estimate sales and production numbers.

Atkins: We start out very methodically by looking at recent history, discussing what we know about current accounts, potential customers, and the general state of consumer spending. Then we add that usual dose of intuition to come up with the best forecast we can.

Granger: I usually take the sales projections as the basis for my projections. Of course, we have to make an estimate of what this year's closing inventories will be, which is sometimes difficult.

Ford: Why does that present a problem? There must have been an estimate of closing inventories in the budget for the current year.

Granger: Those numbers aren't always reliable since Marge makes some adjustments to the sales numbers before passing them on to me.

Ford: What kind of adjustments?

Atkins: Well, we don't want to fall short of the sales projections, so we generally give ourselves a little breathing room by lowering the initial sales projection anywhere from 5 to 10 percent.

Granger: So, you can see why this year's budget is not a very reliable starting point. We always have to adjust the projected production rates as the year progresses; of course, this changes the ending inventory estimates. By the way, we make similar adjustments to expenses by adding at least 10 percent to the estimates; I think everyone around here does the same thing.

Required

a. Marge Atkins and Pete Granger have described the use of budgetary slack.
   1. Explain why Atkins and Granger behave in this manner, and describe the benefits they expect to realize from the use of budgetary slack.
   2. Explain how the use of budgetary slack can adversely affect Atkins and Granger.

b. As a management accountant, Scott Ford believes that the behavior described by Marge Atkins and Pete Granger could be unethical and that he might have an obligation not to support this behavior. Explain why the use of budgetary slack could be unethical.

(CMA Adapted)

Chapter 10

Standard Costs and Performance Reports

LEARNING OBJECTIVES

LO1 Explain responsibility accounting. (p. 330)

LO2 Differentiate between static and flexible budgets for performance reporting. (p. 333)

LO3 Determine and interpret direct materials, direct labor, and overhead cost variances. (p. 337)

LO4 Calculate revenue variances and prepare a performance report for a revenue center. (p. 345)

FINANCIALS: IMPORTANT BUT NOT THE WHOLE STORY

Passed over as successor to Jack Welch as CEO of General Electric, Robert Nardelli left to accept the top job at Home Depot. Believing "facts are friendly," he brought with him a desire to measure almost everything and to hold executives strictly accountable for performance. To enhance financial performance by reducing costs, he replaced thousands of experienced full-time employees with large numbers of part-time employees. Managers not meeting performance targets were also replaced. Indeed, between 2001 and 2007, 98 percent of Home Depot's top 170 executives were new, with more than half coming from outside the company.

Driven by a strategy that included cost cutting, as well as a housing and home improvement boom, Home Depot sales rose from $46 billion in 2000 to $81.5 billion in 2005. Gross profit also increased from 30 percent to 33.8% of sales and profits more than doubled to $5.8 billion. Unfortunately, Home Depot's stock price did not show similar improvements, even though the stock prices of arch rival Lowes continued to build higher. And, the 2000 to 2005 financial improvements may have come with a long-term price.

Employees were alienated by cost cutting and the "replacement" of full-time employees with part-time help. Customers were alienated by the decline in customer service. Do-it-yourself customers complained that the Depot went from great help to "no help." Meanwhile, Lowes was making great strides in customer service and building strong customer relations.

Courtesy of JAM Images

By late 2006, Home Depot and Nardelli were under pressure from sales and profit declines. Nardelli was also under pressure from employees, investors, and financial analysts for what they regarded as his arrogant style, lack of stock performance, and excessive compensation. When Nardelli left in early 2007, employees' cell phones lit up with text-messaged happy-faces. Per Matthew Fassler, a Goldman Sachs analyst, Nardelli's numbers were good but "this retail organization never embraced his leadership style." Harvard Business School professor Boris Groysberg, observing that Nardelli came from General Electric, noted that "GE people are good at getting structure, systems, and strategy right, but they don't always understand soft issues like culture."

Later in 2007, new Home Depot CEO Frank Blake announced plans to commit $2.2 billion to efforts to improve stores, customer service, and sales. According to Blake, "We plan to continue our reinvestment plans for the long-run health of the business, understanding that it will put short-term pressure on earnings."

Understanding and properly using financial performance reports is necessary for the organization to succeed. This chapter introduces the fundamentals of responsibility accounting and the measurement of financial performance. However, as underscored by events at Home Depot, while an understanding of financial performance is necessary for success, it is not sufficient. In addition to financial performance, managers must consider a myriad of quantifiable and non-quantifiable, short-term and long-term factors. Some of these other factors are incorporated into the balanced scorecard, considered in Chapter 11.[1]

[1] "Out at Home Depot," Brian Grow; Dean Foust; Emily Thornton; Roben Farzad; Jena McGregor; Susan Zegal; and Eamon Javers, *Business Week*, January 15, 2007, pp. 56-62. "Being Mean Is So Last Millennium," Diane Brady, *Business Week*, January 15, 2007, p. 62. "Nardelli's Tear-Down Job," John Hollon, *Workforce Management*, January 15, 2007, p. 34. "Home Depot: Blues for Big Orange," *Business Week* Online, May 16, 2007, p. 16.

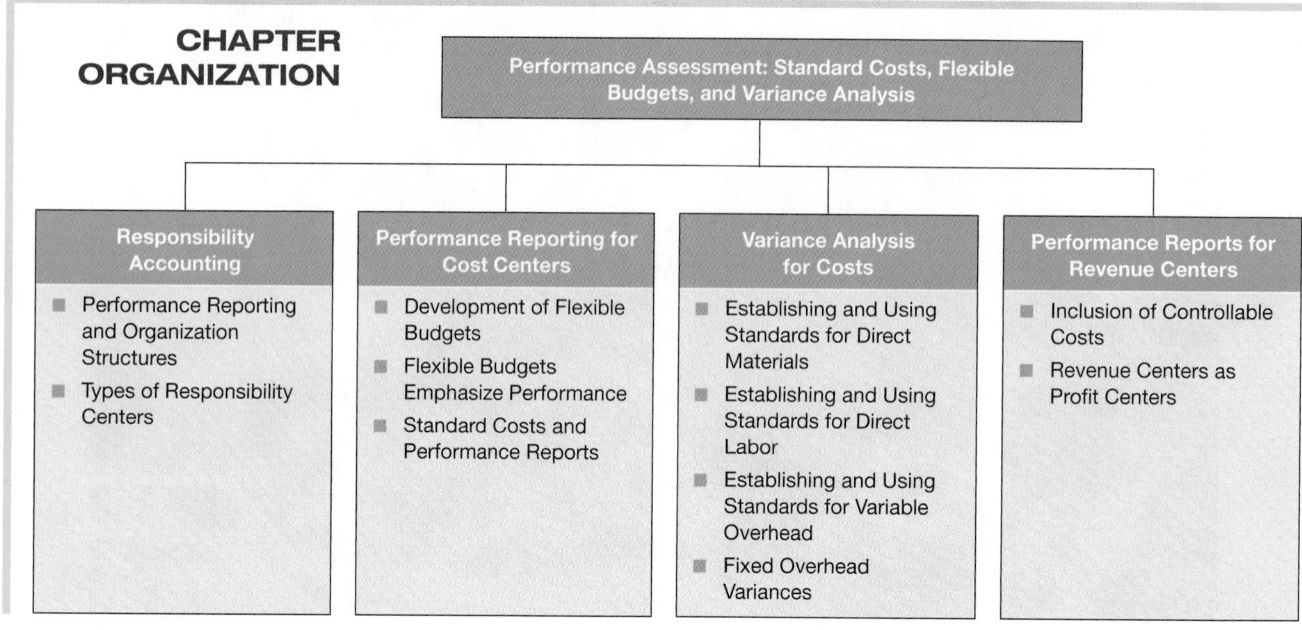

Management accounting tools aid in the assessment of the performance of the firm as a whole and all of its various components. Feedback in the form of performance reports is essential if the benefits of budgeting and other types of planning are to be fully realized. Managers must know how actual results compare with current budgets and standards to control current operations and to improve future operations. These performance reports should be prepared in accordance with the concept of **responsibility accounting**, which is the structuring of performance reports addressed to individual (or group) members of an organization to emphasize the factors they control.

This chapter focuses on responsibility accounting and performance assessment. We examine responsibility accounting and identify various types of responsibility centers. We then take a close look at performance assessment for cost centers. We conclude by considering performance reports for revenue centers. Responsibility accounting for major business segments is considered in Chapter 11.

RESPONSIBILITY ACCOUNTING

LO1 Explain responsibility accounting.

Performance reports that include comparisons of actual results with plans or budgets serve as assessment tools and attention-directors to help managers determine and control activities. According to the concept of *management by exception,* the absence of significant differences indicates that activities are proceeding as planned whereas the presence of significant differences indicates a need to either take corrective action or revise plans. These evaluations and actions are made within the framework of an organization's overall mission, goals, and strategies as discussed in Chapter 1.

Responsibility accounting may focus on specific organization components or various aspects of the value chain that are accountable for the accomplishment of specific activities or objectives. Performance reports are customized to emphasize the activities of each specific organizational unit or value chain element. For example, a financial performance report addressed to the head of a production department contains manufacturing costs controllable by the department head; it does not contain costs (such as advertising, sales commissions, or the president's salary) that the head of the production department cannot control. Including noncontrollable costs in the report distracts the manager's attention from the controllable costs, thereby diluting a manager's efforts to deal with controllable items. Lower-level managers could also become frustrated with the entire performance reporting system if they believe upper-level managers expect them to control costs they cannot influence. However, some companies insist on reporting all related revenues and expenses (controllable and non-controllable) in the same report. When this is the case, the noncontrollable items should be clearly labeled.

A poorly designed responsibility accounting system can lead to unethical practices by managers in key positions. If too much pressure is placed on managers to meet performance targets, they sometimes take actions that are not in the best interest of the organization. The Business Insight that follows presents examples of such actions involving a vice president of Bausch & Lomb and the CEO of Sunbeam who forced sales into one year to the detriment of the companies' sales the following year. The designers of an organization's responsibility accounting system need to be aware of the potential pressures that such a system can place on managers. The decision-making model of the organization should be such that managers are not influenced to make undesirable decisions just to receive bonuses or promotions.

BUSINESS INSIGHT **Ethics and Responsibility Accounting**

A few years ago, the contact lens division of Bausch & Lomb, Inc., was experiencing lower-than-anticipated sales levels. The head of the division called a meeting of its independent distributors and told them that the company had changed its sales strategy. Effective immediately, each distributor would have to boost its inventory of contact lenses if it wanted to remain a distributor of Bausch & Lomb products. The strategy was for distributors to buy only in very large quantities (some as much as a two-year supply) with prices increased by amounts up to 50 percent. Also, the distributors had to place these large orders by year-end. As one distributor stated, "When your No. 1 vendor says you'd better take it or else, what're you going to do?" All but two of Bausch & Lomb's distributors complied with the new sales strategy demands; and those two were subsequently dropped as customers.

Initially the strategy paid off; the sales in the last few days of the year totaled about $25 million and amounted to one-half of the division's profit for the entire year. The division manager was delighted. However, the long-term results were not favorable. By the following mid-year, the company announced that the high inventories of its distributors would severely reduce sales and profits for that year. The profit decline was approximately 37 percent. After the announcement, the company's stock fell from $50 to $32. The manager was forced to step down, and stockholders filed a class-action lawsuit accusing the company of falsely inflating sales and earnings.

History repeated itself when the CEO of Sunbeam followed the Bausch & Lomb plan to force sales to show how well his management style (firing employees and closing plants) was working. Sunbeam instituted a "bill and hold" plan that called for products to be produced in large quantities and sold to customers for delivery at a later date. While this made the financial report for that first year very favorable, it had a detrimental effect on the next year's report. In late March of that following year, Sunbeam acknowledged that first-quarter income would be below expectations, and in fact, a loss. Stockholders quickly filed lawsuits charging deception, and the CEO was fired.[2]

Performance Reporting and Organization Structures

Before implementing a responsibility accounting system, all areas of authority and responsibility within an organization must be clearly defined. Organization charts and other documents should be examined to determine an organization's authority and responsibility structure. **Organization structure** is the arrangement of lines of responsibility within the organization. These structures vary widely. Some companies have functional-based structures along the lines of marketing, production, research, and so forth; other companies use products, services, customers, or geography as the basis of organization. When an attempt is made to implement a responsibility accounting system, management could find instances of overlapping duties, authority not commensurate with responsibility, and expenditures for which no one appears responsible. These circumstances can make the development of a responsibility accounting system difficult. General Electric overcame many of these problems with the use of teams and a new measurement tool as explained in the next Business Insight. (For discussions and examples of organization structures, consult a basic principles of management text.)

[2] "Numbers Game at Bausch & Lomb?" *Business Week*, December 19, 1994, pp. 108–10; and "How Al Dunlap Self-Destructed," *Business Week*, July 6, 1998, pp. 58–61, 64.

BUSINESS INSIGHT **GE's Six Sigma**

General Electric strives to improve quality without ignoring costs and its managers are responsible for controlling the combination of quality and costs. Its responsibility accounting program, called Six Sigma, has increased its annual productivity by over 200 percent and its operating margin by 4 percentage points. Six Sigma, is a means of measuring quality (through errors or defects) for any activity. For each activity, a target for improvement is set and a manager is assigned the responsibility to achieve the target. The reporting system centers on the rate of improvement as measured by reduced defects or errors. The program has five basic steps:

1. *Define:* Teams work to define problems related to a process or service.
2. *Measure:* Determine what is wrong with the existing process or service.
3. *Analyze:* Determine reasons for what is wrong.
4. *Improve:* Define and develop a plan of action.
5. *Control:* Ensure changes are installed and used effectively; keep problems from recurring.

GE is pleased with the system because it improved quality *and* saved millions in operating expenses.[3]

Although performance reports can be developed for areas of responsibility as narrow as a single worker, the basic responsibility unit in most organizations begins with the department and progresses to division and corporate levels. In manufacturing plants, separate performance reports can be used for responsibility centers comprising production or service departments or manufacturing cells. In large universities, separate responsibility centers are set up for individual academic departments (such as accounting, psychology, and mathematics) and staff and service departments (such as human resources, food service, and maintenance). When a large department performs a number of diverse and significant activities, responsibility accounting can be further refined so that a single department contains several responsibility centers with performance reports prepared for each.

Types of Responsibility Centers

Under responsibility accounting, performance reports are prepared for departments, segments of departments, or groupings of departments that operate under the control and authority of a responsible manager. Each organizational unit for which performance reports are prepared is identified as a responsibility center. For the purpose of evaluating their financial performance, responsibility centers can be classified as cost centers, revenue centers, profit centers, or investment centers.

Cost Center

A **cost center** is a responsibility center whose manager is responsible for managing only costs; there is no revenue responsibility. A cost center can be as small as a segment of a department or large enough to include a major aspect of the organization, such as all manufacturing activities. Typical examples of cost centers include the following:

Organization	Cost Center
Manufacturing plant	Tooling department Assembly activities
Retail store	Inventory control function Maintenance department
Hospital	Radiology Emergency room
College	History department Registrar's office
City government.	Public safety (police and fire) Road maintenance

[3]Sridhar Seshadri and Gregory T. Lucier, "GE Takes Six Sigma beyond the Bottom Line," *Strategic Finance,* May 2001, pp. 40–46.

Revenue Center

A **revenue center** is a responsibility center whose manager is responsible for the generation of sales revenues. Even though the basic performance report of a revenue center emphasizes sales, revenue centers are likely to be assigned responsibility for the controllable costs they incur in generating revenues. If revenues and costs are evaluated separately, the center has dual responsibility as a revenue center and as a cost center. If controllable costs are deducted from revenues to obtain some bottom-line contribution, the center is, in fact, being treated more like a profit center than a revenue center.

Profit Center

A **profit center** is a responsibility center whose manager is responsible for revenues, costs, and resulting profits. It could be an entire organization, but it is more frequently a segment of an organization such as a product line, marketing territory, or store. In the context of performance evaluation, the word "profit" does not necessarily refer to the bottom line of an income statement; instead, it likely refers to the profit center's contribution to common corporate costs and profit. Profit is computed as the center's revenues less all costs associated with operating the center. In addition to a center's profits, other measures of performance can include quality assessments, service ratings, and operating efficiencies. Having limited authority regarding the size of total assets, the profit center manager is not held responsible for the relationship between profits and assets.

Investment Center

An **investment center** is a responsibility center whose manager is responsible for the relationship between its profits and the total assets invested in the center. Investment center managers have a high degree of organization autonomy. In general, the management of an investment center is expected to earn a target profit per dollar invested. Investment center managers are evaluated on the basis of how well they use the total resources entrusted to their care to earn a profit. An investment center is the broadest and most inclusive type of responsibility center. Managers of these centers have more authority and responsibility than other managers and are primarily responsible for planning, organizing, and controlling firm activities. Because of their authority regarding the size of corporate assets, they are held responsible for the relationship between profits and assets. Investment centers are discussed further in Chapter 11.

PERFORMANCE REPORTING FOR COST CENTERS

LO2 Differentiate between static and flexible budgets for performance reporting.

Financial performance reports for cost centers include a comparison of actual and budgeted (or allowed) costs and identify the difference as a **variance**. *Allowed costs* in performance reports are the flexible budget amounts for the actual level of activity. The variance is favorable if actual costs are less than budgeted (or allowed) costs and unfavorable if actual costs are more than budgeted (or allowed) costs. These comparisons are made in total and individually for each type of controllable cost assigned to the cost center.

Development of Flexible Budgets

A budget that is based on a prediction of sales and production is called a *static budget*. The operating budget explained in Chapter 9 is a **static budget**. Budgets can also be set for a series of possible production and sales volumes, or budgets can be adjusted to a particular level of production after the fact. These budgets, based on cost-volume relationships, are called **flexible budgets**; they are used to determine what costs should have been for an attained level of activity. For example, if the college cafeteria budgets $15,000 for food during April for 5,000 meals but provides 6,000 meals, the budget needs to be adjusted by the original food budget rate of $3 ($15,000/5,000 meals). Otherwise, the amount spent on food will not be a fair evaluation of the cost per the original budget. If $17,500 was spent on food during the month, the analysis might appear as follows:

Budget Item	Actual	Budget	Difference
Static analysis			
Food.	$17,500	5,000 meals × $3 = $15,000	$2,500 over budget
Flexible analysis			
Food.	$17,500	6,000 meals × $3 = $18,000	$500 under budget

The cafeteria manager is better evaluated based on what actually happened with the flexible budget than with the static budget, especially if the manager had no control over how many student meals were requested.

For a complete example of a flexible budget, assume that McMillan Company, which produces high-quality computer carrying cases, has three departments: Production, Sales, and Administration. The focus in this section is on the development of financial performance reports for the Production Department. The flexible budget cost-estimating equations for total monthly production costs of cases are based on production standards for variable and fixed costs. The standards follow:

Variable costs
- Direct materials—2 pounds per unit at $5 per pound, or $10 per unit
- Direct labor—0.25 hour per unit at $24 per hour, or $6 per unit
- Variable overhead - 2 pounds per unit at $4 per pound, or $8 per unit

Fixed costs—$52,000

If management plans to produce 10,000 cases in July, the budgeted manufacturing costs are $292,000:

MCMILLAN COMPANY Manufacturing Cost Budget For Month of July	
Manufacturing costs	
Variable costs	
Direct materials (10,000 × 2 pounds × $5)	$100,000
Direct labor (10,000 × 0.25 hours × $24).	60,000
Variable overhead (10,000 × 2 pounds × $4).	80,000
Fixed costs	52,000
Total	$292,000

Flexible Budgets Emphasize Performance

If actual production happened to equal 10,000 units the performance of the Production Department in controlling costs could be based on a comparison of actual and budgeted manufacturing costs. If production was at some volume other than that planned in the original manufacturing budget, however, it would be inappropriate to compare actual manufacturing costs with the costs predicted in the original static budget. Doing so would intermix two separate Production Department responsibilities, namely, the manufacturing responsibility for production volume and the financial responsibility for cost control.

The original budget for production volume and related costs was set on the basis of predicted needs for sales and inventory requirements, taking into consideration materials, labor, and facilities constraints and costs. In the absence of any changes, the Production Department is evaluated by comparing the actual and budgeted costs. If, however, production needs change, perhaps due to an unexpected increase or decrease in sales volume, the Production Department should attempt to make appropriate changes.

When the actual production volume is anything other than the originally budgeted amount, the Production Department's financial responsibility for costs should be based on the actual level of production.

For the purpose of evaluating the financial performance of cost centers, a flexible budget is tailored, after the fact, to the actual level of activity. A **flexible budget variance** is computed for each cost as the difference between the actual cost and the flexible budget cost of producing a given quantity of product or service. Assume that actual production for July totaled 11,000 units rather than 10,000 units. Examples of a performance report for July manufacturing costs based on static and flexible budgets are presented in Exhibit 10.1. When the Production Department's financial performance is evaluated using the static budget, the actual cost of producing 11,000 units is compared to the budgeted cost of producing 10,000 units. The result is a series of unfavorable static budget variances totaling $20,000.

EXHIBIT 10.1 Flexible Budgets and Performance Evaluation

McMILLAN COMPANY
Production Department Performance Report
For Month of July

	Based on Static Budget			Based on Flexible Budget		
	Actual	Original Budget	Static Budget Variance	Actual	Flexible Budget*	Flexible Budget Variance
Volume	11,000	10,000		11,000	11,000	
Unit level costs						
Direct materials	$108,000	$100,000	$ 8,000 U	$108,000	$110,000	$2,000 F
Direct labor	70,000	60,000	10,000 U	70,000	66,000	4,000 U
Variable overhead	81,000	80,000	1,000 U	81,000	88,000	7,000 F
Fixed costs	53,000	52,000	1,000 U	53,000	52,000	1,000 U
Totals	$312,000	$292,000	$20,000 U	$312,000	$316,000	$4,000 F

*Flexible budget manufacturing costs: (Actual level × Budgeted unit cost)
Direct materials (11,000 units × 2 pounds × $5)
Direct labor (11,000 units × 0.25 labor hour × $24)
Variable overhead (11,000 units x 2 pounds x $4)

When the Production Department's financial performance is evaluated by comparing actual costs with costs allowed in a flexible budget drawn up for the actual production volume however the results are mixed. Direct materials have a $2,000 favorable variance. Direct labor has a $4,000 unfavorable variance. The variable overhead variance is $7,000 favorable. The fixed overhead variance remains $1,000 unfavorable since the static and flexible fixed budgets stay the same. The net flexible budget variance is $4,000 favorable, a substantial change from the static variance of $20,000 unfavorable.

Flexible budget variances provide a much better indicator of performance than static budget variances that do not consider the increased level of production (11,000 units rather than 10,000 units). When production increases by, say, 10 percent, the static budget variances would be unfavorable. Likewise, when actual production is substantially below the planned level of activity, the static variances are usually favorable. While it is important to isolate and determine the cause of any variation between planned and actual production, the financial-based performance report is not the appropriate place to mix volume-created variances with those related to the actual production levels.

MID-CHAPTER REVIEW

Ron Gilette received the following performance report from the accounting department for his first month as plant manager for a new company. Ron's supervisor, the vice president of manufacturing, has concerns that the report does not provide an accurate picture of Ron's performance in the area of cost control.

	Actual	Budgeted	Variance
Units	10,000	12,000	2,000 U
Costs			
Direct materials	$ 299,000	$ 360,000	$ 61,000 F
Direct labor	345,500	432,000	86,500 F
Variable factory overhead	180,000	216,000	36,000 F
Fixed factory overhead	375,000	360,000	15,000 U
Total costs	$1,199,500	$1,368,000	$168,500 F

Required

Prepare a revised budget that better reflects Ron Gilette's performance.

Solution

The performance report prepared by the accounting department was based on a "static" budget. A better basis for evaluating Ron Gilette's performance is to compare actual performance with a flexible budget. By dividing the budgeted sales and variable costs amounts by 12,000 units, the budgeted unit variable costs amounts can be determined as follows:

Direct materials cost	$360,000 ÷ 12,000 units = $30 per unit
Direct labor	$432,000 ÷ 12,000 units = $36 per unit
Variable factory overhead	$216,000 ÷ 12,000 units = $18 per unit

Using these budgeted unit values, a flexible budget can be prepared as follows:

	Actual	Flexible Budget	Variance
Units	10,000	10,000	
Costs			
Direct materials	$ 299,000	$ 300,000	$ 1,000 F
Direct labor	345,500	360,000	14,500 F
Variable factory overhead	180,000	180,000	
Fixed factory overhead	375,000	360,000	15,000 U
Total plant costs	$1,199,500	$1,200,000	$ 500 F

The plant did not produce the number of units originally budgeted. Therefore, from a cost control standpoint, a flexible budget is a better basis for evaluating Ron's performance because it compares the actual cost of producing 10,000 units with a budget also based on 10,000 units. Based on the flexible budget, his performance is still quite good; however, it is much less favorable than it appeared using a static budget.

Standard Costs and Performance Reports

A **standard cost** indicates what it should cost to provide an activity or produce one batch or unit of product under planned and efficient operating conditions. In a standard costing environment, the flexible budget is based on standard unit costs. Traditionally, standard costs have been developed from an engineering analysis or from an analysis of historical data adjusted for expected changes in the product, production technology, or costs. When standards are developed using historical data, management must be careful to ensure that past inefficiencies are excluded from current standards.

To obtain the full benefit of standard costs, the standards must be based on realistic expectations. The standard cost for direct labor for McMillan Company is $6.00 per unit, (computed as 0.25 direct labor hours × $24 per hour). Some organizations intentionally set "tight" standards to motivate employees toward higher levels of production. The management of McMillan Company might set their standards for direct labor at 0.22 hours per unit rather than at the expected 0.25 hours per unit, hoping that employees will strive toward the lower time and, consequently, the lower cost of $5.28 ($24 × 0.22). The use of tight standards often causes planning and behavioral problems. Management expects them to result in unfavorable variances. Accordingly, tight standards should not be used to budget input requirements and cash flows because management expects to incur more labor costs than the standards allow. The use of tight standards can have undesirable behavioral effects if lower-level managers and employees find that a second set of standards is used in the "real" budget or if they are constantly subject to unfavorable performance reports. These employees could come to distrust the entire budgeting and performance evaluation system, or they may quit trying to achieve any of the organization's standards.

Tight standards are more likely to occur in an imposed budget and less likely to occur in a participation budget for which employees are actively involved in preparing. In a participation budget, the problems may be to avoid loose standards that are easily attained and to avoid overstating the costs required to produce a product. Loose standards may fail to properly motivate employees and can make the company uncompetitive due to costs and prices that are higher than those of competitors.

VARIANCE ANALYSIS FOR COSTS

LO3 Determine and interpret direct materials, direct labor, and overhead cost variances.

To use and interpret standard cost variances properly, managers must understand both the standard-setting process and the framework for computing and analyzing standard cost variances. While these are preliminary tools for decision analysis regarding activities and operations, they nevertheless give managers a starting point in assessing the efficiency (or lack thereof) of activities. The variances alone do not explain, however, why the activity is different from expectations. Underlying causes of variances must be investigated before final judgment is passed on the effectiveness and efficiency of an operation or activity.

Standard cost variance analysis provides a system for examining the flexible budget variance, which is the difference between the actual cost and flexible budget cost of producing a given quantity of product or service. Actual cost is determined from the organization's financial transactions. Flexible budget cost is determined by multiplying standard quantities allowed for the output times the standard price per unit. In other words, the flexible budget can be computed as actual output times the standard unit cost. Recall that standard unit cost represents what it *should* cost to produce a completed unit of product or service under efficient operating conditions. To determine standard unit cost, management establishes separate quantity and price (or rate) standards for each input production component. For a company using activity-based costing, each manufacturing activity could have its own standard costs that focus on underlying concepts and cost drivers, and companies even develop their own set of variances as discussed in the following Business Insight.

Standard cost variance analysis identifies the general causes of the total flexible budget variance by breaking it into separate price and quantity variances for each production component. Two possible reasons that actual cost could differ from flexible budget cost for a given amount of output produced are (1) a difference between actual and standard prices paid for the production components—the price variance—and (2) a difference between the actual quantity and the standard quantity allowed for the production components—the quantity variance. Variances have different names for different cost categories as follows:

Cost Component	Price Variance Name	Quantity Variance Name
Direct materials	Materials price variance	Materials quantity variance
Direct labor	Labor rate variance	Labor efficiency variance
Variable overhead	Variable overhead spending variance	Variable overhead efficiency variance

BUSINESS INSIGHT **Flexibility in Standard Costing**

The variances in this book are not the only ones used by managers. Many companies develop their own variances to meet the needs of their managers when confronted with unusual activities. Such is the case with **Parker Brass**. Two concerns of the production managers at Parker Brass are the timing of product cost information and providing an effective cost control system. As managers were struggling with new and different decisions, they decided that additional information was needed. They developed three new variances: standard run quantity variance, materials substitution variance, and method variance.

The *standard run quantity variance* measures the amount of setup cost that was not recovered because the batch size was smaller than the predetermined optimal batch size. Because the company had been including setup cost with labor, the managers were having difficulty explaining all of the labor variances. By pulling out the amounts related to batch sizes, the remainder of the analysis became easier to explain. The *materials substitute variance* is relevant when the standard materials have to be substituted because of lack of inventory or because a customer wants something different than normal. This often helps explain both materials price variances and usage variances so these two variances do not have to be used to justify all differences between standard and actual cost. The *method variance* is used when different machines or processes can be used to produce the same output. For example, if a process requires three labor hours and two machine hours but due to machine demand by other products, the process can be completed with seven labor hours and one machine hour, the resulting standard versus actual cost variances will be different even when all costs are perfectly controlled.

When managers know that the accounting system is flexible, there is more coordination between those who develop the system and those who use it. Parker Brass modified its standard costing system to better meet the needs of its managers without disrupting the traditional cost accounting system.[4]

Fixed overhead is excluded from the unit standard costs because, within the relevant range of normal activity, it does not vary with the volume of production. To facilitate product costing, however, many organizations develop a standard fixed overhead cost per unit.

In the following sections, we analyze the flexible budget cost variances for materials, labor and variable overhead. Our illustration of variance analysis is based on the following July activity and costs of McMillan Company's Production Department.

McMILLAN COMPANY—PRODUCTION DEPARTMENT Actual Manufacturing Costs For Month of July	
Actual units completed.	11,000
Manufacturing costs	
Unit level costs	
Direct materials (24,000 pounds × $4.50) . .	$108,000
Direct labor (2,800 hours × $25.00)	70,000
Variable overhead	81,000
Fixed overhead costs	53,000
Total	$312,000

Note that detailed information on actual pounds and an actual rate is not provided for variable overhead. That is because variable overhead represents a pool of related costs driven by a number of factors rather than a single cost with a single driver, as is often the case for materials and labor. Although the basis used in budgeting variable overhead may, and should, have a high correlation with actual variable overhead,

[4] David Johnsen and Parvez Sopariwala, "Standard Costing Is Alive and Well at Parker Brass, *Management Accounting Quarterly*, Winter 2000, pp. 12–20.

it is a surrogate for the multiple cost elements that comprise variable overhead. Issues related to variable overhead are discussed in greater detail later in this chapter.

Establishing and Using Standards for Direct Materials

The two basic elements contained in the standards for direct materials are the *standard price* and the *standard quantity.* Materials standards indicate how much an organization should pay for each input unit of direct materials and the quantity of direct materials it allows to produce one unit of output. The standard price per unit of direct materials should include all reasonable costs necessary to acquire the materials. These costs include the invoice price of materials, less planned discounts plus freight, insurance, special handling, and any other costs related to the acquisition of the materials. The standard quantity represents the number of units of raw materials allowed for the production of one unit of finished product. This amount should include the amount dictated by the physical characteristics of the process and the product, plus a reasonable allowance for normal spoilage, waste, and other inefficiencies. The quantity standard can be determined by engineering analysis, professional judgment, or by averaging the actual amount used for several periods. An average of actual past materials usage may not be a good standard because it could include excessive wastes and inefficiencies in the standard quantity.

Direct Materials Variances

The **materials price variance** is the difference between the actual materials cost and the standard cost of actual materials inputs. The **materials quantity variance** is the difference between the standard cost of actual materials inputs and the flexible budget cost for materials. The direct materials variances for McMillan Company follow.

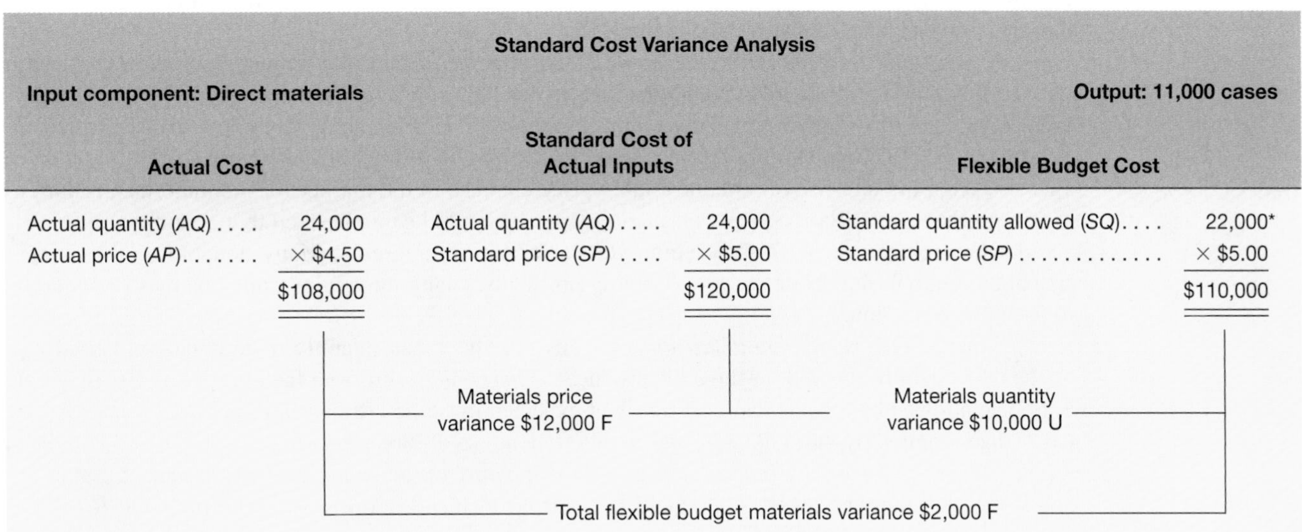

*11,000 units × 2 pounds per unit

McMillan Company had a favorable materials price variance of $12,000 because the actual cost of materials used ($108,000) was less than the standard cost of actual materials used ($120,000). Stated another way, for the materials actually used, the total price paid was $12,000 less than the price allowed by the standards. The price variance can also be viewed as the actual quantity (*AQ*) used times the difference between the actual price (*AP*) and the standard price (*SP*). McMillan Company paid $0.50 per pound below the standard price for 24,000 pounds for a total savings of $12,000. This is readily shown using the formula approach:

$$
\begin{aligned}
\textbf{Materials price variance} &= \textbf{AQ(AP} - \textbf{SP)} \\
&= \textbf{24,000(\$4.50} - \textbf{\$5.00)} \\
&= \textbf{24,000} \times \textbf{\$0.50} \\
&= \textbf{\$12,000 F}
\end{aligned}
$$

The unfavorable quantity variance of \$10,000 occurred because the standard cost of actual materials used, \$120,000 (24,000 × \$5), was higher than the cost of materials allowed by the flexible budget, \$110,000 (22,000 × \$5). A total of 22,000 pounds of materials is allowed to produce 11,000 units of finished outputs. This is computed as 11,000 finished units times 2.0 pounds of direct materials per unit. The materials quantity variance can also be computed as the standard price (*SP*) per pound times the difference between the number of pounds actually used (*AQ*) and the number of pounds allowed (*SQ*). This is also readily shown using the formula approach:

Materials quantity variance = SP(AQ − SQ)
= \$5(24,000 − 22,000)
= \$5 × 2,000
= \$10,000 U

Interpreting Materials Variances

After computing variances, managers must understand how to use them in making decisions relevant to the items being evaluated. A *favorable materials price variance* indicates that the employee responsible for materials purchases paid less per unit than the price allowed by the standards. This could result from receiving discounts for purchasing more than the normal quantities, effective bargaining by the employee, purchasing substandard-quality materials, purchasing from a distress seller, or other factors. Ordinarily, when a favorable price variance is reported, the employee's performance is interpreted as favorable. However, if the favorable price variance results from the purchase of materials of lower than standard quality or from a purchase in more than desirable quantities, the employee's performance would be questionable. Consistent and highly favorable variances could indicate situations that are undermining the responsibility accounting system by building slack into the standards or using incorrect data. These situations should be thoroughly investigated for causes and corrections.

An *unfavorable materials price variance* means that the purchasing employee paid more per unit for materials than the price allowed by the standards. This could be caused by failure to buy in sufficient quantities to receive normal discounts; purchase of higher-quality materials than called for in the product specifications; failure to place materials orders on a timely basis, thereby requiring a more expensive shipping alternative; uncontrollable price changes in the market for the materials; failure to bargain for the best available prices; or other factors. It should be emphasized that an unfavorable variance does not always mean that the employee performed unfavorably. Many noncontrollable factors surround the purchasing function due to timing problems, changing vendors, and changes in materials required by production.

A *favorable materials quantity variance* means that the actual quantity of raw materials used was less than the quantity allowed for the units produced. This could result from factors such as less materials waste than allowed by the standards, better than expected machine efficiency, direct materials of higher quality than required by the standards, and more efficient use of direct materials by employees. An *unfavorable materials quantity variance* occurs when the quantity of raw materials used exceeds the quantity allowed for the units produced. This could result from incurring more waste than provided for in the standards, poorly maintained machinery requiring larger amounts of raw materials, raw materials of lower quality than required by the standards, or poorly trained employees who were unable to use the materials at the level of efficiency required by the standards.

Establishing and Using Standards for Direct Labor

To evaluate management performance in controlling labor costs by using a standard cost system, it is necessary to determine the *standard labor rate* for each hour allowed and the *standard time allowed* to produce a unit. Setting labor rate standards can be quite simple or extremely complex. If only one class of employee is used to make each product and if all employees have the same wage rate, determining the standard cost is relatively easy: Simply adopt the normal wage rate as the standard labor rate. If several different classes of employees are used to make each unit of product, separate efficiency and rate standards could be established for each class.

The standard labor time per unit can be determined by an engineering approach or an empirical observation approach. When using an engineering approach, industrial engineers ascertain the amount of time required to produce a unit of finished product by applying time and motion methods or other available techniques. Normal operating conditions are assumed in arriving at the labor standard. Therefore, allowances must be made for normal machine downtime, employee personal breaks, and so forth. Under the empirical approach, the long-run average time required in the past to produce a unit under normal operating conditions is used as a basis for the standard. Use of normal operating conditions automatically factors inefficiencies such as machine downtime and employee breaks into the standard.

Direct Labor Variances

Using the general variance model that was used for materials, we can compute the labor rate and efficiency variances. The **labor rate (spending) variance** is the difference between the actual cost and the standard cost of actual labor inputs. The **labor efficiency variance** is the difference between the standard cost of actual inputs and the flexible budget cost for labor.

McMillan Company's labor standards provide for 0.25 hour of labor per unit produced at \$24 per hour. During July, 2,800 hours were used at a cost of \$25 per hour. Using these data, the labor rate (price) variance and labor efficiency (quantity) variance can be computed as shown in the following illustration.

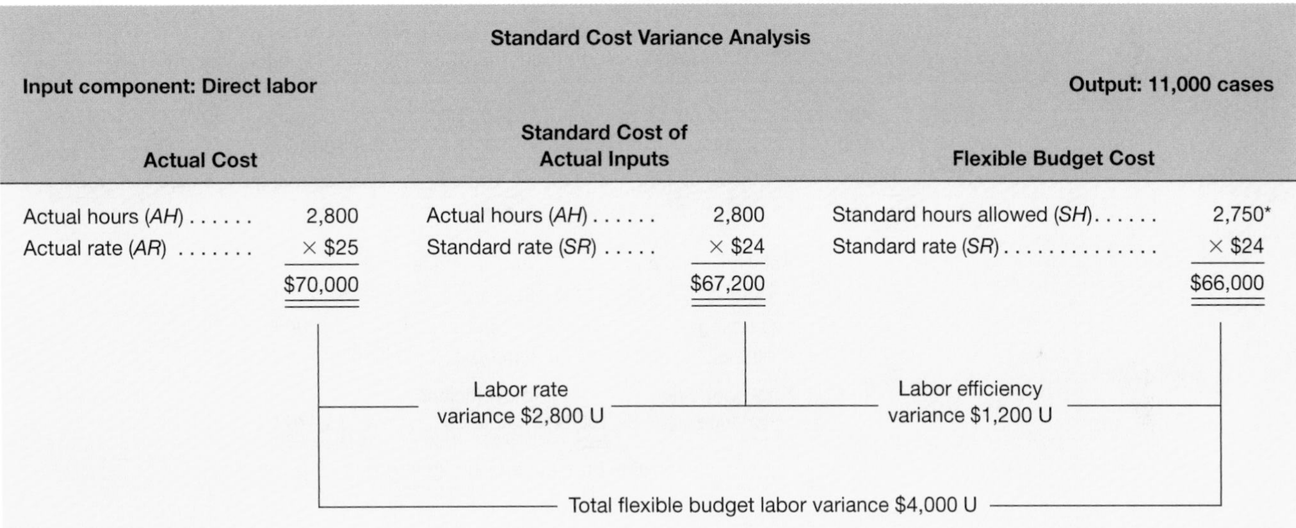

*11,000 units × 0.25 hour per unit

The labor rate variance can also be computed in formula form as the actual number of hours used times the difference between the actual rate and the standard rate. The symbols are the same as in the diagram.

$$\begin{aligned}\textbf{Labor rate variance} &= \textbf{AH(AR} - \textbf{SR)}\\ &= \textbf{2,800(\$25} - \textbf{\$24)}\\ &= \textbf{2,800} \times \textbf{\$1}\\ &= \textbf{\$2,800 U}\end{aligned}$$

This computation of the labor rate variance shows that the company paid \$1 more than the standard rate for each of the 2,800 hours worked.

Since 11,000 units of product were finished during the period and 0.25 hour of labor was allowed for each unit, the total number of standard hours allowed was 2,750. The labor efficiency variance can also be computed as the standard rate times the difference between the actual labor hours and the standard hours allowed for the output achieved:

$$\begin{aligned}\textbf{Labor efficiency variance} &= \textbf{SR(AH} - \textbf{SH)}\\ &= \textbf{\$24(2,800} - \textbf{2,750)}\\ &= \textbf{\$24} \times \textbf{50}\\ &= \textbf{\$1,200 U}\end{aligned}$$

This computation of the labor efficiency variance indicates that the company used 50 more labor hours than the budget permitted for a total of $1,200 more than the standards allowed. Since our illustration avoids the use of more complicated evaluations with multiple drivers, a multiple driver example is provided in the following Business Insight. The approach in this illustration can be used for direct labor or variable overhead.

BUSINESS INSIGHT **Multiple Cost Drivers**

Highly structured activity-based reporting systems usually require the performance reports to indicate all relevant cost drivers associated with the activities being evaluated. This is popular for automated settings such as those of Hewlett-Packard, Advanced Micro Devices, AT&T, and IBM. In these manufacturing environments, labor, as a cost driver, does not dominate. The manufacture and assembly of products are completed in distinct stages, each somewhat independent of others. To illustrate this type of setting, assume that an operating department has three automated processes performing three different tasks. The variances for each activity follow:[5]

Input component: Materials fabrication								**Output: 100 units**
Activity	**Actual Cost**	**Standard Cost of Actual Inputs**			**Flexible Budget Cost**			
Cutting . . .	$ 3,400	160 cuts	× $20.00 =	$ 3,200	150 cuts	× $20.00 =	$ 3,000	
Shaping . .	7,100	8,000 turns	× $ 0.90 =	7,200	8,100 turns	× $ 0.90 =	7,290	
Fitting	18,000	80,000 fittings	× $ 0.20 =	16,000	63,700 fittings	× $ 0.20 =	12,740	
	$28,500			$26,400			$23,030	

Activity spendings		Activity efficiencies	
Cutting	$ 200 U	Cutting	$ 200 U
Shaping	100 F	Shaping.	90 F
Fitting	2,000 U	Fitting	3,260 U
Total spending variance	$2,100 U	Total efficiency. . . . variance	$3,370 U

Total flexible budget variance $5,470 U

Interpreting Labor Variances

The possible explanations for labor rate variances are rather limited. An *unfavorable labor rate variance* can be caused by the use of higher paid laborers than the standards provided. Also, a new labor union contract increasing wages could have been implemented after the standards were set. In this case, the standards should have been revised to account for the wage rate change. In a nonunion situation when a negotiated contract does not control wages, a manager could arbitrarily increase employee wages above the standard rate. This also can cause an unfavorable labor rate variance. A *favorable labor rate variance* occurs if lower paid workers were used or if actual wage rates declined.

Unfavorable labor efficiency variances occur when workers or machines require more than the number of hours allowed by the standards to produce a given amount of output. This could be caused by a management decision to use poorly trained workers or poorly maintained machinery or by downtime resulting from the use of low-quality materials. Low employee morale and generally poor working conditions could also adversely affect the efficiency of workers, resulting in an unfavorable labor efficiency variance.

A *favorable labor efficiency variance* occurs when fewer hours are used than are allowed by the standards. This above-normal efficiency can be caused by the company's use of higher skilled (and higher paid) workers, better machinery, or raw materials of higher quality than the standards provided. High

[5] James M. Reeve, "Projects, Models, and Systems—Where Is ABM Headed?" *Journal of Cost Management*, Summer 1996, pp. 5–16.

employee morale, improved job satisfaction, or generally improved working conditions could also account for the above-normal efficiency of the workers.

Establishing and Using Standards for Variable Overhead

The traditional unit-level approach usually separates overhead costs into fixed and variable elements for control purposes. This separation is necessary because the variance between actual costs and expected costs is caused by different factors for fixed and variable costs. Unlike direct materials costs, which represent specific cost components, manufacturing overhead represents *groups* of different costs. Consequently, setting standards is often more difficult for overhead costs than it is for materials costs. For mixed manufacturing overhead costs (those that have variable and fixed components), an estimation technique, such as the high-low method, regression analysis (least-squares), or scatter diagram, is often used to separate the fixed and variable overhead components. (These techniques were discussed in Chapter 2.) If management concludes that the observations used in estimating variable costs reflect normal operating conditions, managers will probably adopt the estimate as the standard variable cost.

Because it includes many heterogeneous costs, manufacturing overhead poses a unique problem in measuring standard quantity and standard price. Direct materials have a natural physical measure of quantity such as tons, barrels, pounds, and liters. Similarly, labor or assembly is measurable in hours. However, no single quantity measure is common to all overhead items. Overhead is a cost group that can simultaneously include costs measurable in hours, pounds, liters and kilowatts.

The most frequent approach to dealing with the problem of multiple quantity measures in variable manufacturing overhead is to use an artificial (substitute) measure of quantity for all items in a given group. Typical substitute measures are machine hours, units of finished product, direct labor hours, and direct labor dollars. The variable overhead standard is then stated in terms of this single-factor base, and the amount of variable overhead budgeted is based on this artificial activity measure. Alternatively, variable overhead spending and efficiency variances might be developed for two or more of the types of costs included in variable overhead. Although multiple measure approaches may be more accurate they are more complex. Because the concepts are the same as for the single measure approach, only the single measure approach is illustrated.

Variable Overhead Variances

The **variable overhead spending variance** is the difference between the actual variable overhead cost and the standard variable overhead cost for the actual inputs of the measurement base. The **variable overhead efficiency variance** is the difference between the standard variable overhead cost for the actual inputs of the measurement base and the flexible budget cost allowed for variable overhead based on outputs.

For McMillan Company, the actual variable overhead for waterproofing and inspection is $81,000. This represents the actual cost of overhead items such as indirect materials and indirect labor. Since actual variable overhead is expected to vary with pounds of direct materials used, the standard cost of actual inputs is calculated as actual pounds of direct materials (*AP*) times the standard variable overhead rate per pound (*SRP*):

$$\begin{aligned}\textbf{Standard cost of actual inputs} &= \textbf{(AP} \times \textbf{SRP)}\\ &= \textbf{24,000} \times \textbf{\$4}\\ &= \textbf{\$96,000}\end{aligned}$$

The flexible budget cost for variable overhead allowed for the actual outputs is based on the 22,000 pounds of direct materials allowed (*SP*) for the units produced during the period (11,000 units × 2 pounds). The allowed quantities are multiplied by the standard variable overhead rate (*SRP*). The resulting variable overhead flexible budget cost is $88,000:

$$\begin{aligned}\textbf{Flexible budget cost} &= \textbf{(SP} \times \textbf{SRP)}\\ &= \textbf{22,000} \times \textbf{\$4}\\ &= \textbf{\$88,000}\end{aligned}$$

Using these data, the variable overhead spending (price) variance and the variable overhead efficiency (quantity) variance follow.

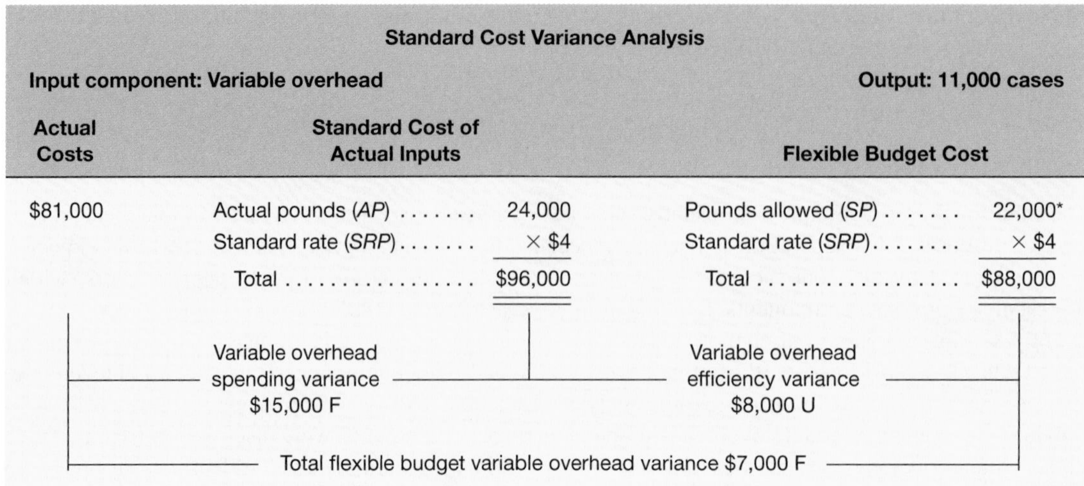

Standard Cost Variance Analysis				
Input component: Variable overhead				**Output: 11,000 cases**
Actual Costs	**Standard Cost of Actual Inputs**		**Flexible Budget Cost**	
$81,000	Actual pounds (*AP*)	24,000	Pounds allowed (*SP*)	22,000*
	Standard rate (*SRP*).......	× $4	Standard rate (*SRP*)........	× $4
	Total	$96,000	Total	$88,000
	Variable overhead spending variance $15,000 F		Variable overhead efficiency variance $8,000 U	
	Total flexible budget variable overhead variance $7,000 F			

*11,000 × 2 lbs.

An alternative to the computation of the variable overhead effectiveness variance follows:

$$\textbf{Variable overhead efficiency variance} = \textbf{SRP(AP} - \textbf{SP)}$$
$$= \textbf{\$4(24,000} - \textbf{22,000)}$$
$$= \textbf{\$8,000 U}$$

This approach emphasizes that the 2,000 extra pounds used should have increased variable overhead by $8,000 at the standard rate of $4 per pound.

Interpreting Variable Overhead Variances

A *favorable spending variance* encompasses all factors that cause actual expenditures to be less than the amount expected for the actual inputs of the measurement base, including consumption and payment. Conversely, an *unfavorable spending variance* results when the actual expenditures are more than expected for the inputs of the measurement base. This is caused by consuming more overhead items than expected, or by paying more than the expected amount for overhead items consumed, or by both. Thus, the term *spending variance* is used instead of *price variance.*

The key to understanding the variable overhead spending variance is recognizing that the amount of variable overhead cost allowed is determined by the level of the measurement bases used. Any deviation from this spending budget—due to uncontrolled or mismanaged variable overhead price or quantity variables—causes a spending variance to occur.

The variable overhead efficiency variance measures the difference between the standard variable overhead cost for the actual quantity of the measurement base and the standard variable overhead cost for the allowed quantity of the measurement base. This variance measures the amount of variable overhead that should have been saved (or incurred) because of the efficient (or inefficient) use of the measurement base. It provides no information about the degree of efficiency in using variable overhead items such as indirect materials and indirect labor. This information is reflected in the spending variance.

MANAGERIAL DECISION **You Are the Vice President of Manufacturing**

Your company has had a practice for many years of budgeting variable overhead costs based on direct labor hours. The managerial accountants have argued that if direct labor hours are controlled, variable overhead costs will take care of themselves since direct labor hours drive variable overhead costs. You (and your plant managers) have become very skeptical of this policy because in recent years variable overhead variances have been very erratic—sometimes being large favorable amounts and other times being large unfavorable amounts. You are beginning to plan for the coming budget year. How do you think you should budget variable overhead and evaluate managers who control these costs? [Answer, p. 353]

Fixed Overhead Variances

By definition, the quantity of goods and services purchased by fixed expenditures is not expected to change in proportion to short-run changes in the level of production. For example, in the short run, the production level does not affect the amount of depreciation on buildings, the number of fixed salaried employees, or the amount of real property subject to property taxes. Whether the organization produces 10,000 or 15,000 cases, the same quantity of fixed overhead is expected to be incurred, as long as the production level is within the relevant range of activity provided by the current fixed overhead items. Therefore, an efficiency variance is ordinarily not computed for fixed overhead costs.

Even though the components of fixed overhead are not expected to be affected by the production activity level in the short run, the actual amount spent for fixed overhead items can differ from the amount budgeted by management. For example, higher than budgeted supervisors' salaries could be paid, longer than normal working shifts could cause heating or cooling costs to exceed budget, and price increases could cause the amounts paid for equipment to be higher than expected. Fixed overhead costs in excess of the amount budgeted are reflected in the fixed overhead budget variance. The **fixed overhead budget variance** is, simply, the difference between budgeted and actual fixed overhead. Using the fixed costs of McMillan Company as an example:

Fixed overhead budget variance = Actual fixed overhead − Budgeted fixed overhead
= \$53,000 − \$52,000
= \$1,000 U

The fixed overhead budget variance is always the same as the total fixed overhead flexible budget variance. Because budgeted fixed overhead is the same for all outputs within the relevant range, the budget variance explains the total flexible budget variance between actual and allowed fixed overhead. Similar to variable overhead, fixed overhead variances can be caused by a combination of price and quantity factors.

PERFORMANCE REPORTS FOR REVENUE CENTERS

LO4 Calculate revenue variances and prepare a performance report for a revenue center.

The financial performance reports for revenue centers include a comparison of actual and budgeted revenues. Controllable costs can be deducted from revenues to obtain some bottom-line contribution margin. If the center is then evaluated on the basis of this contribution, it is being treated as a profit center.

If the organization is to meet its budgeted profit goal for a period, with its budgeted fixed and variable costs, the organization's revenue centers must meet their original revenue budgets. Consequently, the original budget (a static budget) rather than a flexible budget is used to evaluate the financial performance of revenue centers.

Assume that McMillan Company's July sales budget called for the sale of 10,000 units at \$40.00 each. If McMillan Company actually sold 11,000 units at \$38.50 each, the total revenue variance is \$23,500 favorable:

Actual revenues (11,000 × \$38.50)	\$423,500
Budgeted revenues (10,000 × \$40)	(400,000)
Revenue variance.	\$ 23,500 F

The **revenue variance** is the difference between the budgeted sales volume at the budgeted selling price and the actual sales volume at the actual selling price. Because actual revenues exceeded budgeted revenues, the revenue variance is favorable. It can be presented as follows:

Revenue variance = (Actual volume × Actual price) − (Budgeted volume × Budgeted price)

The separate impact of changing prices and volume on revenue is analyzed with the sales price and sales volume variances. The **sales price variance** is computed as the change in selling price times the actual sales volume:

Sales price variance = (Actual selling price − Budgeted selling price) × Actual sales volume

For McMillan, the sales price variance for July follows:

Sales price variance = ($38.50 − $40.00) × 11,000 units
= $16,500 U

The **sales volume variance** indicates the impact of the change in sales volume on revenues, assuming there was no change in selling price. The sales volume variance is computed as the difference between the actual and the budgeted sales volumes times the budgeted selling price:

Sales volume variance = (Actual sales volume − Budgeted sales volume) × Budgeted selling price

For McMillan, the sales volume variance for July follows:

Sales volume variance = (11,000 units − 10,000 units) × $40
= $40,000 F

The net of the sales price and the sales volume variances is equal to the revenue variance:

Sales price variance	$16,500 U
Sales volume variance	40,000 F
Revenue variance	$23,500 F

Interpretation of these variances is subjective. In this case, we could say that if the increase in sales volume had not been accompanied by a decline in selling price, revenues would have increased $40,000 instead of $23,500. The $1.50 per unit decline in selling price cost the company $16,500 in revenues. Alternatively, we might note that a $1.50 reduction in the unit selling price was more than offset by an increase in sales volume. An economic analysis could explain the relationship as volume being sensitive to price (price elasticity).

In any case, variances are merely signals that actual results are not proceeding according to plan. They help managers identify potential problems and opportunities. An investigation into their cause(s) could even indicate that a manager who received a favorable variance was doing a poor job, whereas a manager who received an unfavorable variance was doing an outstanding job. Consider McMillan Company's favorable revenue variance. This occurred because actual sales exceeded budgeted sales by 1,000 units (10 percent), which on the surface indicates good performance. But what if the total market for the company's products exceeded the company's forecast by 15 percent? In this case, McMillan Company's sales volume falls below its expected percentage share of the market; the favorable variance could occur (despite a poor marketing effort) because of strong customer demand that competitors could not fill. As detailed in the following Business Insight, budgeting an erroneously high sales volume can lead to excess production, high inventory levels, errors in developing standard costs, unanticipated financial losses, and cash flow problems.

Inclusion of Controllable Costs

Controllable costs should also be considered when evaluating the overall performance of revenue centers. A failure to consider costs could encourage uneconomic selling practices, such as excessive advertising and entertaining, and spending too much time on small accounts. The controllable costs of revenue centers include variable and fixed selling costs. These costs are sometimes further classified into order-getting and order-filling costs. **Order-getting costs** are incurred to obtain customers' orders (for example, advertising, salespersons' salaries and commissions, travel, telephone, and entertainment). **Order-filling costs** are incurred to place finished goods in the hands of purchasers (for example, storing, packaging, and transportation).

The performance of a revenue center in controlling costs can be evaluated with the aid of a flexible budget drawn up for the actual level of activity. Assume that the McMillan Company's July budget for the Sales Department calls for fixed costs of $10,000 and variable costs of $5 per unit sold. If the actual

BUSINESS INSIGHT **Chrysler Hits Financial Pothole Because of Sales Variances**

When **Cerberus Capital** management acquired an 80.1 percent controlling ownership interest in Chrysler from the former **DaimlerChrysler** AG in August of 2007, analysts speculated that their goal was to "spiff up" the company and sell it or its shares for at a profit. One of the new owner's first actions was to appoint Robert Nardelli (see the introduction to this chapter, pages 328–329), chief executive officer.

Nardelli found a mess that required his structure and systems skills as well as his focus on financial performance. Cost savings efforts were falling short of their targets. The company lagged on improving fuel efficiency, and the characteristics of some models (e.g wind noise and the use of plastic) was unacceptable to Nardelli. Worst of all, although Chrysler had significant unfavorable sales valiances, it was not adequately adjusting production volume and costs.

Chrysler's 2007 sales budget anticipated sales of approximately 2.8 million cars while, by late October 2007, actual sales were running at an annual rate of 2.6 million units, for an unfavorable sales volume variance of 200,000 units. What's more, to even achieve the 2.6 million unit volume, Chrysler increased sales (at lower prices) to rental companies, a tactic that reduces future resale values of automobiles sold to traditional customers.

As a consequence of the unfavorable sales variances, Chrysler was not generating the cash required to finance current operations, upgrade current vehicles, and develop new vehicles, especially vehicles using hybrid technology. Other consequences included facilities and costs geared to a higher level of production than appropriate for current sales (that is, the fixed costs were appropriate for a production volume significantly higher than the actual sales volume), and excess inventories with related inventory carrying costs.

Using a more people-oriented approach than at Home Depot, Nardelli worked with managers, employees, dealers, and others to implement what he regarded as needed changes, including: revised sales forecasts, union agreements allowing Chrysler to significantly reduce labor costs, eliminating some unprofitable product, and eliminating shifts at five plants. To further reduce fixed costs and obtain cash to support operations and invest in innovation, Nardelli plans to sell plant, property, and equipment with a book value of more than $1 billion. Commenting on the planned sale, he noted that publically held companies hesitate to dispose of assets at less than book value because of the resulting book loss. However, because Chrysler is privately owned by Cerberus Capital, "cash is king." Looking ahead, Nardelli believes, "We have a solid strategic direction to return the company to long-term profitability."[6]

fixed and variable selling expenses for July are $9,500 and $65,000, respectively, the total cost variances assigned to the Sales Department, detailed in Exhibit 10.2, are $9,500 unfavorable. In evaluating the Sales Department's performance as both a cost center and a revenue center, management would consider these cost variances as well as the revenue variances. Although the revenue variances are based on the original budget, the cost variances are based on the flexible budget.

Revenue Centers as Profit Centers

Even though we have computed revenue and cost variances for McMillan's Sales Department, we are still left with an incomplete picture of this revenue center's performance. Is the Sales Department's performance best represented by the $23,500 favorable revenue variance, by the $9,500 unfavorable cost variance, or by the net favorable variance of $14,000 ($23,500 F − $9,500 U)? Actually, it is inappropriate to attempt to obtain an overall measure of the Sales Department's performance by combining these separate revenue and cost variances. The combination of revenue and cost variances is appropriate only for a profit center; so far, we have left out one important cost that must be assigned to the Sales Department before it can be treated as a profit center. That cost is the *standard variable cost of goods sold*.

[6] "Chrysler Faces Financial Pinch, Sees Asset Sales," Josée Valcourt and Neal E. Boudette, *The Wall Street Journal*, December 21, 2007, pp. A1, A10; "Chrysler CEP Reassures on Financial Health," *The Wall Street Journal*, December 24, 2007, p. A8.

EXHIBIT 10.2 Sales Department Performance Report for Controllable Costs

McMILLAN COMPANY
Sales Department Performance Report for Controllable Costs
For Month of July

	Actual	Based on Flexible Budget: Flexible Budget*	Flexible Budget Variance
Units	11,000	11,000	
Selling expenses			
Variable	$65,000	$55,000	$10,000 U
Fixed	9,500	10,000	500 F
Total	$74,500	$65,000	$ 9,500 U

* Flexible budget formulas:
Variable selling expenses ($5 per unit)
Fixed selling expenses($10,000 per month)

As a profit center, the Sales Department acquires units from the Production Department and sells them outside the firm. Its total responsibilities include revenues, the standard variable cost of goods sold, and actual selling expenses. The Sales Department is assigned the *standard,* rather than the *actual, variable cost of goods sold.* Because the Sales Department does not control production activities, it should not be assigned actual production costs. Doing so results in passing the Production Department's variances on to the Sales Department. Fixed manufacturing costs are not assigned to the Sales Department because short-run variations in sales volume do not normally affect the total amount of these costs.

To evaluate the Sales Department as a profit center, the net sales volume variance must be computed. The **net sales volume variance** indicates the impact of a change in sales volume on the contribution margin given the budgeted selling price *and* the standard variable costs. It is computed as the difference between the actual and the budgeted sales volumes times the budgeted unit contribution margin.

Net sales volume variance = (Actual volume − Budgeted volume) × Budgeted contribution margin

Using the $40 budgeted selling price, the standard variable manufacturing costs, and the standard variable selling expenses, the budgeted contribution margin is $11.00:

Sales		$40.00
Direct materials	$10.00	
Direct labor	6.00	
Variable manufacturing overhead	8.00	
Selling	5.00	(29.00)
Contribution margin		$11.00

The net sales volume variance is computed as follows:

Net sales volume variance = (11,000 − 10,000) × $11.00
= $11,000 F

As a profit center, the Sales Department has responsibility for the sales price variance, the net sales volume variance, and any cost variances associated with its operations. As shown in Exhibit 10.3, the Sales Department variances, as a profit center, net to $10,000 unfavorable:

[6] "Chrysler Faces Financial Pinch, Sees Asset Sales," Josée Valcourt and Neal E. Boudette, The Wall Street Journal, December 21, 2007, pp. A1, A10; "Chrysler CEP Reassures on Financial Health," The Wall Street Journal, December 24, 2007, p. A8.

EXHIBIT 10.3 Sales Department Profit Center Performance Report

McMILLIAN COMPANY Sales Department Profit Center Performance Report For Month of July	
Sales price variance	$16,500 U
Net sales volume variance	11,000 F
Selling expense variance	9,500 U
Sales Department variances, net	$15,000 U

In an attempt to improve their overall performance, managers often commit themselves to unfavorable variances in some areas, believing that these variances will be more than offset by favorable variances in other areas. When the Sales Department is evaluated as a revenue center, the favorable sales volume variance more than offsets the price reductions and the higher selling expenses. The more complete evaluation of the Sales Department as a profit center (with a $15,000 unfavorable variance) gives a very different impression than the evaluation of the Sales Department as a pure revenue center (with a $23,500 favorable variance) or as a revenue center responsible only for its own direct costs with net favorable variances of $14,000, computed as $23,500 F minus $9,500 U.

CHAPTER-END REVIEW

The flexible budget performance report for Sunset Enterprises Inc. for March follows. The company manufactures only one product, folding chairs.

	Actual Costs	Flexible Budget Cost	Flexible Budget Variances
Output units	5,000	5,000	
Direct materials	$104,125	$100,000	$ 4,125 U
Direct labor	82,400	75,000	7,400 U
Variable manufacturing overhead			
Category 1	31,000	30,000	1,000 U
Category 2	18,000	20,000	2,000 F
Fixed manufacturing overhead	42,000	40,000	2,000 U
Total	$277,525	$265,000	$12,525 U

The standard unit cost for folding chairs follows:

Direct materials (4 pounds × $5.00 per pound)	$20
Direct labor (1.25 hours × $12.00 per hour)	15
Variable overhead, Category 1 (1.25 hours × $4.80)	6
Variable overhead, Category 2 ($4 per finished unit)	4
Total standard variable cost per unit	$45

Actual cost of materials is based on 21,250 pounds of direct materials purchased and used at $4.90 per pound; actual cost of assembly is based on 7,000 labor hours. Variable overhead is applied on labor hours for Category 1 and finished units for Category 2.

Required

a. Calculate all standard cost variances for direct materials and direct labor.

b. Calculate all standard cost variances for variable manufacturing overhead.

Solution

a.

Standard Cost Variance Analysis

Input component: Direct materials — **Output: 5,000 units**

Actual Cost		**Standard Cost of Actual Inputs**		**Flexible Budget Cost**	
Actual quantity (*AQ*)	21,250	Actual quantity (*AQ*)	21,250	Standard quantity allowed (*SQ*)	20,000*
Actual price (*AP*)	× $4.90	Standard price (*SP*)	× $5.00	Standard price (*SP*)	× $5.00
	$104,125		$106,250		$100,000

Materials price variance $2,125 F

Materials quantity variance $6,250 U

Total flexible budget materials variance $4,125 U

*5,000 units × 4 pounds per unit produced

Input component: Direct labor — **Output: 5,000 units**

Actual Costs	**Standard Cost of Actual Inputs**		**Flexible Budget Cost**	
$82,400	Actual hours (*AH*)	7,000	Standard hours allowed (*SH*)	6,250*
	Standard rate (*SR*)	× $12	Standard rate (*SR*)	× $12
	Total	$84,000	Total	$75,000

Labor rate variance $1,600 F

Labor efficiency variance $9,000 U

Total flexible budget labor variance $7,400 U

*5,000 units × 1.25 hours per unit

b.

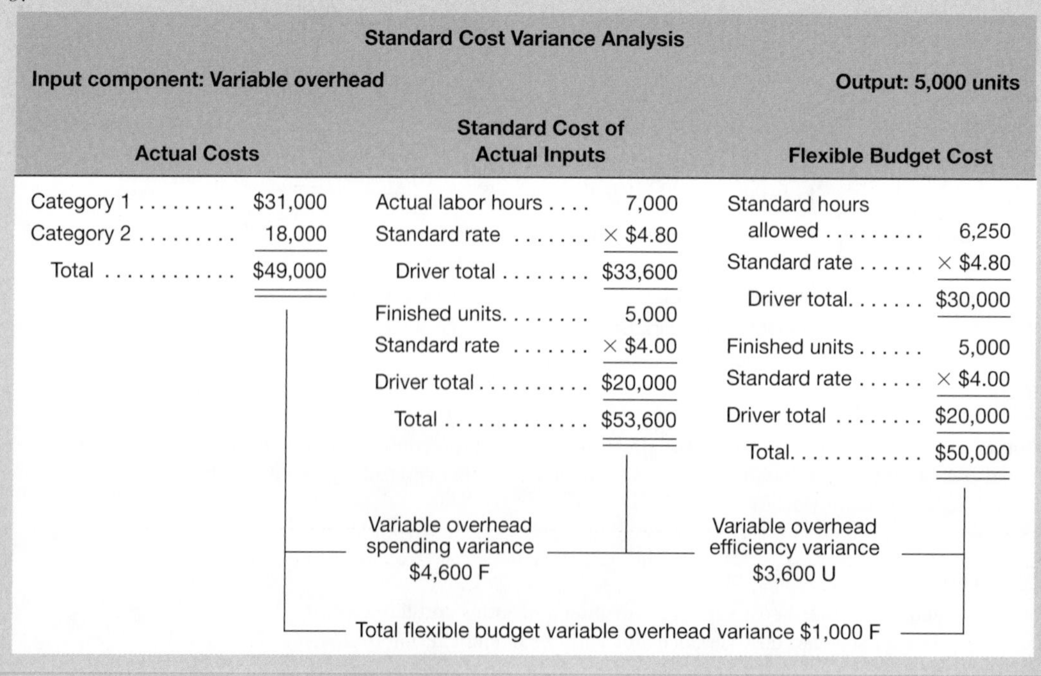

Standard Cost Variance Analysis

Input component: Variable overhead — **Output: 5,000 units**

Actual Costs		**Standard Cost of Actual Inputs**		**Flexible Budget Cost**	
Category 1	$31,000	Actual labor hours	7,000	Standard hours allowed	6,250
Category 2	18,000	Standard rate	× $4.80	Standard rate	× $4.80
Total	$49,000	Driver total	$33,600	Driver total	$30,000
		Finished units	5,000	Finished units	5,000
		Standard rate	× $4.00	Standard rate	× $4.00
		Driver total	$20,000	Driver total	$20,000
		Total	$53,600	Total	$50,000

Variable overhead spending variance $4,600 F

Variable overhead efficiency variance $3,600 U

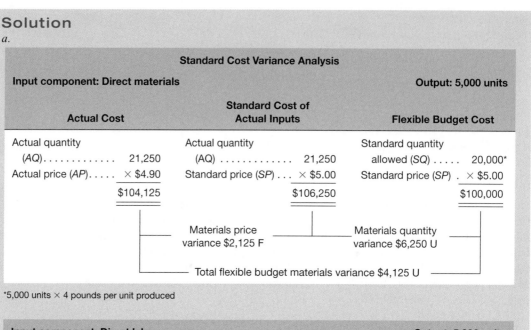

Total flexible budget variable overhead variance $1,000 F

APPENDIX 10A: Fixed Overhead Variances

By definition, the quantity of goods and services purchased by fixed expenditures is not expected to change in proportion to short-run changes in the level of production. For example, in the short run, the production level does not affect the amount of depreciation on buildings, the number of fixed salaried employees, or the amount of real property subject to property taxes. Whether the organization produces 10,000 or 15,000 cases, the same quantity of fixed overhead is expected to be incurred, as long as the production level is within the relevant range of activity provided by the current fixed overhead items. Therefore, an effectiveness variance is ordinarily not computed for fixed overhead costs.

Even though the components of fixed overhead are not expected to be affected by the production activity level in the short run, the actual amount spent for fixed overhead items can differ from the amount budgeted by management. For example, higher than budgeted supervisors' salaries could be paid, longer-than-normal working shifts could cause heating or cooling costs to exceed budget, and price increases could cause the amounts paid for equipment to be higher than expected. Fixed overhead costs in excess of the amount budgeted are reflected in the fixed overhead budget variance. The fixed overhead budget variance is the difference between budgeted and actual fixed overhead. Using the facility-level fixed costs of McMillan Company as an example:

Fixed overhead budget variance = Actual fixed overhead − Budgeted fixed overhead
= $31,000 − $32,000
= $1,000 F

The fixed overhead budget variance is always the same as the total fixed overhead flexible budget variance. Because budgeted fixed overhead is the same for all outputs within the relevant range, the budget variance explains the total flexible budget variance between actual and allowed fixed overhead. Similar to variable overhead, fixed overhead variances can be caused by a combination of price and quantity factors.

Recall that predetermined overhead rates are computed by dividing the predicted overhead costs for the period by the predicted activity of the period. The motivation for using a standard fixed overhead rate is the same as the motivation for using a predetermined overhead rate; namely, quicker product costing and assigning identical fixed costs to identical products, regardless of when they are produced during the year.

When a standard fixed overhead rate is used, total fixed overhead costs assigned to production behave as variable costs. As production increases, the total fixed overhead assigned to production increases. Because total budgeted fixed overhead does not vary, differences arise between budgeted and assigned fixed overhead, and managers often inquire about the cause of the differences.

The standard fixed overhead rate is computed as the budgeted fixed costs divided by some budgeted standard level of activity. Assume McMillian applies fixed manufacturing overhead on the basis of machine hours and that 0.40 machine hours are required to produce one carrying case. Further assume that the budgeted production is 10,000 carrying cases per month, a level that requires 4,000 (10,000 × 0.40) machine hours. The standard fixed overhead rate per machine hour is $8.

Standard fixed overhead rate = Budgeted total fixed overhead ÷ Budgeted activity level
= $32,000 ÷ 4,000 hours
= $8 per machine hour

The total fixed overhead assigned to production is computed as the standard rate of $8 multiplied by the standard hours allowed for the units produced. Therefore, the assigned fixed overhead cost equals the budgeted monthly fixed overhead cost only if the allowed activity equals the budgeted activity of 4,000 hours. If the company operates less than 4,000 hours, the fixed overhead assigned to production is less than the $32,000 budgeted; if it operates more than 4,000 hours, the fixed overhead assigned to production is more than the amount budgeted.

Even though total fixed overhead is not affected by production below or above the standard activity level, the fixed overhead assigned to production increases at the rate of $8 per allowed machine hour. The difference between total budgeted fixed overhead and total standard fixed overhead assigned to production is called the **fixed overhead volume variance**. This variance is sometimes referred to as the **capacity variance**, a term that emphasizes the maximum output of an operation. The fixed overhead volume variance indicates neither good nor poor performance by the production personnel. Instead, it indicates the difference between the activity allowed for the actual output and the budget level used as the denominator in computing the standard fixed overhead rate.

To explain the difference between actual fixed overhead and standard fixed overhead assigned to production, two fixed overhead variances are computed: the fixed overhead budget variance and the fixed overhead volume variance. The fixed overhead budget variance represents the difference between actual fixed overhead and budgeted fixed overhead. The budget variance is caused by a combination of price and quantity factors related to the use of fixed overhead goods and services (e.g., depreciation, insurance, supervisors' salaries). The $1,000 favorable budget variance for McMillan was caused either by using fewer quantities of fixed overhead goods and services, or by paying lower prices than expected for those items, or both.

The volume variance represents the difference between budgeted and assigned fixed overhead and is caused by a difference between the activity level allowed for the actual output and the budgeted activity used in computing the fixed overhead rate. For McMillan, actual July output of 11,000 units resulted in 4,400 allowed machine hours and applied fixed overhead of $35,200 (11,000 units × 0.40 hours × $8). The $3,200 favorable fixed overhead volume variance (budgeted costs of $32,000 minus applied costs of $35,200) indicates that the activity level allowed for the actual output was more than the budgeted activity level. As previously stated, this variance ordinarily cannot be used to control costs. If the budgeted activity is based on production capacity, an unfavorable variance alerts management that facilities are underutilized, and a favorable variance alerts management that facilities are utilized above their expectations. A summary standard cost variance analysis for fixed costs is shown below.

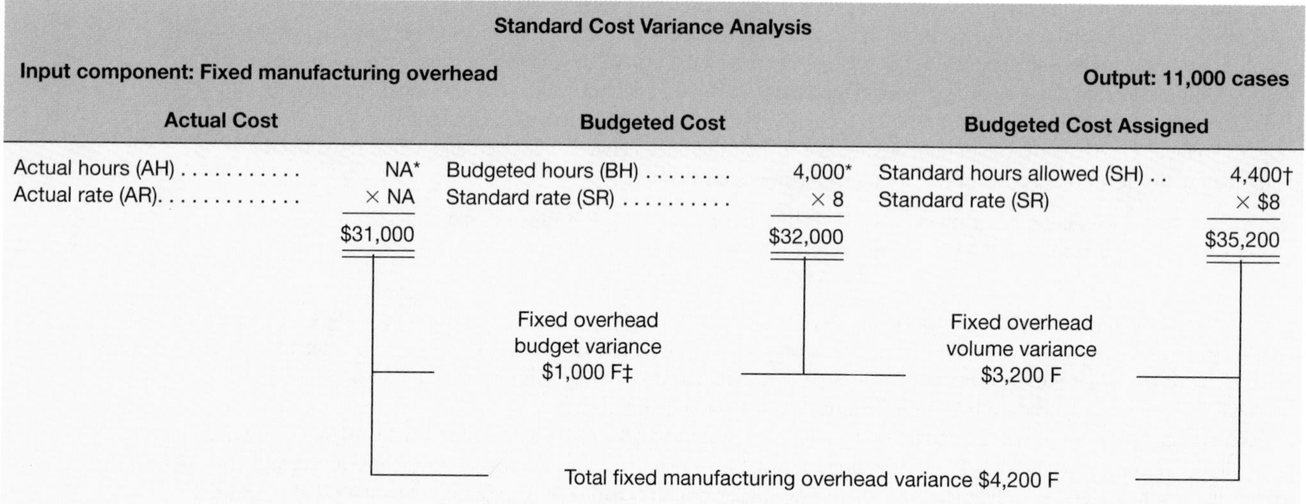

* Not applicable

†11,000 units × 0.40

‡Also the flexible budget fixed overhead variance

APPENDIX 10B: Reconciling Budgeted and Actual Income

Using a contribution format, it is possible to reconcile the difference between budgeted and actual net income for an entire organization. This is done by assigning all costs and revenues to responsibility centers and summarizing the financial performance of each responsibility center. McMillan Company's budgeted and actual income statements, in a contribution format, for July are presented in Exhibit 10.4.

EXHIBIT 10.4 Budgeted and Actual Income Statements: Contribution Format

McMILLAN COMPANY
Budgeted Income Statement
For Month of July

Sales (10,000 units × $40)			$400,000
Less variable costs			
Variable cost of goods sold			
Direct materials (10,000 units × $10)	$100,000		
Direct labor (10,000 units × $6)	60,000		
Manufacturing overhead (10,000 × $8)	80,000	$240,000	
Selling (10,000 units × $5)		50,000	(290,000)
Contribution margin			110,000
Less fixed costs			
Manufacturing overhead		52,000	
Selling		10,000	
Administrative		4,000	(66,000)
Net income			$ 44,000

continued

continued from previous page

EXHIBIT 10.4 Budgeted and Actual Income Statements: Contribution Format

McMILLAN COMPANY
Actual Income Statement
For Month of July

Sales (11,000 units × $38.50)			$423,500
Less variable costs			
Variable cost of goods sold			
Direct materials	$108,000		
Direct labor	70,000		
Manufacturing overhead	81,000	$259,000	
Selling		65,000	(324,000)
Contribution margin			99,500
Less fixed costs			
Manufacturing overhead		53,000	
Selling		9,500	
Administrative		3,800	(66,300)
Net income			$ 33,200

McMillan Company contains three responsibility centers: a Production Department, a Sales Department, and an Administration Department. The Sales Department variances in Exhibit 10.3 net to $15,000 U. The Production Department's variances in Exhibit 10.1 net to $4,000 F. The only variance for the Administration Department is the $200 difference between actual and budgeted fixed administrative costs ($3,800 actual − $4,000 budget). Because the Administration Department is a discretionary cost center, this variance is best identified as being underbudget. For consistency in the performance reports, however, it is labeled favorable. By assigning all variances to these three responsibility centers, the reconciliation of budgeted and actual income is as shown in Exhibit 10.5.

EXHIBIT 10.5 Reconciliation of Budgeted and Actual Income

McMILLAN COMPANY
Reconciliation of Budgeted and Actual Income
For Month of July

Budgeted net income	$44,000
Sales department variances (Exhibit 10.3)	15,000 U
Production department variances (Exhibit 10.1)	4,000 F
Administration department variances ($3,800 actual − $4,000 budgeted)	200 F
Actual net income	$33,200

GUIDANCE ANSWER

MANAGERIAL DECISION **You Are the Vice President of Manufacturing**

It appears that direct labor hours may no longer be a reliable basis for budgeting variable overhead in your company. If actual variable overhead costs do not appear to correlate closely with direct labor hours, this could be an indication that the components of variable overhead have changed since direct labor hours was selected as the cost driver. Your cost accountants should consider other unit-level cost drivers for budgeting variable overhead costs. However, an activity-based costing method using multiple overhead cost pools with separate cost drivers might provide a more reliable basis for budgeting and controlling variable overhead costs.

DISCUSSION QUESTIONS

Q10-1. What is responsibility accounting? Why should noncontrollable costs be excluded from performance reports prepared in accordance with responsibility accounting?

Q10-2. How can responsibility accounting lead to unethical practices?

Q10-3. Responsibility accounting reports must be expanded to include what nonfinancial areas? Give some examples of nonfinancial measures.

Q10-4. What is a cost center? Give some examples.

Q10-5. How is a cost center different from either an investment or a profit center?

Q10-6. What problems can result from the use of tight standards?

Q10-7. What is a standard cost variance, and what is the objective of variance analysis?

Q10-8. Standard cost variances can usually be broken down into two basic types of variances. Identify and describe these two types of variances.

Q10-9. Identify possible causes for (1) a favorable materials price variance; (2) an unfavorable materials price variance; (3) a favorable materials quantity variance; and (4) an unfavorable materials quantity variance.

Q10-10. How is standard labor time determined? Explain the two ways.

Q10-11. In the standard cost system, what is the appropriate treatment of a change in wage rates (per new labor union contract) that dominate the cost of labor?

Q10-12. Explain the difference between the revenue variance and the sales price variance.

Q10-13. Explain the net sales volume variance and list its components.

Q10-14. Explain the difference between how the *actual costs* and the *standard cost of actual inputs* are computed in variable overhead analysis.

Q10-15. Explain what the net sales volume variance measures.

MINI EXERCISES

M10-16. Flexible Budgets and Performance Evaluation (LO2)

Presented is the January performance report for the Production Department of Dover Company.

DOVER COMPANY Production Department Performance Report For Month of January			
	Actual	Budget	Variance
Volume	30,000	28,000	
Manufacturing costs			
Direct materials	$ 89,600	$ 82,000	$ 7,600 U
Direct labor	165,000	140,000	25,000 U
Variable overhead	62,000	56,000	6,000 U
Fixed overhead	27,500	28,000	500 F
Total	$344,100	$306,000	$38,100 U

Required

a. Evaluate the performance report.

b. Prepare a more appropriate performance report.

E10-17 Materials Variances (LO3)

North Wind manufactures decorative weather vanes that have a standard materials cost of two pounds of raw materials at $1.50 per pound. During September 10,000 pounds of raw materials costing $1.55 per pound were used in making 4,800 weather vanes.

Required

Determine the materials price and quantity variance.

M10-18. Materials Variances (LO3)

Assume that Lenscrafters uses standard costs to control the materials in its made-to-order sunglasses. The standards call for 2 ounces of material for each pair of lenses. The standard cost per ounce of material is $15. During July, the Palm Beach location produced 4,800 pairs of sunglasses and used 8,800 ounces of materials. The cost of the materials during July was $15.20 per ounce, and there were no beginning or ending inventories. Lenscrafters

Required

a. Determine the flexible budget materials cost for the completion of the 4,800 pairs of glasses.
b. Determine the actual materials cost incurred for the completion of the 4,800 pairs of glasses and compute the total materials variance.
c. How much of the total variance was related to the price paid to purchase the materials?
d. How much of the difference between the answers to requirements (a) and (b) was related to the quantity of materials used?

M10-19. Direct Labor Variances (LO3)

Assume that Nortel manufactures specialty electronic circuitry through a unique photoelectronic process. One of the primary products, Model ZX40, has a standard labor time of 0.5 hour and a standard labor rate of $13.50 per hour. During February, the following activities pertaining to direct labor for ZX40 were recorded: Nortel (NT)

Direct labor hours used	2,180
Direct labor cost.	$34,000
Units of ZX40 manufactured . . .	4,600

Required

a. Determine the labor rate variance.
b. Determine the labor efficiency variance.
c. Determine the total flexible budget labor cost variance.

M10-20 Significance of Direct Labor Variances (LO3)

The Morgan Company's April budget called for labor costs of $125,000. Because the actual labor costs were exactly $125,000, management concluded there were no labor variances.

Required:

Comment on management's conclusion.

M10-21 Variable Overhead Variances (LO3)

Assume that the best cost driver that Sony has for variable factory overhead in the assembly department is machine hours. During April, the company budgeted 480,000 machine hours and $5,000,000 for its Texas plant's assembly department. The actual variable overhead incurred was $5,200,000, which was related to 500,000 machine hours. Sony

Required

a. Determine the variable overhead spending variance.
b. Determine the variable overhead effectiveness variance.

M10-22. Sales Variances (LO4)

Presented is information pertaining to an item sold by Winding Creek General Store:

	Actual	Budget
Unit sales	150	125
Unit selling price.	$26	$25
Unit standard variable costs.	(20)	(20)
Unit contribution margin.	$ 6	$ 5
Revenues	$3,900	$3,125
Standard variable costs	(3,000)	(2,500)
Contribution margin at standard costs.	$ 900	$ 625

Required

Compute the revenue, sales price, and the sales volume variances.

M10-23[A] Fixed Overhead Variances (LO3)

Phillips Petroleum

Assume that Phillips Petroleum uses a standard cost system for each of its refineries. For the Tulsa refinery, the monthly fixed overhead budget is $21,000,000 for a planned output of 10,000,000 barrels. For September, the actual fixed cost was $22,000,000 for 10,800,000 barrels. The Tulsa refinery's capacity is 11,900,000 barrels.

Required

a. Determine the fixed overhead budget variance.
b. If fixed overhead is applied on a per-barrel basis, determine the volume variance.

M10-24[B] Reconciling Budgeted and Actual Income

Upstate Supply Company has three responsibility centers: sales, production, and administration. The following information pertains to the November activities of Upstate Supply:

Budgeted contribution income	$16,000
Actual contribution income	27,000
Sales price variance	$24,000 F
Sales volume variance	40,000 F
Net sales price variance	6,000 F
Sales department variable expense variance	18,000 U
Sales department fixed expense variance	1,000 U
Administration department variances	0
Production department variances	0

Required:
Prepare a reconciliation of budgeted and actual contribution income.

EXERCISES

E10-25. Direct Labor Variances (LO3)

Springs Industries, Inc.

Assume that Springs Industries, Inc., operates its Charlotte plant using a combination of hourly and incentive wage programs for production employees. The guaranteed minimum wage is $14 per hour but with incentive outputs, the wage can increase to $22 per hour. For dye processing, the standard output per hour is 1,000 pounds of yarn processed and dyed. During June, the dye process had an average wage rate of $16 with 920,000 pounds of dyed yarn completing production. Production hours totaled 950.

Required

a. Compute rate and efficiency variances using the minimum wage as the standard.
b. Compute rate and efficiency variances using the maximum wage with incentives as the standard.
c. Why does changing the standard used for the hourly rate change the efficiency variance?
d. Explain which set of variances is most useful for management.

E10-26. Variable Overhead Variances (LO3)

India Leaf Company bases standard variable overhead cost on direct labor hours as the cost driver. Standard variable overhead cost has been set at $15 per unit of output based on $5 of variable overhead per direct labor hour for 3 hours allowed to produce 1 finished unit. Last month, 4,300 direct labor hours were used, and 1,400 units of output were manufactured. The following actual variable overhead costs were incurred:

Indirect materials	$ 4,500
Indirect labor	8,400
Utilities	5,800
Miscellaneous	3,600
Total variable overhead	$22,300

Required

a. Determine the variable overhead spending variance.
b. Determine the variable overhead efficiency variance.
c. How is the variable overhead efficiency variance related to labor efficiency?
d. If the company used smaller quantities of indirect materials than those reflected in the standards, in which variance would the resulting cost savings be reflected? Explain.

E10-27. Causes of Standard Cost Variances (Comprehensive) (LO3)

Following are ten unrelated situations that would ordinarily be expected to affect one or more standard cost variances:

1. A salaried production supervisor is given a raise, but no adjustment is made in the labor cost standards.
2. The materials purchasing manager gets a special reduced price on raw materials by purchasing a train carload. A warehouse had to be rented to accommodate the unusually large amount of raw materials. The rental fee was charged to Rent Expense, a fixed overhead item.
3. An unusually hot August caused the company to use 25,000 kilowatts more electricity than provided for in the variable overhead standards.
4. The local electric utility company raised the charge per kilowatt-hour. No adjustment was made in the variable overhead standards.
5. The plant manager traded in his leased company car for a new one in July, increasing the monthly lease payment by $150.
6. A machine malfunction on the assembly line (caused by using cheap and inferior raw materials) resulted in decreased output by the machine operator and higher than normal machine repair costs. Repairs are treated as variable overhead costs.
7. The production maintenance supervisor decreased routine maintenance checks, resulting in lower maintenance costs and lower machine production output per hour. Maintenance costs are treated as fixed costs.
8. An announcement that vacation benefits had been increased resulted in improved employee morale. Consequently, raw materials pilferage and waste declined, and production efficiency increased.
9. The plant manager reclassified her secretary to administrative assistant and gave him an increase in salary.
10. A union contract agreement calling for an immediate 5 percent increase in production worker wages was signed. No changes were made in the standards.

Required

For each of these situations, indicate by letter which of the following standard cost variances would be affected. More than one variance will be affected in some cases.

a. Materials price variance.
b. Materials quantity variance.
c. Labor rate variance.
d. Labor efficiency variance.
e. Variable overhead spending variance.
f. Variable overhead efficiency variance.
g. Fixed overhead budget variance.

E10-28 Sales Variances (LO4)

Assume that Casio Computer Company, LTD. sells handheld communication devices for $110 during August as a back-to-school special. The normal selling price is $150. The standard variable cost for each device is $70. Sales for August had been budgeted for 400,000 units nationwide; however, due to the slowdown in the economy, sales were only 350,000.

Casio Computer Company, LTD.

Required

Compute the revenue, sales price, sales volume variance, and net sales volume variance.

E10-29^A Fixed Overhead Variances (LO3)

Huntsville Company uses standard costs for cost control and internal reporting. Fixed costs are budgeted at $7,500 per month at a normal operating level of 10,000 units of production output. During October, actual fixed costs were $8,000, and actual production output was 9,500 units.

Required

a. Determine the fixed overhead budget variance.
b. Assume that the company applied fixed overhead to production on a per-unit basis. Determine the fixed overhead volume variance.
c. Was the fixed overhead budget variance from requirement (a) affected because the company operated below the normal activity level of 10,000 units? Explain.
d. Explain the possible causes for the volume variance computed in requirement (b). How is reporting of the volume variance useful to management?

PROBLEMS

P10-30. Multiple Product Performance Report (LO2)

Storage Products manufactures two models of DVD storage cases: regular and deluxe. Presented is standard cost information for each model:

Cost Components	Regular		Deluxe	
Direct materials				
Lumber	2 board feet × $3	= $ 6.00	3 board feet × $3	= $ 9.00
Assembly kit		= 2.00		= 2.00
Direct labor.	1 hour × $4	= 4.00	1.25 hours × $4	= 5.00
Variable overhead. .	1 labor hr. × $2	= 2.00	1.25 labor hrs. × $2	= 2.50
Total		$14.00		$18.50

Budgeted fixed manufacturing overhead is $15,000 per month. During July, the company produced 5,000 regular and 3,000 deluxe storage cases while incurring the following manufacturing costs:

Direct materials	$ 80,000
Direct labor.	36,000
Variable overhead.	14,000
Fixed overhead.	17,500
Total	$147,500

Required

Prepare a flexible budget performance report for the July manufacturing activities.

P10-31. Computation of Variable Cost Variances (LO3)

The following information pertains to the standard costs and actual activity for Tyler Company for September:

Standard cost per unit	
Direct materials.	4 units of material A × $2.00 per unit
	1 unit of material B × $3.00 per unit
Direct labor	3 hours × $8.00 per hour
Activity for September	
Materials purchased	
Material A	4,500 units × $2.05 per unit
Material B	1,100 units × $3.10 per unit
Materials used	
Material A	4,150 units
Material B	1,005 units
Direct labor used	2,950 hours × $8.20 per hour
Production output.	1,000 units

There were no beginning direct materials inventories.

Required

a. Determine the materials price and quantity variances.
b. Determine the labor rate and efficiency variances.

P10-32. Variance Computations and Explanations (LO3)

Outdoor Company manufactures camping tents from a lightweight synthetic fabric. Each tent has a standard materials cost of $20, consisting of 4 yards of fabric at $5 per yard. The standards call for 2 hours of assembly at $12 per hour. The following data were recorded for October, the first month of operations:

Fabric purchased	9,000 yards × $4.90 per yard
Fabric used in production of 1,700 tents	7,000 yards
Direct labor used	3,600 hours × $12.50 per hour

Required

a. Compute all standard cost variances for materials and labor.
b. Give one possible reason for each of the preceding variances.
c. Determine the standard variable cost of the 1,700 tents produced, separated into direct materials and labor.

P10-33. Determining Unit Costs, Variance Analysis, and Interpretation (LO2, 3)
Big Dog Company, a manufacturer of dog food, produces its product in 1,000-bag batches. The standard cost of each batch consists of 8,000 pounds of direct materials at $0.30 per pound, 48 direct labor hours at $8.50 per hour, and variable overhead cost (based on machine hours) at the rate of $10 per hour with 16 machine hours per batch. The following variable costs were incurred for the last 1,000-bag batch produced:

Direct materials	8,300 pounds costing $2,378 were purchased and used
Direct labor	45 hours costing $450
Variable overhead	$225
Machine hours used	18 hours

Required

a. Determine the actual and standard variable costs per bag of dog food produced, separated into direct materials, direct labor, and variable overhead.
b. For the last 1,000-bag batch, determine the standard cost variances for direct materials, direct labor, and variable overhead.
c. Explain the possible causes for each of the variances determined in requirement (b).

P10-34. Computation of Variances and Other Missing Data (LO3)
The following data for O'Keefe Company pertain to the production of 300 units of Product X during December. Selected data items are omitted.

Direct materials (all materials purchased were used during period)
- Standard cost per unit: (a) pounds at $3.20 per pound
- Total actual cost: (b) pounds costing $5,673
- Standard cost allowed for units produced: $5,760
- Materials price variance: (c)
- Materials quantity variance: $96 U

Direct labor
- Standard cost: 2 hours at $7.00
- Actual cost per hour: $7.25
- Total actual cost: (d)
- Labor rate variance: (e)
- Labor efficiency variance: $140 U

Variable overhead
- Standard costs: (f) hours at $4.00 per direct labor hour
- Actual cost: $2,250
- Variable overhead spending variance: (g)
- Variable overhead efficiency variance: (h)

Required
Complete the missing amounts lettered (a) through (h).

P10-35 Flexible Budgets and Performance Evaluation (LO3)
Anna Van Degna, supervisor of housecleaning for Hotel Dell, was surprised by her summary performance report for March given below.

HOTEL DELL Housekeeping Performance Report For the Month of March			
Actual	**Budget**	**Variance**	**%Variance**
$164,423	$154,000	$10,423 U	6.768% U

Anna was disappointed. She thought she had done a good job controlling housekeeping labor and towel usage, but her performance report revealed an unfavorable variance of $10,423. She had been hoping for a bonus for her good work, but now expected a series of questions from her manager.

The cost budget for housekeeping is based on standard costs. At the beginning of a month, Anna receives a report from Hotel Dell's Sales Department outlining the planned room activity for the month. Anna then schedules labor and purchases using this information. The budget for the housekeeping was based on 8,000 room nights. Each room night is budgeted based on the following standards for various materials, labor, and overhead:

Shower supplies.	3 bottles @ $0.25 each
Towels*	1 @ $2.00
Laundry	10 lbs. @ $0.35 a lb.
Labor	½ hour @ $12.00 an hour
VOH	$6.00 per labor hour
FOH	$4 a room night (based on 8,000 room nights)

*Replacements for towels evaluated by housekeeping as inappropriate for cleaning and reuse.

With 8,900 room nights sold, actual costs and usage for housekeeping during April were:

$6,890 for 26,500 bottles of shower supplies.
$15,563 for 7,900 towels.
$31,329 for 88,500 lbs. of laundry.
$51,591 for 4,350 labor hours.
$25,839 in total VOH.
$33,211 in FOH.

Required:

a. Develop a complete budget column for the above performance report presented to Anna. Break it down by expense category. The following format, with additional lines for expense categories, is suggested:

Account	Actual	Budget	Variance
Shower Supplies	$ 6,890	?	?
...	...	...	...
Total	$164,423	$154,000	$10,423 U

b. Evaluate the usefulness of the cost center performance report presented to Anna.

c. Prepare a more logical performance report where standard allowed is based on actual output. Also, split each variance into its price/rate/spending and quantity/efficiency components (except fixed of course). The following format, with additional lines for expense categories, is suggested:

Account	Actual	Flexible Budget	Total Variance	Price/Rate/ Spending Variance	Quantity/ Efficiency Variance
Shower Supplies	$ 6,890	?	?	?	?
...	—	—	—		
Total	$164,423	?	?		

d. Explain to Anna's boss what your report suggests about Anna's department performance.

e. Identify additional non-financial performance measures management might consider when evaluating the performance of the housekeeping department and Anna as a manager.

P10-36 Flexible Budget Performance Evaluation with Process Costing (LO3)

Note: This problem requires knowledge of process costing concepts covered in Chapter 5

The Waldorf Company produces a single product on a continuous basis. On July 1, 400 units, 75 percent complete as to materials and 50 percent complete as to conversion, were in process. During January, 1,000 units were started and 1,200 units were completed. The July 31 ending work-in-process inventory contained 200 units, 50 percent complete as to materials and 25 percent complete as to conversion.

Waldorf uses standard costs for planning and control. The following standard costs are based on a monthly volume of 800 equivalent units with fixed budgeted at $6,000 per month.

Direct materials [(2 square meter per unit × $8.00 per meter) × 800]	$12,800
Direct labor [(1.5 hours per unit × $20 per hour) × 800]	24,000
Variable overhead [(1.5 labor hours per unit × $5.00 per hour) × 800]	6,000
Fixed manufacturing overhead	6,000

Actual July production costs were:

Direct materials	$20,800
Direct labor	31,400
Manufacturing overhead	11,250

Required:

a. Determine the equivalent units of materials and conversion manufactured during July.

b. Based on the July equivalent units of materials and conversion, prepare a July performance report for the Waldorf Company.

c. Explain the treatment of overhead in the July performance report.

P10-37. Measuring the Effects of Decisions on Standard Cost Variances (Comprehensive) (LO3)

The following five unrelated situations affect one or more standard cost variances for materials, labor (assembly), and overhead:

1. Lois Jones, a production worker, announced her intent to resign to accept another job paying $1.20 more per hour. To keep Lois, the production manager agreed to raise her salary from $7.00 to $8.50 per hour. Lois works an average of 175 regular hours per month.
2. At the beginning of the month, a supplier of a component used in our product notified us that, because of a minor design improvement, the price will be increased by 15 percent above the current standard price of $100 per unit. As a result of the improved design, we expect the number of defective components to decrease by 80 units per month. On average, 1,200 units of the component are purchased each month. Defective units are identified prior to use and are not returnable.
3. In an effort to meet a deadline on a rush order in Department A, the plant manager reassigned several higher-skilled workers from Department B, for a total of 300 labor hours. The average salary of the Department B workers was $1.85 more than the standard $7.00 per hour rate of the Department A workers. Since they were not accustomed to the work, the average Department B worker was able to produce only 36 units per hour instead of the standard 48 units per hour. (Consider only the effect on Department A labor variances.)
4. Rob Celiba is an inspector who earns a base salary of $700 per month plus a piece rate of 20 cents per bundle inspected. His company accounts for inspection costs as manufacturing overhead. Because of a payroll department error in June, Rob was paid $500 plus a piece rate of 30 cents per bundle. He received gross wages totaling $1,100.
5. The materials purchasing manager purchased 5,000 units of component K2X from a new source at a price $12 below the standard unit price of $200. These components turned out to be of extremely poor quality with defects occurring at three times the standard rate of 5 percent. The higher rate of defects reduced the output of workers (who earn $8 per hour) from 20 units per hour to 15 units per hour on the units containing the discount components. Each finished unit contains one K2X component. To appease the workers (who were irate at having to work with inferior components), the production manager agreed to pay the workers an additional $0.25 for each of the components (good and bad) in the discount batch. Variable manufacturing overhead is applied at the rate of $4 per direct labor hour. The defective units also caused a 20-hour increase in total machine hours. The actual cost of electricity to run the machines is $2 per hour.

Required

For each of the preceding situations, determine which standard cost variance(s) will be affected, and compute the amount of the effect for one month on each variance. Indicate whether the effect is favorable or unfavorable. Assume that the standards are not changed in response to these situations. (Round calculations to two decimal places.)

P10-38[A]. Fixed Overhead Budget and Volume Variance

Lucky Seven Company assigns fixed overhead costs to inventory for external reporting purposes by using a predetermined standard overhead rate based on direct labor hours. The standard rate is based on a normal activity level of 10,000 standard allowed direct labor hours per year. There are five standard allowed hours for each unit of output. Budgeted fixed overhead costs are $200,000 per year. During 2009, the company produced 2,200 units of output, and actual fixed costs were $210,000.

Required

a. Determine the standard fixed overhead rate used to assign fixed costs to inventory.
b. Determine the amount of fixed overhead assigned to inventory in 2009.
c. Determine the fixed overhead budget variance.

P10-39[B]. Profit Center Performance Report

Record Rack is a store that specializes in the sale of recordings of classical music. Due to a recent upsurge in the popularity of J. S. Bach's works, Record Rack has established a separate room, Bach's Concert Room, dealing only in recordings of Bach music. The CDs are purchased from a wholesaler for $4.25 each. Although the standard retail price is $7.75 per CD, the manager of Bach's Concert Room can undertake price reductions and other sales promotions in an attempt to increase sales volume. With the exception of the cost of CDs, the operating costs of Bach's Concert Room are fixed. Presented are the budgeted and the actual August contribution statements of Bach's Concert Room.

RECORD RACK—BACH'S CONCERT ROOM
Budgeted and Actual Contribution Statements
For Month of August

	Actual	Budget
Unit sales	4,200	4,000
Unit selling price	$7.25	$7.75
Sales revenue	$30,450	$31,000
Cost of goods sold	(17,850)	(17,000)
Gross profit	12,600	14,000
Operating costs	(5,000)	(6,000)
Contribution to corporate costs and profits	$ 7,600	$ 8,000

Required

Compute variances to assist in evaluating the performance of Bach's Concert Room as a profit center. Was the performance satisfactory? Explain.

P10-40[B]. Profit Center Performance Report

Taco Town operates fast food restaurants in the food courts of shopping malls. It's main product is a burrito that requires beans (direct material) and food preparation (direct labor). The April budget for Taco Town's Riverside Mall restaurant was:

- Sales 21,000 burritos at $0.99 each
- Standard food cost of $0.20 per burrito (1/3 pound @ $0.60 per pound)
- Standard direct labor of $0.30 per burrito (1/30th hour @ $9.00 per hour)
- Fixed occupancy expenses (equip and rent) of $7,000

Actual April performance of the Riverside Mall restaurant was:

- Sales 18,000 burritos at $1.02 each
- Food cost of $3,136 for 5,600 pounds
- Direct labor cost of $6,720 for 800 hours
- Fixed occupancy expenses of $7,200

In early May, the manager received the following financial performance report:

TACO TOWN— RIVERSIDE MALL Performance Report For the Month of April	Actual	Budgeted	Variance
Revenues	$18,360	$20,790	$2,430 U
Food Cost	(3,136)	(4,200)	1,064 F
Labor Cost	(6,720)	(6,300)	420 U
Occupancy	(7,200)	(7,000)	200 U
Profit	$ 1,304	$ 3,290	$1,986 U

Required:

a. Partition variance into variances for 1) selling price and net sales volume, 2) food variances for price and quantity, and 3) labor variances for rate and efficiency.

b. Using the results of your analysis, prepare an alternative reconciliation of budgeted and actual profit. Be sure to include the occupancy variance.

c. Explain why the total variances for sales, food, and labor in your reconciliation differ from those originally presented to the restaurant manager.

P10-41[B]. Comprehensive Performance Report

Presented are the budgeted and actual contribution income statements of International Books Ltd. for October. The company has three responsibility centers: a Production Department, a Sales Department, and an Administration Department. Both the Production and Administration Departments are cost centers, and the Sales Department is a profit center.

INTERNATIONAL BOOKS, LTD.
Budgeted Contribution Income Statement
For Month of October

Sales (900 × $300)			$270,000
Less variable costs			
Variable cost of goods sold			
Direct materials (900 × $50)	$45,000		
Direct labor (900 × $20)	18,000		
Manufacturing overhead (900 × $30)	27,000	$ 90,000	
Selling (900 × $70)		63,000	(153,000)
Contribution margin			117,000
Less fixed costs			
Manufacturing overhead		40,000	
Selling		50,000	
Administrative		10,500	(100,500)
Net income			$ 16,500

INTERNATIONAL BOOKS, LTD.
Actual Contribution Income Statement
For Month of October

Sales (1,000 × $330)			$330,000
Less variable costs			
Cost of goods sold			
Direct materials	$50,000		
Direct labor	25,000		
Manufacturing overhead	35,000	$110,000	
Selling		100,000	(210,000)
Contribution margin			120,000
Less fixed costs			
Manufacturing overhead		38,000	
Selling		65,000	
Administrative		22,000	(125,000)
Net income (loss)			$ (5,000)

Required

a. Prepare a performance report for the Production Department that compares actual and allowed costs.
b. Prepare a performance report for selling expenses that compares actual and allowed costs.
c. Determine the sales price and the net sales volume variances.
d. Prepare a report that summarizes the performance of the Sales Department.
e. Determine the amount by which the Administration Department was over or under budget.
f. Prepare a report reconciling budgeted and actual net income. Your report should focus on the performance of each responsibility center.

CASES

C10-42. Discretionary Cost Center Performance Reports (LO1)

TruckMax had been extremely profitable, but the company has been hurt in recent years by competition and a failure to introduce new consumer products. In 2006, Tom Lopez became head of Consumer Products Research (CPR) and began a number of product development projects. Although the group had good ideas that led to the introduction of several promising products at the start of 2008, Lopez was criticized for poor cost control. The financial performance reports for CPR under his leadership were consistently unfavorable. Management was quite concerned about cost control because profits were low, and the company's cash budget indicated that additional borrowing would be required throughout 2008 to cover out-of-pocket costs. Because of his inability to exert proper cost control, Lopez was relieved of his responsibilities in 2008, and Gabriella Garcia became head of Consumer Products Research. Garcia vowed to improve the performance of CPR and scaled back CPR's development activities to obtain favorable financial performance reports.

By the end of 2009, the company had improved its market position, profitability, and cash position. At this time, the board of directors promoted Garcia to president, congratulating her for the contribution CPR made to the revitalization of the company, as well as her success in improving the financial performance of CPR. Garcia assured the board that the company's financial performance would improve even more in the future as she applied the same cost-reducing measures that had worked so well in CPR to the company as a whole.

Required

a. For the purpose of evaluating financial performance, what responsibility center classification should be given to the Consumer Products Research Department? What unique problems are associated with evaluating the financial performance of this type of responsibility center?
b. Compare the performances of Lopez and Garcia in the role as head of Consumer Products Research. Did Garcia do a much better job, thereby making her deserving of the promotion? Why or why not?

C10-43. Developing Cost Standards for Materials and Labor (LO2)

After several years of operating without a formal system of cost control, DeWalt Company, a tools manufacturer, has decided to implement a standard cost system. The system will first be established for the department that makes lug wrenches for automobile mechanics. The standard production batch size is 100 wrenches. The actual materials and labor required for eight randomly selected batches from last year's production are as follows:

Batch	Materials Used (in pounds)	Labor Used (in hours)
1	504.0	10.00
2	508.0	9.00
3	506.0	9.00
4	521.0	5.00
5	516.0	8.00
6	518.0	7.00
7	520.0	6.00
8	515.0	8.00
Average	513.5	7.75

Management has obtained the following recommendations concerning what the materials and labor quantity standards should be:

- The manufacturer of the equipment used in making the wrenches advertises in the toolmakers' trade journal that the machine the company uses can produce 100 wrenches with 500 pounds of direct materials and 5 labor hours. Company engineers believe the standards should be based on these facts.
- The accounting department believes more realistic standards would be 505 pounds and 5 hours.
- The production supervisor believes the standards should be 512 pounds and 7.75 hours.
- The production workers argue for standards of 522 pounds and 8 hours.

Required

a. State the arguments for and against each of the recommendations, as well as the probable effects of each recommendation on the quantity variance for materials and labor.

b. Which recommendation provides the best combination of cost control and motivation to the production workers? Explain.

C10-44. Behavioral Effect of Standard Costs (LO1, 2, 3)

Delaware Corp. has used a standard cost system for evaluating the performance of its responsibility center managers for three years. Top management believes that standard costing has not produced the cost savings or increases in productivity and profits promised by the accounting department. Large unfavorable variances are consistently reported for most cost categories, and employee morale has fallen since the system was installed. To help pinpoint the problem with the system, top management asked for separate evaluations of the system by the plant department manager, the accounting department manager, and the personnel department manager. Their responses are summarized here.

Plant Manager—The standards are unrealistic. They assume an ideal work environment that does not allow materials defects or errors by the workers or machines. Consequently, morale has gone down and productivity has declined. Standards should be based on expected actual prices and recent past averages for efficiency. Thus, if we improve over the past, we receive a favorable variance.

Accounting Manager—The goal of accounting reports is to measure performance against an absolute standard and the best approximation of that standard is ideal conditions. Cost standards should be comparable to "par" on a golf course. Just as the game of golf uses a handicap system to allow for differences in individual players' skills and scores, it could be necessary for management to interpret variances based on the circumstances that produced the variances. Accordingly, in one case, a given unfavorable variance could represent poor performance; in another case, it could represent good performance. The managers are just going to have to recognize these subtleties in standard cost systems and depend on upper management to be fair.

Personnel Manager—The key to employee productivity is employee satisfaction and a sense of accomplishment. A set of standards that can never be met denies managers of this vital motivator. The current standards would be appropriate in a laboratory with a controlled environment but not in the factory with its many variables. If we are to recapture our old "team spirit," we must give the managers a goal that they can achieve through hard work.

Required

Discuss the behavioral issues involved in Delaware Corp.'s standard cost dilemma. Evaluate each of the three responses (pros and cons) and recommend a course of action.

C10-45[B]. Evaluating a Companywide Performance Report

Mr. Micawber, the production supervisor, bursts into your office, carrying the company's 2009 performance report and thundering, "There is villainy here, sir! And I shall get to the bottom of it. I will not stop searching until I have found the answer! Why is Mr. Heep so down on my department? I thought we did a good job last year. But Heep claims my production people and I cost the company $31,500! I plead with you, sir, explain this performance report to me." Trying to calm Micawber, you take the report from him and ask to be left alone for 15 minutes. The report is as follows:

CRUPP COMPANY, LIMITED
Performance Report
For Year 2009

	Actual	Budget	Variance
Unit sales	7,500	5,000	
Sales	$262,500	$225,000	$37,500 F
Less manufacturing costs			
Direct materials	55,500	47,500	8,000 U
Direct labor	48,000	32,500	15,500 U
Manufacturing overhead	40,000	32,000*	8,000 U
Total	(143,500)	(112,000)	(31,500) U
Gross profit	119,000	113,000	6,000 F
Less selling and administrative expenses			
Selling (all fixed)	60,000	40,000	20,000 U
Administrative (all fixed)	55,000	50,000	5,000 U
Total	(115,000)	(90,000)	(25,000) U
Net income	$ 4,000	$ 23,000	$19,000 U
Performance summary			
Budgeted net income			$23,000
Sales department variances			
Sales revenue	$ 37,500 F		
Selling expenses	20,000 U	$17,500 F	
Administration department variances		5,000 U	
Production department variances		31,500 U	19,000 U
Actual net income			$ 4,000

*Includes fixed manufacturing overhead of $22,000.

Required

a. Evaluate the performance report. Is Mr. Heep correct, or is there "villainy here"?

b. Assume that the Sales Department is a profit center and that the Production and Administration Departments are cost centers. Determine the responsibility of each for cost, revenue, and income variances, and prepare a report reconciling budgeted and actual net income. Your report should focus on the performance of each responsibility center.

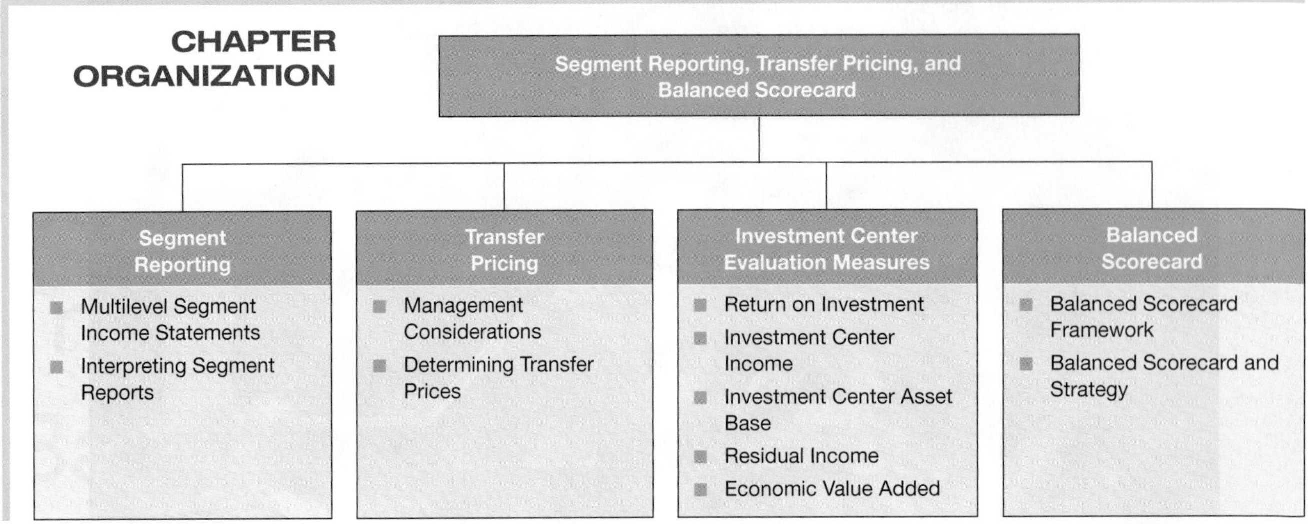

Organizations that maintain multiple product lines or that operate in several industries or in multiple markets often adopt a decentralized organization structure in which managers of major business units or strategic segments enjoy a high degree of autonomy. Examples of strategic business segments include the Chrysler Group of DaimlerChrysler and the Asia Pacific Group of The Coca-Cola Company. Sometimes companies establish segments within segments such as at Coca-Cola, whose Asia Pacific Group has separate business units for individual countries (Japan, Korea, etc.). In organizations such as DaimlerChrysler and Coca-Cola, upper management typically sets specific performance and profitability objectives for each segment and allows the manager of the segment the decision-making freedom to achieve those objectives.

This chapter explains the ways that an organization evaluates strategic business segments. It also considers transfer pricing and some of the problems that occur when one segment provides goods or services to another segment in the same organization.

STRATEGIC BUSINESS SEGMENTS AND SEGMENT REPORTING

LO1 Define a strategic business segment, and prepare and use segment reports.

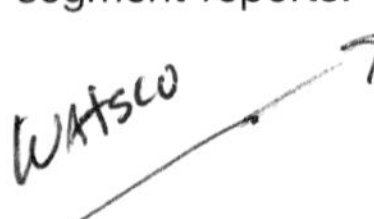

A **strategic business segment** has its own mission and set of goals. Its mission influences the decisions that top managers make in both short-run and long-run situations. The organization structure dictates to a large extent the type of financial segment reporting and other measures used to evaluate the segment and its managers. In decentralized organizations, for example, the reporting units (typically called *divisions*) normally are quasi-independent companies, often having their own computer system, cost accounting system, and administrative and marketing staffs. With this type structure, top management monitors the segments to ensure that these independent units are functioning for the benefit of the entire organization.

Although segment reports are normally produced to coincide with managerial lines of responsibility, some companies also produce segment reports for smaller slices of the business that do not represent separate responsibility centers. These parts of the business are not significant enough to be identified as "strategic" business units as defined, but management could want information about them on a continuing basis.

For example, AT&T has several strategic business units, including residential, small business, enterprise, and wireless. Financial reports are prepared for each of these units. Within the residential division, AT&T can also prepare segment reports on a more detailed basis to determine the profitability of its smaller segments, such as single-line and multi-line customers.

The point is that segment reporting is not constrained by lines of responsibility. A segment report can be prepared for any part of the business for which management believes more detailed information is useful in managing that portion of the business.

Segment reports are income statements for portions or segments of a business. Segment reporting is used primarily for internal purposes, although generally accepted accounting principles also require some disclosure of segment information for public corporations. Even though there are many different types of segment reports, at least three steps are basic to the preparation of all segment reports:

1. Identify the segments.
2. Assign direct costs to segments.
3. Allocate indirect costs to segments.

The format of segment income statements varies depending on the approach adopted by a company for reporting income statements internally. The income statement formats illustrated earlier in this text, including the functional format and the contribution format, can be used for segment reporting. Data availability can, however, dictate the format used. Regardless of the format adopted, it is essential that costs be separable into those directly traceable to the segments and those not directly traceable to segments.

Determining the segment reporting structure is often a more difficult decision than choosing the format for the segment income statements. Companies must decide whether to structure segment reporting along the lines of responsibility reporting, and whether segment reports will be prepared only on one level or on several levels.

For example, consider the hypothetical case of Digital Communications Company (DCC) that has two market divisions, three products, and two geographic territories. DCC's two divisions include the National Division (serving large national accounts) and the Regional Division (serving smaller regional and local accounts). DCC's three product lines are fiber optic cable, twisted pair cable, and coaxial cable. The company is organized into two geographic territories, Atlantic and Pacific. If DCC were using only a single-level segment reporting approach for all three groupings, one report would show the total company income statement broken down into the two divisions, a second report would show the total company income statement broken down into the three products, and a third report would show the total company income statement broken down into the two geographic territories.

Multilevel Segment Income Statements

If top management of DCC wants to know how much a particular product is contributing to the income of one of the two divisions or how much income a particular product in one of its two geographic territories contributes, it is necessary to prepare multilevel segment income statements. Since DCC sells three products and operates through two divisions in two territories, many combinations of divisions, products, and territories could be used in structuring the company's multilevel segment reporting. The goal is not to slice and dice the revenue and cost data in as many ways as possible but to provide useful and meaningful information to management. Therefore, deciding what type of reporting structure is most useful in managing the company is important.

This decision will be constrained to a great extent by data availability and cost. If there were no data constraints, DCC could look at the company's net income for every possible combination of division, product, and territory. The more data required to support a reporting system, however, the more costly it is to maintain the system, so management must determine the value and the cost of the additional information and make an appropriate cost-benefit judgment.

Panel A of Exhibit 11.1 illustrates multilevel segment reporting for DCC in which the first level shows the total company income statement segmented into the two market divisions, National Accounts and Regional Accounts. Panel B of Exhibit 11.1 shows a second-level report for DCC in which the National Division's segment income statement is broken down into its three product lines, fiber optic cable, twisted pair cable, and coaxial cable. Panel C then provides a third-level income statement for the National Division's fiber optic sales in each of the company's two geographic territories, the Atlantic and Pacific territories. The example in Exhibit 11.1 shows only part of the segment reports for DCC. The complete three-level set of segment reports would also break down the Regional Accounts Division into its product lines and all product lines for both divisions into geographic territories.

In the DCC example in Exhibit 11.1, the first reporting level is the company's divisions, its second reporting level is product lines, and the third is geographic territories. Another approach could be to structure the segment reports with product lines as the first level, geographic territories as the second level, and divisions as the third level. Still another approach would be to make product lines the first level, divisions the second level, and geographic territories the third level.

EXHIBIT 11.1 Multilevel Segment Reports

Panel A: First-Level Segment Report of Digital Communications Company—For Divisions (in thousands)

	Segments (Divisions)		
	National Accounts	Regional Accounts	Company Total
Sales	$100,000	$ 200,000	$300,000
Less variable costs	(55,000)	(95,000)	(150,000)
Contribution margin	45,000	105,000	150,000
Less direct fixed costs	(20,000)	(60,000)	(80,000)
Division margin	25,000	45,000	70,000
Less allocated segment costs	(10,000)	(25,000)	(35,000)
Division income	$ 15,000	$ 20,000	35,000
Less unallocated common costs			(12,000)
Net income			$ 23,000

Panel B: Second-Level Segment Report of the National Division—For Products (in thousands)

	Segments (Products)			
	Fiber Optic	Twisted Pair	Coaxial	National Accounts Total
Sales	$30,000	$40,000	$30,000	$100,000
Less variable costs	(15,000)	(19,000)	(21,000)	(55,000)
Contribution margin	15,000	21,000	9,000	45,000
Less direct fixed costs	(9,000)	(4,000)	(2,000)	(15,000)
Product margin	6,000	17,000	7,000	30,000
Less allocated segment costs	(5,000)	(4,000)	(1,000)	(10,000)
Product income	$ 1,000	$13,000	$ 6,000	20,000
Less unallocated common costs				(5,000)
National Division income				$ 15,000

Panel C: Third-Level Segment Report of the Fiber Optic Product Line in the National Division—For Geographic Territories (in thousands)

	Segments (Territories)		
	Atlantic	Pacific	Fiber Optic Total
Sales	$20,000	$10,000	$30,000
Less variable costs	(11,000)	(4,000)	(15,000)
Contribution margin	9,000	6,000	15,000
Less direct fixed costs	(3,000)	(4,000)	(7,000)
Territory margin	6,000	2,000	8,000
Less allocated segment costs	(2,000)	(3,000)	(5,000)
Territory income	$ 4,000	$(1,000)	3,000
Less unallocated common costs			(2,000)
Fiber optic income			$ 1,000

Regardless of how many different ways the company segments the income statements, at least one set of segment reports follows the company's responsibility reporting system; therefore, one of the segment reports has the operating divisions as the first level. If each division has a product manager for each product, the division segment reports are broken down by products. Finally, if each product within each division has a territory manager, the product segment reports are broken down by territories.

Interpreting Segment Reports

Exhibit 11.1 reports costs in four categories: variable costs, direct fixed costs, allocated common costs, and unallocated common costs. Variable costs vary in proportion to the level of sales and are subtracted from sales in calculating contribution margin. **Direct segment fixed costs** are nonvariable costs directly traceable to the segments incurred for the specific benefit of the respective segments. **Segment margin** equals the contribution margin minus the direct segment fixed costs. For DCC, segment margins are referred to as *division margins, product margins,* and *territory margins.* Segment margins represent the amount that a segment contributes directly to the company's profitability in the short run.

Common segment costs are incurred for the common benefit of all related segments shown on a segment income statement. In some cases, allocating some common costs is reasonable even though they cannot be directly traced to the various segments based on benefits received. For example, if segments share common space, allocating all space-related costs to the segments based on building space occupied could be appropriate. If there is no reasonable basis for allocating common costs, they should not be allocated to the segments. In Panel C of Exhibit 11.1, if advertising costs to promote the company's fiber optic products on national television could not be reasonably allocated to the two geographic territories, they would be charged to the fiber optic product line as an unallocated common cost, not to the individual territories.

If some portion of common costs can be reasonably allocated to the segments, those allocated costs are subtracted from the segment margins to determine segment income. Hence, **segment income** represents all revenues of the segment minus all costs directly or indirectly charged to it.

To properly interpret segment income, we should ask whether segment income represents the amount by which net income of the company will change if that segment is discontinued. For example, if DCC discontinues the coaxial product line in the National Division, does this mean that DCC's net income will decrease by $6 million? Also, does it mean that if the National Division stops selling fiber optic cable in the Pacific territory, DCC's net income will increase by $1 million?

The answer to these questions depends on whether the costs allocated to the segments are avoidable. **Avoidable common costs** are allocated common costs that eventually can be avoided (that is, can be eliminated) if a segment is discontinued. If all allocated common costs are avoidable, the effect of discontinuing the segment on corporate profitability equals the amount of segment income. In most cases, the short-term impact of discontinuing a segment equals the segment margin because allocated costs are capacity costs that cannot be adjusted in the short run. Over time, the company should be able to adjust capacity and eliminate some, or possibly all, of the allocated common costs or find productive uses for that capacity in other segments of the business. The unallocated common costs cannot be changed readily in the short term or the long term without causing major disruptions to the company and its strategy. Therefore, over the long term, the impact of discontinuing a segment should be, approximately, it's segment income.

If DCC discontinues selling fiber optic cable in the Pacific territory (see Exhibit 11.1, Panel C) the short-term effect on the company's profits will probably be a $2 million reduction of profits, which equals the Pacific territory's margin. The revenues and costs that make up the Pacific territory margin would all be lost if fiber optic sales were discontinued in the Pacific territory, but the $3 million of common costs allocated to the Pacific territory would continue, at least in the short term. Over the long term, however, after adjusting the capacity for selling this product in the Pacific territory and eliminating the $3 million of allocated common costs, the effect of discontinuing fiber optics in the Pacific territory on profits should be an increase of about $1 million, which is the amount of the segment loss for fiber optics in the Pacific territory.

To summarize, generally, segment margin is relevant for measuring the short-term effects of decisions to continue or discontinue a segment; however, segment income is relevant for measuring the long-term effects of decisions to continue or discontinue.

MID-CHAPTER REVIEW

Refer to the Digital Communications (DCC) example in Exhibit 11.1, Panel B. The following additional information is provided for the Coaxial product line in the National Division:

Sales—Atlantic territory	$12,000
Sales—Pacific territory	18,000
Direct fixed cost—Atlantic territory	500
Direct fixed cost—Pacific territory	800
Allocated segment costs—Atlantic territory	200
Allocated segment costs—Pacific territory	600

Required:

a. Prepare a geographic territory segment report of the Coaxial product line in the National division.

b. Explain why the total of the Territory Margins for geographic segments of the Coaxial product line does not equal the product margin of the Coaxial product segment in Panel B of Exhibit 11.1.

Solution

a.

	Segments (Territories)		Coaxial
	Atlantic	Pacific	Total
Sales	$12,000	$18,000	$30,000
Less variable costs	(8,400)	(12,600)	(21,000)
Contribution margin	3,600	5,400	9,000
Less direct fixed costs	(500)	(800)	(1,300)
Territory margin	3,100	4,600	7,700
Less allocated segment costs	(200)	(600)	(800)
Territory income	$ 2,900	$ 4,000	6,900
Less unallocated common costs			(900)
Fiber optic income			$ 6,000

b. The Product Margin for the Coaxial product line in Panel B was $7,000 and reflected $2,000 of direct fixed costs that were attributable to that product line in the National Division. However, when the Coaxial product segment income statement is further segmented into geographic segments, only $1,300 of the $2,000 could be directly traced to the two geographic territories. Therefore, $700 of costs that were direct costs at the product segment level became common costs (either allocated or unallocated) at the territory segment level. This reflects the general notion that as segmentation is extended down to lower and lower levels, the total amount of common costs increase and direct costs decrease. Hence, segmentation rarely is extended to more than three levels.

Not a reallocation of profit

TRANSFER PRICING

LO2 Explain transfer pricing and assess alternative transfer-pricing methods.

To determine whether each division is achieving its organizational objectives, managers must be accountable for the goods and services they acquire, both externally and internally. When goods or services are exchanged internally between segments of a decentralized organization, the way that the transferor and the transferee will report the transfer must be determined, either by negotiations between the two segments or by corporate policy. A **transfer price** is the internal value assigned a product or service that one division provides to another. The transfer price is recognized as revenue by the division providing goods or services and as expense (or cost) by the division receiving them. Transfer-pricing transactions normally occur between profit or investment centers rather than between cost centers of an organization; however, managers often consider cost allocations between cost centers as a type of transfer price. The focus in this chapter is on transfers between responsibility centers that are evaluated based on profits.

Management Considerations

The desire of the selling and buying divisions of the same company to maximize their individual performance measures often creates transfer-pricing problems. Acting as independent units, divisions could take actions that are not in the best interest(s) of the organization as a whole. The three examples that follow illustrate the need for organizations to maintain a *corporate* profit-maximizing viewpoint while attempting to allow *divisional* autonomy and responsibility.

OmniTech, Inc., has five divisions, some of which transfer products and product components to other OmniTech divisions. The BioTech Division manufactures two products, Alpha and Beta. It sells Alpha externally for $50 per unit and transfers Beta to the GenTech Division for $60 per unit. The costs associated with the two products follow:

	Product	
	Alpha	Beta
Variable costs		
Direct materials	$15	$14
Direct labor	5	10
Variable manufacturing overhead	5	16
Selling	4	0
Fixed Costs		
Fixed manufacturing overhead	6	15
Total	$35	$55

An external company has just proposed to supply a Beta substitute product to the GenTech Division at a price of $52. From the company's viewpoint, this is merely a make or buy decision. The relevant costs are the differential outlay costs of the alternative actions. Assuming that the fixed manufacturing costs of the BioTech Division are unavoidable, the relevant costs of this proposal from the company's perspective are as follows:

Buy		$52
Make		
Direct materials	$14	
Direct labor	10	
Variable manufacturing overhead	16	(40)
Difference		$12

From the corporate viewpoint, the best decision is for the product to be transferred since the relevant cost is $40 rather than to buy it from an external source for $52. The decision for the GenTech Division management is basically one of cost minimization: Buy from the source that charges the lowest price. If BioTech is not willing to transfer Beta at a price of $52 or less, the GenTech management could go to the external supplier to maximize the division's profits. (Although GenTech's managers are concerned about the cost of Beta, they are also concerned about the quality of the goods. If the $52 product does not meet its quality standards, GenTech could decide to buy from BioTech at the higher price. For this discussion, assume that the internal and external products are identical; therefore, acting in its best interest, GenTech purchases Beta for $52 from the external source unless BioTech can match the price.)

Prior to GenTech's receipt of the external offer, BioTech had been transferring Beta to GenTech for $60. BioTech must decide whether to reduce the contribution margin on its transfers of Beta to GenTech and, therefore, lower divisional profits or to try to find an alternative use for its resources. Of course, corporate management could intervene and require the internal transfer even though it would hurt BioTech's profits.

As the second example, assume that the BioTech Division has the option to sell an equivalent amount of Beta externally for $60 per unit if the GenTech Division discontinues its transfers from BioTech. Now the decision for BioTech's management is simple: Sell to the buyer willing to pay the most. From the corporate viewpoint, it is best for BioTech to sell to the external buyer for $60 and for GenTech to purchase from the external provider for $52.

To examine a slightly different transfer-pricing conflict, assume that the BioTech Division can sell all the Alpha that it can produce (it is operating at capacity). Also assume that there is no external market for Beta, but there is a one-to-one trade-off between the production of Alpha and Beta, which use equal amounts of the BioTech Division's limited capacity.

The corporation still regards this as a make or buy decision, but the costs of producing Beta have changed. The cost of Beta now includes an outlay cost and an opportunity cost. The outlay cost of Beta is its variable cost of $40 ($14 + $10 + $16), as previously computed. Beta's opportunity cost is the net benefit foregone if the BioTech Division's limited capacity is used to produce Beta rather than Alpha:

Selling price of Alpha		$50
Outlay costs of Alpha		
Direct materials	$15	
Direct labor	5	
Variable manufacturing overhead	5	
Variable selling	4	(29)
Opportunity cost of making Beta		$21

Accordingly, the relevant costs in the make or buy decision follow.

Make		
Outlay cost of Beta	$40	
Opportunity cost of Beta	21	$61
Buy		$52

From the corporate viewpoint, GenTech should purchase Beta from the outside supplier for $52 because in this case it costs $61 to make the product. If there were no outside suppliers, the corporation's relevant cost of manufacturing Beta would be $61. This is another way of saying that the GenTech Division should not acquire Beta internally unless its revenues cover all outlay costs (including the $40 in the BioTech Division) and provide a contribution of at least $21 ($61 − $40). From the corporate viewpoint, the relevant costs in make or buy decisions are the external price, the outlay costs to manufacture, and the opportunity cost to manufacture. The opportunity cost is zero if there is excess capacity.

Determining Transfer Prices

As illustrated, the transfer price of goods or services can be subject to much controversy. The most widely used and discussed transfer prices are covered in this section. See the following Business Insight box for a discussion of transfer pricing. Although a price must be agreed upon for each item or service transferred between divisions, the selection of the pricing method depends on many factors. The conditions surrounding the transfer determine which of the alternative methods discussed subsequently is selected.

Although no method is likely to be ideal, one must be selected if the profit or investment center concept is used. In considering each method, observe that each transfer results in a revenue entry on the supplier's books and a cost entry on the receiver's books. Transfers can be considered as sales by the supplier and as purchases by the receiver.

Market Price

When there is an existing market with established prices for an intermediate product and the transfer actions of the company will not affect prices, market prices are ideal transfer prices. If divisions are free to buy and sell outside the firm, the use of market prices preserves divisional autonomy and leads divisions to act in a manner that maximizes corporate goal congruence. Unfortunately, not all product transfers have equivalent external markets. Furthermore, the divisions should carefully evaluate whether the market price is competitive or controlled by one or two large companies. When substantial selling expenses are associated with outside sales, many firms specify the transfer price as market price less selling expenses. The internal sale may not require the incurrence of costs to get and fill the order.

BUSINESS INSIGHT **Citigroup's Transfer-Pricing Problems**

Fortune magazine interviewed the CEO of **Citigroup** in connection with its annual "Fortune 500" article. Citigroup is a diversified financial company that includes such major financial brands as Primerica, Salomon Smith Barney, Citibank, and Travelers. Following is an excerpt from that article discussing some problems of decentralization and transfer pricing at Citigroup.

> In a company of Citi's size and complexity, there are dozens of issues—business overlaps, competitive threats, regulations—that cut across divisions. In an institution that promotes cross-selling, for example, there is always the question of how the financial spoils are divided up between the two divisions—a matter that goes under the name "transfer pricing." For example, suppose that a Salomon Smith Barney financial consultant sells a mutual fund "manufactured" by Citi's investment management division. What's the price that the IM division receives? The answer, since it determines profit, is extremely important to executives getting paid (and paying their people) according to what their own bottom line looks like . . . . [The CEO] says testily that he wishes people "would think about doing the business first, and worry about who gets the credit second." But, trying to mediate, he also has his financial people studying plans for internally double-counting revenues, so as to make profits (or losses) accrue to both parties involved in a cross-selling event.[1]

To illustrate using the OmniTech example, assume that product Alpha of the BioTech Division can be sold competitively at $50 per unit or transferred to a third division, the Quantum Division, for additional processing. Under most situations, the BioTech Division will never sell Alpha for less than $50, and the Quantum Division will likewise never pay more than $50 for it. However, if any variable expenses related to marketing and shipping can be eliminated by divisional transfers, these costs are generally subtracted from the competitive market price. In our illustration in which variable selling expenses are $4 for Alpha, the transfer price could be reduced to $46 ($50 − $4). A price between $46 and $50 would probably be better than either extreme price. To the extent that these transfer prices represent a nearly competitive situation, the profitability of each division can then be fairly evaluated.

Variable Costs

If excess capacity exists in the supplying division, establishing a transfer price equal to variable costs leads the purchasing division to act in a manner that is optimal from the corporation's viewpoint. The buying division has the corporation's variable cost as its own variable cost as it enters the external market. Unfortunately, establishing the transfer price at variable cost causes the supplying division to report zero profits or a loss equal to any fixed costs. If excess capacity does not exist, establishing a transfer price at variable cost would not lead to optimal action because the supplying division would have to forego external sales that include a markup for fixed costs and profits. If Beta could be sold externally for $60, the BioTech Division would not want to transfer Beta to the GenTech Division for a $40 transfer price based on the following variable costs:

Direct materials	$14
Direct labor	10
Variable manufacturing overhead	16
Total variable costs	$40

The BioTech Division would much rather sell outside the company for $60, which covers variable costs and provides a profit contribution margin of $20:

Selling price of Beta	$60
Variable costs	(40)
Contribution margin	$20

[1] Carol J. Loomis, "The Fortune 500, No. 6 Sandy Weill's Monster," *Fortune*, April 16, 2001

Variable Costs Plus Opportunity Costs

From the organization's viewpoint, this is the optimal transfer price. Because all relevant costs are included in the transfer price, the purchasing division is led to act in a manner optimal for the overall company, whether or not excess capacity exists.

With excess capacity in the supplying division, the transfer price is the variable cost per unit. Without excess capacity, the transfer price is the sum of the variable and opportunity costs. Following this rule in the previous example, if the BioTech Division had excess capacity, the transfer price of Beta would be set at Beta's variable costs of $40 per unit. At this transfer price, the GenTech Division would buy Beta internally, rather than externally at $52 per unit. If the BioTech Division cannot sell Beta externally but can sell all the Alpha it can produce and is operating at capacity, the transfer price per unit would be set at $61, the sum of Beta's variable and opportunity costs ($40 + $21). (Refer back two pages.) At this transfer price, the GenTech Division would buy Beta externally for $52. In both situations, the management of the GenTech Division has acted in accordance with the organization's profit-maximizing goal.

There are two problems with this method. First, when the supplying division has excess capacity, establishing the transfer price at variable cost causes the supplying division to report zero profits or a loss equal to any fixed costs. Second, determining opportunity costs when the supplying division produces several products is difficult. If the problems with the previously mentioned transfer-pricing methods are too great, three other methods can be used: absorption cost plus markup, negotiated prices, and dual prices.

Absorption Cost Plus Markup

According to absorption costing, all variable and fixed manufacturing costs are product costs. Pricing internal transfers at absorption cost eliminates the supplying division's reported loss on each product that can occur using a variable cost transfer price. Absorption cost plus markup provides the supplying division a contribution toward unallocated costs. In "cost-plus" transfer pricing, "cost" should be defined as standard cost rather than as actual cost. This prevents the supplying division from passing on the cost of inefficient operations to other divisions, and it allows the buying division to know its cost in advance of purchase. Even though cost-plus transfer prices may not maximize company profits, they are widely used. Their popularity stems from several factors, including ease of implementation, justifiability, and perceived fairness. Once everyone agrees on absorption cost plus markup pricing rules, internal disputes are minimized.

Negotiated Prices

Negotiated transfer prices are used when the supplying and buying divisions independently agree on a price. As with market-based transfer prices, negotiated transfer prices are believed to preserve divisional autonomy. Negotiated transfer prices can lead to some suboptimal decisions, but this is regarded as a small price to pay for other benefits of decentralization. When they use negotiated transfer prices, some corporations establish arbitration procedures to help settle disputes between divisions. However, the existence of an arbitrator with any real or perceived authority reduces divisional autonomy.

Negotiated prices should have market prices as their ceiling and variable costs as their floor. Although frequently used when an external market for the product or component exists, the most common use of negotiated prices occurs when no identical-product external market exists. Negotiations could start with a floor price plus add-ons such as overhead and profit markups or with a ceiling price less adjustments for selling and administrative expenses and allowances for quantity discounts. When no identical-product external market exists, the market price for a similar completed product can be used, less the estimated cost of completing the product from the transfer stage to the completed stage.

Dual Prices

Dual prices exist when a company allows a difference in the supplier's and receiver's transfer prices for the same product. This method allegedly minimizes internal squabbles of division managers and problems of conflicting divisional and corporate goals. The supplier's transfer price normally approximates market price, which allows the selling division to show a "normal" profit on items that it transfers internally. The receiver's price is usually the internal cost of the product or service, calculated as variable cost plus opportunity cost. This ensures that the buying division will make an internal transfer when it is in the best interest of the company to do so.

In most cases, a market-based transfer price achieves the optimal outcome for both the divisions and the company as a whole. As discussed earlier, an exception occurs when a division is operating below full capacity and has no alternative use for its excess capacity. In this case, it is best for the company to have an internal transfer; therefore, to ensure that the receiving division makes an internal transfer, the company must require the internal transfer as long as its price does not exceed the established market rate. The only time an external price is more attractive when excess capacity exists is when the external price is below the variable cost of the providing internal division, and that scenario is highly unlikely.

A potential transfer-pricing problem exists when divisions exchange goods or services for which no established market exists. For example, suppose that a company is operating its information technology (IT) service department as a profit center that transfers services to other profit center departments using a cost-plus transfer price. If the departments using IT services can choose to use those services or to replicate them inside their departments, users might not make a decision that is best for the company. It could be best for the company to have all IT services come from the IT department, but other profit centers could believe that they can provide those services for themselves at lower cost. In this case, the company must decide how important it is to maintain the independence of its profit center. In the interest of maintaining a strong profit center philosophy, top management can decide that it is acceptable to suboptimize by allowing profit centers to provide IT services for themselves.

The ideal transfer-pricing arrangement is seldom the same for both the providing and receiving divisions for every situation. In these cases, what is good for one division is likely not to be good for the other division resulting in no transfer, even though a transfer could achieve corporate goals. These conflicts are sometimes overcome by having a higher-ranking manager impose a transfer price and insist that a transfer be made. Managers in organizations that have a policy of decentralization, however, often regard these orders as undermining their autonomy. Therefore, the imposition of a price could solve the corporate profit optimization problem but create other problems regarding the company's organization strategy. Transfer pricing thus becomes a problem with no ideal solutions.

The previous discussion has focused on the challenges of establishing transfer prices that motivate managers to make decisions that are beneficial to their divisions as well as the overall company. However, recent research, discussed in the following Research Insight box, concluded that there are often price benefits when dealing with outside vendors, if the company has the option of acquiring the goods or services internally.

RESEARCH INSIGHT **Transfer Pricing and External Competition**

Researchers found that a firm can glean benefits from discussing transfer-pricing problems with external suppliers. Though transfer prices above marginal cost introduce interdivision coordination problems, they also reduce a firm's willingness to pay outside suppliers. Knowing that costly internal transfers will eat into demand, the supplier is more willing to set lower prices. Such supplier discounts can make decentralization worthwhile for the firm. The benefit of decentralization is shown to be robust in both downstream and upstream competition.[2]

INVESTMENT CENTER EVALUATION MEASURES

LO3 Determine and contrast return on investment, residual income and economic value added.

Three of the most common measures of investment center performance, return on investment, residual income, and economic value added, are discussed in the following sections. Several supporting components of these measures that help clarify the applications are also presented.

Return on Investment

Return on investment (ROI) is a measure of the earnings per dollar of investment. (This assumes that financing decisions are made at the corporate level rather than the division level. Hence, the corporation's investment in the division equals the division's asset base. The return on investment of an investment center is computed by dividing the income of the center by its asset base (usually total assets):

$$\text{ROI} = \frac{\textbf{Investment center income}}{\textbf{Investment center asset base}}$$

[2] "Anil Arya and Brian Mittendorf, "Interacting Supply Chain Distortions: The Pricing of Internal Transfers and External Procurement," *The Accounting Review*, May 2007.

ROI can be disaggregated into investment turnover times the return-on-sales ratio:

$$\textbf{ROI} = \textbf{Investment turnover} \times \textbf{Return-on-sales}$$

where

$$\textbf{Investment turnover} = \frac{\textbf{Sales}}{\textbf{Investment center asset base}}$$

and

$$\textbf{Return-on-sales} = \frac{\textbf{Investment center income}}{\textbf{Sales}}$$

When investment turnover is multiplied by return-on-sales, the product is the same as investment center income divided by investment center asset base:

$$\textbf{ROI} = \frac{\textbf{Sales}}{\textbf{Investment center base}} \times \frac{\textbf{Investment center income}}{\textbf{Sales}} = \frac{\textbf{Investment center income}}{\textbf{Investment center asset base}}$$

Once ROI has been computed, it is compared to some previously identified performance criteria. These include the investment center's previous ROI, overall company ROI, the ROI of similar divisions, or the ROI of nonaffiliated companies that operate in similar markets. The breakdown of ROI into investment turnover and return-on-sales is useful in determining the source of variance in overall performance.

To illustrate the computation and use of ROI, the following information is available concerning the 2009 operations of North American Steel:

Division	Net Assets	Sales	Divisional Income
Maine	$8,000,000	$12,000,000	$1,440,000
Alberta	4,000,000	8,000,000	960,000
Missouri	7,500,000	5,000,000	1,650,000
Tijuana	3,800,000	5,700,000	1,026,000

Using this information and the preceding equations, a set of Dupont performance measures can be presented as shown in Exhibit 11.2. To illustrate, Maine Division earned a return on its investment base of 18 percent ($1,440,000 ÷ $8,000,000), consisting of an investment turnover of 1.50 ($12,000,000 ÷ $8,000,000) and a return-on-sales of 0.12 ($1,440,000 ÷ $12,000,000). Using such an analysis, the company has three measurement criteria with which to evaluate the performance of Maine Division: (1) ROI, (2) investment turnover, and (3) return-on-sales.

For 2009, North American chose to evaluate its divisions based on company ROI and its interrelated components of investment turnover and return-on-sales. Because each division is different in size, the company evaluation standard is not a simple average of the divisions but is based on desired relationships between assets, sales, and income.

Based on ROI, the Tijuana Division had the best performance, the Alberta Division excelled in investment turnover, and the Missouri Division had the highest return-on-sales. From Exhibit 11.2, the Tijuana Division clearly had the best year because it was the only division that exceeded each of the company's performance criteria. For 2009, each division equaled or exceeded the minimum ROI established by the company even though the component criteria of ROI were not always achieved.

To properly evaluate each division, the company should study the underlying components of ROI. For the Maine Division, management would want to know why the minimum investment turnover was exceeded while the return-on-sales minimum was not. The Maine Division could have incurred unfavorable cost variances by producing inefficiently. As a result of inefficient production, the return-on-sales declined to a point below the minimum desired level. Evaluating a large operating division based on one financial indicator is difficult. Management should select several key indicators of performance when conducting periodic reviews of its operating segments.

A similar analysis of ROI and its components is useful for planning. In developing plans for 2010, management wants to know the possible effect of changes in the major elements of ROI for the Maine

EXHIBIT 11.2 Performance Evaluation Data

NORTH AMERICAN STEEL
Performance Measures
For Year Ending June 30, 2009

	Performance Measures		
	Investment Turnover ×	**Return-on-Sales** =	**ROI**
Operating unit			
Maine	1.50	0.12	0.18
Alberta	2.00	0.12	0.24
Missouri	0.67	0.33	0.22
Tijuana	1.50	0.18	0.27
Company performance criteria			
Projected minimums	1.20	0.15	0.18

Division. Sensitivity analysis can be used to predict the impact of changes in sales, the investment center asset base, or the investment center income.

Assuming the investment base is unchanged, a projected ROI can be determined for the Maine Division for a sales goal of \$16,000,000 and an income goal of \$1,600,000:

$$\begin{aligned}\textbf{ROI} &= \frac{\textbf{Sales}}{\textbf{Investment center asset base}} \times \frac{\textbf{Investment center income}}{\textbf{Sales}} \\ &= \frac{\$16{,}000{,}000}{\$8{,}000{,}000} \times \frac{\$1{,}600{,}000}{\$16{,}000{,}000} \\ &= 2.0 \times 0.10 \\ &= 0.20, \text{ or 20 percent.}\end{aligned}$$

ROI increased from 18 to 20 percent, even though the return-on-sales decreased from 12 to 10 percent. The change in turnover from 1.5 to 2.0 more than offset the reduced return-on-sales.

Sensitivity analysis can involve changing only one factor or a combination of factors in the ROI model. When more than one factor is changed, it is important to analyze exactly how much change is caused by each factor.

Statistics such as ROI, investment turnover, and return-on-sales mean little by themselves. They take on meaning only when compared with an objective, a trend, another division, a competitor, or an industry average. Many businesses establish minimum ROIs for each of their divisions, expecting them to attain or exceed this minimum return. The salaries, bonuses, and promotions of division managers can be tied directly to their division's ROI. Without other evaluation techniques, managers often strive for ROI maximization, sometimes to the long-run detriment of the entire organization.

Investment Center Income

Despite the relevance and conceptual simplicity of ROI, a division's ROI cannot be determined until management decides how to measure divisional income and investment. Divisional income equals divisional revenues less divisional operating expenses. Determining divisional revenues is usually a relatively easy task since revenues are typically generated and recorded at the division level, but determining total operating expenses for divisions is more complicated. Because many expenses are incurred at the corporate level for the common benefit of the various operating divisions and to support corporate headquarters operations, the cost assignment issues discussed early in this chapter affect investment center income.

Direct division expenses are always included in division operating expenses, but there are conflicting viewpoints about how to deal with common corporate expenses. In corporate annual reports, many companies are required to provide segment revenues and expenses segmented by product lines, geographic territories, customer markets, and so on. Companies also show operating income for their various segments in their annual reports, but they include a category called *corporate* or *unallocated* for company expenses that cannot be reasonably allocated to the various segments. For example, the Ericsson, Inc. annual report for a recent year includes the following breakdown of its operating income by segments (stated in millions of Swedish kronas):

Networks	17,398 SEK
Professional Services	6,394
Multimedia	(135)
Phones	7,108
Unallocated	(119)
Total operating income	30,646 SEK

"Unallocated" typically includes costs for corporate staffs, certain goodwill writeoffs, and nonoperational gains and losses.

For internal segment reporting, some companies do not allocate corporate costs that cannot be associated closely with individual segments. Other companies insist on allocating all common corporate costs to the operating divisions to emphasize that the company does not earn a profit until revenues have covered all costs. Some top managers believe that since only operating divisions produce revenues, they should also bear all costs, including corporate costs. These managers want to ensure that the sum of the division income for the various segments equals the total income for the company.

Division managers do not control corporate costs; therefore, these costs are seldom relevant in evaluating a division manager's performance. To deal with this conflict, some companies allocate some, or possibly all, common corporate costs in reporting segment operating income, but for ROI calculation purposes exclude allocated corporate costs that are not closely associated with the divisions. These companies include in the ROI calculation costs that represent an identifiable benefit to the divisions but not general corporate costs that provide no identifiable benefits to the divisions. In practice, the treatment of corporate costs for division performance evaluation varies widely.

Investment Center Asset Base

Because the primary purpose for computing ROI is to evaluate the effectiveness of a division's operating management in using the assets entrusted to them, most organizations define *investment* as the average total assets of a division during the evaluation period. For most companies, the *investment base* is defined as each division's operating assets. These normally include those assets held for productive use, such as accounts receivable, inventory, and plant and equipment. Nonproductive assets, such as land for a future plant site, are not included in the investment base of a division but in the investment base for the company.

General corporate assets allocated to divisions should not be included in their bases. Although the divisions might need additional administrative facilities if they were truly independent, they have no control over the headquarters' facilities. The joint nature and use of corporate facility-level expenses make any allocation arbitrary.

Other Valuation Issues

Once divisional investment and income have been operationally defined and ROI computations have been made, the significance of the resulting ratios can still be questioned. Return on investment can be overstated in terms of constant dollars because inflation as well as arbitrary inventory and depreciation procedures cause an undervaluation of the inventory and fixed assets included in the investment center asset base. Asset measurement is particularly troublesome if inventories are valued at last-in, first-out (LIFO) cost and fixed assets were acquired many years ago. A division manager could hesitate to replace an old, inefficient asset with a new, efficient one because the replacement could lower income and ROI through an increased investment base and increased depreciation.

To improve the comparability between divisions with old and new assets when computing ROI, some firms value assets at original cost rather than at net book value (cost less accumulated depreciation). This procedure does not reflect inflation, however. An old asset that cost $120,000 ten years ago is still being compared with an asset that costs $200,000 today. A better solution could be to value old assets at their replacement cost, although obtaining replacement costs are often difficult to determine.

MANAGERIAL DECISION **You are the Division Vice President**

Division managers in your company are evaluated primarily based on division return on investment, and you recently received financial reports for your division for the most recent period and discovered that the ROI for your division was 14.5%; whereas, the target ROI for your division set by the CFO and the CEO was 15%. What action can you take to try to avoid missing your performance target for the next period? [Answer, p. 391]

Residual Income

Residual income is an often-mentioned alternative to ROI for measuring investment center performance. **Residual income** is the excess of investment center income over the minimum rate of return set by top management. The minimum rate of return represents the rate that can be earned on alternative investments of similar risks, which is the opportunity cost of the investment.

The minimum dollar return is computed as a percentage of the investment center's asset base. When residual income is the primary basis of evaluation, the management of each investment center is encouraged to maximize residual income rather than ROI. To illustrate the computation, assume that a company requires a minimum return of 12 percent on each division's investment base. The residual income of a division with an annual net operating income of $2,000,000 and an investment base of $15,000,000 is $200,000 as computed here:

Division income	$2,000,000
Minimum return ($15,000,000 × 0.12)	(1,800,000)
Residual income.	$ 200,000

Economic Value Added

A variation of residual income, referred to as **economic value added** or **EVA®**, is also often used as a basis for evaluating investment center performance. (The term EVA is a registered trademark of the financial consulting firm of Stern Stewart and Company.) EVA is equal to income after taxes less the cost of capital employed. The three significant changes from the residual income computation in applying EVA are the use of an organization's weighted average cost of capital as the minimum return, net assets as the evaluation base, and after-tax income. **Weighted average cost of capital** is an average of the after-tax cost of all long-term borrowing and the cost of equity[3]; **net assets** are total assets less current liabilities. Economic value is added only if a division's taxable income exceeds its net cost of investing.

Using the preceding situation, assume that the company has a cost of capital of 10 percent, $1,800,000 in current liabilities, and a 30 percent tax rate. The economic value-added is $80,000, computed as follows:

Division income after taxes ($2,000,000 × 0.70)	$1,400,000
Cost of capital employed [($15,000,000 − $1,800,000) × 0.10]	(1,320,000)
Economic value added.	$ 80,000

Another differentiating characteristic of the EVA model is that it usually corrects for potential distortions in economic net income caused by generally accepted accounting principles (GAAP). In calculating EVA, the user can abandon any accounting principles that are viewed as distorting the measurement of wealth creation. In practice, EVA consultants have identified up to 150 different adjustments to GAAP income and equity that must be made to restore equity and income to their true economic values. Most

[3] Weighted Average Cost of Capital computations are covered in introductory corporate finance textbooks.

companies use no more than about five adjustments (such as the capitalization of research and development cost and the elimination of goodwill write-offs).

Proponents of EVA argue that it is the best measure of managerial performance from the standpoint of maximizing the market value added to a firm through managerial decisions. They maintain that **market value added (MVA)**, which is the increase in market value of the firm for the period, is the definitive measure of wealth creation and that MVA is maximized by maximizing EVA. By maximizing the excess of economic net income over the cost of all outside capital invested in the firm, the firm should maximize its MVA in the long run.

One might ask why we should use EVA to estimate managerial contribution to the maximization of MVA, when we could simply measure how much market value has been added to the firm by considering changes in stock prices. In theory, measuring market success on stock price changes would work, but in practice this does not work well because of short-run changes in market prices caused by overall market factors, not just firm-specific factors. Also, many firms are not publicly traded, which makes determining market value changes difficult. Finally, companies want to measure managerial performance over specific segments of a firm, as well as the firm as a whole, but market values for individual segments are seldom available.

EVA provides a good operational metric for assessing managers' performance in terms of maximizing MVA over time. An advantage of EVA is that it is a model that can also be used to guide managerial action. Companies that use EVA for evaluating performance use it in making a broad range of decisions such as evaluating capital expenditure proposals, adding or dropping a product line, or acquiring another company. Only alternatives that provide economic value are accepted. The following Research Insight box discusses the impact of adopting an EVA financial management system on performances.

RESEARCH INSIGHT **Evidence Supports EVA**

Research has focused on the effectiveness of EVA in driving companies to superior performance. Stern Stewart and Company tested the relationship between EVA and MVA for the largest companies in the United States and found that EVA statistically explains about 50 percent of the total movement in company MVA, whereas accounting earnings and cash flow explained about 18 percent and 22 percent respectively. Another study found that low MVA and EVA numbers more than double the chance that a company's CEO will be fired. For firms with MVAs above the median, 8.6 percent had fired their CEO, but for firms with MVAs below the median, the firing rate was 20.0 percent. Also, the CEO turnover rate was 9.0 percent when EVA was above the median and 19.3 percent when it was below the median.[4]

Which Measure Is Best?

Many executives view residual income or EVA as a better measure of managers' performance than ROI. They believe that residual income and EVA encourages managers to make profitable investments that managers might reject if being measured exclusively by ROI.

To illustrate, assume that three divisions of Color Company have an opportunity to make an investment of $100,000 that requires $10,000 of additional current liabilities and that will generate a return of 20 percent. The manager of the Paint Division is evaluated using ROI, the manager of the Ink Division is evaluated using residual income, and the manager of the Dye Division is evaluated using economic value added. The current ROI of each division is 24 percent. Each division has a current income of $120,000, a minimum return of 18 percent on invested capital, and a cost of capital of 14 percent. If each division has a current investment base of $500,000, current liabilities of $40,000, and a tax rate of 30 percent, the effect of the proposed investment on each division's performance is as follows:

[4] Al Ehrbar, "Using EVA to Measure Performance and Assess Strategy," *Strategy & Leadership*, May/June 1999.

	Current	+	Proposed	=	Total
Paint Division					
Investment center income / Asset base	$120,000 / $500,000		$ 20,000 / $100,000		$140,000 / $600,000
ROI	24%		20%		23.3%
Ink Division					
Asset base	$500,000		$100,000		$600,000
Investment center income	$120,000		$ 20,000		$140,000
Minimum return (0.18 × base)	(90,000)		(18,000)		(108,000)
Residual income	$ 30,000		$ 2,000		$ 32,000
Dye Division					
Assets	$500,000		$100,000		$600,000
Current liabilities	(40,000)		(10,000)		(50,000)
Evaluation base	$460,000		$ 90,000		$550,000
Investment center income	$120,000		$ 20,000		$140,000
Income taxes (30%)	(36,000)		(6,000)		(42,000)
Income after taxes	84,000		14,000		98,000
Cost of capital (0.14 × base)	(64,400)		(12,600)		(77,000)
Economic value added	$ 19,600		$ 1,400		$ 21,000

The Paint Division manager will not want to make the new investment because it reduces the current ROI from 24 percent to 23.3 percent. This is true, even though the company's minimum return is only 18 percent. Not wanting to explain a decline in the division's ROI, the manager will probably reject the opportunity even though it could have benefited the company as a whole.

The Ink Division manager will probably be happy to accept the new project because it increases residual income by $2,000. Any investment that provides a return more than the required minimum of 18 percent will be acceptable to the Ink Division manager. Given a profit maximization goal for the organization, the residual income method is preferred over ROI evaluations because it encourages division managers to accept all projects with returns above the 18 percent cutoff. The same is true for the Dye Division manager, although the EVA increase is not as high as that of the residual income because it has a different base. However, the EVA is often considered a better evaluation tool than residual income because it is believed to be a better measure of economic profit.

The primary disadvantage of the residual income and EVA methods as comparative evaluation tools is that they measure performance in absolute terms. Although they can be used to compare period-to-period results of the same division or with similar-size divisions, they cannot be used to compare the performance of divisions of substantially different sizes. For example, the residual income of a multimillion dollar sales division should be higher than that of a half-million-dollar sales division. Because most performance evaluations and comparisons are made between units or alternative investments of different sizes, ROI continues to be extensively used. The following Business Insight box discusses the use of multiple evaluation models for assessing IT projects.

BALANCED SCORECARD

LO4 Describe the balanced scorecard as a comprehensive performance measurement system.

Although financial measures have been emphasized throughout this text, several sections stress that other measures, specifically qualitative measures, are important in evaluating managerial performance. This section examines one popular method of performance evaluation using *both* financial and nonfinancial information.

We might ask: why not use just financial measures? First, no single financial measure captures all performance aspects of an organization. More than one measure must be used. Second, financial measures have reporting time lags that could hinder timely decision making. Third, financial measures might not accurately capture the information needed for current decision making because of the delay that sometimes

BUSINESS INSIGHT **Methods used to Evaluate IT Projects at Harrah's**

A recent article in *Computer World* discusses the methods used to evaluate IT project proposals by IT managers and corporate executives. The article outlines the differences between "operational projects" aimed at saving money, and "strategic projects" aimed at making money. Harrah's Entertainment was one of several companies cited in the article.

Harrah's Entertainment Inc. uses three metrics to prioritize IT projects: net present value, internal rate of return, and economic value added. "Increased sales is usually the key benefit to be measured, but the business sponsor of a project works with IT to measure softer benefits such as increased guest visits at Harrah's hotels and casinos, customer satisfaction, and even employee satisfaction."

Using more than one metric has pros and cons, says Harrah's CIO Tim Stanley. "Using multiple criteria to assess a project provides a robust framework for decisions," he says. "Each tool takes into consideration the investment and the expected business value or return, and we are not limited to a single point of view." But, he adds, "the prospect of sophisticated financial analyses can inhibit some people from submitting ideas for consideration."[5]

occurs between making financial investments and receiving their results. For example, building a new nuclear power plant can take several years with the investment in total assets increasing the entire time without generating any revenues.

Balanced Scorecard Framework

look@ using this →

Comprehensive performance measurement systems are one suggested solution. The basic premise is to establish a set of diverse key performance indicators to monitor performance. The **balanced scorecard** is a performance measurement system that includes financial and operational measures related to a firm's goals and strategies. The balanced scorecard comprises several categories of measurements, the most common of which include the following:

- Financial
- Customer satisfaction
- Internal processes
- Innovation and learning

A balanced scorecard is usually a set of reports required of all common operating units in an organization. To facilitate the periodic evaluation of performance, a cover sheet (or sheets for a large operation) can be used to summarize the performance of each area using the established criteria for each category.

For example, a chain of bagel shops might have a balanced scorecard that looks something like the one in Exhibit 11.3. This balanced scorecard uses four categories for evaluation and includes financial and nonfinancial information. Each category being monitored has information from the previous period and the standard related to the category. The report should always include the current period, at least one previous period, and some standard. Each store manager should attach documentation and an appropriate explanation as to the change in the measurements during the reporting period.

In making assessments with the evaluation categories, it is important to consider both trailing and leading performance measures. *Trailing measures* look backward at historical data while *leading measures* provide some idea of what to expect currently or in the near future. For example, in the financial category, ROI is a trailing indicator while a budget of production units and costs for the next period is a leading indicator. In the customer category, the number of sales invoices per store might tell us whether each store is maintaining its customer base (a trailing indicator) while the number of product complaints per 1000 invoices might be a leading indicator of customer satisfaction, quality control problems, and future sales.

[5] Gary Anthes, "What's Your Project Worth? Figuring it out isn't easy. But you can't manage what you don't measure," *Computer World*, March 10, 2008.

EXHIBIT 11.3 Balanced Scorecard Illustration

	Standard	Prior Period	Current Period
Key financial indicators			
Cash flow	$ 25,000	$ 28,000	$ 21,000
Return on investment (ROI)	0.18	0.22	0.19
Sales	$4,400,000	$4,494,000	$4,342,000
Key customer indicators			
Average customers per hour	75	80	71
Number of customer complaints per period	22	21	17
Number of sales returns per period	10	8	5
Key operating indicators			
Bagels sold/produced per day ratio	0.96	0.93	0.91
Daily units lost (burned, dropped, etc.)	25	32	34
Employee turnover per period	0.10	0.07	0.00
Key growth and innovation indicators			
New products introduced during period	1	1	0
Products discontinued during period	1	1	1
Number of sales promotions	3	3	2
Special offers, discounts, etc.	4	5	3

The use of balanced scorecard systems to monitor and assess managerial and organizational performance is increasing worldwide. The following Research Insight box provides more information on the types of key performance indicators used by a group of firms.

RESEARCH INSIGHT **Balanced Scorecard Yields Results**

A survey of firms found that a balanced scorecard is more widely used by larger firms. Also, firms having a higher proportion of new products are more likely to include in their scorecard measures related to new products. However, no relation was found between market share of companies and whether or not they used the balanced scorecard. Yet, results indicated that usage of the balanced scorecard is associated with improved performance of companies regardless of company size, stage of product life cycle, or market position. The following were the most commonly used key performance indicators of the surveyed firms:[6]

Financial perspective:
- Operating income
- Sales growth
- Return on investment

Customer perspective:
- Customer satisfaction
- Number of customer complaints
- Market share
- Percentage of shipments returned due to poor quality
- On-time delivery
- Warranty repair cost
- Customer response time
- Cycle time from order to delivery

Internal perspective:
- Labor efficiency variance
- Rate of material scrap loss
- Material efficiency variance
- Manufacturing lead time
- Ratio of good output to total output
- Percentage of defective products shipped

Innovation and learning perspective:
- Number of new product launches
- Number of new patents
- Time to market new products

A balanced scorecard gives management a perspective of the organization's performance on a recurring set of criteria. Since each reporting unit knows what reports are expected, no one is surprised

[3] Zahirul Hoque and Wendy James, "Linking Balanced Scorecard Measures to Size and Market Factors: Impact on Organizational Performance," *Journal of Management Accounting Research*, Vol. 12, 2000.

by changing monthly requests for data. Because the multiple perspectives provide management a broad analysis of the organization's performance, it allows them to determine how and where the goals and objectives are either being achieved or not achieved.

For most management teams, the balanced scorecard highlights trade-offs between measures. For example, a substantial increase in customer satisfaction can result in a short-run decrease in ROI because the extra effort to please customers is expensive, thereby reducing ROI. A balanced scorecard can be filtered down the organization with successively lower-level operating units having their own scorecards that mimic those of the higher-level units. This provides all levels of management an opportunity to evaluate operations from more than just a financial perspective.

As with all management tools and techniques, the use of the balanced scorecard must be incorporated with the other information sources within the organization. Just as the accounting information system cannot stand alone in managing a business, neither can the balanced scorecard. Some areas could need extensive accounting information in great detail to make the best possible decision while other areas need great detail in production or service integration to be at the right place at the right time. By using a multifaceted approach to managing, the organization should be able to better establish an operating strategy that coincides with its overall goals and objectives.

Balanced Scorecard and Strategy

When a balanced scorecard system is fully utilized to monitor and evaluate an organization's progress, it becomes a system for operationalizing the organization's strategy. Having a goal to maximize shareholder value or generate a certain income does not constitute a strategy. Maximizing shareholder value can be an overarching corporate goal, but it will not likely be realized without a well-developed strategy that identifies and establishes a balanced set of goals on various dimensions of performance.

A balanced scorecard can be the primary vehicle for translating strategy into action and establishing accountability for performance. The balanced scorecard identifies the areas of managerial action that are believed to be the drivers of corporate achievement. If the corporate goal is to increase ROI or EVA, the balanced scorecard should include key performance indicators that drive ROI or EVA.

An interesting parallel to the successful management of a company can be drawn by considering the key performance indicators the manager of a professional baseball team uses in setting goals and evaluating progress. The manager of the New York Yankees does not just tell his players and managers at the beginning of the baseball season that the team's goal is to win the World Series or even a certain number of ball games. The win-loss record is only one metric used to set goals and evaluate performance for a baseball team. The manager looks at many different drivers of success related to hitting, pitching, and fielding, including the earned-run averages of the pitchers, the batting and on-base averages of hitters, the number of errors per game by fielders, and the number of bases stolen by base runners. At the end of the season, the manager measures success not just by whether the Yankees won the World Series, but also by the batting average, number of home runs, and number of bases stolen by individual players, and whether or not a team member won a Golden Glove award or the Cy Young award. These are all measures by which to evaluate achievement and strategic accomplishment. By achieving the goals for each of these areas of the game, the win-loss ratio will take care of itself. If the win-loss results are not acceptable, then the manager adjusts his strategic goals with respect to the key performance indicators (or the manager is dismissed).

Like a baseball team, a company can use a balanced scorecard to develop performance metrics for managers from the top of the company to the lowest-level department. The scorecard becomes a vehicle for communicating the factors that are key to the success of managers, factors that upper management will monitor in evaluating the success of lower managers in carrying out the corporate strategy. To make balanced scorecards more user friendly, several software companies have developed performance monitoring **dashboards**, which are software programs that tabulate and display scorecard results using graphics that mimic the instrument displays on an automobile dashboard.

The following Business Insight box shows a sample dashboard for a company's balanced scorecard results.

BUSINESS INSIGHT **Balanced Scorecard Software**

Ergometrics LTD is a company from New Zealand that was formed to develop and market dashboard software. Ergometrics has developed performance monitoring dashboards that present balanced scorecard results. The following sample is for a hypothetical utility company:

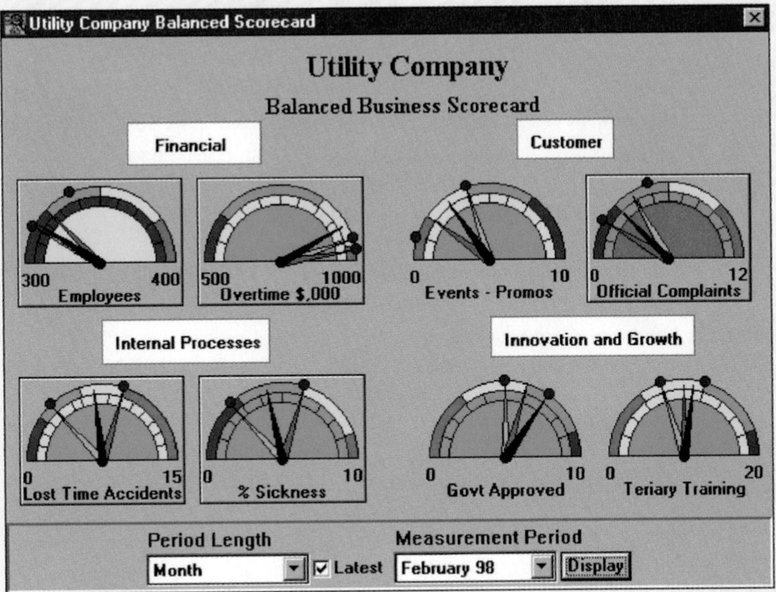

By clicking on any of the four scorecard indicators, the manager monitoring performance can drill down for more detail. Note that the period being examined can be changed to view performance for any period in the dashboard database.[7]

CHAPTER-END REVIEW

Pareto International, a decentralized organization that manufactures specialty construction products, has three divisions, Commercial, Industrial, and Residential. Corporate management desires a minimum return of 15 percent on its investments and has a 20 percent tax rate with an average cost of capital of 12 percent. The divisions' 2009 results follow (in thousands):

Division	Income	Investment	Current Liabilities
Commercial	$30,000	$200,000	$10,000
Industrial..........	50,000	250,000	30,000
Residential	22,000	100,000	5,000

The company is planning an expansion project in 2010 that will cost $50,000,000 and return $9,000,000 per year. It will result in a $10,000 increase in current liabilities.

Required

a. Compute the ROI for each division for 2009.
b. Compute the residual income for each division for 2009.
c. Compute the economic value added for each division for 2009
d. Rank the divisions according to their ROI, residual income, and EVA.
e. Assume that other income and investments will remain unchanged. Determine the effect of the project by itself. What is the effect on ROI, residual income, and economic value added if the new project is added to each division?

[7] As presented at http://www.ergometrics.com/balscore3.htm

Solution

a.

$$\text{Return on investment} = \frac{\text{Investment center income}}{\text{Investment center asset base}}$$

Commercial Division = \$30,000 ÷ \$200,000
= 0.15, or 15 percent
Industrial Division = \$50,000 ÷ \$250,000
= 0.20, or 20 percent
Residential Division = \$22,000 ÷ \$100,000
= 0.22, or 22 percent

b. **Residual income = Investment center income − (Investment center asset base × Minimum return)**

Commercial Division = \$30,000 − (0.15 × \$200,000)
= \$0.00
Industrial Division = \$50,000 − (0.15 × \$250,000)
= \$12,500
Residential Division = \$22,000 − (0.15 × \$100,000)
= \$7,000

c. **EVA = After tax income − (Net assets × Weighted average cost of capital)**

Commercial Division = (\$30,000 × 0.80) − [(\$200,000 − \$10,000) × 0.12]
= \$1,200
Industrial Division = (\$50,000 × 0.80) − [(\$250,000 − \$30,000) × 0.12]
= \$13,600
Residential Division = (\$22,000 × 0.80) − [(\$100,000 − \$5,000) × 0.12]
= \$6,200

d. ROI ranks the Residential Division first, the Industrial Division second, and the Commercial Division third. Residual income ranks the Industrial Division first, the Residential Division second, and the Commercial Division third. Because the investments for each division are different, it is somewhat misleading to rank the divisions according to residual income. The Industrial Division had the highest residual income, but it also had the largest investment. The Residential Division's residual income was 56 percent of the Industrial Division's income but only 40 percent of the investment of the Industrial Division. This fact, along with the best ROI ranking, probably justifies the Residential Division being evaluated as the best division of Pareto Company.

e. Return on investment:

Investment = \$9,000 ÷ \$50,000
= 0.18, or 18 percent
Commercial Division = (\$30,000 + \$9,000) ÷ (\$200,000 + \$50,000)
= 0.156, or 15.6 percent
Industrial Division = (\$50,000 + \$9,000) ÷ (\$250,000 + \$50,000)
= 0.1967, or 19.67 percent
Residential Division = (\$22,000 + \$9,000) ÷ (\$100,000 + \$50,000)
= 0.2067, or 20.67 percent

ROI will increase for the Commercial Division but decrease for the Industrial and Residential Divisions, even though the project's ROI of 18 percent exceeds the company's minimum return of 15 percent.

Residual income:

Commercial Division = (\$30,000 + \$9,000) − [0.15 × (\$200,000 +\$50,000)]
= \$1,500
Industrial Division = (\$50,000 + \$9,000) − [0.15 × (\$250,000 + \$50,000)]
= \$14,000
Residential Division = (\$22,000 + \$9,000) − [0.15 × (\$100,000 + \$50,000)]
= \$8,500

Because the project's ROI exceeds the company's minimum return, the residual income of all divisions will increase.

Economic value-added:

Commerical Division = [(\$30,000 + \$9,000) × 0.80] − [(\$200,000 + \$50,000 − \$20,000) × 0.12]
= \$3,600
Industrial Division = [(\$50,000 + \$9,000) × 0.80] − [(\$250,000 + \$50,000 − \$40,000) × 0.12]
= \$16,000
Residential Division = [(\$22,000 + \$9,000) × 0.80] − [(\$100,000 + \$50,000 − \$15,000) × 0.12]
= \$8,600

The EVA does not shift the same way the residual income does because of the additional relationships between the level of current liabilities and the tax rate. However, in this situation, all divisions have an increase in EVA when the new investment is made.

GUIDANCE ANSWER

MANAGERIAL DECISION **You are the Division Vice President**

ROI is primarily a measure of the profitability of a division's assets, which is in turn a measure of how effectively the investment in assets was used to generate sales, and how profitable those sales were. ROI is driven by investment (or asset) turnover (which is division sales divided by assets) and return on sales (which is division net income divided division sales). Therefore, increasing ROI is similar to a simultaneous balancing act involving controlling sales, expenses, and asset investment. You can increase ROI by increasing sales more than expenses, while holding asset investment constant, or by other combinations of these three variables that ultimately increase ROI. If you adjust one of these variables, at the same time you must keep your eye on the other two variables or you may not achieve your goal of increasing ROI.

DISCUSSION QUESTIONS

Q11-1. What is the relationship between segment reports and product reports?

Q11-2. What is a reporting objective? How is it determined?

Q11-3. Can a company have more than one type of first-level statement in segment reporting?

Q11-4. Explain the relationships between any two levels of statements in segment reporting.

Q11-5. Distinguish between direct and indirect segment costs.

Q11-6. What types of information are needed before management should decide to drop a segment?

Q11-7. In what types of organizations and for what purpose are transfer prices used?

Q11-8. What problems arise when transfer pricing is used?

Q11-9. When do transfer prices lead to suboptimization? How can suboptimization be minimized? Can it be eliminated? Why or why not?

Q11-10. For what purpose do organizations use return on investment? Why is this measure preferred to net income?

Q11-11. What advantages does residual income and EVA have over ROI for segment evaluations?

Q11-12. Contrast the difference between residual income and EVA.

Q11-13. Explain how a balanced scorecard helps with the evaluation process of internal operations.

Q11-14. How can a balanced scorecard be used as a strategy implementation tool?

MINI EXERCISES

M11-15. Multiple Levels of Segment Reporting (LO1)

Gormet Appliances manufactures four different lines of household appliances: cooking, cleaning, convenience, and safety. Each of the product lines is produced in all of the company's three plants: Abbeyville, Bakersville, and Charlottesville. Marketing efforts of the company are divided into five regions: East, West, South, North, and Central.

Required

a. Develop a reporting schematic that illustrates how the company might prepare single-level reports segmented on three different bases.

b. Develop a segment reporting schematic that has three different levels. Be sure to identify each segment's level. Briefly explain why you chose the primary-level segment.

M11-16. Income Statements Segmented by Territory (LO1)

Script, Inc., has two product lines. The September income statements of each product line and the company are as follows:

SCRIPT, INC. Product Line and Company Income Statements For Month of September	Pens	Pencils	Total
Sales.	$25,000	$30,000	$55,000
Less variable expenses	(10,000)	(12,000)	(22,000)
Contribution margin	15,000	18,000	33,000
Less direct fixed expenses.	(9,000)	(7,000)	(16,000)
Product margin.	$ 6,000	$11,000	17,000
Less common fixed expenses			(6,000)
Net income.			$11,000

Pens and pencils are sold in two territories, Florida and Alabama, as follows:

	Florida	Alabama
Pen sales	$15,000	$10,000
Pencil sales	9,000	21,000
Total sales.	$24,000	$31,000

The preceding common fixed expenses are traceable to each territory as follows:

Florida fixed expenses	$2,000
Alabama fixed expenses	3,000
Home office administration fixed expenses.	1,000
Total common fixed expenses	$6,000

The direct fixed expenses of pens, $9,000, and of pencils, $7,000, cannot be identified with either territory. The company's accountants were unable to allocate any of the common fixed expenses to the various segments.

Required

a. Prepare income statements segmented by territory for September, including a column for the entire firm.

b. Why are the direct expenses of one type of segment report not necessarily the direct expenses of another type of segment report?

M11-17. Income Statements Segmented by Products (LO1)

Clay Consulting Firm provides three types of client services in three health-care-related industries. The income statement for July is as follows:

CLAY CONSULTING FIRM Income Statement For Month of July		
Sales.		$900,000
Less variable costs.		(605,000)
Contribution margin		295,000
Less fixed expenses		
Service	$70,000	
Selling and administrative.	65,000	(135,000)
Net income.		$160,000

The sales, contribution margin ratios, and direct fixed expenses for the three types of services are as follows:

	Hospitals	Physicians	Nursing Care
Sales	$350,000	$250,000	$300,000
Contribution margin ratio	30%	40%	30%
Direct fixed expenses of services	$ 20,000	$ 18,000	$ 16,000
Allocated common fixed services expense	$ 1,000	$ 1,000	$ 1,500

Required

Prepare income statements segmented by client categories. Include a column for the entire firm in the statement.

M11-18. Internal or External Acquisitions: No Opportunity Costs (LO2)

The Van Division of MotoCar Corporation has offered to purchase 180,000 wheels from the Wheel Division for $42 per wheel. At a normal volume of 500,000 wheels per year, production costs per wheel for the Wheel Division are as follows:

Direct materials	$15
Direct labor	10
Variable overhead	6
Fixed overhead	18
Total	$49

The Wheel Division has been selling 500,000 wheels per year to outside buyers at $58 each. Capacity is 700,000 wheels per year. The Van Division has been buying wheels from outside suppliers at $55 per wheel.

Required

a. Should the Wheel Division manager accept the offer? Show computations.

b. From the standpoint of the company, will the internal sale be beneficial?

M11-19. Transfer Prices at Full Cost with Excess Capacity: Divisional Viewpoint (LO2)

Wholesome Dairy's Cheese Division produces cheese that sells for $10 per unit in the open market. The cost of the product is $8 (variable manufacturing of $5, plus fixed manufacturing of $3). Total fixed manufacturing costs are $210,000 at the normal annual production volume of 70,000 units. The Overseas Division has offered to buy 15,000 units at the full cost of $8. The Producing Division has excess capacity, and the 15,000 units can be produced without interfering with the current outside sales of 70,000 units. The total fixed cost of the Cheese Division will not change.

Required

Explain whether the Cheese Division should accept or reject the offer. Show calculations.

M11-20. Transfer Pricing with Excess Capacity: Divisional and Corporate Viewpoints (LO2)

Boyett Art Company has a Print Division that is currently producing 100,000 prints per year but has a capacity of 150,000 prints. The variable costs of each print are $30, and the annual fixed costs are $900,000. The prints sell for $40 in the open market. The company's Retail Division wants to buy 50,000 prints at $28 each. The Print Division manager refuses the order because the price is below variable cost. The Retail Division manager argues that the order should be accepted because it will lower the fixed cost per print from $9 to $6.

Required

a. Should the Retail Division order be accepted? Why or why not?

b. From the viewpoints of the Print Division and the company, should the order be accepted if the manager of the Retail Division intends to sell each print in the outside market for $42 after incurring additional costs of $10 per print?

c. What action should the company take, assuming it believes in divisional autonomy?

M11-21. ROI and Residual Income: Impact of a New Investment (LO3)

The Mustang Division of Detroit Motors had an operating income of $900,000 and net assets of $4,000,000. Detroit Motors has a target rate of return of 16 percent.

Required

a. Compute the return on investment.

b. Compute the residual income.

c. The Mustang Division has an opportunity to increase operating income by $200,000 with an $850,000 investment in assets.

1. Compute the Mustang Division's return on investment if the project is undertaken. (Round your answer to three decimal places.)
2. Compute the Mustang Division's residual income if the project is undertaken.

M11-22. ROI: Fill in the Unknowns (LO3)

Provide the missing data in the following situations:

	North American Division	Asian Division	European Division
Sales	?	$5,000,000	?
Net operating income	$100,000	$ 200,000	$144,000
Operating assets	?	?	$800,000
Return on investment	16%	10%	?
Return on sales	0.04	?	0.12
Investment turnover	?	?	1.5

M11-23. Selection of Balanced Scorecard Items (LO4)

The International Accountants' Association is a professional association. Its current membership totals 110,000 worldwide. The association operates from a central headquarters in New Zealand but has local membership chapters throughout the world. The local chapters hold monthly meetings to discuss recent developments in accounting and to hear professional speakers on topics of interest. The association's journal, *International Accountant,* is published monthly with feature articles and topical interest areas. The association publishes books and reports and sponsors continuing education courses. A statement of revenues and expenses follows:

INTERNATIONAL ACCOUNTANTS' ASSOCIATION Statement of Revenues and Expenses For Year Ending November 30, 2009		
Revenues		$30,275,000
Expenses		
Salaries	$14,000,000	
Other personnel costs	3,400,000	
Occupancy costs	2,000,000	
Reimbursement to local chapters	800,000	
Other membership services	500,000	
Printing and paper	320,000	
Postage and shipping	114,000	
General and administrative	538,000	(21,672,000)
Excess of revenues over expenses		$ 8,603,000

Additional information follows:

- Membership dues are $200 per year, of which $50 is considered to cover a one-year subscription to the association's journal. Other benefits include membership in the association and chapter affiliation.
- One-year subscriptions to *International Accountant* are sold to nonmembers for $80 each. A total of 2,500 of these subscriptions were sold. In addition to subscriptions, the journal generated $200,000 in advertising revenue. The cost per magazine was $20.
- A total of 30,000 technical reports were sold by the Books and Reports Department at an average unit selling price of $45. Average costs per publication were $12.
- The association offers a variety of continuing education courses to both members and nonmembers. During 2009, the one-day course, which cost participants an average of $75 each, was attended by 34,400 people. A total of 2,630 people took two-day courses at a cost of $125 per person.
- General and administrative expenses include all other costs incurred by the corporate staff to operate the association.

- The organization has net capital assets of $44,000,000 and prefers to maintain a cost of capital of 10 percent.

Required

a. Give some examples of key financial performance indicators (no computations needed) that could be part of a balanced scorecard for the IAA.

b. Give some examples of key customer and operating performance indicators (no computations needed) that could be part of a balanced scorecard for IAA.

EXERCISES

E11-24. Appropriate Transfer Prices: Opportunity Costs (LO2)

Plains Peanut Butter Company recently acquired a peanut-processing company that has a normal annual capacity of 4,000,000 pounds and that sold 2,800,000 pounds last year at a price of $2.00 per pound. The purpose of the acquisition is to furnish peanuts for the peanut butter plant, which needs 1,600,000 pounds of peanuts per year. It has been purchasing peanuts from suppliers at the market price. Production costs per pound of the peanut-processing company are as follows:

Direct materials	$0.50
Direct labor	0.25
Variable overhead	0.12
Fixed overhead at normal capacity	0.20
Total	$1.07

Management is trying to decide what transfer price to use for sales from the newly acquired Peanut Division to the Peanut Butter Division. The manager of the Peanut Division argues that $2.00, the market price, is appropriate. The manager of the Peanut Butter Division argues that the cost price of $1.07 (or perhaps even less) should be used since fixed overhead costs should be recomputed. Any output of the Peanut Division up to 2,800,000 pounds that is not sold to the Peanut Butter Division could be sold to regular customers at $2.00 per pound.

Required

a. Compute the annual gross profit for the Peanut Division using a transfer price of $2.00.

b. Compute the annual gross profit for the Peanut Division using a transfer price of $1.07.

c. What transfer price(s) will lead the manager of the Peanut Butter Division to act in a manner that will maximize company profits?

E11-25. Negotiating a Transfer Price with Excess Capacity (LO2)

The Weaving Division of Carolina Textiles Inc. produces cloth that is sold to the company's Dyeing Division and to outside customers. Operating data for the Weaving Division for 2009 are as follows:

	To the Dyeing Division	To Outside Customers
Sales		
450,000 yards × $5.00	$2,250,000	
300,000 yards × $6.00		$1,800,000
Variable expenses at $2.00	(900,000)	(600,000)
Contribution margin	1,350,000	1,200,000
Fixed expenses*	(750,000)	(500,000)
Net income	$ 600,000	$ 700,000

*Allocated on the basis of unit sales.

The Dyeing Division has just received an offer from an outside supplier to supply cloth at $3.50 per yard. The Weaving Division manager is not willing to meet the $3.50 price. She argues that it costs her $3.67 per yard to produce and sell to the Dyeing Division, so she would show no profit on the Dyeing Division sales. Sales to outside customers are at a maximum, 300,000 yards.

Required

a. Verify the Weaving Division's $3.67 unit cost figure.

b. Should the Weaving Division meet the outside price of $3.50 for Dyeing Division sales? Explain.

c. Could the Weaving Division meet the $3.50 price and still show a profit for sales to the Dyeing Division? Show computations.

E11-26. Dual Transfer Pricing (LO2)

The Greek Company has two divisions, Beta and Gamma. Gamma Division produces a product at a variable cost of $6 per unit, and sells 150,000 units to outside customers at $10 per unit and 40,000 units to Beta Division at variable cost plus 40 percent. Under the dual transfer price system, Beta Division pays only the variable cost per unit. Gamma Division's fixed costs are $250,000 per year. Beta Division sells its finished product to outside customers at $23 per unit. Beta has variable costs of $5 per unit, in addition to the costs from Gamma Division. Beta Division's annual fixed costs are $170,000. There are no beginning or ending inventories.

Required

a. Prepare the income statements for the two divisions and the company as a whole.

b. Why is the income for the company less than the sum of the profit figures shown on the income statements for the two divisions? Explain.

E11-27. ROI and Residual Income: Basic Computations (LO3)

Watkins Associated Industries

Watkins Associated Industries is a highly diversified company with three divisions: Trucking, Seafood, and Construction. Assume that the company uses return on investment, residual income, and economic value added as three of the evaluation tools for division managers. The company has a minimum desired rate of return on investment of 10 percent and a weighted average cost of capital of 7 percent with a 30 percent tax rate. Selected operating data for three divisions of the company follow.

	Trucking Division	Seafood Division	Construction Division
Sales	$1,200,000	$750,000	$900,000
Operating assets	600,000	250,000	350,000
Net operating income	102,000	56,000	59,000
Current liabilities	40,000	10,000	30,000

Required

a. Compute the return on investment for each division. (Round answers to three decimal places.)

b. Compute the residual income for each division.

c. Which divisional manager is doing the best job based on ROI? Based on residual income? Why?

E11-28. ROI and Residual Income, and EVA with Different Bases (LO3)

BMI Company has a target return on capital of 15 percent. The following financial information is available for October ($ thousands):

	Software Division (Value Base)		Consulting Division (Value Base)		Venture Capital Division (Value Base)	
	Book	Current	Book	Current	Book	Current
Sales	$100,000	$100,000	$200,000	$200,000	$800,000	$800,000
Income	12,000	10,000	16,000	17,000	50,000	52,000
Assets	60,000	80,000	90,000	100,000	600,000	580,000
Current liabilities	10,000	10,000	14,000	14,000	40,000	40,000

Required

a. Compute the return on investment using both book and current values for each division. (Round answers to three decimal places.)

b. Compute the residual income for both book and current values for each division.

c. Compute the economic value added income for both book and current values for each division if the tax rate is 30 percent and the weighted average cost of capital is 10 percent.

d. Does book value or current value provide a better basis for performance evaluation? Which division do you consider the most successful?

E11-29. Balanced Scorecard Preparation (LO4)

The following information is in addition to that presented in Mini Exercise 11-23 for the International Accountants' Association. For the year ended November 30, 2009, the organization had set a membership goal of 100,000 members with the following anticipated results:

INTERNATIONAL ACCOUNTANTS' ASSOCIATION Planned Revenues and Expenses For Year Ending November 30, 2009		
Revenues		$28,000,000
Expenses		
Salaries	$13,950,000	
Other personnel costs	3,450,000	
Occupancy costs	1,900,000	
Reimbursement to local chapters	780,000	
Other membership services	525,000	
Printing and paper	300,000	
Postage and shipping	103,000	
General and administrative	550,000	(21,558,000)
Excess of revenues over expenses		$ 6,442,000

Additional information follows:

- Membership dues were increased from $180 to $200 at the beginning of the year.
- One-year subscriptions to *International Accountant* were anticipated to be 2,400 units.
- Advertising revenue was budgeted at $225,000. Each magazine was budgeted at $18.
- A total of 28,000 technical reports were anticipated at an average price of $40 with average costs of $11.
- The budgeted one-day courses had an anticipated attendance of 32,000 with an average fee of $80. The two-day courses had an anticipated attendance of 3,000 with an average fee of $125 per person.
- The organization began the year with net capital assets of $40,000,000 with a planned cost of capital of 10 percent.

Required

a. Prepare a balanced scorecard for IAA for November 2009 with calculated key performance indicators presented in two columns for planned performance and actual performance—include key financial, customer, and operating performance indicators.

b. Which of the evaluation areas you selected indicated success and which indicated failure?

c. Give some explanations of the successes and failures.

E11-30. Balanced Scorecard (LO4)

The following alphabetically ordered list of financial and nonfinancial performance metrics is provided for BS, Inc.

Average call wait
Average customer survey rating
Employee turnover ratio
Expense as a % of revenue
Expense variance %
Fulfillment %
Headcount growth
Industry quality rating
Job offer acceptance rate
Market share
New customer count
New customer sales value
New product acceptance rate
New product revenue
New product ROI
Net profit
Net profit margin
Number of complaints
Number of defects reported
Service error rate
Time to market on new products
Unique repeat customer count
Year over year revenue growth

Required:

a. Assign the above metrics to the four balanced scorecard categories of (1) Financial Success, (2) Customer Satisfaction and Brand Improvement, (3) Business Process Improvement, (4) Learning and Growth of Motivated Workforce.

b. Comment on the use of balanced scorecard versus a single financial measure such as ROI or EVA.

PROBLEMS

P11-31. Multiple Segment Reports (LO1)

World Products Incorporated sells throughout the world in three sales territories: Europe, Asia, and the Americas. For July, all $50,000 of administrative expense is traceable to the territories, except $10,000, which is common to all units and cannot be traced or allocated to the sales territories. The percentage of product line sales made in each of the sales territories and the assignment of traceable fixed expenses follow:

	Sales Territory			
	Europe	Asia	The Americas	Total
Cookware sales	40%	50%	10%	100%
China sales	40	40	20	100
Vases sales	20	20	60	100
Fixed administrative expense	$15,000	$15,000	$10,000	$ 40,000
Fixed selling expense	$30,000	$60,000	$60,000	$150,000

The manufacturing takes place in one large facility with three distinct manufacturing operations. Selected product-line cost data follow.

	Cookware	China	Vases	Total
Variable costs	$ 9	$ 9	$ 5	
Depreciation and supervision	15,000	15,000	12,000	$ 45,000*
Other mfg. overhead (common)				10,000
Fixed administrative expense (common)				50,000
Fixed selling expense (common)				150,000

*Includes common costs of $3,000

The unit sales and selling prices for each product follow.

	Unit Sales	Selling Price
Cookware	10,000	$10
China	20,000	15
Vases	15,000	20

Required

a. Prepare an income statement for July segmented by product line. Include a column for the entire firm.

b. Prepare an income statement for July segmented by sales territory. Include a column for the entire firm.

c. Prepare an income statement for July by product line for The Americas sales territory. Include a column for the territory as a whole.

d. Discuss the value of multilevel segment reporting as a managerial tool. Compare and contrast the benefits of the reports generated in parts *a*, *b*, and *c*.

P11-32. Segment Reporting and Analysis (LO1)

Milwaukee Bakery Incorporated bakes three products: donuts, pies, and cakes. It sells them in the cities of Chicago and Milwaukee. For March, the following income statement was prepared:

MILWAUKEE BAKERY, INCORPORATED Territory and Company Income Statements For Month of March	Chicago	Milwaukee	Total
Sales	$2,100	$500	$2,600
Cost of goods sold	(1,500)	(300)	(1,800)
Gross profit	600	200	800
Selling and administrative expenses	(400)	(100)	(500)
Net income	$ 200	$100	$ 300

Sales and selected variable expense data are as follows:

	Products		
	Donuts	Pies	Cakes
Fixed baking expenses	$200	$140	$100
Variable baking expenses as a percentage of sales	50%	50%	60%
Variable selling expenses as a percentage of sales	4%	4%	5%
City of Chicago, sales	$800	$900	$400
City of Milwaukee, sales	$200	$100	$200

The fixed selling expenses were $260 for March, of which $160 was a direct expense of the Chicago market and $100 was a direct expense of the Milwaukee market. Fixed administrative expenses were $130, which management has decided not to allocate when using the contribution approach.

Required

a. Prepare a segment income statement for each sales territory for March. Include a column for the entire firm.

b. Prepare segment income statements for each product. Include a column for the entire firm.

c. If the cake line is dropped and fixed baking expenses do not change, what is the product margin for donuts and pies?

d. What other type of segmentation might be useful to Milwaukee Bakery. Explain.

P11-33. Segment Reporting and Analysis (LO1)

Accounting Publishers, Inc. has prepared income statements segmented by divisions, but management is still uncertain about actual performance. Financial information for May is given as follows:

	Textbook Division	Professional Division	Company Total
Sales	$180,000	$410,000	$590,000
Less variable expenses			
Manufacturing	32,000	205,000	237,000
Selling and administrative	4,000	20,500	24,500
Total	(36,000)	(225,500)	(261,500)
Contribution margin	144,000	184,500	328,500
Less direct fixed expenses	(15,000)	(220,000)	(235,000)
Net income	$129,000	$(35,500)	$ 93,500

Management is concerned about the Professional Division and requests additional analysis. Additional information regarding May operations of the Professional Division is as follows:

	Accounting	Executive	Management
Sales.	$140,000	$140,000	$130,000
Variable manufacturing expenses as a percentage of sales.	60%	40%	50%
Other variable expenses as a percentage of sales.	5%	5%	5%
Direct fixed expenses.	$50,000	$75,000	$50,000
Allocated common fixed expenses	$5,000	$2,000	$7,000

The professional accounting books are sold to auditors and controllers. The current information on these markets is as follows:

	Sales Market	
	Auditors	Controllers
Sales.	$30,000	$110,000
Variable manufacturing expenses as a percentage of sales.	60%	60%
Other variable expenses as a percentage of sales.	16%	2%
Direct fixed expenses.	$ 5,000	$ 25,000
Allocated common fixed expenses	$ 7,000	$ 8,000

Required

a. Prepare an income statement segmented by product for the Professional Division. Include a column for the division as a whole.

b. Prepare an income statement segmented by market for the accounting books of the Professional Division.

c. Evaluate which accounting books the Professional Division should keep or discontinue in the short run.

d. What is the correct long-run decision? Explain fully, including any possible risks associated with your recommendation.

P11-34. Segment Reports (LO1)

The Entertainment Corporation produces and sells three products. The three products, CDs, DVDs, and videotapes, are sold in a local market and in a regional market. At the end of the first quarter of 2009, the following income statement was prepared:

ENTERTAINMENT CORPORATION
Territory and Company Income Statements
First Quarter of 2009

	Local	Regional	Company
Sales.	$1,000,000	$300,000	$1,300,000
Cost of goods sold.	(775,000)	(235,000)	(1,010,000)
Gross profit.	225,000	65,000	290,000
Selling expenses	60,000	45,000	105,000
Administrative expenses	40,000	12,000	52,000
Total	(100,000)	(57,000)	(157,000)
Net income.	$ 125,000	$ 8,000	$ 133,000

Management has expressed special concern with the Regional Market because of the extremely poor return on sales. This market was entered a year ago because of excess capacity. Management originally believed that the return on sales would improve with time, but after a year, no noticeable improvement could be seen from the results as reported in the preceding quarterly statement. In attempting to decide whether to eliminate the Regional Market, the following information has been gathered:

	Products		
	CD	DVD	Videotape
Sales	$600,000	$500,000	$200,000
Variable manufacturing expenses as a percentage of sales	60%	70%	60%
Variable selling expenses as a percentage of sales	3%	2%	2%

	Sales by Markets	
Product	Local	Regional
CD	$450,000	$150,000
DVD	350,000	150,000
Videotape	150,000	50,000

All administrative expenses and fixed manufacturing expenses are common to the three products and the two markets; these expenses are fixed for the period. The remaining selling expenses are fixed for the period and separable by market. All fixed expenses are based on a prorated yearly amount.

Required

a. Prepare the quarterly income statement showing contribution margins by market (territories). Include a column for the company as a whole.

b. Assuming there are no alternative uses for Entertainment Corporation's present capacity, would you recommend dropping the regional market? Why or why not?

c. Prepare the quarterly income statement showing contribution margins by product. Include a column for the company as a whole.

d. It is believed that a new product can be ready for sale next year if Entertainment Corporation decides to go ahead with continued research. The new product can be produced by simply converting equipment now used to produce videotapes. This conversion will increase fixed costs by $10,000 per quarter. What must be the minimum contribution margin per quarter for the new product to make the changeover financially feasible?

(CMA Adapted)

P11-35. Segment Reports and Cost Allocations (LO1)

Pacific Products, Inc. has three sales divisions. One of the key evaluation inputs for each division manager is the performance of his or her division based on division income. The division statements for August are as follows:

	Kiwi	Queensland	Hawaii	Total
Sales	$400,000	$500,000	$450,000	$1,350,000
Cost of sales	200,000	240,000	230,000	670,000
Division overhead	100,000	110,000	110,000	320,000
Division expenses	(300,000)	(350,000)	(340,000)	(990,000)
Division contribution	100,000	150,000	110,000	360,000
Corporate overhead	(70,000)	(90,000)	(80,000)	(240,000)
Division income	$ 30,000	$ 60,000	$ 30,000	$ 120,000

The Hawaii manager is unhappy that his profitability is the same as that of the Kiwi Division and one-half that of the Queensland Division when his sales are halfway between these two divisions. The manager knows that his division must carry more product lines because of customer demands, and many of these additional product lines are not very profitable. He has not dropped these marginal product lines because of idle capacity; all of the products cover their own variable costs. After analyzing the product lines with the lowest profit margins, the divisional controller for Hawaii provided the following to the manager:

Sales of marginal products		$90,000
Cost of sales	$50,000	
Avoidable fixed costs	20,000	(70,000)
Product margin		20,000
Proportion of corporate overhead		(16,000)
Product income		$ 4,000

Although these products were 20 percent of Hawaii's total sales, they contributed only about 13 percent of the division's profits. The controller also noted that the corporate overhead allocation was based on a formula of sales and divisional contribution margin.

Required

a. Prepare a set of segment statements for August assuming that all facts remain the same except that Hawaii's weak product lines are dropped and corporate overhead is allocated as follows: Kiwi, $80,000; Queensland, $95,000; and Hawaii, $65,000. Does the Hawaii Division appear better after this action? What will be the responses of the other two division managers?

b. Suggest improvements for Pacific Products' reporting process that will better reflect the actual operations of the divisions. Keep in mind the utilization of the reporting process to assist in the evaluation of the managers. What other changes could be made to improve the manager evaluation process?

P11-36. ROI and Residual Income: Impact of a New Investment (LO3)

Business Equipment Inc. is a decentralized organization with four autonomous divisions. The divisions are evaluated on the basis of the change in their return on invested assets. Operating results in the Retail Division for 2009 follow:

BUSINESS EQUIPMENT INC.—RETAIL DIVISION
Income Statement
For Year Ending December 31, 2009

Sales	$3,125,000
Less variable expenses	(1,562,500)
Contribution margin	1,562,500
Less fixed expenses	(1,000,000)
Net operating income	$ 562,500

Operating assets for the Retail Division currently average $2,500,000. The Retail Division can add a new product line for an investment of $300,000. Relevant data for the new product line are as follows:

Sales	$800,000
Variable expenses (% of sales)	0.60
Fixed expenses	$275,000
Increase in current liabilities	$ 20,000

Required

a. Determine the effect on ROI of accepting the new product line. (Round calculations to three decimal places.)

b. If a return of 6 percent is the minimum that any division should earn and residual income is used to evaluate managers, would this encourage the division to accept the new product line? Explain and show computations.

c. If EVA is used to evaluate managers, should the new product line be accepted if the weighted average cost of capital is 8 percent and the investment tax rate is 40 percent?

P11-37. Valuing Investment Center Assets (LO3)

Six Flags Theme Parks, Inc., operates theme parks in the United States, Mexico, and Europe. One of its first theme parks, Six Flags over Georgia, was built in the 1960s in Atlanta on a large tract of land that has appreciated enormously over the years. Although most of the rides and other attractions have a fairly short life, some of the major buildings that are still in use on the property have been fully depreciated since they were built. Assume that Six Flags over Georgia operates as an investment center with total assets that have a book value of $150 million and current liabilities of $20 million. Assume also that in 2009, this particular theme park had sales of $60 million and pretax division income of $20 million. The replacement cost of all the assets in this park is estimated to be $250 million. The company's cost of capital is 16 percent, and it has a 35 percent tax rate.

Six Flags Theme Parks, Inc. (SIX)

Required

a. Calculate the ROI, residual income, and EVA for Six Flags over Georgia using book value as the valuation basis for the investment center asset base.

b. Repeat requirement (a) using replacement cost as the investment center asset value.

c. Which valuation, accounting book value or replacement cost do you think the company uses to evaluate the managers of its various theme parks? Discuss.

P11-38. Transfer Pricing with and without Capacity Constraints (LO2)

National Carpet Company has just acquired a new backing division that produces a rubber backing, which it sells for $2.10 per square yard. Sales are about 1,200,000 square yards per year. Since the Backing Division has a capacity of 2,000,000 square yards per year, top management is thinking that it might be wise for the company's Tufting Division to start purchasing from the newly acquired Backing Division. The Tufting Division now purchases 600,000 square yards per year from an outside supplier at a price of $1.90 per square yard. The current price is lower than the competitive $2.10 price as a result of the large quantity discounts. The Backing Division's cost per square yard follows.

Direct materials	$1.00
Direct labor	0.20
Variable overhead	0.25
Fixed overhead (1,200,000 level)	0.10
Total cost	$1.55

Required

a. If both divisions are to be treated as investment centers and their performance evaluated by the ROI formula, what transfer price would you recommend? Why?

b. Determine the effect on corporate profits of making the backing.

c. Based on your transfer price, would you expect the ROI in the Backing Division to increase, decrease, or remain unchanged? Explain.

d. What would be the effect on the ROI of the Tufting Division using your transfer price? Explain.

e. Assume that the Backing Division is now selling 2,000,000 square yards per year to retail outlets. What transfer price would you recommend? What will be the effect on corporate profits?

f. If the Backing Division is at capacity and decides to sell to the Tufting Division for $1.90 per square yard, what will be the effect on the company's profits?

P11-39. Transfer Pricing and Special Orders (LO2)

New England Electronics has several manufacturing divisions. The Pacific Division produces a component part that is used in the manufacture of electronic equipment. The cost per part for July is as follows:

Variable cost	$ 90
Fixed cost (at 2,000 units per month capacity)	60
Total cost per part	$150

Some of Pacific Division's output is sold to outside manufacturers, and some is sold internally to the Atlantic Division. The price per part is $180. The Atlantic Division's cost and revenue structure follow.

Selling price per unit.		$1,000
Less variable costs per unit		
Cost of parts from the Pacific Division	$180	
Other variable costs	400	(580)
Contribution margin per unit		420
Less fixed costs per unit (at 200 units per month).		(100)
Net income per unit		$ 320

The Atlantic Division received an order for 10 units. The buyer wants to pay only $500 per unit.

Required

a. From the perspective of the Atlantic Division, should the $500 price be accepted? Explain.

b. If both divisions have excess capacity, would the Atlantic Division's action benefit the company as a whole? Explain.

c. If the Atlantic Division has excess capacity but the Pacific Division does not and can sell all of its parts to outside manufacturers, what would be the advantage or disadvantage of accepting the ten-unit order at the $500 price to the Atlantic Division?

d. To make a decision that is in the best interest of the company, what transfer-pricing information does the Atlantic Division need?

P11-40. Balanced Scorecard (LO4)

The First Street Community Bank recently decided to adopt a balanced scorecard system of performance evaluation. Below is a list of primary performance goals for four major performance categories that have been identified by corporate management and the board of directors.

1. Financial Perspective–Maintain and grow the bank financially
   - *a.* Increase customer deposits
   - *b.* Manage financial risk
   - *c.* Provide profits for the stockholders
2. Customer Perspective – Maintain and grow the customer base
   - *a.* Increase customer satisfaction
   - *b.* Increase number of depositors & customer retention
   - *c.* Increase quality of deposits
3. Internal Perspective – Improve internal processes
   - *a.* Achieve best practices for processing transactions
   - *b.* Improve employee satisfaction
   - *c.* Improve employee promotion opportunities
4. Learning and Innovation – Improve market differentiation
   - *a.* Beat competitors in introducing new products
   - *b.* Become first mover in establishing customer benefit for customers
   - *c.* Become recognized as an innovator in the industry

Required:

a. For each of the 12 goals above suggest at least one measure of performance to measure the achievement of the goal.

b. At what level of the organization should the balanced scorecard be implemented as a means of evaluating performance? Explain.

CASES

C11-41. Transfer Price Decisions (LO2)

IBM Corporation (IBM)

The Consulting Division of IBM Corporation is often involved in assignments for which IBM computer equipment is sold as part of a systems installation. The Computer Equipment Division is frequently a vendor of the Consulting Division in cases for which the Consulting Division purchases the equipment from the Computer Equipment Division. The Consulting Division does not view itself as a sales arm of the Computer Equipment Division but as a strong competitor to the major consulting firms of information systems. The Consulting Division's goal is to maximize its profit contribution to the company, not necessarily to see how much IBM equipment it can sell. If the Consulting Division is truly an autonomous investment center, it has the freedom to purchase equipment from competing vendors if the consultants believe that a competitor's products serve the needs of a client better than the comparable IBM product in a particular situation.

Required

a. In this situation, should corporate management be concerned about whether the Consulting Division sells IBM products or those of other computer companies? Should the Consulting Division be required to sell only IBM products?

b. Discuss the transfer-pricing issues that both the Computer Equipment Division manager and the Consulting Division manager should consider. If top management does not have a policy on pricing transfers between these two divisions, what alternative transfer prices should the division managers consider?

c. What is your recommendation regarding how the managers of the Consulting and Computer Equipment Divisions can work together in a way that will benefit each of them individually and the company as a whole?

C11-42. Transfer Pricing at Absorption Cost (LO2)

The Fabrication Division of Metro Sign Company produces large metal numbers that are sold to the Sign Division. This division uses the numbers in constructing signs that are sold to highway departments of local governments. The Fabrication Division contains two operations, stamping and finishing. The unit variable cost of materials and labor used in the stamping operation is $100. The fixed stamping overhead is $800,000 per year. Current production (20,000 units) is at full capacity. The variable cost of labor used in the finishing operation is $12 per number. The fixed overhead in this operation is $340,000 per year. The company uses an absorption-cost transfer price. The price data for each operation presented to the Sign Division by the Fabrication Division follow.

Stamping		
Variable cost per unit	$100	
Fixed overhead cost per unit ($800,000 ÷ 20,000 units)	40	$140
Finishing		
Labor cost per unit	12	
Fixed overhead cost per unit ($340,000 ÷ 20,000 units)	17	29
Total cost per unit		$169

An outside company has offered to lease machinery to the Sign Division that would perform the finishing part of the number manufacturing for $200,000 per year. With the new machinery, the labor cost per number would remain at $12. If the Fabrication Division transfers the units for $140, the following analysis can be made:

Current process		
Finishing process costs (20,000 × $29)		$580,000
New process		
Machine rental cost per year	$200,000	
Labor cost ($12 × 20,000 units)	240,000	(440,000)
Savings		$140,000

The manager of the Sign Division wants approval to acquire the new machinery.

Required

a. How would you advise the company concerning the proposed lease?

b. How could the transfer-pricing system be modified or the transfer-pricing problem eliminated?

C11-43. Transfer Pricing Dispute (LO2)

MBR Inc. consists of three divisions that were formerly three independent manufacturing companies. Bader Corporation and Roper Company merged in 2008, and the merged corporation acquired Mitchell Company in 2009. The name of the corporation was subsequently changed to MBR Inc., and each company became a separate division retaining the name of its former company.

The three divisions have operated as if they were still independent companies. Each division has its own sales force and production facilities. Each division management is responsible for sales, cost of operations, acquisition and financing of divisional assets, and working capital management. The corporate management of MBR evaluates the performance of the divisions and division management on the basis of return on investment.

Mitchell Division has just been awarded a contract for a product that uses a component manufactured by the Roper Division and also by outside suppliers. Mitchell used a cost figure of $3.80 for the component manufactured by Roper in preparing its bid for the new product. Roper supplied this cost figure in response to Mitchell's request for the average variable cost of the component; it represents the standard variable manufacturing cost and variable selling and distribution expenses.

Roper has an active sales force that is continually soliciting new prospects. Roper's regular selling price for the component Mitchell needs for the new product is $6.50. Sales of this component are expected to increase. The Roper management has indicated, however, that it could supply Mitchell the required quantities of the component at the regular selling price less variable selling and distribution expenses. Mitchell's management has responded by offering to pay standard variable manufacturing cost plus 20 percent.

The two divisions have been unable to agree on a transfer price. Corporate management has never established a transfer-pricing policy because interdivisional transactions have never occurred. As a compromise, the corporate vice president of finance suggested a price equal to the standard full manufacturing cost (i.e., no selling and distribution expenses) plus a 15 percent markup. The two division managers have also rejected this price because each considered it grossly unfair.

The unit cost structure for the Roper component and the three suggested prices follow.

Standard variable manufacturing cost.	$3.20
Standard fixed manufacturing cost	1.20
Variable selling and distribution expenses.	0.60
	$5.00
Regular selling price less variable selling and distribution expenses ($6.50 − $0.60)	$5.90
Standard full manufacturing cost plus 15% ($4.40 × 1.15).	$5.06
Variable manufacturing plus 20% ($3.20 × 1.20).	$3.84

Required

a. What should be the attitude of the Roper Division's management toward the three proposed prices?

b. Is the negotiation of a price between the Mitchell and Roper Divisions a satisfactory method of solving the transfer-pricing problem? Explain your answer.

c. Should the corporate management of MBR Inc. become involved in this transfer-price controversy? Explain your answer.

(CMA Adapted)

Chapter 12

Capital Budgeting Decisions

LEARNING OBJECTIVES

After completing this chapter, you should be able to:

LO1 Explain the role of capital budgeting in long-range planning. (p. 411)

LO2 Apply capital budgeting models, such as net present value and internal rate of return, that consider the time value of money. (p. 413)

LO3 Apply capital budgeting models, such as payback period and accounting rate of return, that do not consider the time value of money. (p. 419)

LO4 Evaluate the strengths and weaknesses of alternative capital budgeting models. (p. 421)

LO5 Discuss the importance of judgment, attitudes toward risk, and relevant cash flow information for capital budgeting decisions. (p. 423)

LO6 Determine the net present value of investment proposals with consideration of taxes. (p. 430)

DIFFERENT MARKET PREDICTIONS LEAD TO DIFFERENT STRATEGIC INVESTMENTS

Predictions of future costs and revenues are key to managers' decisions on capital expenditures. In both the airline and aircraft manufacturing markets, estimates are that air travel will grow by 5 percent per year over the next decade or two. By 2025, airline fleets are expected to exceed 35,000 airliners, or more than double the current number. In this growth environment for commercial aviation, the two world leaders in the production of large airliners—Airbus and Boeing—have different expectations about the next generation of jet aircraft.

Airbus, predicting the worldwide market for jumbo passenger jets at about 1,500 planes, launched the development of the A380 in the year 2000. The double-deck A380 will carry 525 passengers up to 8,200 nautical miles (approximately 9,400 U.S. miles). Airbus states that the A380 will carry 30 percent more passengers, use 20 percent less fuel, and fly quieter than the Boeing 747-400—the only current plane in this size class. Yet, with a wingspan of 262 feet and outboard engines that hang beyond the 150-foot standard width of airport runways, there are limitations on the number of airports that can accommodate this massive jumbo jet.

The first A380 (recall development started in 2000) was delivered to Singapore Airways in late 2007. By 2008 the development costs of the A380 were reported as $17.1 billion and Airbus stated that it needed to sell 420 units of the plane, that has a list price of $319.2 million, to break even. At the time there were 177 firm orders for the A380, with the largest orders from Emirates, Quantas, Singapore Airways, Lufthansa, and Air France.

Courtesy of Getty Images

Boeing Company has different expectations. It estimates that the airliner market in the next two or three decades will require only about 500 jumbo jets. Forecasting a demand for smaller, fuel-efficient, long-range aircraft that would provide increased opportunities for direct service between smaller distant cities, Boeing formally launched development of the 787 Dreamliner in 2003. Unique in its use of composite materials to reduce weight and improve passenger comfort, some experts claim the 290 passenger aircraft will have the same fuel efficiency as a car carrying three passengers, but traveling at ten times the speed. Depending on configuration, the list price of the 787 varies between $200 and $279 million. Its 208-foot wingspan will allow the 787 to access more airports than the A380.

The first 787 is slated for delivery to All Nippon Airways in early 2009. By early 2008 Boeing had orders for more than 800 Dreamliners from 55 customers, which Boeing claimed to be the "fastest-selling start for any commercial airplane program."

As these decisions of Airbus and Boeing illustrate, managers face high stakes in capital expenditure decisions. Expectations and plans often depend on marketing research information and unproved technology. No analytical tools eliminate the inherent uncertainty of such decisions. Still, executives can use management accounting methods to organize information about a particular decision to better evaluate the alternatives.[1]

[1] Mike Blair, "Barrelling Along," *Economist*, September 29, 2007; Pat Shanahan, "Boeing's Dreamliner: Back on Course?," *Business Week Online*, December 12, 2007, p.1.; David Churchill, "The Giant Arrives," *Business Travel World*, November 2007, p.11.; Thomas Geoffrey, "Nothing But Blue Skies for 787," *Air Transport World*, August 2007, pp. 24-26; Carol Matlack, "Airbus A380: In Business at Last," *Business Week Online*, October 16, 2007, p.9.; "Hold that Takeoff," *Business Week*, January 28, 2008; www.airbus.com; and www.boeing.com.

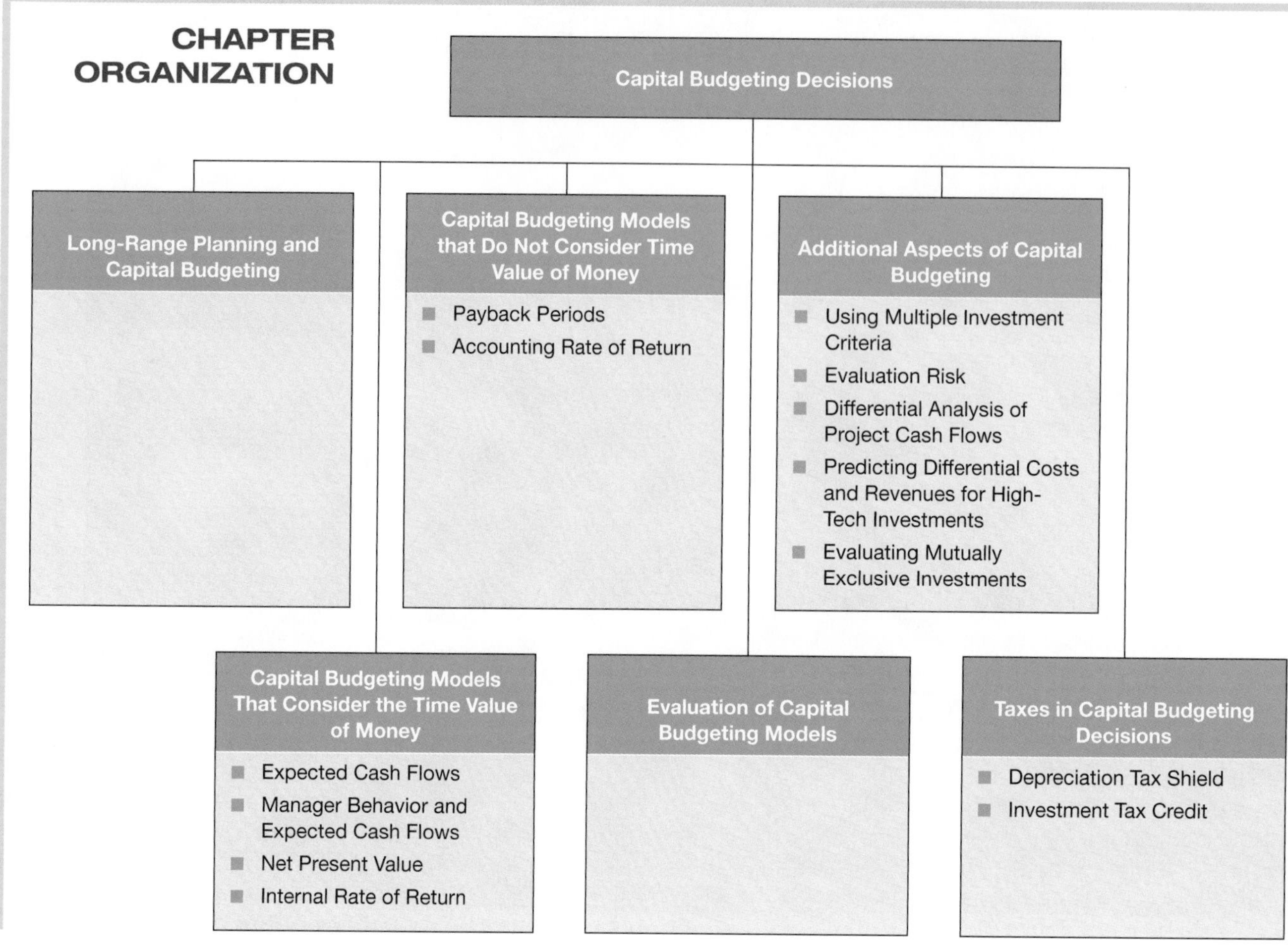

Capital expenditures are investments of financial resources in projects to develop or introduce new products or services, to expand current production or service capacity, or to change current production or service facilities. Capital expenditures are made with the expectation that the new product, process, or service will generate future financial inflows that exceed the initial costs. Capital expenditure decisions affect structural cost drivers. They are made infrequently but once made are difficult to change. They commit the organization to the use of certain facilities and activities to satisfy customer needs. In making large capital expenditure decisions, such as for the Airbus A380 or the Boeing 787, management is risking the future existence of the company.

Although capital expenditure decisions are fraught with risk, management accounting provides the concepts and tools needed to organize information and evaluate the alternatives. This systematic organization and analysis is the essence of capital budgeting. This chapter introduces important capital budgeting concepts and models, and it explains the proper use of accounting data in these models.

Capital budgeting is a process that involves identifying potentially desirable projects for capital expenditures, evaluating capital expenditure proposals, and selecting proposals that meet minimum criteria. A number of quantitative models are available to assist managers in evaluating capital expenditure proposals.

The best capital budgeting models are conceptually similar to the short-range planning models used in Chapters 3 and 4. They all emphasize cash flows and focus on future costs (and revenues) that differ among decision alternatives. The major difference is that capital budgeting models involve cash flows over several years, whereas short-range planning models involve cash flows for a year or less. When the cash flows associated with a proposed activity extend over several years, an adjustment is necessary to make the cash flows comparable when they are expected to occur at different points in time.

The *time value of money concept* explains why monies received or paid at different points in time must be adjusted to comparable values. The time value of money is introduced in Appendix A to this chapter.

LONG-RANGE PLANNING AND CAPITAL BUDGETING

LO1 Explain the role of capital budgeting in long-range planning.

Most organizations plan not only for operations in the current period but also for the longer term, perhaps 5, 10, or even 20 years in the future. Most planning beyond the next budget year is called *long-range planning*.

Increased uncertainty and business alternatives add to the difficulty of planning as the horizon lengthens. Even though long-range planning is difficult and involves uncertainties, management must make long-range planning and capital expenditure decisions. Capital expenditure decisions will be made. The question is: How will they be made? Will they be made on the basis of the best information available? Will care be taken to ensure that capital expenditure decisions are in line with the organization's long-range goals? Will the potential consequences, both positive and negative, of capital expenditures be considered? Will important alternative uses of the organization's limited financial resources be considered in a systematic manner? Will managers be held accountable for the capital expenditure programs they initiate? The alternative to a systematic approach to capital budgeting is the haphazard expenditure of resources on the basis of a hunch, immediate need, or persuasion—without accountability by the person(s) making the decisions.

The steps of an effective capital budgeting process are outlined in Exhibit 12.1. A basic requirement for a systematic approach to capital budgeting is a defined mission, a set of long-range goals, and a business strategy. These elements provide focus and boundaries that reduce the types of capital expenditure decisions management considers. If, for example, KFC's goal is to become the largest fast-food restaurant chain in North America, its management should not consider a proposal to purchase and operate a bus line.

A well-defined business strategy will likewise guide capital expenditure decisions. If Cisco Systems is following a strategy to obtain technological leadership, it might seriously consider a proposal to meet customer needs by investing in innovative production facilities but would not consider a proposal to purchase and refurbish used (but seemingly cost-efficient) equipment. In the following Business Insight Heineken identified reducing energy consumption as a strategic goal, thereby drawing attention to an aspect of business that might otherwise go unnoticed.

EXHIBIT 12.1 Capital Budgeting Procedures

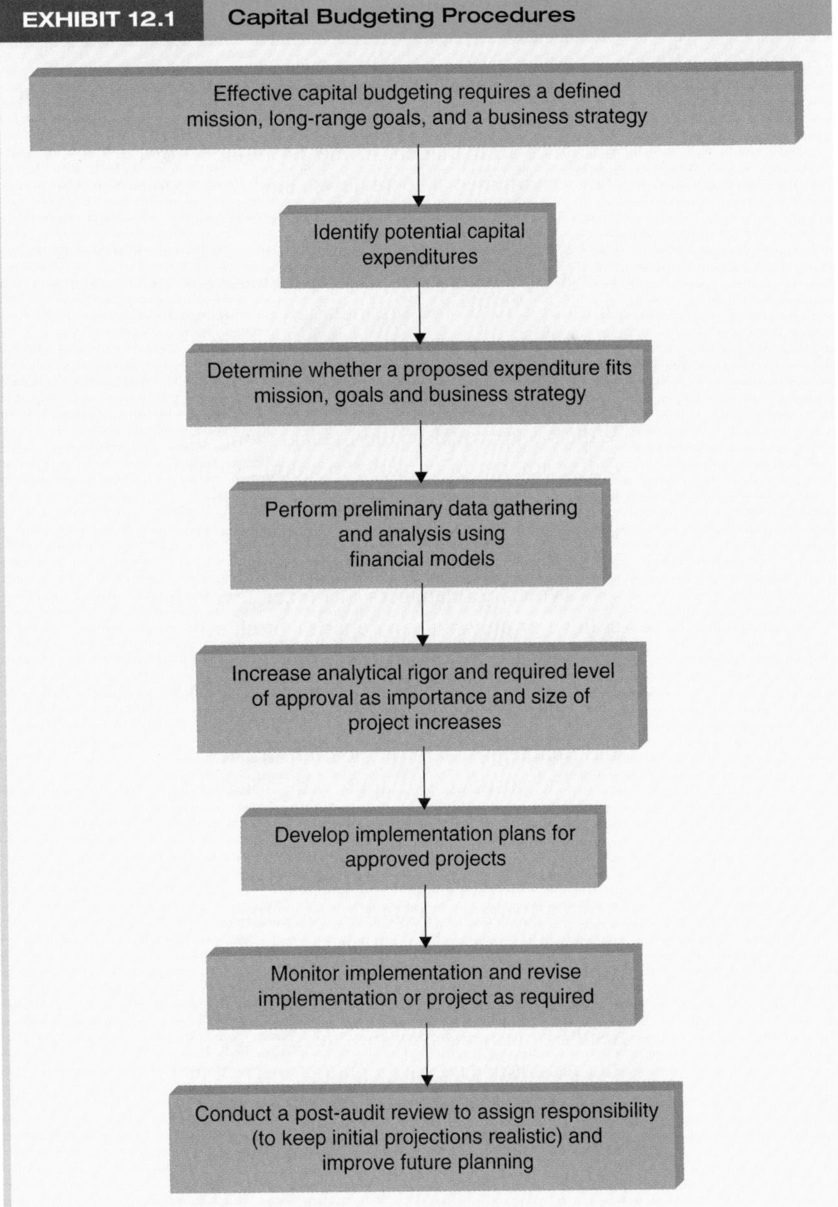
Effective capital budgeting requires a defined mission, long-range goals, and a business strategy
Identify potential capital expenditures
Determine whether a proposed expenditure fits mission, goals and business strategy
Perform preliminary data gathering and analysis using financial models
Increase analytical rigor and required level of approval as importance and size of project increases
Develop implementation plans for approved projects
Monitor implementation and revise implementation or project as required
Conduct a post-audit review to assign responsibility (to keep initial projections realistic) and improve future planning

BUSINESS INSIGHT **Energy Reduction as a Corporate Goal Fosters Green Investments**

With the manufacturing sector accounting for more than one-third of global energy use and energy prices soaring, there are countless opportunities for green investments that reduce energy consumption and costs. Yet, according to energy-expert Paul Waide of the **International Energy Agency**, corporate structure can be an obstacle. No one person is in charge of minimizing energy use. "The purchasing department might be looking for the cheapest motor to install in terms of upfront costs . . . The energy bill gets paid out of some other budget, so unless the company as a whole focuses on the issue, nothing gets done."

Netherlands-based **Heineken**, Europe's largest beer maker, overcame this obstacle by establishing corporate goals for reducing energy consumption. The company plans to use 15 percent less energy in 2010 than it used in 2002. This direction from the top has been important in focusing attention on projects that reduce energy consumption, according to Jasko Bakker, who leads environmental initiatives for Heineken.

HSBC Holdings, an international bank, has committed $90 million to become more energy efficient, with a seven percent targeted reduction in power consumption. HSBC investments to support this goal include software that automatically turns off desktop computers if employees leave them on at night and replacing computer monitors with more efficient models.[2]

Management should also develop procedures for the review, evaluation, approval, and post-audit of capital expenditure proposals. In a large organization, a capital budgeting committee that provides guidance to managers in the formulation of capital expenditure proposals is key to these procedures. This committee also reviews, analyzes, and approves or rejects major capital expenditure proposals. Major projects often require the approval of top management and even the board of directors. The capital budgeting committee should include persons knowledgeable in capital budgeting models; financing alternatives and costs; operating procedures; cost estimation and prediction methods; research and development efforts; the organization's goals and basic strategy; and the expectations of the organization's stockholders or owners. A management accountant who is generally expert in data collection, retrieval, and analysis is normally part of the capital budgeting committee.

Not all capital expenditure proposals require committee approval or are subject to formal evaluation. With the approval of top management, the committee might provide guidelines indicating the type and dollar amount of capital expenditures that managers at each level of the organization can make without formal evaluation or committee approval, or both. The guidelines might state that expenditures of less than $20,000 do not require committee approval and that only expenditures of more than $100,000 must be evaluated using capital budgeting models.

Typically, managers at higher levels have greater discretion in making capital expenditures. In a college or university, a department chairperson could have authority to purchase office and instructional equipment with a maximum limit of $10,000 per year. A dean may have authority to renovate offices or classrooms with a maximum limit of $50,000 per year, but the conversion of the power plant from one fuel source to another at a cost of $400,000 could require the formal review of a capital budgeting committee and final approval of the board of trustees.

The post-audit of approved capital expenditure proposals is an important part of a well-formulated approach to capital budgeting. A *post-audit* involves the development of project performance reports comparing planned and actual results. Project performance reports should be provided to the manager who initiated the capital expenditure proposal, the manager assigned responsibility for the project (if a different person), the project manager's supervisor, and the capital budgeting committee. These reports help keep the project on target (especially during the initial investment phase), identify the need to reevaluate the project if the initial analysis was in error or significant environmental changes occur, and improve the quality of investment proposals. When managers know they will be held accountable for the results of projects they initiate, they are likely to put more care into the development of capital expenditure proposals and take a greater interest in approved projects. Problems can occur when decision makers are rewarded for undertaking major projects but are not held responsible for the consequences that occur several years later.

[2] Leila Abboud and John Biers, "Business Goes on an Energy Diet," *Wall Street Journal*, August 27, 2007, pp. R1, R4.

A post-audit review of approved projects also helps the capital budgeting committee do a better job in evaluating new proposals. The committee might learn how to adjust proposals for the biases of individual managers, learn of new factors that should be considered in evaluating proposals, and avoid the routine approval of projects that appear desirable by themselves but are related to larger projects that are not meeting management's expectations. As summarized in the following Research Insight, an analysis of the findings of post-audit reviews reveals that sales forecasting is the most error-prone element in the financial analysis of capital budgeting.

RESEARCH INSIGHT **Where the Errors Are**

After conducting a study of post-audits of capital expenditures, Professors Sores, Coutinho, and Martins reached the following conclusions:

- Forecasts of operating costs were remarkably accurate.
- There was a high degree of variability in the actual investments when compared to budgeted investments, which may be related to delays in the execution of projects.
- Forecasts of sales were overstated seventy percent of the time, with actual sales, on average, being nine percent below forecasted sales.[3]

MANAGERIAL DECISION **You Are the Vice President of Finance**

You have recently accepted the position of VP of finance for a rapidly growing biotech company. Last year the company made capital expenditures of $10 million and you anticipate that annual capital expenditures will exceed $30 million in a couple of years. You believe it is time to develop a more formal approach to making capital expenditure decisions. Where do you begin? [Answer p. 442]

CAPITAL BUDGETING MODELS THAT CONSIDER TIME VALUE OF MONEY

LO2 Apply capital budgeting models, such as net present value and internal rate of return, that consider the time value of money.

The capital budgeting models in this chapter have gained wide acceptance by for-profit and not-for-profit organizations. Our primary focus is on the *net present value* and the *internal rate of return models*, which are superior because they consider the time value of money. Later discussions will consider more traditional capital budgeting models, such as the payback period and the accounting rate of return that, while useful under certain circumstances, do not consider the time value of money. Although we briefly consider the cost of financing capital expenditures, we leave a detailed treatment of this topic, as well as a detailed examination of the sources of funds for financing investments, to books on financial management.

Expected Cash Flows

The focus of capital budgeting models that consider the time value of money is on future cash receipts and future cash disbursements that differ under decision alternatives. It is often convenient to distinguish between the following three phases of a project's cash flows:

- Initial investment
- Operation
- Disinvestment

All cash expenditures necessary to begin operations are classified as part of the project's *initial investment phase*. Expenditures to acquire property, plant, and equipment are part of the initial investment.

[3] Joao Oliveira Sores, Maria Cristina Coutinho, and Carlos V. Martina, "Forecasting Errors in Capital Budgeting: A multi-firm Post-audit Study, *The Engineering Economist*, Vol 52, 2007, pp. 21-39.

Less obvious, but equally important, are expenditures to acquire working capital to purchase inventories and recruit and train employees. Although the initial investment phase often extends over many years, in our examples, we assume that the initial investment takes place at a single point in time.

Cash receipts from sales of goods or services, as well as normal cash expenditures for materials, labor, and other operating expenses, occur during the operation phase. The *operation phase* is typically broken down into one-year periods; for each period, operating cash expenditures are subtracted from operating cash receipts to determine the net operating cash inflow or outflow for the period.

The *disinvestment phase* occurs at the end of the project's life when assets are disposed of for their salvage value and any initial investment of working capital is recovered. Also included are any expenditures to dismantle facilities and dispose of waste. Although this phase might extend over many years, in our examples, we assume disinvestment takes place at a single point in time.

To illustrate the analysis of a project's cash flows, assume the management of Mobile Yogurt Shoppe is considering a capital expenditure proposal to operate a new shop in a resort community in the Ozark Mountains. Each Mobile Yogurt Shoppe is located in a specially constructed motor vehicle that moves on a regular schedule throughout the community it serves. The predicted cash flows associated with the project, which has an expected life of five years, are presented in Exhibit 12.2.

EXHIBIT 12.2 Analysis of a Project's Predicted Cash Flows

Initial investment (at time 0)		
Vehicle and equipment		$ 90,554
Inventories and other working capital		4,000
Total		$ 94,554
Operation (per year for 5 years)		
Sales		$175,000
Cash expenditures		
Food	$47,000	
Labor	65,000	
Supplies	9,000	
Fuel and utilities	8,000	
Advertising	4,000	
Miscellaneous	12,000	(145,000)
Net annual cash inflow		$ 30,000
Disinvestment (at the end of 5 years)		
Sale of vehicle and equipment		$ 8,000
Recovery of investment in inventories and other working capital		4,000
Total		$ 12,000

Manager Behavior and Expected Cash Flows

Accurately predicting the cash flows associated with a capital expenditure proposal is critical to properly evaluating the proposal. Managers might be overly optimistic with their predictions, and they are sometimes tempted to modify predictions to justify capital expenditures. Perhaps they are interested in personal rewards. They might also want to avoid a loss of prestige or employment for themselves or to keep a local facility operating for the benefit of current employees and the local economy. Unfortunately, if a major expenditure does not work out, not only the local plant but also the entire company could be forced out of business. For example, under pressure to increase current sales, automobile leasing companies could be tempted to overstate cash receipts during the disinvestment phase of a lease. The following Business Insight considers the financial consequences of overstating residual values for automobile leases.

BUSINESS INSIGHT **Manager Behavior and Expected Vehicle Value**

To increase demand for their products, managers of automobile leasing companies have incentives to lower monthly lease rates. Important factors in setting vehicles' lease rates include vehicle cost, interest rate, lease period, and the residual value of the vehicle at lease-end. The most difficult item to predict is residual value. That value, the future selling price of the vehicle, is a function of its condition, economic climate, actions of competitors, and its popularity when the lease expires. If residual values are predicted to be high, the monthly lease can be set low enough to attract customers and still earn a profit. Favorable lease terms help bring down monthly payments of popular Ford Explorers and Jeep Grand Cherokees. With the profitability of leases substantially determined by residual values, a small decrease in market prices of used vehicles can yield a substantial loss.[4]

Net Present Value

A project's **net present value**, usually computed as of the time of the initial investment, is the present value of the project's net cash inflows from operations and disinvestment less the amount of the initial investment. Chapter Appendix A contains an introduction to the time value of money, including net present value fundamentals. In computing a project's net present value, the cash flows occurring at different points in time are adjusted for the time value of money using a **discount rate** that is the minimum rate of return required for the project to be acceptable. Projects with positive net present values (or values at least equal to zero) are acceptable, and projects with negative net present values are unacceptable. Two methods to compute net present value follow.

Table Approach

Assuming that management uses a 12 percent discount rate, the net present value of the proposed investment in a Mobile Yogurt Shoppe is shown in Exhibit 12.3 (a) to be $20,400. Since the net present value is more than zero, the investment in the Mobile Yogurt Shoppe is expected to be profitable, even when adjusted for the time value of money.

We can verify the amounts and computations in Exhibit 12.3. Start by tracing the cash flows back to Exhibit 12.2. Next, verify the 12 percent present value factors in Tables A.1 and A.2 in chapter Appendix A. The initial investment is assumed to occur at a single point in time (identified as time 0), the start of the project. In net present value computations, all cash flows are restated in terms of their value at time 0. Hence, time 0 cash flows have a present value factor of 1. To simplify computations, all other cash flows are assumed to occur at the end of years 1 through 5, even if they occurred during the year. Although further refinements could be made to adjust for cash flows occuring throughout each year, such adjustments are seldom necessary. Observe that net operating cash inflows are treated as an *annuity*, whereas cash flows for the initial investment and disinvestment are treated as *lump-sum amounts*. If net operating cash flows varied from year to year, we would treat each year's cash flow as a separate amount.

Spreadsheet Approach

Spreadsheet software contains functions that compute the present value of a series of cash flows. With this software, simply enter a column or row containing the net cash flows for each period and the appropriate formula. The discount rate of 0.12 is entered as part of the formula. Sample spreadsheet input to determine the net present value of the proposed investment in a Mobile Yogurt Shoppe is shown on the left in Exhibit 12.3 (b). The spreadsheet output is shown on the right, in Exhibit 12.3 (b).

Two cautionary notes follow:

1. The spreadsheet formula for the net present value assumes that the first cash flow occurs at time "1," rather than at time "0." Hence, we cannot include the initial investment in the data set analyzed by the spreadsheet formula when computing the net present value. Instead, the initial investment is subtracted from the present value of future cash flows.
2. Arrange the cash flows subsequent to the initial investment from *top* to bottom in a column, or *left* to right in a row.

---

[4] Kathleen Lansing, "Painful Math for Leasing Companies," *Business Week*, May 19, 1997, p. 38.

EXHIBIT 12.3 Net Present Value of a Project's Predicted Cash Flows

(a) Table approach:

	Predicted Cash Inflows (outflows) (A)	Year(s) of Cash Flows (B)	12% Present Value Factor (C)	Present Value of Cash Flows (A) × (C)
Initial investment	$(94,554)	0	1.000	$ (94,554)
Operation	30,000	1–5	3.605	108,150
Disinvestment	12,000	5	0.567	6,804
Net present value of all cash flows				$ 20,400

(b) Spreadsheet approach:

Input:

	A	B
1	Year of cash flow	Cash flow
2	1	$30,000
3	2	30,000
4	3	30,000
5	4	30,000
6	5	42,000
7	Present value	=NPV(0.12,B2:B6)
8	Initial investment at time 0	(94,554)
9	Net present value	=B7+B8

Output:

	A	B
1	Year of cash flow	Cash flow
2	1	$ 30,000
3	2	30,000
4	3	30,000
5	4	30,000
6	5	42,000
7	Present value	$114,952.41
8	Initial investment at time 0	(94,554.00)
9	Net present value	$ 20,398.41

Internal Rate of Return

The **internal rate of return (IRR)**, often called the **time-adjusted rate of return**, is the discount rate that equates the present value of a project's cash inflows with the present value of the project's cash outflows. Other ways to describe IRR include: (1) The minimum rate that could be paid for the money invested in a project without losing money, and (2) The discount rate that results in a project's net present value equaling zero.

All practical applications of the IRR model use a calculator or spreadsheet. Thus, we illustrate determining an IRR with a spreadsheet. A table approach to determining a project's internal rate of return is illustrated in Appendix B of this chapter.

With spreadsheet software, simply enter a column or row containing the net cash flows for each period and the appropriate formula. Spreadsheet input for Mobile Yogurt Shoppe's investment proposal is shown in Exhibit 12.4. The spreadsheet formula for the IRR assumes that the first cash flow occurs at time "0."

The spreadsheet approach requires an initial prediction or guess of the project's internal rate of return. Although the closeness of the prediction to the final solution affects computational speed, for textbook examples almost any number can be used. We use an initial estimate of 0.08 in all illustrations. Because the IRR formula assumes that the first cash flow occurs at time 0, the initial investment is included in the data analyzed by the IRR formula. Again, we must order the cash flows from top to bottom in a column or left to right in a row. As shown on the right column in Exhibit 12.4, the spreadsheet software computes the IRR as 20 percent.

Although a project's IRR should be compared to the discount rate established by management, such a discount rate is often unknown. In these situations, computing the IRR still provides insights into a project's profitability.

EXHIBIT 12.4 Spreadsheet Approach to Determining Internal Rate of Return

Input:

	A	B
1	Year of cash flow	Cash flow
2	0	$(94,554)
3	1	30,000
4	2	30,000
5	3	30,000
6	4	30,000
7	5	42,000
8	IRR	=IRR(B2:B7,0.08)*

Output:

	A	B
1	Year of cash flow	Cash flow
2	0	$(94,554)
3	1	30,000
4	2	30,000
5	3	30,000
6	4	30,000
7	5	42,000
8	IRR	0.20

**The formula is "=IRR(Input data range, guess)." The guess, which is any likely rate of return, is used as an initial starting point in determining the solution. We use 0.08 in all illustrations.*

The calculated internal rate of return is compared to the discount rate established by management to evaluate investment proposals. If the proposal's IRR is greater than or equal to the discount rate, the project is acceptable; if it is less than the discount rate, the project is unacceptable. Because Mobile Yogurt Shoppes has a 12 percent discount rate, the project is acceptable using the IRR model.

Although a computer and appropriate software quickly and accurately perform tedious computations, computational ease increases the opportunity for inappropriate use. The ability to plug numbers into a computer or calculator and obtain an output labeled NPV or IRR could mislead the unwary into believing that capital budgeting models are easy to use. This is not true. Training and professional judgment are required to identify relevant costs, to implement procedures to obtain relevant cost information, and to make a good decision once results are available. Capital budgeting models are merely decision aids. Managers, not models, make the decisions. To better illustrate underlying concepts, all subsequent textbook illustrations use a table approach.

Cost of Capital

When discounting models are used to evaluate capital expenditure proposals, management must determine the discount rate (1) used to compute a proposal's net present value or (2) used as the standard for evaluating a proposal's IRR. An organization's cost of capital is often used as this discount rate.

The **cost of capital** is the average cost an organization pays to obtain the resources necessary to make investments. This average rate considers items such as the:

- Effective interest rate on debt (notes or bonds).
- Effective dividend rate on preferred stock.
- Discount rate that equates the present value of all dividends expected on common stock over the life of the organization to the current market value of the organization's common stock.

The cost of capital for a company that has no debt or preferred stock equals the cost of equity capital, computed as follows:

$$\textbf{Cost of equity capital} = \frac{\textbf{Current annual dividend per common share}}{\textbf{Current market price per common share}} + \textbf{Expected dividend growth rate}$$

Procedures for determining the cost of capital for more complex capital structures are covered in finance books. Investing in a project that has an internal rate of return equal to the cost of capital should not affect the market value of the firm's securities. Investing in a project that has a return higher than the cost of capital should increase the market value of a firm's securities. If, however, a firm invests in a project that has a return less than the cost of capital, the market value of the firm's securities should fall.

The cost of capital is the minimum return acceptable for investment purposes. Any investment proposal not expected to yield this minimum rate should normally be rejected. Because of difficulties encountered in determining the cost of capital, many organizations adopt a discount rate or a target rate of return without complicated mathematical analysis.

MID-CHAPTER REVIEW

Consider the following investment proposal:

Initial investment	
Depreciable assets	$27,740
Working capital	3,000
Operations (per year for 4 years)	
Cash receipts	25,000
Cash expenditures	15,000
Disinvestment	
Salvage value of plant and equipment	2,000
Recovery of working capital	3,000

Required

Determine each of the following:

a. Net present value at a 10 percent discount rate.

b. Internal rate of return. (Refer to Appendix 12B if using the table approach.)

Solution

Basic computations:

Initial investment	
Depreciable assets	$27,740
Working capital	3,000
Total	$30,740
Operation	
Cash receipts	$25,000
Cash expenditures	(15,000)
Net cash inflow	$10,000
Disinvestment	
Sale of depreciable assets	$ 2,000
Recovery of working capital	3,000
Total	$ 5,000

a. Net present value at a 10 percent discount rate:

	Predicted Cash Inflows (outflows) (A)	Year(s) of Cash Flows (B)	10% Present Value Factor (C)	Present Value of Cash Flows (A) × (C)
Initial investment	$(30,740)	0	1.000	$(30,740)
Operation	10,000	1–4	3.170	31,700
Disinvestment	5,000	4	0.683	3,415
Net present value of all cash flows				$ 4,375

b. Internal rate of return:
Using a spreadsheet, the proposal's internal rate of return is readily determined to be 16 percent:

	A	B
1	Year of cash flow	Cash flow
2	0	$(30,740)
3	1	10,000
4	2	10,000
5	3	10,000
6	4	15,000
7	IRR	0.16

The table approach requires additional analysis. Because the proposal has a positive net present value when discounted at 10 percent, its internal rate of return must be higher than 10 percent. Through a trial-and-error approach, the internal rate of return is determined to be 16 percent.

	Predicted Cash Inflows (outflows) (A)	Year(s) of Cash Flows (B)	16% Present Value Factor (C)	Present Value of Cash Flows (A) × (C)
Initial investment	$(30,740)	0	1.000	$(30,740)
Operation	10,000	1–4	2.798	27,980
Disinvestment	5,000	4	0.552	2,760
Net present value of all cash flows				$ 0

CAPITAL BUDGETING MODELS THAT DO NOT CONSIDER TIME VALUE OF MONEY

LO3 Apply capital budgeting models, such as payback period and accounting rate of return, that do not consider the time value of money.

Years ago, capital budgeting models that do not consider the time value of money were more widely used than discounting models. Although most large organizations use net present value or internal rate of return as their primary evaluation tool, they often use nondiscounting models as an initial screening device. Further, as discussed in the following Research Insight, nondiscounting models remain entrenched in small businesses. We consider two nondiscounting models, the *payback period* and the *accounting rate of return.*

Payback Period

The **payback period** is the time required to recover the initial investment in a project from operations. The payback decision rule states that acceptable projects must have less than some maximum payback period designated by management. Payback emphasizes management's concern with liquidity and the need to minimize risk through a rapid recovery of the initial investment. It is frequently used for small expenditures having such obvious benefits that the use of more sophisticated capital budgeting models is not required or justified.

When a project is expected to have equal annual operating cash inflows, its payback period is computed as follows:

$$\textbf{Payback period} = \frac{\textbf{Initial investment}}{\textbf{Annual operating cash inflows}}$$

For Mobile Yogurt Shoppe's investment proposal, outlined in Exhibit 12.2, the payback period is 3.15 years:

$$\textbf{Payback period} = \frac{\$94{,}554}{\$30{,}000}$$
$$= \textbf{3.15}$$

RESEARCH NSIGHT **Size and Education Matter in Capital Budgeting**[5]

Danielson and Scott, after surveying the owners of small business, concluded that small businesses (an average of ten employees) use much less sophisticated methods in making capital expenditure decisions than recommended by theory. In their survey the most frequently used approach to making capital expenditure decisions was "gut feel" followed by payback period and the accounting rate of return, with few firms using discounted cash flow methods. Commenting on their results, Danielson and Scott observed that:

- Many small business owners have limited formal education and limited staff support. What's more, the investments made by small business are often not discretionary. The firm either makes the investment, say in a new delivery truck, or goes out of business.
- The use of payback appears to increase with the formal education of the business owner as well as the use of basic budgeting techniques such as forecasting cash flows.
- The use of the accounting rate of return increases with the growth or expansion plans of small firms, especially if the firm is required to provide banks with periodic financial information.
- Small businesses with owners having advanced degrees are most likely to use discounted cash flow approaches. They are also most likely to have written business plans and most likely to consider the tax implications of decisions.

Graham and Harvey surveyed chief financial officers (CFOs) of Fortune 500 firms as well as CFOs of smaller firms belonging to the Financial Executives Institute (FEI). CFO's and members of the FEI are likely to have formal education in capital budgeting and they are likely to network with finance professionals through organizations such as the FEI.

Of the CFOs responding to the survey, 46 percent were at firms with sales of more than $1 billion. The majority of respondents to the Graham-Harvey survey used multiple capital budgeting models:

- 75.7 percent used internal rate of return.
- 74.9 percent used net present value.
- More than 50 percent used payback.
- Approximately 20 percent used the accounting rate of return.

Even though the firms included in the Graham-Harvey study were much larger than those in the Danielson-Scott study, Graham and Harvey also noted that "small firms" (firms with sales of less than $100 million) are less likely to use net present value than large firms.

Determining the payback period for a project having unequal cash flows is slightly more complicated. Assume that Alderman Company is evaluating a capital expenditure proposal that requires an initial investment of $50,000 and has the following expected net cash inflows:

Year	Net Cash Inflow
1	$15,000
2	25,000
3	40,000
4	20,000
5	10,000

To compute the payback period, we must determine the net unrecovered amount at the end of each year. In the year of full recovery, the net cash inflows are assumed to occur evenly and are prorated based on the unrecovered investment at the start of the year. Full recovery of Alderman Company's investment proposal is expected to occur in Year 3:

[5] Morris G. Danielson and Jonathan A. Scott, "The Capital Budgeting Decisions of Small Businesses." *Journal of Applied Finance*, Fall/Winter 2006, pp. 45-56. John R. Graham and Campbell R. Harvey, "The Theory and Practice of Corporate Finance: Evidence from the Field," *Journal of Financial Economics*, May-June, 2001, pp: 187-243

Year	Net Cash Inflow	Unrecovered Investment
0	$ - 0	$50,000
1	15,000	35,000
2	25,000	10,000
3	40,000	0

Therefore, $10,000 of $40,000 is needed in Year 3 to complete the recovery of the initial investment. This provides a proportion of 0.25 ($10,000 ÷ $40,000) and a payback period of 2.25 years (2 years plus 0.25 of Year 3). This project is acceptable if management specified a maximum payback period of three years. Because they occur after the payback period, the net cash inflows of Years 4 and 5 are ignored.

Accounting Rate of Return

The **accounting rate of return** is the average annual increase in net income that results from the acceptance of a capital expenditure proposal divided by either the initial investment or the average investment in the project. This method differs from other capital budgeting models in that it focuses on accounting income rather than on cash flow. In most capital budgeting applications, accounting net income is approximated as net cash inflow from operations minus expenses not requiring the use of cash, such as depreciation.

Consider Mobile Yogurt Shoppe's capital expenditure proposal whose cash flows were outlined in Exhibit 12.2. The vehicle and equipment cost $90,554 and have a disposal value of $8,000 at the end of five years, resulting in an average annual increase in net income of $13,489:

Annual net cash inflow from operations.	$30,000
Less average annual depreciation [($90,554 − $8,000) ÷ 5].	(16,511)
Average annual increase in net income	$13,489

Considering the investment in inventories and other working capital, the initial investment is $94,554 ($90,554 + $4,000), and the *accounting rate of return on initial investment* is 14.27 percent:

$$\text{Accounting rate of return on initial investment} = \frac{\text{Average annual increase in net income}}{\text{Initial investment}} = \frac{\$13{,}489}{\$94{,}554} = 0.1427$$

The average investment, computed as the initial investment plus the expected value of any disinvestment, all divided by 2, is $53,277 [($94,554 + $12,000) ÷ 2]. The *accounting rate of return on average investment* is 25.32 percent:

$$\text{Accounting rate of return on average investment} = \frac{\text{Average annual increase in net income}}{\text{Average investment}} = \frac{\$13{,}489}{\$53{,}277} = 0.2532$$

When using the accounting rate of return, management specifies either the initial investment or average investment plus some minimum acceptable rate. Management rejects capital expenditure proposals with a lower accounting rate of return but accepts proposals with an accounting rate of return higher than or equal to the minimum.

EVALUATION OF CAPITAL BUDGETING MODELS

LO4 Evaluate the strengths and weaknesses of alternative capital budgeting models.

As a single criterion for evaluating capital expenditure proposals, capital budgeting models that consider the time value of money are superior to models that do not consider it. The payback model concerns merely how long it takes to recover the initial investment from a project, yet investments are not made with the objective of merely getting the money back. Indeed, not investing has a payback period of 0. Investments are made to earn a profit. Hence, what happens after the payback period is more important than is the payback period itself. The payback period model, when used as the sole investment criterion, has a fatal flaw in that it fails to consider cash flows after the payback period. Despite this flaw, payback is a rough-and-ready approach to getting a handle on investment proposals. Sometimes a project is so attractive using payback that, when its life is considered, no further analysis is necessary.

For total life evaluations, the accounting rate of return is superior to the payback period because it does consider a capital expenditure proposal's profitability. Using the accounting rate of return, a project that merely returns the initial investment will have an average annual increase in net income of 0 and an accounting rate of return of 0. The problem with the accounting rate of return is that it fails to consider the timing of cash flows. It treats all cash flows within the life of an investment proposal equally despite the fact that cash flows occurring early in a project's life are more valuable than cash flows occurring late in a project's life. Early period cash flows can earn additional profits by being invested elsewhere. Consider the two investment proposals summarized in Exhibit 12.5. Both have an accounting rate of return of 5 percent, but Proposal A is superior to Proposal B because most of its cash flows occur in the first two years. Because of the timing of the cash flows when discounted at an annual rate of 10 percent, Proposal A has a net present value of $1,140 while Proposal B has a negative net present value of $(10,940).

EXHIBIT 12.5 Evaluating Capital Budgeting Models with Differences in Cash Flow Timing

Accounting rate of return analysis of Projects A and B

	Project A	Project B
Predicted net cash inflow from operations		
Year 1	$ 50,000	$ 10,000
Year 2	50,000	10,000
Year 3	10,000	50,000
Year 4	10,000	50,000
Total	120,000	120,000
Total depreciation	(100,000)	(100,000)
Total net income	$ 20,000	$ 20,000
Project life	÷ 4 years	÷ 4 years
Average annual increase in net income	$ 5,000	$ 5,000
Initial investment	÷ 100,000	÷ 100,000
Accounting rate of return on initial investment	0.05	0.05

Net present value analysis of Project A

	Predicted Cash Inflows (outflows)	Year(s) of Cash Flows	10% Present Value Factor	Present Value of Cash Flows
Initial investment	$(100,000)	0	1.000	$(100,000)
Operation	50,000	1–2	1.736	86,800
Operation	10,000	3–4	3.170−1.736	14,340
Net present value of all cash flows				$ 1,140

Net present value analysis of Project B

	Predicted Cash Inflows (outflows)	Year(s) of Cash Flows	10% Present Value Factor	Present Value of Cash Flows
Initial investment	$(100,000)	0	1.000	$(100,000)
Operation	10,000	1–2	1.736	17,360
Operation	50,000	3–4	3.170−1.736	71,700
Net present value of all cash flows				$ (10,940)

The net present value and the internal rate of return models both consider the time value of money and project profitability. They almost always provide the same evaluation of individual projects whose acceptance or rejection will not affect other projects. (An exception can occur when periods of net cash outflows are mixed with periods of net cash inflows. Under these circumstances, an investment proposal could have multiple internal rates of return.) The net present value and the internal rate of return models, however, have two basic differences that often lead to differences in the evaluation of competing investment proposals:

1. The net present value model gives explicit consideration to investment size. The internal rate of return model does not.
2. The net present value model assumes that all net cash inflows are reinvested at the discount rate; the internal rate of return model assumes that all net cash inflows are reinvested at the project's internal rate of return.

These differences are considered later when we discuss mutually exclusive investments.

ADDITIONAL ASPECTS OF CAPITAL BUDGETING

LO5 Discuss the importance of judgment, attitudes toward risk, and relevant cash flow information for capital budgeting decisions.

The capital budgeting models discussed do not make investment decisions. Rather, they help managers separate capital expenditure proposals that meet certain criteria from those that do not. Managers then focus on those proposals that pass the initial screening.

Using Multiple Investment Criteria

In performing this initial screening, management can use a single capital budgeting model or multiple models, including some we have not discussed. Management might specify that proposals must be in line with the organization's long-range goals and business strategy, have a maximum payback period of three years, have a positive net present value when discounted at 14 percent, and have an initial investment of less than $500,000. The maximum payback period might be intended to reduce risk, the present value criterion might be to ensure an adequate return to investors, and the maximum investment size might reflect the resources available for investment.

Nonquantitative factors such as market position, operational performance improvement, and strategy implementation often play a decisive role in management's final decision to accept or reject a capital expenditure proposal that has passed the initial screening. Also important at this point are top management's attitudes toward risk and financing alternatives, their confidence in the professional judgment of other managers making investment proposals, their beliefs about the future direction of the economy, and their evaluation of alternative investments. In the following sections, we will focus on evaluating risk, differential analysis of project cash flows, predicting differential costs and revenues for high-tech investments, and evaluating mutually exclusive investments.

Evaluating Risk

All capital expenditure proposals involve risk, including risk related to

- Cost of the initial investment.
- Time required to complete the initial investment and begin operations.
- Whether the new facilities will operate as planned.
- Life of the facilities.
- Customers' demand for the product or service.
- Final selling price.
- Operating costs.
- Disposal values.

Projected cash flows (such as those summarized for the Mobile Yogurt Shoppe proposal in Exhibit 12.2) are based on management's best predictions. Although these predictions are likely to reflect the professional judgment of economists, marketing personnel, engineers, and accountants, they are far from certain.

Many techniques have been developed to assist in the analysis of the risks inherent in capital budgeting. Suggested approaches include the following:

- *To adjust the discount rate for individual projects based on management's perception of the risks associated with a project.* A project perceived as being almost risk free might be evaluated using a discount rate of 12 percent; a project perceived as having moderate risk may be evaluated using a discount rate of 16 percent; and a project perceived as having high risk might be evaluated using a discount rate of 20 percent.
- *To compute several internal rates of return and/or net present values for a project.* For example, a project's net present value might be computed three times: first assuming the most optimistic projections of cash flows; second assuming the most likely projections of cash flows; and third assuming the most pessimistic projections of cash flows. The final decision is then based on management's attitudes toward risk. A project whose most likely outcome is highly profitable would probably be rejected if its pessimistic outcome might lead to bankruptcy.
- *To subject a capital expenditure proposal to sensitivity analysis*, a study of the responsiveness of a model's dependent variable(s) to changes in one or more of its independent variables. Management might want to know, for example, the minimum annual net cash inflows that will provide an internal rate of return of 12 percent with other cost and revenue projections being as expected.

Consider the situation presented in Exhibit 12.2 and analyzed using the net present value and the internal rate of return models in Exhibits 12-3 and 12-4. This proposal has a positive net present value when its cash flows are discounted at 12 percent and an expected IRR of 20 percent. Assuming that Mobile Yogurt Shoppes has a 12 percent discount rate, management might wish to know the minimum annual net cash inflow that will meet this criterion.

In Exhibit 12.3, disinvestment cash inflows have a net present value of $6,804. When this amount is subtracted from the initial investment, $87,750 ($94,554 − $6,804) of the initial investment must be recovered from operations. If this amount is to be recovered over a five-year period with equal annual net cash inflows and a 12 percent discount rate, the factor 3.605 (see Exhibit 2 in the chapter Appendix A) must equate the annual net cash inflows with the portion of the initial investment to be recovered from operations. Hence, the minimum annual net cash inflows must be $24,341:

$$\textbf{Minimum annual net cash inflow} = \frac{\$87{,}750}{3.605}$$
$$= \$24{,}341$$

If management could then predict the probability of annual net cash inflows being more than or equal to $24,341, this would be the likelihood of the project meeting or exceeding a 12 percent discount rate. Again, the ultimate decision to accept or reject the proposal rests with management and their attitudes toward risk.

Notice the similarity of determining the minimum annual net cash inflows and that of determining the break-even point in Chapter 3. In effect, $24,341 in annual net cash inflows is a time-adjusted break-even point.

Differential Analysis of Project Cash Flows

All previous examples assume that capital expenditure proposals produce additional net cash inflows, but this is not always the case. Units of government and not-for-profit organizations might provide services that do not produce any cash inflows. For-profit organizations might be required to make capital expenditures to maintain product quality or to bring facilities up to environmental or safety standards. In these situations, it is impossible to compute a project's payback period, accounting rate of return, or internal rate of return. It is possible, however, to compute the present value of all life cycle costs associated with alternative ways of providing the service or meeting the environmental or safety standard. Here, the alternative with the smallest negative net present value is preferred.

Capital expenditure proposals to reduce operating costs by upgrading facilities might not provide any incremental cash inflows. Again, we can use a total cost approach and calculate the present value of the costs associated with each alternative, with the low-cost alternative being preferred. Alternatively, we can perform a differential analysis of cash flows and, treating any reduced operating costs as if they were cash inflows, compute the net present value or the internal rate of return of the cost reduction proposal. Recall from Chapter 4 that a relevant cost analysis focuses on the costs that differ under alternative actions. Once the differential amounts have been determined, they can be adjusted for the time value of money. To illustrate the differential approach, we consider an example introduced in Chapter 4.

Elektra, Inc. produces a variety of electronic components, including 10,000 units per year of a component used in wireless headsets. The machine currently used in manufacturing the headset components is two years old and has a remaining useful life of four years. It cost $90,000 and has an estimated salvage value of zero dollars at the end of its useful life. Its current book value (original cost less accumulated depreciation) is $60,000, but its current disposal value is only $35,000.

Management is evaluating the desirability of replacing the machine with a new machine. The new machine costs $80,000, has a useful life of four years, and a predicted salvage value of zero dollars at the end of its useful life. Although the new machine has the same productive capacity as the old machine, its predicted operating costs are lower because it requires less electricity. Furthermore, because of a computer control system, the new machine will require less frequent and less expensive inspections and adjustments. Finally, the new machine requires less maintenance.

An analysis of the cash flows associated with this cost reduction proposal, separated into the three phases of the project's life, are presented in Exhibit 12.6. Because the proposal does not have a disposal value, this portion of the analysis could have been omitted. (A detailed explanation of the relevant costs included in this analysis is in Exhibit 4.1 and the accompanying Chapter 4 discussion of relevant costs.) Assuming that Elektra, Inc. has a discount rate of 12 percent, the proposal's net present value (computed in Exhibit 12.7) is $2,681, and the proposal is acceptable.

EXHIBIT 12.6 Differential Analysis of Predicted Cash Flows

	Differential Analysis of Predicted Cash Flows		
	Keep Old Machine (A)	Replace with New Machine (B)	Difference (income effect of replacement) (A) − (B)
Initial investment			
Cost of new machine		$80,000	$80,000
Disposal value of old machine		(35,000)	(35,000)
Net initial investment			$45,000
Annual operating cash savings			
Conversion			
Old machine (10,000 units × $5)	$50,000		
New machine (10,000 units × $4)		$40,000	$10,000
Inspection and adjustment			
Old machine (10 setups × $500 per setup)	5,000		
New machine (5 setups × $300 per setup)		1,500	3,500
Machine maintenance			
Old machine ($200 per month × 12 months)	2,400		
New machine ($200 per year)		200	2,200
Net annual cost savings			$15,700
Disinvestment at end of life			
Old machine	$ 0		
New machine		$ 0	

EXHIBIT 12.7 Differential Analysis of Predicted Cash Flows

	Predicted Cash Inflows (outflows) (A)	Year(s) of Cash Flows (B)	12% Present Value Factor (C)	Present Value of Cash Flows (A) × (C)
Initial investment	$(45,000)	0	1.000	$(45,000)
Operation	15,700	1–4	3.037	47,681
Disinvestment	0	4	0.636	0
Net present value of all cash flows				$ 2,681

Predicting Differential Costs and Revenues for High-Tech Investments

Care must be taken when evaluating proposals for investments in the technological innovations such as flexible manufacturing systems and computer integrated manufacturing. The three types of errors to consider are: (1) investing in unnecessary or overly complex equipment, (2) overestimating cost saving, and (3) underestimating incremental sales.

Investing in Unnecessary or Overly Complex Equipment

A common error is to simply compare the cost associated with the current inefficient way of doing things with the predicted cost of performing the identical operations with more modern equipment. Although capital budgeting models might suggest that such investments are justifiable, the result could be the costly and rapid completion of non-value-added activities. Consider the following examples.

- A company invests in an automated system to speed the movement of work in process between workstations without first evaluating the plant layout. The firm is still unable to compete with other companies having better organized plants that allow lower cycle times, lower work-in-process inventories, and lower manufacturing costs. Management should have evaluated the plant layout before investing in new equipment. They may have found that rearranging the factory floor would have reduced materials movement and eliminated the need for the investment.
- A company invests in an automated warehouse to permit the rapid storage and retrieval of goods while competitors work to eliminate excess inventory. The firm is left with large inventories and a large investment in the automated warehouse while competitors, not having to earn a return on similar investments, are able to charge lower prices. Management should have evaluated the need for current inventory levels and perhaps shifted to a just-in-time approach to inventory management before considering the investment in an automated warehouse.
- A company hires staff to perform quality inspections while competitors implement total quality management and seek to eliminate the need for quality inspections. While defective products or services are now identified before they affect customers, they still exist. Furthermore, the company has higher expenditures than competitors, resulting in a less competitive cost structure. The inspections might not have been needed if management had shifted from inspecting for conformance to an emphasis on "doing it right the first time."
- A company invests in automated welding equipment to more efficiently produce printer casings while competitors simplify the product design and shift from welded to molded plastic casings. Although the cost of producing the welded casings might be lower, the company's cost structure is still not competitive.

All of these examples illustrate the limitations of capital budgeting models and the need for good judgment. *In the final analysis, managers, not models, make decisions.* Management must carefully evaluate the situations and determine whether they have considered the proper alternatives and all important cash flows.

Overestimating Cost Savings

When a number of activities drive manufacturing overhead costs, estimates of overhead cost savings based on a single activity cost driver can significantly overestimate cost savings. Assume, for example, that a company containing both machine-intensive and labor-intensive operations develops a cost-estimating equation for overhead with labor as the only independent variable. Because of this, all overhead costs are associated with labor. The predicted cost savings can be computed as the sum of predicted reductions in labor plus predicted reductions in overhead; the predicted reductions in overhead are computed as the overhead per direct labor dollar or labor hour multiplied by the predicted reduction in direct labor dollars or labor hours. Because a major portion of the overhead is driven by factors other than direct labor, reducing direct labor will not provide the predicted savings. Capital budgeting models might suggest that the investment is acceptable, but the models are based on inaccurate cost data.

Management should beware of overly simplistic computations of cost savings. This is an area in which management needs the assistance of well-trained management accountants and engineers.

Underestimating Incremental Sales or Cost Savings

In evaluating proposals for investments in new equipment, management often assumes that the baseline for comparison is the current sales level, but this might not be the case. If competitors are investing in equipment to better meet customer needs and to reduce costs, a failure to make similar investments might result in uncompetitive prices and declining, rather than steady, sales. Hence, the baseline for sales without the investment is overstated, and the incremental sales of the investment is understated. Not considering the likely decline in sales understates the incremental sales associated with the investment and biases the results against the proposed investment.

Investments in manufacturing technologies, such as flexible manufacturing systems (FMS) and computer integrated manufacturing (CIM), do more than simply allow the efficient production of current products. Such investments also make possible the rapid, low-cost switching to new products. The result is expanded sales opportunities.

Such investments might also produce cost savings further down the value chain, either within or outside the company. Elektra's decision to acquire a new machine might have the unanticipated consequence of reducing customer warranty claims or increasing sales because customers are attracted to a higher-quality product.

Unfortunately, because such opportunities are difficult to quantify, they are often ignored in the evaluation of capital expenditure proposals. The solution to this dilemma involves the application of management's professional judgment, a willingness to take risks based on this professional judgment, and recognition that certain investments transcend capital budgeting models in that they involve strategic as well as long-range planning. At this level of planning, qualitative decisions concerning the nature of the organization are at least as important as quantified factors. The following Business Insight examines the difficulty Aetna Life and Casualty Company encountered in evaluating strategic investments in information technology.

BUSINESS INSIGHT **Investment Returns Are Not Always Quantifiable**

After spending a year trying to determine how to measure the return from investments in information technology, the senior vice president of information and technology at Aetna Life & Casualty Company gave up, calling it "an exercise in futility." He observed that while there appears to be a correlation between investments in information technology and reductions in cost, it is difficult to say that one caused the other. Aetna has a complex computer system that links a collection of central databases with computer networks around the country. The system provides up-to-date information so that agents can immediately respond to customer questions. The complexity of the system makes it difficult to evaluate proposals for additional investments in the system. The vice president's frustration came from the fact that "once a business unit implemented a new technology solution, the [business and technology] became so integrated that you couldn't tell them apart." Aetna managers now make the case for additional investments in technology on the basis of business objectives such as customer satisfaction and product improvements.[6]

[6] "Magic Formula," *Wall Street Journal*, November 14, 1994, p. R18.

Evaluating Mutually Exclusive Investments

Two or more capital expenditure proposals are **mutually exclusive investments** if the acceptance of one automatically causes the rejection of the other(s). Perhaps a builder with a tract of land on the outskirts of Paris is trying to determine the most profitable use of the land. Because of the size of the tract and zoning requirements, the land can be used for only one of three purposes: a shopping center, a housing development, or an office park.

When faced with mutually exclusive investments, management must determine which one to accept. The decision is relatively easy if only one of the proposals meets the organization's investment criteria. If, however, two or more proposals pass the initial screening performed by the investment criteria, management faces the task of selecting the best of the acceptable proposals. To help in this determination, management could request that the proposals be ranked on the basis of some criterion such as net present value or internal rate of return. Unfortunately, while these models almost always lead to identical decisions when used to evaluate individual investment proposals, they frequently produce different rankings of acceptable proposals. Assume that management can select only one of three mutually exclusive investment proposals. Relevant information is summarized in Exhibit 12.8.

EXHIBIT 12.8 Ranking Capital Budgeting Proposals

($ thousands)	Proposal A	Proposal B	Proposal C
Predicted cash flows			
Initial investment	$(26,900)	$(55,960)	$(30,560)
Operation			
Year 1	10,000	20,000	20,000
Year 2	10,000	20,000	20,000
Year 3	10,000	20,000	0
Year 4	10,000	20,000	0
Disinvestment	0	0	0
Investment criterion			
Net present value at 12%	$ 3,470	$ 4,780	$ 3,240
Internal rate of return	18%	16%	20%
Present value index	1.129	1.085	1.106
Ranking by investment criterion (read across)			
Net present value	2	1	3
Internal rate of return	2	3	1
Present value index	1	3	2

Assuming that the organization has a 12 percent cost of capital, all projects have a positive net present value and an internal rate of return in excess of 12 percent. Therefore, all are acceptable. The problem is to determine which of these acceptable proposals is most desirable. Ranking the proposals by their net present value indicates that Proposal B is best, while ranking by IRR indicates that Proposal C is best.

A frequent criticism of using net present value to rank investment proposals is that it fails to adjust for the size of the proposed investment. To overcome this difficulty, managers can rank projects on the basis of each project's **present value index**, which is computed as the present value of the project's subsequent cash flows divided by the initial investment:

$$\textbf{Present value index} = \frac{\textbf{Present value of subsequent cash flows}}{\textbf{Initial investment}}$$

For Proposal A, the present value of the subsequent cash flows, discounted at 12 percent, is $30,370,000 ($10,000,000 × 3.037), and the present value index is 1.129:

$$\textbf{Present value index} = \frac{\$30{,}370{,}000}{\$26{,}900{,}000}$$
$$= \textbf{1.129}$$

Using this criterion, projects that have a present value index of 1.0 or higher are acceptable, and the project with the highest present value index is preferred. Ranking the proposals in Exhibit 12.8 on the basis of their present value index results in Proposal A being ranked number 1.

We now have three acceptable proposals, three criteria, three different rankings, and the task of selecting only one of the three proposals. Many managers would select Proposal C because it has the highest IRR or Proposal A because it has the highest present value index. Either selection provides a satisfactory, but not an optimal, solution to the dilemma. If the true cost of capital is 12 percent and other investment opportunities return only 12 percent, the net present value criterion provides the proper choice. This is illustrated in Exhibit 12.9 by evaluating the additional return earned on the differences between Proposals B and A and on the differences between Proposals B and C.

EXHIBIT 12.9 Analysis of Incremental Investments

($ thousands)	Proposal B	Proposal A	Difference B – A
Predicted cash flows			
Initial investment	$(55,960)	$(26,900)	$(29,060)
Operation			
Year 1	20,000	10,000	10,000
Year 2	20,000	10,000	10,000
Year 3	20,000	10,000	10,000
Year 4	20,000	10,000	10,000
Disinvestment	0	0	0

Net present value of difference (B – A)

	Cash Inflows (outflows)	Year(s) of Cash Flows	12% Present Value Factor	Present Value of Cash Flows
Initial investment	$(29,060)	0	1.000	$(29,060)
Operation	10,000	1–4	3.037	30,370
Disinvestment	0	4	0.636	0
Net present value				$ 1,310

	Proposal B	Proposal C	Difference B – C
Predicted cash flows			
Initial investment	$(55,960)	$(30,560)	$(25,400)
Operation			
Year 1	20,000	20,000	0
Year 2	20,000	20,000	0
Year 3	20,000	0	20,000
Year 4	20,000	0	20,000
Disinvestment	0	0	0

Net present value of difference (B – C)

	Cash Inflows (outflows)	Year(s) of Cash Flows	12% Present Value Factor	Present Value of Cash Flows
Initial investment	$(25,400)	0	1.000	$(25,400)
Operation	20,000	2–4	3.037 – 1.690	26,940
Disinvestment	0	4	0.636	0
Net present value				$ 1,540

The difference in the net present value and internal rate of return rankings results from differences in their reinvestment assumptions. The net present value model assumes that all net cash inflows from a project are reinvested at the discount rate; the internal rate of return model assumes that all net cash inflows from a project are reinvested at the project's internal rate of return. If unlimited funds are available at the discount rate, marginal investments are made at this rate, and the assumption underlying the net present value model is the correct one. Returning to Exhibit 12.9, if all funds not invested in the chosen project and all funds recovered from the chosen project can earn only the discount rate, the firm is $1,540,000 better off by selecting Proposal B rather than Proposal C.

The present value index eliminates the impact of size from net present value computations. However, size is an important consideration in evaluating investment proposals, especially if funds not invested in a project can earn only the discount rate. In Exhibit 12.9, we see that if funds not invested in the chosen project can be invested only at the discount rate, the firm is $1,310,000 better off by selecting Proposal B rather than Proposal A.

TAXES IN CAPITAL BUDGETING DECISIONS

LO6 Determine the net present value of investment proposals with consideration of taxes.

To focus on capital budgeting concepts, we deferred consideration of the impact of taxes. Because income taxes affect cash flows and income, their consideration is important in evaluating investment proposals in for-profit organizations.

The cost of investments in plant and equipment is not deducted from taxable revenues in determining taxable income and income taxes at the time of the initial investment. Instead, the amount of the initial investment is deducted as depreciation over the operating life of an asset. To illustrate the impact of taxes on cash flows, assume:

- Revenues and operating cash receipts are the same each year.
- Depreciation is the only noncash expense of an organization.

Depreciation Tax Shield

Depreciation does not require the use of cash (the funds were spent at the initial investment), but depreciation is said to provide a "tax shield" because it reduces cash payments for income taxes. The **depreciation tax shield** (the reduction in taxes due to the deductibility of depreciation from taxable revenues) is computed as follows:

Depreciation tax shield = Depreciation × Tax rate

The value of the depreciation tax shield is illustrated using Mobile Yogurt Shoppe's capital expenditure proposal summarized in Exhibit 12.2. Assuming a tax rate of 34 percent, the annual net income and after-tax cash flows for this investment without depreciation and with straight-line depreciation are shown in Exhibit 12.10. Examine this exhibit, paying particular attention to the lines for depreciation, income taxes, and net annual cash flow.

Mobile Yogurt Shoppe's annual depreciation tax shield, using straight-line depreciation, is $6,158, computed as annual depreciation of $18,111 ($90,554 investment in depreciable assets ÷ 5-year life) multiplied by an assumed tax rate of 34 percent. Without the depreciation tax shield, annual cash payments for income taxes would be $6,158 more, and after-tax cash flows would be $6,158 less.

The U.S. Tax Code contains guidelines concerning the depreciation of various types of assets. (Analysis of these guidelines is beyond the scope of this text.) Tax guidelines allow organizations a choice in tax depreciation procedures between straight-line depreciation and an accelerated depreciation method detailed in the Tax Code. Because of the time value of money, profitable businesses should usually select the tax depreciation procedure that provides the earliest depreciation. To illustrate the effect of accelerated depreciation on taxes and capital budgeting, we use double-declining balance depreciation rather than the

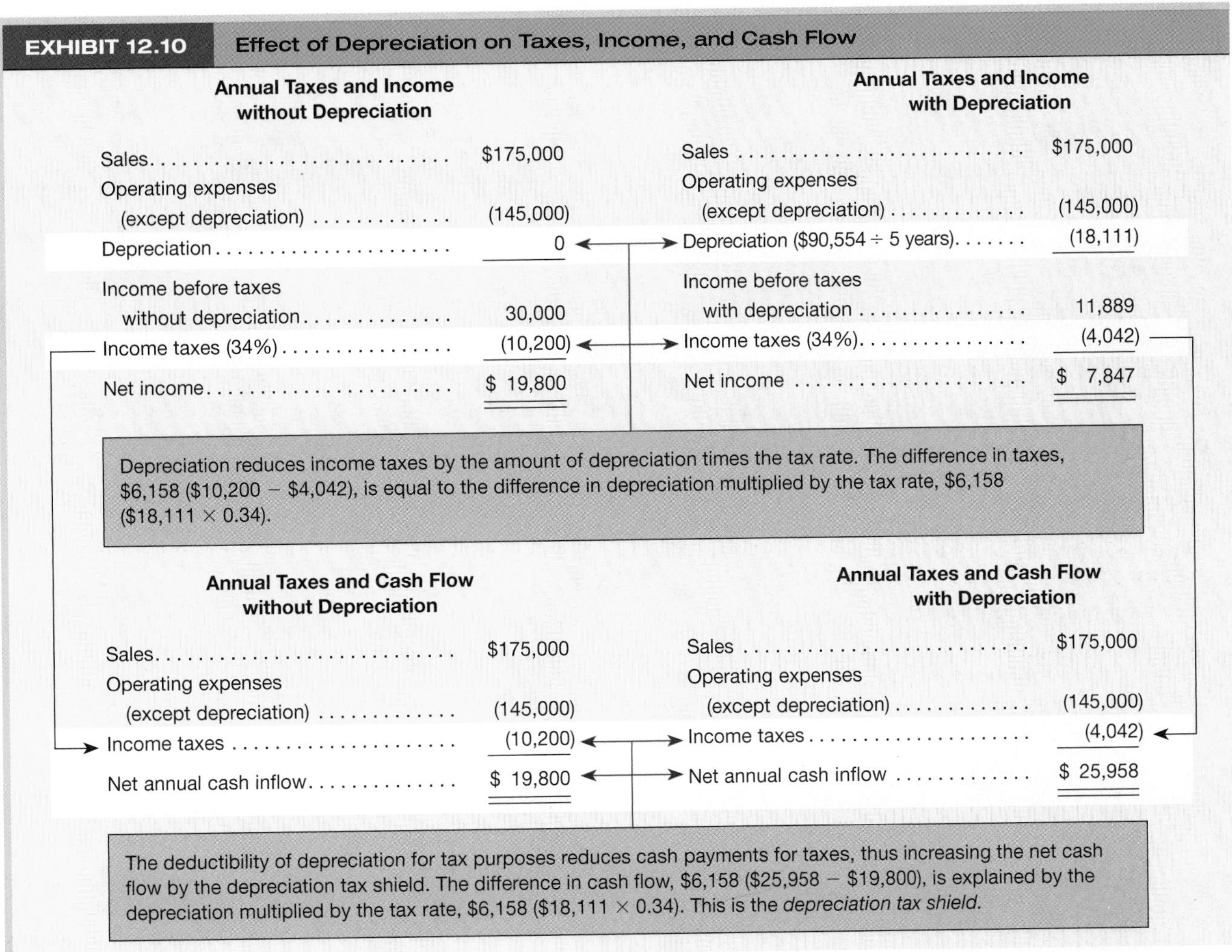

EXHIBIT 12.10 Effect of Depreciation on Taxes, Income, and Cash Flow

Annual Taxes and Income without Depreciation		Annual Taxes and Income with Depreciation	
Sales	$175,000	Sales	$175,000
Operating expenses (except depreciation)	(145,000)	Operating expenses (except depreciation)	(145,000)
Depreciation	0	Depreciation ($90,554 ÷ 5 years)	(18,111)
Income before taxes without depreciation	30,000	Income before taxes with depreciation	11,889
Income taxes (34%)	(10,200)	Income taxes (34%)	(4,042)
Net income	$ 19,800	Net income	$ 7,847

Depreciation reduces income taxes by the amount of depreciation times the tax rate. The difference in taxes, $6,158 ($10,200 − $4,042), is equal to the difference in depreciation multiplied by the tax rate, $6,158 ($18,111 × 0.34).

Annual Taxes and Cash Flow without Depreciation		Annual Taxes and Cash Flow with Depreciation	
Sales	$175,000	Sales	$175,000
Operating expenses (except depreciation)	(145,000)	Operating expenses (except depreciation)	(145,000)
Income taxes	(10,200)	Income taxes	(4,042)
Net annual cash inflow	$ 19,800	Net annual cash inflow	$ 25,958

The deductibility of depreciation for tax purposes reduces cash payments for taxes, thus increasing the net cash flow by the depreciation tax shield. The difference in cash flow, $6,158 ($25,958 − $19,800), is explained by the depreciation multiplied by the tax rate, $6,158 ($18,111 × 0.34). This is the *depreciation tax shield.*

accelerated method detailed in the Code. When making capital expenditure decisions, managers should, of course, refer to the most current version of the Tax Code to determine the specific depreciation guidelines in effect at that time.

Exhibits 12.11 and 12.12 illustrate the effect of two alternative depreciation procedures, straight-line and double-declining balance, on the net present value of Mobile Yogurt Shoppe's proposed investment. We assume that the asset is fully depreciated for tax purposes during its five-year life and is sold for a taxable gain equal to its predicted salvage value. The cash flows for this investment were presented in Exhibit 12.2, and the effect of taxes on the investment's annual cash flows were examined in Exhibit 12.10. Ignoring taxes, the investment was shown (in Exhibit 12.3) to have a positive net present value of $20,400 at a discount rate of 12 percent. With taxes, the investment has a positive net present value of $4,287 using straight-line depreciation and $6,084 using double-declining balance depreciation. Although taxes and cash flows are identical over the entire life of the project, the use of double-declining balance depreciation for taxes results in a higher net present value because it results in lower cash expenditures for taxes in the earlier years of an asset's life.

Investment Tax Credit

From time to time, for the purpose of stimulating investment and economic growth, the U.S. federal government has implemented an investment tax credit. An **investment tax credit** reduces taxes in the year a new asset is placed in service by some stated percentage of the cost of the asset. In recent years tax credits,

EXHIBIT 12.11 Analysis of Capital Expenditures Including Tax Effects: Straight-Line Depreciation

	Predicted Cash Inflows (outflows) (A)	Year(s) of Cash Flows (B)	12% Present Value Factor (C)	Present Value of Cash Flows (A) × (C)
Initial investment				
Vehicle and equipment	$(90,554)	0	1.000	$ (90,554)
Inventory and other working capital	(4,000)	0	1.000	(4,000)
Operations				
Annual taxable income without depreciation	30,000	1–5	3.605	108,150
Taxes on income ($30,000 × 0.34)	(10,200)	1–5	3.605	(36,771)
Depreciation tax shield*	6,158	1–5	3.605	22,200
Disinvestment				
Sale of vehicle and equipment	8,000	5	0.567	4,536
Taxes on gain on sale ($8,000 × 0.34)	(2,720)	5	0.567	(1,542)
Inventory and other working capital	4,000	5	0.567	2,268
Net present value of all cash flows				$ 4,287

*Computation of depreciation tax shield:

Annual straight-line depreciation ($90,554 ÷ 5)	$18,111
Tax rate	× 0.34
Depreciation tax shield	$ 6,158

such as the credits for purchasing hybrid automobiles, have been used to stimulate investments that reduce the emission of greenhouses gases. Typically, this is done without reducing the depreciation base of the asset for tax purposes. An investment tax credit reduces cash payments for taxes and, hence, is treated as a cash inflow for capital budgeting purposes. This additional cash inflow increases the probability that a new asset will meet a taxpayer's capital expenditure criteria.

EXHIBIT 12.12 Analysis of Capital Expenditures Including Tax Effects: DDB Depreciation

	Predicted Cash Inflows (outflows) (A)	Year(s) of Cash Flows (B)	12% Present Value Factor (C)	Present Value of Cash Flows (A) × (C)
Initial investment				
Vehicle and equipment	$(90,554)	0	1.000	$ (90,554)
Inventory and other working capital	4,000	0	1.000	(4,000)
Operations				
Annual taxable income without depreciation	30,000	1–5	3.605	108,150
Taxes on income ($30,000 × 0.34)	(10,200)	1–5	3.605	(36,771)
Depreciation tax shield*				
Year 1	12,315	1	0.893	10,997
Year 2	7,389	2	0.797	5,889
Year 3	4,434	3	0.712	3,157
Year 4	2,660	4	0.636	1,692
Year 5	3,990	5	0.567	2,262
Disinvestment				
Sale of vehicle and equipment	8,000	5	0.567	4,536
Taxes on gain on sale ($8,000 × 0.34)	(2,720)	5	0.567	(1,542)
Inventory and other working capital	4,000	5	0.567	2,268
Net present value of all cash flows				$ 6,084

*Computation of depreciation tax shield:

Year	Depreciation Base[†] (A)	Annual Rate (B)	Annual Depreciation (C) = (A) × (B)	Tax Rate (D)	Tax Shield (E) = (C) × (D)
1	$90,554	2/5	$36,222	0.34	$12,315
2	54,332	2/5	21,733	0.34	7,389
3	32,599	2/5	13,040	0.34	4,434
4	19,559	2/5	7,824	0.34	2,660
5	11,735	balance	11,735	0.34	3,990

[†]The depreciation base is reduced by the amount of all previous depreciation. The annual rate is twice the straight-line rate. For simplicity, we depreciated the remaining balance in the fifth year and did not switch to straight-line depreciation when the straight-line amount exceeds the double-declining balance amount. This would happen in the fourth year, when $19,559 ÷ 2 = $9,780.

CHAPTER-END REVIEW

Consider the following investment proposal:

Initial investment	
Depreciable assets	$27,740
Working capital	3,000
Operations (per year for 4 years)	
Cash receipts	25,000
Cash expenditures	15,000
Disinvestment	
Salvage value of plant and equipment	2,000
Recovery of working capital	3,000

Required

Determine each of the following:

a. Payback period.

b. Accounting rate of return on initial investment and on average investment.

Solution

Basic computations:

Initial investment	
Depreciable assets	$27,740
Working capital	3,000
Total	$30,740
Operation	
Cash receipts	$25,000
Cash expenditures	(15,000)
Net cash inflow	$10,000
Disinvestment	
Sale of depreciable assets	$ 2,000
Recovery of working capital	3,000
Total	$ 5,000

a. Payback period = $30,740 ÷ $10,000
= 3.074 years

b. Accounting rate of return on initial and average investments:

Annual net cash inflow from operations	$10,000
Less average annual depreciation [($27,740 − $2,000) ÷ 4]	(6,435)
Average annual increase in net income	$ 3,565

Average investment = ($30,740 + $5,000) ÷ 2
= $17,870

$$\text{Accounting rate of return on initial investment} = \frac{\$3,565}{\$30,740}$$
= 0.1160, or 11.6%

$$\text{Accounting rate of return on average investment} = \frac{\$3,565}{\$17,870}$$
= 0.1995, or 19.95%

APPENDIX 12A: Time Value of Money

When asked to choose between \$500 today or an IOU for \$500 to be paid one year later, rational decision makers choose the \$500 today. Two reasons for this involve the time *value of money* and the *risk*. A dollar today is worth more than a dollar tomorrow or at some future time. Having a dollar provides flexibility. It can be spent, buried, or invested in a number of projects. If invested in a savings account, it will amount to more than one dollar at some future time because of the effect of interest. The interest paid by a bank (or borrower) for the use of money is analogous to the rent paid for the use of land, buildings, or equipment. Furthermore, we live in an uncertain world, and, for a variety of reasons, the possibility exists that an IOU might not be paid.

Future Value

Future value is the amount that a current sum of money earning a stated rate of interest will accumulate to at the end of a future period. Suppose we deposit \$500 in a savings account at a financial institution that pays interest at the rate of 10 percent per year. At the end of the first year, the original deposit of \$500 will total \$550 (\$500 × 1.10). If we leave the \$550 for another year, the amount will increase to \$605 (\$550 × 1.10). It can be stated that \$500 today has a future value in one year of \$550, or conversely, that \$550 one year from today has a present value of \$500. Interest of \$55 (\$605 − \$550) was earned in the second year, whereas interest of only \$50 was earned in the first year. This happened because interest during the second year was earned on the principal plus interest from the first year (\$550). When periodic interest is computed on principal plus prior periods' accumulated interest, the interest is said to be *compounded*. Compound interest is used throughout this text.

To determine future values at the end of one period (usually a year), multiply the beginning amount (present value) by 1 plus the interest rate. When multiple periods are involved, the future value is determined by repeatedly multiplying the beginning amount by 1 plus the interest rate for each period. When \$500 is invested for two years at an interest rate of 10 percent per year, its future value is computed as \$500 × 1.10 × 1.10. The following equation is used to figure future value:

$$\mathbf{fv = pv(1 + i)^n}$$

where:

$$\begin{aligned} fv &= \text{future value amount} \\ pv &= \text{present value amount} \\ i &= \text{interest rate per period} \\ n &= \text{number of periods} \end{aligned}$$

For our \$500 deposit, the equation becomes:

$$\begin{aligned} \textbf{fv of \$500} &= \mathbf{pv(1 + i)^n} \\ &= \mathbf{\$500(1 + 0.10)^2} \\ &= \mathbf{\$605} \end{aligned}$$

In a similar manner, once the interest rate and number of periods are known, the future value amount of any present value amount is easily determined.

Present Value

Present value is the current worth of a specified amount of money to be received at some future date at some interest rate. Solving for *pv* in the future value equation, the new present value equation is determined as follows:

$$\mathbf{pv = \frac{fv}{(1 + i)^n}}$$

Using this equation, the present value of \$8,800 to be received in one year, discounted at 10 percent, is computed as follows:

$$\begin{aligned} \textbf{pv of \$8,800} &= \mathbf{\frac{\$8,800}{(1 + 0.10)^1}} \\ &= \mathbf{\frac{\$8,800}{(1.10)}} \\ &= \mathbf{\$8,000} \end{aligned}$$

Thus, when the discount rate is 10 percent, the present value of \$8,800 to be received in one year is \$8,000. The present value equation is often expressed as the future value amount times the present value of \$1:

$$\mathbf{pv = fv \times \frac{\$1}{(1 + i)^n}}$$

Using the equation for the present value of \$1, the present value of \$8,800 to be received in one year, discounted at 10 percent, is computed as follows:

$$\begin{aligned} \text{pv of \$8,800} &= \$8{,}800 \times \frac{\$1}{(1 + 0.10)^1} \\ &= \$8{,}800 \times 0.909 \\ &= \$8{,}000 \end{aligned}$$

The present value of \$8,800 two periods from now is \$7,273, computed as [\$8,800 ÷ $(1.10)^2$] or [\$8,800 × \$1 ÷ $(1.10)^2$].

If a calculator or computer with spreadsheet software is not available, present value computations can be done by hand. Tables, such as Table 12A.1 for the present value of \$1 at various interest rates and time periods, can be used to simplify hand computations. Using the factors in Table 12A.1, the present value of any future amount can be determined. For example, with an interest rate of 10 percent, the present value of the following future amounts to be received in one period are as follows:

Future Value Amount		Present Value Factor of \$1		Present Value
\$ 100	×	0.909	=	\$ 90.90
628	×	0.909	=	570.85
4,285	×	0.909	=	3,895.07
9,900	×	0.909	=	8,999.10

To further illustrate the use of Table 12A.1, consider the following application. Alert Company wants to invest its surplus cash at 12 percent to have \$10,000 to pay off a long-term note due at the end of five years. Table 12A.1 shows that the present value factor of \$1, discounted at 12 percent per year for five years, is 0.567. Multiplying \$10,000 by 0.567, the present value is determined to be \$5,670:

$$\begin{aligned} \text{pv of \$10,000} &= \$10{,}000 \times \text{Present value factor for \$1} \\ &= \$10{,}000 \times 0.567 \\ &= \$5{,}670 \end{aligned}$$

Therefore, if Alert invests \$5,670 today, it will have \$10,000 available to pay off its note in five years.

Managers also use present value tables to make investment decisions. Assume that Monroe Company can make an investment that will provide a cash flow of \$12,000 at the end of eight years. If the company demands a rate of return of 14 percent per year, what is the most it will be willing to pay for this investment? From Table 12A.1, we find that the present value factor for \$1, discounted at 14 percent per year for eight years, is 0.351:

$$\begin{aligned} \text{pv of \$12,000} &= \$12{,}000 \times \text{Present value factor for \$1} \\ &= \$12{,}000 \times 0.351 \\ &= \$4{,}212 \end{aligned}$$

If the company demands an annual return of 14 percent, the most it would be willing to invest today is \$4,212.

Annuities

Not all investments provide a single sum of money. Many investments provide periodic cash flows called *annuities*. An **annuity** is a series of equal cash flows received or paid over equal intervals of time. Suppose that \$100 will be received at the end of each of the next three years. If the discount rate is 10 percent, the present value of this annuity can be determined by summing the present value of each receipt:

Year 1 \$100 × \$1 ÷ (1 + 0.10)1 =	**\$ 90.90**
Year 2 \$100 × \$1 ÷ (1 + 0.10)2 =	**82.65**
Year 3 \$100 × \$1 ÷ (1 + 0.10)3 =	**75.13**
Total.	**\$248.68**

Alternatively, the following equation can be used to compute the present value of an annuity with cash flows at the end of each period:

TABLE 12A.1 Present Value of $1

$$\text{Present value of \$1} = \frac{1}{(1+r)^n}$$

Periods (n)	Discount rate (r) 6%	8%	10%	12%	14%	16%	18%	20%	22%	24%	26%	28%	30%
1	0.943	0.926	0.909	0.893	0.877	0.862	0.847	0.833	0.820	0.806	0.794	0.781	0.769
2	0.890	0.857	0.826	0.797	0.769	0.743	0.718	0.694	0.672	0.650	0.630	0.610	0.592
3	0.840	0.794	0.751	0.712	0.675	0.641	0.609	0.579	0.551	0.524	0.500	0.477	0.455
4	0.792	0.735	0.683	0.636	0.592	0.552	0.516	0.482	0.451	0.423	0.397	0.373	0.350
5	0.747	0.681	0.621	0.567	0.519	0.476	0.437	0.402	0.370	0.341	0.315	0.291	0.269
6	0.705	0.630	0.564	0.507	0.456	0.410	0.370	0.335	0.303	0.275	0.250	0.227	0.207
7	0.665	0.583	0.513	0.452	0.400	0.354	0.314	0.279	0.249	0.222	0.198	0.178	0.159
8	0.627	0.540	0.467	0.404	0.351	0.305	0.266	0.233	0.204	0.179	0.157	0.139	0.123
9	0.592	0.500	0.424	0.361	0.308	0.263	0.225	0.194	0.167	0.144	0.125	0.108	0.094
10	0.558	0.463	0.386	0.322	0.270	0.227	0.191	0.162	0.137	0.116	0.099	0.085	0.073
11	0.527	0.429	0.350	0.287	0.237	0.195	0.162	0.135	0.112	0.094	0.079	0.066	0.056
12	0.497	0.397	0.319	0.257	0.208	0.168	0.137	0.112	0.092	0.076	0.062	0.052	0.043
13	0.469	0.368	0.290	0.229	0.182	0.145	0.116	0.093	0.075	0.061	0.050	0.040	0.033
14	0.442	0.340	0.263	0.205	0.160	0.125	0.099	0.078	0.062	0.049	0.039	0.032	0.025
15	0.417	0.315	0.239	0.183	0.140	0.108	0.084	0.065	0.051	0.040	0.031	0.025	0.020
16	0.394	0.292	0.218	0.163	0.123	0.093	0.071	0.054	0.042	0.032	0.025	0.019	0.015
17	0.371	0.270	0.198	0.146	0.108	0.080	0.060	0.045	0.034	0.026	0.020	0.015	0.012
18	0.350	0.250	0.180	0.130	0.095	0.069	0.051	0.038	0.028	0.021	0.016	0.012	0.009
19	0.331	0.232	0.164	0.116	0.083	0.060	0.043	0.031	0.023	0.017	0.012	0.009	0.007
20	0.312	0.215	0.149	0.104	0.073	0.051	0.037	0.026	0.019	0.014	0.010	0.007	0.005

$$\text{pva} = \frac{a}{i} \times \left[1 - \frac{1}{(1 + 0.10)^n}\right]$$

where:

pva = present value of an annuity (also called the annuity factor)
i = prevailing rate per period
n = number of periods
a = annuity amount

This equation was used to compute the factors presented in Table 12A.2 for an annuity amount of $1. The present value of an annuity of $1 per period for three periods discounted at 10 percent per period is as follows:

$$\text{pva of \$1} = \frac{1}{0.10} \times \left[1 - \frac{1}{(1 + 0.10)^3}\right]$$
$$= 2.4868$$

Using this factor, the present value of a $100 annuity can be computed as $100 × 2.4868, which yields $248.68. To determine the present value of an annuity of any amount, the annuity factor for $1 can be multiplied by the annuity amount.

To further illustrate the use of Table 12A.2, assume that Red Kite Company is considering an investment in a piece of equipment that will produce net cash inflows of $2,000 at the end of each year for five years. If the company's desired rate of return is 12 percent, an investment of $7,210 will provide such a return:

$$\text{pva of \$2,000} = \$2,000 \times \begin{array}{c}\text{Present value factor for an annuity of}\\ \text{\$1 for five periods discounted at 12\%}\end{array}$$
$$= \$2,000 \times 3.605$$
$$= \$7,210$$

Here, the $2,000 annuity is multiplied by 3.605, the factor for an annuity of $1 for five periods found in Table 12A.2, discounted at 12 percent per period.

Another use of Table 12A.2 is to determine the amount that must be received annually to provide a desired rate of return on an investment. Assume that Burnsville Company invests $33,550 and desires a return of the investment plus interest of 8 percent in equal year-end payments for ten years. The minimum amount that must be received each year is determined by solving the equation for the present value of an annuity:

$$\text{pva} = a \times (\text{pva of \$1})$$

$$a = \frac{\text{pva}}{\text{pva of \$1}}$$

From Table 12A.2, we see that the 8 percent factor for ten periods is 6.710. Dividing the $33,550 investment by 6.710, the required annuity is computed to be $5,000:

$$a = \frac{\$33,550}{6.710}$$
$$= \$5,000$$

Unequal Cash Flows

Many investment situations do not produce equal periodic cash flows. When this occurs, the present value for each cash flow must be determined independently because the annuity table can be used only for equal periodic cash flows. Table 12A.1 is used to determine the present value of each future amount separately. To illustrate, assume that the Atlanta Braves wish to acquire the contract of a popular baseball player who is known to attract large crowds. Management believes this player will return incremental cash flows to the team at the end of each of the next three years in the amounts of $2,500,000, $4,000,000, and $1,500,000. After three years, the player anticipates retiring. If the team's owners require a minimum return of 14 percent on their investment, how much would they be willing to pay for the player's contract?

To solve this problem, it is necessary to determine the present value of the expected future cash flows. Here we use Table 12A.1 to find the $1 present value factors at 14 percent for Periods 1, 2, and 3. The cash flows are then multiplied by these factors:

TABLE 12A.2 Present Value of an Annuity of $1

Present value of an annuity of $1 $= \frac{1}{r}\left[1 - \frac{1}{(1+r)^n}\right]$

Discount rate (*r*)

Periods (*n*)	6%	8%	10%	12%	14%	16%	18%	20%	22%	24%	25%	26%	28%	30%
1	0.943	0.926	0.909	0.893	0.877	0.862	0.847	0.833	0.820	0.806	0.800	0.794	0.781	0.769
2	1.833	1.783	1.736	1.690	1.647	1.605	1.566	1.528	1.492	1.457	1.440	1.424	1.392	1.361
3	2.673	2.577	2.487	2.402	2.322	2.246	2.174	2.106	2.042	1.981	1.952	1.923	1.868	1.816
4	3.465	3.312	3.170	3.037	2.914	2.798	2.690	2.589	2.494	2.404	2.362	2.320	2.241	2.166
5	4.212	3.993	3.791	3.605	3.433	3.274	3.127	2.991	2.864	2.745	2.689	2.635	2.532	2.436
6	4.917	4.623	4.355	4.111	3.889	3.685	3.498	3.326	3.167	3.020	2.951	2.885	2.759	2.643
7	5.582	5.206	4.868	4.564	4.288	4.039	3.812	3.605	3.416	3.242	3.161	3.083	2.937	2.802
8	6.210	5.747	5.335	4.968	4.639	4.344	4.078	3.837	3.619	3.421	3.329	3.241	3.076	2.925
9	6.802	6.247	5.759	5.328	4.946	4.607	4.303	4.031	3.786	3.566	3.463	3.366	3.184	3.019
10	7.360	6.710	6.145	5.650	5.216	4.833	4.494	4.192	3.923	3.682	3.571	3.465	3.269	3.092
11	7.887	7.139	6.495	5.938	5.453	5.029	4.656	4.327	4.035	3.776	3.656	3.544	3.335	3.147
12	8.384	7.536	6.814	6.194	5.660	5.197	4.793	4.439	4.127	3.851	3.725	3.606	3.387	3.190
13	8.853	7.904	7.103	6.424	5.842	5.342	4.910	4.533	4.203	3.912	3.780	3.656	3.427	3.223
14	9.295	8.244	7.367	6.628	6.002	5.468	5.008	4.611	4.265	3.962	3.824	3.695	3.459	3.249
15	9.712	8.559	7.606	6.811	6.142	5.575	5.092	4.675	4.315	4.001	3.859	3.726	3.483	3.268
16	10.106	8.851	7.824	6.974	6.265	5.669	5.162	4.730	4.357	4.033	3.887	3.751	3.503	3.283
17	10.477	9.122	8.022	7.120	6.373	5.749	5.222	4.775	4.391	4.059	3.910	3.771	3.518	3.295
18	10.828	9.372	8.201	7.250	6.467	5.818	5.273	4.812	4.419	4.080	3.928	3.786	3.529	3.304
19	11.158	9.604	8.365	7.366	6.550	5.877	5.316	4.844	4.442	4.097	3.942	3.799	3.539	3.311
20	11.470	9.818	8.514	7.469	6.623	5.929	5.353	4.870	4.460	4.110	3.954	3.808	3.546	3.316

Year	Annual Cash Flow		Present Value of $1 at 14 Percent		Present Value Amount
1	$2,500,000	×	0.877	=	$2,192,500
2	4,000,000	×	0.769	=	3,076,000
3	1,500,000	×	0.675	=	1,012,500
Total					$6,281,000

The total present value of the cash flows for the three years, $6,281,000, represents the maximum amount the team would be willing to pay for the player's contract.

Deferred Returns

Many times, organizations make investments for which they receive no cash until several periods have passed. The present value of an investment discounted at 12 percent per year, which has a $2,000 return only at the end of Years 4, 5, and 6, can be determined as follows:

Year	Amount		Present Value of $1 at 12 Percent		Present Value Amount
1	$ 0	×	0.893	=	$ 0
2	0	×	0.797	=	0
3	0	×	0.712	=	0
4	2,000	×	0.636	=	1,272
5	2,000	×	0.567	=	1,134
6	2,000	×	0.507	=	1,014
Total					$3,420

Computation of the present value of the deferred annuity can also be performed using the annuity tables if the cash flow amounts are equal for each period. The present value of an annuity for six years minus the present value of an annuity for three years yields the present value of an annuity for Years 4 through 6.

Present value of an annuity for 6 years at 12 percent: $2,000 × 4.111 =	$8,222
Present value of an annuity for 3 years at 12 percent: 2,000 × 2.402 =	(4,804)
Present value of the deferred annuity	$3,418*

*The difference between the $3,420 above and the $3,418 here is due to rounding.

APPENDIX 12B: Table Approach to Determining Internal Rate of Return

We consider the use of present value tables to determine the internal rate of return of a series of cash flows with (1) equal net cash flows after the initial investment and (2) unequal net cash flows after the initial investment.

Equal Cash Inflows

An investment proposal's internal rate of return is easily determined when a single investment is followed by a series of equal annual net cash flows. The general relationship between the initial investment and the equal annual cash inflows is expressed as follows:

$$\text{Initial investment} = \text{Present value factor for an annuity of \$1} \times \text{Annual net cash inflow}$$

Solve for the appropriate present value factor as follows:

$$\text{Present value factor for an annuity of \$1} = \frac{\text{Initial investment}}{\text{Annual net cash inflows}}$$

Once the present value factor is calculated, use Table 12A.2 and go across the row corresponding to the expected life of the project until a table factor equal to or closest to the project's computed present value factor is found. The corresponding percentage for the present value factor is the proposal's internal rate of return. If a table factor does not exactly equal the proposal's present value factor, a more accurate answer can be obtained by interpolation (which is not discussed in this text).

To illustrate, assume that Mobile Yogurt Shoppe's proposed investment has a zero disinvestment value. Using all information in Exhibit 12-2 (except that for disinvestment), the proposal's present value factor is 3.152:

$$\begin{aligned}\textbf{Present value factor for an annuity of \$1} &= \frac{\textbf{Initial investment}}{\textbf{Annual net cash inflows}} \\ &= \frac{\$94{,}554}{\$30{,}000} \\ &= 3.152\end{aligned}$$

Using Table 12A.2, go across the row for five periods; the closest table factor is 3.127, which corresponds to an internal rate of return of 18 percent.

Unequal Cash Inflows

If periodic cash flows subsequent to the initial investment are unequal, the simple procedure of determining a present value factor and looking up the closest corresponding factor in Table 12A.2 cannot be used. Instead, a trial-and-error approach must be used to determine the internal rate of return.

EXHIBIT 12B.1 Internal Rate of Return with Unequal Cash Flows

First trial with a 24 percent discount rate

	Predicted Cash Inflows (outflows) (A)	Year(s) of Cash Flows (B)	24% Present Value Factor (C)	Present Value of Cash Flows (A) × (C)
Initial investment	$(94,554)	0	1.000	$(94,554)
Operation	30,000	1–5	2.745	82,350
Disinvestment	12,000	5	0.341	4,092
Net present value of all cash flows				$ (8,112)

Second trial with a 16 percent discount rate

	Predicted Cash Inflows (outflows) (A)	Year(s) of Cash Flows (B)	16% Present Value Factor (C)	Present Value of Cash Flows (A) × (C)
Initial investment	$(94,554)	0	1.000	$(94,554)
Operation	30,000	1–5	3.274	98,220
Disinvestment	12,000	5	0.476	5,712
Net present value of all cash flows				$ 9,378

Third trial with a 20 percent discount rate

	Predicted Cash Inflows (outflows) (A)	Year(s) of Cash Flows (B)	20% Present Value Factor (C)	Present Value of Cash Flows (A) × (C)
Initial investment	$(94,554)	0	1.000	$(94,554)
Operation	30,000	1–5	2.991	89,730
Disinvestment	12,000	5	0.402	4,824
Net present value of all cash flows				$ 0

The first step is to select a discount rate estimated to be close to the proposal's IRR and to compute the proposal's net present value. If the resulting net present value is zero, the selected discount rate is the actual rate of return. However, it is unlikely that the first rate selected will be the proposal's IRR. If the computation results in a positive net present value, the actual IRR is higher than the initially selected rate. In this case, the next step is to compute the proposal's net present value using a higher rate. If the second computation produces a negative net present value, the actual IRR is less than the selected rate. Therefore, the actual IRR is between the first and the second rates. This trial-and-error approach continues until a discount rate is found that equates the proposal's cash inflows and outflows. For Mobile Yogurt Shoppe's investment proposal outlined in Exhibit 12-2, the details of the trial-and-error approach are presented in Exhibit 12B.1.

In Exhibit 12B.1 the first rate produced a negative net present value, indicating that the proposal's IRR is less than 24 percent. To produce a positive net present value, a smaller rate was selected for the second trial. Since the second rate produced a positive net present value, the proposal's true IRR must be between 16 and 24 percent. The 20 percent rate selected for the third trial produced a net present value of zero, indicating that this is the proposal's IRR.

GUIDANCE ANSWER

MANAGERIAL DECISION **You Are the Vice President of Finance**

There is no single correct response to this question. It is useful to start by learning how other companies in similar circumstances handle capital expenditure decisions. This might be done through personal contacts or through professional organizations, such as the Financial Executives Institute. Another starting point might be the formation of a small capital budgeting committee, which could be expanded as necessary once formal procedures were in place. Early tasks of the committee might include developing guidelines for the size of expenditures at various organizational levels subject to committee review and developing guidelines for the criteria used in formal reviews. You would want to ensure that the CEO is in agreement with these proposals. If the company has a board of directors, you would also want some mutual understanding of the board's role in the approval of capital expenditures. Finally, you would want to make clear the importance of a post-audit review.

Superscript A denotes assignments based on Appendix.

DISCUSSION QUESTIONS

Q12-1. What is the relationship between long-range planning and capital budgeting?

Q12-2. What tasks are often assigned to the capital budgeting committee?

Q12-3. What purposes are served by a post-audit of approved capital expenditure proposals?

Q12-4. Into what three phases are a project's cash flows organized?

Q12-5. State three alternative definitions or descriptions of the internal rate of return.

Q12-6. Why is the cost of capital an important concept when discounting models are used for capital budgeting?

Q12-7. What weakness is inherent in the payback period when it is used as the sole investment criterion?

Q12-8. What weakness is inherent in the accounting rate of return when it is used as an investment criterion?

Q12-9. Why are the net present value and the internal rate of return models superior to the payback period and the accounting rate of return models?

Q12-10. State two basic differences between the net present value and the internal rate of return models that often lead to differences in the evaluation of competing investment proposals.

Q12-11. Identify several nonquantitative factors that are apt to play a decisive role in the final selection of projects for capital expenditures.

Q12-12. In what way does depreciation affect the analysis of cash flows for a proposed capital expenditure?

MINI EXERCISES

M12-13.[A] Time Value of Money: Basics (LO2)

Using the equations and tables in Appendix 12A of this chapter, determine the answers to each of the following independent situations:

a. The future value in two years of $1,000 deposited today in a savings account with interest compounded annually at 6 percent.

b. The present value of $9,000 to be received in four years, discounted at 12 percent.

c. The present value of an annuity of $2,000 per year for five years discounted at 14 percent.

d. An initial investment of $32,010 is to be returned in eight equal annual payments. Determine the amount of each payment if the interest rate is 10 percent.

e. A proposed investment will provide cash flows of $20,000, $8,000, and $6,000 at the end of Years 1, 2, and 3, respectively. Using a discount rate of 20 percent, determine the present value of these cash flows.

f. Find the present value of an investment that will pay $4,000 at the end of Years 10, 11, and 12. Use a discount rate of 14 percent.

M12-14.[A] Time Value of Money: Basics (LO2)

Using the equations and tables in Appendix 12A of this chapter, determine the answers to each of the following independent situations:

a. The future value in two years of $4,000 invested today in a certificate of deposit with interest compounded annually at 10 percent.

b. The present value of $6,000 to be received in five years, discounted at 8 percent.

c. The present value of an annuity of $20,000 per year for four years discounted at 12 percent.

d. An initial investment of $29,480 is to be returned in six equal annual payments. Determine the amount of each payment if the interest rate is 16 percent.

e. A proposed investment will provide cash flows of $6,000, $8,000, and $20,000 at the end of Years 1, 2, and 3, respectively. Using a discount rate of 18 percent, determine the present value of these cash flows.

f. Find the present value of an investment that will pay $6,000 at the end of Years 8, 9, and 10. Use a discount rate of 12 percent.

M12-15. NPV and IRR: Equal Annual Net Cash Inflows (LO2)

Apache Junction Company is evaluating a capital expenditure proposal that requires an initial investment of $9,350, has predicted cash inflows of $2,000 per year for 15 years, and has no salvage value.

Required

a. Using a discount rate of 16 percent, determine the net present value of the investment proposal.

b. Determine the proposal's internal rate of return. (Refer to Appendix 12B if you use the table approach.)

c. What discount rate would produce a net present value of zero?

M12-16. NPV and IRR: Equal Annual Net Cash Inflows (LO2)

Sun Devil Company is evaluating a capital expenditure proposal that requires an initial investment of $32,160, has predicted cash inflows of $7,500 per year for seven years, and has no salvage value.

Required

a. Using a discount rate of 18 percent, determine the net present value of the investment proposal.

b. Determine the proposal's internal rate of return. (Refer to Appendix 12B if you use the table approach.)

c. What discount rate would produce a net present value of zero?

M12-17. Payback Period and Accounting Rate of Return: Equal Annual Operating Cash Flows without Disinvestment (LO3)

Adams is considering an investment proposal with the following cash flows:

Initial investment—depreciable assets	$70,000
Net cash inflows from operations (per year for 4 years)	20,000
Disinvestment	0

Required

a. Determine the payback period

b. Determine the accounting rate of return on initial investment

c. Determine the accounting rate of return on average investment

M12-18. Payback Period and Accounting Rate of Return: Equal Annual Operating Cash Flows with Disinvestment (LO3)

Baker is considering an investment proposal with the following cash flows:

Initial investment—depreciable assets	$120,000
Net cash inflows from operations (per year for 4 years)	40,000
Disinvestment—depreciable assets	20,000

Required

a. Determine the payback period
b. Determine the accounting rate of return on initial investment
c. Determine the accounting rate of return on average investment

M12-19. Payback Period and Accounting Rate of Return: Equal Annual Operating Cash Flows with Disinvestment (LO3)

Charlie is considering an investment proposal with the following cash flows:

Initial investment—depreciable assets	$90,000
Initial investment—working capital	10,000
Net cash inflows from operations (per year for 4 years)	25,000
Disinvestment—depreciable assets	10,000
Disinvestment—working capital	10,000

Required

a. Determine the payback period
b. Determine the accounting rate of return on initial investment
c. Determine the accounting rate of return on average investment

EXERCISES

E12-20. NPV and IRR: Unequal Annual Net Cash Inflows (LO2)

Assume that Goodrich Corporation is evaluating a capital expenditure proposal that has the following predicted cash flows:

Initial investment	$(85,160)
Operation	
Year 1	36,000
Year 2	50,000
Year 3	40,000
Salvage	0

Required

a. Using a discount rate of 12 percent, determine the net present value of the investment proposal.
b. Determine the proposal's internal rate of return. (Refer to Appendix 12B if you use the table approach.)

E12-21. NPV and IRR: Unequal Annual Net Cash Inflows (LO2)

Salt River Company is evaluating a capital expenditure proposal that has the following predicted cash flows:

Initial investment	$(43,270)
Operation	
Year 1	20,000
Year 2	30,000
Year 3	10,000
Salvage	0

Required

a. Using a discount rate of 14 percent, determine the net present value of the investment proposal.
b. Determine the proposal's internal rate of return. (Refer to Appendix 12B if you use the table approach.)

E12-22. Payback Period, IRR, and Minimum Cash Flows (LO2, 3)
The management of Mesquite Limited is currently evaluating the following investment proposal:

	Time 0	Year 1	Year 2	Year 3	Year 4
Initial investment.	$240,000	—	—	—	—
Net operating cash inflows	—	$100,000	$100,000	$100,000	$100,000

Required

a. Determine the proposal's payback period.
b. Determine the proposal's internal rate of return. (Refer to Appendix 12B if you use the table approach.)
c. Given the amount of the initial investment, determine the minimum annual net cash inflows required to obtain an internal rate of return of 14 percent. Round the answer to the nearest dollar.

E12-23. Time-Adjusted Cost-Volume-Profit Analysis (LO2, 3)
Mill Avenue Treat Shop is considering the desirability of producing a new chocolate candy called Pleasure Bombs, Before purchasing the new equipment required to manufacture Pleasure Bombs, Zita Peña, the shop's proprietor performed the following analysis:

Unit selling price.	$1.45
Variable manufacturing and selling costs.	(1.15)
Unit contribution margin.	$0.30
Annual fixed costs	
Depreciation (straight line for 3 years)	$ 20,000
Other (all cash)	25,000
Total	$45,000
Annual break-even sales volume = $45,000 ÷ $0.30 = 150,000 units	

Because the expected annual sales volume is 150,000 units, Zita decided to undertake the production of Pleasure Bombs. This required an immediate investment of $60,000 in equipment that has a life of three years and no salvage value. After three years, the production of Pleasure Bombs will be discontinued.

Required

a. Evaluate the analysis performed by Zita Peña
b. If Mill Avenue Treat Shop has a time value of money of 14 percent, should it make the investment with projected annual sales of 160,000 units?
c. Considering the time value of money, what annual unit sales volume is required to break even?

E12-24. Time-Adjusted Cost-Volume-Profit Analysis with Income Taxes (LO6)
Assume the same facts as given in Exercise E-23.

Required

With a 40 percent tax rate and a 14 percent time value of money, determine the annual unit sales required to break even on a time-adjusted basis.

E12-25. Payback Period and IRR of a Cost Reduction Proposal—Differential Analysis (LO2, LO3)
A light-emitting diode (LED) is a semiconductor diode that emits narrow-spectrum light. Although relatively expensive when compared to incandescent bulbs, they use significantly less energy and last six to ten times longer, with a slow decline in performance rather than an abrupt failure.

New York City currently has 80,000 incandescent bulbs in traffic lights at approximately 12,000 intersections. It is estimated that replacing all the incandescent bulbs with LED will cost $28 million. However, the investment is also estimated to save the City $6.3 million per year in energy costs.[7]

Required:

a. Determine the payback period of converting New York City traffic lights to LEDs.
b. If the average life of an incandescent streetlight is one year and the average life of an LED streetlight is seven years, should the City finance the investment in LED's at an interest rate of five percent per year? Justify your answer.

E12-26. Payback Period and NPV of a Cost Reduction Proposal—Differential Analysis (LO2, LO3)
Mary Zimmerman decided to purchase a new Saturn VUE automobile. Being concerned about environmental issues, she is leaning toward the hybrid VUE Green rather than the completely gasoline four-cylinder model. Nevertheless, as a new business school graduate, she wants to determine if there is an economic justification for purchasing the VUE Green, which costs $1,300 more than the regular VUE. She has determined that city/highway combined gas mileage of the Green VUE and regular VUE models are 27 and 23 miles per gallon respectively. Mary anticipates she will travel an average of 12,000 miles per year for the next several years.[8]

Required:

a. Determine the payback period of the incremental investment if gasoline costs $3.50 per gallon.
b. Assuming that Mary plans to keep the care five years and does not believe there will be a trade-in premium associated with the hybrid model, determine the net present value of the incremental investment at an eight percent time value of money.
c. Determine the cost of gasoline required for a payback period of three years.
d. At $3.50 per gallon, determine the VUE Green combined gas mileage required for a payback period of three years
e. Identify other factors Mary should consider before making her decision.

PROBLEMS

P12-27. Ranking Investment Proposals: Payback Period, Accounting Rate of Return, and Net Present Value (LO2, 3, 4)
Presented is information pertaining to the cash flows of three mutually exclusive investment proposals:

	Proposal X	Proposal Y	Proposal Z
Initial investment	$45,000	$45,000	$45,000
Cash flow from operations			
Year 1	40,000	22,500	45,000
Year 2	5,000	22,500	
Year 3	22,500	22,500	
Disinvestment	0	0	0
Life (years)	3 years	3 years	1 year

Required

a. Rank these investment proposals using the payback period, the accounting rate of return on initial investment, and the net present value criteria. Assume that the organization's cost of capital is 14 percent. Round calculations to four decimal places.
b. Explain the difference in rankings. Which investment would you recommend?

P12-28. Ranking Investment Proposals: Net Present Value and Present Value Index (LO2, 4)
Assume that Nestlé Purina is considering the replacement of its traditional canned dog food with dog food packaged in either resealable plastic containers or in disposable foil-lined pouches. Although either alternative will produce significant cost savings and marketing benefits, limitations on available shelf space in stores require management to select only one alternative. Cash flow information on each alternative follows.

	Plastic Containers	Lined Pouches
Initial investment in necessary equipment	$50,000	$150,000
Increase in annual net cash flows	$20,000	$56,000
Life of equipment (years)	5 years	5 years
Salvage value of equipment	$10,000	$12,000

Nestlé Purina has a 12 percent cost of capital.

Required

a. Evaluate the investment alternatives using the net present value and the present value index criteria.
b. Explain the difference in rankings. Which investment would you recommend?

[7] Based on "Mayors Take the Lead," *Newsweek*, April 16, 2007, pp. 68-73.
[8] Based on Mike Spector, The Economics of Hybrids," *Wall Street Journal*, October 29, 2007, p. R5

P12-29. Ranking Investment Proposals: Net Present Value and Present Value Index (LO2, 4)

Ocean Breeze Cat Sand Company is considering the replacement of its traditional bag packaging of cat sand with either reusable plastic or aluminum pails. Customers would make a refundable deposit on the container each time they purchased cat sand. Because the pails would be reusable, the net cost of cat sand to customers who returned the pail for a refund would be lower than the cost of cat sand sold in bags. Ocean Breeze has a 16 percent cost of capital. Cash flow information on each alternative follows.

	Plastic	Aluminum
Initial investment.	$120,000	$68,000
Increase in annual net cash flows	$ 52,500	$30,000
Life of equipment (years)	4 years	4 years
Disposal value of equipment	$ 12,000	$9,000

Required

a. Evaluate the investment alternatives using the net present value and the present value index criteria.

b. Explain the difference in rankings. Which investment would you recommend if unlimited funds were available at Ocean Breeze's cost of capital?

P12-30. Cost Reduction Proposal: IRR, NPV, and Payback Period (LO2, 3)

JB Chemical currently discharges liquid waste into Calgary's municipal sewer system. However, the Calgary municipal government has informed JB that a surcharge of $4 per thousand cubic liters will soon be imposed for the discharge of this waste. This has prompted management to evaluate the desirability of treating its own liquid waste.

A proposed system consists of three elements. The first is a retention basin, which would permit unusual discharges to be held and treated before entering the downstream system. The second is a continuous self-cleaning rotary filter required where solids are removed. The third is an automated neutralization process required where materials are added to control the alkalinity-acidity range.

The system is designed to process 500,000 liters a day. However, management anticipates that only about 200,000 liters of liquid waste would be processed in a normal workday. The company operates 300 days per year. The initial investment in the system would be $450,000, and annual operating costs are predicted to be $150,000. The system has a predicted useful life of ten years and a salvage value of $50,000.

Required

a. Determine the project's net present value at a discount rate of 14 percent.

b. Determine the project's approximate internal rate of return. (Refer to Appendix 12B if you use the table approach.)

c. Determine the project's payback period.

P12-31. NPV with Income Taxes: Straight-Line versus Accelerated Depreciation (LO2, 6)

John Paul Jones Inc. is a conservatively managed boat company whose motto is, "The old ways are the good ways." Management has always used straight-line depreciation for tax and external reporting purposes. Although they are reluctant to change, they are aware of the impact of taxes on a project's profitability.

Required

For a typical $100,000 investment in equipment with a five-year life and no salvage value, determine the present value of the advantage resulting from the use of double-declining balance depreciation as opposed to straight-line depreciation. Assume an income tax rate of 40 percent and a discount rate of 16 percent. Also assume that there will be a switch from double-declining balance to straight-line depreciation in the fourth year.

P12-32. Payback Period, NPV, and PVI: Taxes and Straight-Line Depreciation (LO2, 3, 6)

Assume that United Technologies is evaluating a proposal to change the company's manual design system to a computer-aided design (CAD) system. The proposed system is expected to save 10,000 design hours per year; an operating cost savings of $40 per hour. The annual cash expenditures of operating the CAD system are estimated to be $200,000. The CAD system requires an initial investment of $500,000. The estimated life of this system is five years with no salvage value. The tax rate is 40 percent, and United Technologies uses straight-line depreciation for tax purposes. United Technologies has a cost of capital of 16 percent.

Required

a. Compute the annual after-tax cash flows related to the CAD project.

b. Compute each of the following for the project:

1. Payback period.
2. Net present value.
3. Present value index.

P12-33. NPV: Taxes and Accelerated Depreciation (LO6)

Assume the same facts as given in P12-32, except that management intends to use double-declining balance depreciation with a switch to straight-line depreciation (applied to any undepreciated balance) starting in Year 4.

Required

Determine the project's net present value.

P12-34. NPV Total and Differential Analysis of Replacement Decision (LO2)

Gusher Petro is evaluating a proposal to purchase a new processor that would cost $120,000 and have a salvage value of $12,000 in five years. Gusher's cost of capital is 16 percent. It would provide annual operating cash savings of $15,000, as follows:

	Old Processor	New Processor
Salaries	$34,000	$44,000
Supplies	6,000	5,000
Utilities	13,000	6,000
Cleaning and maintenance	22,000	5,000
Total cash expenditures	$75,000	$60,000

If the new processor is purchased, Gusher will sell the old processor for its current salvage value of $30,000. If the new processor is not purchased, the old processor will be disposed of in five years at a predicted scrap value of $2,000. The old processor's present book value is $50,000. If kept, the old processor will require repairs predicted to cost $40,000 in one year.

Required

a. Use the total cost approach to evaluate the alternatives of keeping the old processor and purchasing the new processor. Indicate which alternative is preferred.

b. Use the differential cost approach to evaluate the desirability of purchasing the new processor.

P12-35. NPV Total and Differential Analysis of Replacement Decision (LO2)

White Snow Automatic Laundry must either have a complete overhaul of its current dry-cleaning system or purchase a new one. Its cost of capital is 20 percent. White Snow's accountant has developed the following cost projections:

	Present System	New System
Purchase cost (new)	$40,000	$50,000
Remaining book value	15,000	
Overhaul needed	20,000	
Annual cash operating costs	35,000	20,000
Current salvage value	10,000	
Salvage value in 5 years	2,500	10,000

If White Snow keeps the old system, it will have to be overhauled immediately. With the overhaul, the old system will have a useful life of five more years.

Required

a. Use the total cost approach to evaluate the alternatives of keeping the old system and purchasing the new system. Indicate which alternative is preferred.

b. Use the differential cost approach to evaluate the desirability of purchasing the new system.

P12-36. NPV Differential Analysis of Replacement Decision (LO2, 5)

The management of Essen Manufacturing Company is currently evaluating a proposal to purchase a new, innovative drill press as a replacement for a less efficient piece of similar equipment, which would then be sold. The cost of the equipment, including delivery and installation, is $175,000. If the equipment is purchased, Essen will incur a $5,000 cost in removing the present equipment and revamping service facilities. The present equipment has a book value of $100,000 and a remaining useful life of ten years. Because of new technical improvements that have made the present equipment obsolete, it now has a disposal value of only $40,000. Management has provided the following comparison of manufacturing costs:

	Present Equipment	New Equipment
Annual production (units)	400,000	400,000
Annual costs		
Direct labor (per unit)	$0.075	$0.05
Overhead		
Depreciation (10% of asset's book value)	$10,000	$17,500
Other	$48,000	$20,000

Additional information follows:

- Management believes that if the current equipment is not replaced now, it will have to wait ten years before replacement is justifiable.
- Both pieces of equipment are expected to have a negligible salvage value at the end of ten years.
- Management expects to sell the entire annual production of 400,000 units.
- Essen's cost of capital is 14 percent.

Required

Evaluate the desirability of purchasing the new equipment

CASES

C12-37. Payback Period **(LO3, 5)**

In response to a significant increase in energy costs in the fall of 2000, American Energy Systems of Hutchinson, Minnesota, introduced a stove that uses dry-shelled field corn as fuel. Depending on the size of the house and weather conditions, tests indicated that heating an average house requires 15 to 30 bushels of corn per month. The stove sold for $2,170 and, with corn then at a historical low cost of $2 a bushel, heating with corn was ten times cheaper than gas or heating oil and seven times cheaper than electricity.[9]

Required

a. Based on fall 2000 fuel costs determine the range of possible payback periods in months.

b. What other factors should be considered before purchasing a stove that uses corn?

c. Assuming the corn stove has a life of ten years, do you feel comfortable making this decision using only the payback capital budgeting model? Why or why not?

C12-38. Determining Terms of Automobile Leases (Requires Spreadsheet) **(LO2, 5)**

Avant-Garde Motor Company has asked you to develop lease terms for the firm's popular Avant-Garde Challenger, which has an average selling price (new) of $25,000. You know that leasing is attractive because it assists consumers in obtaining new vehicles with a small down payment and "reasonable" monthly payments. Market analysts have told you that to attract the widest number of young professionals, the Challenger must have an initial down payment of no more than $1,000, monthly payments of no more than $450, and lease terms of no more than three years. When the lease expires, Avant-Garde will sell the used Challengers at the automobile's resale market price at that time. It is difficult to predict the future price of the increasingly popular Challenger, but you have obtained the following information on the average resale prices of used Challengers:

Age	Resale Price
1 year	$20,000
2 years	18,500
3 years	16,000
4 years	13,500
5 years	12,500

Avant-Garde's cost of capital is 18 percent per year, or 1.5 percent per month.

Required

a. With the aid of spreadsheet software, develop a competitive and profitable lease payment program. Assume the down payment and the first lease payment are made immediately and that all subsequent lease payments are made at the start of the month. [Hint: Most software packages include a function such as the following: PMT (rate,nper,pv,fv,type), where rate = the time value of money; nper = the number of periods; pv = the present value; fv = the future value; and type = 0 (when the payment is at

[9] Based on Laurie Freeman, "Oil Shock: Throw Another Cob on the Fire," *Business Week*, March12, 2001, p, 16.

the end of the period) or 1 (when the payment is at the beginning of the period). For monthly payments, rate should be set at the annual rate divided by 12, and npr should be set at the number of months in the lease. Here, fv is the residual value. Consider the residual value as a future value and enter it as a negative number, indicating the lessor has not paid the full cost of the car.]

b. Reevaluate the lease program assuming a down payment of $2,000.

c. Reevaluate the lease program assuming a down payment of $1,000 and a $2,000 increase in residual values.

d. Reevaluate the lease program assuming a down payment of $2,000 and a $2,000 increase in residual values.

e. What is your final recommendation? What risks are associated with your recommendation? Are there any other actions to consider?

C12-39. Evaluating Data and Using Payback Period for an Investment Proposal (LO3, 5)

To determine the desirability of investing in a 21-inch monitor (as opposed to the typical 17-inch monitor that comes with a new personal computer), researchers developed an experiment testing the time required to perform a set of tasks. The tasks included the following:

- Setting up a meeting using electronic mail.
- Reviewing meeting requests.
- Checking an on-line schedule.
- Embedding a video file into a document.
- Searching a customer database to find a specific set of contracts.
- Copying a database into a spreadsheet.
- Modifying a slide presentation.

The researchers assumed this was a typical set of tasks performed by a manager. They determined that there was a 9 percent productivity gain using the 21-inch monitor. One test manager commented that the largest productivity gain came from being able to have multiple applications open at the same time and from being able to view several files at once.

Required

Accepting the 9 percent productivity gain as accurate, what additional information is needed to determine the payback period of an investment in one 21-inch monitor that is to be used by a manager? Make any necessary assumptions and obtain whatever data you can (perhaps from computer component advertisements) to determine the payback period for the proposed investment.

C12-40. IRR and NPV with Performance Evaluation Conflict (LO2, 4, 5)

Pepperoni Pizza Company owns and operates fast-service pizza parlors throughout North America. The firm operates on a regional basis and provides almost complete autonomy to the manager of each region. Regional managers are responsible for long-range planning, capital expenditures, personnel policies, pricing, and so forth. Each year the performance of regional managers is evaluated by determining the accounting return on fixed assets in their regions; a return of 14 percent is expected. To determine this return, regional net income is divided by the book value of fixed assets at the start of the year. Managers of regions earning a return of more than 16 percent are identified for possible promotion, and managers of regions with a return of less than 12 percent are subject to replacement.

Mr. Light, with a degree in hotel and restaurant management, is the manager of the Northeast region. He is regarded as a "rising star" and will be considered for promotion during the next two years. Light has been with Pepperoni for a total of three years. During that period, the return on fixed assets in his region (the oldest in the firm) has increased dramatically. He is currently considering a proposal to open five new parlors in the Boston area. The total project involves an investment of $640,000 and will double the number of Pepperoni pizzas sold in the Northeast region to a total of 600,000 per year. At an average price of $6 each, total sales revenue will be $3,600,000.

The expenses of operating each of the new parlors include variable costs of $4 per pizza and fixed costs (excluding depreciation) of $80,904 per year. Because each of the new parlors has only a five-year life and no salvage value, yearly straight-line depreciation will be $25,600 [($640,000 ÷ 5 parlors) ÷ 5 years].

Required

a. Evaluate the desirability of the $640,000 investment in new pizza parlors by computing the internal rate of return and the net present value. Assume a time value of money of 14 percent. (Refer to Appendix 12B if you use the table approach.)

b. If Light is shrewd, will he approve the expansion? Why or why not? (Additional computations are suggested.)

C12-41. NPV and Project Reevaluation with Taxes, Straight-Line Depreciation (LO2, 5, 6)
In 2007, the Bayside Chemical Company prepared the following analysis of an investment proposal for a new manufacturing facility:

Because the proposal had a positive net present value when discounted at Bayside's cost of capital of 12 percent, the project was approved; all investments were made at the end of 2008. Shortly after production began in January 2009, a government agency notified Bayside of required additional expenditures totaling $200,000 to bring the plant into compliance with new federal emission regulations. Bayside has the option either to comply with the regulations by December 31, 2009, or to sell the entire operation (fixed assets and working capital) for $250,000 on December 31, 2009. The improvements will be depreciated over the remaining four-year life of the plant using straight-line depreciation. The cost of site restoration will not be affected by the improvements. If Bayside elects to sell the plant, any book loss can be treated as an offset against taxable income on other operations. This tax reduction is an additional cash benefit of selling.

	Predicted Cash Inflows (outflows) (A)	Year(s) of Cash Flows (B)	12% Present Value Factor (C)	Present Value of Cash Flows (A) × (C)
Initial investment				
Fixed assets	$(800,000)	0	1.000	$ (800,000)
Working capital	(100,000)	0	1.000	(100,000)
Operations				
Annual taxable income without depreciation	300,000	1–5	3.605	1,081,500
Taxes on income ($300,000 × 0.34)	(102,000)	1–5	3.605	(367,710)
Depreciation tax shield	54,400*	1–5	3.605	196,112
Disinvestment				
Site restoration	80,000	5	0.567	(45,360)
Tax shield of restoration ($80,000 × 0.34)	27,200	5	0.567	15,422
Working capital	100,000	5	0.567	56,700
Net present value of all cash flows				$ 36,664

*Computation of depreciation tax shield:

Annual straight-line depreciation ($800,000 ÷ 5)	*$160,000*
Tax rate	*× 0.34*
Depreciation tax shield	*$ 54,400*

Required

a. Should Bayside sell the plant or comply with the new federal regulations? To simplify calculations, assume that any additional improvements are paid for on December 31, 2009.

b. Would Bayside have accepted the proposal in 2008 if it had been aware of the forthcoming federal regulations?

c. Do you have any suggestions that might increase the project's net present value? (No calculations are required.)

C12-42. NPV Analysis of Labor-Saving Investment: Cross-Subsidization (LO2, 5)
Heavy Loading Company's plant has three production departments. Presented are the actual cost functions for each department (DLH = direct labor hour; MH = machine hour):

D1—Total annual overhead = $150,000 + $5DLH + $12MH
D2—Total annual overhead = $185,000 + $2DLH + $10MH
D3—Total annual overhead = $50,000 + $10DLH

The direct labor rate is $12 per hour in all departments. Departments 1 and 2 are machine intensive; Department 3 is labor intensive. The fixed overhead in Departments 1 and 2 is related to building occupancy, machine depreciation, and machine maintenance. The fixed overhead in Department 3 is related to building occupancy.

Required

(The requirements are interrelated and concern a decision to introduce labor-saving equipment into Department 3.)

a. Management is not aware of the actual overhead cost functions. A plantwide overhead rate (based on the historic relationship between the plant's total annual overhead and total direct labor hours) is used to assign overhead to departments and products. Presented are the actual number of direct labor hours and machine hours for a typical year:

	Department 1	Department 2	Department 3
Direct labor hours.	2,000	5,000	10,000
Machine hours	5,000	20,000	0

Determine the plantwide overhead rate per direct labor hour and the annual overhead assigned to Department 3.

b. Management is concerned about the high cost of products subject to Department 3 manufacturing operations. It is evaluating a proposal to invest in a machine that would substantially reduce the labor content of Department 3 operations. The machine would require an initial investment of $500,000. In addition to fixed maintenance costs of $35,000 per year, the machine would have operating costs of $15 per machine hour. It is predicted to operate 4,000 hours during a typical year. Direct labor savings would amount to 7,000 hours per year. The machine is estimated to have a life of five years with no salvage value. Heavy Loading's cost of capital is 16 percent. In evaluating the investment proposal, management included overhead cost savings at the plantwide rate per direct labor hour as determined in requirement (a). Following management's procedures, determine the investment proposal's net present value. Based on this analysis, indicate whether management should accept the proposal.

c. Assuming no change in costs (except in Department 3), determine the plantwide overhead rate per direct labor hour if the proposal is accepted. Why does the rate change from that computed in requirement (a)? Also determine the annual overhead now assigned to Department 3.

d. Evaluate the decision to invest in the new machine. Was this the correct decision? Why or why not? (Provide additional analysis as appropriate.)

e. Assume that Heavy Loading did invest in the machine. Because the machine is a special purpose one, it does not have any resale value, and its scrap value is exactly equal to removal costs. Based on your analysis in requirement (d), what should management do now?

C12-43. Project Screening and Evaluation with Risk: Multiple Criteria **(LO1, 2, 3, 4, 5)**
Transhemisphere uses a capital budgeting committee to evaluate and approve capital expenditure proposals. Because the committee is composed of busy executives, a staff has been assigned to assist the committee in the mechanical aspects of proposal evaluation. As a member of this staff, you have been requested to evaluate five mutually exclusive capital expenditure proposals.

Transhemisphere uses multiple criteria in evaluating capital expenditure proposals. The criteria are designed to consider the time period for which monies invested in a project are unavailable for other purposes, the maximum possible time-adjusted loss on a project, and the time-adjusted relative profitability of a project. To assist in monitoring accepted proposals, the committee also requests information regarding the minimum annual cash flows required for a time-adjusted break-even point. The criteria are applied on a sequential basis, with only proposals that meet the earlier criteria receiving further evaluation. The following specific procedures are to be followed in the evaluation:

1. Only proposals having an expected bailout and/or payback period of three years or less are subject to further evaluation. The bailout period is the time it takes to recover the investment in a project from any source, including disposal.
2. Evaluate the net present value of the pessimistic cash flows associated with each project using Transhemisphere's cost of capital of 16 percent. Projects whose pessimistic cash flows have a negative net present value of $50,000 or more are eliminated from further consideration.
3. Rank the remaining projects on the basis of the internal rate of return of their expected cash flows. (Refer to Appendix 12B if you use the table approach.)
4. For the highest-ranked project, determine the minimum annual net cash inflows needed to provide an internal rate of return equal to the company's cost of capital.

Information pertaining to the five capital expenditure proposals you have been asked to evaluate follows in thousands of dollars (000):

Proposal	Initial Investment	Disposal Value at End of Year 1	2	3	Pessimistic Annual Net Cash Inflow	Pessimistic Life	Expected Annual Net Cash Inflow	Expected Life
A	$196	$150	$100	$ 0	$ 40	7 years	$ 50	10 years
B	500	400	350	0	75	10 years	110	12 years
C	400	300	100	0	40	8 years	50	10 years
D	420	250	200	150	100	7 years	100	10 years
E	250	150	75	0	15	9 years	75	12 years

The nature of the investments is such that none of them has a disposal value after the end of its third year.

Required

a. Following Transhemisphere's capital budgeting procedures, evaluate the five proposals. (Round calculations to the nearest dollar; do not interpolate.)

b. Regardless of Transhemisphere's procedures, which proposal do you recommend and why?

C12-44. Post-Audit and Reevaluation of Investment Proposal: NPV (LO1, 2, 5)

Anthony Company's capital budgeting committee is evaluating a capital expenditure proposal for the production of a high definition television receiver to be sold as an add-on feature for personal computers. The proposal calls for an independent contractor to construct the necessary facilities by December 31, 2010, at a total cost of $250,000. Payment for all construction costs will be made on that date. An additional $50,000 in cash will also be made available on December 31, 2010, for working capital to support sales and production activities.

Management anticipates that the receiver has a limited market life; there is a high probability that by 2017 all new PCs will have built-in high definition receivers. Accordingly, the proposal specifies that production will cease on December 31, 2016. The investment in working capital will be recovered on that date, and the production facilities will be sold for $30,000. Predicted net cash inflows from operations for 2011 through 2016 are as follows:

2011	$100,000
2012	100,000
2013	100,000
2014	40,000
2015	40,000
2016	40,000

Anthony Company has a time value of money of 16 percent. For capital budgeting purposes, all cash flows are assumed to occur at the end of each year.

Required

a. Evaluate the capital expenditure proposal using the net present value method. Should Anthony accept the proposal?

b. Assume that the capital expenditure proposal is accepted, but construction delays caused by labor problems and difficulties in obtaining the necessary construction permits delay the completion of the project. Payments totaling $200,000 were made to the construction company on December 31, 2010, for that year's construction. However, completion is now scheduled for December 31, 2011, and an additional $100,000 will be required to complete construction. If the project is continued, the additional $100,000 will be paid at the end of 2011, and the plant will begin operations on January 1, 2012.

Because of the cost overruns, the capital budgeting committee requests a reevaluation of the project in early 2011, before agreeing to any additional expenditures. After much effort, the following revised predictions of net operating cash inflows are developed:

2012	$120,000
2013	100,000
2014	40,000
2015	40,000
2016	40,000

The working capital investment and disinvestment and the plant salvage values have not changed, except that the cash for working capital would now be made available on December 31, 2011. Use the net present value method to reevaluate the initial decision to accept the proposal. Given the information currently available about the project, should it have been accepted in 2010? (Hint: Determine the net present value as of December 31, 2010, assuming management has not committed Anthony to the proposal.)

c. Given the situation that exists in early 2011, should management continue or cancel the project? Assume that the facilities have a current salvage value of $50,000. (Hint: Assume that the decision is being made on January 1, 2011.)

C12-45. Post-Audit and Reevaluation of Investment Proposal: IRR (LO1, 2, 5)

Throughout his four years in college, Ronald King worked at the local Beef Burger Restaurant in College City. Although the working conditions were good and the pay was not bad, Ron believed he could do a much better job of managing the restaurant than the current owner-manager. In particular, Ron believed that the proper use of marketing campaigns and sales incentives, such as selling a second burger for a 25 percent discount, could increase annual sales by 50 percent.

Just before graduation in 2009, Ron inherited $500,000 from his great uncle. He seriously considered buying the restaurant. It seemed like a good idea because he liked the town and its college atmosphere, knew the business, and always wanted to work for himself. He also knew that the current owner wanted to sell the restaurant and retire to Florida. As part of a small business management course, Ron developed the following income statement for the restaurant's 2008 operations:

Beef Burger Restaurant: College City
Income Statement
For Year Ended December 31, 2008

Sales		$450,000
Expenses		
Cost of food	$150,000	
Supplies	20,000	
Employee expenses	140,000	
Utilities	28,000	
Property taxes	20,000	
Insurance	10,000	
Advertising	8,000	
Depreciation	60,000	436,000
Net income		$ 14,000

Ron believed that the cost of food and supplies were all variable, the employee expenses and utilities were one-half variable and one-half fixed in 2008, and all other expenses were fixed. If Ron purchased the restaurant and followed through on his plans, he believed there would be a 50 percent increase in unit sales volume and all variable costs. Of the fixed costs, only advertising would increase by $12,000. The use of discounts and special promotions would, however, limit the increase in sales revenue to only 40 percent even though sales volume increased 50 percent.

Required

a. Determine
   1. The current annual net cash inflow.
   2. The predicted annual net cash inflow if Ron executes his plans and his assumptions are correct.

b. Ron believes his plan would produce equal net cash inflows during each of the next 15 years, the period remaining on a long-term lease for the land on which the restaurant is built. At the end of that time, the restaurant would have to be demolished at a predicted net cost of $80,000. Assuming Ron would otherwise invest the money in stock expected to yield 12 percent, determine the maximum amount he should pay for the restaurant.

c. Assume that Ron accepts an offer from the current owner to buy the restaurant for $400,000. Unfortunately, although the expected increase in sales volume does occur, customers make much more extensive use of the promotions than Ron had anticipated. As a result, total sales revenues are 8 percent below projections. Furthermore, to improve employee attitudes, Ron gave a 10 percent raise immediately after purchasing the restaurant. Reevaluate the initial decision using the actual sales revenue and the increase in labor costs, assuming conditions will remain unchanged over the remaining life of the project. Was the investment decision a wise one? (Round calculations to the nearest dollar.)

d. Ron can sell the restaurant to a large franchise operator for $300,000. Alternatively, he believes that additional annual marketing expenditures and changes in promotions costing $20,000 per year could bring the sales revenues up to their original projections, with no other changes in costs. Should Ron sell the restaurant or keep it and make the additional expenditures? (Round calculations to the nearest dollar.) (Hint: Ron has just bought the restaurant.)

Appendix A

Managerial Analysis of Financial Statements

LEARNING OBJECTIVES

LO1 Describe the importance of analyzing financial statements for managers. (p. 457)

LO2 Identify factors that influence financial statements and their analysis. (p. 458)

LO3 Specify alternative standards useful in financial statement analysis. (p. 459)

LO4 Describe vertical and horizontal analysis, and their difference. (p. 460)

LO5 Explain the analysis of a firm's solvency. (p. 462)

LO6 Explain the analysis of a firm's performance. (p. 465)

General purpose financial statements are designed to provide information to a large and diverse group of users, including stockholders, creditors, and managers. The objectives of financial statements are broad and, as such, they do not include certain financial measures that specific user groups often need. Through financial statement analysis, however, individual users are able to generate additional useful information and metrics from the statements.

Financial statement analysis is the process of interpreting and evaluating financial statements by using data and disclosures contained in them to produce additional financial measures. Financial statement analysis involves comparing financial statements for the current period with those of previous periods and/or other companies, assessing the internal composition of the financial statements, and measuring relations within and among the financial statements.

The purpose of this appendix is to describe basic measures of financial statement analysis and to consider how managers and others use these measures. For purposes of presentation, assume that the chief financial officer (CFO) of Columbia Corporation is reviewing the financial statements of Berkeley, Inc., a partially-owned subsidiary whose controlling interest is being considered for sale to another conglomerate. The CFO has read several newspaper and magazine articles critical of Berkeley's current operations and its position in the furniture industry. Although Berkeley's sales continue to increase, its profits are relatively flat. This concerns the CFO and she is in the process of gathering additional information about the company and the industry. Her final report will go to the board of directors of Columbia for a decision on the continuation of Berkeley as part of the conglomerate.

Financial statement analysis taps a large amount of useful information that otherwise is not immediately obvious. Credit analysts must evaluate the likelihood that a loan client will make its interest and principal payments on time, stockholders must evaluate the profitability of a firm's assets and the return on investment to various equity holders, and managers must evaluate their overall effectiveness in using the resources entrusted to them by creditors and stockholders.

Two measures often used in financial statement analysis, return on investment (ROI) and residual income, are common to profitability analysis, which was the theme of Chapter 11. Refer to that chapter for a detailed discussion of these measures and how they can also be used for evaluation purposes.

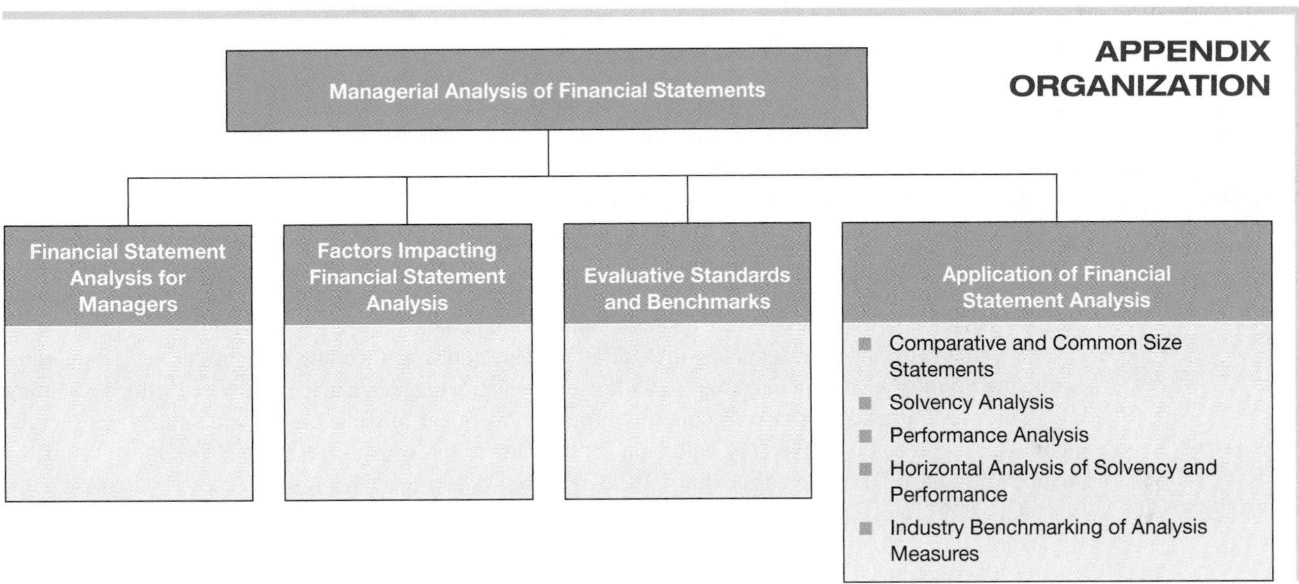

FINANCIAL STATEMENT ANALYSIS FOR MANAGERS

LO1 Describe the importance of analyzing financial statements for managers.

One of the most important reasons for managers to analyze their firm's financial statements is to evaluate the overall performance of the firm, especially as seen by those external to the firm. Managers should be aware of total company performance, not just the performance of their particular areas of responsibility. By analyzing the financial statements for the company as a whole, managers gain a perspective on how the organization is performing *and* how it is perceived.

General purpose financial statements provide the only overall measure of an organization's performance to some managers. The internal reporting system is often limited to reporting component performance, with no report of overall performance provided to managers below the executive level. This reporting limitation excludes many of the financial and nonfinancial sources of information discussed in this book. There is frequently no overall reporting of quality measures, value-added analysis, or activity-based costing between the component level and that of top management.

By evaluating the overall performance of the organization, managers are able to compare their firm with similar firms and to identify potential weaknesses that are worthy of management attention. For example, should managers be alarmed if their firm had a return on equity of 8 percent, while the industry norm is 15 percent? There can be good reasons for the below industry-average return; without financial analysis, however, management may not even be aware of the deficiency or the conditions causing it. Since internal reports of other companies are not available, the only basis for making comparisons with those companies is through their external financial statements and other published materials.

Financial analysis is also necessary for managers whose firms have lending agreements that impose financial restrictions on the organization. Analysis of financial statements is often necessary to determine if restrictions are being met. For example, an agreement may require the debt-to-equity ratio to be maintained below a specified level. Failure to comply could result in a call for immediate liquidation of the debt and could damage the firm's credit rating and its ability to obtain borrowed capital in the future.

A more subtle, but no less important, reason for managers to analyze financial statements is to see their firm as outsiders see it. The financial statements are, in effect, the only window through which many outsiders view the firm. By evaluating the firm's financial statements, managers can better understand outsiders' behavior and attitudes toward the firm and thereby develop a more realistic view of the firm.

FACTORS IMPACTING FINANCIAL STATEMENT ANALYSIS

LO2 Identify factors that influence financial statements and their analysis.

Before learning the procedures for financial statement analysis, it is important to consider several factors that influence the financial statements and the evaluation methods. First, no single financial statement analysis measure can summarize the performance of an organization. This is because each analysis measure is developed to evaluate an operating procedure or a specific area of the organization's performance. For example, sales ratios are used to measure various characteristics or conditions of sales. Although sales ratios help evaluate sales, they do not contribute to the analysis of operating expenses. Before drawing conclusions about the financial condition of an organization, the manager should select several evaluation measures that are germane to the organization being evaluated.

Second, the manager must know which alternative accounting procedures the firm uses. Also, if comparing the results with other companies or with industry standards, the manager must know the accounting procedures each uses. Alternative accounting procedures critical for financial statement analysis include methods of depreciation, inventory valuation (cost or lower of cost or market), and inventory cost flow method (FIFO, LIFO, or average costing). Each of these has an impact on various income statement, cash flow statement, and balance sheet amounts.

Third, inflation, or deflation, can distort the comparisons of financial statements between periods because the statements are based on historical dollars, not on dollars of the same value. Allowances must be made for these effects, or the analysis is distorted. To illustrate, assume that Etson Company has 2007 sales of $100,000 and cost of sales totaling $40,000. During 2008, when inflation is 5 percent, the company's selling prices increase by 5 percent, while its costs have a net increase of only 3 percent due to inventory available at 2007 prices. In 2009, both selling prices and costs go up by 5 percent. Therefore, the company has an increase in 2008 gross profit due primarily to inflation of $3,800 and an increase in 2009 gross profit of $3,190 due solely to inflation.

	2007	2008	2009
Sales	$100,000	$105,000	$110,250
Cost of sales	40,000	41,200	43,260
Gross profit	$ 60,000	$ 63,800	$ 66,990

A manager must be careful to avoid stating that the company has increased operating efficiency when all it did was keep pace with inflation. As a general rule, ignoring inflation produces favorable results when other things remain equal. Inflation can even produce favorable results when actual, constant dollar results are unfavorable. We must remember that external financial statements are presented in historical dollars that have not been adjusted for inflation.

Fourth, changes in the product mix can distort a comparison of financial statements because most products have unique profit margins and their mix influences the firm's profit margin. Assume Wilson Company sells two products, CVT and GHK. During 2009, Wilson sold 100 units of each product; and in 2010, it sold 85 units of CVT and 125 units of GHK. The gross profit for CVT is $10 per unit; for GHK, it is $7 per unit. Total gross profit for 2009 and 2010 follows:

	2009			2010		
	CVT	GHK	Company	CVT	GHK	Company
Gross profit.	$1,000	$700	$1,700	$850	$875	$1,725

Without looking past the total numbers on the financial statements, the analyst might conclude that the company performed better in 2010 than it did in 2009. Total sales units went up from 200 to 210, and profit increased by $25. However, when the individual products are analyzed, another opinion might emerge. Although GHK had increased unit sales of 25 percent, CVT, the product with the higher profit per unit, declined 15 percent. This could signal problems if CVT unit sales continue to decline. For companies with large numbers of products, the changing product mix generally does not have a strong impact. However, companies with only a few products, or with some products that have large profit margins, can have financial results that are difficult to interpret unless the underlying facts are analyzed.

Fifth, changes in organizational structure should be reviewed as part of financial analysis. Today's business environment of mergers, acquisitions, and other changes creates many variations in the financial statements. As organizations are restructured, their accounting procedures change, new information systems are implemented, and many other changes take place that complicate financial analysis.

EVALUATIVE STANDARDS AND BENCHMARKS

LO3 Specify alternative standards useful in financial statement analysis.

Information obtained directly from financial statements and analytical measures derived from statements have little usefulness alone. To be interpreted effectively, this information must be evaluated against some standard. Depending on their objectives, managers can use several different standards. The most common financial analysis standards are: (1) **vertical analysis**, the restatement of amounts in the current financial statements as a percentage of some base measure such as sales; (2) **horizontal analysis**, the comparison of a firm's current financial measures to those of previous periods; (3) **competitor analysis**, the comparison of a firm's financial measures to similar measures for other firms in the industry or to industry averages; and (4) the comparison of a firm's financial measures to its budgeted measures.

Financial statement analysis often begins with an examination of the relations among various accounts. This is normally performed through vertical analysis, where one account, the base account, is set at 100 percent, and all other accounts are presented as a percentage of the base account. In an income statement, sales is typically the base account. After all accounts of a given financial statement are converted into percentages, the statement is known as a **common size statement**. Analysis of common size statements is useful for detecting items that are out of line, that deviate from some preset amount, or that are indicative of other problems. Vertical analysis can be improved by combining it with horizontal analysis and reviewing the common size statements of more than one year. Vertical and horizontal analyses are limited in that they involve comparisons of financial measures only for a single firm. If the firm's performance has been poor or mediocre in the past, these standards do not alert management or the analyst to the need for improvements.

Evaluating financial measures against comparable measures for other firms in the same industry is also beneficial to managers, especially to those in competitive industries. Several financial information services (including Dun and Bradstreet, Standard & Poors, and Moody's) publish averages for commonly used financial measures for all major industries. Failure to perform close to industry norms can signal difficulties in competing with other firms in the future.

When comparing a firm's financial measures with those of other firms, it is necessary to consider any significant differences that might exist among the firms. For example, if one firm is located farther from major suppliers than are other firms in the industry, higher freight costs and possibly lower profits can occur. Differences in accounting practices must also be taken into account in comparing firms; for example, allowances must be made in comparing two firms that use different methods of inventory valuation. Although there are limitations in making intercompany comparisons, looking at other firms' performances is a useful indicator of relative performance.

From management's perspective, the most realistic standard of performance is probably the firm's budgeted performance. Chapter 9 discussed operating budgets and pro forma financial statements, which represent management's most realistic expectations for the period. Managers should compare the analytical measures taken from these statements with the same measures derived from the actual financial statements for the period. For performance evaluation purposes, this comparison is likely to provide managers a useful evaluation of current financial statements.

APPLICATION OF FINANCIAL STATEMENT ANALYSIS

LO4 Describe vertical and horizontal analysis, and their difference.

In addition to the computation of common size statements for vertical and horizontal analysis, financial statement analysis measures include computations that measure the firm's solvency and performance. For a comprehensive analysis of a firm, these measures should be compared to industry norms if available. All of these concepts are illustrated using the 2007, 2008, and 2009 balance sheets and income statements for Berkeley, Inc., which are in Exhibit A.1. The only major economic change in Berkeley's operations during this period occurred in 2009 when it added a new product line. Financial statements for three successive periods are presented because several of the measures require multiple periods or averages. To obtain average information for a period, the beginning and ending balances are summed and divided by 2. Averages computed from values for only two points during the year (beginning and ending) should be used only if monthly or quarterly data are not available. In the following discussions, each analytical measure is presented in general form, along with the measure for Berkeley, Inc. All examples use Berkeley 2009 data unless otherwise noted.

Comparative and Common Size Statements

Converting balance sheets and income statements to common size statements is one of the most direct ways to analyze changes over time. Before the various ratios and account analyses are performed, the manager generally evaluates the income statement and balance sheet using common size statement measures such as sales and total assets. The percentages can also be related to some base period, a month or year, for example. The evaluation of trends in terms of financial statement percentages over time allows for analysis of the underlying movements and shifts in the firm's financial composition.

The percent columns of Exhibit A.1 provide the data needed for this initial evaluation for Berkeley, Inc., for 2009. The computation of common size statements for three to five years allows the manager or analyst to evaluate the activities of the company based on trends of prior periods.

Vertical Analysis

The vertical analysis of the common size statements for Berkeley uses sales from the income statement and total assets from the balance sheet as the bases; these are set at 100 percent. This analysis helps to identify significant changes that have taken place during the period and to determine whether the changes have favorable or unfavorable impacts on solvency and performance.

For example, in evaluating Berkeley's cash needs, the CFO might not be as concerned with the amount of cash as with the percentage of cash to total assets. For Berkeley, the relation of cash to total assets is approximately 17 percent in 2007 and 2008. The decline to 15.2 percent in 2009 could indicate a need to examine the status of cash flows. Before becoming overly concerned with the situation, the CFO would want to compare the status of the 2009 account balances with the company's guidelines or standards and available industry norms. Just because these items deviate from expectations does not indicate a problem. The deviation might indicate improved cash management or changes in credit sales or credit collection policies. The deviation should not be ignored, however, because it might indicate an undesirable trend leading to future difficulties.

Another useful application of common size balance sheet statements is the determination of where shifts occur within major categories. In current assets, for example, the decline in the percentage of cash is offset by increases in accounts receivable and inventories as a percent of total assets. Since the company experienced an increase in sales, it is logical for accounts receivable and inventories to increase. However, if these two accounts had increased and cash had decreased with no corresponding increases in sales, management should be concerned. The latter situation suggests excessive inventory investments and problems collecting accounts receivable.

Vertical analysis is also used with common size income statements. When evaluating the income statement, the manager can use common size measurements to determine quickly whether the company's operating goals are met. If Berkeley's target gross profit margin is 40 percent, attained in 2008 (39.7%),

EXHIBIT A.1 Comparative Financial Statements

BERKELEY, INC.
Comparative Balance Sheets with Common Size Statements
December 31, 2009, 2008, and 2007

($ thousands)	2009		2008		2007	
Assets						
Current assets						
Cash	$1,335	15.2%	$1,341	17.7%	$1,295	17.0%
Marketable securities	250	2.9	200	2.6	228	2.9
Accounts receivable	1,678	19.2	1,386	18.3	1,371	18.0
Inventories	1,703	19.5	1,439	19.1	1,437	18.9
Prepaid items	280	3.2	156	2.1	150	2.0
Total current assets	5,246	60.0	4,522	59.8	4,481	58.8
Property, plant, and equipment	6,934	79.2	6,113	80.9	6,090	80.0
Less accumulated depreciation	3,426	39.2	3,080	40.7	2,955	38.8
Net property, plant and equipment	3,508	40.0	3,033	40.2	3,135	41.2
Total assets	$8,754	100.0%	$7,555	100.0%	$7,616	100.0%
Liabilities and stockholders' equity						
Current liabilities						
Accounts payable	$1,564	17.9%	$1,228	16.3%	$1,243	16.3%
Taxes payable	482	5.5	336	4.4	380	5.0
Accrued expenses payable	202	2.3	178	2.4	152	2.0
Total current liabilities	2,248	25.7	1,742	23.1	1,775	23.3
Long-term Debt	1,208	13.8	1,422	18.8	1,976	25.9
Total liabilities	3,456	39.5	3,164	41.9	3,751	49.2
Stockholders' equity						
Common stock ($1 par)	414	4.7	404	5.3	404	5.3
Additional paid-in capital	531	6.1	270	3.6	270	3.5
Retained earnings	4,353	49.7	3,717	49.2	3,191	41.9
Total stockholders' equity	5,298	60.5	4,391	58.1	3,865	50.7
Total liabilities and equity	$8,754	100.0%	$7,555	100.0%	$7,616	100.0%

BERKELEY, INC.
Comparative Income Statements with Common Size Statements
For Years Ended December 31, 2009, 2008, and 2007

($ thousands, except per share)	2009		2008		2007	
Sales	$9,734	100.0%	$8,028	100.0%	$7,841	100.0%
Cost of goods sold	6,085	62.5	4,843	60.3	4,648	59.3
Gross profit	3,649	37.5	3,185	39.7	3,193	40.7
Operating expenses						
Expenses, excluding depreciation	1,030	10.6	891	11.1	868	11.0
Depreciation	602	6.2	527	6.6	500	6.4
Total expenses	1,632	16.8	1,418	17.7	1,368	17.4
Operating income	2,017	20.7	1,767	22.0	1,825	23.3
Other expenses (revenues)						
Dividend and interest revenue	(80)	(0.8)	(84)	(1.0)	(86)	(1.1)
Interest expense	345	3.5	314	3.9	342	4.4
Gain on sale of investments	(45)	(0.5)	—	—	—	—
Loss on sale of PP&E	35	0.4	—	—	—	—
Total expenses (revenues)	255	2.6	230	2.9	256	3.3
Income before income taxes	1,762	18.1	1,537	19.1	1,569	20.0
Provision for income taxes	599	6.2	523	6.5	533	6.8
Net income	$1,163	11.9%	$1,014	12.6%	$1,036	13.2%
Basis earnings per share	$2.81		$2.51		$2.56	

the manager can readily see that 2009 fell short of the goal by 2.5 percentage points (40% − 37.5%). This suggests that lower prices or items within cost of goods sold were not kept in control. Although the income statement alone cannot provide the answer, it has helped identify the problem and given management a starting point in looking for the cause. Comparable evaluations can be performed on any of the income statement items and, as such, provide a different perspective of evaluation rather than simple reliance on dollar amounts.

Horizontal Analysis

Horizontal analysis is used to evaluate trends in the financial condition of an organization. This analysis allows current year common size statements to be compared to those of prior years and to the organization's goals and objectives. For companies that have few organizational changes and little growth, dollar amounts can be of use for horizontal analysis. However, for companies experiencing major economic changes during the period under evaluation (for example, new product lines, dropping product lines, new sales territories, mergers, or acquisitions), comparisons of dollar amounts are not meaningful. This is true for Berkeley when comparing dollar amounts for 2008 and 2009. Because sales increased substantially when Berkeley added a new product line, it is difficult to evaluate what the dollar amounts should be for most of the other income statement items. In this case, percentages are a better means for comparison.

Using inventories as an item for analysis, we examine how horizontal analysis helps in the evaluation process. From 2007 to 2008, inventories increased by $2,000 ($1,439,000 − $1,437,000), an acceptable change for such a large dollar amount and given that sales increased also. From 2008 to 2009, inventories increased $264,000 ($1,703,000 − $1,439,000), an increase of 18 percent over 2008, which can be alarming without further analysis. However, because the company added a new product line, some increase is expected—but how much of an increase? The current dollar amount seems large. Before rendering judgment, are the percentages from the common size statements just as large? From Exhibit A.1, we see that the percentages for inventory are 18.9%, 19.1%, and 19.5%, respectively, for 2007, 2008, and 2009. Although inventory as a percent of assets has increased, it does not appear unreasonable given the new product line and the overall increase in assets.

After the vertical and horizontal analyses are completed for the common size statements, the manager then begins to make computations concerning other relations within the company's financial reporting system. The most common financial analysis procedures used for financial statement evaluation are considered in the remainder of this appendix.

Solvency Analysis

LO5 Explain the analysis of a firm's solvency.

Solvency refers to the firm's ability to pay its debts as they come due. Primary measures of short-term solvency are the current ratio, acid test ratio, inventory turnover, and days sales in receivables. The debt-to-equity ratio and the times-interest-earned measures are useful in assessing long-term solvency. Information to compute these measures is available in corporate annual reports.

Current Ratio

The **current ratio** measures the relation between current assets and current liabilities. The general equation for the current ratio and the computation for Berkeley, as of December 31, 2009, follow:

Ratio definition: $\textbf{Current ratio} = \dfrac{\textbf{Current assets}}{\textbf{Current liabilities}}$

For Berkeley: $= \dfrac{\$5{,}246{,}000}{\$2{,}248{,}000}$

$= \underline{\underline{2.33}}$

Current assets represent cash and other assets that will be converted into cash (either directly or indirectly) through operations within a reasonably short period of time. Under normal operating conditions, cash is generated by sales of inventory and collection of accounts receivable. Current liabilities are financial obligations that will become due within a relatively short period of time and will be paid from cash currently available and from the pool of cash generated from current assets. Therefore, comparing current assets to current liabilities indicates the extent to which current assets are available to cover current liabilities. Berkeley's current ratio of 2.33 implies that it has $2.33 of current assets for each $1 of current liabilities.

There is no universal guideline for evaluating the current ratio. Although a current ratio of 1.5 is often considered to be the norm, using such an artificial guideline can lead to erroneous conclusions. For example, a current ratio of 1.5 is inadequate for a firm that has 90 percent of its current assets tied up in obsolete or slow-moving inventory, while most of its current liabilities are due in the near-term. The adequacy of a particular current ratio depends on (1) the composition of the current assets and how quickly they will convert to cash, and (2) how soon current liabilities must be paid.

Working Capital

The current asset and current liability accounts are often referred to as current operating, or current working, accounts because assets and liabilities related to operating revenues and expenses normally flow in and out of the balance sheet through these accounts. The difference between current assets and current liabilities is viewed as the net amount of working funds available in the short run. This fund is referred to as **working capital**. Berkeley's December 31, 2009, working capital follows:

Working capital	=	**Current assets**	−	**Current liabilities**
	=	**$5,246,000**	−	**$2,248,000**
	=	**$2,998,000**		

This means that Berkeley has $2,998,000 that it can use as operating funds in the near future. This working capital may be needed if accounts payable continues to increase as a result of the new product line started in 2009.

For a basic illustration as to how working capital is used, consider the following transaction. Assume that during January 2010, Berkeley needs to purchase equipment for $50,000 but does not want to incur a liability. The impact of this transaction is shown as follows:

Working capital	=	**Current assets**	−	**Current liabilities**
	=	**$(50,000)**	−	**$0**
	=	**$(50,000)**		

This leaves a net result of:

Working capital	=	**Current assets**	−	**Current liabilities**
	=	**$5,196,000**	−	**$2,248,000**
	=	**$2,948,000**		

Some transactions affect only current liabilities; others affect both current assets and current liabilities, but by different amounts; others affect both by the same amounts, resulting in no change in working capital; and some transactions have no effect on either. All of an organization's economic transactions—except those that deal solely with the long-term accounts; that is, property, plant and equipment, long-term liabilities, and equity—affect some aspect of the working capital equation.

Acid Test Ratio

Current liabilities are usually paid with cash, not with other current assets. The **acid test ratio** is more specific than is the current ratio as a test of short-term solvency. It measures the availability of cash and other current monetary assets that can be quickly converted into cash to pay current liabilities. Current monetary assets include cash, marketable securities, and current receivables. The general equation for the acid test ratio and the computation for Berkeley, as of December 31, 2009, follow:

$$\textbf{Ratio definition: Acid test ratio} = \frac{\text{Cash} + \text{Marketable securities} + \text{Current accounts receivable}}{\text{Current liabilities}}$$

$$\textbf{For Berkeley:} = \frac{\$1{,}335{,}000 + \$250{,}000 + \$1{,}678{,}000}{\$2{,}248{,}000}$$

$$= \underline{\underline{1.45}}$$

Berkeley's acid test ratio indicates that it has $1.45 of current monetary assets for each $1 of current liabilities. (This ratio is also referred to as the **quick ratio** because it shows the amount of cash that can be obtained relatively quickly for each $1 of current liabilities outstanding.) Many analysts consider an acid test ratio of near 1.0 to be adequate for most businesses. However, as stated earlier in discussing the current ratio, the composition of the ratio components must be considered before deciding what an adequate ratio is. When evaluating the current and acid test ratios, the manager must consider other factors such as seasonal characteristics of the business, the availability of short-term credit lines, the collection terms for accounts receivable, and the payment terms of accounts payable.

As a follow-up to the current and acid test ratios, most analysts evaluate the liquidity of the primary assets in the cash flow stream—namely, inventory and accounts receivable. The inventory turnover and days receivables outstanding are the measures ordinarily used for that purpose.

Inventory Turnover

Inventory turnover indicates the approximate number of times the average stock of inventory is sold and replenished during the year. Inventory turnover is often regarded as both a measure of solvency and a measure of performance. As a solvency measure, inventory turnover reveals how long it takes to convert inventory into current monetary assets. As a performance measure, inventory turnover reveals how well the firm is managing investments in inventory. Inventory turnover is computed as the total cost of the inventory sold during the year divided by the average inventory on hand during the year.

Ratio definition: **Inventory turnover** $= \dfrac{\textbf{Cost of goods sold}}{\textbf{Average inventory}}$

For Berkeley: $= \dfrac{\$6{,}085{,}000}{(\$1{,}703{,}000 + \$1{,}439{,}000)/2}$

$= \underline{\underline{3.87}}$ **times**

During 2009, Berkeley sold inventory costing $6,085,000, and the average inventory for the year was $1,571,000 ([$1,703,000 + $1,439,000]/2). Therefore, the average stock of inventory was sold and replenished 3.87 times during the year. Assuming a 365-day year, the average number of days required for each turnover of inventory was 94.3 days (365 days/3.87). That is, during the year, the average inventory available was sufficient to meet the average sales needs for 94.3 days. Since ending inventory is somewhat higher than is the average inventory for the year, inventory at year-end is sufficient to supply somewhat more than 94.3 days' average sales.

What constitutes an appropriate inventory turnover ratio varies from industry to industry and over time. Obviously, a fast-food restaurant should have a high inventory turnover, whereas a jewelry store typically has a low inventory turnover. Firms adopting just-in-time approaches to inventory management should have an increase in their inventory turnovers. If a firm's competitors' inventory turnovers are increasing, this could indicate that competitors changed their approach to inventory management. The nature of the firm's supply sources, the use of inventory display in selling merchandise, the quickness with which inventory is delivered to customers, and information on the industry should all be considered in interpreting the inventory turnover ratio.

Days Sales in Receivables

Next to cash and marketable securities, receivables are the most liquid assets. They are converted directly into cash in the normal course of business. The **days sales in receivables** ratio measures the number of days, on average, it takes to generate the credit sales uncollected at any point in time. Days sales in receivables is a measure of both solvency and performance. As a measure of solvency, it reveals how many days on average it takes to convert accounts receivable into cash. As a performance measure, days sales in receivables reveals how well the firm is managing the credit extended to customers. The longer the collection period the less cash is available for daily operations. Days sales in receivables is computed as receivables divided by average daily sales.

Ratio definition: **Days sales in receivables** $= \dfrac{\textbf{Accounts receivable}}{\textbf{Average daily credit sales}}$

For Berkeley: $= \dfrac{\$1{,}678{,}000}{\$9{,}734{,}000/365}$

$= \underline{\underline{62.9}}$ **days**

At year-end 2009, Berkeley had receivables equal to the average sales for 62.9 days (assuming all sales are on credit). In evaluating this measure, management should consider the terms under which credit sales are made. For example, if Berkeley sells goods and services on 30-day credit terms, a ratio of 62.9 days probably indicates serious receivables collection problems. This ratio, which is a broad average, is a reliable indicator only if the amount of daily sales was fairly even throughout the year. For more precise information, management should conduct a detailed analysis of year-end receivables to determine their ages and probable collection periods.

Debt-to-Equity Ratio

Most businesses have two basic sources of capital: debt and equity. The balance between the amounts of capital provided by creditors and owners is important in evaluating a business's long-term solvency. Creditors regard equity as a cushion against future operating losses and bankruptcy. The larger the percentage of total assets financed by equity capital, the more secure are the creditors. Aggressive, growth-oriented organizations tend to rely more heavily on debt than on equity, whereas stable, conservative organizations tend to have a larger proportion of equity. The **debt-to-equity ratio** is computed as total liabilities divided by total stockholders' equity.

Ratio definition: Debt-to-equity ratio $= \dfrac{\textbf{Total liabilities}}{\textbf{Total stockholders' equity}}$

For Berkeley: $= \dfrac{\$3{,}456{,}000}{\$5{,}298{,}000}$

$= \underline{\underline{0.65}}$

Berkeley's December 31, 2009, debt-to-equity ratio of 0.65 indicates that its creditors have provided \$0.65 of capital for each \$1 that stockholders provided. Stated another way, for each \$1.65 of asset book values, the company could suffer a \$1 loss and still have total reported assets equal to total liabilities. Although the debt-to-equity ratio is useful as a general indicator of the adequacy of long-term solvency, the amount of long-term debt that a company can justify is primarily related to its ability to repay the funds plus interest.

Times-Interest-Earned

A financially sound business normally pays interest obligations out of current earnings. Accordingly, creditors are interested in the adequacy of earnings to provide payment of interest charges. **Times-interest-earned**, a measure of interest-paying ability, shows the relation between earnings available to pay interest and total interest expense.

Ratio definition: Times-interest-earned $= \dfrac{\textbf{Net income} + \textbf{Interest expense} + \textbf{Income taxes}}{\textbf{Interest expense}}$

For Berkeley: $= \dfrac{\$1{,}163{,}000 + \$345{,}000 + \$599{,}000}{\$345{,}000}$

$= \underline{\underline{6.11}}$ times

In the numerator, interest expense and income taxes are added to net income to determine the pool of earnings from which interest expense is paid. Since interest expense is deducted in computing taxable income, the earnings pool from which interest is paid is income before deductions for interest and taxes. For Berkeley, this pool of earnings for 2009 is 6.11 times the amount of the current year's interest charge on debt.

Performance Analysis

LO6 Explain the analysis of a firm's performance.

Operating performance is related to the broad objective of profitability. The basic activities that characterize a typical for-profit organization follow:

- Generating capital—equity and debt.
- Acquiring assets with capital.
- Using assets to generate sales and profits.
- Using profits to pay the cost of capital.

Primary measures of performance are asset turnover, return on assets, return on equity, and earnings per share. Care must be taken when using ratios for performance evaluation. Several of the measures of solvency discussed previously are also used to assist in the evaluation of these activities. It is quite common to find inventory turnover and days sales in receivables as part of performance evaluation. Common measures of performance are discussed in this section.

Asset Turnover

The **asset turnover** ratio measures the firm's ability to use its assets to generate sales. Asset turnover is computed as sales divided by average total assets.

$$\textbf{Ratio definition:}\quad \textbf{Asset turnover} = \frac{\textbf{Sales}}{\textbf{Average total assets}}$$

$$\textbf{For Berkeley:}\quad = \frac{\$9{,}734{,}000}{(\$8{,}754{,}000 + \$7{,}555{,}000)/2} = \underline{\underline{1.19}}\ \textbf{times}$$

For Berkeley, the asset turnover of 1.19 times indicates that, on the average, each $1 of assets generated $1.19 of sales during 2009. The interpretation of this measure depends largely on the nature of the business. Organizations that are capital-intensive, such as utilities or heavily automated manufacturers, typically have a lower asset turnover than do organizations that are labor-intensive, such as garment manufacturers. Also, firms that generate a small amount of sales with each dollar of assets usually must earn a higher percentage of profit on each sales dollar than do firms that produce a high amount of sales with each invested asset dollar.

Return on Sales

The ability of a firm to generate sales with available assets is important. To be profitable, however, these sales must exceed the cost of generating them. **Return on sales** is a measure of the firm's ability to generate profits from sales produced by the firm's assets. Return on sales is computed by dividing the sum of net income and net-of-tax interest expense by sales.

$$\textbf{Ratio definition:}\quad \textbf{Return on sales} = \frac{\textbf{Net income + Net-of-tax interest expense}}{\textbf{Sales}}$$

$$\textbf{For Berkeley:}\quad = \frac{\$1{,}163{,}000 + \$345{,}000(1 - 0.34)}{\$9{,}734{,}000} = \underline{\underline{0.143}},\ \text{or}\ \underline{\underline{14.3\%}}$$

Interest expense is added to net income because it is not considered an expense of using assets, but rather a cost of providing the capital invested in assets. Since interest expense reduces taxes, it is adjusted for taxes at the company's current effective tax rate of approximately 34 percent. This reveals that, on average, 14.3 percent of each $1 of Berkeley 2009 sales remained as profit after covering all expenses other than interest.

Return on Assets

The **return on assets** ratio combines asset turnover and return on sales to measure directly the firm's ability to use its assets to generate profits. The return on assets computation is derived from the asset turnover and return on sales ratios as follows:

$$\textbf{Ratio derivation:}\quad \textbf{Return on assets} = \textbf{Asset turnover} \times \textbf{Return on sales}$$
$$= \frac{\textbf{Sales}}{\textbf{Average total assets}} \times \frac{\textbf{Net income + Net-of-tax interest expense}}{\textbf{Sales}}$$

$$\textbf{Ratio definition:}\quad \textbf{Return on assets} = \frac{\textbf{Net income + Net-of-tax interest expense}}{\textbf{Average total assets}}$$

$$\textbf{For Berkeley:}\quad = \frac{\$1{,}163{,}000 + \$345{,}000(1 - 0.34)}{(\$8{,}754{,}000 + \$7{,}555{,}000)/2} = \underline{\underline{0.171}},\ \text{or}\ \underline{\underline{17.1\%}}$$

Berkeley's 2009 return on assets is also approximated by multiplying the asset turnover of 1.19 times the return on sales of 14.3 percent. From the previous analyses, we conclude that, on average, each dollar of assets generates $1.19 of sales and $0.171 of income and that each dollar of sales results in $0.143 of income. Return on assets is an important indicator of management's overall performance because it measures management's effectiveness in using the total capital entrusted to them by both creditors and stockholders. A variation of this ratio (return on investment), discussed in Chapter 11, is commonly used for evaluating the performance of divisions in decentralized organizations.

The return on assets ratio measures profitability before deducting capital costs (interest and dividends). Thus, the adequacy of the profitability indicated by this ratio depends on the cost of debt and the return stockholders expect on their investments.

Return on Equity

Return on equity measures the profits attributable to shareholders as a percentage of their equity in the firm. This measure is more specific than is the return on assets ratio in measuring performance because return on equity focuses only on stockholders' profits and investment. The profits available to stockholders consist of net income after deducting all costs and expenses, including interest expense. Return on equity is computed as net income divided by average stockholders' equity.

$$\textbf{Ratio definition: Return on equity} = \frac{\textbf{Net income}}{\textbf{Average stockholders' equity}}$$

$$\textbf{For Berkeley:} \quad = \frac{\$1{,}163{,}000}{(\$5{,}298{,}000 + \$4{,}391{,}000)/2} = 0.240, \text{ or } 24.0\%$$

(If the company also has preferred stock outstanding, then return on equity is computed as the return on *common* equity; where net income is reduced by the amount of annual dividends on preferred stock, and stockholders' equity is reduced by the book value of preferred stock.)

The 2009 return attributable to Berkeley's shareholders was 24 percent, compared to a return on assets of 17.1 percent. The return to shareholders is higher than is its return on assets as a result of financial leverage. **Financial leverage** refers to the use of capital that has a fixed interest or dividend rate. Any time capital can be acquired at a fixed rate, and the return on assets is higher than that fixed rate, the return to the common shareholders is increased through favorable financial leverage. (The interest rate on a variable rate loan can change from period to period as the prime rate changes; however, even in this case, the interest is fixed for a short period of time, and management's ability to generate favorable leverage varies inversely with interest rate changes.) Conversely, if the fixed cost of capital is greater than the return it generates, the shareholders are subsidizing the cost of debt or other fixed rate capital, which reflects unfavorable financial leverage. Berkeley's favorable financial leverage occurred because the return on assets was 17.1 percent, whereas the interest rate as a percent of average total liabilities was 10.4 percent, computed as follows:

$$\text{Average interest rate} = \frac{\textbf{Interest expense}}{\textbf{Average total liabilities}}$$

$$\textbf{For Berkeley} \quad = \frac{\$345{,}000}{(\$3{,}456{,}000 + \$3{,}164{,}000)/2} = 0.104, \text{ or } 10.4\%$$

Berkeley's total debt required a return of only $345 (or 10.4 percent). Therefore, the return above 10.4 percent on the assets acquired with debt increased the return to the shareholders to 24.0 percent.

Earnings per Share

For external reporting purposes, earnings per share amounts are disclosed on the face of the income statement. If a company has gains or losses from extraordinary sources, such as from a natural disaster, or from other unusual and infrequent events, then income and earnings per share figures must be presented separately for income before extraordinary items and for net income. Berkeley's income statement in Exhibit A.1 reported earnings per share of $2.81 in 2009 and $2.51 in 2008. **Earnings per share** is defined as follows:

$$\textbf{Ratio definition: Earnings per share} = \frac{\textbf{Net income}}{\textbf{Average number of common shares outstanding}}$$

$$\textbf{For Berkeley:} \quad = \frac{\$1{,}163{,}000}{414{,}000} = \underline{\underline{\$2.81}}$$

Earnings per share for companies with simple capital structures is computed as net income divided by the average number of shares outstanding for the period. A *simple capital structure* is one consisting only of common stock. The computations are more difficult for a company with a *complex capital structure* that includes preferred stock, convertible bonds, or other types of equity securities. Also, changes in a company's capital structure during the year and over time make it more difficult to compare earnings per share from year to year.

Investors use earnings per share measures as a basis in evaluating the firm's overall profitability. The advantage of the earnings per share measure is that it is reported on the same basis as stock prices—that is, on an individual share basis. Investors often use the **price earnings ratio**, which is the ratio of the current market price divided by the earnings per share of the stock, to arrive at a multiple of earnings.

$$\textbf{Ratio definition: Price earnings ratio} = \frac{\textbf{Market price per share}}{\textbf{Earnings per share}}$$

Some managers use earnings per share as a broad measure of overall performance. However, earnings per share should not be relied on too heavily, nor should it be substituted for other, more detailed profitability ratios that managers can obtain. Other profitability measures are often more useful to managers in evaluating overall management performance. Another reason why managers must monitor earnings per share is to better understand a measure that investors use in making decisions about buying or selling a company's capital stock.

Finally, some managers compute the *dividend payout ratio*, defined as dividends per common share divided by earnings per common share. Companies that have high reinvestment of their earnings would have low dividend payout ratios. Similarly, companies that have few investment opportunities and shareholders that seek dividends would have high dividend payout ratios. Another measure known as the *dividend yield ratio*, defined as dividends per common share divided by market price per common share, reflects the percent of the share market price paid out in cash. A complete summary of the ratios discussed in this chapter is provided at the end of the chapter in Exhibit A.3.

Horizontal Analysis of Solvency and Performance

Horizontal analysis, as already illustrated, provides good measures of performance over time. This analysis can be readily extended to the financial ratios of solvency and performance measures. The annual reports of most companies include several years' data for key items such as gross sales, operating profit margin, net income, earnings per share, dividends paid, and net changes to retained earnings. However, annual reports rarely include financial ratios that are important for evaluation purposes.

Horizontal analysis requires little additional computations because many of the items that provide input for other financial analysis techniques are already computed. A typical analysis often includes the current ratio. Although a measure of solvency in the short run, the current ratio can be a measure of performance when compared over a period of years. For example, if the information for Berkeley is extended back to 2005, a horizontal analysis of the current ratio reveals the following:

	2009	2008	2007	2006	2005
Current ratio	2.33	2.60	2.52	2.56	2.61

It appears that the ratio of current assets to current liabilities has been slowly declining. Such an analysis might alert the manager to take investigative action before the current ratio becomes undesirable. If creditors are using similar analysis, the decline might alert them to be cautious in extending credit to Berkeley.

Horizontal analysis can be performed using both dollars and common size units. However, care must be used when horizontal analysis is based only on dollar amounts. To illustrate, if we refer to Exhibit A.1 and use dollars, horizontal analysis of the income statement reveals that cost of goods sold in 2009 increased substantially over that of 2008 whereas in 2008 and 2007 cost of goods sold were about the same. Is this good or bad, considering 2009 sales also increased substantially? On the other hand, horizontal analysis with common size units reveals another picture—the increase is only 2.2 percent (62.5 percent − 60.3 percent).

Some types of analysis combine both dollars and common size units with two or more sets of data to make performance evaluations using horizontal analysis. Suppose the income statements for Berkeley appeared as follows:

	2009	2008	2007	2006	2005
Sales.	$9,734,000	$8,028,000	$7,841,000	$7,260,000	$7,000,000
Operating income.	2,017,000	1,767,000	1,825,000	1,670,000	1,610,000
Operating income as percent of sales.	20.7%	22.0%	23.3%	23.0%	23.0%

If only the dollars are considered, the trend for Berkeley appears favorable, with sales increasing each year, including substantial growth in 2009. Dollars of operating income are also increasing, except for 2008, with 2009 again showing a substantial increase. However, after adding the common size data to the analysis, the company's performance appears less favorable. After several years of operating with a 23 percent margin, performance slipped to 20.7 percent, even with the large 2009 sales increase.

Another type of horizontal analysis is frequently used when a given point in time has been established as the base year or benchmark for comparison. Using the data above with 2005 as the base year (100%), a horizontal analysis using common size units follows:

	2009	2008	2007	2006	2005
Sales.	139%	115%	112%	104%	100%
Operating income.	125	110	113	104	100

When we add this information to the previous analysis, it appears that the first sign of declining profit was in 2008, when operating income increased much less than did sales. In fact, 2008 operating income was less than that of 2007 by 3 percentage points.

This application is frequently extended by converting an entire financial statement to a base period and computing the change in each account for several financial statements. This allows the manager to examine the movement of all items in relation to a single starting point. Exhibit A.2 reveals the results of holding 2007 as the base year for Berkeley and adjusting all subsequent income statement accounts against those of 2007. To illustrate this application, cost of goods sold showed an increase of 30.9 percent, whereas sales went up only 24.1 percent over the two-year period. Although gross profit increased 14.3 percent over the 2007 base, it did not improve at the same level as sales improved. Therefore, the manager might conclude that the increased sales attributable to the new product do not provide the same profit margin as the other products, or maybe the new product hindered the efficiency of producing existing products. This type of analysis is also applied to base-year comparisons of balance sheets.

Industry Benchmarking of Analysis Measures

Evaluation of a firm's financial condition and performance is incomplete without comparisons to, and benchmarking against, its industry (competitors) during the same operating period(s). Industry comparisons provide insight into the firm's relative financial condition and performance and show whether the firm is keeping pace, moving ahead, or lagging behind competitors. There are several sources, such as Moody's and Standard & Poors, that provide industry benchmarks on key financial analysis ratios and indexes.

Comparative evaluations must be made cautiously. First, avoid generalizations, such as every company should have a current ratio of 2 to 1. This caution was expressed in the section on current ratios.

EXHIBIT A.2 Base Year Common Size Statements

BERKELEY, INC.
Common Size Comparative Income Statements
For Years Ended December 31, 2009, 2008, and 2007

	2009	2008	2007
Sales	124.1%	102.4%	100.0%
Cost of goods sold	130.9	104.2	100.0
Gross profit	114.3	99.7	100.0
Operating expenses			
Expenses, excluding depreciation	118.7	102.6	100.0
Depreciation	120.4	105.4	100.0
Total operating expenses	119.3	103.7	100.0
Operating income	110.5	96.8	100.0
Other expenses and revenues			
Interest and dividend revenue	93.0	97.7	100.0
Interest expense	100.9	91.8	100.0
Gain on sale of investment*	—	—	—
Loss on sale of PPE*	—	—	—
Total other expenses and revenues	99.6	89.8	100.0
Income before income taxes	112.3	98.0	100.0
Provision for income taxes	112.4	98.1	100.0
Net income	112.2	97.9	100.0

*These items are reported only in 2009 and, thus, have no base in 2007.

Second, avoid using industry averages or medians as absolute guidelines for performance measurement. Although industry benchmarks are better than rule-of-thumb generalizations, they do not apply equally to all firms within an industry. The industry benchmark is likely comprised of data from large firms, new firms, growing firms, diversified firms, and numerous other firms that do not match the case of the firm being evaluated. It is helpful if a distribution of the data statistics is provided within industry. (This is provided for many industries in the aforementioned publications.) For example, if the firm being evaluated has a current ratio of 1.6 and the industry average is 2.2, there may be cause for concern. However, if it is known that the firm fits into a category of similar firms within the industry that have an average current ratio of 1.5, cause for concern is lessened.

A third caution relates to the overall industry performance. A firm that is slightly below average in a financially strong industry can be better than one at the top of a financially weak industry. Again, there are business publications that give periodic ratings by industry—for example, the *Wall Street Journal*.

Fourth, a firm must be analyzed as to its diversity or homogeneity. A firm with diversified product lines will often not fit into any group or industry. Various reporting requirements (via government agencies) force companies to classify themselves under some predefined industry classification whether they are diversified or not. Also, diversified firms tend to distort industry benchmarks of firms that have homogeneous product lines and that fit nicely into that particular industry category.

Fifth, size influences how a firm compares to industry benchmarks. Larger firms within an industry should probably be compared to industry benchmarks in a different way than are smaller firms. This is not to imply that large firms are better—in many industries, large firms are the weaker performers.

Each of these cautions should be considered as appropriate when analyzing a firm's financial condition and comparing that analysis to industry benchmarks. Comparing incompatible sets of data can result in managers making incorrect decisions, causing future performance to deteriorate.

Returning to the CFO's analysis of Berkeley, she must render a decision to the board of directors concerning the status of this subsidiary. Assuming her evaluation of Berkeley's position as related to the furniture industry is compatible with the newspaper and magazine articles she read before beginning her analysis, she is left with drawing conclusions about future trends of the company. While the existing current ratio, asset turnover ratio, return on sales, and most other measures are acceptable, the CFO is concerned about the trend evident from the horizontal analysis. That is, the current ratio has been declining, operating income as a percentage of sales has been declining, and the growth of operating income has not kept pace with the growth of sales. It is when faced with such decisions that executives such as this CFO demand timely and relevant information to recommend what is best for the long-run benefits of the company.

EXHIBIT A.3 Summary of Financial Analysis Ratios

Ratio		Formula	Reflects
Solvency			
Working capital	=	Current assets − Current liabilities	Near-term debt-paying ability
Current ratio	=	$\frac{\text{Current assets}}{\text{Current liabilities}}$	Near-term debt-paying ability
Acid test ratio	=	$\frac{\text{Cash} + \text{Marketable Securities} + \text{Current receivables}}{\text{Current liabilities}}$	Near-term debt-paying ability
Accounts receivable turnover	=	$\frac{\text{Net sales}}{\text{Average accounts receivable}}$	Efficiency of receivable collection
Inventory turnover	=	$\frac{\text{Cost of goods sold}}{\text{Average inventory}}$	Efficiency of inventory management
Days sales in receivables	=	$\frac{\text{Accounts receivable}}{\text{Credit sales}} \times 365$	Liquidity of receivables
Days sales in inventory	=	$\frac{\text{Ending inventory}}{\text{Cost of goods sold}} \times 365$	Liquidity of inventory
Debt-to-equity ratio	=	$\frac{\text{Total liabilities}}{\text{Total stockholders' equity}}$	Creditor versus owner financing
Times-interest-earned	=	$\frac{\text{Net income} + \text{Interest expense} + \text{Income taxes}}{\text{Interest expense}}$	Interest-paying ability
Performance			
Asset turnover	=	$\frac{\text{Net sales}}{\text{Average total assets}}$	Efficiency of total assets
Return on sales	=	$\frac{\text{Net income} + \text{Net-of-tax interest expense}}{\text{Sales}}$	Profitability of sales given assets
Gross margin ratio	=	$\frac{\text{Net income} - \text{Cost of goods sold}}{\text{Net sales}}$	Gross profit per sales dollar
Return on assets	=	$\frac{\text{Net income} + \text{Net-of-tax interest expense}}{\text{Average total assets}}$	Profitability of assets
Return on equity	=	$\frac{\text{Net income}}{\text{Average stockholders' equity}}$	Profitability of shareholder investment
Average interest rate	=	$\frac{\text{Interest expense}}{\text{Average total liabilities}}$	Interest rate paid on debt
Book value per share	=	$\frac{\text{Shareholders' equity of common shares}}{\text{Number of common shares outstanding}}$	Liquidation at reported values
Earnings per share	=	$\frac{\text{Net income}}{\text{Average number of common shares outstanding}}$	Income per common share
Price earnings ratio	=	$\frac{\text{Market price per common share}}{\text{Earnings per common share}}$	Market value multiple of earnings
Dividend yield	=	$\frac{\text{Cash dividends per common share}}{\text{Market price per common share}}$	Cash return of market price
Dividend payout	=	$\frac{\text{Cash dividends per common share}}{\text{Earnings per common share}}$	Payout percent of earnings

APPENDIX-END REVIEW: COMPARATIVE COMMON SIZE STATEMENTS AND RATIO ANALYSIS

Comparative 2008 and 2009 income statements and balance sheets for Oxford, Inc., follow.

OXFORD, INC.
Comparative Income Statements
For Years Ended December 31, 2009 and 2008

($ 000s)	2009	2008
Sales	$3,000	$2,500
Cost of goods sold	2,600	2,300
Gross profit	400	200
Operating expenses		
Selling	125	105
General and administrative	70	60
Total operating expenses	195	165
Operating income	205	35
Other expenses (revenues)		
Interest income	(10)	(5)
Interest expense	40	20
Total other expenses	30	15
Income before income taxes	175	20
Provision for income taxes	60	7
Net income	$ 115	$ 13
Earnings per share	$ 1.28	$ 0.19

OXFORD, INC.
Comparative Balance Sheets
December 31, 2009 and 2008

($ 000s)	2009	2008
Assets		
Current assets		
Cash and cash equivalents	$ 375	$ 315
Accounts receivable	325	280
Inventories	400	350
Interest receivable	60	55
Total current assets	1,160	1,000
Property, plant, and equipment	1,500	1,300
Less accumulated depreciation	800	750
Property, plant, and equipment, net	700	550
Other assets	15	12
Total assets	$1,875	$1,562
Liabilities and stockholders' equity		
Current liabilities		
Accounts payable	$ 435	$ 330
Income taxes payable	45	5
Interest payable	50	45
Total current liabilities	530	380
Long-term debt	300	250
Total liabilities	830	630
Stockholders' equity		
Common stock ($1 par)	90	70
Additional paid-in capital	15	10
Retained earnings	940	852
Total stockholders' equity	1,045	932
Total liabilities and equity	$1,875	$1,562

Additional information

- During 2009, operating expenses included $50,000 in depreciation expense.

- Cash dividends of $27,000 are declared and paid during 2009.
- Common stock of $15,000 is issued at par for cash in 2009.
- Equipment costing $200,000 is acquired during 2009 by paying cash of $190,000 and issuing 5,000 shares of common stock worth $10,000.
- During 2009, long-term debt of $20,000 is paid off with cash and new long-term debt of $70,000 is issued for cash.
- The company extended a $3,000 loan to the company president in 2009.

Required

a. Prepare common size statements for 2009 and 2008. Use sales as the base for the income statements and total assets as the base for the balance sheets.

b. What major changes are evident from 2008 to 2009 when horizontal analysis is performed? Explain.

c. Prepare a complete ratio analysis for 2009 including measures of solvency and performance.

Solution to Review Problem

a.

OXFORD, INC.
Common Size Income Statements
For Years Ended December 31, 2009 and 2008

	2009	2008
Sales	100.0%	100.0%
Cost of goods sold	86.7	92.0
Gross profit	13.3	8.0
Operating expenses		
Selling	4.2	4.2
General and administrative	2.3	2.4
Total operating expenses	6.5	6.6
Operating income	6.8	1.4
Other expenses (revenues)		
Interest income	(0.3)	(0.2)
Interest expense	1.3	0.8
Total other expenses	1.0	0.6
Income before income taxes	5.8	0.8
Provision for income taxes	2.0	0.3
Net income	3.8%	0.5%

OXFORD, INC.
Common Size Balance Sheets
December 31, 2009 and 2008

	2009	2008
Assets		
Current assets		
Cash and cash equivalents	20.0%	20.2%
Accounts receivable	17.3	17.9
Inventories	21.3	22.4
Interst receivable	3.2	3.5
Total current assets	61.8	64.0
Property, plant, and equipment:	80.0	83.2
Less accumulated depreciation	42.6	48.0
Net property, plant, and equipment	37.4	35.2
Other assets	0.8	0.8
Total assets	100.0%	100.0%

continued

continued from previous page

OXFORD, INC. Common Size Balance Sheets December 31, 2009 and 2008	2009	2008
Liabilities and stockholders' equity		
Current liabilities		
Accounts payable	23.2%	21.1%
Income taxes payable	2.4	0.3
Interest payable	2.7	2.9
Total current liabilities	28.3	24.3
Long-term debt	16.0	16.0
Total liabilities	44.3	40.3
Stockholders' equity		
Common stock ($1 par)	4.8	4.5
Additional paid-in capital	0.8	0.6
Retained earnings	50.1	54.6
Total stockholders' equity	55.7	59.7
Total liabilities and equity	100.0%	100.0%

b. The common size statements reveal that current assets declined as a percentage of total assets, with the largest decline being inventories (1.1%). The largest change occurred with net property, plant, and equipment, which increased 2.1 percent.

Total liabilities as a group increased by 4.0 percent; taxes payable were the main driver. The primary change in stockholders' equity is retained earnings, which decreased by 4.4 percent.

The substantial increase in dollars of net income can be explained when reviewing the common size statements; cost of goods sold led the way with a 5.3 percent decline. The only items that increased were interest expense and provisions for taxes.

When a company experiences a major change in sales—such as the 20 percent increase for Oxford [($3,000,000 − $2,500,000)/$2,500,000]—it is difficult to assess dollar amounts and tell if every item maintained its proper contribution to the whole. Common size statements permit this analysis and provide evidence as to the degree of change of each item.

c.

Solvency measures:

Current ratio $= \dfrac{\text{Current assets}}{\text{Current liabilities}} = \dfrac{\$1{,}160}{\$530} = 2.19$

Acid test ratio $= \dfrac{\text{Cash} + \text{Current receivables}}{\text{Current liabilities}} = \dfrac{\$375 + \$325}{\$530} = 1.32$

Inventory turnover $= \dfrac{\text{Cost of goods sold}}{\text{Average inventory}} = \dfrac{\$2{,}600}{(\$350 + \$400)/2} = 6.93$ times

Days sales in receivables $= \dfrac{\text{Ending receivables}}{\text{Average daily sales}} = \dfrac{\$325}{\$3{,}000/365} = 39.54$ days

continued

continued from previous page

Debt-to-equity ratio $= \dfrac{\text{Total liabilities}}{\text{Total stockholders' equity}}$

$= \dfrac{\$830}{\$1{,}045}$

$= \underline{\underline{0.79}}$

Times-interest-earned $= \dfrac{\text{Net income + Interest expense + Income taxes}}{\text{Interest expense}}$

$= \dfrac{\$115 + \$40 + \$60}{\$40}$

$= \underline{\underline{5.38}}$ times

Performance measures:

Asset turnover $= \dfrac{\text{Sales}}{\text{Average total assets}}$

$= \dfrac{\$3{,}000}{(\$1{,}562 + \$1{,}875)/2}$

$= \underline{\underline{1.75}}$ times

Return on sales $= \dfrac{\text{Net income + Net-of-tax interest expense}}{\text{Sales}}$

$= \dfrac{\$115 + \$40(1 - 0.34)}{\$3{,}000}$

$= \underline{\underline{0.047}}$, or $\underline{\underline{4.7\%}}$

Return on assets $= \dfrac{\text{Net income + Net-of-tax interest expense}}{\text{Average total assets}}$

$= \dfrac{\$115 + \$40(1 - 0.34)}{(\$1{,}562 + \$1{,}875)/2}$

$= \underline{\underline{0.082}}$, or $\underline{\underline{8.2\%}}$

Return on equity $= \dfrac{\text{Net income}}{\text{Average stockholders' equity}}$

$= \dfrac{\$115}{(\$932 + \$1{,}045)/2}$

$= \underline{\underline{0.116}}$, or $\underline{\underline{11.6\%}}$

DISCUSSION QUESTIONS

QA-1. What is the general purpose for conducting ratio analysis of financial statements?

QA-2. Name three reasons why managers should analyze their firm's financial statements.

QA-3. What is the purpose of evaluation standards (benchmarks) in financial analysis?

QA-4. What types of standards (benchmarks) are probably most relevant for financial analysis by managers?

QA-5. Explain how managers use vertical and horizontal analysis when evaluating financial statements. What changes are usually made in the statements before managers use these techniques?

QA-6. Explain and differentiate the terms solvency evaluation and performance evaluation.

QA-7. Explain the difference between the current ratio and the acid test ratio.

QA-8. Why is it useful to compute inventory turnover and the days sales in receivables? How is each of these measures computed?

QA-9. What are the primary measures of long-term solvency? How are they computed?

QA-10. Which financial statement analysis measure provides information concerning the sales output that a firm's assets produce?

QA-11. Why is interest expense added in the numerator in computing return on assets?

QA-12. Explain the concept of financial leverage. What causes financial leverage to be favorable? Unfavorable?

QA-13. Explain why comparisons to industry norms or averages are important when analyzing financial statements.

QA-14. What cautions should the manager take when using industry norms or benchmarks for comparison?

MINI EXERCISES

MA-15. Short-Term Solvency Ratios (LO5)
Following are financial data from year-end financial statements of York Company for 2011, 2010 and 2009.

	2011	2010	2009
Accounts receivable	$ 153,000	$ 165,000	$ 150,000
Cost of goods sold	1,680,000	1,450,000	1,600,000
Current assets	750,000	600,000	675,000
Current liabilities	525,000	450,000	500,000
Inventory	375,000	275,000	325,000
Sales	1,850,000	2,000,000	1,750,000

Required

a. Compute the following financial ratios for 2010 and 2011. (Round calculations to two decimal places.)
1. Current ratio
2. Acid test ratio
3. Inventory turnover
4. Days receivables outstanding

b. Comment on the short-term solvency of York Company for 2010 and 2011. Did the company's short-term solvency improve or deteriorate during 2011? Explain.

MA-16. Long-Term Solvency Ratios (LO5)
Summary data from year-end financial statements of Palo Alto Company for 2011 follow.

Summary Income Statement Data		
Sales		$8,000,000
Cost of goods sold	$3,425,000	
Selling expenses	625,000	
Administrative expenses	525,000	
Interest expense	1,475,300	
Income tax expense	50,250	6,100,550
Net income		$1,899,450

Summary Balance Sheet Data			
Cash	$ 60,000	Total liabilities	$600,000
Noncash assets	790,000	Stockholders' equity	250,000
Total assets	$850,000	Total liabilities and equity	$850,000

Required

a. Compute the ratio of times-interest-earned. (Round computations to two decimal places.)

b. Compute the debt-to-equity ratio.

MA-17. Measures of Performance and Financial Leverage (LO6)
Following are selected data from year-end financial statements of Nelox Corporation for 2010 and 2009.

	2010	2009
Total assets	$7,349,000	$6,553,000
Interest expense	115,000	102,000
Long-term liabilities	1,220,000	1,239,000
Net income	619,000	563,000
Sales	8,196,000	6,996,000
Stockholders' equity	3,624,000	3,221,000

Required

a. Compute the following performance measurement ratios for 2010. (Round computations to three decimal places and ignore income taxes.)
   1. Asset turnover
   2. Return on sales
   3. Return on assets
   4. Return on equity

b. Is Nelox Company using financial leverage? If so, is the leverage favorable or unfavorable? Explain.

MA-18. Financial Leverage (LO6)
Following are data from McClellan Company and McDonough Company for 2011:

	McClellan	McDonough
Net income	$ 270,000	$ 405,000
Interest expense	120,000	112,500
Total assets, beginning of 2011	3,750,000	6,375,000
Total assets, end of 2011	4,042,500	6,847,500
Stockholders' equity, beginning of 2011	1,594,500	3,703,500
Stockholders' equity, end of 2011	1,689,000	3,832,500

Required

a. Compute the following ratios for McClellan and McDonough Companies at the end of 2011. (Ignore taxes and round calculations to three decimal places.)
   1. Return on assets
   2. Return on equity

b. Comment on the use of financial leverage by these two companies. Which company is the more highly leveraged? Which company's stockholders are benefiting more from the use of leverage?

MA-19. Changes in Working Capital (LO5)
Following is a list of typical financial, investing, and operating transactions. For each transaction indicate whether current assets, current liabilities, and working capital either increased, decreased, or are unchanged. Use the following column headings and relation: **Current assets − Current liabilities = Working capital**.

a. Sold capital stock for cash.
b. Purchased a building for cash.
c. Paid current liabilities with cash.
d. Issued long-term bonds payable for cash.
e. Purchased inventory on account.
f. Purchased a building site by issuing long-term bonds.
g. Sold equipment for a cash amount equal to book value.
h. Sold treasury stock for cash.
i. A long-term note matures next year is reported as a current payable at this year-end.

EXERCISES

EA-20. Effects of Financing Decisions (LO2, 5)
Provo Company has total assets of $2,500,000 and total liabilities of $2,000,000. Provo is considering two alternatives for acquiring additional warehouse space. Under the first alternative, the building would be purchased for $300,000 and financed by issuing long-term bonds. Under the second alternative, the building would be rented with an annual lease cost of $30,000 per year.

Required

a. Compute the company's current debt-to-equity ratio.

b. What effect would the addition of warehouse space have on its debt-to-equity ratio
   1. Assuming the building is purchased by issuing bonds?
   2. Assuming the building is rented on an annual lease basis?

EA-21. Common Size Statements (LO3, 4)
Comparative balance sheets for Albany, Inc., follow for year-end 2011 and 2010. Its president is concerned about the decline in total assets and wants to know where most of the decline took place.

	2011	2010
Cash	$ 220,000	$ 230,000
Accounts receivable	350,000	300,000
Inventory	300,000	450,000
Property, plant, and equipment	1,200,000	1,200,000
Less accumulated depreciation	525,000	475,000
Total assets	$1,545,000	$1,705,000
Accounts payable	$ 260,000	$ 255,000
Long-term note payable	280,000	350,000
Common stock	500,000	500,000
Retained earnings	505,000	600,000
Total liabilities and equity	$1,545,000	$1,705,000

Required

Convert these comparative balance sheets to common size statements. Using the common size statements, explain to the president where the greatest changes occurred.

EA-22. Changes in Working Capital (LO5)

Auckland Industries had a July 31 current asset balance of $31,200 and a current liability balance of $20,800. The following transactions took place in August:

- Sold land for $45,000 cash.
- Collected $80,000 cash on a long-term note receivable.
- Paid $47,000 cash toward outstanding payables.
- Purchased $65,000 of inventory on account.
- Paid $10,000 cash to settle long-term bonds payable two years prior to maturity.

Required

Determine the effects on working capital for each of those transactions and then compute ending working capital. Use the following format (the beginning balances are listed):

	Current assets	–	Current liabilities	=	Working capital
Beginning balance	$31,200		$20,800		$10,400

EA-23. Assessing Inflationary Effects (LO2, 5)

The president of Townville Office Products is pleased with the progress her company has made in recent years, but she cannot understand why the company is always having to borrow funds when sales continually increase. Her office staff is small, and the largest cost outside of merchandise inventory is sales commissions, which are 20 percent of sales. As the cost of merchandise changes, she continually changes retail prices. Thus, she believes the profit margin should remain near the same percentage level for each period. However, even with her best efforts, the company continues to experience cash shortages. After gathering financial data, you prepare the following set of information for the past four years:

	2007	2008	2009	2010
Sales	$240,000	$252,000	$264,600	$277,830
Cost of goods sold	$150,000	$159,000	$168,540	$178,652
Current ratio	1.46	1.34	1.23	1.14
Inventory turnover	4.66	4.65	4.67	4.66
Inflation rate	6.00%	6.00%	6.00%	6.00%

Required

What conclusions can be drawn about the operating condition of Townville Office Products? Explain.

EA-24. Assessing Inflationary Effects (LO2, 6)

The Nova Products Company wants to launch a new product to replace a current product that is technologically inferior. First-year sales for the replacement product are expected to be 100,000 units at a unit selling price of $4.00. The initial cost of the product is $3.00 per unit variable and $100,000 fixed. The expected sales growth is 1,000 units per year, and the expected inflation rate is in a range of 4 to 5 percent for both sales and variable costs.

Required

a. Determine the anticipated profit margin for the new product for the first four years assuming:
   1. No inflation
   2. Inflation at 4 percent

b. Compute the profit margin difference between no inflation and 4 percent inflation. Would this information make a difference in your evaluation of the new product? Explain.

PROBLEMS

PA-25. Comprehensive Financial Analysis (LO5, 6)

Comparative income statements and balance sheets for Seneca Company follow for 2011 and 2010.

SENECA COMPANY
Comparative Income Statements
For Years Ended December 31, 2011 and 2010

	2011	2010
Sales	$11,778,070	$11,241,498
Cost of goods sold	6,615,148	6,395,466
Gross profit	5,162,922	4,846,032
Selling and administrative expenses	3,565,750	3,363,722
Operating income	1,597,172	1,482,310
Other expenses (revenues)		
Interest revenue	(94,034)	(79,060)
Interest expense	76,698	70,204
Total other expenses (revenues)	(17,336)	(8,856)
Income before income taxes	1,614,508	1,473,454
Income taxes	720,368	660,818
Net income	$ 894,140	$ 812,636

SENECA COMPANY
Comparative Balance Sheets
December 31, 2011 and 2010

	2011	2010
Assets		
Cash	$ 241,816	$ 259,370
Marketable securities	437,268	202,802
Accounts receivable	966,982	1,046,246
Inventory	1,501,438	1,620,470
Prepaid expenses	124,988	115,618
Total current assets	3,272,492	3,244,506
Investments and other assets	774,836	604,368
Property, plant, and equipment, net	2,818,912	2,681,680
Trademarks and other intangibles	263,322	281,362
Total assets	$7,129,562	$6,811,916
Liabilities and stockholders' equity		
Notes payable	$ 179,294	$ 175,174
Current maturities of long-term debt	10,030	15,056
Accounts payable and accrued expenses	1,822,326	1,932,930
Total current liabilities	2,011,650	2,123,160
Long-term debt	556,368	539,280
Total liabilities	2,568,018	2,662,440
Common stock	124,778	124,744
Additional paid-in capital	228,388	226,344
Retained earnings	4,208,378	3,798,388
Total stockholders' equity	4,561,544	4,149,476
Total liabilities and equity	$7,129,562	$6,811,916

Required

a. Prepare a comprehensive financial analysis of Seneca for 2011, including the following measures (round all calculations to three decimal places):
  1. Short-term solvency ratios
  2. Long-term solvency ratios
  3. Performance measurement ratios

b. Comment on the financial condition of Seneca with respect to short-term solvency, long-term solvency, and performance.

PA-26. Comprehensive Common Size Statement Analysis (LO3, 4)
After reviewing the financial analyses conducted in Problem A-25, the managers of Seneca Company are still uncertain about the performance of the company during 2011. They believe that common size statements might provide additional insights as to the company's performance.

Required

a. Using the data pertaining to Seneca Company from Problem A-25, prepare common size statements and evaluate the company's performance in 2011 as compared to 2010. For the balance sheets, use total assets as the base; for the income statements, make one set using sales of each year as the base for that year and another set using the year 2010 as the base for both years.

b. Comment on the condition of Seneca drawing on the common size statements.

PA-27. Comprehensive Financial Statement Analysis (LO4, 5, 6)
You are part of the acquisitions committee of Witter Company and are asked to examine the potential acquisition of Dryds, Inc., a merchandising firm. Selected financial statement data from the past two years follow.

DRYDS, INC.
Comparative Balance Sheets
December 31, 2011 and 2010

	2011	2010
Cash	$ 130,000	$ 120,000
Accounts receivable	430,000	370,000
Inventory	400,000	400,000
Property, plant, and equipment	900,000	800,000
Less accumulated depreciation	325,000	250,000
Total assets	$1,535,000	$1,440,000
Accounts payable	$ 300,000	$ 260,000
Long-term note payable	280,000	280,000
Common stock	690,000	690,000
Retained earnings	265,000	210,000
Total liabilities and equity	$1,535,000	$1,440,000

DRYDS, INC.
Income Statement
For Year Ended December 31, 2011

Sales	$2,943,000
Cost of goods sold	2,200,000
Wages expense	350,000
Supplies expense	42,600
Depreciation expense	100,000
Interest expense	22,400
Loss on sale of fixed assets	75,000
Net income before taxes	153,000
Income taxes	52,020
Net income	$ 100,980

Required

a. Compute the following ratios for 2011. (Round calculations to three decimal places.)
   1. Current ratio
   2. Acid test
   3. Inventory turnover
   4. Days receivables outstanding
   5. Debt-to-equity ratio
   6. Times-interest-earned
   7. Asset turnover
   8. Return on sales
   9. Return on assets
   10. Return on equity

b. Prepare common size statements for each of the statements.

c. What is your recommendation regarding the acquisition of Dryds?

CASES

CA-28. Financial Statement Analysis with Actual Annual Report (LO4, 5, 6)
Select a recent annual report or 10-K filing (or use one provided by your instructor) of a publicly held company and perform all of the financial analysis measures discussed in this appendix. Include vertical and horizontal analyses with common size statements. List any of the measures discussed in this appendix that you were unable to perform and state the reasons. Give your evaluation of the company's financial performance and trend, citing financial analysis measures to support your interpretation. If industry data are available, make a comparison of the company under analysis with its industry norms and benchmarks. Evaluate the position the company holds within its industry.

CA-29. Horizontal Analysis and Interpretation (LO3, 4)
Selected 5-year data for the Lexington Company, a manufacturing firm, follow:

	2007	2008	2009	2010	2011
Average cash balance	$ 12,500	$ 18,400	$ 25,600	$ 62,300	$ 88,600
Sales....................	$432,000	$487,000	$539,000	$591,000	$642,000
Operating income..........	$ 3,500	$ 7,850	$ 11,600	$ 94,400	$129,000
Current ratio..............	0.23	0.31	0.56	0.77	0.81
Asset turnover	0.80	0.90	1.00	1.09	1.19

Required
What assessments can be made about this company's performance and operating performance for this five-year period? Explain.

CA-30. Horizontal Analysis and Interpretation (LO3, 4)
El Paso Investment Brokers is considering purchasing Rio Valley. The following data are from recent financial statements of Rio Valley ($ thousands):

	2007	2008	2009	2010	2011
Sales....................	$4,000	$4,300	$4,900	$4,800	$5,100
Operating income..........	$1,100	$1,150	$1,300	$1,285	$1,425
Net income...............	$ 495	$ 520	$ 505	$ 490	$ 513
Current ratio..............	2.33	2.11	2.78	1.96	2.45
Asset turnover	1.01	1.34	1.68	1.73	2.07

Required
Determine the company's strengths and weaknesses as evident from the information provided. Identify one type of common size application for assessing the dollar amounts for your analysis. What do you recommend regarding the purchase of Rio Valley? Explain.

CA-31. Interpreting Financial Analysis Ratios (LO5, 6)

Thorpe Company is a wholesale distributor of professional equipment and supplies. The company's sales averaged about $900,000 annually for the three-year period, 2008-2009. Its total assets at the end of 2009 were $850,000. The president of Thorpe Company asked the controller to prepare a report summarizing the financial aspects of the company's operations for the past three years. This report is to be presented to its Board of Directors at its next meeting. In addition to comparative financial statements, the controller decides to report a number of relevant financial ratios to assist in the identification and interpretation of trends. The controller computes the following ratios for the recent three-year period.

	2010	2009	2008
Current ratio	2.18	2.13	2.00
Acid test ratio	0.97	1.10	1.20
Days receivables outstanding	51.20	42.60	37.60
Inventory turnover	3.80	4.80	5.25
Debt-to-equity ratio	0.61	0.69	0.79
Asset turnover	1.99	1.88	1.75
Sales as a percentage of 2008 sales	1.06	1.03	1.00
Gross profit percent	38.50	38.60	40.00
Return on sales	8.0%	7.8%	7.8%
Return on assets	8.7%	8.6%	8.5%
Return on equity	14.1%	14.6%	15.1%

In preparation of the report, the controller decides first to examine the financial ratios independently of any other data to determine if the ratios themselves reveal any significant trends over this three-year period.

Required

Answer the following questions. Indicate in each case which ratio(s) you used to arrive at your conclusion.

a. The current ratio is increasing, whereas the acid test ratio is decreasing. Using the ratios provided, identify and explain the contributing factor(s) for this apparently divergent trend.

b. In terms of the ratios provided, what conclusion(s) is drawn regarding the company's use of financial leverage during the 2008-2010 period? Explain.

c. Using the ratios provided, what conclusions are drawn regarding the company's ability to generate sales and profits from the assets available to management?

(CMA Adapted)

Glossary

A

absorption costing an approach to product costing that treats both variable and fixed manufacturing costs as product costs.

accelerated cost recovery system (ACRS, MACRS) A system of accelerated depreciation for tax purposes introduced in 1981 (ACRS) and modified starting in 1987 (MACRS); it prescribes depreciation rates by asset classification for assets acquired after 1980

accelerated depreciation method Any depreciation method under which the amounts of depreciation expense taken in the early years of an asset's life are larger than the amounts expensed in the later years; includes the double-declining balance method

access control matrix A computerized file that lists the type of access that each computer user is entitled to have to each file and program in the computer system

account A record of the additions, deductions, and balances of individual assets, liabilities, permanent stockholders' equity, revenues, and expenses

accounting cycle A series of basic steps followed to process accounting information during a fiscal year

accounting entity An economic unit that has identifiable boundaries and that is the focus for the accumulation and reporting of financial information

accounting equation An expression of the equivalency of the economic resources and the claims upon those resources of a specific entity; often stated as Assets = Liabilities + Stockholders' Equity

accounting period The time period, typically one year (or quarter), to which periodic accounting reports are related

accounting rate of return the average annual increase in net income that results from acceptance of a capital expenditure proposal divided by either the initial investment or the average investment in the project.

accounting system The structured collection of people, policies, procedures, equipment, files, and records that a company uses to collect, record, classify, process, store, report, and interpret financial data

accounting The process of measuring the economic activity of an entity in money terms and communicating the results to interested parties; the purpose is to provide financial information that is useful in making economic decisions

accounts payable turnover The ratio obtained by dividing annual cost of goods sold by average accounts payable

accounts receivable aging method A procedure that uses an aging schedule to determine the year-end balance needed in the allowance for uncollectible accounts account

accounts receivable turnover Annual net sales divided by average accounts receivable (net)

accounts receivable A current asset that is created by a sale on a credit basis; it represents the amount owed the company by the customer

accrual accounting Accounting procedures whereby revenues are recorded when they are earned and realized and expenses are recorded in the period in which they help to generate revenues

accruals Adjustments that reflect revenues earned but not received or recorded and expenses incurred but not paid or recorded

accrued expense An expense incurred but not yet paid; recognized with an adjusting entry

accrued revenue Revenue earned but not yet billed or received; recognized with an adjusting entry

accumulated depreciation The sum of all depreciation expense recorded to date; it is subtracted from the cost of the asset in order to derive the asset's net book value

acid test ratio more specific than the current ratio as a test of short-term solvency, the acid test ratio (also known as the quick ratio) measures the availability of cash and other current monetary assets that can be quickly generated into cash to pay current liabilities. The general equation for the acid test ratio is: (Cash + Marketable securities + Current receivables)/Current liabilities.

activities list see operations list.

activity cost drivers specific units of work (activities) performed to serve customer needs that consume costly resources.

activity costing the determination of the cost of specific activities performed to fill customer needs.

activity dictionary a standardized list of processes and related activities.

activity a unit of work.

activity-based budgeting an approach to budgeting that uses an activity cost hierarchy to budget physical inputs and costs as a function of planned activity. It is mechanically similar to the output/input approach to budgeting where physical inputs and costs are budgeted as a function of planned activity.

activity-based costing (ABC) used to develop cost information by determining the cost of activities and tracing their costs to cost objectives on the basis of the cost objective's utilization of units of activity.

activity-based management (ABM) the identification and selection of activities to maximize the value of the activities while minimizing their cost from the perspective of the final consumer.

adjusted trial balance A list of general ledger accounts and their balances taken after adjustments have been made

adjusting entries Entries made at the end of an accounting period under accrual accounting to ensure the proper matching of expenses incurred with revenues earned for the period

adjusting The process of adjusting the historical financial statements prior to the projection of future results; also called recasting and reformulating

aging schedule An analysis that shows how long customers' accounts receivable balances have remained unpaid

allowance for uncollectible accounts A contra asset account with a normal credit balance shown on the balance sheet as a deduction from accounts receivable to reflect the expected realizable amount of accounts receivable

allowance method An accounting procedure whereby the amount of uncollectible accounts expense is estimated and recorded in the period in which the related credit sales occur

Altman's Z-score A predictor of potential bankruptcy based on multiple ratios

amortization The periodic writing off of an account balance to expense; similar to depreciation and usually refers to the periodic writing off of an intangible asset

annuity a series of equal cash flows received or paid over equal intervals of time.

appraisal costs quality costs incurred to identify nonconforming products or services before they are delivered to customers.

articles of incorporation A document prepared by persons organizing a corporation in the United States that sets forth the structure and purpose of the corporation and specifics regarding the stock to be issued

articulation The linkage of financial statements within and across time

assembly efficiency variance the difference between the standard cost of actual assembly inputs and the flexible budget cost for assembly.

assembly rate variance the difference between the actual cost and the standard cost of actual assembly inputs.

asset turnover a measure of performance, the asset turnover ratio measures the firm's ability to use its assets to generate sales. The general equation for asset turnover is: Sales/Average total assets.

asset turnover Net income divided by average total assets

asset write-downs Adjustment of carrying value of assets down to their current salable value

assets The economic resources of an entity that are owned, will provide future benefits and can be reliably measured

audit report A report issued by independent auditors that includes the final version of the financial statements, accompanying notes, and the auditor's opinion on the financial statements

audit An examination of a company's financial statements by a firm of independent certified public accountants

authorized stock The maximum number of shares in a class of stock that a corporation may issue

automatic identification systems (AIS) the use of bar coding of products and production processes that allows inventory and production information to be entered into a computer without writing or keying.

available-for-sale securities Investments in securities that management intends to hold for capital gains and dividend income; although it may sell them if the price is right

average cash cycle Average collection period + modified average inventory days outstanding + modified average payable days outstanding

average collection period Determined by dividing accounts receivable by average daily sales, sometimes referred to as days sales outstanding or DSO

average inventory days outstanding (AIDO) An indication of how long, on average, inventories are on the shelves, computed as inventory divided by average daily cost of goods sold

backflush costing an inventory accounting system used in conjunction with JIT in which costs are assigned initially to cost of goods sold. At the end of the period, costs are backed out of cost of goods sold and assigned to appropriate inventory accounts for any inventories that may exist.

balance sheet A financial statement showing an entity's assets, liabilities, and stockholders' equity at a specific date; sometimes called a statement of financial position

balance sheet a picture of the economic health of an organization at a specific time, showing the organization's assets and the claims on those assets.

balanced scorecard a performance measurement system that includes financial and operational measures which are related to the organizational goals. The basic premise is to establish a set of indicators that can be used to monitor performance progress and then compare the goals that are established with the results.

batch level activity an activity performed for each batch of product produced.

bearer One of the terms that may be used to designate the payee on a promissory note; means the note is payable to whoever holds the note

benchmarking a systematic approach to identifying the best practices to help an organization take action to improve performance.

bill of materials a document that specifies the kinds and quantities of raw materials required to produce one unit of product.

bond A long-term debt instrument that promises to pay interest periodically and a principal amount at maturity, usually issued by the borrower to a group of lenders; bonds may incorporate a wide variety of provisions relating to security for the debt involved, methods of paying the periodic interest, retirement provisions, and conversion options

book value per share The dollar amount of net assets represented by one share of stock; computed by dividing the amount of stockholders' equity associated with a class of stock by the outstanding shares of that class of stock

book value The dollar amount carried in the accounts for a particular item; the book value of a depreciable asset is derived by deducting the contra account accumulated depreciation from the cost of the depreciable asset

borrows at a discount When the face amount of the note is reduced by a calculated cash discount to determine the cash proceeds

bottom-up budget a budget where managers at all levels—and in some cases even non-managers—become involved in the budget preparation.

break-even point the unit or dollar sales volume where total revenues equal total costs.

budget committee a committee responsible for supervising budget preparation. It serves as a review board for evaluating requests for discretionary cost items and new projects.

budget office an organizational unit responsible for the preparation, distribution, and processing of forms used in gathering budget data. It handles most of the work of actually formulating the budget schedules and reports.

budget a formal plan of action expressed in monetary terms.

budgetary slack occurs when managers intentionally understate revenues or overstate expenses in order to produce favorable variances for the department.

budgeted financial statements hypothetical statements that reflect the "as if" effects of the budgeted activities on the actual financial position of the organization. They reflect what the results of operations will be if all the predictions in the budget are correct.

budgeting projecting the operations of an organization and their financial impact on the future.

calendar year A fiscal year that ends on December 31

call provision A bond feature that allows the borrower to retire (call in) the bonds after a stated date

capacity costs see committed fixed costs.

capital budgeting a process that involves the identification of potentially desirable projects for capital expenditures, the subsequent evaluation of capital expenditure proposals, and the selection of proposals that meet certain criteria.

capital expenditures Expenditures that increase the book value of long-term assets; sometimes abbreviated as CAPEX

capital expenditures investments of significant financial resources in projects to develop or introduce new products or services, to expand current production or service capacity, or to change current production or service facilities.

capital lease A lease that transfers to the lessee substantially all of the benefits and risks related to ownership of the property; the lessee records the leased property as an asset and establishes a liability for the lease obligation

capital markets Financing sources, which are formalized when companies issue securities that are traded on organized exchanges; they are informal when companies are funded by private sources

capitalization of interest A process that adds interest to an asset's initial cost if a period of time is required to prepare the asset for use

capitalization The recording of a cost as an asset on the balance sheet rather than as an expense on the income statement; these costs are transferred to expense as the asset is used up

cash (operating) cycle The period of time from when cash is invested in inventories until inventory is sold and receivables are collected

cash and cash equivalents The sum of cash plus short-term, highly liquid investments such as treasury bills and money market funds; includes marketable securities maturing within 90 days of the financial statement date

cash budget summarizes all cash receipts and disbursements expected to occur during the budget period.

cash discount An amount that a purchaser of merchandise may deduct from the purchase price for paying within the discount period

cash equivalents short-term, highly liquid investments that are readily convertible into known amounts of cash and so near their maturity date that they present insignificant risk of change in value from interest or money market rate changes; generally, only investments with original maturities of three months or less are considered as possible cash equivalents.

cash An asset category representing the amount of a firm's available cash and funds on deposit at a bank in checking accounts and savings accounts

cash-basis accounting Accounting procedures whereby revenues are recorded when cash is received from operating activities and expenses are recorded when cash payments related to operating activities are made

centralization when top management controls the major functions of an organization (such as manufacturing, sales, accounting, computer operations, marketing, research and development, and management control).

certificate of deposit (CD) An investment security available at financial institutions generally offering a fixed rate of return for a specified period of time

chained target costing bringing in suppliers as part of the coordination process to attain a competitively priced product that is delivered to the customer in a timely manner.

change in accounting estimate Modification to a previous estimate of an uncertain future event, such as the useful life of a depreciable asset, uncollectible accounts receivable, and warranty expenses; applied currently and prospectively only

changes in accounting principles Cumulative income or loss from changes in accounting methods (such as depreciation or inventory costing methods)

chart of accounts A list of all the general ledger account titles and their numerical code

clean surplus accounting Income that explains successive equity balances

closing procedures A step in the accounting cycle in which the balances of all temporary accounts are transferred to the retained earnings account, leaving the temporary accounts with zero balances

coefficient of determination (R2) a measure of the percent of variation in the dependent variable that is explained by variations in the independent variable when the least-squares estimation equation is used.

commitments A contractual arrangement by which both parties to the contract still have acts to perform

committed fixed costs (capacity costs) costs required to maintain the current service or production capacity or to fill a previous legal commitment.

common cost a cost incurred for the benefit of two or more cost objectives—an indirect cost.

common segment costs costs related to more than one segment and not directly traceable to a particular segment. These costs are referred to as common costs because they are incurred at one level for the benefit of two or more segments at a lower level.

common size statement a financial statement that has had all its accounts converted into percentages. As such, a common size statement is very useful for detecting items that are out of line, that deviate from some present amount, or that may be indications of other problems.

common stock The basic ownership class of corporate capital stock, carrying the rights to vote, share in earnings, participate in future stock issues, and share in any liquidation proceeds after prior claims have been settled

common-size financial statement A financial statement in which each item is presented as a percentage of a key figure such as sales or total assets

comparative financial statements A form of horizontal analysis involving comparison of two or more periods' financial statements showing dollar and/or percentage changes

compensating balance A minimum amount that a financial institution requires a firm to maintain in its account as part of a borrowing arrangement complex capital structure

comprehensive income The total income reported by the company, including net profit and all other changes to stockholders' equity other than those arising from capital (stock) transactions; typical components of other comprehensive income (OCI) are unrealized gains (losses) on available-for-sale securities and derivatives, minimum pension liability adjustment, and foreign currency translation adjustments

computer-aided design (CAD) a method of design that involves the use of computers to design products.

computer-aided manufacturing (CAM) a manufacturing method that involves the use of computers to control the operation of machines.

computer-integrated manufacturing (CIM) the ultimate extension of the CAD, CAM, and FMS concepts to a completely automated and computer-controlled factory where production is self-operating once a product is designed and the decision to produce is made.

conceptual framework A cohesive set of interrelated objectives and fundamentals for external financial reporting developed by the FASB

conservatism An accounting principle stating that judgmental determinations should tend toward understatement rather than overstatement of net assets and income

consistency An accounting principle stating that, unless otherwise disclosed, accounting reports should be prepared on a basis consistent with the preceding period

consolidated financial statements Financial statements reflecting a parent company and one or more subsidiary companies and/or a variable interest entity (VIE) and its primary beneficiary

contingency A possible future event; significant contingent liabilities must be disclosed in the notes to the financial statements

contingent liabilities A potential obligation, the eventual occurrence of which usually depends on some future event beyond the control of the firm; contingent liabilities may originate with such events as lawsuits, credit guarantees, and environmental damages

continuous budgeting budgeting based on a moving time frame that extends over a fixed period. The budget system adds an identical time period to the budget at the end of each period of operations, thereby always maintaining a budget of exactly the same time length.

continuous improvement (Kaizen) budgeting an approach to budgeting that incorporates a targeted improvement (reduction) in costs; management requests that a given process will be improved during the budgeting process. This may be applied to every budget category or to specific areas selected by management. Kaizen budgeting is based upon prior performance and anticipated operating conditions during the upcoming period.

continuous improvement (Kaizen) costing establishing cost reduction targets for products or services that an organization is currently providing to customers.

continuous improvement an approach to activity-based management where the employees constantly evaluate products, services, and processes, seeking ways to do better.

contra account An account related to, and deducted from, another account when financial statements are prepared or when book values are computed

contract rate The rate of interest stated on a bond certificate

contributed capital The net funding that a company receives from issuing and acquiring its equity shares

contribution income statement an income statement format in which variable costs are subtracted from revenues to figure contribution margin, and fixed costs are then subtracted from contribution margin to calculate net income.

contribution margin ratio the portion of each dollar of sales revenue contributed toward covering fixed costs and earning a profit.

contribution margin the difference between total revenues and total variable costs; this amount goes toward covering fixed costs and providing a profit.

controlling the process of ensuring that results agree with plans.

conversion cost the combined costs of direct labor and manufacturing overhead incurred to convert raw materials into finished goods.

convertible bond A bond incorporating the holder's right to convert the bond to capital stock under prescribed terms

convertible securities Debt and equity securities that provide the holder with an option to convert those securities into other securities

copyright An exclusive right that protects an owner against the unauthorized reproduction of a specific written work or artwork

core income A company's income from its usual business activities that is expected to continue (persist) into the future

corporation A legal entity created by the granting of a charter from an appropriate governmental authority and owned by stockholders who have limited liability for corporate debt

cost allocation base a measure of volume of activity, such as direct labor hours or machine hours, that determines how much of a cost pool is assigned to each cost objective.

cost behavior how costs respond to changes in an activity cost driver.

cost center a responsibility center whose manager is responsible only for managing costs.

cost driver analysis the study of factors that influence costs.

cost driver a factor that causes or influences costs.

cost estimation the determination of the relationship between activity and cost.

cost method An investment is reported at its historical cost, and any cash dividends and interest received are recognized in current income

cost objective an object to which costs are assigned. Examples include departments, products, and services.

cost of capital the average cost of obtaining the resources necessary to make investments.

cost of goods sold percentage The ratio of cost of goods sold divided by net sales

cost of goods sold The total cost of merchandise sold to customers during the accounting period

cost of production report used in a process costing system; summarizes unit and cost data for each department or process for each period.

cost pool a collection of related costs, such as departmental manufacturing overhead, that is assigned to one or more cost objectives, such as products.

cost prediction error the difference between a predicted future cost and the actual amount of the cost when, or if, it is incurred.

cost prediction the forecasting of future costs.

cost principle An accounting principle stating that asset measures are based on the prices paid to acquire the assets

cost reduction proposal a proposed action or investment intended to reduce the cost of an activity that the organization is committed to keeping.

cost-volume-profit (CVP) analysis a technique used to examine the relationships among total volume of some independent variable, total costs, total revenues, and profits during a time period (typically a month or a year).

cost-volume-profit graph an illustration of the relationships among activity volume, total revenues, total costs, and profits.

coupon (contract or stated) rate The coupon rate of interest is stated in the bond contract; it is used to compute the dollar amount of (semiannual) interest payments that are paid to bondholder during the life of the bond issue

coupon bond A bond with coupons for interest payable to bearer attached to the bond for each interest period; whenever interest is due, the bondholder detaches a coupon and deposits it with his or her bank for collection

covenants Contractual requirements put into loan or bond agreements by lenders

credit (entry) An entry on the right side (or in the credit column) of any account

credit card fee A fee charged retailers for credit card services provided by financial institutions; the fee is usually stated as a percentage of credit card sales

credit guarantee A guarantee of another company's debt by cosigning a note payable; a guarantor's contingent liability that is usually disclosed in a balance sheet footnote

credit memo A document prepared by a seller to inform the purchaser that the seller has reduced the amount owed by the purchaser due to a return or an allowance

credit period The maximum amount of time, usually stated in days, that the purchaser of merchandise has to pay the seller

credit terms The prescribed payment period for purchases on credit with discount specified for early payment

cumulative (preferred stock) A feature associated with preferred stock whereby any dividends in arrears must be paid before dividends may be paid on common stock

cumulative effect of a change in principle The cumulative effect on net income to the date of a change in accounting principle

cumulative translation adjustment The amount recorded in the equity section as necessary to balance the accounting equation when assets and liabilities of foreign subsidiaries are translated into $US at the rate of exchange prevailing at the statement date

current assets Cash and other assets that will be converted to cash or used up during the normal operating cycle of the business or one year, whichever is longer

current liabilities Obligations that will require within the coming year or operating cycle, whichever is longer, (1) the use of existing current assets or (2) the creation of other current liabilities

current rate method Method of translating foreign currency transactions under which balance sheet amounts are translated using exchange rates in effect at the period-end consolidation date and income statement amounts using the average exchange rate for the period

current ratio A firm's current assets divided by its current liabilities

current ratio a measure of solvency, the current ratio measures the relationship between current assets and current liabilities. The general equation for the current ratio is: Current assets/Current liabilities.

customer level activity an activity performed to obtain or maintain each customer.

customer profitability analysis a presentation showing the profits of individual or categories of customers net of the cost of serving and supporting those customers.

customer profitability profile a graphical presentation showing the cumulative profits from the most profitable to the least profitable customer

cycle efficiency the ratio of value-added to nonvalue-added manufacturing activities.

cycle time the total time required to complete a process. It is composed of the times needed for setup, processing, movement, waiting, and inspection.

D

Dashboards software programs that tabulate and display scorecard results using graphics that mimic the instrument displays on an automobile dashboard

days sales in receivables a measure of both solvency and performance, the days receivable outstanding tells how long it takes to convert accounts receivable into cash or how well the firm is managing the credit extended to customers. The general equation for days receivable outstanding is: Ending receivables/Average daily sales.

days sales in inventory Inventories divided by average cost of goods sold

debenture bond A bond that has no specific property pledged as security for the repayment of funds borrowed

debit (entry) An entry on the left side (or in the debit column) of any account

debt-to-equity ratio a measure of long-term solvency, the debt-to-equity ratio indicates the balance between the amounts of capital that creditors and owners provide. The general equation for the debt-to-equity ratio is: Total liabilities/Total stockholders' equity.

decentralization the delegation of decision-making authority to successively lower management levels in an organization. The lower in the organization the authority is delegated, the greater the decentralization.

declining-balance method An accelerated depreciation method that allocates depreciation expense to each year by applying a constant percentage to the declining book value of the asset

default The nonpayment of interest and principal and/or the failure to adhere to the various terms and conditions of the bond indenture

deferrals Adjustments that allocate various assets and revenues received in advance to the proper accounting periods as expenses and revenues

deferred revenue A liability representing revenues received in advance; also called unearned revenue

deferred tax liability A liability representing the estimated future income taxes payable resulting from an existing temporary difference between an asset's book value and its tax basis

deferred tax valuation allowance Reduction in a reported deferred tax asset to adjust for the amount that is not likely to be realized

defined benefit plan A type of retirement plan under which the company promises to make periodic payments to the employee after retirement

defined contribution plan A retirement plan under which the company makes cash contribution into an employee's account (usually with a third-party trustee like a bank) either solely or as a matching contribution

degree of operating leverage a measure of operating leverage, often computed as the contribution margin divided by income before taxes.

denominator variance see fixed overhead volume variance.

depletion The allocation of the cost of natural resources to the units extracted and sold or, in the case of timberland, the board feet of timber cut

depreciation accounting The process of allocating the cost of equipment, vehicles, and buildings (not land) to expense over the time period benefiting from their use

depreciation base The acquisition cost of an asset less estimated salvage value

depreciation rate An estimate of how the asset will be used up over its useful life—evenly over its useful life, more heavily in the early years, or in proportion to its actual usage

depreciation tax shield the reduction in taxes due to the deductibility of depreciation from taxable revenues.

depreciation The decline in economic potential (using up) of plant assets originating from wear, deterioration, and obsolescence

derivatives Financial instruments such as futures, options, and swaps that are commonly used to hedge (mitigate) some external risk, such as commodity price risk, interest rate risk, or risks relating to foreign currency fluctuations

descriptive model a model that merely specifies the relationships between a series of independent and dependent variables.

design for manufacture explicitly considering the costs of manufacturing and servicing a product while it is being designed.

differential cost analysis an approach to the analysis of relevant costs that focuses on the costs that differ under alternative actions.

diluted earnings per share The earnings per share computation taking into consideration the effects of dilutive securities

dilutive securities Securities that can be exchanged for shares of common stock and, thereby, increase the number of common shares outstanding

direct costing see variable costing.

direct department cost a cost directly traceable to a department upon its incurrence.

direct labor wages earned by production employees for the time they spend working on the conversion of raw materials into finished goods.

direct materials the costs of primary raw materials that are converted into finished goods.

direct method (for cost allocation) a method of allocating service department costs to producing departments based only on the amount of services provided to the producing departments; it does not recognize any interdepartmental services.

direct method (for statement of cash flow) a reporting format for the operating section of the statement of cash flows; where basically, the income statement is reconstructed on a cash basis so that the primary categories of cash inflows and outflows from operating activities are reported.

direct segment fixed costs costs that would not be incurred if the segment being evaluated were discontinued. They are specifically identifiable with a particular segment.

discontinued operations Net income or loss from business segments that are up for sale or have been sold in the current period

discount bond A bond that is sold for less than its par (face) value

discount on notes payable A contra account that is subtracted from the Notes Payable amount on the balance sheet; as the life of the note elapses, the discount is reduced and charged to interest expense

discount period The maximum amount of time, usually stated in days, that the purchaser of merchandise has to pay the seller if the purchaser wants to claim the cash discount

discount rate the minimum rate of return required for the project to be acceptable.

discounted cash flow (DCF) model The value of a security is equal to the present value of the expected free cash flows to the firm, discounted at the weighted average cost of capital (WACC)

discounting The exchanging of notes receivable for cash at a financial institution at an amount that is less than the face value of the notes

discretionary cost center a cost center that does not have clearly defined relationships between effort and accomplishment.

discretionary fixed costs costs set at a fixed amount each period at the discretion of management.

dividend discount model The value of a security today is equal to the present value of that security's expected dividends, discounted at the weighted average cost of capital

dividend payout ratio Annual dividends per share divided by the earnings per share

dividend yield Annual dividends per share divided by the market price per share

dividends account A temporary equity account used to accumulate owner dividends from the business

division margin the amount each division contributes toward covering common corporate expenses and generating corporate profits. It is computed by subtracting all direct fixed expenses identifiable with each division from the contribution margin.

double-entry accounting system A method of accounting that recognizes the duality of a transaction such that the analysis results in a recording of equal amounts of debits and credits

earned capital The cumulative net income (losses) retained by the company (not paid out to shareholders as dividends)

earned When referring to revenue, the seller's execution of its duties under the terms of the agreement, with the resultant passing of title to the buyer with no right of return or other contingencies

earnings per share a measure of performance, earnings per share are disclosed on the income statement. The general equation for basic earnings per share is: Net income less preferred stock dividends/ Weighted average number of common shares outstanding for the period.

earnings quality The degree to which reported earnings represent how well the firm has performed from an economic standpoint

earnings smoothing Earnings management with a goal to provide an earnings stream with less variability

economic profit The number of inventory units sold multiplied by the difference between the sales price and the replacement cost of the inventories (approximated by the cost of the most recently purchased inventories)

economic value-added (EVA) a variation of residual income calculated as income after taxes less the cost of capital employed; specifically, net operating profits after tax less a charge for the use of capital equal to beginning capital utilized in the business multiplied by the weighted average cost of capital.

effective interest method A method of amortizing bond premium or discount that results in a constant rate of interest each period and varying amounts of premium or discount amortized each period

effective interest rate The rate determined by dividing the total discount amount by the cash proceeds on a note payable when the borrower borrowed at a discount

effective rate The current rate of interest in the market for a bond or other debt instrument; when issued, a bond is priced to yield the market (effective) rate of interest at the date of issuance

efficient markets hypothesis Capital markets are said to be efficient if at any given time, current equity (stock) prices reflect all relevant information that determines those equity prices

electronic data interchange (EDI) the electronic communication of data between organizations.

employee severance costs Accrued (estimated) costs for termination of employees as part of a restructuring program

employee stock options A form of compensation that grants a select group of employees the right to purchase a fixed number of company shares at a fixed price for a predetermined time period

enterprise resource planning (ERP) enterprise management information systems that provide organizations an integrated set of operating, financial, and management systems.

equity carve out A corporate divestiture of operating units

equity method The prescribed method of accounting for investments in which the investor company has a significant influence over the investee company (usually taken to be ownership between 20-50% of the outstanding common stock of the investee company)

equivalent completed units the number of completed units that is equal, in terms of production effort, to a given number of partially completed units.

ethics the moral quality, fitness, or propriety of a course of action that can injure or benefit people; also, the values, rules, and justifications that governs one's way of life.

expenses Decreases in stockholders' equity incurred by a firm in the process of earning revenues

external failure costs quality costs incurred when nonconforming products or services are delivered to customers.

extraordinary items Revenues and expenses that are both unusual and infrequent and are, therefore, excluded from income from continuing operations

F

face amount The principal amount of a bond or note to be repaid at maturity

facility level activity an activity performed to maintain general manufacturing or marketing capabilities.

factoring Selling an account receivable to another company, typically a finance company or a financial institution, for less than its face value

file a collection of related records.

Financial Accounting Standards Board (FASB) The organization currently responsible for setting accounting standards for reporting financial information

financial accounting an information processing system that generates general-purpose reports of financial operations (income statement and cash flows statement) and financial position (balance sheet) for an organization.

financial assets Normally consist of excess resources held for future expansion or unexpected needs; they are usually invested in the form of other companies' stock, corporate or government bonds, and real estate

financial leverage The proportionate use of borrowed funds in the capital structure, computed as net financial obligations (NFO) divided by average equity; financial leverage is considered favorable if the return on assets is higher than the fixed rate on borrowed funds and unfavorable if the fixed rate is greater than the return it generates.

financial reporting objectives A component of the conceptual framework that specifies that financial statements should provide information (1) useful for investment and credit decisions, (2) helpful in assessing an entity's ability to generate future cash flows, and (3) about an entity's resources, claims to those resources, and the effects of events causing changes in these items

financial reporting the process of preparing financial statements (income statement, balance sheet, and statement of cash flows) for a firm in accordance with generally accepted accounting principles.

financial statement analysis the process of interpreting and evaluating financial statements by using the data contained in them to produce additional financial measures. Financial statement analysis involves comparing financial statements for the current period with those of the previous periods, studying the internal composition of the financial statements, and studying relationships within and among the financial statements.

financial statement elements A part of the conceptual framework that identifies the significant components—such as assets, liabilities, stockholders' equity, revenues, and expenses—used to put financial statements together

financing activities business activities that involve (1) resource transfers between the entity and its owners and (2) the securement of loans from and the repayment of them to nonowners (creditors).

finished goods inventory The dollar amount of inventory that has completed the production process and is awaiting sale to customers

first-in, first-out (FIFO) method in process costing A costing method that accounts for unit costs of beginning inventory units separately from those started during the current period. The first costs incurred each period are assumed to have been used to complete the unfinished units left over from the previous period.

first-in, first-out (FIFO) method One of the prescribed methods of inventory costing; FIFO assumes that the first costs incurred for the purchase or production of inventory are the first costs relieved from inventory when goods are sold

fiscal year The annual accounting period used by a business firm

five forces of competitive intensity Industry competition, bargaining power of buyers, bargaining power of suppliers, threat of substitution, threat of entry

fixed assets An alternate label for long-term assets; may also be called property, plant, and equipment (PPE)

fixed costs Costs that do not change with changes in sales volume (over a reasonable range); with a unit level cost driver as the independent variable, fixed costs are a constant amount per period of time

fixed manufacturing overhead all fixed costs associated with converting raw materials into finished goods.

fixed overhead budget variance the difference between budgeted and actual fixed overhead.

fixed overhead volume variance the difference between total budgeted fixed overhead and total standard fixed overhead assigned to production.

fixed selling and administrative costs all fixed costs other than those directly associated with converting raw materials into finished goods.

flexible budget variance computed for each cost as the difference between the actual cost and the flexible budget cost of producing a given quantity of product or service.

flexible budgets budgets that are drawn up for a series of possible production and sales volumes or adjusted to a particular level of production after the fact. These budgets, based on cost-volume or cost-activity relationships, are used to determine what costs should have been for an attained level of activity.

flexible manufacturing systems (FMS) an extension of computer-aided manufacturing techniques through a series of manufacturing operations. These operations include the automatic movement of units between operations and the automatic and rapid setup of machines to produce each product.

forecast The projection of financial results over the forecast horizon and terminal periods

foreign currency transaction The $US equivalent of an asset or liability denominated in a foreign currency

foreign exchange gain or loss The gain (loss) recognized in the income statement relating to the change in the $US equivalent of an asset or liability denominated in a foreign currency

for-profit organization an organization that has profit as a primary mission.

franchise Generally, an exclusive right to operate or sell a specific brand of products in a given geographic area

free cash flow This excess cash flow (above that required to manage its growth and development) from which dividends can be paid; computed as NOPAT 2 Increase in NOA

full absorption cost see absorption costing.

full costing see absorption costing.

full costs include all costs, regardless of their behavior patterns (variable or fixed) or activity level.

full disclosure principle An accounting principle stipulating the disclosure of all facts necessary to make financial statements useful to readers

fully diluted earnings per share See diluted earnings per share

functional currency The currency representing the primary currency in which a business unit conducts its operations

functional income statement a type of income statement where costs are classified according to function, rather than behavior. It is typically included in external financial reports.

fundamental analysis Uses financial information to predict future valuation and, hence, buy-sell stock strategies

funded status The difference between the pension obligation and the fair market value of the pension investments

future value the amount a current sum of money (or series of monies) earning a stated rate of interest will accumulate to at the end of a future period.

G

general and administrative expense budget presents the expenses the organization plans to incur in connection with the general administration of the organization. Included are expenses for such things as the accounting department, the computer center, and the president's office.

general journal A journal with enough flexibility so that any type of business transaction can be recorded in it

general ledger A grouping of all of an entity's accounts that are used to prepare the basic financial statements

generally accepted accounting principles (GAAP) A set of standards and procedures that guide the preparation of financial statements

goal a definable, measurable objective.

going concern concept An accounting principle that assumes that, in the absence of evidence to the contrary, a business entity will have an indefinite life

goodwill The value that derives from a firm's ability to earn more than a normal rate of return on the fair market value of its specific, identifiable net assets; computed as the residual of the purchase price less the fair market value of the net tangible and intangible assets acquired

gross margin The difference between net sales and cost of goods sold: also called gross profit

gross profit margin (GPM) (percentage) The ratio of gross profit on sales divided by net sales

gross profit on sales The difference between net sales and cost of goods sold; also called gross margin

H

held-to-maturity securities The designation given to a portfolio of bond investments that are expected to be held until they mature

high-low method of cost estimation utilizes data from two time periods, a representative high activity period and a representative low activity period, to estimate fixed and variable costs.

historical cost Original acquisition or issuance costs

holding company The parent company of a subsidiary

holding gain The increase in replacement cost since the inventories were acquired, which equals the number of units sold multiplied by the difference between the current replacement cost and the original acquisition cost

horizon period The forecast period for which detailed estimates are made, typically 5–10 years

horizontal analysis an evaluative standard, horizontal analysis is the comparison of a firm's current financial measures to those of previous periods. Horizontal analysis is used to evaluate trends in the firm's financial condition covering two or more years.

I

impairment loss A loss recognized on an impaired asset equal to the difference between its book value and current fair value

impairment A reduction in value from that presently recorded

imposed budget see top-down budget.

income statement A financial statement reporting an entity's revenues and expenses for a period of time

income statement a summary of economic events during a period of time, showing the revenues generated by operating activities, the expenses incurred in generating those revenues, and any gains or losses attributed to the period.

incremental budgeting an approach to budgeting where costs for a coming period are budgeted as a dollar or percentage change from the amount budgeted for (or spent during) some previous period.

indirect department cost a cost reassigned, or allocated, to a department from another cost objective.

indirect method (for statement of cash flow) a reporting format for the operating section of the statement of cash flows; wherein net cash flow from operations is computed by entering adjustments to net income from the income statement.

indirect method A presentation format for the statement of cash flows that refers to the operating section only; that section begins with net income and converts it to cash flows from operations

indirect segment costs see common segment costs.

inspection time the amount of time it takes units to be inspected.

intangible assets A term applied to a group of long-term assets, including patents, copyrights, franchises, trademarks, and goodwill, that benefit an entity but do not have physical substance

integer programming a variation of linear programming that determines the solution in whole numbers.

interdepartmental services services provided by one service department to other service departments.

interest cost (pensions) The increase in the pension obligation due to the accrual of an additional year of interest

internal auditing A company function that provides independent appraisals of the company's financial statements, its internal controls, and its operations

internal controls The measures undertaken by a company to ensure the reliability of its accounting data, protect its assets from theft or unauthorized use, make sure that employees are following the company's policies and procedures, and evaluate the performance of employees, departments, divisions, and the company as a whole

internal failure costs quality costs incurred when materials, components, products, or services are identified as defective before delivery to customers.

internal rate of return (IRR) (often called the time-adjusted rate of return) the discount rate that equates the present value of a project's cash inflows with the present value of the project's cash outflows.

inventory carrying costs Costs of holding inventories, including warehousing, logistics, insurance, financing, and the risk of loss due to theft, damage, or technological or fashion change

inventory shrinkage The cost associated with an inventory shortage; the amount by which the perpetual inventory exceeds the physical inventory

inventory turnover (in dollars) often regarded as a measure of both solvency and performance, inventory turnover tells how long it takes to convert inventory into current monetary assets and how well the firm is managing investments in inventory. The general equation for inventory turnover is: Cost of goods sold/Average inventory cost.

inventory turnover (in units) the annual demand in units divided by the average inventory in units.

investing activities business activities that involve transactions related to acquiring and disposing of marketable securities, other long-term investments, and property, plant, and equipment, as well as making and collecting loans unrelated to the sale of goods or services; the acquiring and disposing of resources (assets) that a company uses to acquire and sell its products and services.

investing creditors Those who primarily finance investing activities

investment center a responsibility center whose manager is responsible for the relationship between its profits and the total assets invested in the center. In general, the management of an investment center is expected to earn a target profit per dollar invested.

investment returns The increase in pension investments resulting from interest, dividends, and capital gains on the investment portfolio

investment tax credit a reduction in income taxes of a percent of the cost of a new asset in the year the new asset is placed in service.

invoice price The price that a seller charges the purchaser for merchandise

invoice A document that the seller sends to the purchaser to request payment for items that the seller shipped to the purchaser

IOU A slang term for a receivable

irrelevant costs costs that do not differ among competing decision alternatives.

issued stock Shares of stock that have been sold and issued to stockholders; issued stock may be either outstanding or in the treasury

J

job cost sheet a document used to track the status of and accumulate the costs for a specific job in a job cost system.

job order production the manufacturing of products in single units or in batches of identical units.

job production see job order production.

joint costs all materials and conversion costs of joint products incurred prior to the split-off point.

joint products two or more products simultaneously produced by a single process from a common set of inputs.

journal A tabular record in which business transactions are analyzed in debit and credit terms and recorded in chronological order

just-in-time (JIT) inventory management a comprehensive inventory management philosophy that stresses policies, procedures, and attitudes by managers and other workers that result in the efficient production of high-quality goods while maintaining the minimum level of inventories.

just-in-time (JIT) inventory philosophy Receive inventory from suppliers into the production process just at the point it is needed

K

Kaizen costing see continuous improvement costing.

kanban system see materials pull system.

L

labor efficiency variance the difference between the standard cost of actual labor inputs and the flexible budget cost for labor.

labor rate (spending) variance the difference between the actual cost and the standard cost of actual labor inputs.

land improvements Improvements with limited lives made to land sites, such as paved parking lots and driveways

last-in, first-out (LIFO) method One of the prescribed methods of inventory costing; LIFO assumes that the last costs incurred for the purchase or production of inventory are the first costs relieved form inventory when goods are sold

lean accounting a system of product cost assignment where costs are assigned to value streams of multiple products rather than to individual products

lean production a philosophy of inventory production and management that emphasizes increased coordination throughout the value chain, reduced inventory, reduced production times, increased product quality, and increased employee involvement and empowerment

lease A contract between a lessor (owner) and lessee (tenant) for the rental of property

leasehold improvements Expenditures made by a lessee to alter or improve leased property

leasehold The rights transferred from the lessor to the lessee by a lease

least-squares regression analysis uses a mathematical technique to fit a cost estimating equation to the observed data in a manner that minimizes the sum of the vertical squared estimating errors between the estimated and actual costs at each observation.

lessee The party acquiring the right to the use of property by a lease

lessor The owner of property who transfers the right to use the property to another party by a lease

leveraging The use of borrowed funds in the capital structure of a firm; the expectation is that the funds will earn a return higher than the rate of interest on the borrowed funds

liabilities The obligations, or debts, that an entity must pay in money or services at some time in the future because of past transactions or events

life-cycle budgeting an approach to budgeting when the entire life of the project represents a more useful planning horizon than an artificial period of one year.

life-cycle costs from the seller's perspective, all costs associated with a product or service ranging from those incurred with initial conception through design, pre-production, production, and after-production support. From the buyer's perspective, all costs associated with a purchased product or service, including initial acquisition costs and subsequent costs of operation, maintenance, repair, and disposal.

LIFO conformity rule IRS requirement to cost inventories using LIFO for tax purposes if they are costed using LIFO for financial reporting purposes

LIFO liquidation The reduction in inventory quantities when LIFO costing is used; LIFO liquidation yields an increase in gross profit and income when prices are rising

LIFO reserve The difference between the cost of inventories using FIFO and the cost using LIFO

linear algebra method (reciprocal) method a method of allocating service department costs using a series of linear algebraic equations, which are solved simultaneously, to allocate service department costs both interdepartmentally among service departments and to the producing departments.

linear programming an optimizing model used to assist managers in making decisions under constrained conditions when linear relationships exist between all variables.

liquidation value per share The amount that would be received by a holder of a share of stock if the corporation liquidated

liquidity How much cash the company has, how much is expected, and how much can be raised on short notice

list price The suggested price or reference price of merchandise in a catalog or price list

long-term liabilities Debt obligations not due to be settled within the normal operating cycle or one year, whichever is longer

lower of cost or market (LCM) GAAP requirement to write down the carrying amount of inventories on the balance sheet if the reported cost (using FIFO, for example) exceeds market value (determined by current replacement cost)

M

maker The signer of a promissory note

managed fixed costs see discretionary fixed costs.

management accounting a discipline concerned with financial and related information used by managers and other persons inside specific organizations to make strategic, organizational, and operational decisions.

management by exception an approach to performance assessment whereby management directs attention only to those activities not proceeding according to plan.

management discussion and analysis (MD&A) The section of the 10-K report in which a company provides a detailed discussion of its business activities

managerial accounting The accounting activities carried out by a firm's accounting staff primarily to furnish managers and other employees with accounting data for decisions related to the firm's operations

manufacturers Companies that convert raw materials and components into finished products through the application of skilled labor and machine operations

manufacturing cost budget a budget detailing the direct materials, direct labor, and manufacturing overhead costs that should be incurred by manufacturing operations to produce the number of units called for in the production budget.

manufacturing costs The costs of direct materials, direct labor, and manufacturing overhead incurred in the manufacture of a product

manufacturing margin the result when direct manufacturing costs (variable costs) are deducted from product sales.

manufacturing organizations organizations that process raw materials into finished products for sale to others.

manufacturing overhead all manufacturing costs other than direct materials and direct labor.

margin of safety the amount by which actual or planned sales exceed the break-even point.

marginal cost the varying increment in total cost required to produce and sell an additional unit of product.

marginal revenue the varying increment in total revenue derived from the sale of an additional unit.

market (yield) rate This is the interest rate that investors expect to earn on the investment in this debt security; this rate is used to price the bond issue

market method accounting Securities are reported at current market values (marked-to-market) on the statement date

market segment level activity performed to obtain or maintain operations in a market segment.

market value per share The current price at which shares of stock may be bought or sold

market value The published price (as listed on a stock exchange) multiplied by the number of shares owned

master budget the grouping together of all budgets and supporting schedules. This budget coordinates all the financial and operational activities and places them into an organization wide set of budgets for a given time period.

matching principle An accounting guideline that states that income is determined by relating expenses, to the extent feasible, with revenues that have been recorded

materiality An accounting guideline that states that transactions so insignificant that they would not affect a user's actions or perception of the company may be recorded in the most expedient manner

materials inventory The physical component of inventory; the other components of manufactured inventory are labor costs and overhead costs

materials price variance the difference between the actual materials cost and the standard cost of actual materials inputs.

materials pull system an inventory production flow system in which employees at each station work to replenish the inventory used by employees at subsequent stations. The building of excess inventories is strictly prohibited. When the number of units in inventory reaches a specified limit, work at the station stops until workers at a subsequent station pull a unit from the in-process storage area.

materials push system an inventory production flow system in which employees work to reduce the pile of inventory building up at their work stations. Workers at each station remove materials from an in-process storage area, complete their operation, and place the output in another in-process storage area. Hence, they push the work to the next work station.

materials quantity variance the difference between the standard cost of actual materials inputs and the flexible budget cost for materials.

materials requisition form a document used to record the type and quantity of each raw material issued to the factory.

maturity date The date on which a note or bond matures

measuring unit concept An accounting guideline noting that the accounting unit of measure is the basic unit of money

merchandise inventory A stock of products that a company buys from another company and makes available for sale to its customers

merchandising firm A company that buys finished products, stores the products for varying periods of time, and then resells the products

merchandising organizations organizations that buy and sell goods without performing manufacturing operations.

method of comparables model Equity valuation or stock values are predicted using price multiples, which are defined as stock price divided by some key financial statement number such as net income, net sales, book value of equity, total assets, or cash flow; companies are then compared with their competitors

minimum level budgeting an approach to budgeting that establishes a base amount for all budget items and requires explanation or justification for any budgeted amount above the minimum (base).

minority interest The equity claim of a shareholder owning less than a majority or controlling interest in the company

mission the basic purpose toward which an organization's activities are directed.

mixed costs costs that contain a fixed and a variable cost element.

model a simplified representation of some real-world phenomenon.

modified accelerated cost recovery system (MACRS) See accelerated cost recovery system

movement time the time units spend moving between work or inspection stations.

mutually exclusive investments two or more capital expenditure proposals where the acceptance of one investment automatically causes the rejection of the other(s).

N

natural resources Assets occurring in a natural state, such as timber, petroleum, natural gas, coal, and other mineral deposits

net asset based valuation model Equity is valued as reported assets less reported liabilities

net assets The difference between an entity's assets and liabilities; net assets are equal to stockholders' equity

net book value (NBV) The cost of the asset less accumulated depreciation; also called carrying value

net financial obligations (NFO) net total of all financial (nonoperating) obligations less financial (nonoperating) assets

net income The excess of a firm's revenues over its expenses

net loss The excess of a firm's expenses over its revenues

net operating assets (NOA) Current and long-term operating assets less current and long-term operating liabilities; or net operating working capital plus long-term net operating assets

net operating profit after tax (NOPAT) Sales less operating expenses (including taxes)

net present value the present value of a project's net cash inflows from operations and disinvestment less the amount of the initial investment.

net realizable value The value at which an asset can be sold, net of any costs of disposition

net sales volume variance indicates the impact of a change in sales volume on the contribution margin, given the budgeted selling price and the standard variable costs. It is computed as the difference between the actual and the budgeted sales volumes times the budgeted unit contribution margin.

net sales The total revenue generated by a company through merchandise sales less the revenue given up through sales returns and allowances and sales discounts

net working capital Current assets less current liabilities

nominal rate The rate of interest stated on a bond certificate or other debt instrument

noncash investing and financing activities Significant business activities during the period that do not impact cash inflows or cash outflows

noncurrent liabilities Obligations not due to be paid within one year or the operating cycle, whichever is longer

nonoperating expenses Expenses that relate to the company's financing activities and include interest income and interest expense, gains and losses on sales of securities, and income or loss on discontinued operations

non-value-added activity an activity that does not add value to a product or service from the viewpoint of the customer.

no-par stock Stock that does not have a par value

NOPAT Net operating profit after tax

normal operating cycle For a particular business, the average period of time between the use of cash in its typical operating activity and the subsequent collection of cash from customers

note receivable A promissory note held by the note's payee

notes to financial statements Footnotes in which companies discuss their accounting policies and estimates used in preparing the statements

not-for-profit organization an organization that does not have profit as a primary goal.

not-sufficient-funds check A check from an individual or company that had an insufficient cash balance in the bank when the holder of the check presented it to the bank for payment

O

objective function in linear programming models, the goal to be minimized or maximized.

objectivity principle An accounting principle requiring that, whenever possible, accounting entries are based on objectively determined evidence

off-balance-sheet financing The structuring of a financing arrangement so that no liability shows on the borrower's balance sheet

operating activities business activities that involve transactions that are related to a company's normal income-earning activity (research, develop, produce, purchase, market, and distribute company products and services) and that enter into the calculation of net income on the income statement.

operating asset turnover The ratio obtained by dividing sales by average net operating assets

operating budget detailed plans to guide operations throughout the budget period.

operating cash flow to capital expenditures ratio A firm's net cash flow from operating activities divided by its annual capital expenditures

operating cash flow to current liabilities ratio A firm's net cash flow from operating activities divided by its average current liabilities

operating creditors Those who primarily finance operating activities

operating cycle The time between paying cash for goods or employee services and receiving cash from customers

operating expense margin (OEM) The ratio obtained by dividing any operating expense item or category by sales

operating expenses The usual and customary costs that a company incurs to support its main business activities; these include cost of goods sold, selling expenses, depreciation expense, amortization expense, research and development expense, and taxes on operating profits

operating lease A lease by which the lessor retains the usual risks and rewards of owning the property

operating leverage a measure of the extent that an organization's costs are fixed.

operating profit margin The ratio obtained by dividing NOPAT by sales

operational audit An evaluation of activities, systems, and internal controls within a company to determine their efficiency, effectiveness, and economy

operations list a document that specifies the manufacturing operations and related times required to produce one unit or batch of product.

opportunity cost the net cash inflow that could be obtained if the resources committed to one action were used in the most desirable other alternative.

optimal solution in linear programming models, the feasible solution than maximizes or minimizes the value of the objective function, depending on the decision maker's goal.

optimizing model a model that suggests a specific choice between decision alternatives.

order level activity an activity performed for each sales order.

order-filling costs costs incurred to place finished goods in the hands of purchasers (for example, storing, packaging, and transportation).

order-getting costs costs incurred to obtain customers' orders (for example, advertising, salespersons' salaries and commissions, travel, telephone, and entertainment).

organization chart an illustration of the formal relationships existing between the elements of an organization.

organization costs Expenditures incurred in launching a business (usually a corporation), including attorney's fees and various fees paid to the state

organization structure the arrangement of lines of responsibility within the organization.

organizational cost drivers choices concerning the organization of activities and the involvement of persons inside and outside the organization in decision making.

organizational-based cost systems used for financial reporting, these systems focus on organizational units such as a company, plant, or department rather than on processes and activities.

organizing the process of making the organization into a well-ordered whole.

outcomes assessment see performance measurement.

outlay costs costs that require future expenditures of cash or other resources.

output/input budgeting an approach to budgeting where physical inputs and costs are budgeted as a function of planned unit level activities. The budgeted inputs are a function of the planned outputs.

outsourcing the external acquisition of services or components.

outstanding checks Checks issued by a firm that have not yet been presented to its bank for payment

outstanding stock Shares of stock that are currently owned by stockholders (excludes treasury stock)

owners' equity The interest of owners in the assets of an entity; equal to the difference between the entity's assets and liabilities; also called stockholders' equity

P

packing list A document that lists the items of merchandise contained in a carton and the quantity of each item; the packing list is usually attached to the outside of the carton

paid-in capital The amount of capital contributed to a corporation by various transactions; the primary source of paid-in capital is from the issuance of shares of stock

par (bonds) Face value of the bond

par value (stock) An amount specified in the corporate charter for each share of stock and imprinted on the face of each stock certificate, often determines the legal capital of the corporation

parent company A company owning one or more subsidiary companies

parsimonious method to multiyear forecasting Forecasting multiple years using only sales growth, net operating profit margin (NOPM), and the turnover of net operating assets (NOAT)

participation budget see bottom-up budget.

partnership A voluntary association of two or more persons for the purpose of conducting a business

password A string of characters that a computer user enters into a computer terminal to prove to the computer that the person using the computer is truly the person named in the user identification code

patent An exclusive privilege granted for 20 years to an inventor that gives the patent holder the right to exclude others from making, using, or selling the invention

payback period the time required to recover the initial investment in a project from operations.

payee The company or individual to whom a promissory note is made payable

payment approval form A document that authorizes the payment of an invoice

pension plan A plan to pay benefits to employees after they retire from the company; the plan may be a defined contribution plan or a defined benefit plan

percentage of net sales method A procedure that determines the uncollectible accounts expense for the year by multiplying net credit sales by the estimated uncollectible percentage

percentage-of-completion method Recognition of revenue by determining the costs incurred per the contract as compared to its total expected costs

performance measurement the determination of the extent to which actual outcomes correspond to planned outcomes.

period costs expired costs not related to manufacturing inventory; they are recognized as expenses when incurred.

period statement A financial statement accumulating information for a specific period of time; examples are the income statement, the statement of stockholders' equity, and the statement of cash flows

permanent account An account used to prepare the balance sheet; that is, asset, liability, and equity capital (capital stock and retained earnings) accounts; any balance in a permanent account at the end of an accounting period is carried forward to the next period

physical inventory A year-end procedure that involves counting the quantity of each inventory item, determining the unit cost of each item, multiplying the unit cost times quantity, and summing the costs of all the items to determine the total inventory at cost

physical model a scaled-down version or replica of physical reality.

planning the process of selecting goals and strategies to achieve those goals.

plant assets Land, buildings, equipment, vehicles, furniture, and fixtures that a firm uses in its operations; sometimes referred to by the acronym PPE

pooling of interests method A method of accounting for business combinations under which the acquired company is recorded on the acquirer's balance sheet at its book value, rather than market value; this method is no longer acceptable under GAAP for acquisitions occurring after 2001

position statement A financial statement, such as the balance sheet, that presents information as of a particular date

post-closing trial balance A list of general ledger accounts and their balances after closing entries have been recorded and posted

postdated check A check from another person or company with a date that is later than the current date; a postdated check does not become cash until the date of the check

practical capacity the maximum possible activity, allowing for normal repairs and maintenance.

predetermined manufacturing overhead rate an overhead rate established at the start of each year by dividing the predicted overhead costs for the year by the predicted volume of activity in the overhead base for the year.

preemptive right The right of a stockholder to maintain his or her proportionate interest in a corporation by having the right to purchase an appropriate share of any new stock issue

preferred stock A class of corporate capital stock typically receiving priority over common stock in dividend payments and distribution of assets should the corporation be liquidated

premium bond A bond that is sold for more than its par (face) value

present value index the present value of the project's subsequent cash flows divided by the initial investment.

present value the current worth of a specified amount of money to be received at some future date at some specified interest rate.

prevention costs quality costs incurred to prevent nonconforming products from being produced or nonconforming services from being performed.

price discrimination illegally charging different purchasers different prices.

price earnings ratio a measure of performance, price earnings ratio compares the current market price with earnings per share of stock and arrives at a multiple of earnings represented by the selling price.

price fixing the organized setting of prices by competitors.

price-earnings ratio Current market price per common share divided by earnings per share

pro forma income A computation of income that begins with the GAAP income from continuing operations (that excludes discontinued operations, extraordinary items and changes in accounting principle), but then excludes other transitory items (most notably, restructuring charges), and some additional items such as expenses arising from acquisitions (goodwill amortization and other acquisition costs), compensation expense in the form of stock options, and research and development expenditures; pro forma income is not GAAP

process manufacturing a manufacturing environment where production is on a continuous basis.

process map (or process flowchart) a schematic overview of all the activities required to complete a process. Each major activity is represented by a rectangle on the map.

process reengineering the fundamental redesign of a process to serve internal or external customers.

process a collection of related activities intended to achieve a common purpose.

processing time the time spent working on units.

product costs all costs incurred in the manufacturing of products; they are carried in the accounts as an asset (inventory) until the product is sold, at which time they are recognized as an expense (cost of goods sold).

product level activity an activity performed to support the production of each different type of product.

product margin computed as product sales less direct product costs.

production order a document that contains a job's unique identification number and specifies details for the job such as the quantity to be produced, the total raw materials requirements, the manufacturing operations and other activities to be performed, and perhaps even the time when each manufacturing operation should be performed.

productivity the relationship between outputs and inputs.

profit center a responsibility center whose manager is responsible for revenues, costs, and resulting profits. It may be an entire organization, but it is more frequently a segment of an organization such as a product line, marketing territory, or store.

profitability analysis an examination of the relationships between revenues, costs, and profits.

profit-volume graph illustrates the relationship between volume and profits; it does not show revenues and costs.

project-level activity an activity performed to support the completion of each project.

promissory note A written promise to pay a certain sum of money on demand or at a determinable future time

purchase method The prescribed method of accounting for business combinations; under the purchase method, assets and liabilities of the acquired company are recorded at fair market value, together with identifiable intangible assets; the balance is ascribed to goodwill

purchase order A document that formally requests a supplier to sell and deliver specific quantities of particular items of merchandise at specified prices

purchase requisition An internal document that requests that the purchasing department order particular items of merchandise

purchases budget indicates the merchandise or materials that must be acquired to meet current needs and ending inventory requirements.

Q

qualitative characteristics of accounting information The characteristics of accounting information that contribute to decision usefulness; the primary qualities are relevance and reliability

quality circles groups of employees involved in the production of products who have the authority, within certain parameters, to address and resolve quality problems as they occur, without seeking management approval.

quality costs costs incurred because poor quality of conformance does (or may) exist.

quality of conformance the degree of conformance between a product and its design specifications.

quality of design the degree of conformance between customer expectations for a product or service and the design specifications of the product or service.

quality conformance to customer expectations.

quantitative model a set of mathematical relationships.

quarterly data Selected quarterly financial information that is reported in annual reports to stockholders

quick ratio see acid test ratio; defined as quick assets (cash and cash equivalents, short-term investments, and current receivables) divided by current liabilities.

R

raw materials inventories the physical ingredients and components that will be converted by machines and/or human labor into a finished product.

realized (or **realizable**) When referring to revenue, the receipt of an asset or satisfaction of a liability as a result of a transaction or event

recognition criteria The criteria that must be met before a financial statement element may be recorded in the accounts; essentially, the item must meet the definition of an element and must be measurable

record a related set of alphabetic and/or numeric data items.

registered bond A bond for which the issuer (or the trustee) maintains a record of owners and, at the appropriate times, mails out interest payments

relational (cause-and-effect) cost center a cost center that has clearly defined relationships between effort and accomplishment (cause and effect).

relevance A qualitative characteristic of accounting information; relevant information contributes to the predictive and evaluative decisions made by financial statement users

relevant costs future costs that differ between competing decision alternatives.

relevant range the range of activity within which a linear cost function is valid.

reliability A qualitative characteristic of accounting information; reliable information contains no bias or error and faithfully portrays what it intends to represent

remeasurement The computation of gain or loss in the translation of subsidiaries denominated in a foreign currency into $US when the temporal method is used

residual income for investment center excess of investment center income over the minimum rate of return set by top management. The minimum dollar return is computed as a percentage of the investment center's asset base.

residual net operating income (ROPI) model An equity valuation approach that equates the firm's value to the sum of its net operating assets (NOA) and the present value of its residual operating income (ROPI)

residual operating income Net operating profits after tax (NOPAT) less the product of net operating assets (NOA) at the beginning of the period multiplied by the weighted average cost of capital (WACC)

responsibility accounting the structuring of performance reports addressed to individual (or group) members of an organization in a manner that emphasizes the factors they are able to control. The focus is on specific units within the organization that are responsible for the accomplishment of specific activities or objectives.

retailers Companies that buy products from wholesale distributors and sell the products to individual customers, the general public

retained earnings reconciliation The reconciliation of retained earnings from the beginning to the end of the year; the change in retained earnings includes, at a minimum, the net income (loss) for the period and dividends paid, if any, but may include other components as well; also called statement of retained earnings

retained earnings Earned capital, the cumulative net income and loss, of the company (from its inception) that has not been paid to shareholders as dividends

return on assets A financial ratio computed as net income divided by average total assets; sometimes referred to by the acronym ROA; as a measure of performance, return on assets combines the asset turnover and return on sales ratios to measure directly the firm's ability to use its assets to generate profits

return on common stockholders' equity A financial ratio computed as net income less preferred stock dividends divided by average common stockholders' equity; sometimes referred to by the acronym ROCE

return on equity a measure of performance, the return on equity measures the profits attributable to the shareholders as a percentage of their equity in the firm. The general equation for return on equity is: Net income/Average shareholders' equity; sometimes referred to by the acronym ROE.

return on investment for investment center a measure of the earnings per dollar of investment. The return on investment of an investment center is computed by dividing the income of the center by its asset base (usually average total assets). It can also be computed as investment turnover times the return-on-sales ratio.

return on investment The ratio obtained by dividing income by average investment; sometimes referred to by the acronym ROI

return on net operating assets (RNOA) The ratio obtained by dividing NOPAT by average net operating assets

return on sales a measure of performance, the return on sales measures the firm's ability to generate profits from sales produced by the firm's assets. The general equation for return on sales is: net income divided by net sales; sometimes referred to by the acronym ROS

return The amount earned on an investment; also called yield

revenue center a responsibility center whose manager is responsible for the generation of sales revenues.

revenue recognition principle An accounting principle requiring that revenue be recognized when earned and realized (or realizable)

revenue variance the difference between the budgeted sales volume at the budgeted selling price and the actual sales volume at the actual selling price.

revenues inflows of earned resources from providing goods and services to customers; reflected as increases in stockholders' equity

Robinson-Patman Act prohibits price discrimination when purchasers compete with one another in the sale of their products or services to third parties.

rolling budget see continuous budgeting.

sale on account A sale of merchandise made on a credit basis

sales budget a forecast of sales revenue for a future period. It may also contain a forecast of sales collections.

sales mix the relative portion of unit or dollar sales derived from each product or service.

sales price variance the impact on revenues of a change in selling price, given the actual sales volume. It is computed as the change in selling price times the actual sales volume.

sales volume variance indicates the impact on revenues of change in sales volume, assuming there was no change in selling price. It is computed as the difference between the actual and the budgeted sales volumes times the budgeted selling price.

salvage value The expected net recovery when a plant asset is sold or removed from service; also called residual value

scatter diagram a graph of past activity and cost data, with individual observations represented by dots.

secured bond A bond that pledges specific property as security for meeting the terms of the bond agreement

Securities and Exchange Commission (SEC) The commission, created by the 1934 Securities Act, that has broad powers to regulate the issuance and trading of securities, and the financial reporting of companies issuing securities to the public

segment income all revenues of a segment minus all costs directly or indirectly charged to it.

segment margin the amount that a segment contributes toward the common (indirect) costs of the organization and toward profits. It is computed as segment sales less direct segment costs.

segment reports income statements that show operating results for portions or segments of a business. Segment reporting is used primarily for internal purposes, although generally accepted accounting principles also require disclosure of segment information for some public corporations.

segments Subdivisions of a firm for which supplemental financial information is disclosed

selling expense budget presents the expenses the organization plans to incur in connection with sales and distribution.

semi-variable costs see mixed costs.

sensitivity analysis the study of the responsiveness of a model to changes in one or more of its independent variables.

serial bond A bond issue that staggers the bond maturity dates over a series of years

service cost (pensions) The increase in the pension obligation due to employees working another year for the employer

service costing the process of assigning costs to services performed.

service department a department that provides support services to production and/or other support departments.

service organizations nonmanufacturing organizations that perform work for others, including banks, hospitals, and real estate agencies.

setup time the time required to prepare equipment to produce a specific product.

Sherman Antitrust Act prohibits price fixing.

significant influence The ability of the investor to affect the financing or operating policies of the investee

simplex method a mathematical approach to solving linear programming models containing three or more variables.

sinking fund provision A bond feature that requires the borrower to retire a portion of the bonds each year or, in some cases, to make payments each year to a trustee who is responsible for managing the resources needed to retire the bonds at maturity

solvency refers to the firm's ability to pay its debts as they become due.

source document Any written document or computer record evidencing an accounting transaction, such as a bank check or deposit slip, sales invoice, or cash register tape

special purpose entity (See variable interest entity)

spin-off A form of equity carve out in which divestiture is accomplished by distribution of a company's shares in a subsidiary to the company's shareholders who then own the shares in the subsidiary directly rather than through the parent company

split-off point the point in the process where joint products become separately identifiable.

split-off A form of equity carve out in which divestiture is accomplished by the parent company's exchange of stock in the subsidiary in return for shares in the parent owned by its shareholders

spread The difference between the net financial return (NFR) and the return on net operating activities (RNOA)

standard cost variance analysis a system for examining the flexible budget variance, which is the difference between the actual cost and flexible budget cost of producing a given quantity of product or service.

standard cost a budget that indicates what it should cost to provide an activity or produce one batch or unit of product under efficient operating conditions.

stated value A nominal amount that may be assigned to each share of no-par stock and accounted for much as if it were a par value

statement of cash flows a financial statement that reports the major sources and uses of cash classified into operating, investing, and financing activities and that indicates the net increase or decrease in cash; the statement also includes a schedule of any significant noncash investing and financing activities that occur during the period.

statement of cost of goods manufactured a report that summarizes the cost of goods completed and transferred into finished goods inventory during the period.

statement of financial position A financial statement showing a firm's assets, liabilities, and stockholders' equity at a specific date; also called a balance sheet

statement of owner's equity A financial statement presenting information on the events causing a change in stockholders' equity during a period; the statement presents the beginning balance, additions to, deductions from, and the ending balance of stockholders' equity for the period

static budget a budget based on a prior prediction of expected sales and production.

step costs costs that are constant within a narrow range of activity but shift to a higher level with an increased range of activity. Total step costs increase in a step-like fashion as activity increases.

step method A method of allocating service department costs that gives partial recognition to interdepartmental services by using a methodology that allocates service department costs sequentially to both the remaining service departments and the producing departments.

stock dividends The payment of dividends in shares of stock

stock split Additional shares of its own stock issued by a corporation to its current stockholders in proportion to their current ownership interests without changing the balances in the related stockholders' equity accounts; a formal stock split increases the number of shares outstanding and reduces proportionately the stock's per share par value

storyboard a process map developed by employees who perform the component activities within a process.

straight-line depreciation A depreciation procedure that allocates uniform amounts of depreciation expense to each full period of a depreciable asset's useful life

strategic business segment a segment that has its own mission and set of goals to be achieved. The mission of the segment influences the decisions that its top managers make in both short-run and long-run situations.

strategic cost management making decisions concerning specific cost drivers within the context of an organization's business strategy, its internal value chain, and its place in a larger value chain stretching from the development and use of resources to the final consumers.

strategic plan a guideline or framework for making specific medium-range or short-run decisions.

strategic position analysis an organization's basic way of competing to sell products or services.

strategic position how an organization wants to place itself in comparison to the competition.

strategy a course of action that will assist in achieving one or more goals.

structural cost drivers fundamental choices about the size and scope of operations and technologies employed in delivering products or services to customers. These choices affect the types of activities and the costs of activities performed to satisfy customer needs.

suboptimization when managers or operating units, acting in their own best interests, make decisions that are not in the best interest of the organization as a whole.

subsequent events Events occurring shortly after a fiscal year-end that will be reported as supplemental information to the financial statements of the year just ended

subsidiaries Companies that are owned by the parent company

subsidiary ledger A set of accounts or records that contains detailed information about the items included in the balance of one general ledger account

summary of significant accounting policies A financial statement disclosure, usually the initial note to the statements, which identifies the major accounting policies and procedures used by the firm

sum-of-the-years'-digits method An accelerated depreciation method that allocates depreciation expense to each year in a fractional proportion, the denominator of which is the sum of the years' digits in the useful life of the asset and the numerator of which is the remaining useful life of the asset at the beginning of the current depreciation period

sunk costs costs resulting from past decisions that cannot be changed.

T

T-account An abbreviated form of the formal account in the shape of a T; use is usually limited to illustrations of accounting techniques and analysis

target costing establishes the allowable cost of a product or service by starting with determining what customers are willing to pay for the product or service and then subtracting a desired profit on sales.

temporary account An account used to gather information for an accounting period; at the end of the period, the balance is transferred to a permanent stockholders' equity account; revenue, expense, and dividends accounts are temporary accounts

term loan A long-term borrowing, evidenced by a note payable, which is contracted with a single lender

terminal period The forecast period following the horizon period

theory of constraints every process has a bottleneck (constraining resource), and production cannot take place faster than it is processed through the bottleneck. The theory's goal is to maximize throughput in a constrained environment.

throughput sales revenue minus direct materials costs. See also theory of constraints.

time-adjusted rate of return see internal rate of return.

times interest earned ratio a measure of long-term solvency and interest-paying ability; measured as income before interest expense and income taxes divided by interest expense

top-down budget a budget where top management decides on the primary goals and objectives for the organization and communicates them to lower management levels.

total compensation cost The sum of gross pay, payroll taxes, and fringe benefits paid by the employer

trade credit Inventories purchased on credit from other companies

trade discount An amount, usually based on quantity of merchandise purchased, that the seller subtracts from the list price of merchandise to determine the invoice price

trade name An exclusive and continuing right to use a certain term or name to identify a brand or family of products

trademark An exclusive and continuing right to use a certain symbol to identify a brand or family of products

trading on the equity The use of borrowed funds in the capital structure of a firm; the expectation is that the funds will earn a return higher than the rate of interest on the borrowed funds

trading securities Investments in securities that management intends to actively trade (buy and sell) for trading profits as market prices fluctuate

transfer price the internal value assigned a product or service that one division provides to another.

transitory items Transactions or events that are not likely to recur

translation adjustment The change in the value of the net assets of a subsidiary whose assets and liabilities are denominated in a foreign currency

treasury stock Shares of outstanding stock that have been acquired (and not retired) by the issuing corporation; treasury stock is recorded at cost and deducted from stockholders' equity in the balance sheet

trend percentages A comparison of the same financial item over two or more years stated as a percentage of a base-year amount

trial balance A list of the account titles in the general ledger, their respective debit or credit balances, and the totals of the debit and credit amounts

U

unadjusted trial balance A list of general ledger accounts and their balances taken before adjustments have been made

uncollectible accounts expense The expense stemming from the inability of a business to collect an amount previously recorded as a receivable; sometimes called bad debts expense; normally classified as a selling or administrative expense

unearned revenue A liability representing revenues received in advance; also called deferred revenue

unit contribution margin the difference between the unit selling price and the unit variable costs.

unit level activity an activity performed for each unit of product produced or sold.

unit level approach an approach to analyzing cost behavior that assumes changes in costs are best explained by changes in the number of units or sales dollars of products or services provided for customers.

units-of-production method A depreciation method that allocates depreciation expense to each operating period in proportion to the amount of the asset's expected total production capacity used each period

useful life The period of time an asset is used by an entity in its operating activities, running from date of acquisition to date of disposal (or removal from service)

V

value chain analysis the study of value-producing activities, stretching from basic raw materials to the final consumer of a product or service.

value chain the set of value-producing activities stretching from basic raw materials to the final consumer.

value the worth in usefulness or importance of a product or service to the customer.

value-added activity an activity that adds value to a product or service from the viewpoint of the customer.

value stream consists of the production processes for similar products. Each value stream in a lean company not only has lean processes; it also has a lean accounting system because most costs should be directly traceable to one of the value streams.

variable cost ratio variable costs as a portion of sales revenue.

variable costing an approach to product costing that treats variable manufacturing costs as product costs and fixed manufacturing costs as period costs.

variable costs costs that are an identical amount for each incremental unit of activity. Their total amount increases as activity increases, equaling zero dollars when activity is zero and increasing at a constant amount per unit of activity.

variable costs Those costs that change in proportion to changes in sales volume

variable interest entity (VIE) Any form of business organization (such as corporation, partnership, trust) that is established by a sponsoring company and provides benefits to that company in the form of asset securitization or project financing; VIEs were formerly known as special purpose entities (SPEs)

variable manufacturing overhead all variable costs, except direct labor and direct materials, associated with converting raw materials into finished goods.

variable overhead effectiveness variance the difference between the standard variable overhead cost for the actual inputs and the flexible budget cost for variable overhead based on outputs.

variable overhead spending variance the difference between the actual variable overhead cost and the standard variable overhead cost for the actual inputs.

variable selling and administrative costs all variable costs other than those directly associated with converting raw materials into finished goods.

variance a comparison of actual and budgeted (or allowed) costs or revenues which are usually identified in financial performance reports.

vertical analysis an evaluative standard that restates amounts in the current financial statements as a percentage of some base measure such as sales; focused on one period's statements.

virtual integration the use of information technology and partnership concepts to allow two or more entities along a value chain to act as if they were a single economic entity.

voucher Another name for the payment approval form

waiting time the time units spend in temporary storage waiting to be processed, moved, or inspected.

W

warranties Guarantees against product defects for a designated period of time after sale

wasting assets Another name for natural resources; see natural resources

weighted average cost of capital (WACC) The discount rate where the weights are the relative percentages of debt and equity in the capital structure and are applied to the expected returns on debt and equity respectively; an average of the after-tax cost of all long-term borrowings and the cost of equity

weighted average method in process costing, a costing method that spreads the combined beginning inventory cost and current manufacturing costs (for materials, labor, and overhead) over the units completed and those in ending inventory on an average basis.

work in process inventory The cost of inventories that are in the manufacturing process and have not yet reached completion

work ticket a document used to record the time a job spends in a specific manufacturing operation.

working capital a measure of solvency, working capital is the difference between current assets and current liabilities and is the net amount of working funds available in the short run. The general equation for working capital is: Current assets minus Current liabilities.

work-in-process inventories partially completed goods consisting of raw materials that are in the process of being converted into a finished product.

Z

zero coupon bond A bond that offers no periodic interest payments but that is issued at a substantial discount from its face value

zero-based budgeting a variation of the minimum level approach to budgeting where every dollar of expenditure must be justified.

z-score The outcome of the Altman Z-score bankruptcy prediction model

Index

A

B

C

D

Q

R

S

T